About the author:

W A Sumner studied theology at Hull University and achieved an M Litt from Oxford University. He has spent many years as a teacher and preacher in schools and churches. He is a reader of the Diocese of Birmingham and is also a hospital chaplain.

THE THEOLOGY OF TRUTH

W. A. Sumner

The Book Guild Ltd

First published in Great Britain in 2017 by
The Book Guild Ltd
9 Priory Business Park
Wistow Road, Kibworth
Leicestershire, LE8 0RX
Freephone: 0800 999 2982
www.bookguild.co.uk
Email: info@bookguild.co.uk
Twitter: @bookguild

Typeset in Times

Printed and bound in Great Britain by CPI Group (UK) Ltd, Croydon, CR0 4YY

ISBN 978 1911320 487

British Library Cataloguing in Publication Data.
A catalogue record for this book is available from the British Library.

Contents

Acknowledgements

Peter Turner, Peter Kaye, Evelyn Reston, John Cook, Patricia Bates and William Cooper.

The front cover of my first book, The Theology of Paradox; a design by George Sumner, circa 1965.

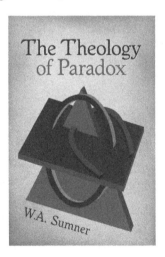 

The front cover of this book, The Theology of Truth; taken from an idea by George Sumner, circa 1965. Additional ideas and amendments by Katie Colclough, George's great granddaughter. The triangle has three messiahs on each corner; Hitler as an evil messiah, Krishna as a meditative messiah and Jesus, as supreme, as the complete and final messiah. The design here is the original and the one of the front cover is a slight adaptation, taking into account people's susceptibilities.

Preface

"What is truth?" asked Pontius Pilate. That is a question that everyone at some time in their lives asks himself. The deep questions about life and death, this world and the next, existence and non-existence, hang over us, regardless of whether we are inclined to one religion or another, or none at all. To consider the world as it is, full of beauty along with its problems, and the heavenly bodies out there in the universe, forces us to ask the question, "what is it all about?"

All religions, and that includes atheism too, attempt to grapple with these questions. There are many answers offered to us, some in agreement with each other, and others not so. But absolute certainty is not available to us; that is unless one is totally committed to some kind of doctrine with an unquestioning faith. Unfortunately, such levels of certainty can come to pieces, leaving one in some kind of spiritual desert.

This book begins with a review of the different types of truth or certainty, ranging from mathematical realities through to theological ideas. It is one thing to say that mathematics and science can tell us all we need to know about life; but most people are not satisfied with that. People want to know what it all means; what is the significance of it all.

The rest of this book is a selection of different scriptural materials from around the world. The writers of these materials would all claim, directly or indirectly to be telling us the truth about life and death. I have taken certain parts of the Bible, Old and New Testament, and placed them alongside each other so that the contrast between them can be seen. It is important not to gain the impression that I undervalue the Bible or rate these other scriptural materials as equal in spiritual authority. One of the problems that anyone would have, is to see these materials in an objective light; I freely admit that I am an Anglican of a traditional stance and cannot avoid assessing these matters without a certain amount of bias. If anyone objects to this, they are perfectly at liberty to write their book taking the same method but seeing it from their stance.

The method I have chosen is as follows; to outline the various forms of truth ranging from mathematics to artistic and on to philosophical and theological, and analyse each book of scripture on that framework. This is done on purpose to achieve a certain degree of objectivity.

The importance of this book lies in this factor; that not every piece of scriptural material is actually of the truth, or spiritually enhancing. If in doubt about this, I strongly suggest that the reader considers my chapter on Mein Kampf (Chapter 4) and Science and Health (Chapter 9). It is so easy for a wrong-headed person to produce a book that has a scriptural appearance and can lead many people astray.

What are the criteria that we should be looking for in a worthwhile piece of scripture? What about God as being the loving Father of all mankind? What about discerning God's ways of speaking to humanity? What about the Messiah? These are the kind of questions that the reader could bear in mind as he reads this book.

The scriptural materials are not in any special order; it was all done at random. But I have tried to choose various types of literature to illustrate the different genres available for conveying the truth. It is the kind of book one can dip into as one's interest moves on.

1

Truth in the telling and imagination

There is a dusty, traffic-ridden street in Central London called Baker Street. It is an unremarkable street by modern standards and may even have been so in late Victorian times. The remarkable thing now is that outside a certain building, number 221, we can often descry a woman in a very attractive crinoline dress or a man in a period policeman's uniform, standing outside as a sort of 'gate-guard' for the intriguing contents of the building, 221b. There is an entire emporium full of 'Holmes-ana' at interesting prices, on the ground floor. Above is an exact replication of Sherlock Holmes' flat, complete with the clutter mentioned in the stories. Attendants will assure you that the main characters, Holmes, Watson and Mrs Hudson, are merely out for the day, probably on some interesting sleuthing – all very realistic and fascinating. There is the need to pinch oneself to recall that Holmes is a literary creation by a certain Arthur Conan Doyle, and never existed in reality. So why is there this establishment in Baker Street now? We can see it on the historical level, in that a group of people went to great lengths to secure the property of 221b Baker Street and transform it into a museum-cum-tourist-trap. This is all very laudable in itself. But there is a deeper level, the level of super-reality, one could call it, in that people love to turn imagination into fact. Do not imagine that this is saying that Sherlock Holmes is a lot of nonsense – very far from it. But it is a genre over and above the literal truth, verging into the realms of mythology. Just how important this has been in succeeding decades can now be briefly indicated.

Conon Doyle actually detested his creation and 'killed off' Holmes at the Reichenbach Falls. This produced an outcry and Holmes mysteriously re-emerged, to the shock of Watson, to continue his sleuthing. But the sleuthing did not cease when Conon Doyle really did come to the end of it; he had, in effect, produced an entirely new genre of literature, the 'who-

1

dunnit', as we see in the works of Dorothy L. Sayer and countless other crime writers and police thrillers, which are eternally popular with the media to this day. It would be tedious to make a list of all the permutations on detection here: *Dixon of Dock Green, Z Cars* and a host of others. Interestingly there are various permutations on Sherlock Holmes himself. As he moved into film and TV productions, we can see all manner of remakes and reinterpretations of the original stories. A long-running recent production with actors Jeremy Brett and Edward Hardwick goes to great lengths to enrich the account with the Victorian costume drama element, and the acting is of the highest order. The penultimate rendition of Holmes, with Benedict Cumberbach, is a way-out interpretation that has little to do with the original stories and is clearly more closely related to another genre, the sci-fi spy thriller idea. The latest version, which appeared on Boxing Day 2015, reverts more to the Victorian costume drama mode with the snobbery element of the big country house. What this all indicates is the hold that Sherlock Holmes has on the popular imagination. Why is this? The answer lies surely as follows: the great detective, with all his idiosyncrasies, flights of genius, and personality disorders, resonates with something deep in human nature. As an interesting side-remark to this, when the Brett-Hardwick series was being produced, someone had an original text on the set and when a 'mistake' cropped up, it was 'corrected' from the original. Literalism on a level above the purely literary; a latter day form of fundamentalism!

The same tendency can be detected in the post-war era with the prevalence of the soap opera. The classic, everlasting one, the *Archers*, has set the genre on a firm basis, and its imitators, *Coronation Street*, *Neighbours*, *Home and Away* and a host of others, are a firmly established feature of modern life. People become well and truly hooked on them. It is interesting that a character like Dan Archer came to command an authenticity and veracity well above the other characters; an influence narrowly accrued by Phil Archer. The same tendency is seen with people like Harold Bishop and many others. People find it difficult to remember that this is all fictional, a script written by a team of writers who have to scratch their heads to bring up new ideas, and sometimes have to rehash old ideas. Many people take the drama quite literally, and send in flowers when there is a funeral. The drama is quite often enhanced by an iconic background: *Home and Away* is set on a shop by the beach in Australia. *Heartbeat* is set in the North Yorkshire Moors with steam trains passing through and the occasional crisis on Whitby harbour. It is another example of how a successful literary invention can become the literal truth for many people. It takes an effort of mind to stand back from it and see the techniques of the scriptwriter at work. Some people do not make the effort. And yet, the success of such material indicates that something in it resonates with certain needs in human nature.

It contains a deeper truth even if the story line is a complete concoction, or even complete nonsense.

It is symptomatic of us that we need to find the truth and yet easily allow ourselves to be led away from the truth. A glance at a public library used to have 'fiction' and 'non-fiction' clearly indicated. Fiction usually meant novels of all kinds including detection thrillers. But although the story line might have been a pure invention on the part of someone like Sexton Blake, as we have seen, there almost always was an element of truth in it, just enough to make it fascinating, challenging and credible. So, for instance, with Holmes we see a heightened level of detection methods before the advent of fingerprinting; Holmes' methods are now standard practice with the CID.

Non-fiction usually meant anything scientific, mathematical, historical, geographical and plain factual. It is worth noting that many of the statements offered to us as 'facts' often turn out to be somewhat less than the truth. Historical material, as we know, is usually written by the winners and we now see other slants emerging that give us a modified view of the losers, such as Richard III. One might suppose that scientific material could be taken as unassailable fact; many people do take scientific findings at face value. Even so we know that the scientists are constantly changing their minds as new discoveries turn up; this applies especially to astrophysics. What about mathematics – straightforward enough? The basics are fair enough, but just look at how high-flown and speculative higher maths have become in recent years. The truth of the matter is that the difference between fiction and non-fiction is not as clear-cut as many would suppose. With every discipline and system of thought there is always the element of distortion; the human mind generally has some sort of primary agenda – whether political, religious or social – and sometimes a secondary or tertiary agenda. Such assumptions usually colour the way we see things. It is a fact of life, unavoidable but real enough.

Areas of knowledge or truth

It is clear that not all knowledge occurs on the same level or in the same dimension. There are various areas that we can assess. Each area has its notable features but they are all subject to the same human impulses and distortions. Everyone has an axe to grind, otherwise we would not put pen to paper. The honest bit comes in realising and admitting to one's bias.

Mathematical Truth

Everyone knows it is possible to score ten out of ten in a maths exam; it is also possible to score nil. But to a large extent, maths is an exact area of truth; when ten plus ten has to make twenty, there is very little room for discussion about it. Even so, the more complicated maths becomes, the more room there is for discussion. To take two examples: the area known as probability, in which we can calculate the chances of such and such an event occurring, is a complete invention. There is no way it can be paraded off as fact, and yet people quote its results as if it is factual. The discipline known as statistics is another highly developed area with all manner of elaborate techniques, but this is just as open to human manipulation as anything else. The old saying is 'there are lies, damned lies, and statistics'. It is very much open to politicians and other campaigners to manipulate statistics to support their theories. A third area, which involves calculating the possibility of 'life' on other, far-away planets, goes in for amazingly complicated equations with all kinds of strange symbols. This is supposed to convince us that there must be little green men tucked away somewhere amongst the stars; it is pure speculation! Even with something as precise as mathematics, there is room for exaggeration, understatement, and colouration of the truth.

Scientific truth

The three main areas, Chemistry, Biology and Physics, though distinct, are nevertheless interrelated and for many are seen as factual and not really open to opinion. This too is a fallacy. As science moves on, not consistently over the many areas available for research, we find constant changes of mind and disagreements amongst what are claimed to be the 'experts'. So, for instance, forensic science is now being given vast amounts of emphasis, while other possibilities are relatively under-researched. It is interesting to hear about 'facts' being discovered about astrophysics. There is a sort of dogmatism going on, shored up with a whole list of gratuitous assumptions, and decorated with sentimental notions of life on other planets; this is all pure speculation and guesswork, and some would say this is not science at all. No one knows for sure what is going on in deep space; at least Patrick Moore was honest enough to tell us that. It is one thing to provide a description of something that is observable; another thing to analyse and explain its workings; another thing to assess it significance and yet a further step to draw moral conclusions from it. A prime example of this would concern 'evolution'. Just because we think we see evolution happening in today's world –for instance, in the Galapagos Islands – that does not have to mean it is a general rule for all of life in all parts of the world, still less, what may or may not have happened millions of years ago. Analysing and explaining its workings is dependent on the truth of the first proposition.

4

Assessing its significance can only work if we can see how it works. To draw moral conclusions from it, assuming it to be true, has resulted in all kinds of cruelties and crazy social ideas. Many people may not be aware that the biological speculators have about half-a-dozen different versions of the theory of evolution, and there is nothing totally certain or proven about it at all. And yet, people talk about it as if it were an unassailable fact!

Historical truth

People are fascinated by the processes of history, and rightly so. It is not possible to understand our present circumstances without a certain amount of information from the past. Often we do not have sufficiently full information to see things in a balanced manner. The past is not just the recent events but matters going back well into pre-history. The influence of ancient Egypt, Israel, Greece, Rome and many others is still with us, regardless of our feelings on the subject. But history is always seen through the colouration of one's spectacles. Facts become blurred with sentimentality and sometimes distaste. A simple example of this would be one's view of the late mediaeval period, a time which has been romanticised and idealised, especially in the late 19th century, but less so in recent times. Tales of Robin Hood, King Arthur and Richard the Lionheart, plus rose-coloured notions about the church before the Reformation, have all given a certain view of that period. It really may have been quite different. And there are certain types of churchmanship, etiquette and attitudes to warfare that are coloured by this view. Taking this into account, it is not easy to isolate what might be termed a 'fact' of history; still less to assess it significance, and even less to assess its significance for us now. One simple example is as follows: FACT: Britain and France declared war on Germany in September 1939. However, this easily conceals the truth that the Second World War had in fact begun much earlier, with the Japanese expansion in the Far East. Also, many countries were involved with German expansion during the late 1930's. Many countries reckon their war as starting in 1940, 1941 and even later and so the significance of 1939 needs comment. Matters had come to a crisis over the invasion of Poland; the British and French had drawn a line in the sand by guaranteeing the state of Poland, but what was the point of doing that? There had to be a 'last straw', otherwise Germany would have gone on unchecked, invading one country after another as the fancy took them. The underlying substratum of this was the highly secret factor that Germany was believed to be developing nuclear power, which could have led to them having an atom bomb. Very few people in the West knew about this, but it explains the urgency to provide a check on German ambitions in 1939, and also, later, the importance of 'Germany first' when

5

the Americans eventually entered the war. History is a pattern of the obvious (facts), interpretation of facts, and often the underlying assumptions in the situation. The significance for us today is that, if Germany had not been checked in 1939-40, the whole world might now be dominated by a ruthless atomic power with no way of countering it. Historical truth is always a matter of debate, emotion and lack of information. The truth is almost always 'plasticined' into serving someone's political agenda.

Geographical truth

If history is about chaps then geography is about maps, so the adage goes. One might think that a map is a straightforward depiction of features on the ground. For the most part, this is true, except that the full truth has to take a back seat in most maps. Have you ever seen a map that includes every feature in a given area? This is impossible, as it would become unreadable and meaningless. Most maps centre on one or a few aspects of a given area and omit anything that is thought to be of less relevance. So for instance, a motorist map (Michelin) will have much detail about roads and certain touristic features, but will be sketchy about other matters. There are many kinds of map: touristic, historical, transport, relief, meteorological, oceanographic and many others. In addition to this there is the matter of depicting a sphere on a flat piece of paper. So, for instance, the Mercator projection of the world is very largely misleading, as the land areas towards the poles are exaggerated. Greenland and Russia appear massive in relation to places on the Equator. There is always the element of interpretation; bare facts can be meaningless, if not misleading.

Linguistic truth

Everyone knows that translation from one language to another is seldom as straightforward as one would hope. The truth is that every language has as its background an entire culture, which is determined by the climate, history and political stance of the people. Each language has its own collection of pejorative words. A simple word-for-word translation almost always loses the flavouring and unspoken assumptions behind such words. We all know what a literal translation sounds like: it is stilted and clumsy, sounding most uncomfortable. At the other extreme is a paraphrase. This will sound natural and like an original text, but may not be quite what the original writer intended. A fair and working translation is usually a compromise between exactitude and interpretation. An important example relevant to theology and philosophy is the Hebrew word *hesed*, usually translated as 'love'. It is the word for God's full and undying loving commitment to his people, the Israelites, in the context of the covenant. It does not mean some sort of passing fancy, or half-baked liking, and still less an erotic attachment. H*esed* is the crucial word for God's deep caring for his people despite all their failings and stupidities. Moving into Greek, *agape* carries something of this meaning, but since Greek culture never had any notion of a covenant of love between the One God and his chosen people, the translation loses something of the implications inherent in *hesed*. Taking it into English, the King James Bible rendered it as CHARITY – what does that imply for us today? Christian Aid, Oxfam, Save the Children? To recover the deep resonance of such words as *hesed* we need to study the Hebrew (and the Greek) and find words or phrases that give a more accurate idea of what is the original intention of the writers.

Translation is always a matter of how the translator approaches it. Here are two versions of the opening verses of the Bhagavad Gita (Chapter 9):

'On the field of truth, on the battle-field of life, what came to pass, Sanjaya, when my sons and their warriors faced those of my brother Pandu?'

'O Sanjaya, tell me what happened at Kurukshetra, the field of dharma, where my family and the Pandavas gathered to fight.'

Both of these are taken from the Sanskrit in the same place, but we can see how differently they can be rendered, as they give rather a different impression. This can be forgiven, as each translator is trying to make it what he thinks is intelligible to an English reader. But there are all kinds of background cultural and theological assumptions in this, which will be explored in Chapter 9.

What is more a matter of contention is the deliberate slanting of a translation to favour a certain theological stance. So for instance a comparison of a Roman Catholic Bible with a Protestant one can reveal some interesting differences which are symptomatic of disagreements over doctrine. Here are two versions of Romans 4:9:

'We say that faith was reckoned to Abraham as righteousness.'

'We said of Abraham that his faith was reckoned to him as uprightness.'

The first quotation is from the RSV (Protestant) Bible and the second one from the Jerusalem Bible (Roman Catholic). There is a difference of opinion over the rendering of 'righteousness'– which in the Greek is *dikaiosune* – a difference that appears in other places in *Romans*. The way it is translated gives a slightly different impression and is parented by dogmas: the Protestants with the emphasis on justification by faith; the Roman Catholics with their emphasis on justification by works.

Another example, which is even more open to contention, is the difference between these two:

'In the beginning was the Word, and the Word was with God and the Word was a God (or 'divine')' (as seen in the footnote).

'In the beginning was the Word, and the Word was with God, and the Word was God.'

The first of these two versions of *John 1:1* is taken from the Jehovah's Witnesses Bible, and the second one is from the RSV Protestant Bible. It all looks reasonable enough until we come to the last four words, which give a noticeably different impression, parented by dogmas. The original Greek for this is *Theos en ho Loyos* (all in capital letters originally). Literally this would be 'God was the Word'. We can leave it to the reader to assess the fairness of these two translations.

Linguistic truth is always open to some kind of background agenda.

Artistic truth

There are many areas of artistry: paintings, sculpture, dance, drama, music and many combinations of these basics. It is an area where interpretation can have much more freedom and legitimacy. It is one thing to do the steps of a dance correctly, and play the music from the score accurately, or to use the right techniques for an oil painting. The mechanics of it are one thing;, the interpretation is quite another. A simple example would be a piece of music, regardless of its technical difficulty can be played absolutely flat by a 'note-producer', but it can be given meaning and interpretation by a gifted musician. Moreover, different interpretations can be given to the piece by the subtle use of phrasing, dynamics and graduation of tempo. Truth is not so much in the actual notes, but in the meaning it conveys to the human soul. The science of vibration and the mathematics of score-writing all play their part, but the reality is on a different level, that of speaking deeper truth to the hearer and the performer. Another example could be taken from the brilliant sculpture of ancient Egypt. In the stylised conception of the New Kingdom, the Pharaoh has an artificial beard. Did they really look like that? The beard was symbolic of divinity and doubtless all the other features such as broad shoulders and enlarged stomachs conveyed something to the Egyptians of that day. Pharaoh is depicted as treading down his enemies and wielding a mace to kill them. Did this actually happen in reality? In a sense, yes, but in literal historical terms he may never have actually killed anyone, personally. It is all about conveying meaning and political agenda. Art, in its various forms, can be a most powerful conveyer of truth to the human soul.

Unfortunately, as we review various scriptural materials, the artistic element in them is very largely understated. It is one thing to discuss the Psalms, but we do not know how they were rendered with music (the same goes for the Zoroastrian material in Chapter 5), yet we know that every religion, and the scriptures that go with them, have had their own art forms as a cultural backdrop.

Literary truth

This is not very different from artistic truth and as far as drama is concerned, it is virtually the same thing. Literature mainly concerns poetry, prose and drama. There is much scope here for conveying truth on a dimension different from science and mathematics, but also more room for divergent opinions. With prose, we see the emergence of the 'novel' in modern times. Are we to assume there was no such thing as a novel in ancient times, that the medium never appears in scriptural material? It is worth considering. But just because a novel is an invention, does not mean it is rubbish. Taking an example from Dickens, the novel *Little Dorrit* is somewhat restrained with regard to Dickens' normal personality exaggeration, and yet the book is so revealing of human nature. In short, William Dorritt was trapped in the Marshalsee debtors' prison and spent his life cadging off anyone who took pity on him. His little daughter idolised him. The second half of the book is a complete about-face, for a kind man went to a lot of trouble to trace William's hidden fortune and so release him from prison and leave him with massive riches. William Dorritt did a complete change of personality; he did not wish to acknowledge anyone who had helped him before, spent money like water, patronised everyone and generally overdid it. His little daughter continued to idolise him. The story is of course a concoction; nevertheless, the debtors' prison with no hope of release was a sad fact of life then. Also, the effect on people's personalities is so true to human nature. The story is real in a deeper sense than just trying to accept it as the literal truth. Any successful novelist will be able to make his account resonate with the realities of human nature. With poetry, we see the free use of figurative language in all its wide applications and permutations. Most of this use of metaphor began its life in ancient Greece and also the poetry of ancient Israel. It is important to remember that the Bible fluctuates from prose to poetry without any warning. A modern translation normally indicates the change, but, as with all poetry, it is foolish to take it as purely literal. Figurative language can convey so much to the human soul. The truth is that we need something on a higher dimension than just plain prose, to lift us into new realities.

Philosophical truth

We are all philosophers in a way; some more than others, but the meaning of life and the basics of existence are questions that any normal, pensive person will engage in somewhere along the line. We think of Plato and others in ancient Greece and yet philosophy can be traced back as far as recorded material can be found (see Chapter 22: Inanna). It is here that the deep truths of life can be discussed but seldom settled to widespread agreement. Philosophy is a gift for those with some sort of political agenda; in fact most political dogmas have attempted to justify themselves by reference to one philosophy or another. Paradoxically sometimes a philosopher will try to support his ideas by adherence to what might seem like a good idea coming from science. There is an element of chicken-and-egg in this, but, whoever is philosophising, has to use human language to express his ideas. There is the literal level where factual description is used to base their ideas. There is the metaphoric level, where interpretation of the world and the universe can only be done with the use of non-literal language. Sometimes a philosopher has to invent new words, and often these new words are not properly understood by others. They have to use language and with that there is always the distortion between hearing and comprehension. Some philosophers are so high-flown that most people cannot understand it. In many ways, philosophy is a secularised attempt at discussing the deep matters of creation and human nature; this does not always work, as theological language and assumptions often find their way into the argument.

We shall find, when reviewing many scriptural texts, that philosophy and theology are so heavily intertwined that it is artificial to try to separate the two modes of truth.

Mythological truth

It is important here to accept that 'mythology' does not mean 'falsehood'. 'Myth' in popular parlance now means 'lie' or 'misapprehension', but this is a misuse of the word. Every culture, ancient or modern, has as its basic assumption, some kind of mythology; an attempt at explaining our origins in the remote past, our circumstances now and even more importantly, our destiny in the future. This is not to say that any given mythology is right or wrong; basically we do not know where we came from or where we are going. But the human mind cannot desist from speculating on these matters. One could say that this is philosophy, however, the difference is that mythology almost always employs high-flown metaphor, poetry and appeals to the emotion, which philosophy ought in theory to avoid. Clearly mythology is heavily influenced by the twists and turns of history; paradoxically, the opposite can happen when mythology can influence the course of events in the present. A simple example of this would be that 120 years ago it was the common assumption, under the influence of 'evolution', that we were gently sliding into a silver-lining type age of peace and wealth and that no one could be so stupid as to spoil this inevitable trend. Two World Wars, culminating in the first use of atomic weapons, has forced us all to rethink and re-evaluate ourselves and to be much more wary about the future. No longer is it an inevitable progress towards some sort of Utopia. But the basic motives that sent the warring nations on their course were mythological, some sort of assumption about racial superiority, territory and magnificent destiny (Chapter 4: *Mein Kampf*) – another chicken-and-egg situation. Mythology is heavily interwoven with our everyday thinking regardless of our religious, political or social stance. As to the truth of these assumptions, who knows? We love to believe what we like the sound of. It is one thing for the scientists to tell us that we all evolved from amoeba (true or false; who knows?) but the human mind is not satisfied with the purely descriptive aspect; we have to assure ourselves that this all means something, not just in the past but pointing to the future as well. This is why mythology and eschatology act as counterparts to one another and can be subsumed under the same title together. The underlying truth in all this is not to do with the facts (?) of creation and destruction; the truth is that mythology tells us all about ourselves, the basics in human nature, our aspirations, our self-evaluation, our fears. In many respects, these factors are the same, the world over.

Mythology works on a completely different level from such matters as mathematics, history and geography. However, so often mythology becomes entangled with scientific speculation. Evolution is a case in point, where a biological theory (true or false, we do not know) has become the myth of the modern age, the be-all and end-all of people's understanding of life.

Theological truth

This area of knowledge is closely related to both philosophy and mythology and is often intertwined with them. In our reviewing of sacred literature, this will be seen repeatedly, and again it is often artificial

11

to attempt to distinguish the one from the other. The difference, with theology is as follows: there is, always has been and always will be some kind of awareness of another world of divinity, or of the spirit, which is not normally obvious from day to day, but is at times to certain people. It is also seen as the end destination when one's earthly life terminates. All manner of modes have been used to express this awareness but the truth is that no one really knows what the next world consists of. Speculation is rife; certainty is somewhat meagre. Theology also involves an understanding of divinity in the sense of God or gods, or spiritual beings. Every culture on earth has, as an accompaniment to its mythology, a system of deity, and that includes the modern secularist systems, communism and Fascism. Polytheism, henotheism, monotheism and even atheism are the commonest patterns, and some of them are interestingly intertwined. Theology is an area where literal and non-literal language are used freely and it is not always obvious which is which in any given context. High-flown metaphor can often be found adjacent to a plain descriptive account, as we see in the Bible repeatedly. Theological truths are a gift for political campaigners and even more so for religious campaigners. But the underlying truth is that the human mind has a deep need for an understanding of divinity; trying to do without it in recent times has been seen not to work. We have seen atheistic states trying to rub out belief; the result has been that someone or something else has had to be promoted to deity. Divinity reasserts itself; theology will not go away.

Finding the truth

From this review of various levels of truth, it can be seen that the *truth* is not just a simple matter of stating the obvious. There is always more to it than what meets the eye. One could conclude, despairingly, that it is impossible to find the pure, unadulterated truth. Even with something as factual and descriptive as mathematics and science, there is always the element of human distortion and egotistic interpretation. The whole thing becomes increasingly opinionated as we move into literature, mythology, art forms, philosophy and theology, but the awareness and need for something that can be termed 'the ultimate truth' is still present in people's minds, just as the awareness of God is a reality. People need to know that truth does exist somewhere; after all, that is what philosophy is all about. Any philosopher who is not seeking the truth is no philosopher. A reference to Job may serve as a useful starting point. *Job 28:12*:

> 'But where shall wisdom be found? And where is the place of discernment (understanding)'.

The philosopher, probably Solomon in this case, has to admit that 'man does not know the way of it'. How true! It is not found in the land of the living. Wisdom is hidden from the eyes of all living (verse 21). Even so, it is highly prized, but beyond price in earthly terms of wealth. No money can buy it, so how or where do we find it? The answer comes in verse 23:

'God understands the way to it and he knows its place.'

This is saying that the ultimate truth is found with God. In other words, the final truth lies not with facts like mathematics and scientific analyses, nor with figurative language like metaphors and mythological speculations. The truth lies in a person, a living spirit. In other words, theology is the true and final avenue for discovering the deep realities of life and death.

This does not mean to say that all other areas of knowledge are wrong, far from it. They all have their elements of truth expressed in their own particular modes, but theology relates to all of these and they are all shot through with theological fundamentals.

One might ask how an atheist would relate to these remarks. After all, if God is the final source of truth, the denial of God might logically entail the denial of the ultimate truth. The fact remains that the human mind has a need not just to describe the world around it, but to have an understanding of it and find some sort of significance. We have yet to see a scientist who confined himself purely and simply to the descriptive level, as they always begin to see and interpret what they see, and then give it some sort of significance, followed by various bits of speculation. A genuine, full-blown atheist is a very rare thing, possibly non-existent. How many people can honestly say they can see absolutely no meaning or destiny in life? Who can say that truth, if it exists, does not matter, and that life is purely physical, mechanical and senseless? Almost everyone sees life in some kind of interpretation and deeper meaning. But as Job points out, that meaning is hidden from our eyes and lives with the ultimate truth, namely God.

The Bible has many obvious and subtle ways of answering its own questions. This is the whole point of the New Testament coming in to complete matters raised in the Old Testament. On the matter of 'truth' or understanding the ultimate issues of life, it is St John who addresses this matter. To study his *Prologue (1:1-18)* makes one realise that in the phraseology of that day and age, John is giving us the Christian answer to the question of ultimate truth (verse 18):

'No one has ever seen God; the only Son who is in the bosom of the Father, he has made him known.'

If we can see beyond the metaphor in this, what is being said is that the truth, which is hidden from our eyes (in God) has been shown to us in the coming of Jesus of Nazareth. The truth actually came embodied as a human being to live with us (verse 14) and enlighten us all about the ultimate truths of life, death and eternity (verse 9). In John 14:6, Jesus actually claims to be the 'Way, the Truth and the Life; no one comes to the Father but by me.'

Taking this totally at face value, as many do, it seems to be saying that the Christian religion is the only one that is correct. But that is the mistake that many people make, to take Biblical citations purely at the literal level. There is a much deeper element to this. The 'way' that he is talking about is our passage through life, but more than that; it is the way that history has developed through to the present and on into the future, mankind's ultimate destiny. This subsumes all those areas of knowledge as seen as already. This includes the descriptive aspect, the interpretative element and the ultimate meaning of life. The truth, which is so elusive to mankind in spite of all the information and speculation that we have, is now to be seen not in some sort of dogma, system of thought or a useful essay from a philosopher; it is embodied in a real living person; a person who is the embodiment of the ultimate truth. And the life? He is not just talking about human existence, although that is included; he is talking about life on another dimension, a raised life, a product of the Resurrection, which was to come. But it made provision for life in this world and the next, something which is available for us all. Sadly, some people seem to reject it. Access to the ultimate truth is through God's own messiah. The argument can be turned round; if one has found the truth in life, it can only have been found through the medium of the messiah. Whether you know him by name or not, is hardly the point. The truth is not merely a list of facts; it is an understanding of the ultimate issues about life and death. God has provided us with a living channel into his eternity. 'No one comes to the Father but through me,' now makes perfect sense.

St John gives us a full array of metaphors as to the significance of Jesus, but the crucial moment comes with his encounter with Pontius Pilate (John 18:37):

'... for this I came into the world, to bear witness to the truth. Everyone who is of the truth hears my voice.'

The final and crashing irony comes in the next verse: 'Pilate said to him, "What is truth?"'

He was staring straight at the ultimate truth but still had to ask that vital question. It may be that he had a notion of the truth since he tried to have Jesus released; it did not work. This is the question that we all have to ask ourselves, some with a certain degree of success and others less so. The question is unavoidable; the answer is to some extent avoidable, as there is none so blind as those who do not wish to see. But for those who are honest with themselves, the final truths about this world and the next are given to us in the ministry and its completion of Jesus of Nazareth.

Thus it can be seen that St John gives us a thorough-going attempt at answering the problem raised in Job, that of the truth being concealed in God. In a sense, it still is, as none of us can give a definition of God without sliding into some kind of idolatry, and that is some kind of distortion of the truth. Paradoxically, the truths about God are shown to us, in terms of human vocabulary and thought-forms, as much as the human soul can cope with in this life. 'No one has ever seen God' is a massive truth and yet, God is made known to us through his messiah. It is no accident that Jesus is described as the 'Word' (logos) of God. This does not mean that John was a gnostic. 'Logos' was a buzzword at that time, and implied wisdom, understanding, scientific insight and much more; all of this background meaning is lost in an English translation. But the implication is that calling Jesus the 'Word', is that he is the substratum, the underpinning and final definition of all forms of knowledge, expression and human enquiry. Now we can see that theology, an understanding of the divine and of deity, is the unavoidable essence at work in all our forms of knowledge, whether it be mathematical, poetic or whatever.

The issue of 'truth' reverberates through into John's epistle. Truth also involves the issue of untruth; John mentions darkness, lies and deception. Essentially, the truth is not in us (1:8) if we maintain that we have no sin. The vital thing is to admit to sin and gain forgiveness. This applies to all forms of knowledge, whether purely descriptive, or interpretative, since human failings can distort any form of knowledge. But admitting to it clears the way to arriving at a balanced account of any account. John's metaphor for repentance is seen in 5:6 where Jesus, who is the truth, came by water and blood, which speaks of cleansing. The Water is at the Baptism and the Blood (with the water) comes at the Crucifixion, but both of them bring forgiveness. Our distortions of the truth can be corrected and given a proper version. The final truth lies in Jesus; not a theory, a description, a philosophical doctrine or some kind of interpretation. The truth is embodied in a living person.

The scope of this book

Finding the truth has always been an issue with regard to the Bible, especially in this modern climate of ultra criticism and scepticism. It will be interesting and helpful to take a selection from various parts of the Bible and see them in the light of our ten areas of knowledge. It would not be realistic to treat every part of the Bible; a representative selection from each type of book is enough. We will see how the biblical writers try to overcome the element of human distortion, and how they succeed remarkably well. A prime example of this would be the provision of four gospels; four different versions of the same events allow each writer to emphasise his areas of particular interest. This way, the ministry of Jesus comes up three-dimensionally. But the gospels are not the only examples of such juxtaposition.

Going further, we are aware of other scriptural works that make some form of claim to be the truth, in the sense that they lay claim to influence and control the mind of mankind. It will be interesting to see how they cope with our ten areas of knowledge and make comparisons with the biblical material. I have selected portions from a wide range of sacred literature, not in any particular order, but they are fairly heavily cross-referenced. The Analects of Confucius, the Book of Mormon, *Mein Kampf*, the Avestas of Zoroaster, Hindu and Buddhist material; I have tried to give a representative sample from each of the main world religions. The reader can select chapters as according to interest. This does not imply that I find them as spiritually authoritative as the Bible, but the reader must draw his own conclusions. I have tried to be as objective as possible; it is not easy to stand back from one's own cultural and theological assumptions; indeed, why should I? It would be senseless to attempt to think like an Indian, a Chinaman, a Persian etc., when I am not. In the final analysis, I am an Englishman brought up with the assumptions of the Anglican tradition, and I make no apologies for it. Even so, a certain degree of objectivity is possible to achieve. This does not mean that I regard all scriptural material as equally valid. I have to say that the Bible stands head and shoulder above all the rest, for reasons that will become clear as the book proceeds.

But there is plenty of scope for the reader to draw his own conclusions as to the location of the truth.

2

The Maccabees

The first and second books of the Maccabees in the Apocrypha

The Old Testament is largely a connected account of the fortunes of the Israelite peoples from Abraham down to the beginning of the post-exilic world, Ezra, Nehemiah and Esther. After that there is a distinct gap, possibly because nothing significant happened until the arrival of the Greeks under Alexander the Great and his offshoots, the Ptolemies in Egypt, and the Seleucids in Antioch. The situation was more complicated than this, as there were other upstart rulers in Asia Minor and Greece itself, but the main focus of attention concerns Palestine. This is where the account of the Maccabees becomes important, as the antics of the Seleucid King Antiochus 4th Epiphanes cause massive disruption and persecution in the land of Israel. The writers of the two books are notably different: 1 Maccabees is almost certainly someone of the Hasmonean persuasion and was writing just after the High Priest Jonathan's reign[1], before the situation began to deteriorate during the later Hasmonean dynasty. The writer has a great admiration for the Maccabees, especially Judas, seeing them as great champions and martyrs of the faith. He was probably not a Hasidic Jew, but was well supported by this group and they were the precursors of the Pharisees; nevertheless, he was a strict adherent of the Mosaic Law and poured scorn on those who attempted any sort of compromise with Greek culture or religion. He was particularly nasty about 'Quislings', who punctuate the story with all manner of treachery. 2 Maccabees is another writer with a slightly different slant, which we shall review later.

We are of course, seeing the whole turbulent situation through the eyes of a persecuted, fanatical, numerically small race, up against the juggernauts of the Greek world. The only relief for them is when the Greeks decide to fight each other or the Romans decide to poke their noses in. Sympathy for the Jews is engendered when we realise that the Seleucids took advantage of the fact that the Jews would not fight on the Sabbath; this had to change to avoid being destroyed altogether. The writer is also a realist as he realises that the Jews had to have allies in order to survive. He records that on several occasions there were overtures to Rome, Cyprus, Cyrene, and Sparta, to name but a few. One wonders if some of this was a bit of wishful thinking; even so, the alliance with Rome did have the effect of tamping down the ambitions of the Greek kings. We begin with a look at 1 Maccabees.

Mathematical realities in 1 Maccabees

This book is interesting because it is full of accurate dating to the year and the month. The datum point, which must have been a relatively new idea at that time, was supposed to have been the first year of Alexander, but calculating it reveals that the system in use in the Maccabees actually relies on the first year of the Seleucid Empire, namely 312 BC when Seleucus 1st took control in Babylon. Before the idea of having a datum point, years were calculated according to the reigns of the kings, but it was the Greeks who brought in this idea of having a datum point, based on Alexander the Great. In the first chapter of 1 Maccabees, we have an anchorage point:

'Antiochus reigned in the 137th year of the kingdom of the Greeks' (1 Maccabees 1:10[2]).

This system prevailed until the Romans enforced their AUC datum point, which referred to the founding of Rome, when they took over the whole of the Hellenistic orient, shortly after this period. There is no reason to question the veracity of these dates and it makes a fairly concise scheme of this piece of history, probably more so than any other Jewish literature, and indeed of any other culture of that age.

What might be a little suspect is the numbers quoted for the opposing armies. The Jews often have to be content with 3,000 soldiers, but the Greeks almost always have vastly superior forces, including elephants, which were the ancient equivalent of the tank. In spite of this the Maccabees almost always win the day with a slaughter running into thousands. One wonders if there is a certain exaggeration going on. One wonders what the Greek version of these events would have been; they appear not to be on record. The mention of 3,000 soldiers recalls certain places in Joshua, Judges and 1

Samuel[3] where armies of the same strength are quoted; is the writer trying to evoke the glory-days of nascent Israel, when everything was going so well?

Geographical realities

From the geographical point of view, 1 Maccabees is fascinating for its mention of place-names. It reads like a complete touristic map, except that some of the place names are not known for certain now, and others appear in deviant spellings that are almost certainly the result of shaky transliteration from Hebrew (Aramaic) into Greek. The writer has to use the Hellenised versions of place names so that his readers, who were Greek speaking, would know what they were. But the Jews were active from Gaza up to Antioch and out into the desert to Nabatea – is this another exaggeration? We can see it as another attempt to recall the glory-days of Solomon, whose kingdom was so extensive. When Judas' army comes up to a certain city in Gilead, he asks permission to pass through; this is refused, with the result that he smashes the place to pieces. This again recalls the early chapters of Deuteronomy when Moses asked for passage through the desert kingdoms.[4] The native kingdoms in these areas may have regarded the Jews as nothing but trouble, and were glad that the Seleucid kings were trying to get them under control. It would not have been easy to produce a unified Seleucid empire with so many tiny fiefdoms with their different customs in that area.

Historical realities

From the point of view of History, 1 Maccabees is very important, even if it is written with a certain slant. Looking at it dispassionately, which is not easy, we marvel at how many times the Greek kings attempted to invade Israel and were fought off with massive losses. Surely they should have learnt their lesson? But there are two substrata at work here. Firstly, Antiochus 4th was trying to bring unity and stability to his empire (1Maccabees 1:41). This was not an easy task, for in contrast with the Ptolemies in Egypt; the Seleucids had a chronically unstable monarchy with all manner of bogus claimants to the throne, plus a vast territory with all manner of different peoples to control. That would entail one system and one religion for all his subjects; the answer was to proclaim himself as 'god'. While some of his subjects might think of that as rather amusing, and others thought it only natural for a king to dub himself as divine, others, namely the Jews, objected violently. The second substratum, not mentioned in the account, but real enough, was as follows. There were, it would seem, two main sources of gold in that region: south of Egypt and at Sardis in Ionia. Up until the battle of Magnesia in 190 BC the Seleucids would have had access to the Sardis gold deposits, but when the Romans claimed that area, they lost the gold. The result was that the Seleucid Empire became progressively short of money; this explains why they were so keen to invade Egypt, and of course, the Jews were in the way. Now we can see the reason for Antiochus' adventures; he was commandeering gold from wherever he could steal it.

In addition to this, there was the policy of Hellenisation. This entailed not just the introduction of Greek gods, but also Greek customs. Such things as circumcision were not politically acceptable. Sports, gymnasia, hippodromes and theatres were socially acceptable. Sport had to be undertaken in the nude; the Greek word *gymnos* means 'naked', hence gymnasium. For the Jews all this was difficult, especially if one had been circumcised. Probably many of the moderate Jews could see no objection to some of this. Some of them may have felt that some sort of compromise at the Temple could be tolerated up to a point; after all, in Samaria (Sebaste) the Temple was dedicated to Zeus[5] and YHWH, which implied that it was one and the same God. We learn that the altar in the Jerusalem Temple had some sort of pagan attachment for some sort of sacrificial act. But the last straw came when Antiochus forced pigs to be sacrificed on God's altar, a deliberate insult to defile the sanctuary. This became known as the Abomination of Desolation, a duty to mention in any crisis material of the time, including the Gospels. Related to this outrage is the presence of the fortress, the Akra, in the heart of Jerusalem, overlooking the Temple. It injures the Jewish heart to have a castle full of heathen troops in the heart of their holy city. It is established in the first chapter and goes on with various vicissitudes to the last chapter, an ongoing irritation and embarrassment. If the Maccabees were so successful in routing the enemy in the countryside, why could they not clear out the heathen presence from the centre of Jerusalem? However, the matter is resolved by the end of the book.

Theological matters

1 Maccabees is important for three crucial matters stemming from Jewish tradition. Firstly there is the matter of covenant. The unspoken thought is that the Jews are the people of the covenant of Sinai, and that that covenant must not be broken as it was in the years leading up to the Exile. They did not want another Exile. The ones who go and make a covenant with the heathen are termed 'wicked men' and 'sold to do mischief'. It is more obviously stated that if one is faithful to God, it will bring its own rewards; this is the main thrust of the Mosaic covenant (1 Maccabees 2:52-60). So we see Judas and his brothers pray fervently before battle and this is rewarded

by victory. Incidentally this illustrates the importance of prayer. In contrast, time and again, the Greeks, especially the Seleucids, are recorded as devious, treacherous and happy to break a solemn promise. The Maccabees soon learn to cope with the flattery, gifts and inducements coming from Antioch; just ignore them as total falsehood. More than once the brothers of Hashmon are lured into a trap and assassinated. The Jews are the ones who stick by their word.

Secondly, there is the issue of the Temple and the City of David. This implies another covenant, that of David, which implied that Jerusalem was inviolate, or should be. The defilement of the Temple registered a deep shock to the Jewish people. We notice, however, that by the end of the book, the matter is resolved, with the Greek king withdrawing his claim on the city and the high priest cleansing the sanctuary. In other words, the 'goodies' won and the 'baddies' had to admit defeat. This is as near to mythology as we come in 1 Maccabees; that right always prevails over wrong.

Thirdly, there is the substratum of the importance of prophecy. Three times it is mentioned that a prophet is expected to come and give guidance over procedural matters. It was a time when military leadership was strong and successful, followed by spiritual leadership, as Jonathan becomes the High Priest with the sponsorship of the pagan King. But prophetic inspiration is missing and very much needed. The writer is harking back to the times of the great prophets of old, like Moses, Samuel, and Elijah, who gave definitive guidelines from God and the future was secure in their hands. When we read the Book of Kings (Chapter 18), we see that prophecy and fulfilment was a very important factor in the faith of Israel; there is much expectation in the Maccabees but only partial fulfilment. The unspoken element obvious to anyone who knew the Hebrew scriptures was that the prophecies of Daniel were coming to reality. The phrase the 'Abomination of Desolation' is clearly borrowed from Daniel and applied to the defilement of the Temple in 167 BC. The pattern of history through the Greek kings was seen closely to match Daniel's outline of the future[6]. It matches so well that scholars in the twentieth century have concluded that Daniel was written after these events and was just describing the past. Although it does not say as much in the Maccabees, there were many at that time who thought that John Hyrcanus was actually the Messiah; events were later to show this as a pre-emptive notion.

But as with most human affairs, in the end it all comes down to money in the final analysis. We see the Maccabees handing over lavish gifts of gold and silver to various kings, including the Romans. But we are left with the original question of why Antiochus 4th burst into the Temple and stole anything he could lay his hands on. The Jerusalem Temple was not the only one he ransacked: there was one in Persia, Elymais (1 Maccabees 6:1), which he thought held a lot of treasure. In the ancient world, violating a temple was seen as really shocking, even if one had promoted oneself to deity. The answer may lie in a little admission that Jonathan had not being paying his taxes:

> 1 Maccabees 13-15: '… for it is for money that he is owing to the king's treasure…'

If that had been going on through that period, failure to pay tribute money to Antioch, which could easily explain why the Greeks persisted in invading Israel. We can see it from what might be the Greek point of view; that the Jews were just tax-dodgers. We can also see it from the Jewish point of view; that the Greeks were just a rabble of worthless idiots who did not deserve to be paid. History is written by the winners; how true in this case!

Literary aspects of 1 Maccabees

As literature, this material does not stand out as anything remarkable. It is all in prose derived from the Greek original. Clearly, it is an attempt at continuing the Deuteronomic history as seen from Joshua down to the Exile, recalling the glory days when the Israelites triumphed:

> 'Call to remembrance what acts our fathers did in their time…' 1 Maccabees 2:51.

It then lists some of the champions of the faith in an abbreviated form, not unlike the famous passage in Ecclesiasticus (Chapter 15).

Although most of the book is a blow-by-blow account of the battles with the Seleucids, the writer occasionally relapses into a bit of sentimentality:

> 'So the princes and elders mourned, the virgins and young men were made feeble, and the beauty of women was changed.' 1 Maccabees 1:26.

Philosophical aspects.

Much of this is included in the theology. But the main offspin from the covenant motif is that the Jews and the Romans came to an agreement. It is heavily emphasised that going back on one's agreement is wrong; treachery is just about the worst thing one can do. That of course, was the normal procedure amongst the Greeks. The writer is full of admiration for the Romans, on account of their success in war but also their method of government, which of course at that stage was the Republic. That would have tied in with the Jewish policy of not having a king. This favourable attitude towards Rome indicates that the book was written before the Roman invasion under Pompey in 63 BC.

2 Maccabees; a slightly different version of the same events.

The writer of 2 Maccabees is clearly a different person with a different style of writing, which indicates a Hellenistic turn of phrase, and a certain amount of different emphasis. His views are not completely different from 1 Maccabees, but different enough to throw a slightly different light on events and their significance. There is some indication that he may have been a Greek sympathetic to the Jews, but also with a certain amount of respect for the Seleucid kings. The scope of the account is much less than 1 Maccabees, starting with the reign of Demetrius. This would be Demetrius 2nd (145-139 BC), Nicator, but harking back to Antiochus 4th[7], and finishing before the death of Judas Maccabeus. The history is far less detailed and sometimes a little inconsistent. He admits to conflating five different written sources, none of which seems to be 1 Maccabees. The book may have been written some time later than the events it describes, which is in contrast to 1 Maccabees. It takes the form of a letter from Jerusalem to the Jews in Egypt, with the purpose of explaining and recommending the feast of Nicanor's Day, 13th Adar (December). The death of Nicanor is mentioned in 1 Maccabees but there is no indication of a feast day being inaugurated to celebrate this victory.

He feels it necessary to mention that the Jews spoke in their own language, which would have been Aramaic, and so this indicates that he was Greek-speaking. He also mentions Greek months; for instance, Xanthicus[8].

Mathematical and geographical issues

There is much less emphasis on dates, even if he is using the same system as 1 Maccabees. Also the numbers involved in the armies are far less heavily emphasised. Also the amounts of money quoted are present but not such a major feature as in 1 Maccabees. The geographical aspect of things is also less precise. Many place names are different and the movement of armies about the country is rather more vague. There is the feeling that the whole account has undergone a degree of précising. This is because the writer's interest is focussed elsewhere, primarily to advocate Nicanor's day.

Historical realities

2 Maccabees is also important for its historical information, even if it is briefer. Several situations in 1 Maccabees, which seem a little strange, are seen in a different light. There is the occasional mention of treachery and trickery, but the main traitors are the 'Quislings' who are jockeying for the post of High Priest; namely, Menelaus and Alcimus. They seem to sink to any trick, bribery and storytelling to gain a mandate from the Seleucid king. Usually their schemes come adrift. The exploits of Antiochus 4th are slightly differently reported. His descent upon Jerusalem is explained as him having heard a rumour that the Jews had revolted, which is untrue. He was let into the Temple by Menelaus whereupon the plundering began. He can hardly have taken all the treasure, as the plundering occurs on other occasions. This is almost but not quite an apology for Antiochus' behaviour. However, he is not to be forgiven for his high-handed behaviour and self-promotion to deity. Later in the book, after he had attacked another temple in Persia, he contracted a frightful illness in his stomach. He gave up the idea of punishing the Jews and gave them freedom and promotion. In spite of being 'converted' to Judaism, he died in agony. This is seen as God smiting him. One wonders what really happened; it is recorded rather less dramatically and painfully in 1 Maccabees 6. 2 Maccabees is happy to relate that the next king, Antiochus 5th Eupater wanted peace with the Jews; sadly, he poisoned himself (or so it is alleged). Again, this is a bit different in 1 Maccabees. The next king, Demetrius, also wanted peace but instructed his envoy, Nicanor, to strike up a friendship with Judas and then arrest him, on the assumption that that will insure peace. Also we have the impression that although the kings wanted to settle matters peacefully with the Jews, some of the local governors and Quislings were doing the opposite, stirring up trouble on purpose. In general terms, the Seleucid kings are seen in a slightly more favourable light.

Another aspect of the matter is that Nicanor has a nasty plan to sell Jews off to Rome to gain tribute money. This is more indirect evidence that at that stage, the Seleucid kingdom was desperately short of cash, and since the Jews had not being paying their taxes, it would balance things up if they were sold as slaves. It also goes a long way to explaining the raids on temples. In those days, a temple would have been seen as not just inviolate but also as the main repository for people's savings and for social welfare as admitted in 2 Maccabees 3:4. It was rather like the Bank of England combined with the dole office. Violating a temple was seen as really atrocious. Although the defilement of the Temple and its cleansing by Judas is mentioned, there is no specific mention of the 'Abomination of Desolation' which caused so much offence. There is also in general terms far less emphasis on prophecy. The emphasis falls far more heavily on the enormity of raiding the Temple and also the atrocities committed in trying to force ordinary people to give up their religion.

Mythology in 2 Maccabees

In contrast to 1 Maccabees, 2 Maccabees gives a fair amount of mythology that enhances the bare historical account. In so many situations, God is seen to be supporting his true followers with apparitions, miracles and claimed wonders from the past. Moses, Solomon, Nehemiah and Jonathan all had an Elijah-type experience as fire spontaneously came from heaven to start the sacrifice. There is also included a claim that the priests at the Exile took fire from the altar and hid it in a pit so that it could be used to start the sacrifices again in the new Temple. When Nehemiah came he found only water in the pit; nevertheless he sprinkled the water on the altar and the miracle occurred just the same. What this is saying, in mythological terms, is that the continuity of the faith from Moses through the first Temple to the second and then the third (with Judas) is real and valid. Judas and Jonathan were standing firmly in the tradition going back to Moses and Elijah that justified the cleansing and the fresh start given by the Maccabees.

On three occasions an apparition of men on horseback appear at the crucial moment to avert disaster. The most dramatic of these is when Heliodorus tries to raid the Temple but is terrified by the vision. He collapses unconscious, and is only revived by the kindness of Onias the High Priest. This is dubbed as a miracle. None of this is mentioned in 1 Maccabees. In various ways 2 Maccabees is more spiritual and symbolic. Almost at the end, Jeremiah appears in a dream, giving a sword to Judas. Not only does this indicate the veneration given to Jeremiah, but it also underscores the legitimacy of Onias as the High Priest, having been displaced by frauds. Jeremiah also appears near the beginning, as the one who hid the ark, the tabernacle and the altar of incense in a cave to avoid them being captured by (presumably) Nebuchadrezzar. Much of this may seem fanciful on a casual reading; however it tells us something of the importance of Jeremiah by this time and more emphatically the need for prophetic guidance which is sadly lacking.

Literary worth

As a piece of literature, 2 Maccabees is more successful. It is not purely and simply a bald account of military victories. It is structured; Jeremiah is referred to at the start and the finish. The implication in that is that the prophets of old are framing the whole course of events. The story comes to a crisis, as Nicanor who sets out to deceive Judas, comes to grief. The chief traitor becomes the subject of a new festival. Also on several occasions, wrong does receive poetic justice, most notably when Antiochus falls ill and dies in agony; a requital for the way he had tortured innocent women and children. 2 Maccabees has a sense of climax and poetic justice, mingled with irony.

Theological matters

There are various important theological strands to be considered. These are not completely different from 1 Maccabees, but are emphasised in different ways. The issue of fighting on the Sabbath appears but is less heavily emphasised. There is a battle on a Friday but the Jews make sure they cease operations in time for 6:00 pm. This allows the enemy to escape and regroup. There are indications that the Jews were rather more integrated with Greek religion than they might have wanted to admit. At one point Onias seeks sanctuary in a pagan temple at Daphne. All the contenders for the High Priesthood have to try to gain a mandate from the Seleucid king; this seems a little strange until we remember that the High Priest was in fact the head of state and therefore a tributary 'king' as far as the Seleucid king was concerned. There is an admission that not just the Temple but also the streets of Jerusalem were full of pagan altars and mini-temples; Judas is the purist who clears the whole lot out and purifies the town. This clearly recalls the days of the two kingdoms, and Judas can be seen as the new Josiah, or possibly Jehu (Chapter 18). After a battle it is discovered that some of the soldiers have stolen silver vessels from a temple in Jamnia; these were collected up and sent to Jerusalem as a sin offering (sacrifice). Always the purism of Judas, who is actually termed a Hasidim, shows through against the compromising attitude of many of his race.

The whole rationale of martyrdom is discussed in 6:12-19. It is for a 'chastening of our nation' and a token of God's goodness. God's mercy is always there and he will never forsake his people. It is a positive view of adversity, underpinned by the reality of the covenant of God. This is underscored by two harrowing accounts: one of Eleazar a principal scribe who refused to eat pork, going so far as to refuse even to pretend to eat a piece. He preferred to die rather than even pretend to give in, it being sheer hypocrisy (6:19). This might imply that some Jews were actually pretending to eat pork just to avoid punishment. This courageous adherence to the Laws of Moses stands in contrast to the two-timing mentality of people like Nicanor and others. The other incident, where a mother and seven brothers had to face the king in a rage, engenders much sympathy from the reader. Even the king begins to feel remorse but cannot afford to back down. The mother's faith in God's mercy and certainty of the resurrection shows through here as in other places. How accurate this story is as history is debatable, but it does show that some of the Jews were absolutely determined not to give in (2 Maccabees 7:1ff).

> 2 Maccabees 7:23: '...the creator of the world... will also of his mercy give you breath of life again as ye now regard not your own selves for his laws' sake...'

As in other places, here is the hint of good deeds earning favour with God, what St. Paul was to call 'works-righteousness.' This is counterbalanced by a strong emphasis on trusting in God, especially before a battle where the odds are stacked against one. Judas is the one with supreme confidence in God; this is contrasted with the antics of people like Nicanor and Antiochus 4th, who eventually get what they are asking for.

The issue of the Temple and the City of David is present in 2 Maccabees but not quite so heavily emphasised. It is interesting that the 'abomination of desolation' is not stated in so many words. The general cleansing of the city is related, done by Judas. Also, the removal of the altar stones and the provision of new ones is also mentioned.

But the underlying assumption, never actually stated openly in 2 Maccabees, is that the prophecies of Daniel had actually come true. It is an assumption running through both books, but was blindingly obvious to anyone living at that time. So striking were the fulfilment of his prophecies that modern scholarship has tried to maintain that Daniel was written after the events and was just a description of history. But this can hardly work for two reasons. Firstly, why did not the Jewish people see Daniel as fraudulent and refuse to take him seriously? Secondly, why did not Daniel make his 'prophecies' more accurate; in other words, make a thorough job of it? As it is, Daniel gives a general impression of the events leading up to and including the Maccabean age, but the details do not quite tally with known events. The contention here is that Daniel was a genuine prophetic work of the early Exile and that explains why Judas and his brothers had the confidence to revolt and contend with vastly superior forces. It also explains why so many literary versions of these events were produced: not just 1 and 2 Maccabees but five books by a certain Jason of Cyrene (2 Maccabees 2:23).

In his last chapter Daniel talks about 'the time of the end'. Did he mean the Messianic age, or the end of the world? We notice that both the books of the Maccabees come to an abrupt end. 2 Maccabees actually says 'and here shall be an end' (right at the end). He does not try to relate all the fortunes of Judas' brothers and the Hasmonean dynasty. Is this intentional? 1 Maccabees does go on to relate the fortunes of Jonathan, Simon and

John. But there is no attempt at labelling any of them as the Messiah. One could say there is a degree of restraint here. 'The end' may simply mean the cessation or victory over the various world empires that were tormenting the Jews. Sadly, this was not to be. This may be one reason why eventually both books of the Maccabees were not accepted for the canon of the Old Testament by the Jews. The Maccabean era was in no way the end of pressure from world empires, neither did the Messiah appear just then.

Josephus – The Antiquities of the Jews: another version.

The famous Jewish historian, Josephus is useful when trying to assess the value of 1 and 2 Maccabees. Josephus was writing about 250 years later in contrast to the Maccabean writers. If his details appear a little careless and even contradictory, the time gap may help to explain this. It is interesting how he uses his source material; his primary source is 1 Maccabees with others such as Nicholas of Damascus and Diodorus worked in. He appears to have no knowledge of 2 Maccabees. Whether this indicates that he did not know it, or that he did not wish to use the material, is difficult to say. He may have felt that his Roman readers would have found the miraculous element in 2 Maccabees a little fantastic. However, with the use of other sources, we see some of the events in a slightly modified light, rendering an explanation for certain, what might have been seen as strange, occurrences.

The scope of Josephus goes much further back than the appearance of Antiochus 4th Epiphanes, in fact the whole background of Hellenistic Egypt and Asia comes up most interestingly. The process of the Jews being integrated into Hellenistic culture would seem to have been gathering pace for some time before Antiochus' assault on Jerusalem. All that happened was that with the encouragement of people like Jason and Menelaus, the claimants to the High Priesthood, the process began to accelerate to the point that the strict Jews began to register concern and serious objection.

The invasion of Egypt by Antiochus 4th turns out to be two separate occasions a year apart. On returning from the first one, he raided the Temple for money; on the second one he took far more spoil, violated a treaty, built the Akra, and defiled the altar. Josephus gives a partial reason for him turning nasty; 'returning from Egypt through fear of the Romans' hints at what we shall learn from Diodorus. Also Antiochus scourged and crucified many, and this is not seen in 1 Maccabees. Additionally, we see Antiochus making a separate deal with the Samaritans in which the temple on Mount Gerizim was dedicated to Zeus Xenios[9] whereas it had been dedicated to the Most High God. Might the compromisers have seen that as just another name for the same thing?

We can learn something of Josephus' slant by what he omits. We notice that Mattathias' speech is remarkably different in the same setting. Josephus omits all mention of the heroes of the past as seen in 1 Maccabees 2:4. Also mention of the Covenant seems not to appear. Is this because Josephus' Roman readers would not really understand these matters? Or was it that Josephus, having turned 'Quisling', wanted to downplay anything specifically Jewish, and emphasise how the Jews and the Romans were allies at this time? However, he does pick out the factor of Daniel's prophesies coming to fulfilment, on the desecration of the Temple. This may be because his readers might not be conversant with Daniel. Additionally, this is something that the Romans would have seen as significant: the importance of prophecy and its fulfilment. The building of a replica Temple in Egypt by Onias 4th is also cited as a fulfilment of Isaiah 19:19. This is something that the purists would have denounced as illegal by the laws in Deuteronomy. But Josephus would like to be seen as a realist, coming to terms with a new situation that cannot be avoided (page 301).

18: '… after stubbornly resisting they might better have done when they were quite unharmed, do they finally choose to do this when once they have been afflicted…' This is a flowery way of saying, 'make peace while you have the chance', something that he might have learned from Jesus. Josephus would almost certainly have had sympathy with the compromisers and those who sought a constructive deal with the Greeks. He is, however, totally out of sympathy with oath-breaking, treachery and pretence, something which is heavily emphasised in the Antiquities.

With Josephus we see more detail of the antics of the Greek kings and the chaos and jockeying for power that characterised the Seleucid empire. So we see how Tryphon had the boy king Antiochus 5th murdered; 'he died under surgery'! Demetrius 1st is lazy, arrogant, reclusive and careless about public affairs. Alexander Balas is the archetypal creep, who lures Jonathan with high honours. But Ptolemy 6th is careful not to accept the crown of Antioch, thus making him the master of both kingdoms at once; the reason being that he 'feared the Romans'.

With this we see the backdrop of the whole scenario. It is only indirectly hinted at in the Maccabees; that Rome was calling the trumps from behind the scenes, not having fully defeated the Greek kingdoms, and yet exerting pressure from Italy. This explains why the region was being destabilised and the sense of panic in the kings. It also explains why the Jews kept sending off envoys to Rome to secure treaties. One sneeze from Rome set them all in a frenzy. Josephus likes to emphasise the fair dealing and honesty of people like Jonathan, in contrast with the Greek kings, and also the fair-dealing of the Romans. He is much in favour of John Hyrcanus who was clearly the most successful of the Jewish leaders. He attained the status of prophet, priest and king, something on the same level as David and Solomon. The Maccabees do not go as far as that, but the Pharisees did. They wanted Hyrcanus to divide the high priesthood from the kingship and be the military man. This is something that Judas Maccabeus never attained, although Josephus states that he had been both for three years, but the Maccabees do not wish to admit to that. But Josephus is not too concerned about kingship in Judaism. Later on we learn that Herod was very much in favour with himself and the Romans. Elsewhere, remarks such as 'the fairness and generosity of the Romans' indicates Josephus' slant.

In this way, Josephus adds much to the historical account in 1 Maccabees with many interesting anecdotes and small political details that help to illuminate the motives of the main characters, often an amusing quip. Such an example would be in the case of Ammonius, who was desperate to escape punishment and dressed up as a woman before riding off to Arabia! As philosophy, there is the occasional moral comment. A good example of that would be his description of the three Jewish schools of thought: the Essenes, the Sadducees and the Pharisees on the subject of free will and predestination. His remarks about the Pharisees inventing rules for the sake of it might have been taken from the words of Jesus. For that reason, some of Josephus' remarks might be taken as slightly anachronistic or even retrojective.

Diodorus: a Roman-orientated historian living in Sicily

It is interesting to add the impression given by Diodorus, of some of the personalities in the Maccabean period. He is not really interested in the plight of the Jews, but likes to comment on the worth of the Greek kings. As history, Diodorus is not rated very highly nowadays; his surviving works are sadly fragmentary. Even so, we see certain individuals in a modified, though not completely different, light. He gives a fair impression of the upheavals and instability in the Empire that Alexander handed on to his generals. The substratum of it, as noted before, was the influence of Rome, acting like a magnet to all aspiring, power-hungry hopefuls in the Orient.

There is the occasional touch of moral philosophy. He begins his Book 21 thus:

'All vice should be shunned by men of intelligence, but especially greed... it brings many great misfortunes not only on private citizens but even on the greatest of kings...'

This thoroughly Roman sentiment is the yardstick by which he judges all the Greek kings and pretenders down to Alexander Balas and Demetrius 2nd. He records their conniving, treacherous, and downright stupid antics in lurid detail, thus providing more background to the attitude of the Greek kings who made life so difficult for the Jews.

As far as mathematics is concerned, Diodorus does not provide much in the way of dating; also, his estimates of the numbers that fell in battle are probably wildly exaggerated. As a biological commentator, he offers a fascinating conclusion to Book 22, where is described the case of a woman turning into a man – what we would call a hermaphrodite. We note that the incident of a 'woman' called Herais who actually gave birth to a son, but later turned into a man and joined the cavalry, is related to a prophecy from an oracle in Cilicia (the sanctuary of Apollo Sarpedonius). This convoluted message concerning 'a two-formed one' only acquired meaning when the case of Herais became known. We see in this that theology and scientific enquiry are not separate matters at all, in fact the one gives rise to the other. Also, this kind of situation with oracles giving out prophecies which were seen to come true, would explain why the Greeks (especially the kings) were convinced that their religion was correct and, that by dint of logic, the Jews were wrong. This is another undercurrent in the whole scenario.

As a literary man, Diodorus can be quite entertaining. His descriptions of the Seleucid kings throws another light on these matters, some of which may not be strictly accurate history. Antiochus 4th is described as embarking on a quixotic mode of life, slipping out of the palace to roam the streets and chum up with anyone, including foreigners. He would gatecrash parties and play the fife. When people realised who it was, they were struck dumb with fear or tried to disappear quickly. Sometimes he would dress up as a Roman, using a toga, and try to persuade people to vote him into some kind of office. He would play at trials in the Roman fashion. How did people see this? Some were deeply perplexed about him; others thought he was mad. How do we assess this sketch of him? Do we take it literally? It could be his attempt at engaging sympathy with the common people, something that most Greek kings would never even have considered. It could be that he was just an exhibitionist, or was he genuinely trying to introduce Roman values into the Orient? At the very least, he comes across as an unstable character, embarking on curious whims quite unexpectedly.

One incident that is helpful to us is the time he invaded Egypt ostensibly to help Ptolemy (but this was just a charade) helps to explain his attitude on coming to Jerusalem. He was on the point of conquering Egypt without a blow, when Popillius the legate appeared and issued him with the Roman senate's decree, ordering him out of Egypt. It was done in a very high-handed manner, giving him no time to think about it, or steal any money. Panic-stricken, and probably in a rage, he backed off to Judea and vented his spleen on the Temple. With regard to this incident, Diodorus only makes passing reference in Book 21:18a:

'He [Antiochus] not only opposed the God in Judea, but also inflamed by the fires of avarice, tried to despoil the temple of Artemis… in Elymais.'

This not only indicates that he was more or less bankrupt, and lacked any sort of scruple, but also that the cause of his last horrific illness (and certain apparitions) were the attack on the pagan temple as opposed to the Jewish one. In other words, poetic justice; he asked for it, but did not realise the true cause of his demise.

In fairness, there was another side to Antiochus: he could be very generous and fair to his captives, doubtless on a whim. Diodorus relates how he would throw massive games and parties and behave like an idiot, running round stark naked in front of all the guests[10]. Diodorus' comment runs:

'... one could not believe that it was possible for such excellence and baseness to exist in one and the same character.'

The Romans would have to wait for the reign of Caligula to be faced with the same kind of problem. The other Greek kings do not come in for such detailed description. This indicates at the very least that Antiochus 4th had a most curious reputation right across the Roman world. Mentally unbalanced, unpredictable, fawning, neurotic, all of these things might have a basis of truth. Was he the first socialist, atheist king, or was he just playing for time, by trying to confuse everyone? But of course the impact on the Jews was devastating and unforgettable; he goes down as one on the same level as Nebuchadrezzar.

Assessing the Maccabean period

It is always difficult to assess exactly what was going on at this time; we always see things through the tint of our own spectacles. Certainly with 1 and 2 Maccabees the tint is heavily in favour of the 'fundamentalist' Jews. Josephus is a more moderate Jew who throws a different light on the situation. Diodorus, a Roman, scornful of the Greek kings, offers another insight. What we do not have is the view of the compromising Jews or the 'Quislings'; still less the view of the Greek kings. We can only guess at that.

A general view, often reading between the lines, might run something like this. The Jews, who had been exiled and managed to regain their homeland, were determined that this should not happen again. The blame was cast on the pre-exilic kings who had disregarded God's laws and compromised with the Assyrians and the Babylonians. The strict Jews could see that this was about to happen again, even if the head of state was the High Priest as opposed to a king.

With the coming of the Greeks came a very different culture that made

Judaism appear antiquated and reactionary. Many Jews could see that to survive in a world dominated by Hellenistic culture there would have to be some degree of compromise and cooperation. Many of the early Greek kings from both Egypt and Antioch had been helpful and respectful towards Judaism and a happy relationship probably emerged. Possibly some of them thought that YHWH equalled Zeus.

The substratum of this was the growing influence of Rome. The Romans did not want a united Greek empire in the orient and were happy to use any method to foster disunity, instability and give encouragement to nuisance enclaves like Judea. The Jews thus became a pawn between three power bases. The Romans probably thought that all of them were hooliganistic, treacherous and egomaniac idiots.

But the final substratum, as ever, is the financial situation. Egypt had the gold. Asia Minor had gold at Sardis but Rome had taken over that part of the world, after the battle of Magnesia. This left the Seleucid Empire with no gold mines, which meant that cash was desperately short and they were prepared to embark on reckless measures to acquire it.

How do we view Antiochus 4th Epiphanes, as calling himself 'God made manifest'? How literally do we take this? A glance at the king-list shows that virtually all of the Greek kings took, or were given, nicknames. Some of them were decidedly comical, such as 'Grypus' (aquiline nose) and 'Physcon' (fat tummy). We see them as humorous but these terms may have been some kind of harking back to the portrayal of the ancient Pharoahs. Others were more complimentary such as 'Nicator' (conqueror), or 'Sidetes' (braveheart or iron heart). Others certainly sounded like deification: 'Soter' (saviour), 'Euergetes' (beneficent) and Epiphanes. Are these to be taken purely at face value? Was 'Epiphanes' to be taken literally as 'god' or just a bit of metaphor, or even humour? We do not seem to see people being forced to worship Antiochus, as did happen in the Roman empire in later years. The strict Jews of course did take it literally, but perhaps not the compromisers. It is difficult to see into the Hellenistic mentality on this matter. One could say that, having taken over the ancient orient, the Greek rulers had to take on board the sacral kingship systems that were traditional in that area, otherwise their subjects might not have taken them seriously. In Egypt, the Pharaoh had for centuries been equated with deity, and if the Ptolemies had not taken on that status, the common people of Egypt would have regarded the new Pharaoh as just a joke. The same situation might have applied in Mesopotamia, although the Semitic kings did not have quite such an acute identification with deity. We do not know whether Antiochus was glad to pose as god or if he was reluctant in the face of public opinion.

Anyway, it is enough to know that the difference in cultures was enough to cause a serious clash in the Maccabean age, and this led to Judea gaining a degree of independence before the Romans eventually took it over. We have to admire the courage and honesty of the Maccabean champions and wonder if the Greek kings really were such inflated, dictatorial scoundrels?

It is always difficult to know how literally any account, which purports to be historical, can be taken. There is always the element of exaggeration, and understatement. There is always the distortion of memory if the account is a long time after the actual events. Also, the author's axe to grind is often a serious twisting of the truth. It is just possible that the reason 1 and 2 Maccabees were rejected from the Old Testament canon was because the Jews were uneasy about the accuracy of some of the claimed events in these books.

In general terms, the two books of the Maccabees are a well-balanced corpus of literature. They include elements from all forms of truth. This is in contrast with some sacred writings that only contain one or a few aspects of truth, and are therefore an unbalanced form of literature.

Notes for Chapter 2: The Maccabees

1. Jonathan, brother of Judas Maccabeaus, was installed as High Priest from 160 to 142 BC. The Hasmonean dynasty continued down to Antigonus by which time the Romans had taken control and Herod the Great was installed, in 37 BC.
2. It was the Greeks who thought of a datum point in history. The Seleucid era was based on 311 BC, when Seleucus Nicator installed himself as king in Babylon. The Romans took the idea but based their datum point (the AUC reckoning) on the founding Rome. Our datum point now is the birth of Jesus Christ, but even that is a matter of some uncertainty.
3. Armies of 3,000 are mentioned in Joshua 7:4 and I Samuel 13:2, for instance.
4. Deuteronomy 3:1-11, when Og the king of Bashan is mentioned.
5. Zeus was the chief god in the Greek pantheon and may have been equated with YHWH by those whose theology was a little approximate.
6. The book of Daniel has been seen as *vaticinium ex eventu* by many modern scholars. The difficulty is that if Daniel was written after the Maccabean uprising, why did the writer not make the historical details coincide exactly. I have argued that Daniel is genuine prophecy, and that explains why the Maccabeans were so confident of defeating the Greeks. The full argument is found in my first book, *The Theology of Paradox*, Chapter 3.
7. A list of the Seleucid kings with their nicknames (or regnal names):
    Seleucus 1 Nicator, 312-280. BC
    Antiochus 1 Soter, 280-262.
    Antiochus 2nd Theos, 261-247.
    Seleucus 2nd 247-226.
    Seleucus 3rd Soter 226-223.
    Antiochus 3rd (the Great) 223-187.
    Seleucus 4th Philopater 187-175.
    Antiochus 4th Ephiphanes 175-163.
    Antiochus 5th Eupator (boy king, murdered) 163-162.
    Demetrius 1st Soter 162-150.

Alexander Balas (imposter) 150-145.
Demetrius 2nd Nicator 145-139.
Antiochus 6th Epiphanes 145-142
Antiochus 7th Sidetes 139-129.
Demetrius 2nd (restored) 129-126.
Antiochus 8th Grypus 125-96.
Antiochus 9th 115-95.
Many of these names indicate 'god', 'saviour', 'god made manifest' and 'loving father'.

8. Xanthicus, the twelfth month in the Seleucid year, equivalent to Adar (Jewish) which
    came before Nisan, round about our Eastertime. The rest of the months are here listed:
    1, Artemisios, 2 Daisios, 3 Panemos, 4 Loos, 5 Gorpaios, 6 Hyperberetaios, 7 Dios, 8
    Apellaios, 9 Audynaios, 10, Peritios, 11 Dystros.

9. Zeus Xenios. The word *xenios* literally means 'gooselike', which is rather a strange
    nickname to give to Zeus. On the other hand *xenios* might be a spelling mistake for
    Zenios. It may be a deliberate spelling mistake to ridicule Zeus. *Zen* was a poetic word
    for Zeus, and *Zenophron* meant 'knowing the mind of Zeus, revealing oracles'. This
    might mean that Sebaste had become a kind of oracle-mongering centre like Delphi.

10. Zeus, and other male Greek gods, were normally portrayed as completely naked.
    Antiochus may have genuinely thought he was a god; otherwise he might have been
    trying to convince people of his 'deity'.

3

Chairman Mao Tse-tung

Quotations from the Little Red Book, 1966

The *Little Red Book,* as published in Peking in 1966, is a selection of sayings of Mao Tse-tung from 1922 to the 1960s. It is interesting that it spans the period from early communism in Russia, through the turbulent period of the 1930s when Japan invaded China, through to the atom bomb and the post-war cold war period with Korea and Vietnam, but stops short well before the collapse of communism in Europe and the modification of communism in China. It would never have occurred to Mao that his ideology could have gone wrong; he was convinced that capitalism would collapse all over the world. The opposite has happened. The point of studying this book is that it purports to be the *truth* about people and politics, was widely held as 'scriptural' by millions, and is still held up by many as some sort of touchstone.

> 'Mao's... thought is Marxism-Leninism of the era in which imperialism is heading for total collapse and socialism is advancing to worldwide victory' – Lin Piao[1].

This is symptomatic of the high regard held for his words, and he is still idolised by millions in spite of the excesses of the Cultural Revolution. When one is convinced of the truth of one's cause, the solution to life's problems becomes very much simplified.

> '... we do not fear criticism because we are Marxists, the truth is on our side and the basic masses, the workers and peasants are on our side' (page 258).

Against the framework of our outline of 'truth' in Chapter 1 it will be instructive to analyse the *Little Red Book*. Some areas of knowledge are virtually non-existent in the book; others receive a disproportionate emphasis. Historical truth, scientific truth, and philosophical truth are the main platform, with the major and fundamental assumption, not evidenced, that Karl Marx must have been right. The book is almost entirely materialistic; there is hardly any mention of religion, in positive or negative mood, mythology, literature or anything else. As such it makes for very banal, repetitive, self-opinionated reading, which on the face of it would seem to be a high ideal. But we know from the implementation of communism in real terms, that it has given itself an atrocious reputation. One wonders if Mao has ever read *Das Kapital*, still less whether he has actually understood it. Even so, he claims to be the 'real' communist in contrast to Khrushchev[2] who is a poseur, 'wearing the cloak of Marxism-Leninism' (page 277).

Mao and historical analysis

Mao includes many remarks about recent history that have shaped the present in China. Strangely he never seems to mention the dynasties of emperors going back many centuries, but the Chinese monarchy had been abolished early in the twentieth century[4]. He is particularly concerned about the imperialists that have interfered with his country in colonial times – the British and the French – who were seen as exploiters. It does not seem to occur to him that it was the Western powers that introduced all manner of technological advances, such as railways, in the nineteenth century. The Japanese and the Americans are all accused of being reactionaries. There was good reason to oppose the Japanese, as they invaded China in the 1930s and committed all manner of atrocities. But for the Americans, who actually helped China in the war and finally finished off the Japanese, there is no word of thanks. He is quite lavish with the phrase 'paper tigers'. All foreign aggressors come in for this label.

'US imperialism has not yet been overthrown... I believe it also will be overthrown. It too is a paper tiger' (page 75).

We can sympathise with his wish to see China free of foreign influences, which have had a corrosive effect on the nation, but to call Hitler and the atom bomb a paper tiger does seem rather strange. His blanket condemnation of imperialism is quite categorical:

'Imperialism will not last long because it always does evil things... and it threatens the peace with atomic war' (page 77).

37

Mao never admits that Russia is an atomic power and is doing 'evil things'; still less does he admit that China is hardly innocent of all manner of cruelties. He is not prepared to admit that the Western powers might do something good or right. It is categorical thinking and a one-sided view of recent history. He has every expectation that the rest of the world will rise up against the reactionaries and the dictatorship of the working class will usher in some sort of utopia. The rest of the world clearly saw things differently.

Within China itself, Mao sees a class struggle that needs to be resolved: the proletariat and the national bourgeoisie, the exploited and the exploiters. The way to resolve this is by discussion, criticism, persuasion and education, and 'not by the method of coercion or repression'. This sounds so idealistic, but the fact remained that there were people in China that did not agree with communism, 'they resist the socialist revolution and are hostile to or sabotage socialist construction and are all enemies of the people'. If there is any doubt about what happens to such people, we must recall the Tiananmen Square incident[3].

But there is another contradiction going on. The enemy is also outside of China. There is no problem in his mind about having a war as long as it is a just war, by which he means a progressive war, which means a war designed to spread communism. 'War has existed ever since the emergence of private property and of classes' (page 58), and so it is quite legitimate to spread communism by force of arms. One wonders if Karl Marx actually advocated this. 'War is the highest form of struggle for resolving contradictions'. This gives rise to a worrying remark, 'every communist must grasp the truth; "political power grows out of the barrel of a gun"'(page 60).

In contrast to these remarks, Mao says he desires peace. 'We stand firmly for peace and against war' (page 67). On the possibility of a third world war, Mao is confident that it will simply result in fewer imperialist countries and many more socialist ones. This will presage the collapse of capitalism altogether. Or so he thinks. Strangely he makes no mention of Korea (1950s) or of Vietnam (1960s), who were aided and abetted by the Chinese and resisted by the Americans only because the local nations asked for assistance.

All this goes to show how history can be written to show one's own side in a sympathetic light and one's enemies in a less favourable light.

Mao and Philosophy

It is clear that Mao is fully espoused to Marxist philosophy. We know it as a nineteenth century socio-economic theory, which by today's standards is definitely dated. It rests on the assumption that there must have been a time when there was no class struggle and that land was held in common and people shared. Only later did exploitation of the workers emerge and the proletariat tyrannised by the bourgeoisie. The assumption goes further; if this system was to be removed, and the proletariat became the dictators, then we should arrive at some sort of utopia. This conceals the massive generalised assumption that all the working class are responsible, generous, altruistic and basically nice; all the upper classes are greedy, cruel, non-caring, and basically nasty. What an assumption!

Mao keeps alluding to the Marxist-Leninist-Stalinist theory as if it were the ultimate truth:

'Marxist philosophy holds that the law of the unity of opposites is the fundamental law of the universe.'

When we compare Mao with Marx, certain differences begin to emerge. Marx talks about 'alienation', which means the workers are not being able fully to participate in the fruits of production; in other words, they are being exploited. Mao's version of this is to bring in the concept of 'contradiction', which we have mentioned before, and which does not mean the same thing. In fact, Mao's version of communism is somewhat of an adaptation of basic Marxism, to match the conditions in the China of the mid-twentieth century. Mao can see that there will be ongoing revolution.

'In any society in which classes exist, class struggle will never end. In classless society the struggle between the new and the old and between truth and falsehood will never end', page 203.

This helps us to understand the five-year plan and the Cultural Revolution[5]. One wonders what he would have thought about China's present situation with its adaptation to capitalism.

He also has scathing remarks to make about liberalism. He sees it as a corrosive element that eats away unity, cohesion and discipline, and alienates the Party and the masses. 'It is an extremely bad tendency'. This means that people pay lip service to Marxism, assuming it to be an 'abstract dogma', and in fact are looking out for themselves all the time. Not obeying orders but giving pride of place to one's own opinion, means we can have democracy as long as we have the same opinion as the Government! And if we hear someone else with the 'wrong' opinion, we are supposed to report it. A nation of informers, just as East Germany became, as well as others. This means that Mao's version of Marxism has got to be right and any other philosophy or socio-economic theory has got to be wrong. This is his version of 'democracy'; it does not have the same meaning as it does in the USA or Britain.

Mao and Theology

Not surprisingly, being thoroughly espoused to Marxist dialectic, Mao has very little that could be called theological. However, there is one passage that is a surprise and may indicate that he was not totally materialistic: page 201.

In Ancient China, a fable tells of the Foolish Old Man who tried to remove two mountains. They were to the south of his house and were blocking the sunlight out. So he decided to dig them up and clear the view. The Wise Old Man came along and said, 'How silly of you to do this; it is impossible to dig up two mountains'. The reply was, 'If we keep on digging – me, my sons and my grandsons – eventually we shall clear them away'. He was unshaken in his conviction. God was moved by this and he sent down two angels who carried the mountains away on their backs.

This is the only mention of God or of anything spiritual in the whole book. But does this really mean that he is a theist? In the next breath, the two mountains become imperialism and feudalism, two massive problems that China needs to be rid of, lying like a dead weight on the Chinese people. Then, he makes out that the Chinese people are God, and they will stand up and dig along with the Communist Party, and clear away China's problems together. At least he did not try to make himself out to be God; although there is a subtle hint in these remarks, that since he is one of the Chinese peasants, then that would be an implication of deity! It is no surprise that now he is dead, his apotheosis is being seen. The same thing happened with Confucius[6]. There are still banners bearing Mao's image all over China, and still there are statues of him being erected, with the implication that he must be venerated. Even so, there are many who regard him as a thing of the past.

In a work that is practically all materialistic, political, economic and tactical, this fable stands out like an oasis of inspiration. This is the clue to what was wrong with communism: it took hardly any notice of the essential needs in human nature. There is greed, fear, and the need for spirituality, destiny, and family values. The communists tried to eradicate religion, even though the *Little Red Book* says nothing on that matter. Greed is the prerogative of the imperialists, but not of the Chinese workers. With the Chinese Red Army there is nothing to fear since it cannot be defeated. Family cohesion came under pressure as part of the policy to break down traditional values and minimise family loyalties. Although there were attempts at providing substitutes for religion, this never really worked. Confucianism[6], Taoism[7] and Buddhism[8] are still a reality in China, and Christianity is infiltrating in many areas. It is not easy to assess the actual situation, but it is probable that religion is one of the factors causing the modification of Communism and of its coming to terms with the Capitalist world.

As a prophet, Mao is just as unsuccessful as Karl Marx was. The rest of the world has not, as yet, gone in for a third world war, very largely because that 'paper tiger' – the atom bomb – has convinced everybody that such a conflict would spell doom to any form of civilisation on this planet. As for communism sweeping through the world and relegating the imperialists to the museum, the opposite is now happening. The tide has turned and it is the Stalinists that are now seen as out-dated, dinosauric and reactionary. We are now left with North Korea as the only outright, full-blown Stalinist country in the world. How long this will continue is hard to say, but already we are seeing a communist 'monarchy'[9] appearing, something that might have had Lenin shaking his head in despair.

A few remarks about *Das Kapital* by Karl Marx

This work, stemming from the mid-nineteenth century in London, has become what might be termed the 'Bible' of Communism. It is a book that people talk about but seldom admit not to have read it. One wonders how many communists actually did read it, and if they did, whether they understood it. It is almost entirely politico-economic theory, and very dry and difficult to follow. There were three volumes of it, most of which never saw the light of day. It was Friedrich Engels[10] who made sure it was noticed and caused it to be influential. If he had not, *Das Kapital* might have fallen by the wayside, and made no impression on world history. As it was, it became a symbol rather than a handbook. It may be that Marx wrote in good faith in the hopes that the lot of the working class could be improved; he had no idea of how it was to be worked out in practicality. It is a lesson to us all, that we need to be cautious in what we write and publish; one does not know how it will be misused or misinterpreted in times to come.

As an economic theory, much of his theories are well and truly dated; some would say obsolete. Like everyone else Marx was a child of his own age. He could see the mass squalor and exploitation of the lower classes in a society where *laissez faire* had had a free reign. Britain had gone through the turbulence of the Industrial Revolution and indeed we are still coping with the reverberations from it now. To be fair to the government and the employers, no one really knew how to cope with this new phenomenon called 'industrialisation'; we are still learning now.

As a political theory, Marx freely advocates the use of force and violence to cure the problems. He could have been more cautious on this issue even then; nowadays we try to rule out violence since we know now of its likely consequences. A glance at the French Revolution tells us that on the one hand there was the desperation of the French peasants and on the other hand the upheaval simply produced someone like Napoleon and a chronically unstable government right into the twentieth century. Once people resort to violence, the situation can so easily go right out of control and not achieve what was originally intended. Many countries have managed to achieve some kind of Welfare State without a violent upheaval and loss of life.

The crux of Marx's theory is the issue of 'surplus value'. What he means by this is that, for instance, the workers in a factory produce a commodity at a certain cost, and the owner of the factory sells it at a profit; the question arises, 'who keeps the profit?' The employer, of course. Marx sees that as unfair; the workers should have the profit. Because the employer, the capitalist, keeps the profit, he then builds up his savings to become a rich man at the expense of the poor.

Marx does not like this.

What Marx does not allow for is this; that that accumulated profit has to pay off any loans that were required to establish the factory, to afford machinery, often updated as technology progresses, to afford raw materials which may go up in price, to cope with competition from other producers and to stave off the threat of bankruptcy. Many people will agree that the one who takes the risk of establishing a firm, the entrepreneur, should be amply rewarded and also take precautions against business failure. Marx does not take into account that there is something in human nature called 'business acumen', and that to discount this is to no one's advantage. As capitalism developed, we have seen the growth of joint stock companies and other arrangements. It is no longer a simple matter of one man, the owner, holding all the assets while everyone else is deprived. Ownership in firms is now spread so that anyone can buy a stake and share in the risk involved in commerce. New enterprises need a capital investment to make anything succeed, and involves people with a keen business sense.

This lesson has been learnt when East Germany went communist in the late 1940s. All the capitalists and entrepreneurs were rounded up, put into Colditz Castle and sent off to Western Germany. The result was a lacklustre economy, with no drive, no forward looking and a serious lack of capital for major investments in such things as infrastructure and new processes. This meant that East Germany, by the 1990s, was miles behind the rest of the world.

Marx, as a prophet, has clearly come unstuck, just like Mao. He thought that the industrial countries of Western Europe would be the first to go communist. In reality, it was Russia, followed by China that went first – two drastically underdeveloped countries. This resulted in massive exploitation of the workers, probably more than the capitalists had done. Also, he thought that the capitalist system would collapse under its own weight, as monopolies would increasingly scoop up all the means of production. If anything, the opposite has happened. Capitalism has for most countries, gradually developed into some sort of balanced situation, in which the government provides for those liable to be exploited and yet retains freedom of expression and initiative for those so gifted. Moreover, there is room for large concerns as well as small ones according to the needs of the situation.

Marx never anticipated the ugly reaction to communism as the Bolshevik threat increased. Many countries saw that fascism, in its various shapes and forms, was the only way of halting the violent and revolutionary policy of the Bolsheviks. Marx clearly saw that violence was the legitimate way of solving the problem of wealth inequality, but would he really have approved of the situation in Russia – and China – where thousands had to die to enforce a totalitarian policy? Would he have agreed with the Cultural Revolution? The end result, after two world wars, has been that most countries are determined to keep the peace, possibly at all costs, since they can imagine what the consequences will be if a third global conflict breaks out. We are now faced with unprincipled violence of another sort; international terrorism. Marx might not have been too pleased with that.

It is unlikely that Marx would have been happy with the suppression of religion and personal opinion in general terms. *Das Kapital* does not remark on religion at all, except indirectly in one or two places. There is no policy of persecution or of withholding personal rights and freedoms. Yet the Bolsheviks and later the Chinese communists embarked on a major policy of persecution.

In fairness, we may admit that Marx's influence has not been totally harmful. Many countries have achieved some form of Welfare State. There are now such things as minimum wage levels, certain standards in housing, compulsory education, prohibition of child labour, universal suffrage, and consideration of not just majority opinions but also of minority ones too. But we all regret the turbulence of the twentieth century which was necessary to arrive at it.

Das Kapital can now be seen as an outdated nineteenth century attempt at coping with economics. Since then other economic theories have come and gone, but none has as yet solved the basic problem of wealth inequality. Moreover, we have seen the effects of rampant inflation since the gold standard has been abandoned. Also the problem of mass unemployment still has no easy solution. There is also the factor of international lending and massive debts, a problem which politicians are wrestling with at the moment. This means that we are living in a totally different economic situation as compared with the mid-nineteenth century. This means that the standoff between working class and capitalist is now to a very large extent irrelevant.

Notes for Chapter 3: Mao Tse-Tung

1. Lin Piao: someone high up in the Chinese government.
2. Nikita Khrushchev: one of the leading commissars in the Second World War and instrumental in defeating the Germans at Stalingrad. He went on to be the Prime Minister of Russia after Stalin's demise.
3. Tiananmen Square: this area is in front of the palace in Peking. A group of students staged a peaceful demonstration in protest at the government's policies. This was put down with force; the world was shocked. This was back in the 1980s.
4. The last emperor was called Piu. He never received a formal, regal name and was deposed in 1911-12, but reinstated as Emperor of Manchuria by the Japanese. This all ended in 1945.
5. The Cultural Revolution was a violent attempt at enforcing communism in China. All manner of cruelties were perpetrated in the name of Marxism. It occurred in the 1980s.
6. Chapter 8: The Analects of Confucius.
7. Chapter 11: The Tao Teh Ching, by Lao Tsu.
8. Chapter 14: The Dhammapada, a Buddhist scripture.
9. Only recently, Kim was succeeded by his son as president of North Korea.
10. Friedrich Engels was a successful businessman in Britain in the mid- to late nineteenth century. He co-authored the *Communist Manifesto* with Karl Marx in 1848.
   The *Communist Manifesto* goes thus, in brief:
   'A spectre is haunting Europe... the spectre of communism. The proletarians have nothing to lose but their chains. They have a world to win. Working men of all countries, unite.'

4

Mein Kampf: 'My struggle'

By Adolf Hitler

This is a work of the early twentieth century, widely regarded as some sort of inspired material, became a sort of Bible for the Nazis and other Fascist-inclined groups. It became more or less compulsory reading during the Third Reich. If Hitler had not strongly resembled a certain Mr Charles Chaplin, an accomplished comedian of the same era, people in the West might have been more inclined to take this book more seriously, and have a clearer idea of what was in store should Hitler ever grasp the levers of power. Sadly, not enough people even bothered to read the book, and still less, realise the implications included in its thinking. It is even now being studied, as a precautionary measure; since its sentiments are very largely evil, it is a warning to us all of what can happen when a twisted mind with an unscrupulous schedule manages to misuse power.

We can understand the background of this book; its setting in history. Germany, with Austria, had just fought a disastrous war on three fronts, had lost millions of young men, and had to admit defeat. Germany was in chaos; the Kaiser had been forced to abdicate, a new republic had been installed, which had had no time in which to settle down or mature. In addition, there were Communist and Fascist groups tussling for control of Germany. There had been strikes, civil unrest, shortages of food and general resentment. It is no surprise that someone like Hitler, a soldier gassed on the western front, should emerge with what must have appeared as a stunningly clever excuse for the failure of the German Army, and a formula for rectifying the situation. This 'clever' idea was to plunge the world into yet another disastrous conflict and end with an even more horrendous result for Germany, topped off by the nuclear threat.

To analyse this work on the same basis as all the others will bring out some interesting points for comparison. But there is no doubt that Hitler and his adherents, had a fanatical commitment to what they saw as the *truth* in these pages. It is worth noting that the first publications of *Mein Kampf* were printed in Gothic script, which we can take as an attempt at giving the book a scriptural appearance. The edition used here is the Pimlico edition, first published in 1992. Since then there have been twenty-four reprints and many previous editions have appeared. This is an indication of the interest and possible hold that this book has on people. One hopes it is not producing a new generation of Fascists. This critique is confined to the actual text of *Mein Kampf* with a few remarks about how it worked out in the course of the Third Reich; there is no attempt to include the content of his speeches, which may have varied a little by comparison with the book.

Mathematical aspects

It is something of a surprise that Hitler hardly ever includes any of this. He is pleased to tell us that the German population is increasing at the rate of 900,000 per year, but there is no mention of the heavy migration of Germans and Austrians to the USA at the same time. Normally, politicians produce masses of statistics to support their arguments, but not so here. This seems rather strange. Does this mean that he does not know or cannot obtain any statistical information? Or does it mean that he would rather not include such material for fear of weakening his argument? One would think that with such a controversial and high-powered political message to disseminate, some actual statistical support (truthful or cooked-up) would have been important.

Scientific Truth

From the point of view of Physics and Chemistry, hardly anything is said; but with Biology, there is a big assumption that is axiomatic to his agenda. It is the issue of BLOOD. When one employs an expression such as 'it's in the blood', we do not intend it to involve any literal or scientific implication. However, Hitler does take it literally, and blood in the biological sense, becomes an issue of the first importance. The Germans have the pure blood, or at least used to have, until they were infiltrated by Jewish schemers who were intent on procuring the downfall of the poor innocent Aryans[1]. The importance of 'pure blood' cannot be understated, in his opinion.

'... is the question of the racial preservation of the nation. In the blood alone, resides the strength as well as the weakness of man. As long as peoples do not recognise and give heed to the importance of their racial foundation, they are like men who would like to teach poodles the qualities of greyhounds... peoples that renounce the preservation of their racial purity renounce with it the unity of their soul in all its expressions...' (page 307).

Hitler is paranoid about the interbreeding of Jews with Germans.

'With Satanic joy in his face, the black-haired Jewish youth lurks in wait for the unsuspecting girl whom he defiles with his blood, thus stealing her from her people. With every means he tries to destroy the racial foundations of the people he has set out to subjugate... he does not shrink from pulling down the blood barriers for others...' (page 295).

Such nonsense would now invite prosecution, but at that time there would have been many who would have been persuaded by such drivel. As we all know, blood is found in certain groups, A or B for instance, and these are distributed around the human race regardless of racial groups. It is true that some blood groups predominate in certain parts of the world, but this has nothing to do with racial characteristics. We have yet to see one blood group associated with any particular physical or mental problem. To say that German blood (which includes all kinds of groups) is tainted by Jewish blood is claptrap. But Hitler was convinced that to allow mixing of races was to invite disaster for the world.

'The result of all racial crossing is therefore in brief the following; (a) lowering of the level of the higher race; (b) physical and intellectual regression and hence the beginning of a slowly but surely progressing sickness. To bring about such a development is, then, nothing else but to sin against the will of the Eternal Creator' (page 260).

Hitler's explanation then, for the decline of all great civilisations of the past, such as Ancient Greece, is because they went in for racial crossing, or interbreeding. Of course, the Germans, whose blood is largely undiluted, are the most superior race in the world, and the evidence for it is thus:

'All the human culture, all the results of art, science and technology that we see before us today, are almost exclusively the creative product of the Aryan... he alone was the founder of all higher humanity... a prototype of all that we understand by the word 'man'. He is the Prometheus[2] of mankind' (page 263).

It would seem that mankind can be divided into three groups: the founders of culture, the bearers of culture, and the destroyers of culture. Only the Aryan can represent the first group. The second group will be people like the Japanese; we can guess what the third group will be!

Hitler tries to strengthen his argument by analogy from animal behaviour: a mouse does not breed with a cat, a dog does not breed with a horse, etc. Therefore different races of mankind ought not to interbreed. This type of naturalistic argument seldom works; it would be true that a dog and a horse could not crossbreed because they have different genes and chromosomes. However some species can produce offspring because their genes are to some extent compatible. Take for instance the 'panther-tiger' or PANTIG[3]; also the LIGER and the TIGON; what about the mule? We know (now) that the genetic make-up of all humans from any part of the world is compatible. The inference from this is that humanity is all of one race, in spite of differences in appearances and cultures. Hitler would doubtless have had a fit on learning this fact. Also, he ignores what we all know about inbreeding. It is healthy for people of different races and genes to interbreed, since it has the effect of strengthening rather than weakening us physically and mentally. We have known for a long time that marrying too close produces offspring with defects.

Thus, as a biological expert, Hitler is a non-starter. He does not properly evidence for us the connection between 'purity of blood', whatever that may mean, and high culture, whatever that may mean, either. It may be true that the white Europeans (termed Aryans) have become more resourceful over the course of history, but like all political and quasi-mythical theories, it is a circular argument. Because of the relative harshness of the climate in northern countries, the constant tussle with nature has forced them to become more resourceful, hard-working, exploitative and larcenous. The historical truth is that 'culture', if by that you mean artistry and technology, was first developed in Mesopotamia, Egypt, Greece and Rome. China had its own, if isolated, cultural development. Only later did these ideas work their way into northern Europe under the influence of Rome. And another circular argument lies beneath the surface here; the anti-Semitic policy, going on for hundreds of years, has forced the Jews to stick together, not just over the issue of diet, but also because of ostracism, which in turn made them an easy target for victimisation. Also they were forced to embark on a lifestyle that was beneath the dignity of the gentiles, namely money-lending. Hitler actually admits that at school there was a Jewish boy in his class; at the time he did not appear to be anything different from the other boys. But there was a certain reserve kept for him; sheer inbuilt prejudice.

Geographical realities

Just as Hitler is obsessive about blood, so too he is obsessive about SOIL. We have already mentioned that the German population was alleged to be expanding at the rate of just under a million a year. This would eventually bring about a crisis of overcrowding and shortage of land area, i.e. soil, which would have implications for food production. Given that Germany's overseas colonies had been confiscated by the Western powers in 1918, it meant that any form of colonisation would have to be at the expense of neighbouring countries in Europe. He would have prefered this policy:

'… such a colonial policy could only have been carried out by means of a hard struggle… to much better purpose, not for territories outside of Europe, but for land on the home continent itself…' (page 128).

He has the idea that England would approve and back such a project, though why the British should agree to such a policy, he does not substantiate. He would allow Britain to ply its overseas colonies and industry and let Germany concentrate on more agriculture in the east. The moral right to appropriate lands in Russia would be the same as when the Teutonic Knights[4] infiltrated Poland and the eastern Baltic states centuries ago. The fact that Russia had just gone over to communism was a signal to Hitler that the time is ripe for an attack. He was able to justify the use of aggression because of course, the master race, being the strongest, has the right to do it. Might is right. He does not pause for a minute to give consideration to Poland as obstructing his line of attack. After all, Poland ought not to exist anyway. In fact there is no thought of the millions who would be dispossessed by the confiscation of their land. All he can think of is Germany's stomach. He wants the soil.

'Germanisation can only be applied to soil and never to people' (page 353).

By this he means that it was no use trying to convert conquered peoples into Germans, just by teaching them to speak German. They will still be Slavs, Poles, Russians etc. He was simply not interested in their fate, except to turn them into a pool of cheap labour.

This policy obviously received a sharpening when the Treaty of Versailles (1919) took away various portions of Germany: Alsace-Lorraine, parts of Schleswig-Holstein, and parts of Silesia. He is tacit on the subject of the Treaties of Brest-Litovsk[5], which set up an independent Ukraine, and various parts of Poland were reshaped; in effect, Poland moved sideways at Germany's expense and Russia's gain. But this was all a part of the melting pot of boundary changes in a territory where there were few natural barriers.

It was the mentality of the age just to redraw national boundaries according to the fancy of the winners. Nowadays this process is seen in an altogether different light; now there is much more sensitivity and consultation over the alteration of boundaries.

'State boundaries are made by man and changed by man... our ancestors had to fight for it... no folkish[6] grace will win soil for us... but only the might of a victorious sword... the right to possess soil can become a duty if without extension of its soil a great nation seems doomed to destruction... (page 597)... we take up where we broke off 600 years ago... we speak of soil in Europe today... we have only in mind Russia and her vassal border states' (page 598).

With this we see the tragic blueprint for World War Two already mapped out in the 1920s. Hitler clearly saw the map of Europe as if it were a massive neurotic chess game, with himself moving all the pieces in accordance with his preconceived racialist fancies.

Historical understanding

Hitler describes how, in his early years at school, he had an exceptionally good history teacher who managed to capture his imagination and give him an abiding fascination for history. It is quite a surprise then to find that *Mein Kampf* does not contain any connected or coherent historical account. There are the occasional mentions of historical events, but there does not seem to be any systematic attempt at an interpretation from a Nazi point of view. For someone who is supposed to be fascinated by history, this is a big gap. He was aware that the German education system was not teaching history properly. Rather than teaching pupils masses of details like dates and names, 'the main value lies in regarding the great lines of development' (page 383).

History is not just about getting to know the past, but it is an 'instructor for the future and for the continued existence of our own nationality'. The normal average man needs that measure of historical insight so that he can cope with the political issues of the day. History is about understanding the past and projecting into the future. The essential strand in a world history as written by the folkish state is the racial question, which must take a dominant position. The broad, clear line that he wants is clearly going to be a political teaching on Nazi lines. Everything will be reinterpreted from a Nazi point of view, which means a racist point of view. That is Hitler's obsession.

Hitler's general overview of history is saturated with his mania that the Jews are trying to gain world domination and the ruination of Germany. He states that they first appeared in Germany when the Romans arrived, presumably 2,000 years ago and went in for commerce (page 280). He does not give actual examples of how the Jews operated, but generalised and slanderous remarks about how they were supposed to have insinuated themselves on the innocent Aryans and became 'blood-suckers', are plentiful. The German princes, always short of cash, persuaded the Jews to lend at usurious rates. In this we see another circular argument: since the Christian population were not allowed to charge interest, but the Jews could, obviously the Jews increasingly slid into that role and gained that kind of reputation. Repeatedly we see the generalised remark, 'the Jew...' as if all of them were equally scheming, lying, conniving agents of the Devil. The suggestion that they cannot speak German without an accent is held up as evidence that they are not really German and their 'blood' is still different, even after 2,000 years. It is tragic that such insane rantings surfaced; even at the time, the authorities took steps to silence Hitler, but this did not succeed. He and his cronies were determined to expose the 'Jewish menace'. Perhaps what really captured people's attention was the claim that it was Jewish infiltration that had brought about the defeat of the German army in 1918, and the imposition of the Treaty of Versailles. And of course the added element of Marxism, a new political theory developed by Karl Marx in the mid-nineteenth century was becoming an increasing threat to the stability of Germany. As it happened, Marx[7] was actually a Jew, though probably not a particularly Zionist one; we would see that as purely coincidental, but Hitler saw it in an altogether different light. He interprets it as a pacifist, proletarian challenge to authority that is dominated by Jews, intent on wrecking German statehood and bringing in some sort of international brotherhood. Jewish-Bolshevism became a complete mania with him and the Nazi programme; but this too caught the public imagination. It resonated with deeply held prejudices and the result was massive political rallies with Hitler ranting and indoctrinating millions of Germans. We would see the logic of that as rather strange; the Jews were largely capitalists, and equating them with the Bolsheviks[8] was a heavy strain on common sense. Added to that, there were many Jews who fought bravely in the war and gained many medals; this was to no avail when introduced to the gas chambers at Auschwitz. But in the fervid atmosphere of political and economic chaos in the inter-war years, any lunatic logic could probably pass for a brilliant new discovery. At least, that is how Hitler and his adherents saw this clever new idea. Hitler was much in favour of the mass meeting with heavy-duty persuaders in attendance, rather than trying to enlighten people by writing books.

'The greatest revolutions in this world have never been directed by a goose-quill... has been the magic power of the spoken word' (page 98).

We can guess which great orator he has in mind to carry the masses along. We can see who he means from this remark:

'Only a storm of hot passion can turn the destinies of peoples, and he alone can arouse passion who bears it within himself'. He never actually specifies himself; we have to guess.

As far as the great events in Germany's history is concerned, Hitler has very little to say. One would have expected a Nazi view of such events as the battle of Blenheim, the French invasion under Napoleon and other important events, but none are forthcoming. Instead he is full of sarcasm about the Hapsburg Monarchy and their policy of slavicisation. This must have been a deliberate plan to integrate the Czechs with the Germanic people of Austria. He is full of scorn for this idea and sees it as the ruination of Austria. But strangely there is no mention of Hungary, which again had a different language[9]. He is repelled by the conglomeration of races in Vienna, but most notably by the Jews. This was his reason for seeing Austria as doomed to die as a Germanic culture and explains his move to Germany where there was much less cultural decline, as he saw it (page 113). The alliance with Austria, he regards as an absurdity; all they wanted was to preserve world peace and yet they were forced into a war (1914) in spite of all their peaceful intentions. He calls Austria 'a mummy of a state' and has no respect for it.

Hitler relates that as a schoolboy he became a National Socialist not for Austria but for Germany, and so he learned to grasp the meaning of history. For him, the meaning of history is the assertion of Germany's greatness. This can hardly be achieved by pacifism; he revels in the idea of a struggle, and knows that to gain more territory will involve aggression. The success of the 1870 attack on France, allowing Germany to annex Alsace-Lorraine, is evidence to him that this policy will work.

The substratum of this is the Pan-German movement of the late nineteenth century, which looked back on the times of Charlemagne[10] with his strong, Holy Roman Empire; it was a sentimental but anachronistic and foolish longing to re-unite German-speaking peoples in central Europe. One of the leading lights in this, Schönerer, was a rabid anti-Semite. Seen from this aspect, Hitler is only a fanatical version of what many Germans were hoping for, and this also helps to explain why his ideas found a ready market.

With regard to recent events, history in continuation, Hitler is quite fulsome, even if it is depicted not just from a Nazi point of view but also in high-flown emotional, melodramatic language. Recent developments in Austria from a political point of view are described, not always as accurately as one might have hoped; the main strand is how the Jews are undermining a great empire. Meanwhile, the German Empire, with Kaiser Wilhelm 2nd, whom he admires, was moving inevitably towards war. Wilhelm was noted for being a sabre-rattler, which must explain Hitler's admiration for him. Wilhelm was not the only warmonger in Germany; in a very real sense, the nation talked itself into a war. Hitler was delighted to join up in the Bavarian regiment and go to the Western front, full of enthusiasm with thousands of other volunteers, convinced of the rightness of their cause and prepared to die for Germany. He relates how while the front held steady with the great courage and heroism of these men, back home there were agitations for peace, strikes in favour of an end to the war, and more disgustingly, hordes of people in politics and commerce who were lining their pockets and undermining the morale of the nation. These people, of course, were the Jews! (*All of them?*). The logic of it is not really so tortuous: if all the Jews are blood-sucking, treacherous scoundrels, then all the blood-sucking, treacherous scoundrels at home must be the Jews. What a wonderful piece of reasoning!

The Kaiser tried to come to some sort of arrangement with the Marxists, presumably as a last ditch attempt to pull things together, but this had no effect:

'... he was the first German emperor to hold out a conciliatory hand to the leaders of Marxism, without suspecting that scoundrels have no honour. While they still held the imperial hand in theirs, the other hand was reaching for the dagger. There is no making pacts with Jews; there can only be the hard either-or' (page 187).

From this we see the doctrine of the 'stab in the back' which was to dominate Nazi rhetoric all through the rallies of the 1920s and 1930s. When talking about scoundrels having no honour, it is ironic, since that is exactly how he behaved when in power, breaking treaties and agreements right, left and centre. He totally fails to mention the courageous Jews who fought for Germany in the war. Also we see the nonsense of 'block-thinking'; a categorical condemnation of a whole section of people that are imagined to be undermining the nation. A remark on these lines is 'there were certain people at home who were undermining the war effort, and making a fortune out of it, and some of them, we suspect, were Jewish'. Even that might be an overstatement. Also he never considers remarking thus: ' in wartime, there are always people who object, and others who make a fortune in the background; these are not necessarily of any particular race.' His dogmatic and damning stance was grossly unfair on vast numbers of loyal German-Jews. When he talks of the Austrian Parliament being riddled with Jews, the truth was that there may have been one or two in it that were actually Jewish. So in this we see his hysterical neurosis about world Zionism; the truth has to take a back seat (see footnote of page 35)[11].

Artistic realities

As a student he came to realise that he had a gift as an artist. Some of his pictures are still on show somewhere, and display a certain degree of merit[12]. In addition he became fascinated with architecture. It is a great pity that he was turned down for the Art College in Vienna; history might have been very different if he had not been so embittered that he embarked on politics. All through his political career there was a fascination for art and architecture, which indicated that he had some sort of idealism. Another aspect of this was his enthusiasm for Wagner's Operas. It would be anachronistic to call Wagner a Nazi, except to say that there may have been certain elements in the operas that would lend encouragement for an impressionable person to take on that kind of politic. There was always the temptation to take certain ideas and allow them to become a documentary for modern statecraft.

Hitler's adherence to something called 'German culture' is a major strand in his thinking. He talks as if no other nation or race had any culture, artistic tradition or technological skill, in the modern world or the ancient world. He is particularly sarcastic about 'cubism'[13] and 'dadism'[14]. This was a new idea coming in at the early stages of the twentieth century, and the main names associated with it were Picasso and Braques. As we know, Picasso's modern art ideas became world famous. That is not to say that everyone ought to like it, as it is a matter for personal taste. Even so, it has its place in the world of art appreciation. However, Hitler manages to tie it in with his favourite bogey-politics, Jewish-Bolshevism!

'Art Bolshevism is the only possible cultural form and spiritual expression of Bolshevism as a whole...' (page 235).

Cubism is the recognised art form of those states that had gone in for communism, and is seen as a symptom of their political decay. He believes that the state has a duty to prevent a people from sliding into such a spiritual madness. He takes the mind-set that if we do not halt it, we shall allow parasitic growths that presage the ruin of our culture. We live in a slowly rotting world; even in Germany we see the debasement of art and culture and we are heading for the abyss. It is the task of the government to take a firm line in removing such lunatic artwork. This of course is what did happen in the Third Reich; anything that was not in accordance with Hitler's taste, had to be removed; anything produced by a Jew also had to be repressed. But nowhere does he actually tell us what is wrong with Cubism or Dadism, or indeed what is wrong with Mendelssohn's music. A proper critical explanation would have made more sense.

Nowhere does he actually define what he means by 'culture', whether good or bad. We have indirect remarks about Schiller, Göethe and Shakespeare (page 236), and we know that Wagner held a deep fascination for him. We can gather that culture means somewhat more than just artistic expression. He includes technology, agriculture and all the other factors of civilisation. To do this, the Aryans had to recruit 'lower beings' to do the hard work, but they did not manage to have any decent ideas of their own.

'The first cultures arose in places where the Aryan in his encounters with lower peoples, subjugated them and bent them to his will. They then became the first technical instrument in the service of a developing culture' (page 268).

Eventually, the subjected people raised themselves up and the dividing line between master and servant became blurred. At that point the Aryan gave up the purity of his blood and hence his culture entered a decline. Even then we are left wondering what actual characteristics are associated with culture and still we are left unclear about why the purity of one's blood is anything to do with cultural achievement. He states that culture has something to do with the 'humanly beautiful and sublime' but again this is a vague statement which could have done with more explanation. It will be lost forever if a 'bastardised and niggerised' world is allowed to prevail:

'Human culture and civilisation on this continent are inseparably bound up with the presence of the Aryan. If he dies out or declines, the dark veil of an age without culture will again descend on this globe' (page 348).

With this we see that, for Hitler, culture and race are inseparably tied up, and that to ensure the advance and correction of culture, the master race must prevail, and that includes by force. Sadly this doctrine was worked out in real terms by art theft on a grand scale, on the assumption that Göring (and his minions) knew how to look after it. Even to this day looted artwork still keeps coming to light.

Literary and linguistic expression in *Mein Kampf*

If Hitler's talent in artistry and architecture had any merit, the same could be said of his literary skills. Admittedly, he does not embark on poetry and drama, but as a work of prose, *Mein Kampf* is quite remarkable. For one who was advised to leave school at fourteen for his poor academic record, it is quite a surprise to find a work of considerable skill emanating from one of probably low intelligence. The work has been criticised for its repetitive style, but this is no more so than many 'holy' books, including the Bible and the Koran. Repetition has its place; it serves to emphasise and help to indoctrinate the reader. Nazism was a severe case of indoctrination. Even though he had an amanuensis, Emil Maurice, there is every indication that the book was all his own work. His use of figurative language is quite elaborate at times and one wonders if he had embarked on a purely literary career, he might have produced some interesting work. Unfortunately, employing high-flown figurative language in what must be regarded as a political tract is ill-conceived and calculated to appeal to the emotions far too much. A political statement has to adhere carefully to verifiable facts, not to go off into exaggerations and inaccuracies as this work does. It is regrettable that so many took his work as literally true and made an entire gospel of it; thus it became the blueprint for the Holocaust. If his literary skill had been channelled into a doctrine of love and positive policy for the world as a whole, then it would have been something to be admired; as it is we have hate, suspicion, and negative thinking, mostly for Jews and others who are thought to be 'inferior', and high-flown ideas about the German people. This optimism is often clearly misplaced.

A good example of emotionally exaggerated language is as follows:

'In a few days the whole mist and swindle of this infamous betrayal of the people had scattered away (1914) and suddenly the gang of Jewish leaders stood there, lonely and forsaken, as though not a trace remained of the nonsense and madness... it was a bad moment for the betrayers of the German working class but as soon as the leaders recognised the danger which menaced them, they rapidly pulled the 'tarn cap' of lies over their ears, and insolently mimicked the national awakening... the time had come to take steps against the whole treacherous brotherhood of these Jewish poisoners of the people... then while Jewish jabber about international solidarity had vanished at one stroke... if the best men were dying at the front, the least we could do was to wipe out the vermin' (page 154).

The 'tarn cap' is a cloak that confers invisibility, in German legends; the term recalls the battle between Siegfried[15] and Brunhilde. It is a clever metaphoric use of the mentality of Wagner's operas. In this passage we see the libellous vocabulary used against the supposed Jewish menace in Germany. Standing back from it, it can be seen as a lot of neurotic, exaggerated claptrap, but expressed in a way to carry conviction with many an impressionable German. As a drama, and complete fiction, it is quite a melodrama; as political accuracy, it is sheer nonsense.

A clever use of pun occurs on page 229 with regard to young men sowing their wild oats.

'...the poor girl will be happy to find one of these WORN-OUT (*enthoernt*) Siegfrieds...'

This is virtually untranslatable into English but in German it is quite effective. 'To sow one's wild oats' in German would be '*sich die Hoerner abstossen*', which means literally, 'de-horned'. Siegfried did not have horns, so it is an allusion is to his horny skin, which made him invulnerable. This is quite a clever use of language using allusions to Wagnerian libretto. Not bad for someone who was advised to leave school at fourteen!

An interesting use of language comes in page 160 when talking about the gap between the working class and the middle class.

'... for here two worlds oppose each other in part naturally and in part artificially divided whose MUTUAL RELATION can only be struggle. The younger will be victorious – and this with Marxism'.

The word *Verhaltungszustand* is the original of 'mutual relation'. This word appears to be a *hapax legomenon,* i.e. a one-use word. Maybe Hitler coined it himself; it appears to mean 'condition of behaviour or attitude' but it could also mean 'suppressed condition,' or even 'repressed attitude'. It is clearly a pejorative word that is not easy to render in English and it has to do with the tense standoff between social classes. In his jaded view, it has to be characterised by violence, with Bolshevism as the prime cause. If this is a fair understanding of *Verhaltungszustand* then we have a creative use of language, a literature; what a shame it was the rhetoric of political hate and violence!

At this point it will be instructive to consider the element of propaganda, an aspect of politics which has dominated the scene for well over a century now and has caused all manner of misapprehensions. Nowadays, it is called 'spin' or 'spin-doctoring'! He discusses propaganda at length in Chapter 6, obviously envious of the Socialist-Marxist parties' mastering of the techniques with astounding skill. He understands the importance of propaganda as a weapon, every bit as effective as guns and bullets, but he stops short of saying that it can be a collection of lies. What he does say is that it can be carefully trimmed and simplified to appeal to the lowest common denominator in intelligence. It is no use directing propaganda at the intellectuals! Is this an admission that they will see through it and point out the falsehoods in it? It must be directed at the masses.

'The art of propaganda lies in understanding the emotional ideas of the great masses and finding, through a psychologically correct form, the way to the attention and thence to the heart of the broad masses' (page 165).

How true! The successful propagandist works out what prejudices and presuppositions are in the minds of working people, and then works on it from there. In this case, it was the augmentation of anti-Semitic feelings in people. He has to admit that there is such a thing as careless or bad propaganda, such as the German Government gave out in 1914, to the effect that the French and the British were all softies and could easily be pushed back. When the German Army was halted and had received a severe lesson in the trenches, it seriously affected the morale of the army, as the government line was seen to be a miscalculation. He admits that the British and American propaganda was sound; it portrayed the Germans as barbaric, and thus the front-line soldiers were not really taken by surprise when encountering a ferocious opposition. He does not venture to comment on the truth or falsehood involved here. His view of propaganda is that as a weapon, anything goes, when it comes to a life-and-death struggle such as the First World War. Moreover that weapon cannot be some sort of debating society; it must be categorical and not allow a loophole for the opposite opinion to creep in. He knows that emotion and feelings dominate people's minds (page 167).

'This sentiment is not complicated, but very simple and of a piece. It does not have multiple shadings; it has a positive and a negative; love or hate; right or wrong; truth or lie; never half this way and half that way, never partially or that kind of thing'.

Thus we see the categorical kind of thinking in his book, a mentality which pervaded virtually every argument. Göbbels managed to exploit this propagandist mentality brilliantly. When the German army was always 'advancing' he did not allow the compass directions to interfere with the main thrust of his statements! This kind of method still prevails today, the spin-doctoring, although mercifully we have the freedom to criticise it. It also surfaces in certain kinds of newspaper with a 'tabloid' mentality. It is in effect an insult to any thinking person; now we know why Hitler does not wish education to be too thorough in case, one can see through some of these claims. He would prefer to concentrate on physical education and muscle-building (in preparation for war).

Also his tactics in propaganda are outlined: it must be repetitious and stick to one line. Even if the posters do alter, the same consistent message should be there. He has a somewhat cynical view of the intelligence of the masses but repeating it 'a thousand times' will eventually make it sink in. It needs to have a 'unified and complete' effect (page 169).

Other examples of his literary expertise are shown below:

'Karl Marx, with the sure eye of the prophet, recognised in the morass of a slowly decomposing world the most essential poisons, extracted them, and, like a wizard, prepared them into a concentrated solution for the swifter annihilation of the independent existence of free nations on this earth. And all this in the service of his race [Jewish]' (page 347).

Here we see the melodramatic, over-stated approach, almost pantomimic in its luridness. As a passage from MacBeth this would be quite acceptable, but as a political statement, it is bunkum.

An example of how exaggerated and inaccurate his remarks could be comes with his scorn for the Hapsburg dynasty in Austria:

'In the north and the south the poison of foreign nations gnawed at the body of our nationality, and even Vienna was visibly becoming more and more of an un-German city. The royal house Czechised wherever possible, and it was the hand of the goddess of eternal justice and inexorable retribution which caused Archduke Francis Ferdinand[16], the most mortal enemy of Austrian-Germanism, to fall by the bullets which he himself had helped to mould. For had he not been the patron of Austria's Slavisation from above?' (page 14).

This is a grossly hyperbolised overview of what was happening in Austria in the first years of the twentieth century. The truth was that the Archduke favoured a reorganisation of the monarchy, which would have given the Slavs equality with the Germans and the Hungarians. Some of the leaders favoured collaboration with the Slavic upper classes and some relief for the oppressed Slavic populations. How much of this did come to pass is uncertain, as the War diverted everyone's attention. But Hitler likes to overstate the matter by inferences about God and eternal justice, which of course must be in favour of German culture! Nowadays we would see it as only fair to allow constituent nationalities of a great empire to have equal treatment and encourage their influence in the capital and the government. It is never easy to run an Empire with three distinct linguistic groups and seventeen different languages, with an admixture of races. But to label the non-Germans as poisonous and a corroding influence on the country just shows how narrow-minded he is. It would probably do as a snatch from a Wagnerian libretto, but this is about all.

Hitler has absolutely no time for the parliaments in either Germany of Austria. This is from first hand observation in Vienna when he visited the parliament building and witnessed the debates. Admittedly he has a great respect for the British parliament, but can only see political debate as the wedge in the door for Communism.

> 'The Western democracy of today is the forerunner of Marxism... it provides this world plague with the culture in which its germs can spread. In its most extreme form, parliamentarianism created a "monstrosity of excrement and fire", in which, however, sad to say, the "fire" seems to me at the moment to be burned out' (page 72).

Here we see an allusion to Göethe's *Faust, Part One*, again emotionally charged language not really appropriate for a sensible political statement. It is quite a reasonable turn of metaphor but his talents could have been directed to a much more worthy cause than condemning anyone who happened not to be a true German. We can tell from other parts of his book that a one-party state with a dictator is the only system he can contemplate. Not that he ever nominates himself as the dictator but the inference is fairly blatant. He can justify this by claiming that the only way to stop creeping Marxism is to have a firm unified lead from the government; in other words, Fascist totalitarianism.

> 'From the millions of men... ONE man must step forward who, with apodictic force, will form granite principles... from the shifting waves of a free thought-world there will arise a brazen cliff of solid unity in faith and will...' (page 346).

And with this we see the blueprint for the Third Reich and all its excesses. This is outlined on page 312. It is anti-parliamentarian; the idea of majority rule means that the leader is degraded to the level of a mere executant of other people's ideas. The leader must be free to exercise unconditional authority, but that involves the highest responsibility as well. In effect, this is a return to mediaeval absolutist monarchy with some sort of parvenu who has managed to grasp the levers of power. With this we see all the abuses of unchecked power in the Fascist system. He does not discuss what happens when a scoundrel manages to inveigle his way into the position of leadership. Hitler goes further to describe the structure from local level to the top; it is a system of little Führers who have unlimited powers and authority; this must mean the withdrawal of rights and freedoms of the individual at all levels.

Relevant to these literary and linguistic matters is the word 'folkish' (*Volkisch*). It is an adjective with much pejorative loading; a simple rendering would be 'nationalist', but it implies a lot more, very largely suggestive of anti-Semitism. It is German folk-lore with a nasty racialist tinge. Hitler is sarcastic about some folkish groups that go in for the dim pre-history of Germany with ancient artefacts and dressing up; he sees it as a distraction from the main target of folkism, that of concentrating on the Jewish problem. Bayer saw folkism as a monarchist attitude; other groups had a variety of different interpretations of it. There were the 'knights of the spiritual sword' (page329). All this Hitler regards as hot air and cowardice. There were various nationalistic groups with an anti-Semitic tinge, but Hitler attacks other rightist groups. Eventually the Nazis managed to scoop up nearly all of them along with just about everything else in Germany.

As far as he is concerned, folkish, though having a wide and vague definition, should involve not the equality of races, but the 'the basic aristocratic idea of Nature', i.e. the superiority of the German people. This philosophy is the innermost will of Nature; this is an indirect way of saying that it is God's intention that... the best of humanity should take over the Earth and be the master race. So 'folkish' becomes more than just a nationalistic adjective; it becomes a worldview. The basis of this, with the Aryans, should be a policy of only allowing the healthy to beget children; thus a highly-bred racial stock will be the result. Hitler sees it as a crime against God for people with diseases and mental illnesses to breed. Breeding of healthy bodies needs plenty of physical training in school; it is a requirement for the preservation of the nation. So from this we see the blueprint for the Nazi euthanasia programme and for the selective breeding programmes.

Another aspect of 'folkish' is the religious element. This is not directly involved in the racial mentality of Nazism; indirectly it is. Hitler sees it as a mistake to allow religious disagreements to interfere with national unity. He boasts that in the Nazi party, he has catholic and protestant sink their differences for the sake of unity of purpose for the national good. Germany has spent too much time on religious quarrels, which has simply played into the hands of Jewish interests, namely, that of destroying the Aryan race. There is no hint at this stage of the situation that did emerge in the Third Reich; namely that, although many churchmen favoured the regime, others objected and formed a confessing church. Many clergymen were sent to the concentration camps.

The selective breeding policy does sound convincing to those who have little knowledge of genetics. Many people were taken in by this policy. But the truth is that fit and intelligent parents do sometimes produce a child that is mentally deficient or physically weak. The opposite is also true: parents with health problems can and do produce a child that is strong and intelligent. The eugenics programme was an inhuman policy that backfired on the Nazis; it was a severe interference with human freedom and dignity. Many churchmen had the courage to stand out against it.

These are the various aspects of the 'folkish' system of thought. It must be seen against the backdrop of the times in Germany in which the word was a sort of buzz-word amongst rightist groups; the difference with Hitler, it would seem, was that he took it far more literally and with a vile element of exaggeration, which resulted in an inhuman social policy.

Theological aspects

It is clear from various indirect remarks early in the book that Hitler was raised as a Roman Catholic and he does not appear to renounce this background anywhere. That is not to say that every Roman Catholic is an anti-Semite of the most violent kind. It must be seen in context; there were plenty of Protestants with equally extreme views. He is clearly in favour of a religious faith, but it needs to be 'clearly delimited'; having endless different groups with opposing ideas is not only worthless for human life, but will hasten the general disintegration of culture which is going on.

He appears to agree that there are various ideas such as the indestructibility of the soul, the eternity of existence, the existence of a higher being. It is clear in places that he believes in God, and related to that, fate, providence and destiny, with himself in the spotlight. Sadly, God is all mixed up with racial purity:

> '... to put an end to the constant and continuous original sin of racial poisoning, and to give the Almighty Creator beings such as He Himself created?'

Is this an indirect claim that Adam and Eve were Aryans?

He often makes rhetorical remarks, such as 'Lord protect us' (page 515) and 'no, by the Living God' (page 13), and 'How thankful I am to this day to the Providence...' (page 27). One wonders how genuine such phrasing is or is it just hot air?

But elsewhere his belief system may be genuine, even if riddled with anti-Semitic backdrop:

> 'The folkish-minded man (anti-Semitic)... has a sacred duty each in his own denomination (talking about different churches), of making people stop just talking superficially of God's will and fulfil God's will, and not let God's word be desecrated. For God's will gave men their form, their essence and their abilities. Anyone who destroys His work is declaring war on the Lord's creation, the divine will' (page 512).

The assumption here is that it is against God to allow Jewish influence and infiltration to persist. So his theology, though basically 'Christian' (or so he would claim), is riddled with racial prejudice. This is something that most people will find difficult to take on board; yet we have seen this sort of thing in South Africa and in the Deep South of the USA, and will see it in the Book of Mormon (Chapter 7). Nowhere in the Bible do we find this sort of 'gospel', in fact, the very opposite. But Hitler believes that 'Eternal Nature avenges the infringement of her commands... I believe that I am acting in accordance with the will of the Almighty Creator; by defending myself against the Jew, I am fighting for the work of the Lord' (page 60).

In his rantings about the Jews, he makes out that 'his spirit is inwardly as alien to true Christianity as his nature two thousand years ago previously, to the great founder of the new doctrine' (page 278). He is of course talking about Jesus as if he were not a Jew himself. He cites Jesus' alleged antipathy to the Jews, by driving them out of the Temple, since their interest in it was only pecuniary. This resulted in the Crucifixion. Hitler seems to be in favour of Jesus; but then he never stops to consider that Jesus was Jewish himself; under the Third Reich, he too would have been introduced to the gas chambers at Auschwitz! Or is Hitler assuming that Jesus was actually an Aryan?! Hitler does not stop to consider that the teachings of Jesus were about caring for people and violence was not included in his thinking. As for Jesus' attitude to the Jewish people, his first disciples were all Jewish, and he appealed to vast numbers of them in the land of Israel. It was certain elements in the Jewish leadership (by no means all of them) that had Jesus condemned to die. Admittedly, St John speaks as if all the Jews hated Jesus, but what he means is that certain elements reacted badly and plotted his downfall. This is another instance of Hitler's categorical thinking which is so unfair and dishonest.

With regard to marriage, Hitler has a high view of its importance for producing the next generation of Aryans. There will be a prohibition on mixed marriages. There will be a citizen's diploma that will admit one to public activity, and also a health certificate confirming one's physical health for marriage. This way, the 'continuous defilement' of the race will be halted and marriage will be able to produce 'images of the Lord' and not 'monstrosities halfway between man and ape.' (page 366). This implies that pure German children will resemble Jesus (the Lord). Has it occurred to him that Jesus was Jewish?

As far as interbreeding is concerned, he sees this as 'the most execrable crime'.

'Anyone who dares to lay hands on the highest image of the Lord commits sacrilege against the benevolent creator of this miracle and contributes to the expulsion from paradise (page 348).

Such language may suggest that Hitler is some sort of Bible fundamentalist; and yet, he does not go on to explain what he means by 'expulsion from paradise'; is it literally what went wrong in the Garden of Eden? How could that be a matter of racial intermixing, if Adam and Eve were of the same race? Or is he talking figuratively about Germany's loss of innocence with the incursion of the Jews and their plan to destroy the nation? As it worked out, it became clear that he was talking figuratively: the Third

Reich was a pattern of intolerance for anyone who was not pure Aryan.

Complementary to a high view of marriage, he has a disgust for prostitution, something that was rampant in most European cities at that time, not least Vienna. He is deeply concerned about the prevalence of syphilis, which is one of the main results of prostitution.

'Prostitution is a disgrace to humanity but cannot be eliminated by moral lectures, pious intentions etc.' (page 228).

The way forward is to remove the causes of it. One of them is that young men find it too difficult to marry early; this should be reversed with a new financial and housing policy. Secondly, education should be shaped so that young men's physical qualities should be developed; a healthy body gives a healthy mind. Free time should be used for physical training rather than hanging around the streets in idleness with no real purpose in life. Thirdly, the poisoning of the soul should be tackled; the content of films, theatre, vaudeville, with debased sexual values advertised, should be stopped. He is concerned about young people's innocence being taken away. 'Public life must be freed from the stifling perfume of our modern eroticism, just as it must be freed from all unmanly prudish hypocrisy' (page 232).

Strange as it may seem, the Jews do not appear to be the target for blame in these matters; however the racial element is never very far beneath the surface; 'the right of personal freedom recedes before the duty to preserve the race'.

It would be fair to say that the Third Reich did succeed in removing prostitution from the streets. That is not to say that the problem itself was actually solved; such people were consigned to the concentration camps, and many of them actually became the guards and staff at these places. As the German army sent its men away from home, military brothels were established, normally supplied with ladies selected from conquered territories, on a compulsory basis. It is thought that Hitler himself was not exactly a stranger to the Viennese brothels and he has been suspected of having contracted syphilis himself. No one knows for sure since he would never allow a proper doctor to examine him.

In general terms, *Mein Kampf* is characterised by its religious tone. How sincere this was, would be an interesting question. If he were genuinely Christian-orientated, one would expect and hope that there would be less inclination to violence and more inclination to caring for people, not just the Germans, but for everyone else, like Jesus.

Philosophical aspects of *Mein Kampf*

Hitler has a lot to say on the subject of Philosophy, in fact he discusses it in the whole of Chapter 1: Philosophy and Party. One might have thought that some attempt would have been made to justify or substantiate his views by reference to the respected philosophers of the past – Plato, Aristotle, Boethius, Aquinas and others – but there is never any mention of such people. Hitler's philosophy is grounded in the mentality of the hooligan: might is right. The winner in any battle has a moral right to be justified and claim what he wants. This was worked out in real terms with the plundering that went on in the conquered territories in the war. He sees the whole of life as a massive struggle 'entirely in keeping with the primal meaning of things' by which the highest humanity, i.e. the Germans, is to be preserved and advanced. It is a truly high mission given by the benevolence of the Almighty.

Hitler has absolutely no time for pacifism. The ultimate aim is peace with the master race ruling the world, but to achieve it, force must be used:

'... what so many blinded today hope to gain by begging, whining, and whimpering; a peace, supported not by palm branches of tearful, pacifist female mourners, but based on the victorious sword of a master people, putting the world into the service of a higher culture' (page 360).

His whole outlook is conditioned by violence, attack, no compromise, no peace conference, no co-operation. The thought of defeat, surrender or even a tactical retreat is not in his terms of reference at all. He quotes Clausewitz[17] to this effect:

'... that the stain of a cowardly submission can never be effaced; that this drop of poison in the blood of a people is passed on to posterity and will paralyse and undermine the strength of later generations...' (page 610).

An admission of defeat means that a nation has lost all honour and character, and will just accept humiliation and slavery without a murmur. Such was the situation in 1918; a situation that Hitler is absolutely convinced he can reverse by kicking new life into a demoralised and confused country. The only way to bring in a new regime and break the slavery of the present situation, is to fight terror with terror, or coercion by coercion.

He has no time for endless political parties which have to make some sort of alignment with others to gain any ground. This was the turbulent situation in the inter-war years in Germany, when there were thirty or more parties vying for power; none of them could muster a majority at an election which meant that it was all down to coalitions and deals to make any headway. We can now see the motive for a one-party state for a country in such a crisis.

'Political parties are inclined to compromises; philosophies never. Political parties even reckon with opponents; philosophies proclaim their infallibility' (page 413).

He would say that all political parties have some sort of philosophy as their basis, whether rightist or leftist. The difference with Nazism is that the philosophy *is* the political party and cannot make deals with any other. He sees the critical issue as between Marxism with its 'internationalist' mentality and the folkish worldview, which as we have seen is all about German superiority with the master race. The only way to resolve it is through armed struggle. He claims that the folkish philosophy agrees with the innermost will of Nature, because it provides for the higher breeding of the best in human nature. Eternal truth, which is a secularised way of saying 'God', is on the side of folkism.

Essential to Hitler's philosophy is his understanding of fate. He uses various expressions for this, varying in emotionalism and theological implications. But what it amounts to is that he believes in Predestination. There is a feeling of inevitability in the recent course of History concerning Germany and Austria. His book is peppered with words such as fate, providence, 'predestined', destiny and others. This is a poetic way of saying that God had it all planned out, and that Hitler was a part of that plan. He never actually claims to be the chosen one of God in so many words, but the implication is never very far beneath the surface. A good example of his hinting claim would be:

'If you believe that you have been chosen by fate to reveal the truth in these matters, do so; but then have the courage to do so, not indirectly through a political party... for this is a swindle; but for today's evil substitute your future good' (page 106).

Strangely, destiny is something that can be challenged. 'If providence had put me in the place of the incapable or criminal incompetents or scoundrels in our propaganda service, our battle with Destiny would have taken a different turn' (page 171).

Here is an element of illogicality in this; how can destiny be fought against? So predestination is not all that it might seem to be. Moreover there is an element of meritology in dealing with the goddess of Destiny; not it would seem for good deeds, but for truth and steadfastness.

'... the inexorable hand of the goddess of destiny begins to weigh peoples and men according to the truth and steadfastness of their convictions... it seemed to me almost a belated act of grace to be allowed to stand as a witness in the divine court of the eternal judge and proclaim the sincerity of this conviction' (page 149). He is talking about the joy of enlisting as a soldier to prove his adherence to the German cause, but not, however to the Austrian one.

In his sarcasm about the hair-brained academics, he can see that only a wave of hot passion can turn the destinies of peoples. The 'cruel Goddess of Distress' is involved here. But it needs someone with the right pitch of conviction and oratory to alter the destiny of Germany. Here comes another hint of his own future:

> '... he alone can arouse the passion who bears it within himself. It alone gives its chosen one the words, which, like hammer blows, can open the gates to the heart of a people. But the man whom passion fails and whose lips are sealed... he has not been chosen by heaven to proclaim its will' (page 98).

Another aspect of this kind of thinking involves Nature as personified, taking revenge on those who transgress, i.e. the mixing of races. The substratum of this, though never clearly stated, is that he takes the theory of evolution very seriously and assumes that the survival of the fittest is the ruling principle, not just in zoology but in every area. This then can justify the dominant race and to thwart this is a crime against 'God'. How literally we take this is debateable; however, many did take it literally and never even questioned it in relation to ethics. The result was the atrocities of the Third Reich.

Essentially he believes in the 'aristocratic idea of Nature', not just on a national level but right down to the last individual. The equality of races is nonsense; the better and stronger must subordinate the weaker and inferior nations, and this is in accordance with the eternal will that dominates the universe (page 348). From this a new and nobler age will emerge, a final, great future for the German people but also for the whole of humanity. He talks as if the subordinated nations of the world will enjoy being tyrannised and exploited by the 'pure Aryans'.

Another aspect of the folkish philosophy, apart from its racialist cant, is the emphasis placed on 'personality'; this is one of the main pillars of its entire edifice. He sees Marxism as denying the importance of the personality. This has been borne out by the procedures in many a communist state, where they all have to wear the same uniform, behave exactly the same and make applause all in unison. But the Nazis can claim to be a philosophy of life because of the emphasis placed on personality. But the way it works out, in his view, is that able men cannot be appointed from above; they must force their way upwards so that the best minds work their way up into leading positions. This is not done by voting and popularity contests, it is done by the ingenuity, force of personality, and possibly also trickery of the individual. This leads on to his philosophy of government; it is nothing to do with electioneering; it is a matter of who manages to push his way into the halls of power, whether at local or national level. And such a person will have the right to make authoritative decisions, and also take the responsibility. Might is right. This is the blueprint for fascist dictatorship.

> 'A philosophy of life which endeavours to reject the democratic mass idea and give this earth to the best people... that is the highest humanity... must logically obey the same aristocratic principle... the leadership and the highest influence in this people fall to the best minds... it builds not upon the idea of the majority but upon the idea of personality' (page 403).

We notice that he does not attempt to define what 'the best' might mean; in practice, it turned out to be the most unscrupulous, power-hungry, and nasty-minded. People like Julius Streicher, the arch Jew-baiter, Heinrich Himmler, the one with no conscience about murdering thousands, and Josef Göebbels, the one who had difficulties in discriminating between the truth and lies. People like this became the leading lights in the Third Reich; a most uncomfortable thought.

> 'By rejecting the authority of the individual and replacing it by the numbers of some momentary mob, the parliamentary principle of majority rule sins against the basic aristocratic principle of Nature...' (page 74).

> 'The Jewish doctrine of Marxism rejects the aristocratic principle of Nature and replaces the eternal privilege of power and strength by the mass of numbers and their dead weight. Thus it denies the value of personality in man, contests the significance of nationality and race, and thereby withdraws from humanity the premise of its existence and its culture' (page 60).

So we see that his whole outlook circulates around racial prejudice and force. 'The world belongs only to the forceful "whole man" and not to the weak "half man" (page 234). Whether any responsible or principled philosopher could ever endorse these views is an awkward question. Possibly someone like Machiavelli[18] would approve of such ideas, but even then he might be stunned at the exaggerated emotionalism and the grandiose scale of its implementation.

Conclusions about *Mein Kampf*

This is an amazing document, and in its day it attracted a lot of attention and acceptance in Germany. It is regrettable that more people from outside Germany did not take note of it. It was translated into forty-five languages. If such a document appeared today, it would almost certainly be laughed off a sheer nonsense, and would probably land the author in court for racially-motivated incitement. That is because we have the luxury of hindsight; we all know what the excesses of the Third Reich led to, namely the Bar of justice at Nuremburg. But we must see *Mein Kampf* in its setting, just as with the Bible and many other 'sacred' literatures. What circumstances produced such a work; what was the substratum of it all?

The reality of it was that Europe had just been through an unprecedented period of change, known as the Industrial Revolution. This had produced massive industrial cities with new classes of factory workers and beneath that, grafting workers living in grinding poverty. At the same time, the emerging industrial nations had been in cut-throat competition to build empires in what is now known as the Third World, partly to obtain resources and partly to park off their superfluous population somewhere abroad. There was also the backtaste of the Napoleonic wars in which the French had rampaged all over Europe and given themselves a bad reputation, especially in Germany. Germany, however, was late in the colonial race and had only managed to acquire a few colonies in Africa, none of which were particularly worthwhile in terms of resources, and so there was envy there. Another factor was that Germany had not become united as a Reich until 1870, was still eyeing up territories that might be annexed to the Reich, and was still finding its feet as a 'democracy'. It was an unstable political situation and also unstable on the issue of boundary settlements. As we know, a democracy needs time and patience to mature; this was not helped by the delusions of grandeur handed out by the Kaisers and Bismarck[19]. The defeat of 1918 caused total dismay in Germany, for they could not see a reason for it, having convinced themselves that they had the best army in the world. This was augmented by the humiliating Treaty of Versailles (1920); that in itself was a formula for trouble in the future, plus the crushing reparations that were imposed. There were thousands of disaffected German soldiers who could not come to terms with this; in fact the whole nation was deeply embittered. Now we see the obvious setting for someone to appear and offer an answer to all these problems.

If it had not been Hitler, it would probably have been someone else with some sort of cheap answer. It was like the Garden of Eden; we have to find someone or something to blame; we cannot look ourselves in the mirror. Hitler had the insight to see two scapegoats just waiting to be roped in – the Jews and the Marxists – then he cleverly managed to merge the two into one. This was the reason for the failure of 1918: the stab in the back.

It was reasonably easy to target the Jews as the villains of the piece: they were a group that tended to stick together with their distinctive customs and diet. It was not quite so easy to define those who were not full-blown Jewish, but the Nuremburg laws[20] set about drawing the line somewhere. There was a lot of anti-Semitic feeling latent in Germany and Austria. The Jews were seen as a 'foreign' influence, many with a distinctive accent. With the Marxists, that would be more difficult as a target because vast numbers of the German working class were, through the trades unions, in favour of what Marx was offering; equality of livelihood and freedom from exploitation. But the clever trick, which seems to be Hitler's own bright idea, was to equate the Jews with the Marxists! How often do we encounter the phrase 'Jew-Bolshevik' in his book? Laughable really, but as a crazy idea, it just happened to carry conviction. We add to that the element of flattery; that seldom fails in politics. He told the German people that they were the best people on earth; their destiny was to rule the world, that would involve force, but it would be worth it for the benefits that would be brought for all the races of the world. There was, however, a corrupting influence at work, undermining the Aryan race, that of the Jews. To restore Germany to its true leading role in world affairs would mean the removal of the Jewish-Marxist influence, thus producing a stronger, healthier, culturally more brilliant master race. Given such a glittering vision of the future, what people could resist such flattery-cum-temptation? Cap that by telling them that God is in favour of this scheme and that Adolf Hitler is doing the will of God, and you have an argument that carries its own conviction.

But implementing these ideas was another matter. Hitler did not believe in any sort of compromise, discussion, trimming of his policies to suit circumstances. Nazism was not really a political party; it was an entire philosophic-religion with a solid doctrine, with himself as the queen-bee. Force had to be used; a gang of ruffians was recruited and sordid punch-ups occurred at many a political rally. In spite of him paying lip service to electioneering in order to gain 'legitimate' power in the Reichstag, there was always the element of unprincipled violence and threat at work. This aggressive attitude coupled with his obsessive, categorical mind-set, was a formula for trouble. This could have been prevented except that by 1930, Germany was in such a state that any solution would carry conviction with a distraught population.

The implementation of these ideas was not going to be easy. With any retrospective legislation comes the moral problem of unfairness. The Nuremburg laws were retrospective in that it applied to people who were already Jewish and could not undo that fact. It was not as if they were given the chance to renounce their racial background. There was also the problem of defining Jewishness; an elaborate scheme was devised so that half-Jews and quarter-Jews were dealt with accordingly. People were then deprived of their civil rights and also duties; a Jew could not serve in the army, but on the other hand, he could serve in the navy! The active persecution gradually grew worse up to the Final Solution and the activities of the Einsatzgruppen in the conquered territories. Behind all this was the categorical thinking of Hitler. All Jews are rotten; all Germans are superb; there are no shades of opinion. All Jews are Marxists; all Marxists are Jews. How simple and straightforward! There was no mention of the thought that, even if one Jew was a conniving rascal, that does not mean that they all are; conversely, if some Germans are superb chaps, that means that they all have to be fantastic. The same goes for communism: just because Karl Marx happened to be Jewish (he might not have been a practicing Jew) that does not have to mean that all Jews are revolutionary Bolsheviks. But that is where the crackpot logic of the obsessive people leads. The false logic of all this finally came home to roost in 1945 with Hitler, still not admitting to having got it wrong, blamed everyone else for treachery, and dodged the responsibility which he himself had delineated, by killing himself with his mistress, Eva Braun.

Now we are left with the legacy of the Third Reich. The vast majority of the world totally rejects anything like a fascist totalitarian state. This is fair enough, except that 'democracy' has gone to such extremes, in reaction, that many countries, including Britain, find it difficult to come to a clear policy or a clean-cut decision on anything. Much time is wasted with endless wrangles. As far as nationalism is concerned, this is often seen as something suspicious, but a positive and peaceful approach to nationalism is no problem. One can be enthusiastic and loyal to one's own country and yet be prepared to co-operate with other countries.

The same goes for the racial question. It is a fact that there are different peoples with different cultures and religions in this world. Just trying to blur over this to make out that we are all the same is misleading. But this does not have to lead to one race proclaiming itself as superior and ready to dominate all the others with what they claim as a superior 'culture'. Far more constructive and respectful is to say that each race and culture has something positive to offer to the general picture; whether it be art forms, technology, sport, religion, and many other fields. To make out that one's own culture is the only one available is nonsense. Then we come to the question of leadership. It is true that some people are more gifted than others; that does not necessarily qualify them to be higher up the social or political ladder than others. Being gifted in one area does not always carry the element of being ambitious. Conversely, being ambitious does not always mean that one is highly gifted.

So we come inevitably to the question of what was Hitler? He thought he was a Christian! He claimed to be doing the will of God, and doing his best for the future of German civilisation. The essential question is whether he was sincere in this, or just systematically deceiving everyone, including himself. Difficult! Some would say he was sincere, even if totally misled.

Others would say he was the anti-Christ, totally riddled with hate and evil. One thing could be said: he was not stupid. He had the native wit of someone who has studied human nature and worked out how to manipulate people's fears and prejudices. As a politician he was highly accomplished; as a military tactician he was a complete amateur. At the beginning of the war he managed to dazzle everyone as being a military genius, then as the war progressed, he made one blunder after another, which in fact played into the hands of the Allies more than he ever realised. It was said that the best general the Allies ever had, was Hitler himself! But did he deliberately set to work to cause so much pain, loss of life and distress? It is just possible that he was carried away by his own dogmas; when it got to the point in the early 1940s that events were not going to work out quite so easily in his favour, in spite of having the master race to make it all happen, he was then trapped in his own delusions of grandeur. This led to the murder of millions, the total collapse of the Third Reich, the triumph of Bolshevism and the rejuvenation of Judaism.

Needless to say, the true values of Christianity as seen in the gospels are all about caring, humility, helping the weak and sick, peace, acceptance of other races in a positive way, and above all, the true form of leadership, that of giving oneself completely for the sake of humanity. These values are the exact opposite of what the Third Reich stood for.

As an artist and a theoretical architect, it would seem that he had a lot to offer. Looking at this literary style in *Mein Kampf*, he had much potential as a dramatist or librettist for the Wagnerian type of opera or melodrama. But sadly his obsessive racism and fascination with some sort of idealised Germanism gave a heavily negative view of everything. It is rather like reading an up-market version of Mr. Alfred Garnett; highly amusing as a drawing room joke session, but disastrous when taken too literally by a people who were in a desperate crisis.

So what conclusions can be drawn from Hitler and Third Reich? It is certainly a warning from history, which, if we become complacent, could happen again. History has a nasty habit of repeating itself.

1. It is very important to ensure that a responsible person, carefully selected and supervised, should be allowed to grasp the levers of power in any country. Allowing someone with no moral scruples to run the government is asking for trouble. There was no official opposition, monarch or president to whom he was answerable, still less anyone who could remove him from office when things began to deteriorate.
2. It is important that each thinking person should stop and evaluate all pronouncements from the government. Believing the propaganda issued by the ruling elite can become disastrous. It is even worse when the ruling echelons begin to believe their own lies, as did happen in the

Third Reich. People must be free to question, criticise, and not be in fear of persecution if they happen to disagree.

3. It is clear that a gospel of hate and persecution generally backfires on one. Although millions of Jews died, it gave them the moral high ground and a wave of sympathy which resulted in the establishment of the modern state of Israel. Judaism is now a major influence in world affairs, and they react quickly to stamp on any outbreaks of anti-Semitism.

4. Deliberately starting a war is foolish; one can never foresee the medium to long-term consequences. Would it have been possible in 1939 to guess how events would turn out by 1945? Hardly! The world was transformed by the Second World War; the net result was a major nuclear stalemate between the Soviet bloc and the Western powers. Now we have nuclear proliferation. We are still living with the consequences of Hitler's attack on Poland. The net result for Germany was a divided nation up to 1990, and a major loss of territory.

5. There were some helpful results from the war. The foundation of the United Nations with the necessary teeth to enforce peace has been a major gain. Co-operation between nations and a determination to make peace work has been a welcome development. Also racial discrimination is now right out of favour; in fact, any kind of discrimination is frowned upon. Equality is now the new gospel. All this is the exact opposite of the theories of Hitler.

6. The importance of being willing to display humility is very relevant to contemporary politics. Hitler was a bad loser; he could not cope with the idea of losing a battle, a tactical withdrawal, an accommodation to someone else, co-operation in general. Even when he made a treaty it was simply a tactic to delay what he actually intended to do. The whole course of history could have been different if he had not had such delusions of grandeur and infallibility; or at least he had managed to moderate things before it got completely out of hand after 1938. But then history is full of 'what-ifs'!

Hitler's thinking in relation to Wagner's operas

Hitler admits that Wagner's operas made a deep impression on him as a young man and remained a major influence on him in his political career. One wonders if there is anything in these operas that would encourage such extreme views and political policies.

In general terms, Wagner's operas contain three important strands: the mythical or legendary plot, the pure love of a woman, and a *Leitmotiv* – a use of typical musical phrases to represent various characters or situations. In addition to this, there is the attempt at a complete artistic experience, with every art form worked in, backed up by a massive orchestra in which all the instruments are multiplied by three. This gives a massive stirring sound. These operas can only be described as the work of a genius, even if they are not to everyone's taste. They are also highly emotional and romanticised; it is very easy to become completely carried away. How is this relevant to Hitler's mentality?

Firstly, the mythological or legendary aspect is a direct appeal to antiquity and the supposed nobility that goes with it. Much of this mythology concerns Germany, but not all. There is always the temptation, especially for those whose intelligence might be a little less acute, to take mythology as the literal truth. This may well be so with Hitler who seems to have been an emotional and impressionable character. Certainly the Nazi ideology as it developed, managed to include all kinds of mythological material, regardless of its historical veracity.

With regard to the complete artistic experience, which can still be sampled at the theatre in Bayreuth, Hitler certainly fancied himself as an artist and also a connoisseur of culture, although he never actually defined the essence of culture for our clarification. It is clear that the overwhelming emotional experience of a Wagner opera could overexcite someone as impressionable as Hitler; the massive orchestra with hordes of singers on the stage would easily translate itself into the massed rallies of Nuremburg, in which people got totally carried away.

But looking at one specific opera, *Die Meistersinger von Nürnberg*[21], there is also much to give one the opposite impression. The opera starts in a church, with a holy ambience and the message is one of Peace. The religious tone keeps reappearing in the opera, with remarks about St.John the Baptist and people being baptised. When a street brawl does occur, someone authoritative comes out and orders them to be peaceful and go home to bed. There is actually a polemic against fighting. Perhaps Hitler could have taken more notice of that strand in this opera! Admittedly, Walther (the main character) is dubbed as a *Ritter*[22], which means some sort of Teutonic Knight, but he does not seem to be a noticeably aggressive character.

As far as Nationalism is concerned, there is a remark made about the *Deutschen Reich* in which we 'treasure the fair and good'. This is not a racist remark; it is a general comment about German culture and art forms. This is fair enough as far as it goes; it is not an incitement to the persecution of other cultures. At the end there is a remark about 'Holy German art'; the implication here is that it refers to the *Meistersingers* and the perfection that they expect of anyone attempting to join their brotherhood.

There is also a remark about the threat of foreign domination, but in such a way as to be non-specific. At that time, in the First Reich, such a thing was far from their minds; it was much the opposite, since Germany had notions about recovering the Holy Roman Empire, and had, in 1870, managed to take a generous portion out of France, namely Alsace and Lorraine.

From this sample of Wagnerian opera, it can be seen that there is very little to fuel a creed as extreme and racist as Nazism. If anything, the contrary ideology can be seen, that of peace. If Hitler had taken more notice of this world history could have been somewhat different. It is easy to see, however, that the grand manner, the big parade, the high emotion, the inflated ideas, backed up by snobbery, could easily put ideas into the head of someone such as Hitler. It is a cautionary factor for us all: the ideas we have now might easily be reinterpreted into something fantastic and totally contradictory by someone in the future who fatally misunderstood one's meaning.

Göethe's *Faust* in relation to Hitler's thinking

Hitler claims to have a great admiration for Göethe as well as Schiller and Shakespeare. Reading through *Faust*, the first part, one is struck by the elevated language and use of metaphor, which is in many ways equivalent to Shakespeare's. The difference is that the play concerns itself mainly with the dubious relationship between Doctor Faust, a high-level teacher who is disillusioned with life, and Mephistopheles, the Devil. The ordinary people at street level only seem to be involved incidentally, with the exception of Margaret, with whom Faust has fallen in love. God, or angels seem only to play a minor role and have hardly any influence. One is struck by the religious tone of the book; the backdrop of it is Roman Catholicism.

It is hard to see how such a work could have engendered the fanatical racist mentality of the Nazis. The Jews are never worked into the plot in any way and there is no racist polemic or sentiment in the entire work. The only remark that could be relevant to this would be:

'The church alone, dear women, can digest ill-gotten gains without a stomach-ache. That is a universal custom; a Jew or a king might do the same'.

This is the sort of throwaway remark which has very little prejudice involved; it is mildly humorous and would have been nothing out of the ordinary in Göethe's day.

With regard to German blood, there is also another throwaway remark which goes:

'A German of true blood can never like the French, but he enjoys their wines a lot'.

This is in the context of a jocular scene in a wine cellar in Leipzig; the sort of remark that no one would take literally.

With regard to acquisition of territory in the east, there is nothing whatsoever mentioned on this subject, nor the Teutonic Knights, or any kind of Ritter. There is nothing here to encourage territorial expansion.

What could be relevant to Hitler's philosophy is the Devil's approach to systems of thought:

> ' In general, put all your faith in words, for then you will surely pass the gate and reach the temple-halls of certainty. But each word should harbour some idea... don't torment yourself too much, because precisely where no thought is present a word appears in proper time. Words are priceless in an argument. Words are building stones of systems. It's splendid to believe in words; from words you cannot rob a single letter'.

If we compare this with Hitler's approach to philosophy and propaganda, we see that the usage of words is very important in constructing systems of thought. Hitler was highly sarcastic about people who just throw words around but never actually do anything with them in reality. This brings us to a very instructive passage in Faust, where the Doctor is doing an exegesis of John 1:1:

> '"In the beginning was the WORD!"... I truly cannot rate the word so high. I must translate it otherwise. I believe the Spirit is inspiring me and I must write: "In the beginning was the MIND"... it is the mind that stirs and makes all things? The text should be, "In the beginning was the POWER!"... the Spirit helps me now. The answer is at hand... "In the beginning was the DEED".'

Mary Baker Eddy (Chapter 10) would doubtless have agreed with the word being the Mind, but Göethe goes further. All of these implications would be a fair deduction from the concept of Logos as in the Ancient World, except that St John intends the Word to be coterminous with the pre-existent Messiah, Jesus. But we can see how a biblical text like this could be taken and misused by those of an extremist nationalist mentality. The concept of power and deed are clearly a concomitant of the word of God; if you are going to have a political theory about rescuing one's nation from degeneration, it is helpful to enlist God as one's ally and use this train of thought. Indeed, Hitler did claim to be doing God's work.

Other than these remarks, there is nothing in *Faust* that could seriously be taken as a blueprint for National Socialism in the form that Hitler devised it.

Notes for Chapter 4: Mein Kampf

1. Aryans. This comes from the Sanskrit *arya* meaning 'noble'. These people originated in Iran and Northern India and the Indo-European languages are thought to come from them. In the nineteenth century there was the theory that the Aryan peoples were morally, culturally and physically superior to other races. This idea was seized upon by Hitler and the Nazis.
2. Prometheus. In the Greek drama, *Prometheus Bound*, the god Prometheus is crucified on a rock and descends into hell because he stole some of Hephaistus' fire and gave humanity all kinds of skills.
3. Pantig, Liger and Tigon. These are crossed versions of lions, tigers etc. The big cats are capable of producing offspring, just as dogs can.
4. The Teutonic Knights were the 'noble' warriors who extended German culture through Poland, and into the Baltic States, in mediaeval times.
5. Brest-Litovsk. This was the peace settlement between Germany and Russia in 1918. It provided for the creation of Poland, Ukraine, Finland and the Baltic States as independent.
6. 'Folkish'. Literally, 'people-ish'; a pejorative adjective that has cultural and racist overtones.
7. Karl Marx. A political and economic theorist of the nineteenth century, living in London. His book, *Das Kapital*, became the touchstone of communism (see Chapter 3).
8. Bolshevik. Meaning 'one of the majority', it was the party led by Lenin, which took over Russia after the October Revolution (1917). They suppressed all other parties and their policy was of violence and confiscation of property. It developed into the Communist Party of Russia.
9. The Austro-Hungarian empire, ruled by the Hapsburg dynasty, was basically Austria, Czechoslavakia and Hungary, but with territories reaching down into Serbia. Although German was supposed to be the basic language, there were in fact seventeen different languages spoken. That must have been a very complicated empire.
10. Charlemagne, AD 742-814. The instigator of the Holy Roman Empire, with Aix-la-Chapelle as its centre. It brought together all the Christian lands in central Europe, mainly in the Low Countries and Germany and parts of France. The Germans had ideas about recreating the Holy Roman Empire. Charlemagne was the centre of a cult in the Middle Ages and was informally beatified.
11. Footnote on page 35 of *Mein Kampf*. Universal suffrage and secret ballot were introduced into Austria in 1906. The Austrian Social Democratic Party was intellectually active and able to tackle the inadequacies of theoretical Marxism. The leading figures were, Adler, Bauer, Renner and Hilferding. Adler was the only Jew among them.
12. There is an art gallery in Linz; Hitler bequeathed his paintings to the town of Linz.
13. Cubism is the term given to the style of Piccasso and Braques.
14. Dadism is another modern art idea; it is a nihilistic movement in art.
15. Siegfried and Brunhilde. Siegfried is a mythological character who killed the monster Brunhilde. He hid in a pit and stabbed the monster from below, and the blood gave him a horny skin. Siegfried appears in various Wagner operas, not least, *Der Junge Siegfried*. Siegfried's name was given to the line of defence running along northern France in the late 1930s.
16. The Archduke Francis Ferdinand was shot by a Serbian nationalist and this precipitated the First World War in the summer of 1914.
17. Clausewitz, 1780-1831. A Prussian general who advocated the concept of 'total war', which meant that not just the army would be involved, but the whole population and its property. He was involved in the Napoleonic Wars and became a military theorist.

18. Machiavelli, 1469-1527, lived in Florence. He wrote a book called *The Prince* in which he propounded the theory that a ruler had the right to hold on to power using all manner of devices which might not be totally ethical (at least by our standards). It became the basis for the rule of many heads of state and the inspiration behind the Fascist mentality of dictatorship.

19. Bismarck, Otto von. He was the chancellor of the First German Reich. He was skilled in foreign policy and in drawing Germanic territories into the Empire. At home, he was the first to institute a social security policy (which we would now call the Welfare State). By 1890 he was failing and had to be sidelined.

20. Nuremberg Laws. In 1935, Göering enacted these infamous laws, depriving the Jews of their German citizenship. Later it became necessary to define Jewishness, and complicated rules were devised for that purpose. Once the Jews were isolated and defined, it was much easier to victimise them.

21. The Mastersingers of Nuremberg; one of Wagner's many operas.

22. *Ritter*, the word used for a German knight. These were the ones who invaded North-Eastern Europe ostensibly to spread Christianity. They were dubbed as 'very noble'.

5

The Gathas

The Hymns of Zoroaster

This is the scriptural basis for the Zoroastrian religion. This became the official religion of the Persian Empire, certainly from Darius 1ˢᵗ (521-485 BC) but possibly of Cyrus and Cambyses, his predecessors. Zoroaster was a prophet who had a Theophanous experience[1], not unlike what we read in the books of Ezekiel and Daniel. It is difficult to date Zoroaster; he is certainly as old as the sixth century BC but may go back much further, even as far as 1000 BC. No one knows for certain when he lived; even so, we are dealing with a real historical person who spoke the Avestan language; the Gathas are written in this language. It is estimated that three quarters of his work is lost. Nevertheless, the material that survives gives a fair impression of his ideas and contribution to the theology of the ancient world. His ideas are well in advance for his age. It is a good question as to which way the influence was: the Old Testament or the Gathas[2]. Much of his work has the tone of the Psalms and the Proverbs and, additionally, there are elements reminding us of the Rig Veda. It is largely a question of dating, which we cannot do. His influence is still with us; partly with the Parsees of Western India, and also the Zoroastrians who still survive, but also the dualism seen in the New Testament is usually accredited to Zoroastrianism. In these seven chapters we are seeing into the mind of a genuine person of spiritual depth, even if the last Yasna (53) is not actually his own work. The net result for the Jews in exile was highly helpful; Cyrus the first Persian emperor was mercifully tolerant to minority religions and encouraged the Jews to return to their homeland. Many did not and it would seem that a Jewish lady, Esther, actually became the queen of Persia[3]. The Jews may have seen Zoroastrianism as something very close to their own monotheism; not exactly the same but certainly an advance on the polytheistic nonsense of nearly all the rest of the Ancient World. The version used here is the work of M.L.West, *The Hymns of Zoroaster* (2010).

From the point of view of mathematics, there is nothing of that nature in these scriptures, not even a date. Geographic and historical information is minimal, although enough to give us an impression of the setting of his work. His homeland appears to be Bactria, Eastern Persia, not far from Afghanistan, a cattle herding culture. This may mean that he was almost certainly nomadic to some extent. His main annoyance is that the local priests persist in rustling cows to be used for sacrifice; this goes against all Zoroaster's finer feelings and provides an important element in his theology. Historically, he fits the era just before the rise of the Persian Empire, and was probably aware of the Assyrian and Babylonian dominations, and this era of excessive violence, cruelty and intolerance may have set him thinking about the opposite conduct. He mentions in passing some of his family members; Djamaaspa, (Yasna 49:9, page 145), Haecataspa, (Yasna 53:3, page 165), and Porucista, (Yasna 53:3, page 165), his daughters whether natural or by adoption is not totally clear. Even so, his background is not of vital importance, for his message is valid in all circumstances.

Linguistic truth

This is a crucial element in understanding the Gathas. It is written in Avesta, an older version of Persian, and is not at all easy to translate. Another factor in this is that the Gathas existed and continued by oral transmission for 1,000 years after Zoroaster. This does not mean that there were distortions, very much the contrary. But what was happening was that those who recited them gradually lost the meaning of much of the material; also the pronunciation was changing. When the material was eventually written down in the Sassanian period, such corruptions of the text appear to have happened with the copying of manuscripts. It was under Khosrow 1st (431-578 AD)[4] that a definitive edition of the Gathas in twenty-one volumes was produced; it required a special alphabet based on Pahlavi but increased to fifty-three characters in order to cover every permutation of pronunciation. Given this history it is amazing that the text is so uniform and not corrupted. This however does not make it easy to translate into modern English; inevitably something of the original flavour and loading of various pejorative words is lost or slightly distorted. Even so, West's rendering of the Gathas is a remarkable attempt and must be the most balanced attempt yet; faithful to the text and yet not sliding into too much paraphrasing.

Literary truth

The Gathas are entirely written in the form of poetry. There is absolutely
no prose in them at all. It is hymns used in a liturgical context and as such
should be understood in the light of the Psalms. This does not have to mean
that Zoroaster knew of the Psalms of David but there is the possibility
that since most if not all of the Hebrew Psalmody had been produced
before his time, he could have had some knowledge of them. In addition
to this, it is on record that King Hezekiah sent choristers off to Assyria
to please Sennacherib[5]; Hebrew Psalmody may well have been known in
other countries. He certainly had knowledge of the Rig Veda, as seen in his
remarks about Soma[6]: 'the wrongful one who makes the resistant juice flare
up', (Yasna 32:14, page 75). The tone of his literature is mostly praise but
many remarks on a theological and philosophical level are mentioned in
passing.

Avestan poetry seems to function largely on a three-line stanza;
sometimes it is a four-line or even a five-line verse. There is evidence of the
use of metre but no rhyming. These are elements that are of help to anyone
memorising the material.

His use of imagery is often quite commendable. Such phrases as 'who
by his intent is a healer of existence... ', (Yasna 44:2, page 103), and, 'what
skilful artificer made the light and the darkness... what skilful artificer
made sleep and waking?', (Yasna 44:5, page 105), and '... to what good
destinations will my soul journey?' (Yasna 44:8, page 107). This all indicates
a literary person of some standing, even allowing for the translator's skills.
But Zoroaster's use of personification is perhaps the most noteworthy. The
importance of the cow cannot be underestimated. This must have dominated
his life as a cattle-herder, but came to be his chief metaphor. In the Bible, it
would have been the sheep and in the modern world it would probably be
the motor car. The cow is not exactly a god, since she was created by Ahura
Mazda, but is an object of deep respect, having a soul and emotions like a
human. It may be a little different with the ox: '...the light of the sun, the
potent of Ox of days,' (Yasna 50:10, page 151) is actually associating the
ox with Ahura Mazda; also '... will those Oxen of days set forth the path
of Right to uphold the world...' (Yasna 46:3, page 121). This has a certain
ring to it, reminding us of the Ancient of Days as seen in Daniel, Chapter 7
(three references).

'... and one that was Ancient of Days took his seat... his throne was
fiery flames... a stream of fire... came forth...' (verse 7).

Zoroaster would have very much approved of this metaphor for God
Almighty, as Ahura Mazda was seen as light, fire, and flames.

Other aspects of his imagery are interesting; often they are taken from the racecourses or speeding horses, and also the house and the path, and the pasture. All of these are basic motifs in the Bible. The house is, of course, the Temple, which very nearly every religion had; paradoxically the Zoroastrians had open-air worship and only later did temples with fire altars appear. The 'path' is a factor deeply embedded in Hebrew thought: 'prepare ye the way of the Lord'[7] and the 'highway' as seen in Isaiah. The 'pasture', hinting of God's providence and also of heaven, 'he shall lead me forth in paths of righteousness...' and '... he makes me lie down in green pastures' (Psalm 23:1-3), and 'I shall dwell in the house of the Lord for ever' (verse 6).

As with all poetic imagery, it is a mistake to take it totally at face value. Many have done this with the Bible, especially books like Daniel, with the result that God is literally seen as an old man sitting on a chair in the sky. But the beauty of Zoroaster's poetry is that he can take experiences from his own ephemeral situation, and paint it on a much wider canvas to open up new vistas of theological understanding in relation to God and faith. This is seen particularly with the cow. The cow represents the innocent soul being fought over by the powers of good and evil. Like most of us who have to make moral decisions every day and can easily be enmeshed in evil, the innocent appeals to the follower of truth and virtue, to come to the rescue. If he had been a sheepherder, he might have used that metaphor, as seen in Ezekiel and Enoch, but he probably had no experience of sheep. As a work of poetic literature, the Gathas stand out as remarkable for that time in history; even so, the Psalms of David and other poetic passages in the Old Testament still stand head and shoulder above the works of Zoroaster.

Theological basics with Zoroaster

This follows on naturally from his use of metaphor in relation to God. It looks very much as though he does not have an actual name for God. Ahura Mazda literally means 'Lord of Light', and this is a result of his Theophanous experience at the start of his ministry. He calls God 'Ahura' and this is as close as he gets to calling God a god. However he has an entire array of metaphors that pass for titles of God. Mindful Lord, Bounteous Will, Right and Good Thought, Best One, Caring One, Lord that Judges, Shaper, Dominion, Good Dispensation, Promoter, Flaming Fire, Creator; all of these give a comprehensive view of God's activity in the world. West has rendered all of these titles in capital letters, but there were no such indications in ancient languages until we come to Greek and Latin. This means that many more titles for God may be lurking in the text but not readily recognised by a modern translator. Many of these titles remind us of the figurative titles for God in the Old Testament, such as *El 'Elyon*, 'God Most High' (Genesis 14:19-20). But Zoroaster does not have a sacred name, analogous to YHWH, nor does he go to the trouble to explain that God is beyond definition. This comes very close to monotheism, except to say that Ahura Mazda is seen to have a daughter called Piety:

'... he has a daughter, who does good deeds, Piety.' (Yasna 45:4, page 117).

As with all poetry, how literally do we need to take this? If we compare this with another passage, it could be seen in a different light:

'The wise man says seize hold of this Good Thought's actions and of Bounteous Piety, knowing her the creator and companion of Right, and of all these excellences, Mindful Lord, they are in thy domain' (Yasna 34:10, page 91).

Elsewhere, Ahura Mazda is seen as the creator, so in effect, Piety, though termed a 'daughter' is not something separate from God. This reminds us of 'Wisdom' in the Wisdom literature of the Old Testament and the Apocrypha, in which Wisdom is personified as a woman; 'The Lord created me at the beginning of his work... wisdom has built her house...' (Proverbs 8:22-9:10). This was always seen as figurative, and never an infringement of monotheism. Perhaps we can take Bounteous Piety as just another metaphor for God? Interestingly, one of the matters raised by Muhammad was the issue of Allah having three daughters; the response to that is that Allah cannot have children, neither can he 'beget'[8], and this has become one of the main matters of disagreement between the Muslims and the Christians.

As far as other gods are concerned, Zoroaster consigns them all to be demons, and not worthy of worship. The term *daeva* is a Vedic word for 'god'; Zoroaster sees them all as bad. Also evil is Angra Mainyu; what we would call Satan or the Devil. There is a paradox going on here; on the one hand Angra Mainyu is seen as the 'twin' of Ahura Mazda; conversely, Angra Mainyu was 'created' by Ahura Mazda. Two quotations will elucidate:

' The two Wills, the twins who in the beginning made themselves heard through dreaming... ' (Yasna 30:3, page 51), and '... vexation to the men of Wrong; of these realms too the Mindful Lord is the creator... ' (Yasna 45:7, page 117).

It is possible that Zoroaster never intended to set out a systematic theology with a deep contradiction like this. Of course, if we take it literally, there is a problem, but this is poetry.

This leads us into an important element is Zoroaster's religion; namely Dualism. There are two wills, rivals, battling for the human soul. This is a cosmic battle and yet it goes on in the minds of humans. Angra Mainyu also has an array of titles: Wrongful One, Evil Thought, Wrong, Contempt, Bad Thought and many others. The Daevas, the demoted gods, are spawned by Angra Mainyu. He too, although of some great spiritual power, is not worthy of worship. In the end, the battle will be won by Ahura Mazda and there will be judgement; Right will prevail. Strangely there is no mention of angels or good spirits in attendance on Ahura Mazda. We can see from this how the eschatological element in Judaism and later with Christianity, almost certainly gained its inspiration from Zoroaster. It is just remotely possible that it is the other way round, but not very likely. But of course the Jews came up with all kinds of imaginative names for the devils: Beelzebub, Belial, Azazel and more which can be seen in the late apocryphal material such as the Testament of the Twelve Patriarchs[9]. Strangely, Daniel does not embark on this type of speculative metaphor. Dualism, as an element in theology, is found in various guises in many religions; it is an attempt at coping with the question of Theodicy 'Why do we have to suffer?' Again, with Zoroaster, there is a certain amount of self-contradiction, for, in spite of Angra Mainyu's antics, it is essentially Ahura Mazda that decides our fate:

'... him who makes our fortune and misfortune at his discretion... ' (Yasna 45:9, page 119).

However, Ahura Mazda is seen as responding to good works. Merits are often mentioned; what St Paul would have called 'works-righteousness'.

'This I ask of thee, tell me straight, Lord; how am I to earn that reward with Right' (Yasna 44:18, page 113).

However, there are two rewards available: one for the good and one for the bad, namely those who have gone in for Angra Mainyu and his wickedness. One needs to make a decision for right or wrong; there seems never to be a grey area in which humans are an admixture of good and bad. It is all black and white and this is slightly unrealistic about life.

'... those two kinds of thought, of speech, of deed, the better and the evil; and between them well-doers discriminate rightly but ill-doers do not. Once these two Wills go into battle, a man adopts life or non-life... ' (Yasna 30:3-4, page 51).

We note here that Zoroaster appears to be the prophet who coins the phrase 'in thought, word and deed'. This reverberates through the epistles of St

Paul, Romans 15:18 and Colossians 3:17, 'whatever you do in word and deed... ' It is now a normal phrase in modern parlance. Zoroaster is aware of two worlds: the material and the spiritual, or 'thought' world. He talks of the next life, continuing life, the soul and even pristine existence, which hints at a kind of golden age in the past, which can be recovered, with many other phrases which hint at the same thing. The cow also has a soul, as indeed all the other animals. This betrays a Hindu influence, which scarcely worked its way into biblical tradition.

Philosophical aspects

It is not easy to separate theology from philosophy in the Gathas; much of philosophy has already been included or referred to. He is not setting out to give a systematic philosophy; it is just ideas included in hymns. He is sure he is speaking the TRUTH:

'It will go best for him who knows and speaks my truth...' (Yasna 31:6, page 59).

It is at this point that the Gathas most resemble the wisdom literature of the Old Testament, such as Proverbs, and later material such as the Wisdom of Solomon. He is quite sure that all reason, discernment and intelligence comes from God and the one who can see this and accept it is on the way to salvation.

'Let the Knowing One speak to the knowing; let the unknowing delude no longer. Be for us Mindful Lord our teacher of good thought' (Yasna 31:17, page 65), and 'the wise man says seize hold of this Good Thought's actions... through the wisdom of Good Thought, Piety together with Right increases... ' (Yasna 34:11, page 91).

This is something that Proverbs would hardly have disagreed with, although he goes into much more detail about what constitutes wisdom and its application to daily life. 'The fool' as in Proverbs is never mentioned in the Gathas, and yet the implication is there: if one makes the wrong decision, one will become involved with Bad Thought, which is another title for Angra Mainyu.

The issue of free will versus predestination is never addressed in the Gathas. Zoroaster would probably have been in favour of free will, since he is clear in his mind that everyone has to make a decision whether to focus on right or wrong. There is nothing about God controlling people's lives; still less the concept of 'election' as seen in the Bible. Even so, there is the concept of God intervening in our lives:

'... him who makes our fortunes and misfortunes at his discretion...' (Yasna 45:9, page 119).

But essentially mankind is seen as a moral being and in the end there will be judgement, assumedly at one's death, but also when the final battle between good and evil is won. There is the mention of 'the Arbiter's crossing' which is a euphemism for the moment of death, i.e. crossing the River Styx, as in Greek thought. But the judge will be waiting to sort out the good from the bad. He does not actually state that hell is waiting for the bad, but the implication is there. 'The worst things' are waiting for the wrong ones. Heaven too is not actually mentioned. This is an interesting case of talking about merit and rewards on an abstract or theoretical level, and less on a literal or physical level. In this regard, Zoroaster is a long way ahead of the thinking of his times; he can think in mythological terms but also in demythologised thought. This makes him very modern in many respects. Also there seems to be no mention of karma, or reincarnation; one lives once and then faces judgement.

He places a heavy emphasis on peace and is very much against violence, something that is also very modern in thought. 'Thou didst establish peace with piety' (page 131), indicates that peace is an attribute of God; it is clear that Wrong is tied up with violence, and that is the antithesis of wisdom;

'Those who in ill wisdom increase violence and cruelty... through whose failure to do good deeds the ill deeds prevail, they establish the Daevas, which is the wrongful religion' (Yasna 49:4, page 141).

This is interesting because the implication here is that one's bad conduct actually encourages the devils. Does this imply that evil does not really have an existence of its own, independent of human activity? Does this mean that the cosmic battle between Ahura Mazda and Angra Mainyu does not have a 'boxing ring' apart from the human soul? If that is the implication, then this is a very modernistic, humanistic thought. Is he saying that God and the Devil only exist in the human mind? Many a modern humanist would probably agree with this. Perhaps this is pushing the interpretation of 'they establish the Daevas' a little too far.

Mythological aspects

Zoroaster does not indulge in elaborate mythological ideas with fanciful names for gods and their grotesque activities. This is in complete contrast with almost every other system of thought in the Ancient World, and places him very close to the Hebrew tradition. He makes mention of Creation but does not go into details of how it came about; Ahura Mazda is the great creator of all, at least of all the good things in life, but there is no attempt at describing the processes by which he did it. It is all very restrained, refined and spiritual.

A trace of pre-existing mythology comes in Yasna 32:8 where he refers to Yima, the son of Vivahvant:

'... Even Yima, who sought to gratify our mortal race by feeding them portions of the cow... ' (Yasna 32:8, page 71).

This may be a reference to Yama, the god of the dead, who presides over the Wheel of Becoming, as in Buddhist thought. But this is not stated as some sort of doctrine, it is just an archaic explanation for the atrocious practice of sacrificing cows.

Another vestigial remark betraying mythology is the mention of 'earth's seventh part'. It appears to mean 'all over the world', where the Daevas have been up to their duplicitous deeds. The Ancient World assumed that the figure seven represented the whole universe: three layers and four corners. We now take this as metaphorical; they almost certainly understood it as literal truth. But it is not an essential element in Zoroaster's thinking.

With the mythological aspects toned down almost to nothing, and theological, philosophical and spiritual aspects given much more prominence, Zoroaster has produced something very acceptable to modern minds. The only serious lack is the missing historical aspect of faith, something that gives the Bible a reality and hold on people's belief in a way which is not seen in Eastern religions. This element could have been supplied, as we know that Zoroaster had a Theophanous experience and there were details of his ministry that were worth including in his scriptures.

As we can see, this work is in complete contrast to such material as *Mein Kampf*, the Book of Mormon, the Book of Kings, and Chairman Mao's *Little Red Book*. It has a firm basis in a specific setting in Bactria before the rise of the Persian Empire, but has an application relevant to all right-minded people in any situation. As we have seen, there is clearly some kind of reciprocal relationship with elements in the Bible and the Apocryphal material. We suspect that the early Hebrew tradition had some influence on the Gathas and, vice versa, there is a lot to suggest that Zoroaster contributed much to later Jewish and Christian thinking.

Elements in the Psalms of David that may be related to Zoroastrianism

One of the main assumptions in Zoroaster's thinking is the matter of judgement; he sees it as a final settlement after the battle between good and evil is over. The Psalms also mention judgement in various places. The best example is in Psalm I:5:

> 'Therefore the wicked will not stand in the judgement, nor sinners in the congregation of the righteous.'

This has just the faintest suggestion of the Day of Judgement, which was to become a major theme in the apocalyptic material. This may be the starting point of that theme. The psalm also emphasises the contrast between the righteous and the wicked, with no suggestion of a grey area in between. This is an assumption seen in the Proverbs (Chapter 15), the Dhammapada (Chapter 14) and in the Gathas. The same motif comes in Psalm 75:2:

> 'At the set time which I appoint, I will judge with equity... but it is God who executes judgement, putting down one and lifting up another...'

This sounds even more like an appointed day of judgement although it does not specify the end of time or the end of the world. In Psalm 149:9 'to execute on the judgement written' sounds even more formal, except that it is now talking about exalting the humble and abasing the proud, such as kings and nobles. This is an ongoing theme in the Psalms and is amply summed up in Psalm 76:9; 'when God arose to establish judgement to save all the oppressed of the earth'. The main thrust of 'judgement' is about God coming to make things fairer for the poor, the downtrodden and the righteous who are being harassed.

Comparing this with the Gathas, we find that in (Yasna 29:4, page 45) it goes... 'He (the Mindful One) is the Lord that judges; it will be as He will'.

Another element found in the Gathas, is the wish for peace. This can be evidenced in Psalm 11:5: '... the Lord tests the righteous and the wicked, and his soul hates him that loves violence... ' and also in Psalm 26:9: '... sweep me not away with sinners, nor my life with bloodthirsty men... '

In general terms, the main thing in common is the personal conversation between the believer and his god. With the Psalm, David (presumably) is seen as very close to YHWH, which is all a part of the Covenant of David. With Zoroaster, he is very close to Ahura Mazda, as all his hymns are addressed to his god. The chief difference is in the quality of the poetry. The Hebrew poetry, which is characterised by superb parallelisms, is among some of the best to be found in the Old Testament or anywhere else; this explains the influence and hold of the Psalms on Jewish and Christian worship to this day. The Gathas of Zoroaster, although they hold much beauty and depth, do not really reach the same standard of spiritual insight as the Psalms do.

Notes for Chapter 5: The Gathas

1. A Theophanous experience: Some are seen the Old Testament, but Zoroaster is understood to have been caught up to heaven to meet Ahura Mazda. This explains his conviction and spiritual insight.
2. The Gathas: a full discussion is given in *The Hymns of Zoroaster* by M.L.West.
3. Herodotus claims that a lady called Amestris was the queen of Artaxerxes, emperor of Persia. We note that 'Esther' is consonantly compatible with Amestris. The full discussion is in my first book, *The Theology of Paradox*, Chapter 6.
4. Khosrow 1st. A Persian king of the Sassanian period, a great reformer and patron of the arts.
5. Sennacharib. The Assyrian king who attacked Jerusalem during the reign of Hezekiah; see Chapter 18, 1 and 2 Kings.
6. Soma: an intoxicating drink consumed at the Yagya celebrations, described in the Rig Veda.
7. Isaiah 40:3.
8. The metaphor of 'begetting' is seen in John 1:14. If this is taken literally, it becomes a problem; if it is taken figuratively, the problem ceases.
9. The Testament of the 12 Patriarchs is a pseudepigraphal work which includes names such a Beliar and Belial as names for Satan.

6

The Revelation: St John

Situated at the end of the Bible, it makes a fitting end to the extraordinary matters recorded so far. It is the only full-blown apocalypse in the New Testament, and relates well with the only apocalypse, Daniel, in the Old Testament. This is not to say that there is no other apocalyptic material in the Bible; the three Synoptic gospels each have a section in which Jesus speaks of the end times; this element is strangely missing from St John's gospel. This may be deliberate. Perhaps St John wanted to keep his gospel calm, quiet, understated and at times even sentimental, whereas his apocalypse is the opposite: it is triumphant, loud, exaggerated and judgemental. This is not to say that both books have to have been written by the same person, but both books, plus the three epistles, are firmly in the Johannine tradition.

Revelation must be seen in relation to the other apocalyptic material of the times. There is a wealth of literature which was sub-canonical, but which can still be studied. Some of it, such as 1 Enoch (Chapter 20)[1], were nearly included in the Old Testament; others such as the Assumption of Moses and the Jubilees never came near it. Even so, they are all a fascinating insight into the thinking of theological writers of that day. They were all convinced that the end of time was about to happen with the coming of the Messiah: there would be a grand judgement day and all the wicked would be damned to hell and the righteous admitted to heaven. The clearest example of this was the Koran, even if it appeared several centuries later. But St John's Revelation stands head and shoulders above all the other eschatological works.

In general terms, people have difficulties with Revelation, and, indeed, all works of that genre. The nub of the matter lies with to what extent we take them literally. There are varying levels of literal interpretation available; none of these would render one a 'heretic'. Unfortunately, this literature has been an encouragement to splinter groups with a doomsday mentality. Others with a more liberal stance still find it difficult because of the implication that there are certain people who are claimed to be damned for ever; also there is plentiful mention of 'wrath', which upsets people nowadays. At the very least, Revelation must be approached with caution, and insight into its genre and mentality is essential.

Where, what and how does eschatology fit with one's theological horizons? We note that the Bible begins with two creation accounts. This is now seen as 'mythology'. This is not to say that it is a complete fabrication. People tend not to realise that virtually every culture or race on earth has some kind of mythology as a basis for its *raison d'etre*. These various world mythologies are not a collection of rubbish, they show us, in exaggerated picture language the basic truths about gods and humans. The first two Chapters of Genesis should be seen in this light: not to be taken literally, but figuratively and symbolically. Eschatology, or the apocalyptic scheme of thought, is the counterpart of mythology. We could call it futuristic mythology. The two elements serve to frame human history, like two bookends. Interestingly, they use the same metaphors, imagery, and exaggerated vocabulary. Seen in this light, the apocalyptic mode can hardly be taken at face value, literally. This is not to say that the material is worthless, as, if carefully evaluated, it contains deep truths about life, death, God and human nature. The mode in which it is expressed can be frightening, but that is being done on purpose. Just as Jesus in his teachings employed high-flown exaggerated language, so too do the apocalyptists, to arrest people's attention and force them to think deeply about what life, death, heaven and hell are all about.

Mathematical aspects

In common with other apocalyptic writers, John goes in for a lot of number symbolism. His method, however, is noticeably different from that of the pseudepigraphal writers; they try to calculate the beginning and end of the world by measuring epochs. John does not embark on this approach at all. After all, the 'end' with the coming of the Messiah is now in the past; now we are expecting the end of all things and the consummation of history. He is content to warn of its imminence: 'Surely I am coming soon', which is only a reinforcement of what Jesus promised in his last days on earth, but there is no attempt at calculating it in terms of mathematics. However, the use of numbers is very important in Revelation; it appears that there is an entire code at work, clearly based on the symbolisms used in previous scriptures. It is an entire mistake to try to take these figures literally; they clearly stand as symbols for something. The problem is that we do not always have the key to the code, but to the early Jewish Christians in Asia Minor, it would almost certainly have been obvious what he was saying. We can attempt to unravel the code but while some of it is fairly straightforward, other parts of it are open to various guesses.

The easiest place to start is with the number seven. This number is a recurring theme from start to finish and in a way, holds the book together across the many scenes. We start with the seven stars and lampstands associated with the seven churches of Asia. Right from the start this infers the hint that seven is symbolic; after all, there must have been many more churches than seven in that part of the world, and as for stars, even in those days, they must have known that there are millions of stars in the sky. What does seven stand for? The assumption in the Ancient World was that the universe had three tiers and four corners, thus making seven. Seven, therefore, implies completeness, wholeness, God having finished his creative work, everything coming to a conclusion. So we have the seven spirits of God, seven thunders, seven angels, seven trumpets, seven scrolls, seven horns, all of this suggests the final thrust, the concluding actions of God. The seven trumpets and thunders not only augment what happened at Sinai, but speaks of the ultimate noise which will silence everything else; God is in the process of overwhelming everything else, and that includes evil, personified by Satan.

A derivation from seven is three and a half, sometimes appearing as forty-two months, which makes three and a half years, and also 1260 days. In one place it is actually three and a half days. All of this is derived from Daniel in his prophecy of the Abomination of Desolation. This was seen to come to fulfilment with the defilement of the Temple under Antiochus 4th Epiphanes in 167 BC[2]. Jesus took up the same phrase but applied it to the future, firstly talking of his own crucifixion and secondly the ruination of the Temple in 70 AD. John never actually mentions the Abomination of Desolation in so many words, but any reader would have immediately connected three and a half with that historical fact and with Jesus' prophecy. A half of seven implies the opposite of completeness; it means things have gone wrong, the Devil has managed some sort of trick, defilement, incompleteness, God's work being interfered with, but the need to put things right.

The use of fractions is also interesting. We have a half, a third, a quarter, and a tenth. This too is suggestive of incompleteness. There seems to be no Old Testament precedent for these, but the impression given is that something has started but not been finished. Thus, a third of the sea is turned to blood; this reminds us of the River Nile turning to blood in Exodus, but the difference is that God has made a start on his warning without giving a complete catastrophe; this gives people yet another chance to think again and repent. The purpose of the plagues of Egypt was to give

Pharaoh yet another chance to change his mind. The use of half an hour, silence in heaven, is used to build up the suspense; God's action is slightly delayed, but will come only too soon, a theme seen right across Revelation but also an important element seen in the parables of Jesus[3].

The number twelve is not too difficult to understand. There were twelve tribes of Israel and twelve apostles; these are clearly being referred to in Revelation. The twelve apostles become the basis for the New Jerusalem, there are twelve kinds of fruit on the tree of life and Mary wears a crown of twelve stars. What is being said here? John is saying that the divine organisation of the tribes and the apostles is now the foundation of the New Testament (not that he ever uses the word 'Testament'). After all, four times three is twelve; multiplying instead of adding; this is a high-powered way of saying perfection, fulfilment. Twelve becomes augmented to twenty-four, which represents the elders and the thrones. This reminds us of the twenty-four elders appointed by Moses in the wilderness. What is this saying? That the pattern laid down by Moses is now coming to completion and the elders are now promoted to being next to God, with regal status as they wear crowns, but of course subservient to God as they throw their crowns down; the Old Testament is glorious but secondary to the New Testament.

The number ten is also important, as recalls the succession of kings in Daniel, something which came to fulfilment with the Seleucid dynasty leading up to the disaster perpetrated by Antiochus 9th Epiphanes[2]. John now transposes this image to the succession of Roman emperors. The beast has seven heads and these symbolise the seven hills upon which Rome was built, and the seven kings, five of which have already fallen. 'One is and one is yet to come'. This is useful as just a little bit of historical anchorage: the five emperors would be Julius, Augustus, Tiberius, Caligula, Claudius, and Nero is actually on the throne. There is a reference to the martyrdom of Christians in 17:6; 'Drunk with the blood of the saints…' which was the first persecution. This would give us a date of about 66 AD. The seventh king is only to remain a little while. How true; it was the year of the three emperors.

The number four, apart from being the four corners of the earth, clearly relate to the four Gospels. In 4:7 there are four living creatures; the lion, the ox, the face of a man, and the flying eagle. These have become the traditional symbols for the four gospel writers; they are pictured as being with the elders round the throne of God. The implication is that Matthew, Mark, Luke and John are very close to the basic realities of God, but are yet to be subservient to him. With their eyes in front and behind, they are constantly giving us insights into God's very self, which is what Jesus actually did. Incidentally, if it is true that Revelation was written about the time of Nero, that would be evidence that all four Gospels had been completed and were in circulation by this time.

The use of 1,000 occurs occasionally, usually in some kind of compound such as 7,000 or 12,000. This is a feature seen often in the Old Testament. It may be that it is an impressionistic way of saying 'a vast number'. If we look at 5:11, it talks of myriads and myriads, and thousands and thousands; in other words, the angels are beyond all calculation. It is no use trying to count them. This brings us to the thorny question of 144,000, which appears twice as the number to be admitted to heaven. This is a case in point of how Revelation has been taken far too literally. This may relate to the 144 cubits in 21:17, which is the measure of the wall of the New Jerusalem. Multiplying it by 1,000 implies that twelve times twelve, the tribes of Israel augmented by the first disciples, augmented by a vast number, means that there is plenty of room for Jews and Christians in heaven. Another possible interpretation of 144,000 is as follows. In the book of Enoch, it is stated that the number of God is 100^4, but there is no reason given for this. A possible approach to it may be to say that just as a human has ten fingers with which he creates things, so ten squared symbolises God as the great creator, but this is just a thought. It may help to explain various things. 144,000 is twelve times twelve times 100 times ten. Is this a way of saying, God, on a grand scale, is now integrated with the tribes of Israel and the Christian disciples? In other words, God is with his people in a special way that was not before, and that is very much the gist of Revelation.

In 20:2 and 20:4 Satan is bound in hell for 1,000 years, only[19] then to be released. Is that a way of saying that Evil will be contained for a long time but not for ever? That, in the end, the problem of evil will be resolved? There may be another side to this. In Zoroastrian thought, a world saviour was expected to appear at the end of every[5] 1,000 years. Is St John saying, indirectly, that there is only going to be one period of a thousand years and then it will all come to a conclusion?

The idea of the number of God being 100 may under lie the statement in 14:20: 'blood flowed from the winepress... for 1,600 stadia.' A stadia was a unit of distance used in the distance of the stadium. 1,600 is four squared times 100. The four corners of the earth are augmented and then 100 augments the whole thing. In other words, the grape harvest of the whole world, on an augmented scale not seen before will have God active in it in a power not seen before. This is just a possibility.

In 11:3 we have two olive trees and two lampstands. This clearly evokes Zechariah, Chapter 4, in which Joshua the High Priest and Zerubbabel are re-establishing the Temple. The thought here is that the new Temple will be established in the New Jerusalem. There is the other implication in the number two that the two Hebrew kingdoms which Ezekiel thought would be reunited, will come together in the end. In other words, the people of God will finally be united in his presence.

This leaves us with 666, the number of the beast in 13:18. This has traditionally been taken as an approximation of two thirds of 1,000. In other words, something wrong, evil, incomplete, faulty. If 1,000 is 100 times ten, in other words, augmented God, then two thirds of God is something incomplete, failed and wrong. John is actually saying in so many words in that passage, that you need to use a bit of common sense; 'this calls for wisdom.'[6] In other words, all these numbers do not have to be taken at face value – use a bit of intelligence. Another approach to 666 is as follows: it is a fact that the letters in the Hebrew alphabet also denote numbers, for instance, aleph, the first letter, stands for one. If we take the name Neron Caesar and turn it into Hebrew numerals, it turns out to be 666[7]. Incidentally Neron is an alternative to Nero. This is how it works:

Nun (n) equals	50	Ingenious; but what happens if we take Shin which is 300 instead of Samekh, or if we take Kaph, which is 20 instead Qoph? As in English there is more than one letter to denote the same sound; for instance, C, K, and Q.
Resh (r) equals	200	
Waw (w)	6	
Nun (n)	50	
Qoph (k)	100	
Samekh (s)	60	
Resh (r)	200	
Total	666	

If this suggestion is true, and it is only a suggestion, it would mean that John was hinting at Nero as being the beast. But it is true that gods and important people were often referred to in some sort of number-code. It is maintained that the code number for Jesus is 888, but this is not clarified. The idea that Nero's number is 666 does not rule out the previous idea about imperfection and wickedness; both ideas may hold water.

Enough has been said to show that number symbolism, often derived from the Old Testament is a major strand in John's method of expression. Sometimes it is being done to avoid being too specific about real historical events. But mostly it is his way of showing that in God's approach to this world, there is nothing that is haphazard, approximate or careless. This comes out most noticeably with his fascination for the Temple and Jerusalem. He is clearly recalling Ezekiel 40 and Zechariah to some extent. A man appears with a measuring rod and takes the measurements of the New Temple. Ezekiel goes into great detail about the symmetry of this temple, as does John in 21:15. But he transposes the reed in Ezekiel to a golden rod, and the angel measures out Jerusalem as 12,000 cubic stadia, enough to contain a vast number of people. Earlier in the book John makes much reference to the Temple as having the presence of the Lord in it; however, paradoxically, the heavenly Jerusalem has no Temple in it since God himself is the divine presence. Even so, the fascination with measurements is an important ingredient. Architecture and builders were much valued by the Jews. Herod the Great was noted as a great builder. What it indicates is that with God, nothing is illogical, haphazard, careless, or badly thought out. The structure of the universe is his wonderful, careful work. But Ezekiel's vision is transposed to a much more magnificent pitch, leading up to the final appearance of the Holy City, and the fulfilment of all believers' hopes.

Mythological aspects

If Mathematical considerations are important in Revelation, then mythology is probably the clue to unlocking almost all of its secrets. We have already seen that eschatology is the futuristic counterpart of mythology; it uses so many of the images, techniques and themes common to mythology the world over. Perhaps the most interesting mythology to compare it with it the Japanese one in the Kojiki, reviewed in Chapter 12. But Revelation makes a great play of linking its thoughts to the two Genesis accounts of Creation; not that St John would have seen them as two accounts, but that is what modern criticism has, almost certainly correctly, decided.

John refers back to Genesis in many ways, with the implication that the Fall is going to be reversed, and that will mean the elimination of all evil, pain, death and every aspect of Satan's works. In Revelation 1:8: it says, 'I am Alpha and Omega, who is and who was and who is to come...' and in 22:13, the whole book is stitched together and framed with 'I am Alpha and Omega, the first and the last, the beginning and the end'. Clearly this evokes, 'in the beginning'. It is no surprise then that the tree of life appears in 22:2 on both sides of the river of the water of life. In terms of logic this is impossible, but we must recall this is visionary and dream-like. This time, the fruit is not forbidden, instead there are twelve kinds of fruit, not just one, and the leaves are for the healing of the nations. In other words, it is all transposed to a higher pitch and augmented so that the whole universe is to be given understanding and life. It is even an upgrading of 2:7: 'I will grant to eat of the tree of life, which is in the Paradise of God...' Also the river that flowed out of Eden, Genesis 2:10, becomes the water of life and the flaming sword of Genesis 3:24 as adapted in various places in Revelation where a sword appears. Sometimes it is a two-edged sword (1:16) which is another example of augmentation. An angelic figure has a two-edged sword issuing from his mouth; if we can decode that, it means that God's hyper-judgements come straight from his minions in heaven. This time, we are not warned off the tree of life; on the contrary, the sword is there to defend the truth and dispatch evil. With regard to the creation of the world, we see that God provides a 'new heaven and a new earth, for the first heaven and the first earth have passed away, and the sea is no more'. The sea is symbolic of the underworld. It contained monsters like Behemoth and Leviathan, which terrified the Jews. This means that everything that had gone wrong in the old world – sin, death, fear, wickedness – is removed and we start afresh. Death and Hades are thrown into the lake of fire. This is a hyperbolised way of saying that the creation will be cleansed and given a new start.

World mythologies have various main features in common. It is interesting that St John draws in many images from world mythology, some of them not seen previously in the Bible. He must have had a profound understanding of human nature. One major theme is the fascination with gold, jewels, crystal, mirrors, glass and translucent stones such as onyx. These are all symbolic of eternity and indestructibility, everlasting life. A classic passage is in Revelation 21 where the Holy City is seen with all manner of precious stones. 'It was built of jasper... the city was pure gold... clear as glass, adorned with every jewel, jasper, sapphire, agate, emerald, onyx, carnelian, chrysolite, beryl, topaz, chrysoprase, jacinth and amethyst... pearls... street was pure gold, transparent as glass.' All this speaks of the glory and permanence of God's presence with his people. It also evokes Exodus 28:17 where Moses makes the breastpiece of judgement for the high priest. It has all these gemstones set in it, and the symbolism is that God's high priest (the true one is Jesus) and his own presence as a judge is there in the New Jerusalem. Strangely we have no mention of diamonds nor of jade: diamonds were known in the Ancient World, but jade, being found in China, might not have been known in the West.

An important symbol in virtually every world mythology is the sword, as it speaks of eternal justice, the righting of all wrongs. Where a sword is absent, a spear or an arrow are used as a substitute. These two do not appear in Revelation, but various swords do in several contexts. In 19:15, the angelic horseman, Faithful and True leads the army of God with a sharp sword to defeat evil. Further on he is called the Word of God, which means that he is Jesus conquering evil. This ties in with a strand in St Matthew's gospel, in which Jesus is portrayed as the eternal judge. Paradoxically, Jesus always tried to avoid condemning people, such as the woman taken in adultery[8]. But the ultimate truth is that people find themselves judged by the standard of the humble servant, the Son of God, who gives himself completely.

Cleansing or purification is another important strand in world mythology. Normally this is achieved either by fire or water as the two principal agents. St John however has a third agent, that of the blood of Jesus, which cleanses us, as explained in his epistle[9]. Revelation makes various mentions of all three agents, and it is symbolic of the purification needed if the world is to start all over again. There are many references to water but the most significant are in 21:6 and 22:1, where the river of the water of life flows from the throne of God.

With regard to fire, in 3:18 we have a remark about gold refined by fire, and this serves to confirm that John is thinking of fire as a refining agent. Every time we have mention of fire, such as the seven torches of fire, angels throwing fire on earth, hail fire and blood, fire smoke and sulphur, the sea of glass and fire, and a lake of fire into which the Devil is thrown, this is speaking of purification. The dross of human failure and wickedness is being smelted out, to leave us with a clear conscience and a fresh start.

With regard to blood, there is the extra element that in the thinking of the ancient world, the blood of an animal is the life in it[10]. But John transposes the blood of Jesus, his essential core of life, to be another cleansing agent. So when in 7:14 we have 'they washed their robes white in the blood of the Lamb', that epitomises John's thinking: Jesus, giving his life, is the final act of cleansing a corrupt world. 19:3 also has the same image, a robe dipped in blood. Every time we have mention of blood in Revelation, it is nothing to do with murder; it is God active in bringing healing and cleansing to the world. So when a third of the sea turns to blood, it is saying that the process of cleansing is under way, with the implication that it will continue. When the moon turns to blood, what is this saying? The moon was, at least in Ephesus, associated with Dianna the moon goddess, and also seen as a sinister influence generally. If the moon is turned to blood, this implies that God is overcoming not just the sinister elements in life but also he is correcting the pagans, baptising their faulty theology. The image of blood, which seems to be peculiar to St John, is a powerful one; there is no way that it can be taken literally.

Another important element in world mythology is the symbol of the snake; it signifies death and, paradoxically, life and fecundity. It bears an uncanny life and seems indestructible. The serpent in Genesis is well known for its temptation, although at that stage, there is no attempt at equating him with Satan. But the snake in Revelation is transposed to a much higher, cosmic level. Now he is clearly associated with Satan or the Devil (20:2), but also augmented to being a dragon. Earlier in Revelation, the locust also comes in as a partial image of the same thing: a great destroyer with a sting in his tail as opposed to his face. Satan is cast into a pit for 1,000 years and chained up. This image could have been derived from 1 Enoch[11] where the fallen angels are chained up. In 12:1-17 the serpent-dragon tries to devour the child being born, which is Jesus born of Mary. This is symbolic of the Temptations and other attempts by Satan to derail the ministry of Jesus. By the end of the book, the Devil is finally defeated and thrown into a lake of fire. Does this mean that he will be destroyed or alternatively redeemed by the refining fire? That is a dilemma that has reverberated through church history, whether or not the Devil and his angels will finally be redeemed. Perhaps there is a profound paradox in this; in one sense, evil will be removed, destroyed and forgotten; on the other hand, human failure, weakness, folly and cruelty will be an unavoidable factor as long as humanity persists in surviving. But St John is convinced that evil will finally be defeated, in a massive confrontation between God and the Devil.

Another important image in world mythology is the tree. Which type of type of tree does not matter; an oak in Germany, a tamerisk in Egypt, an ash tree in Norse mythology, a fig tree in the Gospels, and an ashvattha tree in Hinduism. The point is that the tree is rooted in the ground, reaching down to the underworld, its bole is plain enough to see in this world, and its branches reach up to heaven, thus forming a connection between all three zones of the universe. There are of course other methods of connection cited, such as ladders and rainbows. We have to think of Jacob with his ladder coping with angels moving up and down, and the rainbow actually does appear twice in Revelation. But what is it saying, metaphorically? It is showing that there is a connection, a channel of communication between God, humanity and the dead souls in hell. In Genesis we have the tree of knowledge of good and evil, which bears forbidden fruit, and also the tree of life, which has to be guarded by the cherubim; in Revelation, this is all reversed so that we do have first hand knowledge of God, and the tree of life is available for all.

This brings us to consider angelology, which is a notable feature of apocalyptic literature. There is an awareness in Hebrew thought that although, God is only one, he is not solitary in heaven. The pagan myths have hordes of underling gods doing the chief god's work for him, and sometimes fighting each other. In Jewish thought, these secondary gods are non-existent and yet God has hordes of angels doing the work. Also there are fallen angels who attempt to oppose the good angels. In 1 Enoch and other literature of those times, vast lists of angels with names applied to them make interesting reading, but are pure speculation. Clearly they are a substitute, on a monotheistic principle, for polytheism. In Revelation, however, John is economical with speculation about angels. There are good ones and bad ones, and Michael (in Chapter 12) is the chief; there is a battle but the goodies win, of course. What does this tell us? That justice and truth will win through eventually, and evil will be defeated.

Once we begin to understand Revelation in terms of mythological imagery, it begins to make far more sense. The metaphors are frightening, but they only are imagery. Why does he do it in such a fashion? Surely his motive is to dramatise, augment and excite the reader. The battle between good and evil, as seen with the life of Jesus, was on the mundane level of everyday encounters; but St John is in fact saying that this battle was a cosmic one, applicable to the entire universe. Evil is not just a local mistake; it is a universal distancing between God and Satan. It deserves an elaborate, highly exaggerated mode of expression to do it justice.

Theological truth

The main theme of the Judaeo-Christian theology is the metaphor of covenant. Although St John never actually mentions the word in any of his writings, (with the exception of mentioning the ark of the covenant), there is still the background assumption in his mind. One wonders if the phrase 'New Jerusalem' is not another way of saying the same thing? Of the various covenants in the Old Testament, we begin with the covenant of Noah, which involves a rainbow, the sign of God's caring for all the people of the world, irrespective of how far they go astray. In Revelation 4:3, when there is an open door into heaven, there appears a rainbow round the throne, looking like an emerald. Not only does this speak of access to the presence of God for all people; we can all achieve heaven, but the emerald can symbolise the green of natural growth with the crops, according to the promise that seedtime and harvest will never fail, as long as the earth endures[12]. In 10:1, a mighty angel appears wrapped in a cloud with a rainbow round his head. Is this a way of saying that the cloudy pillar of the Exodus, i.e. the covenant of Moses, is now integrated with the covenant of Noah? The cloud in Hebrew thought symbolises the presence of God.

There is very little to remind us of the covenant of Abraham. 1:17, 'I fell at his feet as though dead but he laid his right hand on me and said, "Fear not..."' reminds us of Abraham falling on his face, Genesis 17:3 and 15:1, 'Fear not, Abraham, I am your shield'. Other than that, it seems that Abraham is seriously understated in Revelation. Indirectly we have mention of Sodom and Egypt, which recall the plight of Lot and Abraham's bargaining session with God in Genesis 18.

The opposite is true for the covenant of Moses and the Sinai event; the whole book is full of allusions to the Exodus. The trumpet blast, the lightning and thunder, the manna, the plagues of Egypt, the darkness and cloud, the ark of the covenant, the tabernacle; all are predominant in the symbolism. What does it mean? It means that the Old Testament, namely the Law, has come home to God's Temple and has pride of place in heaven. The Ten Commandments are not actually mentioned, but in 22:14, we have an indirect reference to doing God's commandments which gives one the right to the tree of life. But the chief link to the Passover is with Jesus being identified with the Lamb, which means the sacrifice which took place on the night of the Passover and which was the crucial phase of God's people being rescued from the tyranny of Egypt. Revelation 11:8 '... the street of the great city, which is allegorically called Sodom and Egypt, where their Lord was crucified'. In one sense this is talking about Rome, which was full of all kinds of debauched behaviour, like Sodom. In another sense it is talking about Jerusalem where Jesus was crucified. The crucifixion is clearly equated with the sacrifice of the Passover Lamb. In his gospel, John has Jesus on the cross at the very moment when the lambs would have been slaughtered in preparation for the Passover meal that evening. The Lamb is the main player in the drama of Revelation, and this indicates that the crucifixion is the nub of the whole matter of salvation, the destruction of evil and the triumph of goodness, and the cleansing of the world. What is the importance of reminding us of the Sinai event? John is saying that this seminal event is now brought to a magnificent conclusion and fulfilment; the plagues, the trumpet soundings, the thunder are now augmented to a much greater pitch. It no longer just concerns just Egypt; it concerns the whole world. God's salvation is now played out on a universal canvas, as opposed to a local one.

Also heavily emphasised is the Davidic covenant, which includes the importance of the Hebrew monarchy, the Holy City and the Temple. It is thoroughly integrated with the previous covenant. Revelation 14:1 '... on Mount Zion stood the Lamb...' means, in other words, the Passover has come home to the Holy City. Also the Law has come home to the Temple. The Exodus has now been tied in with the New Jerusalem (dare we say 'the New Testament'?). Although there is God's Temple in heaven, paradoxically there is no temple in heaven because God himself is the temple; this means that God is with his people, the citizens of the Holy City. The New Jerusalem comes down from heaven to be with mankind. 'Behold the dwelling of God is with men. He will dwell with them and they shall be his people...' God himself will be the true light; they will need no created light such as the sun. This reminds us of Genesis 1 in which light is provided before the creation of the sun and moon. There are indirect references to King David, in such a way as to imply that Jesus is the true heir to the Jewish monarchy (3:7), the Lion of Judah (5:5), and 'I am the root and offspring of David, the bright morning star' (22:16). This again transposes Jesus to being the epitome of royalty; what a contrast with people like Caligula and Herod the Great! Now we have a king who is not just King of the Jews, but the king of the universe. Also there is the paradox of Jesus being a Lion and yet a Lamb. Both are true in their own way; the Lion being the king of beasts, courageous enough to fight anything including evil; the Lamb being humble, vulnerable and the sacrificial victim. The imagery is brilliant and profound.

In case one were wondering whether monarchy is integral to the Judaeo-Christian system of thought, again we have to beware. A literal acceptance of this way of thinking would actually mean that a country ought to have a monarch who is responsible only to God, and that is how many countries in the Christian era worked it out. But we are talking on a figurative, eternal level here. If applied to human government, it means that anyone who is head of state, whether king, president, prime minister or whatever the constitution provides, ought to be responsible to God for his actions, and have the best interests of his people at heart. There is a strong case for humility and taking into account what the public wish; on the other hand, there needs to be the courage to make difficult decisions which may not be the easy way out of any problem. That is the pattern that Jesus gave us for any kind of leadership.

Another theological matter is the issue of **wrath**. This word appears about twelve times in Revelation. It usually has an unfortunate effect on people and it is common procedure to talk oneself out of it and pretend it does not exist. Calvin and others of that way of thinking found it a useful issue to include in their theology. The crux of the matter lies in how literally one takes it, as with just about everything else in the book. The phrase 'the wrath of the Lamb' (16:6) sounds strange; after all, Jesus was not noted for being bad-tempered; there was only one occasion on which he is recorded as losing his temper[13]. Wrath does not have to mean being furious. The Greek word 'thumos' can be translated as 'soul, heart, spirit, courage, positive passion' as well as 'anger or fury'. Has anyone ever translated 'the wrath of the Lamb' as 'the courage of the Lamb'? Even so there are several contexts where anger and fury cannot be avoided. One situation is regarding the future of the Roman Empire, coded as 'Babylon'. In 16:19, Babylon has to drink the cup of wrath. In 18:3 all nations have drunk the wine of her impure passion, which means that all the rulers on earth have compromised themselves with the debauchery of Rome. We have only to read the books by Suetonius and Tacitus[14] to know what was going on in the imperial family. But in 6:16, there comes a king who is superior to them all, and they are in fear and trembling of the wrath of the Lamb. In other words, Jesus, the ultimate judge, will show up their wickedness. But who shall stand when he appears? And who can endure the day of his coming? This is an adaptation of Malachi 3:2.

In other places, wrath is associated with the grape harvest. In 14:10 and 19 it is harvest time – not an earthly harvest, but the harvest of the end times, as seen in many of the parables of Jesus. It is the consummation, and those who are going to be found guilty will have to drink the cup of wrath. That is, they will be caught out and thoroughly embarrassed. In 12:2 it is the devil who hands out the wrath; this makes sense of Satan as he is the great accuser, as seen in Zechariah. As with many of the images in Revelation, wrath is an augmented, hyperbolised way of saying that the moment of judgement is happening, and it is in the hands of Jesus, the tender lamb. Seen like this, it is far less worrying; even so, we all need to be aware of

God's impending day of judgement. This is seen in 1 Enoch and many other apocalyptic writings. But the paradox is that, though there is judgement, there is also acquittal and healing for us all. Wrath has to be taken in its context and balanced with other images in Revelation.

Another important theological issue is that of prophecy. St John calls his book a prophecy and warns that the time is near. This motif appears several times in Revelation, but he very wisely makes no attempt at calculating the end of the world in terms of mathematics. This is an important contrast with nearly all the eschatologists of the BC period. The fact is that he is looking back on the appearance of the Messiah and the final judgement on the world, but paradoxically he is looking forward to the Second Coming. Much more noteworthy is his reference back to the prophets of the Old Testament. He is particularly fascinated by Daniel and Ezekiel, and to some extent Enoch. Daniel is the basis for the Son of Man coming in the clouds of heaven and also the hints surrounding the Abomination of Desolation. With Ezekiel there is the quantity surveying concerning the building of the Temple, not just after the Exile but also for the New Jerusalem. These are his main interests, but there are many minor references, direct or indirect, to other prophets. Isaiah is not forgotten. In Isaiah 22:22 we have 'I will place on his shoulder the key of the house of David; he shall open and none shall shut' .This is applied to the church of Philadelphia in Revelation 3:7. John is soaked in the prophets; one might almost say that prophesying the future is of little interest to him; the real theological meat is already there in the past. If there is anything concerning the future, it could be the general thought that Rome will fall; 'So shall Babylon the great city be thrown down with violence and shall be found no more.' (18:21).

One more theological issue is latent in the Revelation. It concerns the 'interim period'[3] as seen in the Gospels, particularly the Synoptics. In so many of the parables of Jesus the story begins with the master or king setting the men to work, going away, and then coming back to finish things off. The interim period is important for people to have the chance to repent, pull themselves together and be in readiness for the coming of the master. The paradox is that on the one hand, the Kingdom of God has arrived; on the other hand, the Kingdom will arrive with the conclusion of the ministry of Jesus. The message from this is that we should always be at the ready for the coming of Jesus. Traces of this system of thought are found in Revelation. Such phrases as, 'the time is near' (1:3) and 'behold, I am coming soon' (22:7), all indicate the same thing. In John's gospel, it is phrased slightly differently; 'but the hour is coming, and now is...' (John 4:23), but it amounts to the same thing.

Literary and Linguistic issues

Although Revelation is all written in Koine Greek it is clear that John was thinking in Hebrew or Aramaic. It is possible that he had an amanuensis translating his thoughts directly on to paper. It has been noted that the Greek of St John's gospel is quite simplistic and not the same style as Revelation; the Greek writer is different but the Hebrew thinking behind it is the same. Even so, the immediacy, the poetry and the conviction of the Old Testament shines through at all times.

Whatever one may think of the theology of Revelation, it is nevertheless a stunning piece of literature. The main literary aspect is the lavish use of hyperbole, on a scale not seen in other parts of the Bible. It comes close to Daniel and Ezekiel but goes that bit further with its vision of the future. The work of salvation done by the humble carpenter is now writ large with an exaggeration only equal to the backdrop of the entire cosmos. For this reason, Revelation can best be understood in comparison with St John's gospel. In that, the work of Jesus is deliberately kept unspectacular, thoughtful, and at the halfway point, his public ministry abruptly comes to an end. The whole thing is understated in the gospel: quiet, calm, and even sentimental with Mary Magdalene in the garden.

But in Revelation there is a complete contrast, which makes it one of the most stunning works of literature in the world. The use of figurative language with symbolism, in addition to hyperbole, has to be taken into account and appreciated. There is hardly any literal language in the whole book. On this basis, it is folly to attempt to take the work as the literal truth.

A few examples of how John augments scenes and some of the teachings from the ministry of Jesus can be instructive.

In Revelation 4:1 it mentions, 'in heaven, an open door'. If we look at John's gospel, Chapter 10, Jesus states that he is 'the door of the sheep'. 'I am the door and if anyone enters by me, he will be saved...' (v.9). So the metaphor of the door is transposed from being just an earthly sheepfold to the grand entrance to Heaven for all who truly follow Jesus. Jesus is the genuine entry into God's presence.

In Revelation 7:9 we have a vast multitude from every nation in the world, wearing white robes, carrying palm branches and shouting, 'Salvation belongs to our God...' The palm branches immediately remind us of the triumphal entry into Jerusalem. This incident comes in John 12:13, but it could remind us of any of the three Synoptics, which mention the waving of palm branches and the use of the word 'Hosanna' which means 'Please save us'. The incident is thus augmented to include not just the people of Jerusalem, but vast numbers from all over the world. The triumphal entry motif receives another permutation in Revelation 19:10, where a white horse appears and the Word of God, which means Jesus himself, is seated on it and is entitled King of Kings and Lord of Lords. This time, the donkey is augmented into a horse, and Jesus is coming out of heaven as opposed to entering Jerusalem. He is to make war and execute judgement this time; to defeat evil in another way as opposed to being crucified.

In Revelation 7:17, we have 'the Lamb in the midst of the throne will be their shepherd and he will guide them to springs of living water...' This reminds us of John 10:14, 'I am the good shepherd; I know my own and my own know me'. This speaks of Jesus caring for us all to the extent of laying down his life for us, and the universalism in this; 'I have other sheep not of this fold...there shall be one flock, one shepherd'. It also evokes Psalm 23 in which the Lord is our Shepherd who leads us by still waters. We notice that the still waters are augmented into springs of living water.

In Revelation 12:1 we have an augmentation of Mary as she is about to give birth to Jesus. On the one hand, the red dragon represents Herod in his attempt to destroy Jesus; on the other hand the dragon represents the Devil at the Temptations. The whole incident is magnified and dramatised. When it says that her child was caught up to God and his throne, it is talking about the Ascension, but also it reminds us of the assumption of Elijah.

We also have a reference to the crucifixion in Revelation 11:8: '... the great city which is called Sodom and Egypt where their Lord was crucified.' Here we see Jerusalem, and specifically Golgotha allegorised as Sodom, the epitome of disgusting behaviour and Egypt, the archetypal system of slavery and ethnic cleansing. So it was essentially the wickedness of this world that crucified Jesus, rather than the errors made by the Sanhedrin. But the prophets of God, including Jesus came back to life and terrified their persecutors, and were taken up into Heaven in a cloud. There is another possible reference to the crucifixion in Revelation 16:17 where a great voice comes out of the Temple and from the throne, saying, 'It is done'[15]. This reminds us of the last words of Jesus from the cross, 'It is finished'[15] (John 19:30), meaning that everything had come to a completion. In John's gospel we have no earthquakes, that is left to St Matthew (27:51). Revelation augments the whole thing into thunder and lightning and the great city split into three parts, whereas in Matthew, the rocks are split.

All this shows how Revelation takes elements from not just his own gospel but also the others, and magnifies them to a colossal degree: exaggeration on a massive scale. He is trying to say that the work of the humble messiah is not just local and confined to the land of Israel, but is universal.

There are many places where it can only be understood as being Hebrew parallelism, a form of poetry seen in many places in the Old Testament. It is here adapted to the Greek mentality (not that the Greeks ever went in for Hebrew-style poetry). John must have been thoroughly soaked in the mentality and method of the Psalmists. Consider this from Revelation 7:15-17:

> 'Therefore they are before the throne of god,
> And serve him day and night within his temple.
> And he who sits on the throne will shelter them with his presence.
> They shall hunger no more, nor thirst any more.The sun shall not strike them nor any scorching heat.
> For the Lamb in the midst of the throne will be their shepherd
> And he will guide them to springs of living water,
> And God will wipe away every tear from their eyes.

This passage has a wonderful feeling of God's protection and consolation for the hardships that the saints have endured, thinking of the persecutions. But the other aspect is the way it quotes or reminds us of various Old Testament texts; Psalm 121:6, 'the sun shall not strike you by day nor the moon by night...' and Isaiah 49:10, '...they shall not hunger nor thirst...' and other references such as in Ezekiel 34:23 and Isaiah 25:8. John has cleverly worked all these thoughts into an inspirational canticle. Another such situation arises in Revelation 15:3-4, 'Great and wonderful are thy deeds...' clearly linking it to the Song of Moses in Exodus 15:1 and the crossing of the Red Sea. The parallelism is not strictly confined to the snatches of poetry; sometimes it appears as prose, so in Revelation 21:4, '...he will wipe away every tear from their eyes and death shall be no more, neither shall there be mourning nor crying nor pain any more, for the former things have passed away'.

An interesting use of suspense comes in Revelation 8:1, '...there was silence in heaven for half an hour.' The imprecision of 'about half an hour' is masterly; the use of half in Hebrew thought suggests an incomplete number, or things not quite right, or things about to happen. Then we have the complete contrast with angels blowing trumpets, thunder, lightning and earthquakes. Looking at the book as a whole, it is a series of massive contrasts. We begin with the seven churches, which all have their failings, shortcomings and need for correction, but by the end of the book all that is swept away and everything is brought to correction. Another technique for building up the suspense is the way in which the woes and plagues come round almost like repeat shots; this comes round at least four times, each time notching up the fear. In the final Chapter it all comes to a massive climax when God and his people are reconciled and evil is finally swept away. There are so many appeals to human emotion, not least the appearance of the bride adorned for her husband.

Another literary device is the use or invention of names for people or situations. This follows the tradition of Isaiah and other prophets. In Revelation 8:11, 'the name of the star is Wormwood'. The Greek is *apsinthos* or absinthe, a bitter herb, making the water bitter. This is evocative of the Meribah incident in Exodus. In Revelation 9:11 we have a king called Abaddon, which in the wisdom literature is equivalent to *Sheol* or hell. Its meaning is made clear by the Greek translation, *Apollyon* which means 'destroyer'. Also the name Apollyon may be a pun on Apollo, one of the gods especially revered in western Asia Minor. John is in fact saying that this god is a wrecker, very far from being any helper for mankind. In 16:16 we have mention of Armageddon, something that has passed into our language as the frightful destruction of the world. But what did St John intend by it? The etymology of this word is a little uncertain but it may mean something like 'the lion of Megiddo'. The Battle of Megiddo is recorded in Judges 5:19 and *ari* means a lion. It is in the context of the decisive final battle. The battle, which saw the defeat of the Canaanites, was not the only confrontation in the plain of Megiddo. Josiah, one of the good kings, was murdered there by Pharoah when there was a major confrontation between Egypt and Assyria 609 BC. John is in fact saying that there will be a decisive major confrontation between good and evil.

In Revelation 20:7 we have mention of Gog and Magog. No one knows what Gog means; Magog is thought to be the wild terrain between Media and Cappadocia, but it is clearly evoking Ezekiel 38. In this passage, Gog is the chief prince of Meshech and Tubal, but he seems to symbolise all the hordes of marauding armies that will attack Israel. In other words, millions of gentiles from all over the world are assembling for that final confrontation. In Revelation 19:11 we have a horse with someone mounted on it, called Faithful and True, who turns out to be the Word of God, namely Jesus. One wonders if this is not a sarcastic side-swipe at Caligula who named his horse Incitatus[18] and tried to introduce him into the government as a Seanator; in other words, Jesus is far more reliable and truthful than the nonsense going on in the Senate house in Rome. This use of names, whether cryptic or obvious, is an effective way of being suggestive without being too plain . It is almost on the level of giving nicknames.

Another literary device seen in virtually all the apocalyptic works of that era, is the appeal to history. Almost all these works begin or include some kind of historical anchorage. Usually it is the events connected with the defeat of Jerusalem and the Exile. This is evidence of the deep impact this made on Jewish literature. The exceptions to this would be the apocryphal books of Enoch and Moses, in which the historical material concerns the early history of Israel. The History is often fanciful and distorted, twisting Old Testament material to suit the writers' agenda; sometimes it is almost identical to existing historical material, as in 1 Esdras, where 2 Chronicles is often alluded to. With Revelation, recent history is not alluded to but instead we have the historical grounding of the seven churches of Asia. Babylon is mentioned, not in the literal sense but as a code word for Rome. The book then slides off into prophecy, or at least what is dubbed as prophecy, but is in fact a consumme of historical factors from the Old Testament and the ministry of Jesus. In common with most apocryphal books, there are outbursts of poetry, but of a much higher order.

It is important to see that John not only alludes to the past, but also shows how it is all being brought to a fantastic and glorious conclusion. We have the factor of augmentation, already mentioned earlier; we start with a comparatively mundane level with the local churches and it all builds up to a massive climax at the end, with mounting excitement. This is helped by the striking contrasts worked in all through the book: the angels and devils, heaven and hell, glory and destruction, and Jesus being the Lion and the Lamb, and those who are earmarked for salvation or damnation. The redeeming work of the humble carpenter Messiah is writ large against a massive cosmic backdrop.

Philosophical aspects

There is very little that could be called philosophy in Revelation. It is largely bound up with the theology, and only indirectly brings up philosophical matters. One such is the issue over free will and predestination. We notice that the angels unfold scrolls with people's names inscribed inside. This is an idea taken from Enoch and other apocalyptists. The implication in it is that everyone is earmarked beforehand for salvation or damnation. This is an uncomfortable thought which raises the matter of predestination. But if we look at Enoch, one's being recorded in the secret books has something to do with one's conduct in one's earthly life. So keeping the commandments of God is a matter of free will and personal choice; this is another aspect of the 'scroll' image. But the positive side of this imagery is that God is taking a personal interest in everyone's life and future, something that Jesus emphasised: every sparrow that falls to the ground is known about by the Heavenly Father.

The other issue latent in Revelation is over theodicy[16]: the problem of evil. If asked, John would almost certainly say that the answer lies in monotheism with a moderated element of dualism. There is no doubt that he holds God as supreme and in control of everything, even if recent events, such as the persecution, have been so horrific. His explanation for this would be that there is a fallen angel called Satan, who has a coterie of bad angels, like a gang of bandits, trying to undo God's work and spoil things for the Christians. But the same question must arise, as ever, 'How can a good God allow evil to exist in the creation?' Fundamentally, this question is unanswerable from the human point of view. From God's point of view, it is probably the only way in which he can operate a thing called Creation. But the problem of pain is a nagging question in the soul of every thinking person. St John reassures us that, in the end, all this will be resolved and everlasting justice, mercy and healing will prevail.

Geographic-historical aspects

Paradoxically, with the apocalyptic material being futuristic and prophetic, it still has some kind of anchorage in geography and history. This is a pattern seen in Daniel and 1 Enoch, and in fact in most of that genre; some kind of historical pattern or resumé is included somewhere, even if in indirect symbolic terms. John, however, has an interesting permutation on this approach; he is writing a letter to the seven churches of Asia; namely, Ephesus, Smyrna, Pergamum, Thyatira, Sardis, Philadelphia, and Laodicea. The historical situation is that they were the most advanced and prosperous parts of Asia-minor, a hotbed for Christian conversion, but a target for persecution, and a breeding ground for cranky splinter groups. The archaeologists have located all of these towns, and all of them except Smyrna have been excavated, revealing their opulence. Smyrna cannot be unearthed because it is under the modern town of Izmir, a vast city. In this way, the book begins with a clear touch of worldly reality, except of course that there were almost certainly many more nascent Christian churches in that area. Why does John select seven? It would seem to mirror the seven hills of Rome where there was so much wickedness going on; but the churches have the potential of doing far better. How these seven cities relate to Revelation can be seen below.

Ephesus, with its fine theatre in which St Paul had so much trouble, used to be on the coastline but is now seven miles inland as the bay has silted up. One of the streets is called the Curetes Street, and there are notches in the wall where torches used to be ensconced, and they can still be seen to this day. Little girls, called *curetes*, would run about the town at lighting up time, going from one home to another. When John says in 2:5, 'I will remove your lampstand from its place...' this could be a reminder of that custom. A visit to Laodicea reveals that nearby is a place called Hieropolis which has warm springs which are pleasant to bathe in but not pleasant to get in one's mouth; one spits it out. Does this remind us of '...you are neither cold nor hot. Would that you were cold or hot. Because you are lukewarm...I spew you out of my mouth.' 3:15. With the mention of Smyrna being poor, 'but you are rich' 2:9, we recall that that area around Smyrna was one of the main sources of gold ore in the Greco-Roman world. The other sources were Egypt and Spain. Now we know why the Romans invaded those parts!

John is comparing their economic wealth with their spiritual poverty, a strand of thought emphasised by Jesus in his parables. Thyatira had a flourishing metal industry, involving bronze, this could explain the remark '…whose feet are like burnished bronze.' 2:18. Pergamum was an important town, with a royal palace on top of a sheer cliff; also it had a library with cavity walls to keep the damp off the books. Also it had an Asklepion, a hospital complex for treatment of all conditions, including mental cases. It must have been a very sophisticated town by comparison with most places. The mention of Satan's throne is interesting; could this be a reference to the acropolis, which dominates the surrounding countryside? Other than that it is difficult to make a historical grounding with the other towns and details. But there is enough here to show that John is not being totally symbolic; there is historical and geographical anchorage in his first few Chapters. Moreover, he returns with a mention (22:16) of the seven churches. This has the effect of bringing us down to earthly realities once more.

This anchorage in historical realities is fully in accordance with the Hebrew tradition of theology: God is real and imminent in the workings of history. He is not some sort of abstract idea far away, leaving humanity to muddle through as best we can. It is all part of the pattern of history being planned and guided by the Almighty, a factor that is heavily emphasised in Revelation. Also theologically valuable is the claim that each church has its guardian angel, just as each person has. This is something that again goes back to the faith of Jesus. It is a mythological way of saying that God knows exactly what is happening to each and every one of us, and he cares deeply about the course of our lives. See Matthew 18:10.

Concluding remarks on Revelation

A stunning work of literature, this cannot be denied. That does not mean we have to accept every doctrine stated or implied in the book. The problem has been, over the centuries, that people have taken it far too literally, frightened themselves unnecessarily, and then rejected it out of hand. There is no need for this. We have to accept that the symbolisms in the book are often fairly obvious, but also can be very subtle. It is no use pretending that we can understand every detail of it; this account has touched on many matters but there is no claim to have unravelled all of it. It is unlikely that St John was actually trying to give details about the future of mankind and the end of the world. His focus is nearly all backward looking and bringing the whole pattern of salvation to a glorious climax; he is looking back at the crucifixion and the resurrection as accomplished facts. But splinter groups of a doomsday mentality have constantly tried to relate Revelation to actual dates and places in modern history – this is a fool's errand.

Paradoxically, just as we now wish to downplay hell, damnation and the end of the world on a theological level, the astrophysicists on the other hand, assure us that the world will come to an end, as the sun expands into a red giant and everything goes wrong in the solar system. Moreover we have managed to drag hell up to earth level with two major world conflicts and ethnic cleansings on a scale not seen before. There is this urge in human nature to contemplate the END as well as the BEGINNING, and to describe both of them in much the same imagery and high-flown hyperbole.

The Book of 4 Ezra as compared with Revelation

The book of 4 Ezra must not be confused with the Ezra seen next to Nehemiah in the Old Testament. It is regarded as pseudepigraphal, which means that it does not even appear in the Apocrypha. It did appear in the Vulgate, in Latin, as a kind of epilogue, but has never been taken seriously as scriptural. There is some debate as to its age. It is maintained that it had a Hebrew original, and that makes a lot of sense in that it gives us some lovely Hebrew poetry in parallelisms. But the Hebrew original has never been traced; it now appears in Greek, Latin and various eastern languages. If it did have a Hebrew original, this might argue for an early date, perhaps even near to the time of Ezra himself. There is a dating clue in the text; it talks of thirty years after the fall of the city, and also talks of Babylon and the Euphrates, and the loss of the Ark of the Covenant. This would place it about 567 BC, during the Exile. However there are many that think that it is talking about the fall of Jerusalem in AD 70, and that this book could have been written as late as AD 135. It is always difficult with these pseudepigraphal books to be certain of how much imagination and metaphor is being given to us.

The relevance of it to Revelation is thus: there is a passage in 4 Ezra (11:1) that talks about an eagle with twelve feathered wings. This has been taken to refer to the rise of Rome (as the eagle was symbolic of Rome) and twelve to refer to the line of Emperors from Julius onwards. Various attempts have been made to relate the twelve eagles' wings to the names of the Emperors and also the 'anti-wings' to the various plotters and upstarts during the first century AD. If we compare this with Revelation 17, we have a beast with seven heads and ten horns. This is also clearly related to Rome, with its seven hills upon which it was built. But here we have ten horns, which is taken to mean ten Emperors from Julius down to Nero who is the sixth, plus four more to come. From this it has been possible to speculate a date for Revelation, namely about 65 AD.

Leaving aside the fact that Revelation uses the metaphor of a beast, and Ezra the metaphor of an eagle, we can see that they are talking about the same situation in the Julian scheme of the Empire. The difference is that Ezra goes a little further and into more details. This gives the appearance that he is writing after Revelation with more knowledge of historical events, but using the same basic scheme of metaphor or encodement. Both of them entertain the idea that the Messiah will defeat Rome and bring in the messianic kingdom. This comes in Revelation 17:14, where the Lamb conquers and also in 4 Ezra 11:37 where the lion, the Messiah, will defeat Rome. One wonders if this Ezra is a covert Christian of Jewish background.

Even more intriguing is the 'man from the sea' in Ezra 13:1, clearly meant to be the Messiah. In verse 11 this man has sparks and fire issuing from his mouth. We can interpret this in mythological terms as the Messiah cleansing the world and defeating evil. But there was someone who took this totally at face value, one Bar Kochba, an insurgent about 135 AD; an uprising that failed. We do not have a full account of this episode, but one thing we do know, is that Bar Kochba used to put straw in his mouth and light it up, to make it appear that he was spewing fire out of his mouth[17]! This would be a graphic example of a literal interpretation of something that was only figurative. Both ideas appear to be a development of the Messianic prophecy in Isaiah 11:4: 'and with the breath of his lips he shall slay the wicked.'

The relationship between these two eschatological works is not easy to analyse, but there certainly is some relationship. By comparison with Revelation, Ezra is nowhere near as graphic, exciting, and inspired. One could almost call it banal.

It is also possible that 4 Ezra shows a relationship with other elements in the New Testament. In 4 Ezra 13:46 we have mention of a region called Arzareth. One wonders is this is a misspelling of Nazareth? Also in the early Chapters there is mention of 'the first Adam'. Is this a partial quotation from St Paul who spoke of the first and the second Adam? (1 Corinthians 15:45). Also 4 Ezra 7:10 presents us with the metaphor of someone who cannot receive his inheritance unless an heir pass through the danger set before him. This is almost the same thought that occurs in Hebrews, in which the New Testament cannot come into force unless Christ dies first, to make the Will come into action. Could Ezra have derived his idea from Hebrews? It is just possible, or the reverse.

The relationship between 4 Ezra and the New Testament is an interesting one; we may never be able to settle the matter with any certainty unless more evidence appears.

Notes for Chapter 6: Revelation

1. 1 Enoch is discussed in Chapter 20.
2. Antiochus 4th Epiphanes has been described in Chapter 2, the Maccabees. A full list of Greek Seleucid kings is shown in the footnotes to Chapter 2.

3. The 'interim period' is a theme that dominates the parables of Jesus. For a full discussion of this feature, please refer to my previous book, *The Theology of Paradox*.
4. The number code for God is 100; no one explains this, but it is an idea which occurs in Hindu scriptural material also. See my Chapter on 1 Enoch, Chapter 20.
5. This is described in Mary Boyce's Book, *The Zoroastrians*.
6. Revelation 13:18. John is giving a clear indication that he is talking figuratively and to take it literally is foolish.
7. The number of the beast is 666, Revelation 13:18. This scheme of interpretation is taken from Lauria Guy, Making Sense of the Book of Revelation.
8. John 8:1-11, the woman caught in adultery; this passage is not included in some ancient versions. However, it is typical of Jesus not to be too judgemental.
9. 'The blood of Jesus cleanses us from all sin', 1 John 1:7.
10. Leviticus 17:11.
11. See 1 Enoch, as discussed in Chapter 20.
12. The Covenant of Noah; see Genesis: 16-18.
13. The cleansing of the Temple: John 2:13-20. 'Zeal for my house will consume me'. This uses the word *zelos* as opposed to *thumos*, but the meaning is virtually the same.
14. Suetonius; *The Twelve Caesars*. Tacitus: *The Annals of Imperial Rome*.
15. 'It is done' *gegonen*, John 16:7, as compared with 'it is finished' John 19:30 *tetelestai*. But the meaning and intention is the same.
16. For a full discussion of theodicy, refer to my first book, *The Theology of Paradox*. There is also some discussion of it in Chapter 26.
17. *Bar Kochba* (various spellings), literally 'Son of a Star', the last crazy messianic uprising in Palestine. Jerome records him as having lighted straws in his mouth so that he would appear to be spewing forth fire. Jerome; Apology against the books of Rufinus.
18. *Incitatus* means 'Speedy'. The incident is described in Suetonius, *The Twelve Caesars*, p.176.
19. In Greek mythology, souls are thought to go to Hades for 1,000 years to be purged and prepared to be reborn into a new earthly life. This may be an example of how Greek thought has worked its way into Christian thinking.

List of Roman Emperors: relevant to this period

Julius Caesar; Augustus Caesar (27 BC to 14 AD); Tiberias (14-37 AD); Gaius (Caligula), (37 to 41 AD); Claudius (41-54 AD); Nero (54-68 AD); Galba/Otho/Vitellius (68-69 AD); Vespasian (70-79 AD); Titus (79-81 AD); Domitian (81-96 AD).

List of Jewish kings and tetrarchs at the same time

Herod the Great (37-4 BC) ruled all of Israel with permission from Rome. Archelaus (4 B –6 AD) ruled Judea and was deposed for incompetence. Son of Herod. Antipas (4 BC– 39 AD), son of Herod, ruled Galilee. Jesus called him 'that Fox'. Philip (4 BC– 34 AD), son of Herod, ruled Iturea, northern parts of Israel. Agrippa 1st (41–44 AD), grandson of Herod, ruled a united Jewish kingdom. Agrippa 2nd great grandson of Herod, ruled northern areas, (50–100 AD).

7

The Analects of Confucius

The sixth century BC, (probably 552 BC) saw the appearance of a most influential figure, K'ung Ch'iu, with variants on his name, the Latinised version of which is Confucius. Very little is known for certain about his origins and life; this is of little importance, since his message does not really relate to his own personal history or indeed that of the China in which he lived. It is enough to know that the background to the Analects is one of China as separate fiefdoms and local rulers often in contention with one another. As time went on, China became unified under one emperor. The other aspect of it is the importance given to bureaucracy and the training that this involved. As far as religion was concerned, Confucius did not attempt to introduce much in the way of new ideas or reforms. He just assumes the background religion of his day. His main message is very much a this-worldly contribution. He might fairly be termed an agnostic; certainly many a humanist of modern times would find his ideas helpful. Confucius would in today's terms make quite a reasonable civil servant; he hardly comes across as a great religious innovator. Even so, his influence on Chinese culture up to the present day has been profound, and this in spite of the latest twist in its history, that of the communist upsurge. It was later generations that promoted him to deity; he himself would probably have found that most amusing but also misleading.

The Analects were written in the Chinese of Confucius' day and are not easy to translate. Many of his thought-forms do not readily connect with modern Western assumptions. The book was not written by he himself. It takes the form of various disciples asking him questions and he giving various answers or non-answers. As compared with the Bible, the tone and method is very much analogous to the Proverbs and other

114

wisdom literature. After that there is nothing remotely like the personal encounters with God that people like Moses, Elijah or Isaiah experienced; still less is there anything like the Psalms or other poetical works of the Old Testament. The recording must have been done by scribes, who were anxious to preserve his sayings. This method continued with the writings of Mencius, one of his main successors. There is nothing historical recorded, nor geographical, nor scientific, nor mathematical; such remarks that are made on this level are purely incidental and irrelevant to his message. We may start with theological aspects, for although Confucius was not really orientated to this line of thought, Confucianism rapidly became a dominant religion in China, in company with Taoism and Buddhism.

The version of the *Analects* used here is the Penguin Classics by D.C. Lau, published in 1979, using chapter and verse references and giving page numbers.

Theological aspects

For a religious leader, Confucius is remarkably reserved on the subject of gods:

'The topics that Master did not speak of were prodigies, force, disorder and gods' 7:21 (page 88).

He does not indulge in a lot of speculation about deities or the Jade Emperor or any notions about the spirit world. He is suitably vague on these matters. When he uses the term 'heaven' it is in a general and vague sense, a kind of euphemistic synonym for God. 'Destiny' could do as another synonym for it. It could be seen as the Chinese approach to demythologising.

'Heaven is the author of the virtue that is in me' (7:23, page 89).

He had a sense of the world of the spirit giving him the urge for learning and moralising, but after that the whole thing is suitably vague. One would fairly assume that Confucius would have agreed with predestination, but he never elaborates on this. The nearest we come to this would be the words of Tzu-hsia:

'Life and death are a matter of Destiny; wealth and honour depend on Heaven. The gentleman is reverent and does nothing amiss, he is respectful towards others and observant of the rites, and all within the Four Seas are his brothers...' (12:5, page 113).

115

A noble thought indeed about the brotherhood of mankind. Confucius would hardly have disagreed with this. Here we see destiny and heaven used as parallel terms and one's status in life is decided from above. In 20:1 we actually have the use of the term 'the Great Lord'; this is the nearest we come to some sort of definition of God. It is not actually said by Confucius himself, but he would probably have agreed with it. There is nothing specific on the lines of YHWH or Allah or Ahura Mazda in any of these writings.

The mention of the 'rites' is interesting. We would assume, superficially, that that means religious observances, such as sacrifice. But Confucius is somewhat ambivalent about religious observances. He does not exactly condemn them but does not make them a central plank in his teachings.

'Sacrifice as if present is taken to mean sacrifice to the gods as if the gods were present. The Master however said, "Unless I take part in a sacrifice, it is as if I did not sacrifice."' 3:12 (page 69). One could conclude that he personally could manage without the rites, even if others do have a need for them.

'I do not wish to witness that part of the TI sacrifice which follows the opening libation to the impersonator' (3:10, page 68)[1].

This indicates the basis of sacrifice; it was an offering to the dead ancestors. This was, and still is, an important part of the spirituality of China. Tseng Tzu said, 'Conduct the funeral of your parents with meticulous care and let not sacrifices to your remote ancestors be forgotten...' (1:9, page 60).

Confucius probably would not have denied this procedure; however when he visited the Grand Temple (of the Duke of Chou) he asked questions about everything. His remark was 'The asking of questions is in itself the correct rite' (3:15, page 69).

In general terms, Confucius advises people to comply with the rites, as it is all bound up with reverence towards one's parents;

'When your parents are alive, comply with the rites in serving them; when they die, comply with the rites in burying them; comply with the rites in sacrificing to them' (2:5 ,page 63).

But here we see that 'rites' are not purely and simply some kind of religious observance. They are a complete code of conduct. We in the West would probably separate the religious from the secular in this respect; Confucius almost certainly does not. The rites mean one's whole moral conduct in secular life, what a gentleman would normally expect to comply with. These are virtues such as love, kindness, peace, caring for the common people, honesty, and eagerness to learn. The general term for this is 'benevolence', a term which occurs frequently in the Analects.

Confucius seems to have a hierarchy in his mind: first comes the **sage**, then the **good man**, then comes the **gentleman**, and then the **small man.** Confucius has an exalted view of the sage; he himself did not claim to be such. This may be a case of false modesty. In later years, his followers certainly elevated him to the top rank, in fact even higher, to become a god. But the 'gentleman' receives a lot of comment. He is expected to take part in government, as a 'civil servant'. Studying and holding a bureaucratic office are essential attributes of the gentleman; as well as benevolence[2].

'If a man sets his heart on benevolence he will be free from evil' 4:4 (page 72).

Benevolence is a matter for one's own effort. It has a very wide meaning but in general terms it means consideration for others.

'Do not impose on others what you yourself do not desire', 12:2 (page 112).

This comes very close to the New Testament dictum of 'love your neighbour as yourself' though not quite in the same terms. Love for people is definitely involved, but benevolence goes a lot further. It is all about being a responsible administrator, eager to learn, avoiding inflexibility and observing established procedures (the rites). 'In this way you will be free from all ill whether in state or in noble family' (12:2, page 112). However, a gentleman does not behave well purely and simply to earn a salary and merit with heaven. He does it for the sake of benevolence itself; it is morality for its own sake. Also, good leadership will have its effect on the people:

'Just desire the good yourself and the common people will be good. The virtue of the gentleman is like wind; the virtue of the small man is like grass… let the wind blow over the grass and it is sure to bend' (12:19, page 115).

This is what we in the West would call a thoroughly humanistic view of human nature, highly optimistic about the nature of mankind, and with no thought of 'original sin'. It would be a mistake, however, to think that Confucius has no concept of sin. There is a sense of shame and the need to reform oneself.

'When you have offended against Heaven, there is nowhere you can turn to in your prayers' (2:3, page 63). This is a basic problem in humanism; how does one cope with guilt? Confucius seems to ignore the age-old method of performing a sacrifice to clear guilt. But in general terms, he is superficial on the matter of sin, human corruption and wickedness.

Heavily emphasised in the Analects is the concept of 'The Way of Heaven' or 'The Decree of Heaven', or just 'The way'. He claims to have managed to comprehend the Decree of Heaven (2:4 page 61), but does not go into details about what it consists of. We have no such thing as anything like the Ten Commandments or a list of moral precepts. Everything is very broad and vague. This seems to reflect itself in his disciples who appear somewhat confused:

'One cannot get to hear his views on human nature and the Way of Heaven' (Tzu Kung in 5:13, page 78).

We have already detected an element of elitism in Confucius' thoughts; consider this:

'The gentleman stands in awe of three things. He is in awe of the Decree of Heaven. He is in awe of great men. He is in awe of the words of the sages. The small man, being ignorant of the Decree of Heaven, does not stand in awe of it. He treats great men with insolence and the words of the sages with derision' (16:8).

'There are nine things that the gentleman thinks about: firstly, to see clearly when he uses his eyes; secondly, to hear acutely when he uses his ears; thirdly, to appear cordial in his face; fourthly to appear respectful in his demeanour; fifthly, to be conscientious when speaking; sixthly to be reverent in his duties; seventhly, to seek advice when in doubt...' 16:10 (page 141).

Admirable qualities in a bureaucrat; not the sort of thing associated with a domineering pushy sort of person.

The word 'Way' which is a translation of *Tao*[3] has much significance; a pejorative word not just found in Confucianism. It has a very broad application and different schools of thought would interpret it differently. However, for Confucius it seems to mean the sum total of the ultimate truth. We never actually see a word equating to 'truth' in his thoughts, but 'way' might be roughly equivalent. It reminds us of the claim made by Jesus, 'I am the Way, the Truth and the Life'. This does not mean that Jesus was thinking in terms of the Chinese civil service! But this is another aspect in which Confucius is very close to New Testament thinking. Certainly the humility, caring for people, responsibility and service match well with the teachings of Jesus.

With regard to the politics of the local states, the Way is an important element in responsible government. There are some states where the Way is taken seriously and all is well, and other states where the Way is not taken seriously and fades out. A ruler should be conscientious and trustworthy, single-minded and reverent in deed; then even the barbarians will respect him; on the other hand if he fails to observe these criteria he will not even be respected in his own neighbourhood. For anyone in government, whether a king or a civil servant, there are five excellent practices and four wicked practices, 20:2 (page 159).

The excellent ones are: being generous without it costing him anything; works others hard without their complaining; has desires without being greedy; is casual without being arrogant; is awe-inspiring without appearing fierce.

The four wicked practices are: to impose the death penalty without first attempting to reform is cruel; to expect results without first giving warning is tyrannical; to insist on a time limit when tardy in issuing orders is to cause injury; when something has to be given to others anyway, to be miserly in the actual giving is to be officious.

All of this is very good advice to anyone in a position of leadership. These ideas square well with his five good qualities and six faults as discussed in 17:6 and 8 (page 144).

'They are respectfulness, tolerance, trustworthiness in word, quickness and generosity. If a man is respectful he will not be treated with insolence. If he is tolerant, he will win the multitude. If he is trustworthy in word his fellow men will entrust him with responsibility. If he is quick he will achieve results. If he is generous he will be good enough to be put in a position over his fellow men.'

The six faults are also described on page 144:

'To love benevolence without loving learning is liable to lead to foolishness. To love cleverness without loving learning is liable to lead to deviation from the right path. To love trustworthiness in word without loving learning is liable to lead to harmful behaviour. To love forthrightness without loving learning is liable to lead to intolerance. To love courage without loving learning is liable to lead to insubordination. To love unbending strength without loving learning is liable to lead to indiscipline.'

It is all about the Way, the intentions of Heaven and Destiny; three words which mean more or less the same thing for Confucius. It is all a part of being benevolent. As we can sense, God, as an active element in life is not very strong. He is a passive element, and distant. Even so, human conduct is to be lived with Heaven in mind, with humility, consideration, friendliness, service, love and peace. It is humanism with a faint backdrop of deity. One could not actually call it Atheism; agnosticism might be nearer the mark. It is a creed that assumes that humanity is basically good and yet there is still the need for training, which will involve studying and learning all the cultural refinements and social mores. In case one were to think that the precepts of the past were unalterable, that would be a mistake, for Confucius sees the need to be flexible and take account of new circumstances. One of the problems that the Nationalists and the Communists encountered on attempting to bring modernisation to China was that Confucianism was seen as reinforcing the ancient customs, especially about obedience to parents[4]. This was holding back reforms. It would have been interesting to see what Confucius himself would have said about this impasse; maybe he would have agreed with the modification of ancient mores in order to improve the lot of the common people. He might be roughly termed as 'conservative' with a small C; but he was not totally fixated on the rites of the past.

In general terms, on the subject of Theology, the Analects are not some kind of systematic array of theological ideas. They are just a collection of varying ideas uttered by the Master, sometimes actually being slightly contradictory. His whole slant is on the subject of good morality and guidance for anyone who is in a position of leadership. The Analects are at their most similar to the Bible with the Wisdom literature (Chapter 15: Proverbs, and later material that contains advice on good leadership). He has little to say for the peasants or even the 'little man'. Benevolence[2] is his favourite word, and that is in line with the thinking of Heaven.

Mythology in the Analects

There is very little that can be called mythology in the Analects. Confucius does not indulge in elaborate accounts of the antics of gods, spirits and devils. When he uses the term 'heaven' it is a kind of euphemism for God but beyond that there is nothing specific stated. That was left to the Taoists who supplied the spiritual side of Chinese thought; Confucius concentrates on this world and our moral conduct. Even when we have a remark such as this:

'The rule of virtue can be compared to the Pole Star which commands the homage of the multitude of stars without leaving its place' (2:1, page 63).

This can be seen as a demythologised remark. He is in fact saying that the whole universe is ruled by moral standards, a most valuable remark. He does not even attempt to turn the Pole Star into a god or some kind of spiritual entity, as some other religions would have done. The stars offer homage, but is this to be taken literally? It is a superb piece of metaphor containing a great deal of truth: the universe is ordered, moral, consistent and based on all the virtues that a gentleman should exhibit.

We have passing mention of spirits, such as in 6:6: 'would the spirits of the mountains and rivers allow it to be passed over...?' Also in 10:14, '... when the villagers were exorcising evil spirits, he stood in his court robes on the eastern steps.' This may indicate that Confucius stood to one side when such a ritual was being performed; the 'eastern steps' were the place for a host to stand. Also 11:12 may sum up his attitude to the other world. Chi-lu asked how the spirits of the dead and the gods should be served. The Master said, 'You are not able even to serve man. How can you serve the spirits?' and 'May I ask about death?' and the reply, 'You do not understand even life. How can you understand death?'

This is fair indication that Confucius was simply not interested in speculation about the afterlife and the other world. There is no teaching on what happens when we die or where we shall go. Nor is there any mention of Hell. That is left to the Taoists. Confucius is very much a this-worldly thinker.

The Analects as literature

The Analects take the form of various ad hoc conversations between Confucius and his followers. It reminds one a little of Anselm's *Cur Deus Homo?*[5] As a work of literature it is not really outstanding. There is no sense of structuring, climax or anti-climax or chiasmus; all the remarks appear to be disconnected and haphazard; there is no sense of system or progression.

As far as poetry is concerned, there is none. However, Confucius often refers us to the Odes[6], a corpus of poetry that he regards as compulsory reading. This may have been for him his 'Bible'. A good example would be when Nan Jung kept mentioning the 'white jade sceptre', which would have been a symbol of mystical rulership eliciting thoughts about the Jade Emperor, who is seen as God.

'A blemish on the white jade can still be polished away; a blemish on these words cannot be removed at all' – A quotation from Ode 256.

'When the water is deep, go across by wading; when it is shallow, lift your hem and cross' – A proverb taken from Ode 54.

There are places where his use of metaphor is quite apposite and accomplished. A few examples will suffice:

'I do not see how a man can be acceptable who is untrustworthy in word. When a pin is missing in the yoke-bar or a large cart or in the collar-bar of a small cart, how can the cart be expected to go?'

'A piece of rotten wood cannot be carved, nor can a wall of dried dung be trowelled... I used to take on trust a man's deeds after having listened to his words... now having listened to his words I go on to observe his deeds' (5:10).

'Heaven is about to use your Master as the wooden tongue for a bell,' 3:25. This meant that Confucius was about to rouse the Empire.

'The stuff is no different from refinement; refinement is no different from the stuff. The pelt of a tiger or a leopard, shorn of hair, is no different from that of a dog or a sheep' (12:8).

'After all in the course of a year, the old grain having been used up, the new grain ripens, and fire is renewed by fresh drilling.' This was on the subject of how long to mourn one's parents; Confucius is in favour of the traditional three years (17:21).

'The gentleman's errors are like an eclipse of the sun and moon in that when he errs, the whole world sees him doing so, and when he reforms the whole world looks up to him' (19:21).

Many of his metaphors are somewhat obscure as they relate to agricultural life in China 2,500 years ago. Even so, some of them are quite acceptable. One has the feeling that if he had offered much more figurative language, the *Analects* would have been much improved and more colourful. Some of his imagery reminds one a little of the parables of Jesus. It is the same method for conveying eternal truths in metaphor rather than univocal language.

Philosophical truth

It would be fair to say that the thoughts of Confucius can be described as a moral philosophy rather than as a religion. It only became a religion as his followers adapted and applied it in later years. But as far as Confucius is concerned, this would sum it up:

'To work for the things the common people have a right to, and keep one's distance from the gods and spirits, while showing them reverence, can be called wisdom' (6:22).

There are only a few remarks that contain the word 'wisdom', and one is left with the impression that 'benevolence' is almost a synonym for 'wisdom'. Consider this remark;

'The wise find joy in water; the benevolent find joy in mountains. The wise are active; the benevolent are still. The wise are joyful; the benevolent are long-lived.' This appears to be an interesting piece of parallelism, not unlike Hebrew poetry. The implication is that wisdom and benevolence are virtually the same thing.

Being wise very much relates to the everyday business of administration and dealing with ordinary people. Again here, we see wisdom and benevolence meaning virtually the same thing:

'Fan Ch'ih asked about benevolence. The Master said, "Love your fellow men." He asked about wisdom. The Master said, "Know your fellow men." "Raise the straight and set them over the crooked. This can make the crooked straight."' Apart from sounding like something out of Isaiah, it means that moral philosophy is essentially about knowing how to deal with real people in actual situations, rather than some kind of elaborate theory. Wisdom is not a matter of endless discussions and clever remarks; it is about being taciturn:

'The gentleman is judged wise by a single word he utters; equally he is judged foolish by a single word he utters. That is why one really must be careful of what one says. The Master cannot be equalled just as the sky cannot be scaled...' (19:25).

Confucius was noted for not saying a great deal, in fact there were times when he kept his mouth shut. There is nothing said about 'fools' in the Analects, but the implication is that those that prattle on endlessly are stupid. Wisdom resides in being reserved and thinking carefully before making a pronouncement. This thought can be traced in the Proverbs; in fact the tone of the whole book is most closely related to the Wisdom literature of the Old Testament.

'The mark of a benevolent man is that he is loath to speak' (12:3).
'When to act is difficult; is it any wonder that one is loath to speak?'

All of this relates to the Way, the Tao, the ruling principle of the universe, and the gentleman should align himself to that policy. It is a passive view of deity, a demythologised understanding of God, which is different from God in the Wisdom literature of the Old Testament. Here, God is active and plays a dramatic part in the processes of creation, and Wisdom is personified. With Confucius, there is no such personification. Wisdom and Virtue, the same thing, are an essential part of the Way of Heaven; everything circulates around that; that is the core of his philosophy.

Linguistic considerations

There is no doubt that translating from ancient Chinese to a modern language such as English is not a straightforward matter. There are all kinds of historical and cultural assumptions in the Analects, and a literal translation does not really convey the full flavour of the text. A case in point is the use of the word *Tao*, the Way, which is used frequently. In Chinese this is a pejorative word with much loading, and different slants according to who is using it. There is no doubt that Confucius was influenced by Lao Tzu, the chief inspiration behind Taoism. It is believed that they actually met and discussed things. It is clear that many of the terms Confucius used can be traced in the Taoist philosophy: gentleman, benevolence, sage, are just a few terms. But he seems to have given them a fuller meaning and significance. Taoism, as a philosophy, later developed into a religion, as much as Confucianism did. The relationship between the two 'isms' is not always clear, and interdependence must have taken place. The other large influence on Confucius was the Book of Odes.

On a more mundane level, there are passages in the Analects that are obscure and translation is only tentative. We have similar problems with parts of the Bible, Proverbs being a good case in point. One example would be this:

'Do I possess knowledge? No, I do not. A rustic put a question to me and my mind was a complete blank. I kept hammering at the two sides of the question until I got everything out of it' (9:8).

On the face of it, this comes out quite well in English, but we must remember that a certain amount of paraphrasing must have gone into this, and the original might have had quite a different flavour.

Another phrase, which includes a cultural assumption, goes like this;

'If there was a ruler who achieved order without taking any action… there was nothing for him to do but to hold himself in a respectful posture and to face due south' (15:5).

There are various assumptions contained in this that require a certain amount of comment to make any sense to a Western mind. Facing due south was what the Chinese Emperor did when sitting on his throne. It was obviously a gesture of authority and command over what ought to have been a united empire, but at that time was not. If Shun faced south, in one sense he was impersonating the Emperor, which might be a good tactic as long as the Emperor did not take that the wrong way. Also he holds himself in a respectful posture; this is not described, but we can imagine that he was not behaving like an idiot or play-acting. Just to strike a dominating posture might have been all that was required at that time in China, rather than marching out with the troops and causing mayhem. Would this work in the West? Probably not, but it tells us something of the mind-set of the Chinese people. They respected a leader who said little, looked imposing and tried to replicate himself as a mini-emperor. A different world indeed!

Another cultural assumption is as follows:

'When the Master encountered men who were in mourning or in ceremonial cap and robes, or were blind, he would, on seeing them, rise to his feet, even though they were younger than he was, and, on passing them would quicken his step,' (9:10, page 97).

To modern western ears, this makes very little sense; however there are several assumptions contained in this passage, all illustrative of Chinese culture at that time and still to some extent to this day. If you were in mourning, that was expected to last for three years in honour of one's parents. The reason being that if one's mother had suckled one for three years, the least one could do would be to honour them for three years, in addition to sacrificing to their spirits. This is an aspect of ancestor worship. Anyone in ceremonial robes or cap would be performing some sort of religious observance. Confucius debates whether to use silken robes and cap, or just plain linen ones. Being a modest man he goes for linen. Anyone blind would be respected. Confucius rises to his feet, even if they are younger than himself. Normally the older person demands more respect, if not obedience, and the younger man has to stand up first, not the other way round. Then he quickens his step; again another sign of respect, which one would expect a younger man to do, but not this time. Confucius, in some respects, breaks through the social mores and introduces a slightly modified code. There is a lot contained in this little passage which can only be understood by a certain knowledge of ancient Chinese culture.

We have become aware of the 'gentleman' *chun tzu* and the 'small man' *hsiao jen*[8] as referring to the ordinary people. It is the contrast between the rulers and the ruled. However there is much pejorative loading in these terms. They are, for Confucius, essentially moral terms. The gentleman is the one with a cultivated moral character, studious, honest, helpful, a pillar of virtue, setting a good example; the small man is the opposite, and is expected to take his tone from the gentleman. There is just a touch of snobbery in this, at least from a modern western standpoint. Even so, there is nothing to stop the small man setting out to study and elevate himself to the status of gentleman, as indeed Confucius did himself. There are many such pejorative words in the *Analects*, the meaning of which only becomes clear when we research Chinese culture and pre-digested thought. The same is true for many parts of the Bible. All these ancient works of literature can only be properly understood against their cultural and linguistic background. They all include obscure passages. This is because the writers could not anticipate the mentality of readers perhaps twenty centuries later. The linguistic difficulty is probably more acute with ancient Chinese than with many other sacred texts.

The Book of Odes

One of the major influences on Confucius was the Book of Odes; he constantly refers to them in such a fashion as to make one think that this was his book of reference, in other words, his 'Bible'. He must have been influenced by Lao Tzu, the founder of Taoism, but not to such an extent. The Odes, or the Shi King, or Book of Poetry, is only a part of a corpus of literature from ancient China, some going back to about 1750 BC. Confucius himself compiled them and there are thought to be about 300 of them. The edition cited here by L. Cranmer-Byng, the Kissenger Legacy Reprints dated 1909, is only a selection. But they are characterised by great poetic beauty and imagination. It must have been quite a feat of ingenuity to render the ancient Chinese in a modern Western form such as quatrains which rhyme properly. One wonders what form Chinese poetry of that genre took. *The Odes* are very largely love poems, often written from the girl's point of view, which might seem unusual. It would be unnecessary to discuss all of these poems; rather it is of relevance to select the few that directly tie in with the thinking of Confucius, namely, his advice to those in positions of power and influence.

'The Prayer of the Emperor Ching' – Number 1

This short poem has the Emperor asking (presumably Heaven) for guidance in his onerous task of ruling China.

> 'Let me be reverent, reverent, even as the way of Heaven is evident...'
> (page 25)
> This is a word that Confucius would very much have approved of. Responsible rulership with benevolence at its heart is constantly emphasised in the *Analects*, and the last verse is highly appropriate for anyone in authority:
> 'I will hold fast some gleams of knowledge bright. Help me to bear my heavy burden right, and show me how to walk in wisdom's way.'

This reminds us of Solomon as God asked him what he would like, and he replied that he wished to have the wisdom to rule his people aright (1 Kings 3:9).

'The Prayer of the Emperor Ching' – Number 2

It becomes more obvious that he has succeeded to the throne as a child:

'Even as a little helpless child am I, on whom hath fallen the perplexed affairs of this unsettled state…' (page 25).
He is praying to his Father. Given that ancestor worship was and still is a well-established feature of Chinese religion, he is not necessarily praying to a god, but to his actual dead parent, for help. The boy-king is committed to following in the footsteps of his ancestors and is not to be side-tracked from continuing their policies.
'O great and gracious Father, hear and condescend to guard, to cherish, to enlighten me.'

Confucius was not really concerned with the world of the spirits or with sacrificing to one's ancestors. However he would have very much approved of the determination of the young king to do his duty by his country.

'The Princes'

This poem concerns the princes who are coming with harvest gifts to the king, styled as the Son of Heaven. This would imply the Emperor himself. He is expected to renew their rights. This sounds like an annual ceremony:

'May the pleasure and power for my lords increase, may the land yield corn and the years bring peace' (page 38).

The setting and the intention sounds like the annual kingship ceremony in which the Emperor himself performed a sacrifice, which was meant to ensure the success of the harvest and also the security of the nation.

'Good King Wu'

'Good King Wu was a monarch true…' is the chorus. Clearly he had a very high reputation with the people. He used divination to select a site for his palace and, once established, he chose responsible underlings to run the kingdom. All his plans came to fruition and his son inherited a happy and grateful land. Monarchy, in Confucius' eyes is a good thing: a responsible monarch results in a contented public that can see no reason for a *coup d'etat*.

The vast majority of the Odes are love songs, often about a deserted lady or thwarted lover. It would be interesting to compare these with the Song of Solomon. The material in the Hebrew canon is much more erotic and basic; in the Odes, the tenor is on a much higher level. From 'A Wife's Memories' we have:

'Do I not go by dream to you, who cannot come to me?' (page 37).

'Before the Ford' is also interesting:

'If your heart be kind and true, I will ford the stream with you. If your fickle thoughts go straying, come with me no more a-maying…' (page 49).

It would be interesting to know what significance Confucius would have placed on this kind of poem, but he was certain in his own mind that a knowledge of the Odes was the hallmark of a proper Chinese gentleman, cultured, responsible and benevolent.

The Song of Solomon in relation to the Odes

We have already noticed that there are aspects of Confucius' thought which tie in with Solomon, King of Israel. On the face of it, Solomon would have predated Confucius by about four centuries, which would indicate that Hebrew ideas had worked their way through to China; possible but somewhat unlikely. The other issue, that of the love poems, may indicate the opposite. If the *Odes* were in circulated in China before the time of Solomon, then the influence might have been the other way round. Love poetry is unusual in what we regard as sacred literature; the Chinese have the *Odes* of Confucius; the Hebrews have the Song of Solomon. Comparing the two reveals some interesting factors.

The Song of Solomon is a kind of conversation between a king and his chosen queen. Strangely the conversation does not really make one reply after another; the two speakers do not really connect except occasionally.

Girl: 'I am a rose of Sharon, a lily of the valleys.'
Boy: 'As a lily among the brambles so is my love among maidens' (song 2:2).

From time to time there is the hint of the Garden of Eden, although this is never stated plainly. There is much about trees with fruit on them, and it speaks of idyllic innocence.

The poetry in it is of the highest order, with figurative speech and parallelism of the best.

> 'My beloved is all radiant and ruddy; distinguished among ten thousand. His head is finest gold; his locks are wavy, black as a raven... his cheeks are like beds of spices, yielding fragrance. His lips are lilies, distilling liquid myrrh... his body is ivory work encrusted with sapphires' (song 5:10-16).

Many of the passages are what we would now call 'erotica', but in Solomon's day they may never have thought of it like that. In general the poetry is a long way ahead of the *Odes*.

There is the faintest indication that even this poetry is not to be taken literally. 'You have ravished my heart, my sister, my bride... how sweet is your love, my sister, my bride,' (4:9-10). This requires poetic license: he his hardly going to marry his sister, even if the Pharaohs did.

The early Christians quickly saw the Song a prophetic of the love between Jesus Christ and his church. One example would be where Solomon had a vineyard which he let out to keepers and expected a fee from them. This reminds us of the Wicked Tenants. But the best and most profound remark is: 'for love is strong as death, and jealousy is cruel as the grave' (song 8:5).

Notes for Chapter 7: The Analects

1. The 'impersonator'. A boy or girl would be dressed up to look like the dead ancestor, and be the centre of the sacrifice.
2. 'Benevolence' has a very wide range of meaning; it is the whole personality of the gentleman who is a bureaucratic official and responsible to the king and the public.
3. *Tao*, 'the Way', has a wide range of meaning. It is the whole principle and meaning of the universe.
4. 8:2 (page 92) is about affection for one's parents which is the core of Chinese thinking.
5. Anselm, twelfth century archbishop of Canterbury, who wrote *Cur Deus Homo*? 'Why did God become man?' which outlines the sacrificial theory of the Atonement.
6. The Odes, assembled by Confucius, number about 300. They are of great beauty and poetic achievement.
7. Three years of mourning for one's parents was the norm; the reason was that since one's mother suckled one for three years, one should devote three years to mourning.
8. Chun Tzu and Hsiao Jen, 7:37 (page 91). 'The gentleman is easy of mind, while the small man is always full of anxiety.'

8

The Bhagavad Gita

This Hindu text from remote pre-history was allegedly composed by the sage Vyasa, who had been given divine sight so that he could see and report on all 'events' to the blind king Dhritarashtra. In fact it is Dhritarashtra who starts the book off with the question:

'O Sanjana, tell me what happened at the Kurukshetra, the field of dharma, where my family and the Pandavas gathered to fight' (1:1, page77).

The latest and most scholarly version in English, used in this assessment, is found in Eknath Easwaran's version, which gives a balanced translation, faithful to the text and yet not afraid of a little paraphrasing at the appropriate moment. It is difficult to date The Bhagavad Gita, but it must come later than the Rig Veda and the Mahabharata, but predates the upsurge of Buddhism. It may be contemporaneous with the classical Hebrew era. Although the Mosaic covenant probably predates this work, it would be difficult to see any influence. More likely, there could be a small amount of influence from Chinese thinking. Whichever way one sees it, the Gita is a remarkable work, full of sensitivity and yet displaying nearly all the basics of traditional Hindu thought. There is no attempt at producing a systematic pattern of doctrine. There are fluid ideas that move from one heading to another, but nothing hard and fast. The Gita forms a complete contrast with the Analects of Confucius (Chapter 8) and indeed with virtually every other portion of 'scriptural' material. It is the god Krishna holding a conversation with Prince Arjuna and Sanjaya about the essentials of spiritual life and salvation.

Mathematical material

There is nothing in this work that could be called mathematical. Dates, ages, timings, measurements are all simply not mentioned. The only thing that could be seen as mathematical is the remark that the Day of Brahma is 100 yugas, but this is not explained or expanded upon. Strangely, the idea that the number of God is 100 appears in the Hebrew tradition, (Enoch, Chapter 20), but this too is not explained.

Historical material

The book begins with what appears to be a historical battle about to commence, giving a list of kings and champions arrayed ready for the conflict; a mighty build-up, with people roaring like lions and blowing on conch shells, 'echoing throughout heaven and earth'. But the way it is described, in massive heroic terms, carries one above the purely historical level. We are entering the mythological level; the battle is symbolic of the struggle between good and evil. In fact, it may be safe to say that there is no actual history in the Gita. There may be some kind of 'recollection' of a real battle in remote prehistory, since Kurukshetra is actually a real place, but that is not the point. From the point of view of geography, and indeed science, there is nothing solid. The whole work is based on mythological assumptions and internal spirituality.

The storyline, if there is one, develops with a crisis at the start, when Prince Arjuna, the leader of the 'goodies', develops cold feet just before the battle starts. This is because he realises that the opposing army consists of many of his very own relatives. With his mind in a whirl, he cannot bring himself to kill his own brothers and cousins. He would much rather they were to kill him. Is it really so simple to dub them as all evil? This is something that would have astonished everyone in the ancient world {1:47} (page 82):

> 'Overwhelmed by sorrow, Arjuna... cast away his bow and arrows, sat down in his chariot in the middle of the battlefield.'

It sounds like an outburst of Pacifism! But if we take it literally, it would be. And yet, this is not literal; it is symbolic. Arjuna is backing off from contesting with evil. It is the age-old conflict between good and evil. This is something that Zoroaster (Chapter 5) might have learned from Hindu tradition. Even if the Devil is not mentioned, God soon is, and this is, it would seem, the Hindu view of Dualism, which is one answer to the question of theodicy. But Krishna soon sets to work to clarify matters for him, and that takes up the entire book. The battle never seems to start even though Krishna tries to persuade Arjuna to fight the other army. Essentially, Arjuna sees killing his own relations as a sin that will always be a burden of guilt for him. But Krishna maintains that it is a sin not to destroy evil; it is part of his work.

'I am born in every age to protect the good, to destroy evil, and to re-establish the dharma,' 4:7-8 (page 117).

Philosophic-theological content

It is not easy to separate theology from philosophy in Hindu thought, as the two strands are inextricably interwoven. When talking about gods, Brahman is the ultimate unknowable god, roughly analogous to YHWH in Hebrew thought: distant, eternal, but one. It has been maintained that Hinduism is basically another version of monotheism. This may seem rather strange since their holy writings refer to many gods as underlings and offshoots of Brahman – there are literally thousands of them. Even so, a Hindu might claim that they are only differing emanations and manifestations of the one true god. Something of this comes out in the Ramayana (Chapter 22).

This is particularly true of Krishna, who claims to underpin the whole of creation; this clearly associates him with Brahman and there is no real separation between them.

'My true being is unborn and changeless. I am the Lord who dwells in every creature. Through the power of my own maya[1], I manifest myself in a finite form,' (4:6, page 117).

In this, we see the pantheistic element in Hinduism. It might be slightly anachronistic to say that this actually is pantheism[2], but it does come very close to it. This is reinforced by Krishna's claims, which are very widespread.

'I will tell you of my divine powers. I will mention only the most glorious for there is no end to them… I am the true self in the heart of every creature… the beginning, middle and end of their existence,' (10:19, page 185).

At this point it is worth mentioning that this claim reminds us of 'I am Alpha and Omega' as seen in Revelation 1:8, in which it is stated that Jesus is the true beginning and end of everything. But Krishna goes further and makes a massive list, which need not be quoted in full; a sample will do;

'I am Ananta the cosmic serpent, and Varuna the god of water... I am the lion... the eagle... the crocodile... I am Karpanda, the power of sex, and Vasuki the king of snakes... ' (10:29, page 187).

The list is never-ending, but most significantly he claims to be the way into meditation and philosophy.

'Of all the sciences, I am the science of self-knowledge, and I am logic in those who debate. Among the letters, I am A... I am infinite time and the sustainer whose face is seen everywhere... .' 10:33 (page 187-8).

We notice that the use of the word 'science' is not the normally accepted meaning; it does not mean a laboratory with experimentation. It sounds more like what we know as the social sciences, such as psychology and sociology.

'I am the repetition of the holy name and among mountains I am the Himalayas,' (10:25, page 186). The symbol *OM* is the holy name, the sound used to obtain access to God, namely Brahman. These are massive claims; it means that Krishna regards himself as the sum total of all divinity, not just of Brahman but of all the other gods, lesser divinities, and even devils (wicked Daevas). This is in contrast to Jesus whose claims, from himself, were very modest. The clearest claim that he made for himself was the 'servant', and also the 'Son of Man' (which was a two-sided claim). Neither of these appear in Krishna's list. It is not characterised by humility but, more likely, by boasting. Now we can see the extra relevance in St John stating that Jesus is the beginning and the end. Whether St John knew of the Gita is beyond us to say, but this does provide the Christian answer to these claims. In more general terms, Krishna's list also recalls the 'I am... ' passages in St John's gospel: 'I am the light of the world... I am the true vine... ' and others. We notice St John limits it to seven crucial statements about the work of Jesus, and it brings the definition of God to a completion. 'I am that I am' in Exodus 3:14 is now given a full treatment and the work of God in this world is seen in real terms. One could see St John as in effect putting a limit on Krishna with his all-inclusive, all-pervasive claims. After all, if Krishna is in everything, then everything comes to equal everything, and there is no real contrast between good and evil, no values, no right and wrong. But Jesus shows us that the dualism between good and evil is real; that he is not the Devil and his ministry is a constant struggle against temptation to do wrong.

Another important aspect of Hindu theology is that of incarnation. This must not be confused with what is claimed for Jesus. He came as completely human, flesh and blood, was born and died and when he was injured, he really hurt. But the Hindu gods, particularly Krishna, never come as solid, real human beings; they never live a real, down-to-earth human existence. They only appear occasionally, like some sort of apparition, usually to help people, but not to engage themselves in the real turmoil of this world. Krishna never admits to being injured, insulted, or cruelly put to death.

This leads us on to the question of sacrifice, an issue which is basic to virtually every religion. It would be fair to say that the Gita has an elevated view of sacrifice. There seems to be no mention of killing an animal, such as a horse sacrifice as is mentioned in the Ramayana (Chapter 22). It is a transmuted sacrifice on a much higher level.

> 'The process of offering is Brahman; that which is offered is Brahman. Brahman offers the sacrifice in the fire of Brahman... some aspirants offer material sacrifices to the gods, others offer selfless service in the fire of Brahman... some renounce all enjoyment... some offer the workings of the senses and the vital forces through the fire of self-control kindled in the path of knowledge. Some offer wealth...' (4:27-28, page 120).

So we see that Hindu sacrifice is on a much higher and more intellectual level than most in the ancient world, and this would still apply today. He is in effect saying that yoga, in whatever form it is employed, lifts one out of Karma and everyone can reach the eternal Brahman. There is also an element in Hindu thought about a king called Perusha who was sacrificed and thereby gained merit for the whole of mankind. This is mentioned in 8:2 (page 165) but not properly explained:

> '... Perusha, eternal spirit... the supreme sacrifice, is made to me as the Lord in you.'

Perusha was never an historical figure; he was purely mythical. Nevertheless it reminds us of the sacrifice of Christ: God himself provided a sacrifice to clear the sin of the world. The difference here is that Krishna was never a real historical person, nor was Perusha, and neither of them were subjected to a real death like Jesus. For the Hindus it is all in the mind, imaginary, theoretical, like a projection from a cinematograph on a screen. But Jesus brings the whole configuration into reality: the sacrifice is done with all observing and being involved. It is not done over our heads in some faraway, eternal, imaginary location. In this way, Jesus brings the whole Hindu system of sacrifice to a completion in real terms.

One aspect of the Gita, which is very much in agreement with the Bible, is the love of God. Krishna often states that love is essential in all our relationships with him.

'This supreme Lord who pervades all existence, the true Self of all creatures, may be realised through undivided love,' (8:22, page 168).

Love is required both ways. Firstly there is the love of the seeker for Krishna:

'... Give all your love to me... fill all your mind with me; love me, serve me... ' (9:34, page 177).

This is the sure way of coming to Krishna when one dies. This is the way to avoid rebirth and the cycle of Karma, going straight to one's god. Vice versa, Krishna loves anyone who has the following qualities:

'... living beyond the reach of "I" and "mine" , and of pleasure and pain, patient, contented, self-controlled, firm in faith with all their heart and mind given to me... with such as these I am in love' (12:13, page 208).

He goes on to list all the qualities of the faithful adherent, taking several verses, and culminating in the most decisive element for escaping Karma:

'Those who meditate upon this immortal dharma[3] as I have declared it, full of faith and seeking me as life's supreme goal, are truly my devotees, and my love for them is very great' (12:20, page 209).

Sadly, there is no mention of Krishna displaying love for anyone who does not love him. Do we assume that Krishna hates such a person, which would explain why he has to be reborn and have another try at getting it right? But Jesus displayed love for everyone, even the 'baddies'.

In many ways, this passage on love reminds us of St Paul's famous passage in 1 Corinthians 13 on that very subject. He states that it is the supreme gift of the Spirit. But there is an essential difference here; for the Christian, love is basically the gift of God; it is not something that one can conjure up for oneself. With Krishna, however, the implication is that one has to try very hard to achieve it, using one's own efforts.

'Hazardous and slow is the path to the Unrevealed, difficult for physical creatures to tread' (12:5, page 207).

In other words, it is a 'work' rather than a 'grace', or at least that is the impression given. There are many people who fail to achieve it, and when they die, they go to whatever god they have attached themselves to. If it is Krishna they love, they go to him. If it is the daevas, then one goes to the daevas, and the same with the ancestors and the ghosts. One's fate at death is decided by oneself (9:23, page 176). This is not a totally hopeless situation for those who do not go to Krishna; they will be reborn and have another chance, eventually, perhaps after many lifetimes, they will achieve Nirvana, union with Brahman.

On the other hand, paradoxically, Krishna carries a mace and has a wonderful and terrible form. The entire universe shakes in terror before his fearful teeth. This is Vishnu, the frightening aspect of Krishna. He has fearful teeth and mouths burning like fires at the end of time. Does this remind us of Revelation? This is the fierce side of Krishna. 'Your nature and your works confound me,' says Arjuna 11:31 (page 198). Krishna's reply to this is that he is the destroyer of all. All that army that is arrayed for battle, as at the beginning of the book, are already killed. Arjuna might as well fight them because all he will be is Krishna's instrument. We have to remember the mythical element in this, symbolic of overpowering evil. However, the impression is that essentially Krishna is a god of love and cares deeply for anyone who attaches himself to him.

Something that western theology might not agree with, and has been encountered elsewhere, is the notion that one is born for good or evil.

'But attachment to the gunas leads a person to be born for good or evil' (13:21, page 219).

This sounds like the Hindu version of predestination, although it may not be meant in quite the same way. It seems there is plenty of scope for one to decide on the right path in life and lift oneself out of evil. Even so, some people are born with divine tendencies and others with demonic. The divine attributes are as follows: self-control, sincerity, truthfulness, love, desire to serve, vigour, patience, will, and purity. Much of this sounds like passages from the New Testament, especially St Paul. However, those with demonic tendencies display inhuman traits: hypocrisy, arrogance, conceit, anger, cruelty, ignorance, impurity, untruthfulness, pride, and greed. They think that the basis of life is sex and that the gratification of lust is the highest that life can offer. They will deny the existence of God; so atheism is at the root of it; lust anger and greed and the three gates of darkness. When it comes to death, they are reborn into a family of the same mentality, with demonic tendencies. They fall lower and lower until eventually they 'fall into a dark hell'.

There is another analysis at work in the Gita. There are three types of people, and it all depends on what they worship. There is the rajasic type, who worships power and wealth. There is the tamasic type, who worships spirits and ghosts. There is the sattvic type, who worships forms of god. Even their taste in food, the work they do and the disciplines they practise and the gifts they give are all indicators of their personality.

Sattvic people like food that is mild, tasty, substantial, agreeable and nourishing. They perform sacrifices with their mind fixed on the purpose of the sacrifice, without thought of reward. They are honest, non-violent, kindly, helpful, calm, gentle, silent, and self-restrained. This is done without attachment to the results, but in a spirit of great faith. This reminds us of 'to labour but not to ask for any reward[4]'.

Rajasic people like food that is salty, or bitter, hot, sour, or spicy and which promotes discomfort or disease. They perform sacrifices for the sake of show and the good it will bring them. They assume that it will bring them respect, honour or admiration. They are undependable and transitory. When they give something, they expect something in return or expect to receive a favour. This is really describing the pushy sort of person who, because he is rich, thinks he can have everything his own way, and dominate everyone.

The tamasic people like overcooked, stale, leftover and impure food that has lost its taste and nutritional value. They perform sacrifices ignoring the letter and the spirit, and they omit proper offerings, proper food and proper faith. This conduct is practised to gain power over other people. They also torture themselves on the assumption that this is spiritual. Giving at the wrong time and in the wrong situation, and to an unworthy person without respect is tamasic. They worship spirits and ghosts, invent harsh penalties, and torture their innocent bodies. They think and act like demons.

This is an interesting analysis but one wonders if it is just a little simplistic. Surely there are many people who are a combination of some of these traits, and not purely and simply one thing or the other? And with people who are good or evil, is there no grey area in which one might be a mixture of the three? (See Chapter 16: Qitab-i-Aqdas and Chapter 15: Proverbs).

And yet there is another kind of analysis discussed in the Gita: the 'field' and the 'Knower of the field'. It is about the duality of the body and the soul, which is eternal. The field is not just the body but the mind as well. It is the object that the Knower is aware of. The Knower is the Self, and Krishna is the hidden Knower in everyone. Krishna goes into details about the field.

'The field is made up of the following: the five areas of perception, the five elements, the five sense organs and the five organs of action, and the three components of the mind: *manas*[5], *buddhi*[6], and *ahamkara*[7]. In this field arise desire, and aversion, pleasure and pain, the body, intelligence and will' (13:5, page 216).

But the Knower of the field is that eternal element in every creature. It is without a beginning or end. It lives in the body but is not tainted by emotions or actions. Those who recognise this Self have found the way to freedom and to the attainment of the supreme goal. The way to find it is not just one method. One could practise meditation, or go in for Wisdom, while others perform selfless service. Others might find an illuminated teacher. All of these methods would lead to the escape from Karma and union with Brahman. So in one sense, it is the Krishna element in everyone that makes this work; on the other hand, one comes to realise the truth of this self.

The result, if the method is followed carefully, means a certain detachment from the rough and tumble of life.

'Free from selfish attachment, they do not get compulsively entangled even in home and family. They are even-minded through good fortune and bad. Their devotion to me is undivided. Enjoying solitude and not following the crowd, they seek only me. This is true knowledge, to seek the Self as the true end of wisdom always. To seek anything else is ignorance...' 13:9 (page 217).

This self-awareness has many helpful aspects, but one wonders whether too much detachment from real life is likely to cause problems for other people. It is one thing to be 'professional' in the sense of not allowing oneself to become over-emotional about dealing with the realities of life. But turning oneself into a sort of zombie and not registering any emotion is liable to upset people unnecessarily. We can applaud such virtues as being gentle, forgiving, upright, pure, filled with inner strength, and self-control, but spending too much time on meditation may become excessive and counter-productive. Of course, to know oneself and be aware of one's strengths and weaknesses is a valuable thing; but that is perhaps not quite what is being said in the Gita.

Philosophical aspects of the Gita

Much has already been said on this level, since theology and philosophy are closely connected in Hindu thought. Krishna claims to be in possession of the *truth* about life and death, and this is an important basis for any philosophical system.

'Whoever knows me as the Lord of all creation, without birth or beginning, knows the truth and frees himself from all evil' (10:2, page 183).

'O Krishna, I believe that everything you have told me is divine truth' (10:14, page 185).

All the scriptures reviewed in this work make some sort of claim to be the truth, either directly or indirectly. This is why many people are confused about which religion is the right one, where does the truth about life and death really lie? For the Hindus, essentially, this life is an illusion and the reality is the eternal world of Brahman. This general assumption is not regularly stated in the *Gita* but does break the surface in places.

'The impermanent has no reality; reality lies in the eternal' (2:16, page 90).

What it means, by the 'impermanent' is this world. This of course has a strong element of truth for all, regardless of one's religion. The created world must have had a beginning and, by process of logic, must have an end, somewhere. This is augmented by the way that created things change, come and go, die and are born and go round in circles. But to say that this world does not exist; it is just an illusion is not something that everyone can cope with. This strand of thought is a feature of Gnosticism; a philosophical idea that was prevalent in Roman times and still crops up in the modern world (see Chapter 10 with Mary Baker Eddy). It is possible that Hindu influence managed to work its way into the west in Roman times. The difference between the Hindus and the Gnostics appears to be thus: the Gnostics believed that the flesh was beyond redemption, but the Hindus (*Gita*) that there is that element of eternity in every living soul, and it can be realised by working on it. The most successful method involves meditation, which brings a realisation of the Self. We might call that the Ego or possibly the Super-Ego. It is easy to see how Freud could have based his psychological speculations on Hindu philosophy.

'In this world there are two orders of being; the perishable separate creature and the changeless spirit. But beyond these there is another, the supreme Self, the eternal Lord who enters the entire cosmos and supports it from within' (15:16, page 234).

The answer to life is to take wisdom as one's main aim; by this one is lifted away from sin and is purified and attains perfect peace.

'... you could cross beyond all sin by the raft of spiritual wisdom... the fire of knowledge burns to ashes all karma... those who take wisdom as their highest goal, whose faith is deep... attain wisdom quickly and enter into perfect peace...' (4:36-39, page 121).

Understandably, doubt will undo all this; one must put doubts out of one's mind. It is interesting to see what sin consists of. At the start, Arjuna is horrified at the thought of killing his own relatives (1:36) and that will make him a sinner. The family will lose its sense of unity, ancient traditions will be lost and the spiritual foundations of life. Even if they are evil, that would not make it right to kill them. But Krishna keeps on insisting that Arjuna should attack and destroy them. We in the West would agree with Arjuna: even if we are cornered into fighting a war, we still feel bad about killing the enemy. But as far as Krishna is concerned, sin is something else; it is a failure to defeat evil and to indulge in all the destructive aspects of behaviour as listed earlier. If you are rajasic or tamasic then there is the need to become sattvic. There seems to be no notion of sin being disobedience to god; in fact there is no list of moral precepts like the Ten Commandments that would define sin. Sin appears to be something rather superficial and not endemic in human nature. Neither do we see any mention of repentance and everlasting forgiveness.

Mythology

It is rather artificial to make out a separate strand called mythology in the Gita. The whole book is a derivative of mythological assumptions. The battle, which never starts, is never a physical battle; it is a theoretical juxtaposition of the forces of evil and of good. Virtually all the Hindu scriptural material is some form of mythology (see Chapter 22: The Ramayana). There is no actual history in them, which makes them a considerable contrast to the Bible.

However there are a few phrases that make interesting mythological assumptions. In several places it refers to the 'three worlds'.

'I see the three worlds trembling before this vision of your wonderful and terrible form,' 11:220 (page 197).

This would be heaven, earth and hell; the three-tiered system which was the common assumption in the ancient world. Here it is not meant as a command to believe, but as a background assumption.

'There is none equal to you in the three worlds,' 11:43 (page 201).

In other words, Krishna is supreme in all three layers of the universe. Also, there is a connection between the three levels, which is called the ashvattha tree[8]. This is a common notion in world mythology, which describes a connecting chord between all three worlds. The only difference here is that this tree has its roots up in the air and its branches somehow under the soil.

'Sages speak of the immutable ashvattha tree, with its taproot above and its branches below. On this tree grow the scriptures; seeing their source one knows their essence,' 15:1 (page 2320.

An inverted tree may seem an absurd idea. Even so, such a strange thing has been found off the Norfolk coast, the branches stuck in the seabed and the roots sticking up. How it was done is a puzzle, but it must have been achieved a long time ago, presumably by Celtic peoples in the Stone Age. One wonders what the symbolism is in it.

Krishna tells us that there are seven great sages and four ancient ancestors (10:6, page 184) but he does not go into details and tell us the names of these people, which would have been interesting; however, he does let drop that all the creatures of the earth were created through them. Instead he reels off a collection of mythological people and creatures, claiming to be each of them himself. It all begins to sound like a version of Pantheism: everything seems to equal everything else. Arjuna lets drop a few names: Narada[9], Asita[10], Devala[11], and Vyasa[12] are mentioned but no description of their work is offered. With mythical animals more detail is given.

There is Kamadhuk, the cow that fulfils all desires. This is the rationale behind the Hindu myths and the 'sacred cow' mentality. Also there is Ananta, the cosmic serpent; also Yama the god of the dead, who presides over the Buddhist Wheel of Becoming; Vasuki, the king of snakes (snakes are a regular feature of mythology the world over); and Garuda, the eagle.

'I am born from the nectar of immortality as the primordial horse and as Indra's noble elephant' (10:27, page 187).

On a different level, is the concept of the Day and Night of Brahman. The Day of Brahman ends after 100 yugas (4,320 million years) and the Night of Brahman does the same. Every time this happens, multitudes of beings are created and destroyed repetitiously. But above that is a formless state that is eternal.

Although interesting, these mythological references are not of the first relevance to the main theme of the book. It assumes that we know what these people or animals are and their significance. It all adds to the poetry and the mystery of the book.

As literary work of the first order

There is no denying that *the Bhagavad Gita* is one of the world's great classics of literature; this may be said regardless of whether one accepts its teachings or not. Obviously there is a lot here to consider and evaluate, but the standard of expression is superb. The whole tone is one of sympathy and sensitivity for the seeker after the truth. There is the Gayatri metre as in the Vedas, and the language is Sanskrit. The whole work is poetic. This could alert one to the possibility that the material need not be taken completely literally or at face value. That would certainly be true of the 'battle' at the beginning.

The use of figurative language is quite widespread. We have some lovely similes.

'As the heat of a fire reduces wood to ashes, the fire of knowledge burns to ashes all Karma' (4:37, page 121).

'Even as a tortoise draws in its limbs, the wise can draw in their senses at will' (2:58, page 96).

'As the rivers flow into the ocean but cannot make the vast ocean overflow, so flow the streams of the sense world into the sea of peace that is the sage' (2:70, page 97).

'As one abandons worn out clothes and acquires new ones, so when the body is worn out a new one is acquired by the Self, who lives within' (2:22, page 91).

'As the sun lights up the world, the Self dwelling in the field is the source of all light in the field' (13:33, page 220).

There are also some very apt metaphors.

'You could cross beyond all sin by the raft of spiritual wisdom' (4:36, page 121).

'Cut through this doubt in your own heart with the sword of spiritual wisdom' (4:41, page 121).

A sustained metaphor occurs in Chapter 13, where the Field and its Knower is explained in detail. This motif has been discussed above, but a helpful anecdote from Hindu tradition may help to summarise it.

'A wandering holy man is asked what his work in life is. He replies: "I'm a farmer." This seemed somewhat of a surprise, but then he added, "This body of mine is the field. I sow good thoughts and actions, and in my body I reap the results."'

There is a lot of truth in this, though it may not be the entire truth. What we are is what we think; our basic assumptions condition our actions and attitudes.

More important and essential to the thinking in the Gita is the use of paradox in many different ways, but principally in talking about Brahman.

'It is both near and far, both within and without every creature; it moves and is unmoving. In its subtlety it is beyond comprehension. It is indivisible yet appears divided in separate creatures. Know it to be the creator, the preserver, and the destroyer' (13:15, page 218).

A whole string of paradoxes comes in 9:16-17 (page 175).

'I am the ritual and the sacrifice; I am the true medicine and the mantrum. I am the offering and the fire that consumes it, and the one to whom it is offered. I am the father and mother of this universe, and its grandfather too... I am the womb and the eternal seed' (9:17-18, page 175).

Paradox is also used to describe the one whose meditation has lifted him above all earthly entanglements.

'Established within themselves, they are equal in pleasure and pain, praise and blame, kindness and unkindness. Clay, a rock and gold are all the same to them. Alike in honour and dishonour, alike to friend and foe, they have given up every selfish pursuit' (14:24, page 227).

Concluding remarks on the Bhagavad Gita

There are many aspects that are appealing in this work not least the atmosphere of a caring god, Krishna. Consider the atmosphere in this quotation.

'"Do not be troubled; do not fear my terrible form. Let your heart be satisfied and your fears dispelled in looking at me as I was before"... having spoken these words, the Lord (Krishna) once again assumed the gentle form of Krishna and consoled his devotee, who had been afraid.'

There is tenderness, empathy and peace of mind in this; all the essentials that a religion can truly offer. The book is characterised by the love of the god for his believer and the believer's love for his god. There is so much in this that reminds us of Jesus in the New Testament. It is not just the moral or ethical aspects of it, but the closeness and trust. The Bible uses the metaphor of covenant; there is no mention of this concept in the Gita, not even a synonym for covenant, and yet the basics of it are there.

But there are important differences from the Bible. The Judaeo-Christian tradition is insistent that there is only one God. This would be the equivalent of Brahman, except that Brahman is distant and not involved in world affairs. The God of Abraham is imminent and closely involved in the action of history and people. For the Hindus, it is Krishna, or possibly another avatar such as Vishnu who is engaging with people from day to day. It has been claimed that Hinduism is another form of monotheism, in spite of the thousands of gods in their tradition. This claim to monotheism would hold water if the *Bhagavad Gita* were taken at face value; in that Krishna is intertwined and co-terminous with Brahman, in the same way that Jesus is with the Eternal Father. This would involve relegating all the other 'gods' to the level of angels, devils and lesser spirits. This is something that Zoroaster did (Chapter 5) but the main traditions of Hinduism have not.

More importantly, there is a fundamental difference at work here. With Hinduism, history is of no account. A symptom of this is the difficulty in determining the dating and sequence of written material in Hinduism. Life on this earth is not real. The true reality is in the world of eternity, which although it is found in each and every person, does not make this life real. This life is some sort of illusion, a phantom, or even a cinematic projection on a screen. We see this in the *Gita*, where Arjuna is told to do battle and kill all the other army. This will not be counted as murder, since Krishna has already killed them, which means that the battle will simply be an illusion. This kind of thinking is very much to the contrary with the Judaeo-Christian approach. For them, life is real, not just in heaven but on earth too. Obviously there is a massive paradox in this, in that the world of the spirit produces a material world of reality. The Hindus, in saying that this world is an illusion, have rendered the paradox almost to the level of non-paradox, which is rather strange. So many of their attempts at describing Brahman involve some very appropriate usages of paradox, which come near to Lao Tzu's productions (see Chapter 11). This is something that Western religion could learn from without diminishing the value of their theology. The Jews and the Christians see history as real and as a progression from start to finish. God is active and guiding in all of it, whether it be his own people or other peoples yet to be included, or even those who try to deny it. The crux of it comes with the life and ministry of Jesus. The Christians have always maintained that he was a solid, real human being who really died. His life and death was an atonement for the sins of the world, and brought in a new relationship of trust and love between God and mankind. The concept of a god being sacrificed is certainly there in the Gita, but it is Perusha, who is claimed to be another manifestation of Krishna. But crucially, Perusha was never a real historical figure; he is some sort of principle or imaginary god who is sacrificed, and the purpose of it is not entirely clear. It is not clearly claimed that this is the atonement for the sins of the world.

The way that Krishna describes himself as in and through everything and every person sounds very much like Pantheism. This may be somewhat anachronistic, and may not have been meant in quite that way. But the impression given is that the god is in everything, and actually is everything. This is different from the monotheism of the west, for there, God is admittedly involved in everything that goes on in the world, and yet he is totally other. This is the importance of calling him holy. The Hebrew word *qadhosh*, usually rendered as 'holy', essentially means, 'separated, distinct from'. God stands in contradistinction to the world and he judges the world, sifting the good from the bad. This is not at all clear in the Gita.

Notes for Chapter 8: The Bhagavad Gita

1. Maya, the creative power of God (see page 28 in Easwaran's book).
2. Spinoza; the seventeenth century proponent of Pantheism. This philosophy, which equates God with the Creation, can be traced back to the ancient Greek philosophers, such as Plato, but Spinoza is the first modern philosopher to develop the idea. Mainstream Christianity has always maintained that God is other than the Creation.
3. Dharma: here it means 'law, or duty'.
4. The prayer of St Richard.
5. Manas: the mind, or memory (see page 28 in Easwaran's book).
6. Buddhi: understanding, correct view, idea, and purpose.
7. Ahamkara: self-will, separateness.
8. Ashvattha tree: the pipal tree, a kind of fig, often planted in Temple precincts.
9. Narada: a sage and also a divine musician.
10. Asita: a SAGE
11. Devala: a SAGE
12. Vyasa: a sage, an author, the one credited with this work, the Gita.

9

Science and Health – Mary Baker Eddy

Mary Baker Eddy, in the 1870s, made an interesting discovery in the world of philosophy combined with theology and health. She produced a book, *Science and Health,* which among other writings sets forth her convictions. This was the inspiration behind the Church of Christian Science. This all took place at Lynn, Massachusetts. At first, this new movement made a considerable impression and spread to many countries. Nowadays it still persists but in nowhere near the popularity that she had expected. It has always been controversial, and has run up against objections not just from the medical profession but also the mainstream churches. There was probably no faulting her sincerity in wishing to help those with health problems. She herself claims to be a spiritual healer with much success. But most rational people will find her theorisings as cranky, dated, and at variance with science and religion. The book, of about 700 pages, is not particularly well organised. It is rambling, repetitive and crassly dogmatic, and these are features which it has in common with *Mein Kampf*; the difference is that, while Hitler's gospel was one of hate and violence, Eddy's gospel is of love, good health and acceptance of all mankind. As with all these bright ideas, there is always just that little element of truth included somewhere; the mistake comes in fastening on to one idea and placing far too much emphasis on it. Mary would definitely claim to be parading the *truth*; it appears on almost every page. This is particularly emphasised on page 457, where she claims that her book is 'the voice of Truth to this age and contains the full statement of Christian Science, or the Science of healing through the mind'. But since so many other 'scriptural' productions claim to have the truth, one wonders what to make of it. The reader will doubtless form his own opinions as this discussion proceeds.

Theological material

The whole of her thinking revolves around God. He is the Ultimate Principle, the Supreme Ruler, Mind and Spirit. She is a rampant Monotheist and has no time for Pantheism or Polytheism. There is no power apart from God (page 228); he is the one primal cause (page 207); he is the infinite that never began nor will it ever end (page 245); he is the Spirit that is the only intelligence and substance (page 204). But when we come to such phrases as the Ego, does this remind us of the Freudian analysis of human nature? When we have such expressions as 'the All' and 'the All-in-all', this reminds us of certain Eastern religions such as Hinduism and Buddhism and also the Gnostics of the first century AD. There may be some influence here; Eddy does not embark on an explanation of such phrases. A good summary of her theology of God can be quoted thus:

> 'Spirit, bearing testimony, saith: "I am Spirit. Man, whose senses are spiritual, is my likeness. He reflects the infinite understanding, for I am Infinity. The beauty of holiness, the perfection of being, imperishable glory... all are Mine, for I am God. I give immortality to man, for I am Truth. I include and impart all bliss, for I am Love. I give life, without beginning and without end, for I am life. I am supreme and give all, for I am Mind. I am the substance of all, because I AM THAT I AM."' (page 253).

Thus far, most believing people would not find much wrong with this. A few unfamiliar elements now creep in. 'Mind is perpetual motion. Its symbol is the sphere. The rotations and revolutions of the universe of Mind go on eternally,' (page 240). Here we see a slight admixture of possibly Mithraic thinking and also of modern astrophysics. It also reminds us of Taoist philosophy in which the *Tao* is never static but always moving (Chapter 11). Whether she meant this literally is hard to say, but it also suggests a certain Gnostic influence, specifically from the *Corpus Hermeticum*. Another issue raised is that in referring to the Genesis Creation account, she says that, 'His work was *finished*, nothing is new to God, and that it was *good*,' (page 206). But according to Hebrews, on the one hand, God has his Sabbath rest, but, paradoxically, God never rests[1]. In other words, the work of creation goes on perpetually, and new things do appear. Another issue raised is that if there is nothing new to God, what about the New Testament? This is a phrase rarely if ever seen in Eddy's book, and in fact one wonders if she has any idea of its meaning. For one who claims to be so orientated on the Bible, the basic concept of covenant, whether old or new, never seems to receive a mention. The significance of this may be seen later.

In general terms, Eddy has a concept of a God which accords well with philosophical principles and is distant. A possible exception to this could be her statement that there never are any accidents, everything is caused by God:

'Under divine Providence, there can be no accidents, since there is no room for imperfection in perfection' (page 424).

This raises the age-old dilemma of predestination versus free will. Eddy never actually discusses this issue, but the impression given would be that she accepts predestination. If this is so, this makes nonsense of the idea of making a decision to be a Christian Scientist, which for her is so very important.

There is very little to suggest a God who is active and intervening in day-to-day life. This is the Judaeo-Christian understanding of God, as imminent and personal. It would be fair to say that Jesus Christ figures large in her thinking, but there is no attempt at discussing the Incarnation, or how Jesus relates to God. Not that this issue is within the scope of human theorisation, but there is no mention of it.

'Jesus elaborated the fact that the healing effect followed the understanding of the Divine Principle and of the Christ-spirit which governed the corporeal Jesus' (page 141).

What does this mean? Is she talking about the Incarnation? If we look at page 332, we find that there is some kind of dichotomy between Jesus and Christ. Messiah is the true idea, voicing good; he was incorporeal, spiritual, the divine image and likeness. However, the man Jesus was human, corporeal. It sounds very much as if she is saying that there are two persons in the one Jesus Christ. This sounds like one of the early heresies in the early church, which was condemned at the Council of Nicaea[2]. The orthodox party emphasised that Jesus Christ was one person divine and human without any separation, dichotomy or clash. He was genuinely human and divine at the same time. We can see where her idea is leading: if the man Jesus was just human, then he would be just as non-existent as everyone else in creation. She does not appear to go as far as to say that, but that is where the logic of her system would lead. Talking about the Incarnation clearly raises the issue of the Trinity. On the face of it, she appears to agree with it and states it thus:

'Life, Truth and Love constitute the triune Person called God. They represent a trinity in unity, three in one... the same in essence, though multi-form in office: God the Father-Mother; Christ the spiritual idea of sonship; Divine Science or the Holy Comforter' (page 331).

148

So far not too bad, except that the Holy Spirit has been enlisted to encapsulate Christian Science! But it is not as simple as that, since Eddy thinks that the trinity infringes monotheism:

'The theory of three Persons in one God (that is, a personal Trinity or Tri-unity) suggests polytheism, rather than the one ever-present I AM... (God) cannot be understood aright through mortal concepts. The precise form of God must be of small importance in comparison with the ultimate question, What is infinite Mind or divine Love?' (page 256).

If Eddy had taken the trouble to study the early church fathers, she would have been aware that the issue of polytheism did arise and was ably answered by such theologians as Origen and Tertullian. The Trinity only suggests polytheism to those who wish to find fault with it. Saying that God is One, is fine as Monotheism, but he is not monochrome. He acts in different ways. But one way in which he does not act is to regard the created world as non-existent; if he did, why did Jesus Christ come into the world to redeem it? Otherwise, it is a fair question to ask, 'What is infinite Mind or divine Love?' Everyone could honestly ask themselves this question; none of us can really understand or analyse the mind of God. It was Jesus who showed us as much as we can cope with, of the nature of God. That message was one of humility and acceptance of suffering. That rules out pretending that pain does not exist and is only a wrong idea in people's minds.

Here she is talking about ecclesiastical hierarchy and the mention of Jesus is purely coincidental and not some sort of theory. We are left wondering how Jesus relates to God. There is seldom any mention of the Holy Spirit in her book, and hardly any impression of the Spirit as active and influential in the life of the believer. God as mercifully intervening in one's life is played down. The opposite is supposed to happen: one is meant to re-arrange one's thinking so that one can be acceptable for the Divine Science.

'Thought passes from God to man, but neither sensation nor report goes from material body to Mind. The intercommunication is always from God to his idea, man.'

This raises the issue of the validity of prayer. Is it true that man cannot communicate with God; is prayer another bit of self-deception? But if we look at the life of Jesus, we see him, whether as Christ or Jesus, praying to the Father, and advising his followers to do the same. He gave them the Lord's Prayer; was that another bit of illusion? There seems to be some sort of confusion as well as delusion in Eddy's mind.

She has the idea that to gain salvation it is no good seeking pardon; one should reform one's ideas, ignore matter and resort to the spirit (page 285). This makes nonsense of a phrase such as 'forgive us our trespasses' in the Lord's Prayer. To skirt this issue, Eddy renders it as 'forgive us our debts' and the paraphrase goes like this, 'Love is reflected in love' (page 17). This neatly avoids the issue of repentance and forgiveness; this element is a crucial strand in orthodox Christian procedure, but she slides out of it. After all, sin is an illusion, so we do not need to apologise for it!

We now turn to the issue of theodicy, for if God is the only source of power, how are we to understand evil? Does this mean that God causes evil? Eddy's answer is quite ingenious; there is no power or reality in evil! A useful quotation comes from page 186:

'Evil is a negation, because it is the absence of truth. It is nothing, because it is the absence of something. It is unreal, because it presupposes the absence of God, the omnipotent and omnipresent. Every mortal must learn that there is neither power nor reality in evil.'

How very convenient it is to say that evil is non-existent, or some sort of illusion! Satan, it would seem, is an illusive personification (page 187). There is no wickedness or sin, nor disease. All we have to do is focus on God, and all the bad things will melt away. Even so, Eddy can see the dilemma; is it God who causes evil to occur? Consider this quotation:

'... if sin and suffering are realities of being, whence did they emanate? God made all that was made and Mind signifies God... infinity not finity. Not far from infidelity is the belief which unites such opposites as sickness and health, holiness and unholiness, calls both the offspring of the spirit, and at the same time admits that Spirit is God... virtually declaring Him good in one instance and evil in another' (page 229).

'If God causes man to be sick, sickness must be good, and its opposite health, must be evil for all that He makes is good and will stand for ever' (page 229).

'If God makes sin, if good produces evil, if truth results in error, then Science and Christianity are helpless' (page 231).

Here we see the age-old dilemma in the human heart: why is there any evil in the world? It is no use trying to pretend that there is no evil, or that there are no evil spirits. What about Jesus in St Mark casting out devils? Was Jesus working under some sort of delusion? Even if one cannot cope with evil spirits, then what about evil humans such as Hitler and Nazism? Are they also some sort of illusion? One could advise Eddy to read the first chapter of Job, where it clearly depicts God in conversation with Satan about the fate of Job, a righteous man. Eddy would probably find Job chapter one as a problem, for she denies that there is any collusion between God and Satan.

'The ancient error that there is fraternity between pain and pleasure, good and evil, God and Satan' (page 389).

As the book of Job unfolds, it seems that there is a positive side to suffering and evil; that God does it for love and the long-term benefit of the human soul. To say that it is all an illusion caused by error of thinking, is just to duck the issue.

This brings us to the core of Christian Science, that of sickness, sin and death and what it consists of. This is expounded largely in Chapter 7 of *Science and Health* but reappears in many other parts of the book. Essentially it is thus:

"… Suffering and disease are the self-imposed beliefs of mortals, and not the facts of being; that God never decreed disease…" (page 221).

The cause of all disease is false belief: disease is unreal, the soil of disease is the mental mind (page 188). Sickness is a growth of error springing from mortal ignorance or fear. Error rehearses error. This means that the pain you have is not real, it is a product of your own false ideas. One might say that a broken leg is real enough; hardly a figment of one's own imagination. But Eddy says:

'Bones have only the substance of thought which forms them. They are only phenomena of the mind. The so-called substance of bone is formed first by the parent's mind, through self-division…' (page 423-4).

She is actually talking about how a child gains ideas from its parents, but the notion is the same; that bones are not actually real, therefore a broken limb is only a figment of one's imagination. With regard to hereditary diseases, Eddy goes on to tell us:

'The Scientist knows that there can be no hereditary disease, since matter is not intelligent and cannot transmit good or evil intelligence to man,' (page 412).

This means that conditions such as scrofula and tuberculosis (page 424 and 426) can be dispatched by the right sort of mental approach.

'To prevent or to cure scrofula and other so-called hereditary diseases, you must destroy the belief in these ills and the faith in the possibility of their transmission,' (page 424).

It goes further than this and claims that all the physical world is also a illusion. It is not real. The only reality is God. The only way to defeat pain and disease is to allow Mind, God, to take over and effect a cure. Eddy believes that 'matter', by which we assume all created things, has no sensation or power of its own. The only real power is God; everything else is self-delusion.

This is a most bold claim and how it can be maintained in the face of medical facts is a good question. In the 1870s everyone knew about the work of Pasteur, about germs, bacteria and viruses. And yet Eddy can maintain that:

'We weep because others weep, we yawn because they yawn, and we have smallpox because others have it; but mortal mind, not matter, contains and carries the infection' (page 153).

Now that we have managed to control smallpox and encapsulate it in a test-tube in a laboratory, surely this is proof that many diseases are not just a figment of one's imagination, but are caused by tiny organisms that invade the body. Even so, there is that element of truth in what she says, that one can think oneself into an illness just by fear and possibly fashion. Also if one reads a medical journal, it is all too easy to imagine one has caught a disease described; there is this element of fear and fascination. But to say that the whole thing is an illusion, staggers belief. She even goes further to say that old age is an illusion (page 245). Eddy cites the case of a woman who was disappointed in love, became fixated about her boyfriend, and in this mental state remained young, taking no account of the passing years. The end of this story is not related – how she eventually came to die!

It is also fair to say that many conditions are the result of fatigue, stress, guilt, fear, accident and faulty lifestyle. Even Eddy would not deny this, except to say that the whole thing is illusory. To take fatigue: it is not the body that is tired, it is one's own mind, in error, thinking that one is tired.

To say that matter has no power or spirit of its own is also contentious. We can understand her aversion to Pantheism. However, those of a different theological stance will maintain that all physical things have some sort of spiritual element. The shaman understands that everything has a spirit living in it; the Japanese Shintoist might well claim that all things have some sort of *kami* in them. This is a matter of dispute, but many believe that the created universe has some sort of spiritual backing or invisible soul.

These things are difficult to quantify, but it is no use attempting to be too dogmatic about it. Eddy is quite dogmatic.

As far as she is concerned, there are two elements in the equation:

'There are two separate, antagonistic entities and beings, two powers; namely, Spirit and matter... resulting in a third person (mortal man) who carries out the delusions of sin, sickness, and death. The first power is admitted to be good, an intelligence or Mind called God. The so-called second power, evil, is the unlikeness of good. It cannot therefore be called mind, though so called. The third power, mortal man, is a supposed mixture of the first and second antagonistic powers, intelligence and non-intelligence, of Spirit and matter,' (page 204).

This is an interesting version of Dualism, which is relevant to theodicy, and yet even so, to deny that evil has any spiritual force flies in the face of evidence.

The way out of disease, pain and death is Eddy's great discovery. One must accept science, namely Christian Science (page 249). One should change course and do right.

'If you believe yourself diseased, you can alter this wrong belief and action without hindrance from the body' (page 253).

Here is an extreme case of 'mind over matter'. One wonders how one would think oneself out of something like the Black Death or cholera. Both of these are caused by bacteria and, unless the medical skills are available, there is little that can be done to cure them. It is true that people do survive such extreme infections, but that is because we now know that some people have an immunity, which, although they become ill, prevents the disease from becoming fatal. An example of this would be cowpox in relation to smallpox; it was realised that the milk-maids never seemed to contract smallpox. One wonders what Eddy would say in the case of a pandemic; would she ignore instructions from the authorities and pretend there was no infection? In the case of the outbreak of Ebola, would she ignore all the restrictions on travel and allow the infection to spread all over the world? This might lead to such a person being prosecuted for criminal spreading of infection.

With regard to such things as Cancer, we have no comment from Eddy. Cancer has come to the fore only recently, although it has been with us for a long time. Apart from some indication that lifestyle has something to do with it, i.e. smoking in relation to lung cancer, no one really knows the basic cause of it. Why do some people contract it but others not? Is it to do with guilt, or fear or what? One could almost call it a pandemic except that it is not an infection or contagion.

It would be a wonderful thought if we could all think ourselves out of disease but this is not realistic. Infection is a reality, even if the whole of life is an illusion. Going further, the idea that one can lift oneself out of disease just by one's mental attitude is clearly some sort of 'works-righteousness'. It is not a grace. The Christian stance, as outlined by St Paul, is that we are saved by the loving intervention of God, not by some sort of clever philosophy that relies on human ingenuity. But that is what Eddy is in effect saying; that we are saved by our own devices rather than God's love. Not all of us are clever enough or have enough willpower to clear ourselves of disease. Even so, there is an element of truth in what she is saying. If you can think yourself into an illness, you can also think yourself out of it. If one thinks positive about life, and has no time to spare for minor complaints, one can live a healthy active life and never think about being ill. If one goes through life cringing and terrified of what might go wrong, one is likely to fall ill. It is all a matter of morale. It is like soldiers going into battle; if they think they are going to win, there is a much better chance of success than if they think they are going to be beaten. On this level, there is this element of truth in what Eddy is saying. But to blow it up to include every disease regardless of its severity or cause, is sheer folly.

The result, of course, in practical terms, is that Eddy says we should not bother to consult the doctor or the chemist for any sort of drug or medicine.

'The popular doctor believes in his prescription and the pharmacist believes in the power of his drugs to save a man's life... the doctor's and the pharmacist's is a medical mistake' (page 166).

This is where most people will part company with Eddy, if they have not done so already. She believes that it is all a delusion and drugs are of no avail, in fact, counterproductive. Again, there is that tiny element of truth in this assertion. It is so easy to become reliant on drugs, some of which are actually poisons. But in the hands of a responsible medically-trained person, they can solve many problems. Eddy could well do to remember that when God made all things good, that would include the opium poppy and the coca plant. Of course it is so easy to misuse such substances, but they are all there for a purpose. Medical science is still exploring the correct usage of such material which can be of benefit to mankind without ruining people's health. But to say that all drugs and medicines are a mistake is a gross overstatement. And to persuade people to avoid going to the surgery is another mistake, for the local GP is the first safeguard against contracting anything serious. If a complaint is caught in its early stages, almost always something can be done to correct it. This applies to many conditions, since they begin with minor symptoms and then progress. The doctor will be able to recognise the early symptoms and take action. Just pretending that pain does not exist is a gross piece of self-delusion.

In fairness we must say that such things as broken bones should be left to the surgeon:

'It is better for Christian Scientists to leave surgery and the adjustment of broken bones and dislocations to the fingers of a surgeon, while the mental healer confines himself chiefly to mental reconstruction and to the prevention of inflammation' (page 401).

Common sense prevailing, but only just a little. She goes on:

'Christian Science is always the most skilful surgeon but surgery is the branch of its healing which will be last acknowledged. However it is but just to say that the author has already in her possession well-authenticated records of the cure, by herself and her students through mental surgery alone, of broken bones, dislocated joints and spinal vertebrae' (page 402).

Some claim! But as we have seen, bones do not really exist anyway!

But Eddy is particularly sarcastic about medical research.

'Treatises on anatomy, physiology and health, sustained by what is termed material law, are the promoters of sickness and disease... so long as you read medical works, you will be sick' (page 179).

She is actually saying that doctors promote disease as opposed to defeating it. She claims that in the past, before the modern medical mania took hold, they were all a lot healthier because they had no knowledge of what they could contract.

'They were as innocent as Adam, before he ate the fruit of false knowledge, of the existence of tubercles and troches[3], lungs and lozenges' (page 175).

Again there is just that small element of truth in this. Ignorance is bliss. If you don't know what illness to contract, you are quite likely never to contract it. There is a sense in which people talk themselves into illness, largely because they have nothing better to do with their time. But that is not the whole truth.

Eddy is sure that there was a Golden Age in the past, an idea which is often seen in many mythologies around the world. When we come to know the truth, 'man will re-open with the key of Divine Science the gates of

Paradise which human beliefs have closed and will find himself unfallen, upright, pure, and free...' (page 171).

What a lovely thought, all done by reorientating one's mind to Divine Science!

As to the truth of this, one may well have doubts. A study of the Royal Tombs in Egypt, going back 3,000 years, reveals that the population may not have been as healthy as one might have hoped or speculated. It may be that now, in the twenty-first century, humanity has reached a point of good health never seen before, in spite of the disease problems which we are coping with at the moment.

But Eddy is particularly sarcastic about alternative medical approaches, what we might call 'quack' methods. 'Mental medicine' and 'mind-cure' using the earth's magnetic currents, hypnotism, the 'Graham system', mesmerism, fasting, hygiene, and yes, even fresh air are all bogus. She seems to have some time for homeopathy, having used it herself to some good effect, but basically, it is Christian Science that is the answer. Some of these ideas have indeed died the death. Her mention of 'electricity' is interesting. At her time, this was a very new discovery and its potential was only just being explored. We have seen in our own times the electric shock treatment used on mental patients, and this is now going out of favour (thankfully!). She is, however, in favour of the good old placebo! She never stops to consider that her bright idea might be yet another quack method!

On the subject of healing, it would seem that Eddy herself was some sort of spiritual healer. She recounts various cases where she cured people who were considered terminal cases by the doctors. An interesting example is found on page 192, where a Mr Clark of Lynn had been confined to bed for six months with a hip-disease. He was dying. Mary went in to him and in a few moments his face changed, and after a sleep of about ten minutes, he said, 'I feel like a new man; my suffering is all gone.' Soon after he was up and having supper. Shortly afterwards he was back to work. If this is the truth, then so be it. There are such people who can heal by faith; their ability is beyond medical explanation, but it is a reality nevertheless. In her chapter called Fruitage, Eddy cites numerous examples of healing under Christian Science method; if these are the truth, then so be it. And yet one would like to have some sort of verification of these claims. It is to be noted that in the case of Linda Martel, the little child who lived in Guernsey in the late 1960s, that Charles Graves went to some lengths to research and verify the claims made about this little healer[4]. There are tapes, photographs, records of interviews and all manner of information, making it difficult to pour cold water on the claims made for Linda. Obviously in Eddy's day research and recording was not as thorough as it is now. There have been many such people, healing by spiritual means and Jesus is the best-known example; he is very well recorded and verified by the four Gospel writers. Just enrolling oneself as a Christian Scientist does not have to mean that one automatically becomes a faith healer; nor does it mean that all faith healers are Christian Scientists. But Eddy would probably say that any convert could potentially become a healer. The method is a matter of cleansing oneself spiritually, or otherwise it will not work.

'In order to cure his patient, the metaphysician must first cast moral evils out of himself and thus attain the spiritual freedom which will enable him to cast physical evils out of his patient; but heal he cannot while his own spiritual barrenness debars him from giving drink to the thirsty and hinders him from reaching his patient's thought... yea, while mental penury chills his faith and understanding' (page 366).

This would be quite a tall order for any human soul, to make oneself perfect! Yet on page 428, we are told that we are perfect and immortal; the suggestion being that it is not just the Christian Science healer, but everyone:

'The great spiritual fact must be brought out that man IS, not SHALL BE, perfect and immortal.'

Eddy is thinking of the Sermon on the Mount where Jesus tells us to be perfect as our Heavenly Father is perfect. This a case of taking Jesus far too literally; it is hardly possible for any human being to be perfect, as we all have our failings. She is clearly going against the basics of Judaeo-Christian theology, which states that is not possible for one to cleanse oneself, it is the gracious work of God, either through fire or water, that cleanses the human soul. In general about spiritual healing, it is a gift from God not often seen. But to make an entire metaphysical theory of it, which involves boycotting one's local doctor and chemist, is over the top.

Just as Eddy is sarcastic about alternative methods of medicine, she is also damning about other religious groups. Roman Catholic is associated with Satan (whose existence is somewhat dubious anyway); dead faith and ceremonies are wrong. Sectarianism is wrong as worshipping through the medium of matter is paganism. We should worship spiritually, and that means to cease worshipping materially. Baptism and the Eucharist are not to be done literally but spiritually. 'Our Eucharist is spiritual communion with the one God. Our bread "which cometh down from heaven" is Truth. Our cup is the cross. Our wine the inspiration of Love... ' (page 35) 'Our baptism is a purification from all error.' This means in effect, one has to accept Eddy's theories about the illusion of the physical world and the reality of the divine. On this basis, the worship at the Christian Science Church must be very tedious and banal. No colour, no action, no symbolism, no drama, and probably no music. How boring! What she fails to see is that the rituals and symbolisms of the mainstream churches are there for a purpose. They appeal to the basics in human instinct and the five senses. Those senses, by the way, are all wrong, but even so, we have to live with them in this world, and they speak to the soul in ways that mere words and philosophical theories do not.

Eddy is all in favour of the Lord's Prayer; however, it has to have its own special interpretation to suit her theories. The full text can be read up on page 17.

'Our Father which art in heaven' becomes 'our Father-Mother god, all-harmonious.'

'But deliver us from evil,' becomes, 'deliver us from sin, disease and death.'

She cannot bring herself to understand Jesus as wrestling with the powers of evil. Satan has to be demythologised. The Devil is an illusion, what if Jesus was an illusion; what if God himself should be a delusion? If we follow the logic of it through, then everything could be a bit of self-delusion, which means that we are back where we started, with life being a tough show and heaven being a promise.

Eddy is quite well accomplished at reinterpreting the Bible to suit her own theory. Much of her book is taken up with a treatment of the Genesis creation account, juxtaposed with the Book of Revelation. This in itself is an interesting way of seeing the scriptures as a whole, with the Creation and the Apocalypse framing the whole of the history of salvation. Issues raised in Genesis find an answer in Revelation.

The first two chapters of Genesis are reinterpreted in spiritual terms, i.e. scientific in the thought-pattern of Christian Science. It would be fair to say that she could be termed a Bible fundamentalist, but even so she can see that a literal approach to Genesis lands one in various complications. But her version of a figurative interpretation is simply a restatement of her theory. There is no need to cite every detail of her exegesis, for a few examples will be enough; one can read the rest up for oneself in her book.

Genesis 1:1: 'In the beginning God created the heaven and the earth... ' is taken to mean: 'The infinite has no beginning. This word *beginning* is employed to signify *the only*... that is the eternal verity and unity of God and man, including the universe' (page 502).

Genesis 1:2: 'And the earth was without form, and void and darkness was upon the face of the deep. And the spirit of God moved upon the face of the waters... ' This means that the Divine Principle and idea constitute spiritual harmony, heaven and eternity. In the universe

158

of truth matter is unknown. God is All-in-all... hence is the eternal wonder... that infinite space is peopled with God's ideas, reflecting him in countless spiritual forms' (page 503).

This reminds us of various aspects of Gnosticism, and the mention of 'harmony' would also elicit approval from the Taoists.

Genesis 1:16: 'God made two great lights (the sun and the moon)...' Eddy takes the sun as a metaphorical representation of soul outside the body, giving existence and intelligence to the universe. It is to her credit that there is no geological explanation for the Sun. This is still true to this day, for although we can analysis it in terms of hydrogen and helium, there is still no cogent explanation for the Sun either in terms of physics or of theology, and perhaps there never will be. Sadly, the Moon fails to receive a metaphorical interpretation, which is slightly strange. Many people have understood the Moon to be something sinister, but then, Eddy does not believe there is any evil (page 510).

Genesis 1:29: 'And God said, "Behold I have given you every herb bearing seed... and every tree... for meat..."' Eddy does not admit that some of God's provisions include such things as the opium poppy and the cannabis plant. A fair inference from Genesis is that all these created things have some part to play in the general picture and in human needs. Obviously, drugs can be used or misused, and the skill of the medical scientist is an important issue. But Eddy would have trouble bringing herself to admit to such matters, which explains why she makes no comment on it in her book (page 518).

To her credit, Eddy is aware of the second chapter in Genesis being from another source and another author; thus far she takes account of modern scholarship. However, since Chapter One is spiritual and therefore correct, Chapter Two is unspiritual and anthropomorphic, which means that this is where error slides into the picture:

'Genesis 2 contains a statement of this material view of God and the universe, a statement which is the exact opposite of scientific truth as before recorded... the science of the first record proves the falsity of the second. If one is true, then the other is false, for they are antagonistic' (page 522)[5].

So some of the Bible is right and some of it is wrong! How clever to be able to tell the difference! Unfortunately for Eddy, we now see that she has no idea of the issue of paradox. Paradox means that two opposing statements or ideas do not have to be a matter of right and wrong. Both may be true in their own way: paradoxes occur in all areas of life, not least in theology. The major and original paradox is that God who is eternal spirit can produce and influence created matter, the physical world. That is the root problem with Christian Science, there is no concept of the paradox between spirit and created matter, which when the logic of it is followed through, means that the physical world is just an illusion and, going further, evil is non-existent. This comes out in her treatment of the Fall. Also, the belief that God made everything *good* has to mean that anything bad cannot exist. This is another paradox at the heart of the question of theodicy, but since she cannot cope with the concept of paradox, that means that evil is also an illusion.

> 'In the gospel of John... all things were made through the Word of God, and without him was not anything made that was made. Everything good or worthy, God made. Whatever is valueless or baneful, he did not make... hence its unreality' (page 525).

When it comes to the serpent in the Garden of Eden, Eddy manages to make him 'mythical'. Adam is a synonym for error, and represents a belief of material mind. Sadly we do not seem to have an allegorisation for Eve, which might have been quite interesting. The tree of life stands for the idea of Truth, and the sword which guards it is the 'type'[6] of Divine Science. The tree of knowledge stands for the erroneous doctrine that the knowledge of evil is as real... as the knowledge of good (page 526).

One page 528, we have an intriguing case of 'mental midwifery'. As Eve is taken from Adam, one of his ribs, this is the first 'birth', without instruments, which Eddy offers as a useful hint to the medical faculty! We notice that the non-existence of medicine has suddenly become a reality (or do we interpret this wrongly?)

Even if some of this beggars belief, it is worth noting that what might be termed 'a Bible fundamentalist' can see the Genesis accounts as non-literal, mythical and symbolic. This does not have to mean that we accept Eddy's peculiar interpretation of the material, but it does indicate that she can see that truth is not necessarily just plain facts from History. She sees History as a complete fiction from start to finish, which is a shame because that would mean that Jesus himself would be non-existent, presumably? But her method of allegorical interpretation is nothing new. Such methods were common with the early Church Fathers, such as Augustine. The only difference is, that Eddy has managed to impose her idiosyncratic view of 'Science' on to an ancient text, the writers of which might never have guessed the significance of what they were recording.

Strangely, Eddy is somewhat sympathetic to Charles Darwin with the Theory of Evolution. She thinks that Darwin's theory of evolution from a material basis is more consistent than most theories (page 547), with the thought that mankind has ascended through all the lower grades of existence. However evolution does not acknowledge the method of divine

Mind, nor see that material methods are impossible in Divine Science and that all Science is of God, not of man (page 551).

One intriguing exegesis on Genesis 1:26, a key text in Christian theology:

'And God said, "Let us make Man in our own image, after our own likeness… "'

Eddy cleverly brings in the metaphor of a mirror; that mankind is a reflection of the divine nature. 'Now compare man before the mirror to his Divine Principle, God. Call the mirror Divine Science and call man the reflection… .as the reflection of yourself appears in the mirror, so you, being spiritual, are the reflection of God…' (page 515-6).

This reminds us of the mirrors in Japanese mythology, where they are a reminder of immortality and eternity. Also in the Buddhist thinking, the Wheel of Becoming is held up to us, by Yama the god of the dead, to show us what we really are, i.e. circulating between one level of reality and another. Very revealing!

The Book of Revelation comes in for the same method of allegorisation as Genesis. Eddy manages to relate it to the Creation narratives quite successfully, but omits to connect any of it with Ezekiel or Daniel, or even Enoch, which is a major feature of Revelation. She begins at chapter 10, omitting all mention of the seven churches of Asia:

'And I saw another mighty angel come down from heaven…' (page 558).

Eddy sees this angel as the message that comes from God, clothed with a cloud, prefiguring Divine Science. Christian Science does seem obscure to people, hence the mist, but a bright promise crowns its head, which is symbolised by the rainbow. The angel had a book in his hand; this symbolises the revelation of Divine Science. Eddy does not attempt to comment on the other six angels blowing their trumpets before this, the seventh one appeared. The whole passage is redolent of the Sinai event at the Exodus, as trumpets are sounded.

Chapter 12 also attracts Eddy's interpretative skills. She thinks this is highly relevant to the nineteenth century, with the opening of the sixth seal.

Revelation 12:1: 'A woman clothed with the sun, with the moon under her feet… and a crown of twelve stars…' (page 560).

We have the distinct impression that Eddy is going to claim herself to be the woman! However, she holds back from that thought. The woman symbolises 'generic man', the spiritual idea of God; she illustrates the coincidence of God and man as the Divine Principle and the divine idea. The sun symbolises Spirit. The moon under her feet is the radiance of spiritual truth; also this reveals the universe as secondary and tributary to Spirit. The spiritual idea is crowned with twelve stars, the twelve tribes of Israel. They are the lamps of the spiritual heavens of the age, in which the sick and the sinning are enlightened and the night of materialism wanes.

It goes on in this vein. Predictably, the serpent comes in for comment:

'The great dragon was cast down, that old serpent,... Satan... .was cast out... ' (Revelation 12:9, page 567).

This is allegorised to mean 'that false claim... that ancient belief, that old serpent whose name is devil, claiming that there is intelligence in matter either to benefit or to injure man... is pure delusion... is cast out by Christ, Truth, the spiritual idea, and so proved to be powerless...' (page 567)

A final, interesting allegorisation comes with Revelation 21:16: the holy city, the New Jerusalem comes down out of heaven, with its foursquare configuration. This represents the light and glory of Divine Science. The four sides symbolise the Word, Christ, Christianity and Divine Science. The city is wholly spiritual. To the north, the gates open to the North Star, the Word, the polar magnet of Revelation; eastward to the star seen by the Magi; southward to the tropics with the Southern Cross, as at Calvary; westward to the grand realisation of the golden shore of love and the peaceful sea of harmony. How elaborate. Did St John really think in these terms when he wrote the Revelation?

It is good, however, to see Eddy trying to find allegorical and figurative meanings in such a book. Far too many people have tried to take Revelation purely at face value with some rather strange results. We think of the Jehovah's Witnesses. But Eddy appears not to be carried away with the apocalyptic mentality. She seems never to mention the end of the world or the Second Coming of Christ. Revelation would seem to be purely figurative.

As we have seen from a detailed analysis of Revelation (chapter 6) there is much imagery and symbolism, which would have meant a lot to a Jewish Christian of the first century AD, but which is now largely lost on us. But Eddy is happy to foist her own special theory on to the Revelation, a theory that would almost certainly have meant nothing to St John.

For those who cannot aspire to become Christian Science healers, there is a crumb of comfort that just reading her book will be beneficial:

'A thorough perusal of the author's publications heals sickness. If patients seem worse while reading this book, the change may either arise from the alarm of the physician, or it may mark the crisis of the disease. Perseverance in the perusal of this book has generally completely healed such cases' (page 446).

The truth of the matter is, for most rational people, that if one were to stop worrying about one's illness, it would, in general terms, aid recovery. Again there is that smattering of truth in this, but not the total truth. How can reading Eddy's book cure something like AIDS?

Scientific information

The word science as it is used in the book *Science and Health* is not the normal usage of that word. In our state of knowledge at the moment, Science means such areas as Biology, Chemistry, Physics and their subsidiary areas, including Astrophysics. Also the social sciences are included: Psychology, Sociology, Anthropology and many other areas. What they have in common is that they all attempt, through research and experimentation, to discover the workings of the natural world and render some kind of explanation. As far as this world is concerned, they still have a long way to go, for there are vast areas of this planet that are not properly explored or described. The same can be said for the social sciences; they too have a long way to go. With astrophysics, they are still only just scratching the surface.

What has this to do with Christian Science? Nothing whatsoever. The word 'science' is a misnomer. In one context, Eddy actually uses the word LOGOS. This Greek word was a buzz word in the ancient world; translated, it is literally 'word' but it had all manner of connotations. It was a pejorative word; it conveyed much more than just the English 'word'. It meant 'knowledge, metaphysic, understanding of spiritual matters, relationship to God, the key to understanding all things'. St John uses it as a metaphor for Jesus Christ, and indeed it is very apt. But the Gnostics and others used the word in their own theorising:

'Spirit, God, has created all in and of Himself. Spirit never created matter. There is nothing in Spirit out of which matter could be made, for as the Bible declares, without the Logos, the Aeon or Word of God, "nothing was made that was made"' (page 335).

We notice that *Logos* (Word) is used as a synonym with *Aeon*. This word, meaning Age or Epoch, was actually deified by the Greeks and the Mithraic religion. Aeon was pictured as a lion with serpents around him and four arms, not unlike an Indian god. Apart from this, most rational people will see a deep contradiction in this quotation. First she says that

God, the Spirit, created all; then she says that Spirit never created matter. That sounds rather strange until we recall that Eddy does not believe that matter exists anyway. Even so, there is a strange contradiction in this passage. Eddy claims never to contradict herself:

> 'In this volume of mine there are no contradictory statements, at least none which are apparent to those who understand its propositions well enough to pass judgment on them' (page 345).

How convenient one cannot comment on her views, contradictory or otherwise, unless one has that special insight of Christian Science!

We can understand Eddy's choice of the word 'science' for her bright idea. She was living in an age when scientific advances appeared to be overwhelming religious beliefs. One simple example would be the Theory of Evolution, which appeared about this time and appeared to cancel out the creation accounts in Genesis; but this was not the only spiritual crisis going on between science and religion. It might seem like a bright idea to link science and Christianity with something that she calls PROOF. That word appears rather often in her book, and one wonders what she means by 'proof'. Is there any certainty in her claims? But we all know that scientific knowledge and theological knowledge are on different levels. Science explores and describes the observable world; theology explores and attempts to describe matters concerning the divine, the unseen world, which people have an awareness of but find it hard to conceptualise. The mistake comes when the scientists try to pose as theologians and vice versa the theologians try to pose as scientists. That way, so many issues are confused and people find their faith is unnecessarily disrupted. The scientist should concentrate on how things come about; the theologian should consider why things occur, not in the physical sense but in the realms of ultimate meaning and fulfilment. To force an equation between Christianity and Science is to confuse the issue. There is nothing scientific about her claims.

Is this theory 'Christian'? Many would say no. If Christian means something to do with helping people, alleviating their problems, giving them hope, how does this square with Christian Science? To tell someone in pain that it is an illusion and one can think oneself out of it could be disastrous for them. The first resort is one's local doctor, after that the specialist. If they cannot cope with it, then spiritual healing may lend some help. To cross out the doctor is crass folly. Jesus himself is reported as telling the leper, when he was cured, to go and see the health inspector (the priest); do not miss out the basic common sense element when dealing with illness. Eddy denies that Jesus ever recommended attention to the laws of health (page 369), but it is plain enough in St Mark's Gospel. In addition to this, it is a part of church tradition that St Luke himself was a doctor. The best doctors of that time tended to be Greeks; they had all kinds of interesting methods in action, many of which are lost to us today. Doubtless Eddy would say they were all quackery, as she is sarcastic about the Asclapium[7], which was a kind of Greek sanatorium.

Eddy can now be seen as a child of her age and unaware of true scientific procedures. She claims that 'heredity is not a law' (page 178). We know now that heredity is a reality, having discovered genes and chromosomes, and the fact that certain diseases are inherited from parents. With this we are a bit nearer to 'proof' than she is. As a mathematician Eddy is a non-starter; she has no time for dates, chronology or figures:

'The measurement of life by solar years robs youth and gives ugliness to age... ..never record ages. Chronological data are no part of the vast forever. Time-tables of birth and death are so many conspiracies against manhood... life is eternal' (page 246).

According to this, we have no need of calendars, calculation of years, and the course of history. This becomes obvious, as her book has no historical material in it at all, and nothing remotely like mathematics. This is at variance with the Judaeo-Christian tradition, as laid down in the Bible. The course of history is the pattern of salvation, and a progression from elementary religion with Noah and Abraham, through to Jesus and into the Church. Part of Christian teaching is that history is real and is guided by God, not just the main events but each person's life and destiny.

Another aspect of her teachings is that evolution is wrong, in spite of what she says elsewhere:

'Theorising about man's development from mushrooms to monkeys and from monkeys into men amounts to nothing in the right direction and very much in the wrong' (page 172).

'The human mortal mind, by an inevitable perversion, makes all things start from the lowest instead of from the highest mortal thought. The reverse is the case with all the formations of the immortal divine Mind' (page 189).

At that time, when Darwin's theory was still rocking the civilised world, we can understand this outburst. Of course, if everything in the created world is an illusion, it will make no difference how species developed, if they developed at all. Looking back on the progress of human thought, we now see that the concept of evolution is endemic in virtually every area of knowledge and few people can think themselves out of it. There are a few lone voices who are calling it into question, and they may increase in volume. But Eddy is right in a sense, that we should not reduce everything to the lowest common denominator; rather we should look up, and trace how we are inspired by God and lifted above the physical world. Obviously she would now be called a Bible fundamentalist, but back in the 1870s it would not have been as simple as labelling her as such.

Literary ability in The Science and Health

There is no poetry in Eddy's book, except for a few quotations from elsewhere. However, there are the occasional outbursts of figurative language that can be quite apt and poetic:

> 'Nature voices natural, spiritual law and divine love, but human belief misinterprets nature. Arctic regions, sunny tropics, giant hills, winged winds, mighty billows, verdant vales, festive flowers, and glorious heavens... all point to Mind, the spiritual intelligence they reflect. The floral apostles are hieroglyphs of Deity. Suns and planets teach grand lessons. The stars make night beautiful, and the leaflet turns naturally towards the light' (page 240).

What a shame it is all illusory! There is a lot of good metaphor and imagery in this, and it is perfectly true that the glories of Nature indicate to us the wonders of God; no one would object to this piece of literature. What a shame she thinks the human race will misinterpret it all! Perhaps some people do, but most thinking people will appreciate the beauties of nature and see God in them.

> 'The lame, the deaf, the dumb, the blind, the sick, the sensual, the sinner, I wished to save from the slavery of their own beliefs and from the educational systems of the Pharaohs, who today as of yore, hold the children of Israel in bondage. I saw before me the awful conflict, the Red Sea and the wilderness; but I pressed on through faith in God, trusting Truth, the strong deliverer, to guide me into the land of Christian Science, where fetters fall and the rights of man are fully known and acknowledged' (page 226).

This is a very apt piece of sustained metaphor using the image of the Exodus. No one would deny that we are in slavery to sin and need to be released. This was the whole thrust of the ministry of Jesus. But to spoil it all and say that this slavery is purely caused by one's own erroneous beliefs and to equate the land of Canaan with the Utopia of Christian Science, is asking a lot of our credibility. To her credit, she is talking largely about freeing the slaves in this context. The American Civil War would just have ended at this stage, and Eddy is emphatically in favour of emancipation:

'The rights of man were vindicated in a single section and on the lowest plane of human life, when African slavery was abolished in our land... the voice of God in behalf of the African slave was still echoing in our land, when the voice of the herald of this new crusade sounded the keynote of universal freedom, asking a fuller acknowledgement of the rights of man as a Son of God...' (page 226).

Whereupon she goes off into Christian Science indoctrination again, and spoils it all. But her turn of phrase and use of imagery is good. The image of the trumpet announcing a crusade is very apt in relation to the Biblical use of the trumpet.

As one can see, Eddy has a habit of bending every apt remark to support her theory. She is prolific in her quotations from the Bible, in both Testaments. But the aptness of her quotations sometimes leave us a little puzzled. One example comes on page 242 where she quotes John 19:24 about the soldiers apportioning the garments of Jesus. His tunic was woven as one piece and could not be shared between four soldiers, so they cast lots for it. Eddy makes out that this symbolises the integrity of Divine Science. St John, who must have been a figment of everyone's imagination, including himself, was hardly thinking of this subtle interpretation. More likely he was hinting at the unity of Christian people, a theme he is most keen on, and the folly of disagreements between Christ's followers. Had it occurred to Eddy that this thought is a criticism of herself and others like her with a cranky splinter-group agenda? The Psalmist (22:19) is crying to God for help, feeling that he has been deserted, and then receives encouragement. This is highly appropriate for the crucifixion, but has nothing to do with Science and Health.

Isaiah 40:6-8 receives a rather strange treatment. Eddy manages to render it somewhat differently from the normal translations. 'As for man, his days are as grass... ' (page 190). Isaiah is pointing out, most poetically, the contrast between the eternal word of our God, which will stand for ever, and the ephemeral nature of the created world. In that context he is talking about the world being prepared for the coming of the Lord to give peace to his people, and when God makes a promise like that, he means what he says unlike the uncertainties of mankind. Eddy makes out that this means that 'this mortal seeming is temporal; it never merges into immortal being... ' (page 190). This is a perfectly straightforward and beautiful passage bent round to evidence the illusion of the physical world and the reality of the Divine. Hardly what Isaiah intended.

On page 181 we have a quotation from Genesis 3:9 where Adam and

Eve have just eaten the fruit and realised they were naked, and had to hide from God in the bushes. Eddy takes the words, 'Adam, where art thou?' and applies it to those who prefer error to trusting in truth. But that is totally out of context. The Genesis passage is about being tempted by the serpent and the first beginnings of guilt and a breakdown in the relationship between God and mankind. Adam throws the blame on to Eve; she blames the serpent. But they are still guilt-ridden and because of their disobedience, all the problems of life ensue from that. Sin is clearly not some kind of illusion or self-delusion. It is real; that is what the passage is basically saying. The passage has nothing to do with the physical world being an illusion. It is a clever adaptation of a scriptural text to suit a cranky theory, but not very convincing.

A quotation from St Paul in 2 Corinthians 6:15, 'What accord has Christ with Belial?' Here St Paul is talking about marrying the wrong person, a believer mated with a non-believer. 'What fellowship has light with darkness?' He goes on to say that, 'We are the Temple of the Lord'. Quite how this relates to Eddy's theories is a puzzle. The way she quotes it is quite out of context. She says, 'Evil would appear to be the master of good, and sickness to be the rule of existence, while health would seem the exception, death the inevitable, and life a paradox'. Eddy does not go so far as to comment on 'We are the Temple of the Lord'. It means that the Christian people are the visible means for God to be present in this world. Would she say that God could be present in a world and amongst a people that were illusory and non-existent?

A quotation from St Mark on the subject of Jesus casting out demons (page 252). 'If a kingdom is divided against itself, that kingdom cannot stand' Mark 3:24. This is in the context of the Pharisees alleging that Jesus is possessed by the Devil. Jesus must have been infuriated by this notion, and ends his tirade by saying that they are guilty of an eternal sin, which will not receive forgiveness. It is the sin against the Holy Spirit. What is St Mark trying to say? That you can't remove dirt by applying dirt; you can't solve a problem for someone by making the problem worse? He is stating that Jesus is the true healer of all illnesses, both physical and mental with his divine power. This is the opposite of what Satan does. The Pharisees have clearly got the whole thing the wrong way round. It means that their theology is upside down. But Eddy bends this to mean that 'ignorance, like intentional wrong, is not Science. Ignorance must be seen and corrected before we can attain harmony' (page 251). With this we lose the context and the original intention of St Mark.

But the most crass misuse of the Hebrew Scriptures comes on page 338[8]:

'The word ADAM is from the Hebrew ADAMAH, signifying the red colour of the ground, dust, nothingness... '

So far, not too bad. *Adamah* does mean soil, but also land, territory, country, but the thought of it being 'red' is not included. The idea of it being 'nothingness' is nonsense; the writer clearly intends that mankind, which is included in the name Adam, came from the earth, which is a reality. The name Adam is a pun on it, though why it should signify 'nothingness' is a stretch of the imagination. For most people, the soil of the earth is real enough, and hardly any fiction. The Hebrew word *dam* means 'blood' and this will involve the notion of redness, but she never says this. She goes on:

'... Divide the name Adam into two syllables and it reads A DAM, or obstruction. This suggests the thought of something fluid, of mortal mind in solution... here a dam is not a mere play on words; it stands for obstruction, error, even the supposed separation of man from God...' (page 338).

The Hebrew writer would hardly have been thinking of a dam in the modern sense of a barrage. Though there were such features in the ancient world, the imagery does not really involve barrages. We notice that her favourite word 'error' creeps in. The mention of 'soil', whether red or any other colour, does not involve thoughts of a mistake. The separation of man from God was real enough but she stops short of calling it sin; after all, sin is supposed to be an illusion. Perhaps the tree with its fruit, the serpent, and Eve herself were all a figment of Adam's fertile imagination! Perhaps Adam was non-existent too! But this example of the misuse of scripture is perhaps the most palpable.

Thus it can be seen that Eddy's literary skills in relation to the quotation of the Bible is not particularly satisfactory. One wonders if she could not have based her appeal to authority on other scriptural texts. After all, some of her ideas are clearly inspired by Hinduism and Buddhism. The reference to 'harmony' reminds us of the philosophisings of Lao Tzu, the founder of Taoism (Chapter 10). On that basis, it is an attempt at combining eastern religion with Christianity. Unfortunately, it is not very convincing.

One disturbing element in Eddy's ideas is the close connection between sin and disease. In St John's gospel, we are confronted with the blind man and the question raised was 'who sinned? Was it he himself or his parents?' This is the age-old assumption that disease is a punishment for sin. We hear this assumption very often from anyone who is seriously ill; 'what have I done to deserve this?' Eddy repeatedly reinforces this connection by juxtaposing sin and disease in the same breath, sometimes adding 'death'. Page 379 makes a definite linkage between sin and disease:

'If disease can attack and control the body without the consent of mortals, sin can do the same, for both are errors, announced as partners in the beginning.'

The truth is that this connection is part of the Old Testament configuration, as seen in parts of the Pentateuch. But Jesus in the New Testament deliberately breaks this connection and association. The blind man was blind not because of any sin on anyone's part, but for an opportunity to demonstrate the glory of God. 'I am the light of the world' was to be shown in real terms; this man's gaining of sight. This was something that the Old Testament people found beyond their comprehension. There are of course instances where Jesus states that someone's sins are forgiven, when doing a healing, but not in every case. It is true that some conditions are the result of wickedness, misuse of substances, and downright carelessness. But Jesus comes into our world with forgiveness, freeing up of troubled consciences, release from all forms of captivity, even self-imposed ones. Disease is not necessarily tied up with sin; it may be in some cases but not always. Eddy's categorical connection between the two is misleading and potentially harmful for those who worry about such things.

General Remarks about Christian Science

What has been the legacy of Christian Science over the last 140 years? We have seen our own times how drug-taking can be so drastically abused and there is an element of truth in using severe restraint with such substances. It can be seen that doctors are now far more careful about prescribing medicines. We have had the thalidomide[9] scare and other situations where use of drugs should not always be the first resort. It would be fair to say that Christian Science has had its effect on the world, but not in quite in the way that Eddy had expected.

'A grain of Christian Science does wonders for mortals...' (page 449).

Prophetic words. Her main contribution to philosophy and medical practice has been to engender an atmosphere of caution and responsibility about the use of drugs, and also, more importantly, the tendency to resort to quackery when conventional medicine is thought not to have the answers. But to take every idea of Eddy's completely literally and rely totally on her version of spiritual healing, is asking for trouble.

It is also fair to say that medical research and practice has moved on into vast new territories over the last centuries. We now have routine procedures that were thought impossible in Eddy's day. The discovery of penicillin and other antibiotics has altered so many factors. Also the fact that the indiscriminate use of such material will reduce its effectiveness, a factor that would tend to favour Eddy's views. It would be fair to say that many more diseases can be treated; even so, there remains a hard core of conditions that are hard to analyse or control. It is also a fact that as one problem is largely solved (smallpox), another one comes to prominence. This might indicate the spiritual side of disease; disease is not just purely and simply a physical matter.

Finally, as an analysis of Eddy's philosophic-theological ideas, her religion comes across as yet another interesting version of Gnosticism. The Gnostics of the Roman Empire claimed that the body was beyond redemption and yet the soul of man could be redeemed by discovering that special insight, a gnosis, which would render him saved and fit for heaven. Eddy's views are not so very different from this. Her denial of the reality of the physical world is interesting, and reminds us of certain Hindu theorists. It is one thing to say that God is real and everything else is some sort of fantasy; but in the final analysis, we have to cope with the world as we see it, real or unreal, or whatever adjective one applies to it. Simply denying its reality is a sort of cop-out; it means that we do not have to take the realities of life at all seriously, if they in fact do not exist. But most rational people will know that life is there as a challenge and as a preparation for the next world. Jesus told us to take up the cross; not dodge out of it with some sort of fiction. That means that the hard side of life is there for a purpose, not just something to be escaped from.

Notes for Chapter 9: Science and Health

1. Hebrews: Chapter 23.
2. One of the early heresies in the Early Church was to say that there were two people in the one Jesus, the human person and the spiritual person. This emerged in some of the Gnostic theorisings and later in Arianism.
3. Troche: some sort of circular pill in common use at that time.
4. *The Legend of Linda Martel*, by Charles Graves.
5. Eddy has no notion of paradox. A full discussion of paradox in relation to contradiction is found in my previous book, the Theology of Paradox, Chapter 1.
6. A full discussion of the concept of 'type' comes in Hebrews (Chapter 23).
7. The Asclapium was a centre for healing, in Ancient Greece. There is one preserved at Pergamum but there were many others. It must have been a sort of sanatorium.
8. The name Adam appears in Genesis 5:22, before that he was called 'the man'.
9. Thalidomide, a drug that produced deformed babies when given to pregnant mothers. This scandal had the effect of making doctors far more cautious about administration of drugs, especially to pregnant women.

10

Tao Teh Ching

Lao Tzu

This is the sacred literature of the Taoists, and may rank as one of the earliest scriptural materials ever produced. Its author, Lao Tzu, whose spiritual title is 'Most Exalted One', is one of China's greatest sages, hailing from about the time of Confucius; in fact they are thought to have conversed with one another. The edition used is that of Hua-Ching Ni 1979, rendering this ancient text in intelligible English. Again this book claims to portray the truth, but it is notably different from anything discussed earlier in this work. The word *Tao* can be rendered 'Way', but it has a wealth of meaning, the integral truth of the universe. It might even be seen as analogous to the concept of *logos* as seen in St John and the Gnostics of the Roman era. *Teh* means virtuous application of such high, subtle knowledge, and *Ching* means serious spiritual guidance, and that involves this holy book. It is all about philosophy and theology; there is nothing about mathematics, geography, history, while language and literature are purely coincidental. Even so, it forms a complete contrast with Mary Baker Eddy (Chapter 9) and also with Japanese mythology (The Kojiki: Chapter 12). As things worked out, Taoism concentrated on the spiritual side of religion in China, while Confucius talked almost entirely about ethics with scant mention of theology. There are many aspects of Taoist thinking which will strike a chord with twenty-first century mankind. It is not just the way in which it has been translated; its basic concepts are, or should be of some value to thinking people today. This is not the least true for Lao Tzu's advice for those in positions of leadership or control. A lot of his material relates directly to successful tactics in government, something that modern governments could take into consideration.

Theology and Philosophy

As with many scriptural materials, it is not at all easy to separate these two strands of truth. The chief focus of this thinking is the Tao[1]. It is not a god, in the Western way of thinking, and yet it is roughly analogous to YHWH, or God the Father. It is the subtle origin of all things. Even if it seems weak, its power is inexhaustible (4, page 11), it is the unfailing fountain of life (6, page 13). It is the Primal Female and the subtle origin (6) and the Mother (20, page 31). The Tao cannot be described or conceived. 'It subtly and gently generates without exhausting itself' (6, page 13). Life is constantly renewing itself, as indeed so is truth. If it did not, and ground to a halt, then truth would die. The Tao produces existence and non-existence, and they give birth to one another. This is interesting, as only in recent years have the scientists begun to consider the question of 'anti-matter'.

'The subtle virtue of the universe is wholeness, it regards all things as equal' (5, page 12).

With this goes the concept of harmony; there should be, or at least was at one time, a happy integration between the Tao and the created world. 'The Tao gave birth to a world of peace and order. It responds to the order and harmony of all beings and things without needing to talk to them' (73, page 94).

We now consider the factors of Heaven and Earth. Heaven is everlasting and Earth is perpetual. They were both formed, before time began (21, page 32) and also divinity was formed. Later Taoism was to think in terms of hell, but this does not appear in the Tao Teh Ching. The Tao is the ultimate in creation and also in non-creation (21, page 32), and brings all into being. This is interesting as we see a subtle interplay between literal and figurative language here. On the one hand the world is 'born' but on the other hand the creation comes 'into being'. As with many sacred writings, the boundary between literal and figurative language is not very sharp.

'Before Heaven and Earth are born, there is something formless and complete in itself. Impalpable and everlasting, silent and undisturbed, standing alone and unchanging, it exercises itself gently and generates itself inexhaustively in all dimensions. It may be regarded as the mother of all things. Far beyond humankind's relative conception, it cannot be referred to by a specific name, yet it may be identified as the subtle essence of the universe' (25, page 36). This is a most apt description of the Tao. As a way of describing God the Father, it goes a long way. The difference is that God the Father in Western thought is not just a remote principle, or silent factor underpinning all of creation; he is also active, a spiritual force in the physical world, directing and inspiring people in their daily lives. Even so, 'the subtle essence of the universe is omnipresent... thus it may be recognised as 'the Great' (25).

This could be seen as a form of monotheism. There may be pantheistic elements in it but that might be somewhat anachronistic to call Lao Tzu a pantheist. There is the occasional mention of divine spirits such as 'Divine spirits attained the subtle essence of the universe and became powerful... ' (39, page 55), but that does not mean they are seen as gods. They could be regarded as the equivalent of angels, as seen in Biblical thinking.

The whole point of this philosophy is to find, achieve or maintain the harmony between heaven and earth, the world of the spirit and the physical world. We now see how human life relates to the Tao.

'In the natural flow of energy transformation, human life becomes one of the four great expressions of the Tao. It is the way of subtle integration. Humankind conforms to earth, earth conforms to the sky, the sky conforms to the Subtle Origin, the subtle origin conforms to its own nature' (25, page 37).

The natural way of life is harmony and integration between all aspects of life, human, divine and everything else. At some stage in the past, this went wrong:

'When humankind strayed from the natural way of life... when disharmony manifested in family relations... when chaos prevailed in the country' (18, page 28).

Lao Tzu advises everyone to return to their true nature. It requires love, kindness, wisdom, family harmony, and loyalty. That way people will regain the natural virtue of wholeness and the world will be naturally ordered' (18, page 28).

If this sounds like the Eastern version of the Fall, as described in Genesis, this could be a fair way of assessing it. But Lao Tzu does not have a story like Adam and Eve in the Garden of Eden; it is only mentioned in general terms that mankind somehow went wrong, which destroyed the harmony between heaven and earth. He thinks that that harmony can be regained by everyone trying hard to be nice. It would be a wonderful thing if everyone did make such an effort, but unfortunately life is not as simple as that. There are certain people who are bent on being aggressive, selfish and exploitative. The Humanistic view that mankind can save itself by its own efforts is a vain hope. The truth of the matter is that the problem requires the active intervention of a loving God, to re-establish the harmony between heaven and earth. Such a concept is lacking in Chinese thought generally, and specifically missing from the Tao Teh Ching.

But Lao Tzu's advice to everyone is to cultivate humility and reduce selfishness.

'He, too, dissolves all consciousness of self and lives as the universe. By putting himself behind others, he finds himself foremost. By not considering his own personal ends, his personal life is accomplished. He finds himself safe, secure and preserved. Because he does not hold a narrow concept of self, his true nature can fully merge with the Tao' (7, page 14).

Lao Tzu goes further than this: 'One with the wholeness of virtue... is kind to the kind. He is also kind to the unkind... he is faithful to the faithful and also faithful to the unfaithful... ' (49, page 67). This is indeed a high ethic, something we see in the Sermon on the Mount.
We notice the paradoxes in this; not claiming to be anything superior, one actually does become superior. One should be like water; it always finds the lowest place and yet it is vital for all aspects of life (8, page 15). The genuine Taoist is peaceful, not argumentative, and sincere. So it is no surprise to find Lao Tzu advocating pacifism.

'Weapons are instruments of killing and destruction which are contrary to the nature of life... only when one has no other choice may one resort to using them... and even so one must employ calmness and restraint... even in victory there is no cause for excitement and rejoicing... .he who delights in killing and destruction cannot be expected to thrive for long in the world' (31, page 44).

Lao Tzu can see that warfare is in the end self-defeating:

'It is generally the nature of weapons to turn against their wielders' (30, page 43). How true! The course of history has shown us that those who start a war almost invariably finish off defeated in the long run. Even the Romans, who were militarily brilliant, descended into chaos when they decided to fight each other. Aggression is in the end, self-defeating.
It almost sounds like 'he who lives by the sword shall die by the

175

sword'[2]. 'What the ancients have taught, I also shall teach; "a man of force and violence will come to a violent end."' Lao Tzu has to admit that war has to occur in certain circumstances, although he does not go into details about the righteous war. But normally, to be in harmony with the Tao, one should avoid all violence, killing and cruelty. These are astonishing words for someone who is potentially a citizen of the Iron Age, but as we have seen from the Bhagavad Gita, there were others who felt that warfare was morally wrong. Nowadays this pattern of thought is taken as axiomatic by most responsible governments. But as ever, the problem is to convince everyone of this truth of pacifism; then it would work.

Here comes sound advice for anyone thinking of starting a war: 'There is no greater mistake than to underestimate the power of an opponent' (69, page 90). How true! Virtually all wars start because the aggressor has convinced himself that he cannot fail to win.

Lao Tzu appears to believe in an afterlife in heaven, at least for those who try to keep harmony with the Tao.

'To be heavenly is to be one with the Tao. To be one with the Tao is to enjoy everlasting life. Such a one will be preserved even after the dissolution of his physical body' (16, page 26).

But for those who cannot behave according to the Tao, there is extinction. He does not go into details as to what happens. On this matter he is not very specific:

'Extinction happens to one who violates his true nature... without maintaining their potency, spirits would disperse' (39, page 56).

So this applies to divinities as well as humans. Later Taoist thinking made out that there was hell for those who fail to connect with the Tao, for those who are deliberately aggressive, cruel and selfish. That aspect of Taoism was to creep in later.

Lao Tzu is prepared to admit that there are people who cannot take the Tao on board, but he does not seem to have a way of talking them round:

'When mediocre people hear of the Tao they are unimpressed. When people who are low hear of the Tao they break into loud laughter. If it were not laughed at it would not be the Tao' (41, page 58).

This could be the Taoist equivalent of being 'a fool for Christ's sake' and reminds us of 1 Corinthians 1:25: 'For the foolishness of God is wiser than men, and the weakness of God is stronger than men.'

Literary expertise

The Tao Teh Ching can be lauded for its sustained use of paradox. Whether there was a word for this feature of literature at that time is not known. We believe that the concept and identification of paradox begins with the philosophers of ancient Greece. But Lao Tzu is in fact using this literary technique quite extensively; the nearest he comes to giving it a name is 'contradictory concepts and images' (65, page 85). He does this on purpose in order 'to maintain the natural state of simplicity'. This is largely what is wrong with the world; that people have gone in for increasing complications, arguments and distractions. He states that a complicated mind is the source of all calamities. A leader who has simplicity is the source of all blessing. Lao Tzu uses paradox not just in describing the Tao but in other areas too, quite extensively.

> 'Confront it and you do not see its face; follow it and you do not see its back. It does not appear bright when viewed at the zenith. Nor does it appear dark when viewed at the nadir. There is nothing that can make the Tao distinct. When you try to make it clear to yourself, it evasively reverts to Nothingness' (14, page 21).

Profound! If this sounds somewhat like the incident when Moses[3] 'saw' God's back, this would be fair. That was as much of God as Moses could stand. Any attempt to define God, pin him down, turn him into terms of human expression, all fall apart. This might be a helpful remark for the Atheist who would like to find God. God does revert to non-existence if one tries to force preconceived ideas on to him, making him conform to human notions.

A string of paradoxes can be applied to the one who integrates with the Tao:

> 'Because he does not flaunt his brightness, he becomes enlightened; because he is not self-important, he becomes illustrious; because he does not boast of his accomplishments, he becomes successful; because he is not self-assertive, he becomes supreme...' (22, page 33).

Lao Tzu is talking about the ideal leader, who must elicit the respect of his subjects. We notice that this is the exact opposite of what we read in *Mein Kampf* (Chapter 4), where the leader forces his way into power, using bullying, deceit and cruelty to attain control of other people. It would indeed be an ideal world if all leaders had this responsible idea of humility in their posts, but unfortunately, the reality of life is not so. We have unscrupulous, dominating and dishonest people very often in the halls of greatness. Lao Tzu does not really have a solution for dealing with such people.

Another string of paradoxes is reminiscent of something in the Bible:

'There is a time for things to move ahead, and a following time for things to retreat; a time to withdraw internally, and a following time to expand externally; a time to grow luxuriantly; and a following time to decay; a time to rise up; and a following time to sink down' (29, page 42). This is so like that famous passage in Ecclesiastes[4]: ' a time to be born and a time to die... etc.'. One might almost think that Solomon, if he wrote it, had actually influenced Chinese thinking. It is not out of the question.

Consider this string of paradoxes:

'The yielding are preserved whole, the crooked become straight. The empty become filled. The depleted are renewed. What has little will gain. What has much will become confused' (22, page 33).

The crooked becoming straight reminds us of that famous passage in Isaiah[5] where every valley will be filled in and equality will arrive with the coming of the Messiah. The difference here is that Lao Tzu has no idea of God sending a Messiah to bring about harmony between heaven and earth. Other than that, there is so much in the *Tao Teh Ching* that sounds like Biblical thinking, and especially of the New Testament.

'When the government does not interfere, the people are simple and happy. When the government does interfere, the people are tense and cunning. Disaster is what blessing perches on. Blessing is where disaster abides' (58, page 77).

These comments could so aptly be applied to our circumstances today in which there is far too much government control in just about every area of life. It is true that the people just develop ways and means of dodging governmental interference. The final paradoxical comments, that disaster is what blessing perches on, could easily have come from the book of Job, which again is not out of the question.

Two good examples of sustained simile come in (74, page 95).

'To become the executioner of artificial righteousness is like the inexperienced lad who would brandish a sharp axe of a master carpenter. He can seldom escape cutting himself'.

'One whose virtue is deep treats the world as if he were the debtor... he willingly repays the world through serving his fellow man... one who is partially virtuous treats the world as if he were the creditor... he thinks the world owes him something and should repay him...' (79, page 100).

We notice that Lao Tzu does not go so far as to talk about anyone being bad; he has a high estimation of human nature, perhaps a little over-optimistic.

Mythology

The Tao Teh Ching is a remarkable document for its age. It forms a complete contrast to the Japanese holy writings in which mythology goes to extremes of crudity and anthropomorphism about how the gods produced the world and mankind. Lao Tzu's work could be described as the first demythologised account of Heaven and Earth. He pictures the Tao as 'giving birth' to all things, but this does not descend to the crudity seen in other mythologies. One wonders if he meant 'birth' in a non-literal sense, just as the Christians would say that 'the only begotten Son of the Father' is only figurative.

> 'The Tao gave birth to One, One gave birth to Two, Two gave birth to Three. Three gave birth to the myriad things. All lives have their backs to the yin and embrace the yang' (42, page 60).

With this we see a kind of Trinity, even if it is completely different from the Christian conception of Father Son, and Holy Spirit. One of these is the Jade Emperor, as it was worked out later. But he is never mentioned in the Tao Teh Ching. The mention of the yin and yang is interesting. Lao Tzu only once mentions this configuration but does not go into details about it. This was also to come later, with a complete philosophy of physics to go with it.

Interestingly, Lao Tzu never broaches the subject of reincarnation. It would seem this was not an original element in Taoist thought. It is now; it looks as if multi-life worked its way into Chinese thinking with the coming of the Buddhists.

He mentions in passing the 'Valley of the Universe' (page 55) but does not go into details about what it actually means. We might speculate that he saw the living space of mankind as surrounded by mountains. The term 'Central Territory, ' though not appearing in the Tao Teh Ching, refers to the full extent of China as we know it today. Further out from that would seem to be something of a vague concept for the Taoists and the Chinese in general.

The Hua Hu Ching

This too is a scriptural work of Lao Tzu, but, since there were attempts at destroying it, only fragments of it now survive to this day. Any discussion of it has to be dependent on speculation and analysis. However it does not, it seems, introduce anything particularly new. This corpus of writing had its influence on Manichaeism[7] and also Mahayana Buddhism, and also Sufism. Hua Ching Ni's compilation and realisation of it is a commendable work, even if it is clearly couched in modern paraphraseology. There is no need to embark on a detailed analysis of its thoughts; a few useful remarks may help to see the Tao Teh Ching in a slightly modified light. The Hua Hu Ching takes the form of a conversation between Lao Tzu and a certain unnamed prince; they seem to agree on virtually everything.

The unity of life and of the universe is still a major theme. One should not hold any antagonism or discrimination for anything; one harmonious wholeness is the ideal. That includes colour, nationality, family or social conditions. This may be phrased in terms of modern ideas on equality, but it is consistent with the Tao Teh Ching. Being selfless and extending virtue to the world unconditionally is the way to dissolve the self-created agony, misery and tragedy in one's life.

At this point we have passing mention of 'many lifetimes' (page 111). How original this is to Lao Tzu's essential thinking is open to question, but of course reincarnation has become a major strand in the theology of eastern religions.

On the issue of merit as opposed to grace, which is a major factor in western thinking, the same strand appears in the Hua Hu Ching (page 114). The master asked the prince if one amassed a big worldly treasure and then gave it away to those in need, would he derive blessings in proportion to the amount he gave away. The answer to this is yes, which means in effect, one can buy blessings from God. However, Lao Tzu goes on to say that anyone who treasures these teachings and instructs others to carry them out, his blessings will be far greater. But that is not the essence of life; once we start to worry about blessings, they cease to be blessings. One should give spontaneously without thought of reward. How much of this reminds us of Jesus telling the rich man to give it all away, of Martha and Mary, and also of 'to labour and not to ask for any reward'[8]?

It is interesting that the master embarks on what we would now call astrophysics. He talks of small particles that make up the universe, and how vast the universe is. But then, paradoxically, the universe is not vast, nor its particles numerous. It is just one's relative mind that labels them so. In other words, he has realised that big and small are only relative, and in fact value judgements.

'Each small particle is an entire world in itself. The worlds are the conjoint movement of small particles. There is no real difference between small particles and the vast world, but they are differently named because of the relative concepts of small and vast' (32, page 138).

In our own times we have become aware of atoms and molecules and also of the immense distances in outer space, measured in light years. Also he talks of invisible particles of energy (page 179) and of energy rays, both positive and negative. These are factors only recently analysed in modern scientific atomic theory. Lao Tzu has an amazing awareness of these matters. How much of this is Hua Ching Ni's realisation as opposed to the master's original thought is debateable; even so, it is consistent with the Tao Teh Ching.

Lao Tzu also has an awareness of the dilemma between design and descent. He says that basically it makes no difference if one can see the real essence of things:

'Nor are there any grounds for commenting on whether those movements are the mischief of blind, mechanical, physical nature, or the wonderful creation of an artistic, universal mind. It is all the same when one has the insight to see the deep nature of things'(32, page 138). This is an amazing thought, which has only really surfaced in modern times.

The whole issue of putting a label on God also surfaces. Can one imagine the Tao as having any kind of wonderful form? The answer is no, because the Tao is not *real* in the sense of being a physical thing or person; he is just labelled as such. In other words, we can only talk of the Tao in terms of human metaphor. If we label the Tao as subtle and transcendental, then it ceases to be the true integral oneness; if we reduce it to a mental sphere it is no longer the undistorted reflection of the universal truth of one life. This amounts to an understanding of idolatry. As in Western thought, the minute one creates a picture of God, whether mental or an artistic rendition, one has reduced God to human canons of thought and conception. Asking the question, does the Tao have a beautiful physical appearance, the answer would be 'no', because that would mean he has no form. 'Beautiful physical appearance' is only a matter of labelling and value judgement. However it is possible to observe the appearance of the Tao in all kinds of beautiful forms. Conversely, if one sees the Tao in a particular form, one will never actually see him. It will descend into sorcery and fail altogether. Lao Tzu is a very profound thinker and hardly a child of his age. The issue of God's faculties now surfaces; does he have eyes, in the physical sense? (20, page 126). The answer is yes, but not just physical ones. Spiritual, wise, perceiving, incomparable eyes. There is nothing that escapes his perception; he is omnipresent.

The issue of defining culture also surfaces; can beauty or perfection or the integral truth be put into words? (page 136). The answer is that they cannot be put into words, but they simply speak for themselves. We notice that this comes close to one of the 'proofs' for the existence of God, as outlined by Aquinas, the Cosmological argument which means, briefly, that we are all aware of beauty but never perfect beauty in this world; we can only find it in the world of divinity, God being the ultimate beauty. Lao Tzu does not need to embark on anything like a 'proof' for the existence of the Tao; such a thought might have seemed irrelevant to him.

With regard to mythology, the Hua Hu Ching raises the question of how humanity came into existence. The prince cites the legend of Old Pan Kou; this name literally means 'big round drum', since the universe was believed to be a sealed round drum made of stone. Here we see an attempt at interpreting the metaphor; does this mean that the first human beings were shaped like drums, or that the first human beings were like someone living in a drum, not knowing what goes on outside? (38, page 146). In reply, Lao Tzu sings the song of Pan Kou, which describes how he fashioned the world and people. One minute it is anthropomorphic; the next minute it is transcendental. 'The genesis of the world is the exercise of his mind;' and 'he swings his axe and chisels rhythmically' (page 146). But Lao Tzu is not really interested in such accounts. He is content to say that 'the named was born from the unnamed'. The describable world comes from the indescribable Source. In this way, creation is portrayed purely in philosophical, demythologised terms. 'That which creates things is itself uncreated'.

At this point he goes on to talk of the 'mystical opening and closing of the gate of Origin which performs the Mystical Intercourse of the Universe' (page 149). It is the mysterious relationship between yin and yang, which is a gentle, subtle, perpetual movement that is the root of universal life. At this point we can include comments on the Three Main Categories (62, page 197)[9], or the Three Great Treasures: heaven, earth and mankind. Each one has its own purity, as listed in the footnotes. This is where Yin and Yang become relevant to the theory of human nature. Yang stands for heaven, yin stands for Earth and the subtle combination of the two produces humanity[10]. It is interesting that the same configuration appears in the Genesis Creation stories; that God took some clay and formed mankind; this is saying the same thing in anthropomorphic terms while Lao Tzu is saying it in metaphysico-philosophical terms. It amounts to the same thing, that mankind is a subtle combination of basic earth and the essentials of divinity. Lao Tzu goes further and says that if one lives one's life according to the Tao, one in effect becomes a divinity.

> ' A person of truth is a living divinity. He is not only above his mind, but he can be above the laws of physical nature. He actually becomes one with all. When he moves, the universe moves. When he sleeps the universe sleeps… ' (77, page 223).

The master then goes on to discuss the Five Subtle Phases and the Eight Great Manifestations, which can be seen in the diagram[11]. There are four cardinal virtues[12], five great blessings[13], five great relationships, and eight great treasures[14]. Virtue is the mother of all blessings and anyone who practises virtue will receive heaven's reward. This is where the health aspect of Taoism comes in, for it contains a complete scheme of holistic healing called the Yi Yau (55, page 173). A complete theory of illness appears: moving is normal, stagnation is sickness. This is something inherent in the understanding of the Tao. Another aspect of this is 'so-called pain and happiness are merely conditions'; is this a claim that pain does not really exist? If so, this would indicate a source for Mary Baker Eddy's theory of disease, i.e. it is non-existent (46, page 158).

The claim is that all truth is contained within the T'ai Chi, which is portrayed by the well-known Yin-Yang symbol. There are various versions of this, and a whole collection of fascinating diagrams to elucidate such matters as the Three Treasures of the multi-universe, the Five Great Performers, the unmanifested and the manifested sphere, and also the Four Forces and the Eight Great Manifestations, which lead on to the Sixty-Four Dimensions. All this can be related to a Time Sequence, using the Chinese months and times of day. To go into detail here would be unnecessary, but it is astonishing that a philosopher of the Iron Age could produce something as subtle and what we would call 'modern' as this psycho-physical theory. Obviously some elements in this would seem somewhat hair-brained, but essentially, Lao Tzu is pointing out the spiritual underpinning and dimension of the entire universe. To say that this is the entire truth is quite a bold claim; it is to be noted that Lao Tzu does not go along with religious theories or dogmas; even so, this system of thought looks suspiciously like such a thing. The element of truth in it is surely the portrayal of the Yin-Yang sign; that life is a balancing act between light and darkness, good and evil, weak and strong. This is his main contribution to the question of theodicy, whether he realised it or not is irrelevant. But this is a strand in theology that has teased the human mind since the dawn of civilisation and still we do not have a clear-cut, simple solution. Why is there evil in the world? Why does the innocent have to suffer, or indeed why does anyone have to suffer?

But essentially the Universal Integral Way, the Tao, is simple to understand and easy to follow. It is possible to get carried away with all kinds of elaborate theories and teachings, but the key to life is very straightforward. It is all about simplicity, not getting too tied up with the frenzy of life, keeping calm, not becoming involved with too much materialism. This would be the hallmark of the Taoist, and it has a lot to offer to the modern world. It would also coincide well with the teachings of Jesus, and other matters raised in the Bible. The major element missing from these Taoist sacred writings is the issue of Messianism, which means in effect God coming into this world in real human terms to show us what he is really like.

Clearly this rendition is an achievement of Hua Ching Ni. It does raise the question of how much this is a modern paraphrase of Lao Tzu's original thoughts. There are many modernistic terms and phrases used in this work. A full list would not be necessary, but telekinesis, clairaudience, telepathy, sublimation and revitalisation strike one as the product of modern psychology or even parapsychology. One wonders what the original Chinese of these words could have been! Even so, the Hua Hu Ching is a fascinating book to read and clearly lifts Taoism out of the poor reputation that it had acquired and sanitised it for the twenty-first century seeker of truth.

Notes for Chapter 10: Tao Teh Ching

1. The Tao: this has a wide range of meaning but is usually rendered as 'the subtle essence of the universe' or 'the deep nature of the universe' or 'subtle way of the universe' and many other variants on it.
2. 'For all who take the sword shall perish by the sword,' Matthew 26:52.
3. Exodus 33:21-23; the incident on Mount Sinai when God showed himself to Moses.
4. Ecclesiastes 3:1-8; 'For everything there is a season... a time to be born and a time to die... '
5. Isaiah 40:4-5 and 42:16.
6. John 1:14 '... the only Son from the Father.'
7. Manichaeism: a dualistic religion with affinities to Gnosticism founded in Persia in 3rd Century AD, by someone called Mani.
8. The Prayer of St Richard.
9. Each of the three Main Categories has its own purity: one who achieved himself spiritually attained the range of Yu Ching; one who achieved himself by attaining the wisdom that is connected with universal mindedness... attained the range of Shan Ching; one who achieved himself by refining his sexual energy attained the range of T'ai Ching. If one achieved all three, expressed in an integral and virtuous life, then he would achieve the Tao.
10. Explained on page 187 with symbols to elucidate.
11. Five Subtle Changes and Eight Great Manifestations as shown in the diagram on page 190. The result is that the Eight Great Manifestations are Heaven, Earth, Water, Fire, Thunder, Lake, Wind and Mountain. These then generate sixty-four hexagrams with 384 lines, which display all the possible combinations of yin and yang. With this system being based on the figure eight, one wonders if this has any relevance to the number eight, which holds so much significance in Japanese mythology.
12. Four cardinal virtues: natural piety, natural sincerity, gentleness, natural supportiveness.
13. Five great blessings: *Fuh*, happiness that makes no demands; *Su*, longevity; *Kang*, health that is free from abuse; *Ning*, peace which is not disturbing; *Fui*, wealth honestly gained.
14. Eight Great Treasures. Again we see the emphasis on eight, which ties in with Japanese thinking; eight as a symbol of completeness, wholeness (see Chapter 12). This also reminds us of the Eight Immortals as in Chinese mythology.

11

The Book of Mormon

Joseph Smith

This corpus of literature has an almost unique provenance. A certain Joseph Smith of New York State, USA, claims he was given a collection of brass plates engraved with a curious language. He translated them with the aid of a special pair of spectacles. The result was the Book of Mormon and is the inspiration and scripture for the Church of Christ of Latter Day Saints. The Mormons also accept the Bible as scriptural. The authenticity of the plates is very difficult to establish; only a few people claim[1] to have seen them and now they are not available for inspection. We have only the word of a few people of the Mormon persuasion, that the plates actually did exist and only Smith's word that he actually did translate this unknown language.

In assessing the genuineness of the Book of Mormon, the only way it can be done is by internal examination. It is notable that there are various anachronisms that cast a serious doubt on its authenticity. In 1 Nephi 16:18 we have mention of 'fine steel' of which his bow was made. The date involved was well within the Iron Age (600 BC), but at that time the technology for making a bow of fine steel was unknown. It was only in Mediaeval Europe that Toledo steel was developed for use with the rapiers. Bows were made of wood, usually yew. 'A sword made of the most precious steel' appears in 1 Nephi 4:9. Such a thing would have been unknown in those days. Added to that, in Alma 43:18, we have people armed with 'swords and cimeters and all manner of weapons of war', and in many other places. We know that in this context in America, steel was unknown, also iron. It is fair to say that the Indians knew about gold and silver, but essentially, they were still in the Stone Age. Iron and steel was unknown until the coming of the Spaniards in the sixteenth century. A scimitar (correct spelling) is an Arabic weapon and can hardly have been found among the Indians. Alma 24:12-15 and other references make various mentions of swords, assumedly made of steel, if they were 'bright'.

In Nephi 18:12 we have mention of a 'compass' that did cease to work but in verse 21 it decides to work again. This is how the Nephites managed to navigate the Atlantic Ocean and find the Promised Land in America. In Alma 37:38 this compass is described in more detail:

'... the thing which our fathers call a ball or director, or our fathers called it Liahona[2]... a compass; and the Lord prepared it.'

It goes on to mention its workings, with spindles to point the way to go. Compasses were unknown until the late Medieval period; before that a gadget called a 'astrolabe'[3] was used for navigation. In this land of promise, all kinds of animals were found including horses, cows, donkeys, and goats; all of these are European animals. Horses were unknown in the New World until the Spaniards arrived in the sixteenth century. When the Aztecs saw men on horseback, they thought it was all one animal. The horse only ran wild in America when the European settlers introduced them; before that the Indians had never seen a horse.

In this promised land it is claimed they built all kinds of temples, synagogues and churches. Alma 16:13-15 is one such place but there are many others. No such trace or evidence has been found of such buildings by the archaeologists. As for churches, they are a specifically Christian structure meaning 'gathered together', or 'ecclesia', which only has meaning after the coming of Jesus. In 78 BC, Jesus is still in the future. The first verifiable church building has been found in Tiberius, the house of Peter's mother-in-law, an octagonal building of the first century AD.

Linguistically, there is a problem in Alma 7:20. '... Turning from the right to the left or from that which is right to that which is wrong.' This is a sort of pun; quite amusing in English, but puns do not readily translate from a strange antique language into a modern language. One wonders what the original would have been! Also the occurrence of 'adieu' in Jacob 7:27 is a give-away; this is a word from modern French; hardly something from the Ancient World. Also we have the term 'en fine' used quite often; it is clearly a corruption of *enfin* in French, which means 'at last' or 'eventually'.

Even more strange, in 2 Nephi 29:3 we have people demanding to have a Bible. In its setting, 559 BC, no one could talk of there being a Bible. The Old Testament itself was at that time probably only half complete and the New Testament was about 600 years in the future. The word itself is clearly of Greek derivation[4] and the Greeks did not have any influence in

Israel until about 300 BC. It is quite likely that the Bible, as we know it, as a complete book, only appeared quite late in the Christian era, possibly at the Reformation when printing made it realistic to issue all the books of the Bible together in one production. Before that, it was almost certainly circulated in separate portions, referred to as 'scriptures' or 'gospels'.

Also there are several words or phrases which have a modern ring to them, hardly the mentality of the genuine Biblical writers. 'Liberal' (Jacob 5:), and 'frenzied mind' (Alma 30:16) and 'preparatory' (Alma 13:3) and many others. Such vocabulary would not have been found in Semitic languages (Hebrew or Aramaic), which presumably would have been the basis of this strange language on the plates[5]. The same goes for the idea that the language was 'reformed Egyptian', whatever that was. It might conceivably be the product of Greek thought, but then the Greeks did not enter the picture until the coming of Alexander the Great, 300 years after the alleged departure to the New World. Just remotely possible as a product of Greek thought is the reference to the planets in Alma 30:44:

'... even the earth and all things that are on the face of it... its motion...
.all the planets which move in their regular form... '

It was the Greeks, not the Hebrews, that were interested in the motions of the planets. In addition, there is the hint that the earth and the planets move in orbits, 'their regular form', something that was not realised until relatively modern times. In the Ancient World it was assumed that the earth was the centre of the universe and did not move about, as we now know it does.

In various places we have mention of 'cement'. In Helaman 3:7 it is claimed that people built houses of cement because there was not enough wood. America well endowed with timber; areas to the north have massive forests (Helaman 3:10). Cement however was a medium developed by the Romans at a place called Potsuoli in Italy; it was unknown to the Egyptians, Persians and Greeks. Apparently it occurred naturally at Potsuoli and the Romans discovered how to make it artificially from limestone, and clay. It was unknown in America until the Spaniards arrived.

The main and inescapable anachronism in the Book of Mormon is the fact that in 600 BC everyone thought that the world was flat and that to go too far out in the Atlantic Ocean was to invite falling off the edge into a void. No one dared go out too far; hardly out of sight of land. It is possible that the Mithraians thought that the world was a sphere, but the vast majority of people thought otherwise. Columbus thought he had found somewhere in what we now call the East Indies and that explains why the West Indies are so called, because he thought it was 'the Indies'. Only later did they discover the Pacific Ocean.

Back in 600 BC, it is highly unlikely that the Jews escaping from the doomed city of Jerusalem had any idea of finding a new territory across the Atlantic Ocean. More likely, following the impression we gain from the Old Testament, is the fact that they were terrified of dreadful sea monsters like Leviathan and Behemoth, and the sea symbolised the forces of evil and destruction. They had ships, but they mostly plied the Red Sea and the Mediterranean. The Book of Mormon does not explain why or how these Jews would have known that there was land to be colonised hundreds of miles out across the Atlantic Ocean. In addition to this, the second contingent would not have been informed of the first contingent landing in 'America', since the first contingent did not return to the Old World, as Columbus did.

The whole account in the Book of Mormon presupposes that the Americas were known about in pre-history and that the two expeditions of Jews leaving Palestine for a better life somewhere else were confident of finding land far out across the Atlantic Ocean. This is the chief anachronism concerning the Book of Mormon, but there are many other minor ones which will emerge as this discussion proceeds.

There is enough here to make one suspicious of the authenticity of the Book of Mormon; one may fairly conclude that it is a forgery. However, that does not necessarily invalidate it as a work of literature, or of philosophy or of theology. Just as Shakespeare's *Julius Caesar* has a clock striking, it does not alter the fact that the play is of the highest value as drama and literature.

With this in mind, it could be reasonable to say that we are looking at Joseph Smith's personal concoction and fantasies. Even so, a study of the book can reveal factors of value for our knowledge of faith and how it relates to other sacred writings.

Literary criticism

One notable feature of the Book of Mormon is that it has integrity; it is all of one piece and appears to have been written by just one author. This is in spite of it being arranged in fifteen separate books, most of which flow from one to another without much of a break. This is in contrast to the Bible: here we have a collection of books spanning many centuries, with an array of different authors, each with his own view of matters and theological axe to grind. Added to that, these books display a wide variety of literary genre: prose, poetry, hymnody, mythology, epistles, prophecy, and wisdom literature. The Book of Mormon, in contrast, is very much a 'one-genre' book. It is true that epistles are worked in in places, and also large chunks of quotation from the Bible, including Isaiah and the Sermon on the Mount. Otherwise it is a catalogue of alleged historical events, becoming very tedious as one battle after another is described. It resembles rather the Odyssey, with its endless violence; the difference being that Homer ascribes it all to the pagan gods; J. Smith has God always on the side of the righteous Jewish-Christians. This is the Nephites, initially, and then the Lamanites (the Indians) as they turn to Christ.

As a literary work, it is a reasonable attempt at imitating the classic accounts of Israel's history in the books of Samuel and the Kings. Sadly, it is slightly overdone. The phrase 'and it came to pass' occurs rather too often, to the point of being annoying. Nowhere do we get the personal encounters such as David and Jonathan, Elijah and the Shunamite woman, Samson and Delilah, which make the account so real. Admittedly there are some elements that recall features in the Old Testament. The early settlement of the Nephites was ruled by Judges, clearly a revamp of the situation as seen in the book of Judges, though none of them have the personality of people like Gideon and Deborah. Recalling Daniel and the fiery furnace comes in Helaman 5:44; also 2 Nephi 28:21-22, and 4 Nephi 1:32-33. Nephi and Lehi are in prison but encircled with a pillar of fire, and also a cloud of darkness. This also recalls the Exodus. There are many references to the Garden of Eden and the Fall, including the Tree of Life and the cherubim with a flaming sword.

We can see that the attempt to copy the language of the Authorised Version is intended to evoke the feeling of antiquity and authority. If it had been phrased in modern English, it would not have helped to carry conviction. It is a feature of scriptural material that it has to evoke the authority of the past; God is seen as ancient, so any language relevant to him must be antique and verging on obsolete. On that basis, it is a shame that Smith did not make an attempt at some Hebrew poetry, but he may not have understood what that was. It is only recently that we have become aware of the nature of Hebrew poetry as a very special genre. The same goes for wisdom literature: there is nothing like Job, Proverbs or Ecclesiastes that delve into the deeper questions of life, such as theodicy and predestination. It would indeed have required a literary genius to make a really convincing pastiche of Biblical literature in its full range. Smith is not of that calibre.

Another aspect of dealing with the Bible is the element of textual criticism. Since the Bible grew over many centuries and was the work of copyist scribes, long before the age of printing, we have various minor versions with textual aberrations. This is only to be expected and indicates that the work is a human document as well as of divine inspiration. Very few of the textual differences make any real difference to the main gist of the message. But with the Book of Mormon, there are no textual deviations. It is all one work from start to finish, and solidified by being put into print straight away. There is no tradition of development here. It is the work of just one man. The implication in this is that one has to make one's mind up whether Smith was genuinely inspired by God or whether he was just a plain fraud. Just talking about the brass plates is irrelevant here; the evidence is in the book itself.

In general, the literary style is unnecessarily repetitive, which recalls the style of Ezekiel at times, but otherwise it is a serious waste of space. This is something that the Biblical writers could not afford to do; papyrus was expensive and there was a limit on how long a scroll could be. Clearly the Book of Mormon does not have this problem to contend with; these brass plates must have been very large, about the size of a tennis court to have contained all of this book!

Mathematic information

There is much use of figures in the Book of Mormon, mainly concerning dates. It begins at 600 BC, which forms a kind of datum point for the Mormon separation from Jerusalem. In 1 Nephi 10:4 we have '... 600 years from the time that my father left Jerusalem, a prophet would the Lord God raise up among the Jews, even a Messiah... a saviour of the world.' The scheme of dating is kept up consistently by footnotes through the 'historical' developments, including the sea voyage to America in 588 BC. When we come to the reign of the Judges, when the Nephites and the Lamanites begin to fight each other, 91 BC is cited. The years of the judges are carefully cited until we come to the birth of Jesus Christ. Nine years later the Nephites begin to reckon their time from when the sign was given (3 Nephi 5:8). Thus we see the need for a datum point in history, finding that 600 BC is superseded. This claim in effect means that America had delineated 1 AD as the start of the Christian era long before the Council of Nicaea had addressed itself to the question. Smith does not indicate whether all these dates were on the brass plates or whether they were his own calculations added at the bottom of each page.

Ironically, as the Old World made its calculations a slight mistake is thought to have crept in. Dennis Exiguus is believed to have slipped up by four years, which means that we now reckon Jesus to have been born in 4 BC, or possibly even earlier! Smith does not come to grips with this issue.

Another interesting mathematical aspect is the citation of weights and measures. Alma 11:5-19 goes into some detail about gold and silver values in relation to commodities. So we hear about a 'senine of gold, a seon, a shum and a limnah' and a whole list of others. This is all very fascinating but almost certainly pure fiction. None of these values appear in the Old Testament; moreover, we would expect the mention of shekels, minas, and ephahs, if these people were really a Jewish contingent from the Old World. The partial explanation is given in verse 4, where 'the Nephites did not reckon after the manner of the Jews' but changed them 'according to the minds and circumstances of the people... having been established by King Mosiah.' The truth is that quantities like this were not known in the New World until the coming of the Europeans in the sixteenth century. It can be seen as an attempt, by Smith, to give realism and detail to an otherwise rather tedious and repetitive account of one battle after another.

Geographical information and the relationship to known places

Jerusalem is the only place that is recognisable from both the Bible and the Book of Mormon. After that, we are left with a vague impression of how the escapees arrived at the Atlantic seaboard; was it via North Africa or via Europe? Once in America there are many interesting place names cited, none of which bear any relationship to known places now. 'The city of Nephehah', 'the waters of Sebus' and the 'city of Zarahemla' are all very fascinating but are probably the product of a fertile imagination. The lands to the north, which receive repeated expeditions to explore them, are never described in sufficient detail to make out if this is Hudson Bay or Alaska or even Newfoundland.

Historical material and its relationship to known events

The Book of Mormon is nearly all historical account. Dates are provided as a footnote all the way through, starting about 600 BC and finishing about 421 AD. The gist of it is that in the last days before Jerusalem was defeated by the Babylonians, a contingent of Jews set off into the wilderness in order to avoid what was going wrong in the city and start again somewhere else. Somehow they built a ship and managed to cross the Atlantic Ocean and start a colony on the eastern coast of America. After many tussles with the Indians (called Lamanites) they were eventually all destroyed. In addition to this, it is also claimed that another expedition set out for America some time after the first one. The date, in the time of King Mosiah, about 130 BC, has a contingent of Jaredites building eight barges to cross the Atlantic. The way they are described reminds us of the first submarines which began to appear in the nineteenth century. They were built 'tight' so that the people inside were sealed in; this way the barges could be covered with water and not sink. One would hardly think that that the technology for such a boat was available in the Ancient World. The book does not explain how the passengers could avoid being suffocated. Strangely, the Jaredites and the Nephites, though landing on the same part of America, never seem to encounter one another. However, certain brass plates with writing on,

191

recording these events, were hidden and remained so until Joseph Smith, by angelic guidance, rediscovered them in 1821. He translated the plates, behind a curtain, and only a few people saw them. Their names are recorded in the Preface of the Book of Mormon. We are not able to inspect the plates, assess their quality, or still less try to analyse the strange writing upon them.

In Mormon 9:32-33 it discusses the language on the plates, but we are still none the wiser:

> '... we have written this record according to our knowledge in the characters which are called among us the reformed Egyptian, being handed down and altered by us, according to the manner of speech. And if our plates had been sufficiently large we would have written in Hebrew, but the Hebrew hath been altered by us... none other people knoweth our language... '

Just what 'reformed Egyptian' is, is an interesting question. We are familiar with hieroglyphics, and also that they were changed into a kind of cursive in the later years, as is seen on the Rosetta Stone[5]. That was discovered some time before Smith's literary production. Just what he means by Hebrew 'being altered by us' is an interesting question; is he talking about Aramaic? But that would have taken up as much space of the plates, as the alphabet was the same. Unless we can have sight of these 'alleged plates' we cannot really decide on what strange language this was.

The connection with the last days of Judah is obviously an attempt to give these accounts some sort of basis of truth. We know that there were contingents of Jews that escaped off to Egypt, taking Jeremiah with them, to avoid the Exile. But that is where the Mormon story grows in incredulity. Would it have been possible at that time in history, to construct a ship capable of crossing the Atlantic? Highly unlikely! The Mormons themselves have to admit that there is no independent evidence such as archaeological findings or references in other written material. The idea that there was a full-blown Jewish community, complete with synagogues, temples and 'churches', located in America long before the arrival of Columbus, is highly unlikely. When assessing the Bible, we are accustomed to be able to relate many remarks to actual findings in Israel and further afield. This has had the effect of corroborating many aspects of the Bible, but not so with the Book of Mormon. The best the Mormons can do is to refer to the alleged discovery of a stone box (an ossuary) near Persepolis. It contained gold and silver plates, inscribed in three languages. They claim it relates to Darius 1st, 588 BC, but this date is wrong: Darius came after Cyrus in 521 BC. It would seem that Smith found a similar stone box with his plates inside; this is held to corroborate their authenticity. But of course it does not. Ossuary boxes like this were commonplace in the Ancient World, although they did not normally contain gold plates.

It may be true that the witnesses saw the plates, but that does not mean that they were genuine. Smith could have forged them himself. We are left with the feeling that the whole 'history' is an elaborate concoction, complete with a number of fairly obvious anachronisms.

Another aspect of the Book of Mormon is what might be called the 'single account method'. In the Bible we often have two or more accounts of the same events, placed side by side. Clearly different authors are involved. An example of this is the J, E, D and P analysis of the Pentateuch. The same thing happens in the books of Samuel and the Kings. With Maccabees it appears in two separate books. The gospels appear in four separate versions. This means that each writer can describe things in his own way and from his own viewpoint. This way, the whole thing is much more honest and open for people to come to their own conclusions. None of this occurs in the Book of Mormon; we are only seeing the view of one man, namely Joseph Smith.

Theological considerations

The basic question with Mormonism is that of an additional corpus of scripture, the assumption being that the Bible is not enough. This dilemma is tackled, rather shakily, in 2 Nephi 29:3-12. We are accustomed in the Judaeo-Christian tradition to assume a feature called 'canon-closure' by which we mean that the Bible has been limited to certain selected books and cannot be added to. The Council of Jamnia in 90 AD settled the Old Testament; the Council of Laodicea in 420 AD decided on the New Testament.

However, the justification for the book of Mormon is tackled by Smith:

'Many of the Gentiles shall say, "A Bible! A Bible! We have got a Bible, and there cannot be any more Bible"' (2 Nephi 29:3).

But Smith goes on to say, in verse 10, '… because ye have a Bible ye need not suppose that it contains all my words; neither need ye suppose that I have not caused more to be written.' He goes on to say that God is capable of inspiring all manner of people to 'write all the words which I speak unto them' (2 Nephi 23:6). ' I shall speak unto the Jews and they shall write it; I shall speak unto the Nephites and they shall write it.' The same goes for the other tribes of Israel that have gone into Exile, and also all the nations of the world. He does not go on to specify, but this could be a vague way of saying that all the other sacred writings of the world have their validity. Does this mean that the

Koran, the Rig Veda, and the Avestas are all valid as scripture? Interesting!

One implication in this is that the Nephite writings and the Bible issue basically the same theological teachings. Although there is certain degree of truth in this, it is not the entire truth. The Book of Mormon is an attempt at a pastiche of the Bible, but in some respects fails to understand the essentials of Judaeo-Christian teaching. In many respects it has the tone of the Koran.

This is most clearly seen in the concept of the covenant, a metaphor that is essential for any understanding of the Bible. The word occurs several times in the Book of Mormon, usually referring to an agreement between people or individuals. In Alma 44:14 we have a remark which goes 'and depart with a covenant of peace', clearly borrowed phraseology from Ezekiel[6]. But on one occasion it is claimed that the Nephites made a covenant with God: 'Now this was the covenant which they made... we covenant with our God that we shall be destroyed... if we shall fall into transgression' Alma 46:22. This is actually contrary to the covenant procedure in the Bible. In all the covenants described, that of Noah, Abraham, Moses, David and of Jesus, it is God who initiates the agreement: the believer does not but only accepts and gives thanks. Smith has misunderstood a vital part of Biblical theology.

With regard to belief in God, there is a passage in Alma 18:18-30 where the reality of God is discussed, and it is similarly discussed in the whole of Chapter 18. King Lamoni, who appears to be one of the Indians, mistakes Ammon for the 'Great Spirit'. This is a touch of reality, since the Indians did call God the 'Great White Spirit'. However, Ammon assures Lamoni that there is a God, not Ammon himself. Now belief in God as the great creator is brought out and in verse 36, goes on to discuss the creation of Adam and the Fall. It would be slightly anachronistic to call Smith a Bible fundamentalist, since at that time practically everyone took Genesis 1-2 at face value, the theory of Evolution not having been proposed by Darwin (see also 2 Nephi 2:18-23). In other places there is frequent mention of the Holy Spirit as inspiring the prophets and also of the Son of God as imminent but also working with the Father in creation from eternity. This is fair enough as Trinitarian theology; moreover, nowhere does Smith go into analytical details as to how this worked. The relationship between Father, Son and Holy Spirit is left undiscussed (3 Nephi 11:27). This is in contrast to what happened in the early church: they became embroiled in Trinitarian disputes, which eventually led to the formulation of the major creeds. There is nothing here equivalent to the creeds. What it does imply is that the New World had a Trinitarian understanding of God long before the Old World did. Is that realistic? But we are reassured that the Father, Son and Holy Spirit are a unity, very much the orthodox Christian position (3 Nephi 11:27).

'... that the Father Son and Holy Ghost are one; and I am in the Father, and the Father in me, and the Father and I are one.' This is said by the risen

Jesus as he appeared to the Nephites in America. As far as the Incarnation is concerned, Smith does not go into details about that, except to give us an indication of Jesus' humanity, even after he is risen:

'... and when he had done this he wept again...' This is Jesus blessing the children. In 3 Nephi 11:14, the crowd are invited to touch his body, feeling his wound and the nail marks. This can hardly have been done with a phantom or apparition. So the Incarnation is a reality, not some sort of pretence as the Gnostics would have maintained.

In contrast with this there is a passage that sounds almost like some sort of Gnosticism, although it does not directly concern Jesus. In 3 Nephi 29:36-40, we have three special 'apostles' who are not to die but carry on until Christ appears again. The remark '... I know not whether they are cleansed from mortality to immortality... there must needs be a change wrought upon their bodies or else... they must taste death.' As we know, the Gnostics believed that the flesh was corrupt and could not be redeemed; is Smith admitting that human flesh is in need of cleansing? This may be a slight touch of Gnostic thought, though not very thoroughgoing.

In Ether 3:16 Jesus appears again to the Jaredites. This appears to be an attempt at explaining the Incarnation:

'Behold this body which ye now behold is the body of my spirit; and even as I appear unto thee to be in the spirit I will appear to my people in the flesh.'

It is claimed that it was the 'same body' with which he showed himself to the Nephites. This appears to be a rather crude attempt at discussing the Incarnation. But nowhere does Smith appear to deny the reality of Christ's flesh.

One of the problems with Christianity is the question of particularity. This issue concerns the fact that Jesus Christ came to the Incarnation at a specific time and place in history, namely the Land of Israel in the period 1–33 AD or thereabouts. This has seemed unfair not only for those who lived before his time in the BC era, but also those who lived in far away countries where they did not have a chance to know about Jesus. The Book of Mormon and indeed the whole mentality of Mormonism tackles this problem in its own way. In effect it is saying that Jesus Christ was known in the Americas at the same time as in Israel, and even before. There seems to be no concern about other far-flung countries such as Australia, Japan, Oceania and many others. But it is probably a part of the American hubris that Jesus had to have been involved with their early development, actually before he did arrive. The crucial passage is in Helaman 16:18:

'... it is not reasonable that such a being as a Christ shall come; if so, and he be the Son of God,... why will he not show himself unto us as well as unto them who shall be at Jerusalem[1]?, and verse 20: '... for we cannot witness with our own eyes that they be true... '

Smith does not really answer this question at this point, except to say that such ideas are foolish and vain; he does not actually say why. What he does do is describe remarkable signs of the Saviour's coming in 3 Nephi 1:15-21. One day, at evening, there was no darkness all through that night, and people began to realise that the prophecies were coming true, and that the Christ would shortly appear. Also 'a new star did appear'; this is clearly a reference to the Star of Bethlehem. Also, in 32 AD we have a massive storm with thunder and earthquakes, and three hours of darkness; 3 Nephi 8:1-9ff. Also there was a prophet called Samuel who did miracles in the name of Jesus (verse 1). Smith goes to some length to emphasise the truth of this; 'we know our record to be true, for behold it was a just man who did keep the record.' All these disasters are seen to coincide with the crucifixion – all this had been prophesied by the prophet Samuel.

But the full answer comes in 3 Nephi 11:1-10. Firstly there is a voice coming from heaven, three times over. Then the crowd saw a man in white descending from heaven and announcing himself as Jesus Christ, the Light of the World. This happened three times with vast numbers of people seeing him. Also, he spoke specifically to twelve disciples and delineated three of them never to die. Also the name of the church is discussed and decided upon. This is quite a massive claim, that the risen Christ appeared to the Americans at the same time as the resurrection appearances were happening in the land of Israel. However, it is not out of the question. The only problem with it is whether Smith is just inventing it. But it is his answer to the problem of particularity.

All this had been prophesied by the prophet Samuel the Lamanite: the star, the three days of darkness. Helaman 14:1-17 goes into detail about how the death and resurrection of Jesus will bring salvation to all mankind.

'... the resurrection of Christ redeemeth mankind, yea, even all mankind, and bringeth them back into the presence of the Lord' (3 Nephi 14:17).

This is not the only place where universality of salvation is outlined. Consider Helaman 3:28, '... we see that the gate of Heaven is open to all.'

The only caveat in this is that although everybody is redeemed from the first death (the spiritual death), there is also the second death if one fails to be repentant and accept God's salvation. What went wrong in the Garden of Eden is reversed by the death and resurrection of Jesus Christ. However, it is now up to everyone to accept it and repent, otherwise they will be damned. So while we have an attempt at answering the question of particularity, we are still left with the problem of people coming to know about the salvation provided for them. Smith has the Americans going in for repentance; he does not mention the thought that there are millions of people in other parts of the world who have not had these amazing signs and wonders. This of course explains the Mormon missionary zeal in attempting to inform people all over the world of the message.

The concept of 'first death' and 'second death' may not be a major New Testament concept, as Smith portrays it. The phrase is only found in Revelation, in four references[7]. It seems to refer firstly to the conversion to Christ when one becomes a priest or a king to God. One then has no fear of the second death, which it seems is one's earthly death. Revelation goes in for high drama and exaggeration, but Smith is taking it all literally, about hellfire and damnation. What he fails to see is that there is a profound paradox at work here; on the one hand, the whole of humanity is saved by the life and death of Jesus, and that applies to all, regardless of whether they have actually heard or understood what he came to show us. On the other hand, there is judgement and everyone has to face up to God and account for his deeds. This paradox is beyond human explanation; it has however confused many Christians and many a non-Christian over the centuries. Even so, this is an example of how Smith has taken an element from a certain context in the New Testament, namely Revelation, and turned it into a major strand. And yet this is balanced by a much gentler and more sensitive remark in Helaman 12:1:

'… we can behold how false, and also the unsteadiness of the hearts of the children of men; yea, we can see that the Lord in his great infinite goodness doth bless and prosper those who put their trust in him.'

We can see this as another major paradox: although there is judgement and the tough side of God, he is also very much aware of human frailty and takes these matters into consideration. Judgement and mercy are always juxtaposed; the paradox is not easy for us to cope with. Only God can analyse it.

Another major strand in the Bible is the roles of prophet, priest and king; all these are intermediaries between mankind and God. Smith has very little time for priests; he is very much in favour of equality, and priesthood would imply some sort of inequality. Priests only receive scant mention. The same goes for kings; he has very little time for them, in fact, they are seen in a negative light, with sarcastic remarks made about them. But prophets are the dominant aspect of the Book of Mormon. He begins by roping in the early prophets such as Isaiah and Jeremiah. He quotes vast amounts of Isaiah on the subject of the Suffering Servant. People like Ezekiel and Daniel are not mentioned: rightly so, since they came after the departure from Jerusalem in 600 BC. All the same, there is probably an allusion to Daniel with the fiery furnace when Nephi and Lehi were in the midst of a flaming fire, which did not harm them (Helamen 5:44). This reminds us of the three holy children in the fiery furnace[8].

This heavy emphasis on prophecy gives a rather unbalanced view of truth. In the Bible, the three elements of prophet, priest and king are subtlety balanced and interplay with each other. Moses and Aaron are a case in point; also Abraham and Melchizedek; also David and his entourage of prophets. As we know from Jeremiah, the factor of false prophecy was, and still is, a matter of concern. There is only one context in which 'a false prophet' is mentioned but Smith does not discuss it, and still less does he consider that it might apply to himself. As we know, there can be false prophets and false kings; but the interplay and balancing between the three elements of leadership in faith, manage to stabilise the situation. A good example of that would be King David, as a brilliant charismatic leader of men, champion of the faith and spiritually gifted, and yet committed the Bath Sheba incident; it took a prophet called Nathan to correct him on that matter. We all have our failings; we all need correction from somewhere. That is the relevance of mercy as juxtaposed with judgement.

If we understand this passage in Helaman 5:10, it sounds as if we have to be repentant of sin before Jesus will come and save us.

'... the Lord surely should come to redeem his people, but that he should not come to redeem them IN their sins but to redeem them from their sins... '

This runs the risk of contradicting the New Testament. St Paul says that 'God shows his love for us in that while we were yet sinners, Christ died for us... while we were enemies, we were reconciled to God by the death of his Son...' (Romans 5:8-10).

In other words, God did not wait for us to get it right before Jesus came; he came in mercy beforehand and effected his salvation for us all, whether we knew about it, wanted it or were inclined to accept it. If he had waited for us all to be repentant in advance, he would have had a long wait, as is evidenced in the events in the Book of Mormon!

With regard to prophecy, it is interesting that in Alma 9:21 we have an outline of the gifts of the spirit, very much in line with New Testament thinking:

'... visited by the spirit of God... having the spirit of prophecy, and the spirit of revelation, and also many gifts, the gift of speaking with tongues, and the gift of preaching, and the gift of the Holy Ghost, and the gift of translation.'

Here we see that the phenomenon of glossolalia[9], which is now reappearing in the Church in recent times, is mentioned in 82 BC long before the first Whit Sunday. Is this another anachronism? The corrective to this lies in St Paul's classic passage in 1 Corinthians:

'If I speak in the tongues of men and angels, but have not love, I am a noisy gong or a clanging cymbal... love never ends. As for prophecies, they will pass away; as for tongues they will cease; as for knowledge it will pass away... so faith, hope and love abide, these three; but the greatest of these is love.'

It is a matter of regret that these three are rather meagre in their mention in the Book of Mormon, though not entirely absent. Love, of God and of believing souls, is really quite scarce. There is much emphasis on threat, violence, damnation and all the worrying aspects of faith. One wonders if this 'prophet' actually does love God and man?

With regard to theodicy, Smith is quite at home with the traditional notion of heaven, hell and the Devil. This is actually discussed in 2 Nephi 28:22 where there is the possibility of there being no hell and no devil. This is pure deception, in his opinion. Satan is mentioned in many places in the Book of Mormon, which indicates that Dualism, as seen in the New Testament, is his answer to the problem of pain and death. Verse 23 mentions that all those that have been seized by the Devil will 'go into the place prepared for them, even a lake of fire and brimstone, which is endless torment.' This is clearly a quotation from Revelation and indicates that Smith took this work purely at face value and literally. This could be seen as the reassertion of dualistic values in the face of the so-called 'Age of Reason', which involved the denial or serious questioning of Calvinistic ideas and literalistic acceptance of the mythology of the Bible.

With regard to the sacraments, Smith is in favour of just two: Baptism and the Eucharist. In 3 Nephi 18:1-9 we have Jesus instituting the Communion, using bread and wine. It is a scene recalling the Feeding of the Five Thousand. We notice that wine is used, not water. The Mormons now use water; they are very strict about the use of drugs, alcohol being one of them. Nowhere in the Book of Mormon is there any comment about drugs. There is great strictness about people receiving communion unworthily; anyone who is wicked is to be excommunicated and ejected from the Church. There is also a certain strictness about Baptism. This is specified in Moroni 6:1-5. People were not accepted for Baptism unless 'they brought forth fruit meet that they were worthy of it.' In other words, one had to merit it. With regard to child baptism, Smith is very much against it. In Moroni 8:9 Smith says, 'it is a solemn mockery before God that ye should baptise little children.' He thinks little children do not need to repent since they cannot have committed any sin. They are innocent. 'Little children are alive in Christ'. With this we see that there is no suggestion of original sin. Does this mean that Smith was originally a Baptist? With regard to other ceremonies and procedures at church, Smith has very little to say, except in tones that recall the church of Rome, he says, 'come unto me; and for your money you shall be forgiven your sins.' Is this a reference to Indulgences, a problem that sparked off the Reformation in 1519? (Mormon 8:32). Also in 8:37 he talks about 'fine apparel' and the 'adorning of your churches'. Is this a reference to high-churchmanship?

With regard to marriage, which Smith does not appear to class as a sacrament, he says very little. In Ether 10:5, he is very condemnatory about a man who had many wives and concubines:

'... Riplakish did not do that which is right in the sight of the Lord, for he did have many wives and concubines... and did lay that upon men's shoulders...'

Other than that there is no mention of polygamy in the Book of Mormon, which is strange, since the early Mormons did embark on polygamy, only to have to stop it when Utah wanted to join the USA. Even so, there are isolated incidents of it still prevailing in Utah, but not on an official basis.

Philosophical aspects

It is something of a surprise that bits of logic and philosophy are worked into the Book of Mormon, but as with all human literature, it must be seen against the background of its day, and in this case, it is the early nineteenth century, as opposed to the mentality of a supposed Jewish community in contention with the American Indians.

In 2 Nephi 2:13, we have an interesting piece of chop logic. To quote in full:

'... if we say there is no law... there is no sin... if there is no sin... there is no righteousness... if there is no righteousness there be no happiness... and if there be no righteousness nor happiness there be no punishment nor misery. And if these things are not, there is no God. And if there is no God we are not, neither the earth for there could have been no creation of things, neither to act nor to be acted upon, wherefore all things must have vanished away.'

This interesting compound syllogism corners us into believing in God, but of course, most of it is entirely circular (meaning 'begging the question').

200

At least two 'proofs' for the existence of God are involved here. Firstly the Kantian idea that happiness is to be equated with moral correctitude. At that time, Kant would have been a novelty in the world of theology and philosophy and this passage is a reverberation of this thinking. It would hardly have been the thought of Jewish settlers in America about 570 BC. Also the teleological argument by Aquinas is hinted at; how could there be anything at all unless there were a God to start things off? Needless to say, the Bible never embarks on this line of argument. This passage assumes the philosophy of Greece as it was embellished and adapted through the Middle Ages, into the Enlightenment and to Smith's own times, when it was felt necessary to attempt to 'prove' the existence of God.

On the issue of free will as opposed to predestination, Smith points out that we have the freedom to make a choice between good and bad (2 Nephi 2:27):

> '... men are free according to the flesh... they are free to choose liberty and eternal life... or to choose captivity and death.'

On the other hand, Smith makes frequent mention of 'a plan of redemption', which has been prepared 'from the foundation of the world'. He does not seem to use the word 'predestination' as Calvin would have, but we have much mention of God's foreknowledge. An example of this would be in Alma 13:3-10 – this is tantamount to talking about predestination. St Paul would have termed it such, but Smith seems to have toned it down just a little. This may be under the influence of the liberalistic ideas of the Enlightenment.

This leads us on to the question of 'liberty', a red-hot issue in Smith's day. He makes frequent mention of liberty and often in a context that implies that the opposite involves having a king. Alma 52:5-6 juxtaposes free government with monarchy:

> '... those who were desirous that Pahoran should be dethroned from the judgement seat were called 'King men' for they wanted to overthrow the free government and have a king over the land... '

The ones who wanted to keep Pahoran as chief judge called themselves 'freemen... because they wanted their rights and privileges of their religion by a free government.' The outcome of this was that the freemen won the argument and there was no monarchy. Elsewhere, the 'king men' are shown in a rather jaded light. Alma 60:16 has them being blamed for all the bloodshed; they wanted to take power and authority over the Nephites rather than uniting the people against their enemies, the Lamanites. The phrase 'a friend to liberty' occurs often, and 'a free people' too. Clearly Smith is talking with the backdrop of the American War of Independence, which had only recently been settled, and also the French Revolution in which an absolutist king had been deposed and a republic declared. The Enlightenment did serve as a basis for such 'free thinking'. This shows through in the Book of Mormon. Of course, nowadays, monarchy in a constitutional setting is seen as a guarantee of religious and political freedom. It just shows how times and people's views alter with circumstances.

Another strand or assumption in the Book of Mormon is the racist attitude. It is a background assumption but occasionally breaks the surface. Having a black skin is taken to mean that one is under a curse. This is spelt out in 2 Nephi 5:21-25:

> '... .and he caused a cursing to come upon them (the Lamanites) wherefore as they were white and exceedingly fair and delightsome ... the Lord did cause a skin of blackness to come upon them... .'

Moreover, intermarriage with coloured people is inviting a curse:

> '... and cursed be the seed of him that mixeth with their seed, for they shall be cursed... and because of their cursing... they became an idle people full of mischief and subtlety...'

Are black people inclined to be idle and corrupt? What a prejudice! In 2 Nephi 30:6, we have the strange idea that as people are converted to Christ, their blackness fades out and they become white. 'They shall become a white and delightsome people.' It does not seem to occur to Smith that the Jews would hardly have been 'white', more likely coffee-coloured, and that Jesus himself would hardly be termed 'white'. But then those of a racist mentality find it difficult to think of Jesus as anything other than white European, or Aryan. This was a trait seen in *Mein Kampf*.

In Jacob 3:8 we have the prospect of the Lamanites becoming whiter than the Nephites, since they are more inclined to repent. We also have the equation between blackness and filthiness in verse 9, which exemplifies the depth of prejudice that white people have over a dark skin. To his credit, Smith says we should no longer revile them because of their skin, since they inherit it from their fathers, so it cannot be their fault. Rather, we should be aware of our own filthiness.

In 3 Nephi 2:15, we have the interesting and incredible situation where the Lamanites, as they repent and join in with the Nephites, that 'their skin became white like unto the Nephites; their young men and their daughters became exceedingly fair and they were numbered among the Nephites.' This meant that the 'curse' was removed from them. This is a step higher up than Mein Kampf; Hitler would have said that one cannot alter race, since it is literally in the blood, not the outward appearance.

It is not clear whether Smith was thinking of the black American slave population of the eastern states when he wrote about them being under a curse and filthy. Of course it is easy to condemn people for being dirty if they have no chance of having proper washing facilities, and have to live in a cabin like 'Uncle Tom'. It is another circular argument; racism usually does thrive on begging the question. But we can see this element in context in the 1820s: black slavery was still the norm in the USA and was one of the basic aspects of the Civil War which was forty years in the future. To think that black people were in America in the years before Christ is a crazy anachronism, since we know that they were shipped across the Atlantic in slave ships in the eighteenth century. Smith does not seem to discuss the fact that the Indians (the Lamanites?) were redskins, but he probably regarded them as coloured too. But the basic assumption that only white people can be proper Christians is total rubbish. Mormonism has had this racist undercurrent; still does to this day to some extent. Needless to say, the Bible has none of this attitude; there is no mention of colour as a method of segregation. St Paul goes so far as to say that there is no slave nor free, Jew nor Greek etc. Moreover, it is quite likely that Simon of Cyrene was a black man and he was accepted by Jesus to carry his cross. This also, indirectly, may indicate that someone from Cyrene, in the deep south of Egypt, could be accepted as Jewish at the Passover observances.

Related to racial discrimination is class-consciousness. In 4 Nephi 4:25-26, we see the Nephites becoming too rich for their own good and this results in them having 'their substance no more in common among them; and they began to be divided into classes'. It was all about gain and greed, forgetting the essentials of Christianity, namely sharing. Clearly Smith is in favour of social equality. This is again a symptom of the American constitution; all have equal right, except of course for the African Americans!

Just in case one were to think that the Nephites were interlopers in America, Smith provides a justification for their invasion and settlement which must have deprived the Lamanites of their lands. In 3 Nephi 15:13, he has Jesus saying to them:

'... this is the land of your inheritance, and the Father has given it to you...'

This notion is repeated, giving it emphasis. So in 3 Nephi 16:16 he says 'the Father hath commanded me... that I should give unto this people this land for their inheritance.' It has further ramifications, as in 3 Nephi 21:23-24, this land of inheritance will have a new Jerusalem built, and it will attract all the people of God scattered about the earth, including the tribes of Israel that have been lost (from the Northern Kingdom?). The idea is that there will be one church with Christians united, a noble thought, but not helped by Smith starting up a new denomination with a cranky 'Bible' as its basis. Smith does not go on to specify whether this New Jerusalem will be Salt Lake city in Utah, but that is where the Mormons did establish themselves and their central headquarters are there to this day. This is of course evidence that the white settlers in America had the thought at the back of their minds that they did not have a particularly firm claim on the land. To make out that Jesus had given it to them would have been really quite reassuring!

In contrast to thoughts about 'liberty' (Ether 13:18), Smith comes out with some strange remarks about 'secret society'. Ether 11:22 is one such place; also 2 Nephi 9:9. He talks about 'secret combinations', which seems strange for these people in 559 BC. Is he talking about political parties, or possibly something like the Ku Klux Klan? Smith does not like disagreements or arguments. It is possible that he is thinking about the political situation in America as their democracy is developing. He does not like kings; nor political parties; he seems to want a theocratic arrangement with 'judges' ruling the community. In Helaman 1:2 there is a dispute over who is to be the next judge; it caused three divisions among the people. In the end some sort of election settled the matter, but the loser was dissatisfied. In the end he had to be condemned to death because 'he had sought to destroy the liberty of the people'. Even then the matter was not resolved without bloodshed. We can sense that Smith would have liked all this to have been settled conclusively without bloodshed.

Mythological aspects

There is very little that can be taken as mythological in the Book of Mormon; at least what we would call mythological. It is true that Smith often refers to the Creation and the Garden of Eden, but then he is taking it literally and would probably not have understood it being classed as 'myth'. The same is true for the eschatological element, which is the counterpart of creation mythology. He has a strong impression of the end of time, the day of the Lord. Mormon 8:26-34 is a prime example of it, but nothing like as vivid as anything in the gospels or Revelation. Again, he would be taking this as literal truth and not mythological. For us, it might be possible to take the two ships as crossing the Atlantic as mythical; Smith would be taking it literally, but we can see all manner of problems with the practicality of it. All the same, these voyages do recall Noah's Ark and also the Moses basket in the Nile: the faithful are saved by boats and water. The same configuration occurs in the Gospels, where Jesus and the disciples take a boat-trip on the Sea of Galilee. Other than that, the mythological element is greatly understated, which gives the impression that the message of Mormonism is just a historical development as opposed to a cosmically important scheme enacted by the world of the spirit. Perhaps this is a symptom of the Enlightenment with its liberalistic ideas.

Conclusions on the Book of Mormon

Essentially, Mormonism justifies itself with reference to John 10:16, which says: 'I have other sheep that are not of this fold; I must bring them also and they will heed my voice.' Normally we take that to mean that Jesus is talking about the Gentile world in general; the 'other sheep' are the non-Jews in the Ancient World. The Book of Mormon stretches the meaning of this to mean the two contingents of Jews who sailed across the Atlantic and started up a colony in the BC period. We have to decide whether or not this is a fair interpretation.

Smith would doubtless say that this book is the TRUTH. A useful quotation comes in Moroni 10:4-5:

'... he will manifest the truth of it unto you by the power of the Holy Ghost... .ye may know the truth of all things.'

Coming near the end, this is balanced by another remark at the beginning: 1 Nephi 1:3; 'I know that the record I make is true... '

On the face of it, this is quite a claim, but as we know, truth comes at varying levels and quantities. An important question for us all is whether this book is the literal truth or the figurative truth. We can see that the Bible is a mixture of many elements of truth; much of it can be taken as metaphoric; some of it is clearly historical truth. The Bible does not tell us when it switches from the one to the other. Is it possible to view the Book of Mormon in the same light? The Mormons will doubtless take both books completely at face value; what is now known as Bible fundamentalism. Is it realistic to accept that two contingents of Jews managed to land in America and establish a colony with synagogues, churches and temples?

Is it possible to see the Book of Mormon from the point of view of what it is actually saying? In theological and philosophical terms it has a lot to say; not that one would necessarily agree with it. Much of this has been discussed before. But the essentials of it could be listed as follows.

Firstly, the remnant element. This is an important strand in Old Testament thinking. When the people of God have gone astray, there is always the faithful few who refuse to be taken in by falsehood. They are the ones who make a fresh start. This is a recurring theme in the Scriptures. With the Book of Mormon we see two contingents of Jews who did not wish to be corrupted, set out to start afresh somewhere else. Does this actually work? What happened in the end was that although Jesus came to visit them in America, they all faded out, leaving the brass plates buried, only to be found by Joseph Smith in 1820. This is an interesting permutation on the remnant theology. Doubtless the Mormons will claim that they are the true remnant, with the true Jerusalem in Salt Lake City. What does that mean for all the other Christian churches in the world: they too are just as clear in their minds about their adherence to Christ.

Going further, it is clear that Smith is a strong supporter of his version of 'liberty'. On the face of it, no one would object to that as a political theory based on certain philosophical basics. However, he cannot see liberty as working with monarchy. Is he saying that true Christianity is essentially connected with republicanism? Is he taking into account that many countries work with a monarchy that guarantees the Christian faith? In that regard, he is a child of his age, the age of a newly emerging republic in the USA.

A hint as to the importance of this newly-emerging civilisation could be seen in the fact that the Jaredites, at the time of King Mosiah (130 BC), had encounters with Jesus, both in the Old World and the New. Is this a symbolic way of saying that the Americans anticipated the coming of Jesus and were actually ahead of the Jews and Christians in Palestine? This does not quite work with regard to the Nephites who had encounters with Jesus at the same time as the crucifixion and resurrection. What is this saying? It could be that it is saying that their version of Christianity is just as valid as that found in the Old World; possibly more valid since the Americans were not encumbered with kings and emperors.

An important element in Christianity is 'justification by faith', as described by St Paul[10]. This does not appear to figure in Smith's thinking. He is heavily involved with the Mosaic covenant mentality; do good and you are blessed; do bad and you are cursed. This takes no account of the important Biblical strand, that God loves all mankind and blesses them, even if they have gone wrong. In this way, Smith is deeply involved with Old Testament thinking; this is in spite of all he has to say about Jesus Christ being a reality in the life of these settlers. It looks very much as if he does not really understand the New Testament. Is this essentially yet another version of Judaism, with Messianism tacked on? It may be symptomatic that Smith does not actually mention the term 'New Testament'.

So what would be the point of having Jesus appear in the New World? The substratum of the whole book is that there has to be some sort of justification for the settlers taking the land from the Indians (Lamanites?). Obviously there must have been some sort of conscience about dispossessing the native population. If it could be shown that Jesus had sanctioned and blessed the Jewish settlers from the Old World that would give some sort of justification for it. Now we see the point of tacking on Messianism. Also we see the point of the plates being hidden for so many centuries, only to be found by Smith just at the moment when the American continent was being rapidly colonised by European immigrants; they could rest assured that God had sanctioned the invasion and also had been in agreement with cutting loose from British rule which involved monarchy.

Unfortunately, the whole matter is confused by the alleged plates with their strange antique language, as well as the two fantastic trips across the Atlantic. But if we see beyond this bit of superstructure, the motives and the real message of the Book of Mormon can be analysed. It is then up to the individual believer to decide on where the basic truth really lies.

Notes for Chapter 11: The Book of Mormon

1. A list of names is given in the Book of Mormon; Christian Whitmer, Jacob Whitmer, Peter Whitmer, John Whitmer, Hiram Page, Joseph Smith senior, Hyrum Smith, Samuel Smith. Many if them appear to be related, some to Joseph Smith. The plates were found on 23rd September 1823.
2. Liahona; this appears to be the invention of Smith.
3. The astrolabe was used in the 15th century by mariners, followed by the use of the sextant.
4. The Bible, as a complete work, only appeared quite late in the Christian era, probably with the coming of printing, which made it possible to include all the books in one volume. The word Biblos in Greek means a book.
5. The Rosetta stone; this has three lots of writing on it; Egyptian hieroglyphics, Egyptian demotic, and Greek. It hails from about 205 to 180 BC, during the reign of Ptolemy 5th Epiphanes. It was discovered at Rosetta near Alexandria, in 1799 and enabled scholars to decipher Egyptian hieroglyphics as seen on the tombs of the Pharaohs. It is possible that Smith had heard of this stone and gained the idea of writing a book based on 'reformed Egyptian'.
6. Ezekiel's mention of a 'convenant of peace' is found in Ezekiel 34:25 and 37:27
7. 'The second death'; Revelation 2:11, 20:6, 20:14 and 21:8.
8. The Three Holy Children; Daniel 3:1-25.
9. Glossolalia; 'speaking in tongues', one of the gifts of the Holy Spirit, see Acts 2:1-13.
10. Justification by faith; this is described in details by St.Paul in Romans 5:1 principally.

12

The Holy Kojiki and the Yengishiki

This is the oldest known document in the Japanese language and dates from the eighth century. It is also known as the 'Records of Ancient Matters', the official story of the Japanese peoples, the creation, the gods and how this relates to humans. The Kojiki is almost entirely mythology; this does not mean that it is all nonsense. It certainly speculates on the creation of the world, but also tells us much about human nature and how the Japanese people see themselves in relation to their gods. The Yengishiki is all liturgical as opposed to mythological, but again tells us much about human nature. This material can be seen as underpinning the Shrine Shinto traditions and to a small extent what came to be known as State Shinto, the Japanese understanding of their emperor, the Mikado. There is a certain amount of geographical information, but this is much bound up with the mythology. All references are from the Cosimo Classics publication of 2007.

Geographical information

It is interesting that amongst so much mythological material there is frequent mention of place names. The place that stands out as significant is Ise, one of the most important Shinto shrines in Japan, and the way in which it is worked into the story. Another place name that relates to reality is Anaba, a place on the north west coast. Also Cape Keta, which means 'north cape'[1]. Beyond that, nearly all the places mentioned are imaginary or antique names, which fit in with the mythological method of the work. It lends a certain touch of reality to the fantastic, dramatic and frightening antics of the gods as they fashion the Japanese lands and peoples. The unspoken geographical aspect is of course that Japan, as an island, has

208

been isolated from the land mass of Asia and in fact the rest of humanity. Whereas virtually all the other world religions have had some knowledge of each other and interchange of ideas, Shinto was the recipient of ideas coming from China, such as Buddhism, but not the other way round. There was a noted tendency for the Japanese to think of themselves as the only people on earth and their island the only territory.

Mythological Sagas

We start with the beginning of heaven and earth and the birth of the first god, the Master-of-the-August-Centre-of-Heaven. Other gods with compound names like this are produced, by birth, but there is no explanation for how they were 'born'. They seem to emanate from one another in a series. We begin with five deities and then there is another series of seven divine generations. The last two, Izanagi (the Male-who-invites) and Izanami (the Female-who-invites) will become significant for the creation of Japan itself and eventually the people.

We notice that the theologically significant numbers, five and seven are being used. Seven betokens the three levels of heaven, earth and hell, with the four corners of the earth. Seven is seen as a lucky number in Japan (just as three is in British thinking). At this point, hell is not being mentioned; that will appear later. Hell might appear to be an afterthought when death begins to creep into the story. We notice that the gods come in a series, rather like some of the Gnosticism as seen in the first century Roman Empire. They all have interesting and descriptive compound names, suggestive of their roles. The term 'August' is freely applied to many of them. Some of these names are quite amusing: Oh-Awful-Lady and Mud-Earth-Lord. Comparing this with the first two Chapters of Genesis is interesting. There we have one God, and the account begins before heaven and earth are actually formed. There is water and the Spirit of God moves over them. With the Japanese account, the water, the ocean is assumed rather than specified.

The actual formation of the land is performed by Izanagi and Izanami. They are commanded to stand on the Bridge of Heaven and push a jewelled spear down into the water, stir it up, pull it up, and the drips are piled up and form the island of Onogoro, which we take to be Japan.

There is no mention of any other land; Japan is assumed to be the central land in the world. The Bridge of Heaven, which seems to float on the water, can be assumed as the connection between heaven and earth. This idea of the connection between heaven and earth is a common feature in world mythologies; how do the gods contact humanity and vice versa. Here it is a bridge. In Ancient Rome, too, it was a bridge, and the word Pontiff meant 'bridge-builder', which is a metaphorical way of saying that the Roman

Emperor was himself the connection between the gods and humanity. Also we see the allusion to a spear with jewels. The spear (and sometimes a sword) betokens truth, putting everything to rights, the defeat of evil. Jewels are symbolic of eternity, indestructible life and the avoidance of death. This too is a common feature in world mythologies.

Izanagi and Izanami came down to earth and put up a pillar and a hall, and decided to have children. They went round the pillar and met up on the other side to copulate. She made the mistake of speaking first, 'Ah what a fair and lovable youth'. The result of this union was the 'leech-child' Hiroku. Even at the age of three he could not stand up straight. So they made him a reed boat and let him float away. They also produced the island of Aha.

This is interesting, for it gently introduces the problem of theodicy. Why is there anything wrong with the world? How do gods produce something which is not excellent, first class and fully healthy? The mistake was that the goddess spoke first – is this a way of asserting male dominance? They erect a pillar, which is suggestive of an erection. We notice that being brother and sister, this is actually incestuous, but the Kojiki does not comment on this, let alone give it as a reason for Hiroku's weakness. They stop short of murdering him; they send him off in a boat to seek his fate. Does this remind us of Moses being found in a boat in the bulrushes? We notice also that they build a hall; is this some sort of temple? We may assume it to be some sort of residence for the two gods in their 'marriage'.

Wishing to discover why Hiroku was weak, they go to the heavenly deities to enquire. They go in for divination and discover that it was because the goddess spoke first. They are advised to try again, with the god speaking first. It worked; they produced various islands, eight in number, and then another six, all of which are offshore of Japan. The number eight becomes important later on[2], appearing all kinds of permutations. In Japanese thinking, eight is auspicious, and seen as a firm base for opportunity, and also prosperity. They then go in for producing a collection of deities, thirty-five in total, by which time Izanami is literally burnt out and dies. Izanagi buries her on Mount Heba. The last god that they produce, The Shining-Elder, has his head cut off by his father using a sabre. The blood splatters around, and produces more gods, eight in number. It becomes cruder when from the corpse of the Shining-Elder emanate more gods from his belly, his private parts, his left and right hand, left and right feet. All these are symbolic of various parts of Japan.

We notice that the gods in heaven do not know the answer to the question until they use divination. Again we see the emphasis on the priority of the male over the female, a feature that is seen in the Genesis account. We have a goddess who dies; is this possible since gods are supposed to be immortal? Perhaps we are dealing with entities that are not fully divine, halfway to being human? We have the first murder; not that it is dubbed as such, but the father beheads his last son, the Fire God. Perhaps this is a roundabout way of saying that Japan is such a wonderful land, the product of the Shining-Elder. Interestingly, the first murder comes with Cain and Abel, in Genesis. The crudities compare well with Greek mythology.

Izanagi misses his 'sister-cum-wife' so he goes down into Hades to persuade her to come back. He says that the work of creation is not complete and there is more work to be done. She goes to enquire of the hell-gods and tired of waiting, he goes in to find her, only to discover that she is rotting, with maggots all over her, and she has produced eight thunder deities. He runs off back to escape hell, but she sends the Ugly-Female-of-Hades to pursue him. He manages to stave her off, but then there are 1,500 warriors of Hades chasing him. He takes out his sabre and attacks; they all flee back. He takes three peaches that are growing at the Even-Pass-of-Hades; he designates them as the Great-Divine-Fruit. Then Izanami comes out and blocks the way to hell with a massive rock.

We notice that there is no account of how Hades came into existence, but it is peopled with nasty gods and goddesses, including thunderous ones. Izanami is 'dead' and yet alive, and capable of escaping from hell with the help of her 'husband-cum-brother'. Again we note that incest is not an issue here. Here an important god is getting hell under control and fighting evil and raising a goddess who has been claimed by hell. The peach, in China, is symbolic of eternity, and so in Japan it seems to indicate everlasting life and the defeat of death.

Izanagi feels the need for purification, so he bathes in a river. No less than fourteen gods emanate from his clothing and person, the last three coming from his two eyes and nose. The first is Amaterasu, the sun goddess. The second is the moon god, and the third, from his nose, the storm god. Izanagi gives his jewel string to Amaterasu. But the storm god is not a very good boy. He pouts and wants to go and see his mother's land, the Nether-Distant-Land. Izanagi is furious and banishes him, so he goes up to heaven making an awful noise. Amaterasu guesses that he has bad intentions and makes him assure her of his good intentions. They agree to have children, so another series of gods appears by this incestuous union. She claims all the males as hers and relinquishes all the females to him. One of his sons, Prince-Lord-of-Heaven, becomes the ancestor of the rulers of various lands, such as Ki, Tanaka, and Amuchi[3].

The need for purification is a very common urge, often done by bathing in a river. We think of the River Jordan and John the Baptist and also the River Ganges and the Hindus. But Izanagi does not appear to feel defiled over his incestuous behaviour. Now we see Amaterasu, the sun goddess being given charge of the sky during the day. The moon god does not seem to be sinister, but the storm god is devious and scheming. Here again we see a subtle approach to theodicy: why is there any evil in the world? Now we see the divine series blending into human realities, as the local rulers of various territories begin to appear. Mythology is now sliding into human history, and the same thing is seen to happen in Genesis.

The storm god's behaviour gets progressively worse and eventually he frightens Amaterasu so much that she shuts herself into a rock dwelling for safety. All the world goes dark. Eventually, the gods manage to coax her out of her cave by using a mirror with various jewels. She is surprised to see that the world has light even though she has been hidden. Someone fetches her out completely so that the whole earth lights up again. For behaving so badly, the Storm god is banished, but in his pique he kills the goddess who offers him food.

Here we have an understanding of darkness: even if the sun goes in, there is still light. This is a paradox seen in Genesis. God creates the light but it is not the same as the sunshine or the moonshine. Not only jewels but mirrors enter the story. A mirror is often seen on the altar of a Shinto shrine. It again indicates eternity, everlasting life, as the jewels do. Again the undercurrent of theodicy is at work; the storm god's behaviour deteriorates to the point where he has to be banished.

After his banishment, the Storm god goes off to the land of Idzumo. There he meets an old man and a woman with a girl; they were earth deities. They were weeping because every year an eight-headed snake comes and carries off one of their daughters, and they are down to the last one. The storm god wants the girl for a wife. He instructs them to brew up an eightfold-refined liquor and places it in eight vats on a fence with eight gates. When the snake comes and sticks his heads into the liquor, he gets so drunk that he falls asleep. The storm god takes his sword and chops him up. He finds a sword concealed inside the snake's insides. He shows it to Amaterasu. It is called the Herb-Quelling-Sabre; this will appear later in another myth. Then, looking for a place to build his palace, he chooses Suga. A mist comes out and rises up.

This is one of the most lurid accounts but also highly symbolic. The snake clearly symbolises evil and death, and yet paradoxically, life. Handing over one daughter a year is clearly some sort of sacrifice to propitiate evil. Sacrifice is not normally mentioned in the Kojiki in so many words. We notice the heavy emphasis on the number eight, often drawn into many accounts. Again this is symbolic; an auspicious number which appears to indicate completeness, perfection, righteousness and victory. Evil is evenly balanced by the clever method of sending it off to sleep and then carving it up. The concealment of the sword inside the snake almost certainly betokens that out of evil good can come; out of sacrifice, things can be put right, or justified. Out of falseness can come truth. This is another aspect of theodicy. We recall the serpent in Genesis, the agent of temptation. The building of a temple produces a mist, or clouds. This is symbolic of the presence of God. We recall the dedication of Solomon's Temple, when it was filled with smoke; also the cloud at the Ascension.

A most intriguing account concerns the White Hare of Inaba[4]. The storm god produces eighty deities and they all want to marry the Princess Yakami in Inaba So they set off, making the last god, Great-Name-Possessor, carry the luggage. When they arrive at Cape Keta, they find a naked hare lying on the ground. The eighty deities give him unsound advice, to go and bathe in the sea and then lie out on a mountain slope; soon he was weeping with pain. Great-Name-Possessor comes along and asks him why he is weeping. He had played a trick on the crocodiles and the last one had stripped him of his clothing and this was compounded by the bad advice of the eighty gods. Great-Name-Possessor advises him to bathe in a river and roll in pollen. With this he is restored, and promises the god that he will get the princess, and not the other eighty. When the eighty realise that the princess has chosen Great-Name-Possessor, they are furious and vow to kill him. They hurl a red hot stone at him and he dies. His mother seeks help from heaven and he is restored as a beautiful young man. The eighty gods again play a trick on him: they take him up a mountain, cleave a tree and insert him in the cleft, thus torturing him to death. Again his mother rescues him and restores him to life. So now he has to run off quickly as the eighty are preparing their bows and arrows to shoot him.

In this account we are coming much closer to real human situations. The last boy in the line, the fag, is actually chosen by the princess. This reminds us of David, the last of Jesse's sons, being chosen to be king. The hare must symbolise something, perhaps humanity, because he is naked. He is clearly distressed at being deprived of his clothing. It is the old question of nakedness, a theme which appears in the Garden of Eden. The eighty gods are furious that the fag has merited the princess. Their intention to kill him is matched by the incident in Genesis where Joseph is left in a pit and his father is informed of his death. His brothers were jealous of his popularity. We notice there are three attempts on his life but he escapes. The cleft tree configuration also occurs in the *Tempest*, where Caliban is thus trapped by Prospero. The appearance of the god as a beautiful young man reminds us of Adonis, who was raised from the dead. Always, the motif of resurrection is woven into the story, often several times over.

Great-Name-Possessor is advised to go off to the Nether-Distant-Land and seek advice. As he arrives, Forward-Princess comes out and they fall in love and get married. When she tells his father, he takes a dislike to him and makes him sleep in the snake house. His wife gives him a snake-scarf that keeps the snakes at bay. The same happens with the centipedes and the wasps. After another trial on the burning moor, he manages to steal his father-in-law's sword, arrows and lute, taking his wife with him. The old man is enraged, but instructs him to defeat his enemies. So Great-Name-Possessor attacks his eighty half-brothers and defeats them and sweeps them into every river.

Here we see the transference of loyalty by a daughter from her father to her husband, an element seen in the Garden of Eden. Again we have the snakes, symbolic of evil and death; they can be kept at bay with the right sort of charm. This theme is often seen in mythology; that of gods fighting each other and a champion hero emerges as the winner.

A few conclusions can be drawn from this account. It is a more or less connected account from the very beginning, through a series of gods, down to the beginnings of humanity. There seem to be myriads of gods inhabiting every natural feature. This is a concept very close to Shamanism; where everything has some sort of spirit in it. Human relationships and failings are projected into the skies; there seems to be no guilty conscience over murder, incest, theft or deception. The idea of a god being deceptive may seem strange to Western ears, but the serpent in the Garden of Eden was the great deceiver and accused God of being deceptive. Also we see the ancestors of the Japanese rulers being gods; the local rulers and also the Mikado are descended from Amaterasu the sun goddess. In a roundabout way, this is saying that the Japanese people are somehow divine and their rulers are gods. The Mikado was regarded as a god until 1945, when he had to renounce his status. There is lavish use of snakes, jewels, swords, spears, arrows, and peaches. All of these are heavily loaded with symbolism, mainly to do with eternity, the defeat of death and hell, everlasting life and resurrection. But the age-old question of Theodicy is the substratum of so many of these incidents; why is there evil in the world; why do we have to suffer; why does the innocent have to be punished?

The myths continue into another dimension; namely, contact with humans. Prince Wo-usu is sent to teach his elder brother a lesson for not coming to the party. He rips him up. He is then sent to teach the Kumaso Braves a lesson. He dresses up as a woman and infiltrates their camp. The Braves quite like him, but he thrusts his sword through the one's chest and the other's buttock. This was because the Braves were indomitable and disrespectful. The second one gave him the name Yamato-Take. He goes on to subdue all the river and mountain gods. Then there is the Idzumo brave; he makes friends with him but secretly makes a sword of oak. They go swimming in the river and afterwards Yamato teases him into swapping swords, which they do. Predictably, the Idzumo Brave is killed. Yamato goes on to subdue the rest of the Braves and bring order to the country.

It looks very much as though Wo-usu, being a god, is in contention with human bullies. Again we see the element of deception on two occasions. The Japanese must see their gods as deceitful and tricky, just like some humans. The Braves are punished because they are disrespectful; this is an element in

Japanese society that involves bowing and showing deference. It is quite an offence to omit this kind of ritual. There is also the element of bathing, for purification, and the use of swords for the righting of all wrongs. The Idzumo Brave is actually killed with his own sword; in other words, foisted with his own petard. Yamato stands out as a hero god, bringing order to chaos.

After this success, he is sent to subdue the people of the East and visit his aunt at Ise. He is afraid of being killed, but his aunt gives him the Herb-Quelling-Sabre, which came from the eight-headed snake, and a bag with something helpful in it. On the way to the East he gets betrothed to a Princess called Miyadzu. He goes on to control all the unruly deities. But there is one who deceives him, claiming that in the moor is a lagoon with a really violent god. When Yamato goes on the moor, the ruler of Sagamu sets fire to the moor, hoping to kill our hero. Not so: he uses the sword to knock down the grass and then opens the bag to find a fire-striker. With that he fights fire with fire and escapes. Then he goes on and kills all the rulers of that land.

Again we see a god coming into contact with human rulers: myth sliding into history. The sabre, which has come from the snake, can be seen as evil countering evil, and good prevailing in the face of a dirty trick.

A postscript to this account comes as Yamato's aunt took a ship to cross the sea of Hashiri-Midzu. The god of that crossing raised a storm. But his aunt spread eight thicknesses of sedge rugs, eight skins of rugs, and eight of silk rugs on the waves and that calmed it down. Here we see an incident sounding rather like the stilling of the storm in the Gospels. There is no reason why this story could not have been based on a real historical incident in Japan. Again we see the use of the number eight, a significant number in Japanese thinking[5].

The Kojiki is thus characterised by bloodshed, violence and tough-guy exploits. There is romantic love, but otherwise, nothing that would equate to the love of God as explained in the Bible. All too clear is the projection of human traits into the skies.

The Yengishiki

There are seven recorded rituals designed for various occasions, such as the Harvest, Fire, and Purification. They are not like the Psalms, even if they are liturgical in character; in fact that are unlike anything else in sacred literature. They are not in the form of poetry. The priest gets up and says a formula of words, asking for the god's help.

The ritual to the sun goddess, Amaterasu, takes place at dawn on the seventeenth day of the sixth moon of the year (probably early June), at the shrine at Ise. It relates especially to the Mikado and his family.

'So that she deign to bless his [the Mikado's] life as a long life and his age as a luxuriant age eternally… may deign to bless the children that are born to him…' (page 55).

It continues with an interweaving of offerings:

'And deigning to cause to flourish the five kinds of grain which the men of a hundred functions and the peasants of the countries in the four quarters of the region under Heaven long to peacefully cultivate and eat…' (page 55).

Sacral kingship has been a strong element in Japanese culture, though its involvement in fertility has not been as strong as it has been in some cultures. The territorial nature of Shinto is stressed here; the culture and mythology does not really extend beyond the shores of Japan. Other parts of the world would appear to be irrelevant to Japanese mythology and mind-set.

Another aspect of the Mikado's role concerns the purification of the nation. In the myths, some of the gods feel the need for purification, and bathe in a river. This time, it is not done by water or even fire, but by the priest taking a broom made from grass and sweeping away the sins into the sea, where several deities are waiting to disperse the sins of the nation. One of them, the Maiden-of-the-Swift-Cleansing, who lives in the sea, gulps them down. The nature of the sins may seem strange to us, but they are divided into two categories: the heavenly offences, such as breaking the ridges, filling the watercourses, opening sluices, flaying and dunging. We notice that the the storm god did this sort of thing. Earthly offences are cutting flesh, leprosy, incest between mother and child, bestiality, using incantations. We notice that incest between brother and sister are not mentioned. It is interesting that leprosy is seen as an offence rather than as a disease. When this ritual is repeated, the heavenly gods will push open heaven's eternal gates and cleave a path through the clouds. Again, clouds and mist are involved, indicating the presence of gods.

This cultural ritual, which concerns the sins of commission and of ignorance, reminds us of the Scapegoat ritual in Leviticus where two goats are selected and one is sent off into the wilderness, carrying away the sins of the nation. It is significant that here in Japan there is an understanding of corporate or national guilt, as in Israel. There is, however, no mention of personal guilt as there is in the Bible. We notice also that the gods are found to be guilt-ridden just as humans are. This strengthens the feeling that the gods and the humans are not very far apart in reality. Human nature is projected into the skies and, vice versa, the gods descend in a series into human society.

It is interesting that in spite of Japan's isolation from the rest of the world, various features appear in common in their mythology. Even the thought of a god dressing up as a woman to deceive people is noted in Norse mythology (see Chapter 22: Ramayana) where Thor does the same thing. Not mentioned in the Kojiki is the motif of the rainbow as the bridge between heaven and earth; this is found in Japanese thought as well as Norse thinking. It may be that there was some exchange of thinking in the remote past; more likely, it is something instinctive in human nature.

Literary worth

In common with many other sacred writings of the world, the Kojiki is characterised by quite a lot of repetition. The word 'August', in the sense of majestic or illustrious, comes over with almost every title of each god. But the Kojiki can rise to some flights of literary expression, loaded with symbolism and imagination. Take this passage:

> '... and take cherry bark from the Heavenly Mount Kagu, and perform divination, and pulling up by pulling its roots a true cleyera japonica with five hundred branches from the Heavenly Mount Kabul, and taking and putting upon its upper branches the augustly complete string of curved jewels eight feet long... of five hundred jewels... and taking and tying to the middle branches the mirror eight feet long, and taking and hanging upon its lower branches the white pacificatory offerings and the blue pacificatory offering of his Augustness Grand-Jewel, taking these things and holding them together with the grand august offerings... ' (page 26).

We notice the element of exaggeration. Would anyone have had a mirror eight feet long in those times? Additionally, there is the reference to sacrifice, and the tautological aspect of it, perhaps intended to convey emphasis. At has a style all of its own, and reflects the many folk traditions of the many parts of Japan. The number symbolisms too are worked in all through, especially eight which holds so much significance. It reflects an almost totally different culture from Western thinking.

Footnotes for Chapter 12: The Holy Kojiki and the Yengishiki

1. Keta can also mean 'come'. This is one of the few place names that can be recognised today. Suga, Sagamu, Idzumo, Tanaka, Ki, Aha are some of the places cited which cannot be traced today.

2. Eight is symbolic for 'a firm base for opportunity' and ' prosperity' the future is wide open. The Japanese character for eight reflects this concept. / \ is the sign for eight.
3. Amuchi means 'sticky rice'. These lands appear to be imaginary and mythological. The equivalent in English thinking might be 'Avalon' or possibly 'Lionness'.
4. Here we have a place recognisable on today's maps; Inaba which is found on the North West Coast. It may indicate that each area has its own collection of folklorist myths.
5. The number eighty-eight is seen as very auspicious. The Kojiki uses eight in all kinds of permutations.

13

Deuteronomy

The Fifth Book of the Pentateuch

The Pentateuch has always been of the highest authority for the Jewish faith. The first five books of the Bible are claimed to be the work of Moses, and it may well be true that much of it is. However, with Deuteronomy we must pose a question mark; towards the end – Chapter 31 and onwards – it clearly displays the work of another writer as the life of Moses comes to an end. Scholars have raised the very real possibility of Deuteronomy being some kind of 'fraud'. This may be putting it rather too strongly. This is because in 2 Kings 22-23 we have a report of the Josianic reform, in which a book of the law was found in the Temple during various renovations. It registered a considerable shock with everyone including the King Josiah. It is thought, probably correctly, that the book in question was actually Deuteronomy, and that it may have been planted there on purpose to stimulate a return to pure Jewish religion. Josiah went to considerable extremes to remove all manner of pagan accretions in Jerusalem, and from the whole country generally. This view can receive support from the fact that the manner of phraseology in Deuteronomy, which is quite distinctive in places, also recurs in the books of the Kings and also, most notably in the book of Jeremiah. This prophet actually includes a large section of 2 Kings in his prose section; there has to be some sort of relationship between Jeremiah and Deuteronomy; the wording and phraseology is so similar, particularly in Deuteronomy 28.

Much speculation has gone into attempting to date Deuteronomy; some see it as early, others as late. At all events, it must surely have been in existence before the Exile, otherwise it would never have accrued the authority and spiritual command that it did, along with the other four books in the Pentateuch. If it is a 'fraud' one would expect to find anachronisms, such as we find in the Book of Mormon (Chapter 7). It is difficult to see into the world of Ancient Israel and identify such features. But three times we have the mention of **iron** (Og the king of Bashan had an iron bedstead Deuteronomy 3:11). We are accustomed to think of the Iron Age coming to Palestine with the Philistines, a generation later than Moses. At least the Israelites were still, assumedly, in the Bronze Age at this stage. This could be some sort of retrojection or anachronism and could indicate that Deuteronomy was written, or at least finalised in the early years of Samuel. But there is nothing certain about this at all.

Deuteronomy literally means 'second law' in Greek and that is a fair description. It is a resumé of the Wilderness period, a reiteration of the Ten Commandments and a restatement, somewhat simplified and modified, of the laws seen in Exodus and Leviticus. It ends with the completion of the ministry of Moses and the continuation of it under Joshua. It is interesting to see the differences between the two law codes; Deuteronomy shows evidence of the realities of living in the land of Canaan. Either Moses was genuinely seeing into the future right down to the Exile and beyond, or someone, such as Samuel, was adapting the basics of the Mosaic Law to the situation as the Israelites rubbed shoulders with the Canaanites and Philistines. There may be an element of truth in both these propositions.

As a corpus of literature, Deuteronomy is a remarkably well-balanced work, unlike many other sacred books. It has historical, geographical, legal material; also amongst the prose are sections of poetry and semi-poetry. Theology is of course paramount, but philosophy also is touched on in places. Even mathematics, in the form of dating, is included. Just because it is suspected of being a 'fraud' does not mean that it is worthless; Deuteronomy has much that is of spiritual value to Jews, Christians and Moslems, not least the heavy emphasis on the Old Testament configuration of thought. Although it differs in certain respects from Exodus and Leviticus, it is a fair summary of Mosaic thinking, and underscores the towering influence of Moses in the history of religious thought.

Mathematical information

The book begins by telling us that it is eleven days journey from Horeb to Kadesh Barnea. As with all number work in Hebrew thought, we must consider that there may be a symbolic element included here, as is seen in the Revelation (Chapter 6). Is it possible that eleven is suggestive of 'not quite ready'; nearly twelve as with the tribes of Israel, the complete picture? Eleven days' journey might seem a little excessive to go from Sinai to the borders of Canaan, but the writer is also saying in a roundabout way, that it need not have taken forty years for the Israelites to arrive at the Promised Land if they had been responsive to God's wishes. So, in the fortieth year, on the first day of the eleventh month, the Israelites arrived at their jumping off point for invading the land of Canaan. Also it ends with the thirty days of mourning for Moses before Joshua actually got to work. This is a well-known tradition that it took forty years of wandering in the Wilderness before the people were ready to move on into their new home. But this is typical of the method in the Old Testament; the writers are emphatic that dates, ages and time-spans are to be mentioned, as we have seen in the Maccabees (Chapter 2). The one thing lacking here is a datum point in history; that was to come later when the Greeks arrived with Alexander. If we had had a datum point, it might have been possible to identify the Pharaoh of the Exodus[1].

Historical information

The book begins with an anchorage in history. The first five chapters are a potted history of the Israelites' progress through the desert kingdoms. We hear about Og the king of Bashan, and Sihon king of Heshbon, the Moabites, the Edomites, the Ammonites, and the Amelekites. All this is fascinating history and there is no reason to cast doubt upon it, except to say that various details seen in Numbers have been toned down or omitted altogether. There is no mention of the Balak and Balaam incident[2]. The effect is that the faith of Israel is deeply grounded not on high-flown theories, but on real places and persons. It is all about the mentality of possession. It seems that it was perfectly acceptable to invade another territory and expel the inhabitants; Israel was only doing what was thought to be normal at the time. Nowadays we have more subtle ways of invading other countries, usually not quite so violent but still causing consternation to the natives. It used to be called 'imperialism'; now we call it 'immigration'. Adolf Hitler, who advocated force, called it finding 'lebensraum'. The Jews had the idea that the land of Canaan was theirs by right, from God, and of course they still think that now, with the establishment of the modern state of Israel. Joseph Smith decided that the land of America was the 'promised land' for the European settlers (Chapter 7). The historical information in Deuteronomy is full and reliable; many of the events relate well to the places mentioned. Deuteronomy concludes with another section of historical realities as Moses dies and Joshua prepares for the invasion.

Geographical information

This ties in well with the historical narrative. We begin with Horeb. This is another name for Mount Sinai, which takes centre stage in Exodus. There have been attempts at identifying this mountain, without much certainty. But many of the place names cited can be identified nowadays, such as Mount Nebo, the plains of Moab, and Jericho; others are less certain. Again the effect is to give reality to the faith of Israel. It is not a clever philosophical theory, as we see in many eastern religions. It is a down-to-earth, day-to-day, relationship with a living God who has a definite plan for his people. The land of Canaan is seen as God's favoured territory and moreover he will select a special place for his name to dwell, which means, the Temple in Jerusalem, or at least that it how it was interpreted in later times. We are constantly reminded of the Egypt period when the Israelites were in slavery and in danger of ethnic cleansing, the miraculous event of the Passover and the Crossing of the Red Sea. All this is fundamental to Judaism and Christianity. It is unfortunate that the Pharaoh's actual name is not mentioned; attempts have been made at identifying him but with not much success. The faith of Israel is firmly grounded in historical events and geographical realities. Sadly there is not much in the way of archaeological material to tie in with this period.

Theological aspects of Deuteronomy

As with virtually all of the Old Testament, it is impossible to make any sense of it unless one takes in the concept of covenant. The book constantly reminds us of this element. The covenant of Noah is not mentioned, but the one pertaining to Abraham and his children, is constantly referred to. But principally, the covenant of Sinai is rammed home, and just because later generations might try to disassociate themselves from it, Deuteronomy stresses that it applies to all of the Israelites going on into the future;

Deuteronomy 5:2: 'The Lord our God made a covenant with us in Horeb. Not with our fathers did the Lord make this covenant, but with us, who are all of us alive this day.'

The concept of national and family continuity is assumed here. This element in Deuteronomy could be taken to indicate that the book was written well after the Wilderness period when memories of the Sinai event were fading and the people were drifting away into other religions. But this is by no means totally certain.

With the establishment of the covenant of Moses goes the giving of commandments and laws. The basic thrust of it comes with the Ten Commandments, found in Deuteronomy 5:6ff. Because God has rescued them from Egypt, they must respond by observing his rules. The essential one, at the top of the list, 'thou shalt have no other gods before me,' is essential to the Jewish faith. This is monotheism, revealed in a world where everyone else had hundreds of gods and images of them. The Hebrews are forbidden to indulge in idolatry. That monotheism was not totally unknown in the Bronze Age can be evidenced by the religion of Akhenaten, the Pharaoh who departed from normal Egyptian practice and enforced the worship of the Sun (Aten) as the one god. This Pharaoh lived just before Tutankhamun and it is likely that his reign was more or less contemporaneous with King David, which means that Akhenaten may have taken the idea from Moses. Other than that, we have to wait for the Persian period for a religion coming anywhere near monotheism, namely Zoroastrianism (Chapter 5).

It is worth noting that there is another, presumably earlier version of the Ten Commandments in Exodus 20. The two versions are very much the same, but one notable difference is the rationale behind observing the Sabbath (Saturday). In Exodus, God blesses the Sabbath because in six days he created the entire universe but then rested on the seventh. In Deuteronomy, the author returns to his main theme:

> 'Remember that you were a servant in the land of Egypt and the Lord your God brought you out with a mighty hand and outstretched arm; therefore the Lord commanded you to keep the Sabbath day' Deuteronomy 5:15.

This brings us to the fundamental understanding of God's nature. Essentially God is a god of love who cares for his people.

> 'Know therefore that the Lord your God is God, the faithful God who keeps covenant and steadfast love with those who love him and keep his commandments, to a thousand generations... ' Deuteronomy 7:9.

The word used here is *hesed*, (love). This is not some sort of sentimental, vapid, superficial love; it is a deep caring which endures and continues however frayed the relationship might become. God cares; what about his people? The counterpart of it is that we are commanded to love God in return.

Deuteronomy 6:4: 'Hear O Israel, the Lord your God is one Lord, and you shall love the Lord your God with all your heart, and with all your soul, and with all your might... '

This would seem to be an amazing statement at that time in history. With the pagans terrified of their gods, attempting to bribe them with gifts, not trusting them an inch, the thought that God was not only singular but deeply caring for humanity, would have seemed very strange. But that is the important contribution that Moses gives us in the development of theology.

Towards the end of Deuteronomy there is mention of establishing another covenant, on the assumption that the Sinai agreement has collapsed.

This would not be a new covenant, such as we see with the covenant of David, or that of Jesus. It is simply the same arrangement restarted on the original assumptions. Interestingly we see King Josiah (2 Kings 23:3) do just that; he reinitiates the covenant of Sinai; he may have taken this idea from Deuteronomy. The basic thread of thought in the Sinai covenant is as follows.

God decided to save the people of Israel from bondage in Egypt. He rescued them and brought them to Sinai. He chose them, not the other way round. He then gave them a raft of legal material to observe; if they kept the laws, all would go well for them; if they ignored the laws, it would all go wrong. If however, they realised they had gone wrong and repent, the covenant is still there and there is forgiveness. It can all be put right. This is the gist of the Old Testament; it taps into the basic instinctive assumption in every human mind; 'if I do good, God will be pleased with me; if I do wrong, the opposite will happen.' This applies to every human soul in no matter what religion. The essential difference here is that Moses is saying that no matter how far wrong you go, and however unpleasant life becomes as a result, underneath it all is still that everlasting love of God. That is what marks Judaism out from every other faith in the world; by implication Christianity continues in this mould.

Essential to the thought pattern of Judaism is the legalism, which begins with the Ten Commandments but then continues, going into much detail about conduct in everyday life. It is worth remarking that many of these laws are far in advance in their humanitarian mentality, as compared with the conduct of the surrounding nations. A few examples will suffice. In Deuteronomy 20:1-10, when a battle is impending, the officer will ask the soldiers if anyone has just built a new house, or planted a vineyard, or taken a wife; that soldier will be allowed to go home and enjoy his acquisitions. Even the ones lacking 'moral fibre' are allowed to go home! Did that happen in the Second World War? In Deuteronomy 20:19-20 we have the situation where the Israelites might invade another country. The temptation is to cut down all their trees, including the fruit trees. This is forbidden; they can cut down ordinary trees to use as armaments, but the fruit trees, which take years to mature, must not be destroyed.

In the community, there is also a strong feeling of conscience over the poor and underprivileged. In Deuteronomy 15:1 there is the year of release for slaves; at the end of every seven years all slaves should be given the chance to have their freedom; all debts are to be cancelled. This seven-year rule still applies in British law to this day, even if it relates to unclaimed property. In 15:7 there is an injunction to help the poor; a sort of welfare state long before such a thing was devised in 1948. There is a moratorium on sacrificing one's children, a practice that was widespread in the Ancient World, especially amongst the Canaanites (Deuteronomy 18:9). In Deuteronomy 21:15 a rule about inheritance is given: if a man has two wives, one the favourite, the first born son receives his due inheritance regardless of whether his mother was in favour or not. If one finds a bird sitting on a nest, one can take the eggs, but one must allow the mother hen to run away. The famous injunction, 'an eye for an eye and a tooth for a tooth' may seem barbaric by today's standards, but in that setting it would have been remarkably restrained. It would be normal for revenge to be far more thorough and cruel, especially with the Assyrians who were really sadistic. In general terms Deuteronomy is developing and elaborating on what we find in the laws in Exodus and Leviticus, and some of them may be seen as natural developments in a settled agricultural milieu, which again suggests that Deuteronomy was written or at least completed well after the time of Moses.

An important aspect of Israelite theology is the phenomenon of prophecy. Moses is seen as a towering figure, as stated plainly in the last verse:

> Deuteronomy 34:10: 'And there has not arisen a prophet since in Israel like Moses whom the Lord knew face to face; none like him for all the signs and wonders which the Lord sent him to do in the land of Egypt, to Pharaoh and to all his servants and to all his land, and for all the mighty power and all the great and terrible deeds which Moses wrought in the sight of all Israel.'

This sounds as if the writer has not experienced the age of Elijah and Elisha. Even so, some of the laws regulating prophecy have a certain ring to them, which might suggest an even later age. The passage Deuteronomy 18:9-22 discusses the issue of false or true prophets. It is in the context of ruling against divination, necromancy and spiritualism in general. God promises to raise up another prophet like Moses, 'I will put my words in his mouth' (verse 18). This reminds us of Isaiah and Jeremiah. But the issue of false prophecy arises and the difficulty of knowing who is speaking truthfully and who is not. The answer is that one has to wait and see whether the prediction comes true or not (verse 22). This issue of course arose in the time of Jeremiah, and eventually his predictions came uncannily true. It is unlikely that Deuteronomy was written as late as the age of Jeremiah; more likely that Jeremiah read and was influenced by this legal code. A very strong indication of this comes in Deuteronomy 24:1-4 in which a man having divorced his wife, may not marry her again; a law that does not appear earlier in the Pentateuch. Jeremiah is clearly referring to this in one of his passages.

> Jeremiah 3:1: 'If a man divorces his wife and she goes from him and becomes another man's wife, will he return to her?'

Another theologically important matter connecting Deuteronomy with Jeremiah is the spiritual meaning of circumcision. Deuteronomy 10:16: says 'Circumcise therefore the foreskin of your heart, and be no longer stubborn.' This means that circumcision is not just a matter of physically cutting off a bit of flesh in a kind of token sacrifice; it is about humility and taking note of what God says, rather than objecting. In Jeremiah 4:4 we have a direct adaptation: 'circumcise therefore the foreskin of your hearts... ' Here it has a slightly different meaning: 'break up your fallow ground', which means make a fresh start and a new beginning; ' sow not among thorns', which means 'don't just try to amend things by raking over old ground full of weeds. By this he means that they should remove their false gods and not just try to patch things up with some sort of compromise with paganism. This has less to do with humility and more to do with a completely fresh start.

To sum up on the legal aspects of Deuteronomy, this law code (and other parts of the Pentateuch) stands out as unique in that milieu in history. It would be true that the surrounding nations had law codes, but nothing like the covenant framework, which gives it such a strong rationale. Generally speaking, the Israelite culture was far in advance of anything at that time. Many of its provisions still dominate modern law codes. For Hitler to say that the Jews are the destroyers of culture is total nonsense (Chapter 4); the Jews initiated a humane, enlightened and considerate attitude towards their fellow men; not just within their own nation but towards foreigners too. It is interesting that both Christianity and Islam have both followed suit and produced copious law codes of their own, often connected directly to the Mosaic law. Other religions too have borrowed from Moses, notably the Buddhists with their Noble Eightfold Path.

Philosophical aspects of Deuteronomy

There is very little that could be seen as wisdom literature or philosophy in Deuteronomy. It can fairly be said that there is a certain amount of assumption behind the material. On the issue of freewill and predestination there is an interesting paradox unfolding. On the one hand, the Israelites are chosen by God and rescued from Egypt; there is no free will involved here at all. The covenant is installed without asking their opinion, and the whole scheme is designed and executed by God, regardless of their objections. The element of prophecy itself implies predestination. If the future can be foretold by a far-sighted person like Moses, what space is there left for freedom of will?

Deuteronomy 31:16: '... the Lord said to Moses... "... this people will rise and play the harlot after the strange gods of the land... and they will forsake me and break my covenant... ."'

This of course is exactly what did happen. The implication in it is that predestination is a reality. On the other hand, in several places the Israelites are given a choice:

Deuteronomy 30:15: 'Behold I have set before you this day life and good; death and evil... I have set before you life and death, blessing and curse... therefore choose life.'

The implication in this is that there is the freedom to make moral choices and avoid ruining one's life. This means that there is a tension going on here between free will and predestination; it is not something that can be rationalised or explained. It amounts to a deep paradox; that on the one hand God guides people's lives, but on the other hand we have free will and can make important choices.

Another quasi-philosophical element comes in Deuteronomy 30:11-14. God is talking about where the truth can be found. It is not some kind of high-flown theory up in the skies; nor is it miles away, which would require someone to fetch it over. 'But the word is very near to you; it is in your mouth and in your heart, so that you can do it.'

To transpose this into the thought form of later ages, when philosophy began to emerge, it is in effect saying, that one's religious faith is not something terrifically complicated, abstruse and a matter of mental gymnastics. One's faith is very simple and basic, instinctive; if you do good, you will prosper; if you do bad, the opposite will happen. Deuteronomy emphasises this in many places. But it is true of human nature that the Old Testament grows out of this instinctive response in humanity. As we all know, life is not always quite as simple as that; the book of Job takes on the difficult task of trying to delve into the question of Theodicy; why does the innocent have to suffer?

As far as the genre of wisdom literature as seen in the Old Testament, is concerned, there is very little to be found in Deuteronomy. However, a tiny passage in 32:28 contains this:

'For they are a nation void of counsel, and there is no understanding in them. If they were wise they would understand this, they would discern their latter end.'

This is in the context of the Israelites behaving foolishly by not admitting to the saving power of God in their history. The vocabulary of the wise men, such as Proverbs (Chapter 15) and Ben Sirach is used; some would maintain that this indicates a late date for this passage, while others would say that it is evidence that this genre actually began to emerge early in Israel's history. As with all these matters, arguments can be circular; nevertheless the Hebrew Wisdom (Proverbs Chapter 15) element is the nearest thing that they come to philosophising. It is all very basic and this-worldly, a contrast to what we see in Èastern religions, and with their scriptural material.

Deuteronomy as literature

Most of the book is in prose, and somewhat repetitive at that. This is a normal feature of sacred writings; it is a way of emphasising one's message. Towards the end, however, there are two major poems, The Song of Moses and the Blessing of Moses, which are on a par with what we read in the Psalms. One might have thought that they would have been included in the Psalter; however, there is a different feel about them which almost certainly rules out the possibility of their being written by David or his imitators. It is thought, by scholars, that these songs, along with the song recorded in Exodus 15, and the Blessing of Jacob in Genesis 49, and the Song of Deborah in Judges 5, and the Song of Hannah in 1 Samuel 2, are probably the earliest written material in the Bible. Certainly the standard of Hebrew poetry in Deuteronomy is of the highest quality. A few examples will demonstrate the parallelism at work.

> Deuteronomy 32:2: 'May my teaching drop as the rain; my speech distil as the dew; as the gentle rain upon the tender grass; and as the showers upon the herb.'

> Deuteronomy 33:13: 'Blessed by the Lord be his land, with the choicest gifts of heaven above, and of the deep that couches beneath; with the choicest fruits of the sun and the rich yield of the months, with the finest produce of the ancient mountains, and the abundance of the ancient hills; with the best gifts of the earth and its fullness; and the favour of him that dwelt in the bush...'

This is a good example of sustained parallelism; the alternation between synonym and antonym. The blessing of Moses mirrors the Blessing of Jacob, even if the twelve tribes cited are in a different order. It all goes to emphasise the importance of the twelve tribes, their heritage and their interrelationship. Incidentally, Moses talks of the tribe of Joseph in its capacity of leadership among his brothers and only latterly mentions the division into the tribes of Ephraim and Manasseh, a fact forced on them because they became far more numerous and influential.

Theologically the poems are significant. There is the metaphor of God being a 'Rock'.

Deuteronomy 32:4: 'The Rock, his work is perfect; for all his ways are justice; a God of faithfulness and without iniquity; just and right is he.'

Genesis 49:24: '... by the name of the Shepherd, the Rock of Israel...'

The poetry, use of metaphor, is stunning and of spiritual help to us all.

Deuteronomy 33:26: 'There is none like God, O Jeshurun, who rides through the heavens to your help, and in his majesty through the skies. The Eternal God is your dwelling place, and underneath are the everlasting arms.'

This is a reassurance to us all that no matter how hard life may become, beneath it all, and above, is a God of Love who cares deeply for us all.

In general terms the poems do not introduce any new element in contrast to the message of the prose section. Deuteronomy is very much a unified message, even if different writers may have had a hand in its production.

To balance these important poems at the end, Deuteronomy utilises vestiges of an ancient poem in the first few chapters. It concerns Israel's relationship with the kingdoms in the Wilderness. The poem can be reconstructed from fragments in this way:

> '*Let me pass through thy land,*
> *I will not turn into a field or a vineyard,*
> *I will not drink the water of a well,*
> *I will go on the way of the king,*
> *I will not turn right or left,*
> *Food thou shalt sell me for silver, and I shall eat,*
> *And water thou shalt give me for silver and I shall drink,*
> *Only let me pass through on foot.*'

This reconstruction has four parallelisms in a chiastic[3] arrangement.

A: Plea for passage.
B: Pilfering food and water.
C: Keeping straight on the road.
B: Buying food and water.
A: Plea for passage.

Chiasmus is a form found in prose as well as poetry in Hebrew literature. It is a deliberate attempt at shaping and giving meaning to the material. Having noted the scheme ABCBA in the quasi-poetry of the approach to the various kingdoms of the Wilderness, it is now possible to discern the same ground plan in the whole of Deuteronomy. It begins with a historical resume located in the plains of Moab before the river Jordan; in the last chapters, the same situation reappears, as Moses comes to the end of his ministry and life. Then come the Ten Commandments and the Shema', essential elements in the faith of Judaism; this is balanced by another list of laws, twelve in number, to reflect the twelve tribes Deuteronomy 27. Both of these summary law codes have a blessing and cursing addendum to reinforce their importance. Then comes the main detailed laws of Judaism, many of which are a resume of what is seen in Exodus and Leviticus; also there are new elements and adaptations which are important for a settled agricultural nation. In between these main elements there are various exhortations to adhere to God's laws, and the reason behind it; gratitude for God's love in rescuing Israel from Egypt. So the chiasmus, not quite as clear as in some examples but there nevertheless, goes as follows:

A: historical resume Deuteronomy 1-3.

B: The Ten Commandments with exhortations and blessing and cursing Deuteronomy 4-11.

C: The main law code starting at 'these are the statutes... .' Deuteronomy 12-26.

B: Another version of the Commandments, twelve this time with blessing and cursing Deuteronomy 27-30.

A: historical section concluding the Pentateuch and the life of Moses in the plains of Moab Deuteronomy 31-34.

From this we see that the book is structured and purposeful, even if the chiasmus is somewhat blurred by the sermonising and exhortation to keep the laws and the consequences of not doing so. It indicates that these early Hebrew writers were not just throwing ideas down on paper, but carefully presenting their material schematically. It all ties in with the basic assumption in Judaism and later in Christianity, that history is planned, structured and determined by the Almighty hand, and that nothing is just haphazard, accidental or meaningless.

Linguistic matters

The book is of course written entirely in the Hebrew of the classical age. The Deuteronomist has his own particular favourite phrases and his style is evidenced in many places in the Pentateuch; also through Joshua, Judges and through to the major histories of the Kings. No one knows for sure who this writer was, but such persons as Isaiah and Jeremiah are possible candidates. That does not mean that Deuteronomy has to be a product of their times; they could have just used earlier source material and rephrased it in their own idiom. Anyone who writes a book has to use source material, and occasionally in Hebrew literature we have mention of such works which have been lost to history.

The Hebrew of Deuteronomy is not particularly antique or abstruse. In fact it is very plain indeed and for a purpose; the writer wanted to make it crystal clear that there was no mistake about God's claim on his people's allegiance. There are however a few words and phrases which are difficult to interpret in today's world.

A few examples will suffice. In Deuteronomy 11:30 we have mention of the oak of Moreh. This remark may seem strange to modern ears, except that it was Canaanite practice to have an *asherah*, a tree planted beside the altar, as a symbol of the Astarte, or the female principle which was the co-relative of Baal the male deity, symbolised by a stone pillar.

Deuteronomy 16:21: 'You shall not plant any tree as an Asherah beside the altar of God... you shall not set up a pillar which the Lord... hates.'

We notice that the writer does not wish to quote the name 'Baal'.

Elsewhere Israel is instructed to destroy all such pagan apparatus. In 14:21 we are ordered not to 'seethe a kid in its mother's milk'. Again, to modern ears this is meaningless, but in that day, it referred to some sort of pagan practice that was not acceptable to God.

Also we have the laws of consanguinity, forbidding one to marry relatives that are too close, such as brother and sister, father and daughter. To us now, who have taken this as a natural assumption it seems pretty obvious; but that was not so in those days. We know that the Pharaohs were more or less obliged to marry all their female relatives in order to prevent a rival claim being made on the throne. The result of course was inbreeding and the decline of one dynasty after another. They were not to know this, but we now know the realities of inbreeding as a result of marrying too close.

Another aspect of sexual relations comes in Deuteronomy 23:17:

'There shall be no cult prostitute of the daughters of Israel, neither shall there be a cult prostitute of the sons of Israel. You shall not bring the hire of a harlot or the wages of a *dog* into the house of the Lord...'

God says that this is an abomination. It must be remembered that normal Canaanite practice was sacral prostitution. It was all a part of the rituals relating to fertility and the harvest. The pagans almost certainly saw it as essential to stimulate the produce from the land. Here, God is saying it is totally wrong and disgusting. The alternative rendering of 'dog' is 'sodomite', and we know from the Sodom and Gomorrah incident in Genesis that God is not pleased with such behaviour.

Mythology

There is very little that could be called mythology in Deuteronomy. One might almost say that Deuteronomy is the most demythologised book in the Bible, or indeed in any scriptural material. There seems to be hardly any reference to any Creation accounts, neither any thought about eschatology. Deuteronomy is a very this worldly, down-to-earth document, dealing with day-to-day conduct and the rationale behind it. Even at the end, when Moses dies, this concludes on something of an anti-climax. 'No one knows his sepulchre' and a very understated view of his demise. Later generations were to take this to mean that he was 'assumed' which means taken up into heaven, in the same way as Elijah was. The book, the Assumption of Moses, works on this idea. The idea of Moses seeing the Promised Land but not being allowed to enter it with the people has captured the imagination of many people, and also their sympathy, after all the ground-breaking work that he had done.

Concluding remarks on Deuteronomy

As compared with other books in the Bible, Deuteronomy stands out as the least incredible of all; there is no challenge to credulity, no miracles, nothing fantastic. It sets out the epitome of Old Testament thinking, crystallising the material seen earlier in the Pentateuch and looking forward to the situation in the Promised Land. Even so, there is the awkward question of literality; how literally do we take some of these laws? One instance of this comes in Deuteronomy 12:15; 'you shall not eat the blood'. How strictly do we have to take this? The Jews and Muslims have their methods of draining the blood out of the animal; it is impossible to remove every drop of it. Do we have to refuse a blood transfusion? The Christians regard this type of law as obsolete and unnecessary. 'You shall not seethe a kid in its mother's milk'; does this have any meaning for us today, given that it is some sort of ancient pagan practice? The Jews take this to extremes; they will not drink milk at the same time as eating meat. Many will say that this is taking it rather too far. If, after seven years, a slave is offered his freedom, but decides to stay on, do we really have to pin his ear to the doorpost with an awl? Deuteronomy must be seen against the background of its situation in history. Many of these laws were not just valid but of considerable importance at that time; now, some of them are of no relevance at all; others are still of considerable moment; others may be seen as symbolic as is discussed in the Epistle of Barnabas (Chapter 24).

An issue that arose in Israel and later Judaism, was the location of the Temple. Deuteronomy instructs us to have one place where sacrificing may be done; otherwise it was banned. There is the insistence on just one place, where God would make his name to dwell. That of course came to be Jerusalem, but before that there were shrines at Shiloh and other places. This could be taken to indicate that this law in Deuteronomy had not yet been framed; on the other hand, it could indicate that since David had not yet captured Jerusalem, they were obliged to have a shrine somewhere else. When the divided monarchy arose, the Northern Kingdom had its own temples and sacrificial system, in defiance of the Jerusalem Temple. In the Maccabean age, a temple was built in Egypt, again ignoring the Deuteronomic law. The law went further and ordered everyone to congregate at the one Temple three times a year for the great feasts. Was this realistic? Surely Deuteronomy was assuming a relatively small nation and land area, in which it would be easy for everyone to gather together? But as the Jews spread out into more and more distant parts of the Orient and to Rome and then Germany, it became impossible to fulfil this law. Even with the Temple ruined and a remnant called the Western Wall surviving, Jews from all over the world appear to worship there. This is probably the origin of the concept of 'pilgrimage,' something that the Christians and Muslims also practise. To obey this law today, it would mean something like, all the Christians converging on St Peter's Rome three times a year (or possibly St Paul's Cathedral!). Not realistic. The Muslims do converge on Mecca, but not all at once and at the same time; even so, it is quite a crowd and quite an experience.

As with so many aspects of the Bible, one has to use a certain generous helping of common sense as applied to modern circumstances. Those who do try to take everything totally at face value and literally, give themselves all manner of problems. A case in point is the Jehovah's Witnesses' insistence on not to have a blood transfusion. This also is a case of taking that law about eating blood far too literally; God does not want anyone to die unnecessarily, just because a pint of blood will save one's life. A literal interpretation may be useful in some circumstances, but not always. Jesus would probably have said something the effect that saving life is far more important than fussing over the details of an archaic rule.

The Assumption of Moses: an apocalyptic work of the Post-Exilic period

This work is regarded as very late, possibly almost into New Testament times; even so it is almost certain that parts of the New Testament are reliant on the Assumption of Moses, particularly Jude. It is thought that it had a Hebrew original, which no longer survives; it is now only known in Greek and Latin, and some of that text is lost. The theology is very much in line with Deuteronomic thought, and there is no serious departure from the mind-set of early Israel. Consistent with this is the omission of any mention of the coming of the Messiah; such ideas only really came in with Isaiah and his imitators. The writer does not agree with an armed uprising to bring in the Kingdom of God; he is insistent that rather than give in to the enemy, he would hide in a cave and die there.

The book does not purport to have been written by Moses, but just as Deuteronomy is almost certainly a pastiche, the Assumption is even more likely to be such. Even so one can admire that sense of balance in the work. We begin with a historical reference to the handing on to Joshua, with calculations of years and dates, and ends on the same subject. In between we have a more detailed 'prophecy' of the course of Israel's history with the two kingdoms, the Exile, the apostasy in the later kingdom of Judah, the Return and the reign of the Herods. Strangely there is no allusion to the Maccabees and their uprising and kingdom; this could be because the writer disapproved of armed struggle to bring in the kingdom? Alternatively it could be evidence that the book was written before the Maccabean era. Even so there is mention of a certain Eleazar, a chief scribe and priest, who was martyred rather than eat any pork. This account appears in 2 Maccabees 6:18 (Chapter 2).

In harmony with Deuteronomy there is a poetic section in Chapter 10. The style is nowhere near as majestic as the songs in Deuteronomy; they are rather banal and there is an attempt at parallelism that is nowhere near as high-flown. It is here that a certain element of mythology creeps in, though nothing like as full and picturesque as in a book like Daniel or Revelation.

With regard to the 'assumption' of Moses, he expects to 'sleep with his fathers', which is the normal Old Testament way of euphemising one's funeral and burial, almost certainly in a tomb. However it is only in the title itself that 'assumption' is mentioned; that would imply being bodily lifted up into heaven. Even though the assumption is not described in detail, as it was with Elijah, there is an admission that Moses is in heaven with God;

'The Lord hath on their behalf appointed me to pray for their sins and make intercession for them' (Assumption of Moses 12:6).

This means that the idea of Jesus making intercession, and also of the Virgin Mary doing the same, is not a new idea at all. Moses was seen as fulfilling this role after his earthly life.

All this is symptomatic of the towering influence that Moses had, and still does have, with the people of Israel, and also by implication the Christians and the Muslims.

Notes for Chapter 13: Deuteronomy

1. 1 Kings 6:1 tells us that Solomon began to build the Temple 480 years after the Exodus. If we reckon Solomon's reign to be about 960 BC, then the Exodus would be 1440 BC, at about the time when the Egyptian Book of the Dead (Ani's version) was in use (see Chapter 25). This might mean that the Pharaoh of the Exodus was Amenhotep 2nd or 3rd, or Thothmes 4th. Akhenaten might be later than the Exodus, and Tut-ankh-amon even later still.
2. An incident related in Numbers 22; this does not appear in Deuteronomy.
3. Chiasmus; a literary feature often used in Hebrew writing, following a pattern such as ABCDCBA.

14

The Dhammapada

A Section of the Buddhist Scriptures

We do not know for certain who wrote the Dhammapada; it may have been a developing tradition within the early Buddhist movement. Some of the material almost certainly stems from Siddhartha himself[1]; some of it from before but used by him; other material may be the early realisations amongst his followers. But 2,500 years ago, contemporaneous with Ezra the scribe and the Return of the Jews from Exile, there was a new development in the Indian subcontinent, that of the Enlightenment of Siddhartha, who claimed to have rediscovered the way to escape from the pain and misery of this world by attaining Nirvana. The text used is the latest translation by Gil Fronsdal, an experienced and committed Buddhist himself. Traditionally, the Dhammapada was mostly known and used by the Bhikkhus (monks and nuns) in their monasteries, but in recent times there have been attempts to render the Dhammapada in other languages so that ordinary Buddhists and others of different religions can learn from it. It was written in Pali, which at the time was the modern language that Siddhartha preferred. Now, Pali is antique and obsolete and needs careful translating and paraphrasing to make it intelligible to modern ears. Even in translation, the Dhammapada is a book of great beauty and spiritual value, regardless of one's feelings about Buddhism itself. There is absolutely no mathematical, geographical, historical or factual material in it at all; this is a stark contrast to Western scriptural material, which anchors itself in places, events and dates. All the material is theologico-philosophical and ethical with mild touches of mythology. One of its most notable features is its command of literary expression;

236

figurative language is of great importance in conveying eternal truths, as we see from certain parts of the Bible.

Theology/Philosophy

It would be artificial and misleading to attempt to separate theology and philosophy in the Dhammapada; they are closely interwoven and form the main gist of Buddhist thinking. In contrast with many other religions, it does not start with any statement about God; this book is strangely silent on that subject. It begins with the core of Buddhism, that of controlling one's own spiritual destiny, the impetus for which must come from oneself; the idea of a loving merciful God rescuing people is simply not mentioned. This is how its starts:

> 'All experience is preceded by mind, led by mind, made by mind. Speak or act with a corrupted mind, and suffering follows... speak or act with a peaceful mind, and happiness follows... ' (1:1-2, page 1).

Essentially this is the Buddhist answer to the question of theodicy; why do we have to suffer? The answer is that if we do evil, we suffer in this world and the next; if we do good we accrue merit and gain happiness. A clear statement of this comes thus:

> 'One who does evil grieves in this life, grieves in the next... one who makes merit rejoices in this life, rejoices in the next... seeing one's own pure acts brings joy and delight. One who does evil is tormented in this life,... reborn in realms of woe, he is tormented all the more... ' (1:14-16, page 4).

We can see here that this has something in common with Krishna's remarks in the Bhagavad Gita[2]; in fact, Buddhism is heavily reliant on traditional Hindu thought, especially on the matter of Karma[3]. Unfortunately, there is no admission that sometimes the wicked person can prosper in this life and vice versa, a virtuous person can fall on misfortune, as we see in the book of Job. The Dhammapada would probably agree with the Deuteronomic view of life, that you get what you deserve. But Buddhism contains no mention of any covenant between God and the believer, nor any other metaphor which might amount to the same thing. After all, if God is not included in one's system, then there cannot be a covenant with him.

It would be misleading to say that there are no gods in Buddhism. This is where the concept of samsaric realms becomes important. The Dhammapada talks of heaven and hell; the gods live in heaven and the moral failures live in hell. Strangely there is no mention of the other four states in the samsaric realms of the Wheel of Becoming[4]; it looks as though that was a later development and possibly not a part of Siddhartha's original teachings. But the gods in heaven are not the ones who created the world; that matter is left unstated.

> 'Some are reborn in a womb; evildoers are reborn in hell. People of good conduct go to heaven; those without toxins are fully released in Nirvana' (9:126, page 33).

So Nirvana is not the same as heaven; from heaven one could be demoted to something worse, like hell, or from hell be promoted to heaven. But Nirvana is a permanent state of release from this inexorable round of rebirth and suffering; something that can be attained in this life as well as the next.

> 'Absorbed in meditation, persevering, always steadfast, the wise touch Nirvana, the ultimate rest from toil' (2:23, page 6).

Nirvana could be seen as roughly analogous to the Christian heaven, but the way it is conceived is clearly different. At this point, it can be seen that achieving Nirvana is not just a matter of good conduct. There is a stark dichotomy between the wise and the fool. The wise person has a disciplined mind, which brings happiness:

> 'Through effort, vigilance, restraint, and self-control, the wise person can become an island no flood will overwhelm. Unwise, foolish people give themselves over to negligence... vigilant and absorbed in meditation one attains abundant happiness... a sage observes the sorrowing masses as someone standing on a mountain observes fools on the ground below' (2:26-28, page 7).

There is a certain amount of spiritual superiority in this, which is at variance with the Christian gospel. The book looks down on the fools who cultivate desire and pride. Chapter five is all about such people:

> 'Fools with no sense go about as their own enemies, doing evil deeds that bear bitter fruit... fools will want unwarranted status, authority in monasteries... homage from good families... such are the thoughts of a fool who cultivates desire and pride. The way to material gain is one thing, the path to Nirvana another... ' (5:66-73, page 17).

But the wise, or the sages, let go of this world:

238

'There they should seek delight, abandoning sensual desires, having nothing. Sages should cleanse themselves of what defiles the mind. Those who fully cultivate the Factors of Awakening, give up grasping, enjoy non-clinging and have destroyed the toxins, are luminous and completely liberated in this life' (6:87-89, page 23).

This is the core value in Buddhism; that desire is the basic problem in humanity. From desires spring all the pain, problems and disappointments. The way to escape this is to remove desire; this has to be done by oneself.

'Longing gives rise to grief; longing gives rise to fear... affection gives rise to grief... Infatuation gives rise to grief... sensual craving gives rise to grief... craving gives rise to grief... for someone released from craving there is no grief... ' (16:212-216, page 57).

It is not just sexual attraction that is included in desire; it is any form of desire. The answer to the problem is to disentangle oneself from wanting anything. This seems to rule out any positive or helpful desire that one might have; it also goes against human instinct, in that we all need to love and be loved; we all have fears and centres of interest. But the renunciant that can remove himself from any form of attraction, wish or ambition is the one who will arrive at Nirvana. One might ask, 'what about friends and family; can't we have love for them?' Buddhism does not rule that out completely. Even so, there is a negative feeling about family. Symptomatic of this is the fact that the Buddhists have no marriage ceremony, which is unusual in religions.

'Neither mother nor father, nor any other relative can do one as much good as one's own well-directed mind' (3:43, page 11).

This is a down-playing of family values. Even so, one is enjoined to respect one's parents, a value probably gleaned from the Ten Commandments.

'Happiness is having friends when need arises. Happiness is contentment with whatever there is. Happiness is merit at the end of one's life. Happiness is the abandoning of all suffering. In the world, respect for one's mother is happiness as is respect for one's father. In the world, respect for renunciants is happiness as is respect for Brahmins... ' (23:331, page 87).

With this we see that the monastic arrangement becomes equivalent to family life, and this explains why Buddhism is so heavily centred on monastic community life. One could say that this is a weakness in

Buddhism, the understatement of the value of family life. Most other religions place a heavy emphasis on positive family relationships, particularly the Jews and the Confucianists. In fact when Buddhism arrived in China, it was initially not well received for that very reason; it has little positive to say about family coherence.

Another important theological issue in Buddhism is the gaining of merit.

'Having done something meritorious, repeat it, wish for it; merit piled up brings happiness' (9:118, page 31).

'One who makes merit is delighted in this life, delighted in the next, is delighted in both worlds. Here she is delighted, knowing, "I have made merit". Reborn in realms of bliss, she delights all the more' (1:17-18, page 5).

There is no attempt at explaining with whom the merit is supposed to be valid. It is not directed at God, since God (if he exists) is not relevant to the situation. Neither is it directed at any kind of supernatural being, or even human beings. One wonders exactly what is meant by 'merit'. It ought to mean, in Western thinking, an accumulation of plusses that will have purchasing power with someone, whether in this world or the next. But the way it is put in verse 17-18, it could simply mean feeling pleased with oneself. This could mean some kind of spiritual superiority complex not unlike the Phariseeism that Jesus criticised so heavily. It comes out even more acutely when one is told not to associate with bad people:

'Do not associate with evil friends; do not associate with the lowest of people. Associate with virtuous friends; associate with the best of people' (6:78, page 20).

Jesus did the very opposite of this; he said that those who are well do not need a doctor; those who are sick certainly do. That raises the question of how anyone who has gone wrong in life can be helped to do right, unless someone with moral firmness comes to the rescue.

St Paul would almost certainly have condemned this attitude as 'works-righteousness'. Essentially the Christian believes that not by one's own efforts at being good are we saved, but by God's merciful and loving gift, regardless of how virtuous one thinks one is. But of course, if there is no God available, then salvation by faith in God does not mean a great deal.

As far as ethics is concerned, the Dhammapada is more detailed than the Hindu writings. The Noble Eightfold Path has various commandments in common with the Ten Commandments[5]. These laws do not appear in

240

a codified form in the Dhammapada, but scattered remarks give us a fair impression of the ideal Buddhist conduct. One must not kill or harm anyone, in fact violence of any kind is forbidden. Even one's speech is to avoid hostility (10:133) (page 36). Speaking the truth is advised (17:223) (page 59) and not speaking falsehoods. Adultery is wrong (22:309-310) (page 80). Stealing is wrong. One is advised to avoid greed and observe moderation in eating. Envy is wrong. Virtue is advised, although there is no attempt at defining virtue. This would be a fair estimate of the Buddhist ethic:

'Conquer anger with non-anger; conquer wickedness with goodness; conquer stinginess with giving and a liar with truth' (17:223, page 59).

For one whose conduct is in line with this, there is the expectation of heaven. We must recall that heaven is not the same as Nirvana. But all this conduct will accrue merit. There are some who do not even cling to merit; they are the ones who are heading for Nirvana.

'For one who is awake, whose mind isn't overflowing, whose heart isn't afflicted, and who has abandoned both merit and demerit, Fear does not exist' (3:39, page 11).

We notice that there is no concept of temptation by adverse spiritual powers; no mention of repentance and amendment of life. One appears to be either good or bad; there is no notion of people being an admixture of the two, with a constant battle between right and wrong going on inside them (as one would expect from Zoroastrianism). All this about good conduct is purely one's own effort.

So we see that the Buddhist ethic, while being laudable and in many ways in line with the New Testament, is inextricably bound up with Karma and merits. This, of course, is fair enough as far as it goes, but it does not address the problem of human corruption and the issue of correcting it, at least, not in this life.

In common with much of the wisdom literature of the Old Testament, the Dhammapada gives us a sharp dichotomy between the wise and the foolish.

'Unwise, foolish people give themselves over to negligence. The wise protest vigilance as the greatest treasure' (2:26, page 7).

The fool is the one who fastens on to earthly values, such as wealth, large family, ambition, status and influence, pride; they are their own worst enemies. It all finishes off with grief and they are destined for hell. It is

241

not always a matter of appearances, for sometimes a person wearing the saffron robe in a monastery can be a pure hypocrite and be in line for hell.

'Many who wear the saffron robe have evil traits and lack restraint. By their evil deeds are these wicked people reborn in hell' (22:307, page 79).

By contrast the wise have a disciplined mind. The sage will be able to disentangle himself from bad behaviour.

'Virtuous people always let go. They don't prattle about pleasures and desires. Touched by happiness and then by suffering, the sage shows no sign of being elated or depressed' (6:83, page 21).

There is that sense of distancing oneself from the values of this world, and this can be achieved in the monastic community. Also it can be a matter of becoming a recluse, and practising one's meditation alone.

'If you do not find an intelligent companion, a fellow traveller of good conduct and wise, travel alone, like a king renouncing a conquered kingdom... travel alone, at ease, doing no evil like the elephant Matanga in the forest' (23:329-330, page 85)[6].

Siddhartha himself went through this phase, giving up a comfortable life in a palace and living as a mendicant on his own for a long time until he come to his Enlightenment and rediscovered Nirvana. This is the opposite of the Christian ideal. Although there have been and still are Christian hermits, the main tenor of Christianity is 'the Church' by which is meant the gathering of the faithful to worship together, in community.

The qualities of a Brahmin, someone who has found the right formula for happiness, are described in Chapter 26. He will keep his temper, banish all evil, copes with abuse, assault, imprisonment, has no craving, has nowhere to live, is absorbed in meditation, is not a hypocrite.

'Whoever is untied and free of distress, and for whom neither a "beyond" a "not-beyond", nor a "both beyond-and-not-beyond" exist, I call a Brahmin' (26:385, page 99).

This brings us to the question of existence or non-existence. There is that sense in eastern religions that the physical world is purely an illusion. It is likely that Mary Baker Eddy gleaned this idea when trying to make out that everything is in the mind.

'One for whom nothing exists, in front, behind, and in between, who has no clinging, who has nothing, I call a Brahmin' (26:421, page 107).

'If one sees the world as a bubble, if one sees it as a mirage, one won't be seen by the king of Death' (13:170, page 46)[7].

Here it is not stated so much as a doctrine as much as an assumption. It is one thing to maintain that the world does not exist, but the realities of life are still the same. We all need to eat, sleep, and earn something for a living, even if it is all an illusion. But there seem to be some people who can excuse themselves from these realities. To say that they are not hypocrites is rather strange, since if they sit back and meditate all day, how do they earn a living? The answer is that they have to rely on the kindness of other people who have to do the work. Most Christian monastic communities have some kind of method for earning an income so that they are not dependant on the local community.

Mythology

We know that Buddhism has a lot of distinctive mythology in its traditions; one example is the Wheel of Becoming. But the Dhammapada does not have much in the way of mythology. Certainly there is no Creation myth, in contrast with most world religions. Also there is no eschatology, which is the futuristic counterpart of myth. There are scattered references to Indra and Brahma, Hindu gods, not so much as a doctrine but as an assumption. More thorough is the mention of Yama, the king of Death, who presides over the Wheel of Becoming[7].

'You are now like a yellowed leaf; Yama's henchmen are standing by. You stand at the door of death... you're headed for Yama's presence with no resting place along the way, no provisions for the journey... be quick in making effort, be wise... you'll experience birth and old age no more' (18:235-237, page 62).

This is the person approaching death; the angels of death are waiting to carry him off to another rebirth, possibly to something worse, like hell. Now is the time to pull oneself together before it is too late, and renounce everything.

We also have references to Mara the god of death. How he differs from Yama is not clear; possibly Yama is the eastern equivalent of 'the grim reaper'. But Mara can be defeated. He is not the Devil, as in western thought. Mara does not come to plague us with temptations or make life difficult for

243

us. He is passive, and perhaps we can see him as a personification of death, rather than an active force.

'This is the path for purifying one's vision; there is no other. Follow it, you'll bewilder Mara. Follow it, you'll put an end to suffering... ' (20:273, page 71).

'Those who delight in calming their thoughts... will bring an end to craving. They will cut Mara's bonds' (24:349-350, page 90).

Literary merit

The Dhammapada, even in translation, shines out as a work of literary merit. Some of the figures of speech are of great spiritual value and enhance the work enormously. It is not a drab, plain statement in univocal language; there is much to stimulate the imagination and appeal to the soul of mankind.

We begin with a selection of similes:

'As rain penetrates an ill-thatched house, so lust penetrates an uncultivated mind. As rain does not penetrate a well-thatched house, so lust does not penetrate a well-thatched house' (1:13-14, page 4).

'Even a young Bhikkhu (monk) lights up this world, like the moon set free from a cloud' (25:382, page 98).

'Speak or act with a corrupted mind, and suffering follows as the wagon wheel follows the hoof of the ox... speak or act with a peaceful mind and happiness follows like a never-departing shadow' (1:1-2, page 1).

There is imagination and poetry in this, which makes the work attractive. The use of metaphor is every bit as apt:

'Cut down the forest (of desire), not (real) trees. From the forest (of desire), fear is born. Having cut down both the forest and the underbrush, monks, be deforested (of desire)' (20:283, page 73).

'Weeds are the ruin of fields; ill will is the ruin of people. So offerings to those free of ill will bear great fruit' (24:357, page 92).

'The one who keeps anger in check as it arises, as one would a careening chariot, I call a charioteer. Others are merely rein-holders' (17:222, page 59).

'When, with tranquillity and insight, the Brahmin reaches the other shore, then for that "knowing one" all fetters come to their end' (26:384, page 99).

This is of course talking about arriving in Nirvana and casting off all pain, fear and worldly cares. More noteworthy in the Dhammapada is the use of antitheses, often with some kind of recurring chorus.

'Whoever lives focused on the pleasant, senses unguarded, immoderate with food, lazy and sluggish, will be overpowered by Mara, as a weak tree is bent in the wind. Whoever lives focused on the unpleasant, senses guarded, moderate with food, faithful and diligent, will not be overpowered by Mara, as a stone mountain is unmoved by the wind' (1:7-8, page 3).

'Sorrow grows like grass after rain, for anyone overcome by this miserable craving and clinging to the world. Sorrow falls away like drops of water from a lotus, for anyone who overcomes this miserable craving and clinging to the world' (24:335-336, page 87).

A recurring chorus is often used. A good example would be 'there is no grief; and 'from where would fear come?' This comes round five times in 16:212-216, page 57. It is easy to imagine the monks chanting this and the chorus is an aid to memorisation. Sometimes the repetition is slightly altered as the verses proceed. So for instance in 8:100, page 27 we have 'Better than a thousand meaningless statements is one meaningful word, which having been heard brings peace' and then it graduates to 'one meaningful line of verse' and then to 'one line of Dharma' (8:102, page 27)[8].

The Dhammapada is rather short of paradoxes, which is a surprise, but a good one occurs in 26:385, page 99.

'Whoever is united and free of distress and for whom neither a"beyond", a "not-beyond", nor a "both beyond-and-not-beyond" exist, I call a Brahmin.'

This is talking about Nirvana; elsewhere there is the contrast between this world and the next, using the metaphor of a sea-shore:

'Few are the people who reach the other shore. Many are the people who run about on this shore' 6:85, page 22.

In 2:26, page 7 the metaphor is developed a little further.

'Through effort, vigilance, restraint and self-control, the wise person can become an island no flood will overwhelm.'

This ties in with the impression of a meditator being a hermit not necessarily needing a monastic community to work with.

Another feature, not quite a paradox but certainly a contradiction is the use of balancing contrasts. Chapter one dubs them as 'dichotomies'. Each pair of verses uses much the same expression but are opposites, good and evil. So for example 1:3-4, page 2.

'"He abused me, attacked me, defeated me, robbed me!" For those carrying on like this, hatred does not end.'
"She abused me, attacked me, defeated me, robbed me!" For those not carrying on like this, hatred ends.'

Many of the verses in the Dhammapada follow this kind of pattern.

In general terms, the figurative language in the Dhammapada is of a high quality, using much imagination; this can be admired, regardless of one's feelings about Buddhism in general.

Linguistic considerations

As this work is written in Pali, an ancient language of India and now not normally spoken, there are problems in translation, which Gil Fronsdal has coped with admirably. The word *Dharma* (which is the same as *Dhamma*) is a key word found in the title, the Dhammapada, but is not easy to translate because, being a pejorative word, it has a whole range of implications[8].

'Live the Dharma, a life of good conduct... ' (13:169, page 45).

This is a simplistic use of the word, but it also implies much more. Religious teaching, religious truth, justice, virtue, even experience, and mental states. It could be left untranslated since any attempt at rendering it in English inevitably distorts its meaning somehow.

The word *Yamaka* means 'pairs or twins' but is rendered as 'dichotomies' as discussed above. The effect of this is to bring out the contrast between good and bad.

Sometimes we have a word that is not clear at all. *Yamamase* is taken to mean 'we here must die' (1:6, page 2); it could be rendered 'others do not realise that we should be restrained'. If however it is read as *Yama-amase*, it may refer to Yama the king of death and would then mean 'going into the presence of Yama.'

The word *Amata* is a key word with powerful overtones in Buddhist scriptures. It means 'deathless' and is a euphemism for Nirvana, the state one achieves if one does not have to be reborn into yet another unpleasant life. *Amata* stands in contrast to the frequent mention of *Mara*, which is a personification of Death.

In 26:388, page 100 we have a word-play between *pabbajeti* and *pabbajati*. The first one means 'drives out, makes go away, banishes' and the second word means 'goes forth into the renunciate life'. Also there is another word-play between *samacariya* and *samano*. The first word means 'living peacefully' and the second means 'renunciant'. So the sense is as follows:

'Having *banished* evil, one is called a Brahmin. *Living peacefully,* one is called a renunciant. *Having driven out* one's own impurities, one is called "one who has *gone forth.*"'

All this indicates that in translation many of the nuances are lost.

Often we have remarks that seem obscure and can only be explained by knowledge of general Buddhist thought. So, for instance in 25:370, page 95 it talks about the five fetters and the five faculties. These can be explained as follows:
The five lower fetters are:

1. Views pertaining to self or what belongs to self
2. Doubt
3. Grasping at precepts and practices
4. Sensual passion
5. Ill will.

The higher fetters are:

1. Attachment to phenomena or form
2. Attachment to the formless phenomena
3. Conceit
4. Restlessness
5. Ignorance

The five faculties are:

1. faith
2. effort
3. mindfulness
4. concentration
5. wisdom or insight.

If a monk manages to achieve all this, he will be termed 'one who has crossed the flood', which is a metaphor for Nirvana.

This is just a sample of the linguistic considerations in the Pali of the Dhammapada. An experienced Buddhist might well say that every time he reads this book, another aspect or nuance may become apparent. It is like the Bible, in that different matters occur to different people and different situations may bring out other implications. The work is a work of genius, even if it is a compilation of Siddhartha's thoughts. From the Western point of view, the missing ingredient is the Almighty merciful God who cares for mankind and invites them to be reconciled with him. This is not mentioned in the Dhammapada, but Buddhist philosophy later came to speculate on all kinds of principles and bodhisattvas[9] stretching back in time and into the future. All very theoretical and abstruse; the opposite of Deuteronomy which says 'the word is very near to you... '

Concluding remarks about the Dhammapada

This book is a remarkable document which is seminal to the religion of Buddhism. It could fairly be said to be the Buddhist statement of truth. Claims to be the truth are found in virtually all the selected scriptural material and one is left wondering which one is correct. A quotation from 20:273, page 71 sums it up quite well:

'The best of paths is the Eightfold Path; the best of truths, the Four Noble Truths. The best of qualities is dispassion; and the best among gods and humans is the one with eyes to see.'

We have seen that some of this ties in with other systems of thought. It is not that Buddhism is a totally different theory of truth. It simply varies according to emphasis. The emphasis is not on Almighty God, the Creator. The emphasis is firmly on self-help and the accruing of merit. As with every aspect of theology, there is that element of truth and also of falsehood. We see in the teachings of Jesus that there is a sense in which there are rewards waiting for those who make a commitment to right behaviour and the Kingdom of God. There is a sense in which the believer makes an approach to God and God listens. On the other hand, there is the sense that God selects people, cleanses them and puts their lives right. This is a paradox that does not emerge in Buddhism. The emphasis is heavily on the individual deciding to gain wisdom, the correct approach to life and morality. It may be that later generations of Buddhists sensed this imbalance and found theoretical ways of addressing it.

One such aspect is the phenomenon of Amida[10], a king who is imagined to have accrued so much merit that it was transferable to poor languishing souls who could not manage to accrue merit. One simply had to appeal to the merits of Amida. Amida was never a real historical person; he was purely theoretical and mythological. He is never mentioned in the Dhammapada.

What is mentioned in passing is the existence of 'buddhas', which implies that Siddhartha was by no means the only one. These buddhas are believed to have appeared at other times in the past and will appear in the future to bring the message of the truth to those whose minds are darkened by wrong ideas. In a way this is their answer to the problem of particularity; if the Buddha appeared at a certain time and place in history, that would be unfair on earlier generations who could not have heard his teachings. The Zoroastrians had another way round the problem; that every thousand years a 'world saviour' would appear. The Christians had another way round it; that although Jesus Christ only needed to come once, his message would continue into the future via the Holy Spirit and backwards into the past since he visited the languishing souls in hell and gave them relief.

'... purifying one's mind; this is the teaching of the buddhas. Patient endurance is the supreme austerity. The buddhas say that Nirvana is supreme' 14:183-4, page 49.

Notes for Chapter 14: The Dhammapada

1. The title of the book, Dhammapada. *Pada* means 'path, foot, way' and *Dhamma* means teachings, truth, justice, virtue and even experience. It had a very wide range of meaning, a pejorative word which is hard to translate without some sort of paraphrase. It is the equivalent of Dharma (Sanskrit).
2. Bhagavad Gita. (Chapter 9). This is an important Hindu scripture, which describes the relationship between Krishna and the believer, in this case Arjuna.
3. Karma; this is the Hindu-Buddhist doctrine of reincarnation. It is a basic assumption in India and countries under that influence.
4. The Wheel of Becoming. This is usually six samsaric realms through which one passes from one life to another. To escape from it one needs to aim for Nirvana. The symbol for Buddhism is the Wheel of Becoming.
5. Clearly the Ten Commandments are being used, in part, to define good conduct in the Buddhist life. The Noble Eightfold Path includes five rules; not to kill (that includes animals), no stealing, adultery is wrong, drugs or alcohol are forbidden.
6. Matanga; this was an elephant who became disillusioned with life in the herd and went off to live a solitary life.
7. Mara, the King of Death. This is rather like Yama, a frightening skull figure that presides over the Wheel of Becoming and holds it up like a mirror to show us what we really are.
8. Dharma, the same as Dhamma as described in number one.
9. Bodhisattvas: these are spiritual beings like the Buddha who come in mercy to help mortals to find Nirvana. There are thought to have been hundreds of them.
10. Purusha or Perusha. This is the Hindu equivalent of Amida (or Amidaba), the king who accrued so much merit that lesser mortals could appeal to him and benefit from it.

15

The Proverbs

A book that has affinities with the Dhammapada (Chapter 14) is the book of
Proverbs in the Old Testament. One wonders if Siddhartha knew of it and
gleaned ideas from it. It is probably one of the least well-known books in
the Bible and yet indirectly it has a lot to show us about life and thought
in the Hebrew world. No one knows when it was written; opinions vary
widely about its dating. It may have been like Deuteronomy, an ongoing
collection, and the product of a succession of authors. Some of the language
is difficult and obscure to translate; this may indicate an early date for it,
but not necessarily. The first verse, which ascribes the Proverbs to King
Solomon, the son of David, may not mean quite what it would appear to
mean. It is true that Solomon was the father of Hebrew wisdom but that
does not have to mean that he wrote every bit of it. It may mean that it was
written in the tradition of Solomon's patterns of thought. In Chapter10:1
there is a title stating 'the Proverbs of Solomon' and in 25:1 there is another
claim that the following are the proverbs of Solomon copied by the men of
Hezekiah, king of Judah (which would be some 200 years after Solomon's
time). In 30:1 the following are stated as the 'words of Agur son of Jakeh
of Massa' (which might also mean 'the oracle'). In 31 we have 'the words
of Lemuel king of Massa which his mother taught him'. This is enough to
show that the book is not from a single author but an ongoing collection
probably from the time of Solomon down to the late Monarchic times. To
support this view, there is the book The Wisdom of Solomon, a post-exilic
work of the Apocrypha; clearly 'Solomon' does not literally mean the man
himself, but his tradition. Having said this, there is a certain unity of thought
and connected message in Proverbs. It is not as if one writer contradicts
another. A few words will be said about the Solomonic corpus of literature
as a postscript to this analysis.

Historical aspects

There is no historical account in Proverbs whatsoever. This is unusual in the Old Testament and the Bible generally, since the faith of Israel is anchored in historical realities. We may see the mention of David, Solomon, Hezekiah and others as an attempt at rectifying this matter. Even if the book has no story line, it still draws in real historical characters. The same goes for geographical realities. Scientific matters only receive indirect remarks, such as the 'pillars of the earth'. Also there is nothing mathematical such as dates, and measurements. The only thing that could be seen as mathematical is the so-called 'number Proverbs' which will be discussed later.

Mythology

As a kind of corrective for the lack of historical material, there are various references to mythology. These are not plentiful, but are essential for the thought patterns of the Wisdom writers. This is where philosophy and mythology merge to give a rationale for the phenomenon of Wisdom. While the surrounding nations produced the wisdom literature as the bright ideas of their own magi, the Hebrew version of it is clearly related to the creative genius of the one true God. Wisdom is personified as a woman; the first thing that God produced at the beginning of Creation.

'The Lord created me at the beginning of his work, the first of his acts of old. Ages ago I was set up, at the first, before the beginning of the earth... when he established the heavens, I was there. When he drew a circle on the face of the deep... then I was beside him, like a master workman, and I was daily his delight...' (Proverbs 8:22).

It is strange that this fundamental thought does not appear until Chapter 8; even so, 1:7 lays down the theological basis of Wisdom.

'The fear of the Lord is the beginning of knowledge; fools despise wisdom and knowledge' (Proverbs 1:7).

In 3:19, in a less poetic tone, Wisdom is mentioned almost as a tool used in Creation.

'The Lord by wisdom founded the earth; by understanding he established the heavens; by his knowledge the deeps broke forth...'

We can see that 'understanding' and 'knowledge' are synonyms for skill, ingenuity and brilliance.

The personification of Wisdom does not infringe the concept of monotheism. The Hebrews would hardly have taken it literally, but as high-flown poetic expression. But of course, later generations were to conceive of wisdom as a separate entity. The Christians quickly equated wisdom with Jesus Christ, even if it was expressed in feminine terms.

In addition to an understanding of Creation, which incidentally presupposes the early parts of Genesis, we also have the mythological concept of the three-tiered universe: heaven, earth and hell. At that time, people almost certainly took it completely literally. Also it was generally thought that since the sky was blue, that meant there was an ocean arching over the sky and this was called the 'firmament'. That word itself never occurs in Proverbs, but 'heavens' do appear. Far more heavily emphasised is Sheol or 'the Pit', which is an early understanding of Hell. This was the Hebrew understanding of the underworld; we see this assumption in the Epic of Inanna in Chapter 22. The idea that hell was fires of torment only came in later under Zoroastrian influence. Sheol was the fate of those who were sinners.

'... like Sheol let us swallow them alive... like those who go down to the Pit' (Proverbs 1:12).

Another word for Sheol is Abaddon (27:20). It would appear that Sheol was not the inevitable destination for everyone; it could be avoided, but there is no real explanation for what the alternative could be, unless one were of the stature of Enoch, Moses or Elijah, who were 'assumed'.

'If you beat him with a rod, you will save his life from Sheol' (Proverbs 23:14).

'The wise man's path leads upward to life, that he may avoid Sheol beneath' (Proverbs 15:24).

The mention of a wise man's path reminds us of the Dhammapada (Chapter 14), which means the path of wisdom, and the connection to Buddhist thought is reinforced by this.

'Her house is the way to Sheol; going down to the chambers of death' (Proverbs 7:27).

Here we see Sheol as virtually a personification of death in the way that Yama and Mara are described in the Dhammapada. But Proverbs does not go so far as to state that the wise go to heaven; that would be the inference from 'leads upwards to life', but that is never explained or clarified. This stands in contrast to the Egyptian ideas about the afterlife, (Chapter 25) which were highly elaborate. When we look at the Book of the Dead, we see highly developed ideas about funerary procedures and one's condition in the next world[1].

Theological factors

It hardly needs remarking that Proverbs has a thorough acceptance of the One God. There is never any mention of other gods, even in a negative context. Neither is there any mention of evil spirits or Satan. This might indicate an early date but it is not total proof. We are enjoined to trust in God and this will be true insight and wealth (Proverbs 3:5 and 28:25).

With regard to the question of theodicy, the problem of pain, there is no attempt at an explanation. A few stray remarks may give some kind of indirect indication but there is nothing definite offered:

> 'The rich and the poor meet together; the Lord is the maker of them all' (Proverbs 22:2).

This is a brief thought on the question of poverty versus wealth; ultimately, it is God who creates the difference.

> 'Who has woe? Who has sorrow? Who has strife? Who is complaining? Who has wounds without cause? Who has redness of eyes?' (Proverbs 23:29).

This raises the question of why people suffer when they have not deserved it, the most poignant aspect of theodicy. There is no clear answer to this. Proverbs goes on to skirt the question by blaming it on drunkenness, which means people losing control of themselves. There may be an indirect reference to the serpent as in the Garden of Eden, '... at the last it bites like a serpent, and stings like an adder'. But this is talking about the drink rather than temptation coming from an evil influence.

There is only one use of the word 'covenant' in Proverbs 2:17 and in a context which is not very relevant to the main thrust of Old Testament theology. However, the main covenants are assumed rather than referred to. With the book accredited to David and Solomon, this brings to mind the Davidic covenant, the kingship arrangement that God made with David, that his heirs would continue to reign and be guided by the Almighty. Solomon's dream, as a continuation of that thought, is described in 1 Kings 3:10, in which God gave him a wise and discerning mind to rule the Israelites, and because he had not asked for wealth, God promised him wealth as well as wisdom. Also the Mosaic covenant is assumed rather than stated plainly:

> 'My son, do not forget my teaching but let your heart keep my commandments; for length of days and years of life and abundant welfare will they give you. Let not loyalty and faithfulness forsake you, bind them about your neck and write them on the tablet of your heart[2]. So you will find favour and good repute in the sight of God and man' (Proverbs 3:1-4).

This is the assumption from Deuteronomy 28 and other places, that if one keeps God's laws, then all will go well and one will prosper. There is no attempt at discussing the sad situation where a righteous man falls into misfortune, as with Job. This may indicate that Job was written some time after the book of Proverbs, but not necessarily so. Also writing up the commandments reminds us of the writing on the two tables of stone as seen in Exodus and Deuteronomy. There is no mention, direct or indirect, of the covenants of Noah or of Abraham.

The dilemma over free will and predestination receives a brief but poignant airing in two references:

> 'A man's steps are ordered by the Lord; how then can man understand his way?' (Proverbs 20:24).

This clearly states that God directs people's lives but then the question inevitably arises as to how much freedom we have. 'How can a man understand his way?' could be a confused way of saying, 'We don't know where we are going but we appear to have free choices'.

Another reference is even more illuminating:

> 'A man's mind plans his way, but the Lord directs his steps' (Proverbs 16:9).

This is in effect saying that God predetermines the pattern of one's life, but even so one makes choices and takes certain courses. This is a stunning paradox, which philosophers have failed to take on board; on the one hand there is predestination but on the other hand there is free will. This is a contradiction that cannot be explained by the human mind, and probably never will be. But this actually provides the answer to this dilemma and it presupposes the existence of the Almighty who decides and controls everything.

> 'The lot is cast into the lap, but the decision is wholly from the Lord' (Proverbs 16:33).

In effect this is saying that things may appear to happen by chance, like tossing a coin, but it is God who brings the outcome. This is a perceptive comment on the dilemma over free will and predestination.

The theology of the Old Testament is inextricably bound up with moral standards as a vital element in the Mosaic covenant. Proverbs does not actually cite the Ten Commandments but refers to them indirectly. There is no attempt at commenting on the ritual prescriptions of Exodus and Deuteronomy, except to say:

'To do righteousness and justice is more acceptable to the Lord than sacrifice' (Proverbs 21:3).

'The sacrifice of the wicked is an abomination' (Proverbs 21:27).

This gives rather a negative feel to the ritual injunctions of the Mosaic laws. It is interesting that the first quotation is actually looking forward to the Christian era, in which it was realised that the ritual material could be omitted and a greater emphasis laid on morality.

But there are indirect references to the Ten Commandments:

'A false witness will not go unpunished, and he who utters lies will not escape' (Proverbs 19:5; also 19:9 which is almost the same).

This is referring to 'thou shalt not bear false witness against thy neighbour', but it is intensified to include lying. There are several remarks about lying, which amount to the same thing. This trend to intensification is seen in the teachings of Jesus, in the Sermon on the Mount.

'There are six things that the Lord hates, seven which are an abomination to him; haughty eyes, a lying tongue, and hands that shed innocent blood, a heart that devises wicked plans, feet that make haste to run to evil, a false witness that breathes out lies, and a man who sows discord among brothers' (Proverbs 6:16-19).

'If a man is burdened with the blood of another, let him be a fugitive until death...' (Proverbs 28:17).

This time we have a reference to 'thou shalt not commit murder'. In 22:22 we have a reference to theft, 'do not rob the poor because he is poor or crush the afflicted at the gate...'. Other than that we seem not to have much mention of 'thou shalt not steal'.

Of course, the whole book is based on the advice of a father to his son. So often we hear this kind of exhortation:

'Hear my son, your father's instruction and reject not your mother's teaching' (Proverbs 1:8).

This clearly involves the fifth commandment, 'honour your father and mother'. This motif has the strongest emphasis in the book, followed closely by the order to tell the truth.

There is no direct allusion to 'thou shalt not commit adultery', however there is much said about marriage and sexual relations. In Proverbs 31:10 we have a picture of the ideal wife:

'A good wife, who can find? She is far more precious than jewels. The heart of her husband trusts in her... she opens her mouth with wisdom and the teaching of kindness is on her tongue... '

This takes a positive look at family life and cohesion, which is an advance on the negative feel of the eighth commandment. This is contrasted very strongly with the foolish woman who does not have any restraint:

'A foolish woman is noisy; she is wanton and knows no shame. She sits in the door of her house... calling to those who pass by... ' (Proverbs 9:13).

'For the lips of a foolish woman drip honey, and her speech is smoother than oil...' (Proverbs 5:3).

It gets worse, for now we have various references to prostitutes seducing young men. The passage 7:6-27 presents the picture of a prostitute peering out and spotting a young innocent man in the twilight. She goes out to seduce him, with promises of luxury and delight, while her husband is away. The wise man cautions us against this sort of thing that can only end in disaster, and a visit to Sheol. The purpose of this lurid passage is to make the contrast with Wisdom, personified as a woman. One wonders if this element in Proverbs is not meant figuratively just as the female Wisdom is not to be taken literally.

'Say to Wisdom, "You are my sister" and call insight your intimate friend; to preserve you from the loose woman and from the adventuress with her smooth words' (Proverbs 7:4-5). There are several other places where a warning is given against prostitution. This reminds us of the prophet Hosea, who had to bring his erring wife back; it was a parable for Israel deserting the true God[3]. Possibly prostitution is not meant literally here; it is an attempt at persuading people to be true to the Wisdom of God. Then in Chapter 8 comes the famous and axiomatic statement of Wisdom being the 'right hand man' of God in Creation.

'Does not Wisdom call? Does not understanding raise her voice?' (Proverbs 8:1-31).

This is another woman who calls out to people and tries to draw them, not unlike a prostitute, but for a completely opposite purpose, that of instilling decent conduct and morality. The contrast is a powerful one, and explains why wisdom is personified as a female as opposed to a male. There is also the implication that God has a female counterpart in his workings; this is in a way a response to the pagan, Canaanite notion that Baal has a consort, Astarte, the stone pillar and the wooden pillar[4]. But this is pure speculation; it is never alluded to directly in Proverbs.

A natural development of the wisdom genre is sound advice to kings and rulers. This is where Proverbs is related to the Analects of Confucius, (Chapter 8); whether the one knew of the other is impossible to be certain, but it is not out of the question. More likely, the Dhammapada of Buddhism (Chapter 14) knew of Proverbs and included some comments about rulership.

'By me (Wisdom) kings reign and rulers decree what is just, by me princes rule and nobles govern the earth' (Proverbs 8:15).

There are various comments on methods of ruling and how one should approach a king. It must be remembered that this was an age when the king had absolute power and in many nations was actually seen as a god. The Hebrews were the exception to this and never regarded any of their kings as gods; more likely they described all their shortcomings and blamed them for the fall of both Hebrew kingdoms. But at this stage, there is a certain degree of idealisation of kingship, which again might argue for an earlier date.

'In the light of a king's face there is life, and his favour is like the clouds that bring the spring rain' (Proverbs 16:15).

'The king's heart is a stream of water in the hand of the Lord; he turns it wherever he will' (Proverbs 21:1).

'By justice a king gives stability to the land, but one who exacts gifts ruins it' (Proverbs 29:4).

There is an awareness that not all kings are honest and caring for their people:

'Like a roaring lion or a charging bear is a wicked ruler over a poor people. A ruler who lacks understanding is a cruel oppressor' (Proverbs 28:15-16).

As today, rulers and governments vary greatly in their policies; some caring and humanitarian, others ruthless, exploitative and dishonest. In many places, Proverbs is advising decency and integrity in the use of power over the peoples of the nations.

In general terms, Proverbs is supportive of the Mosaic legal system and it is interesting how many times an obscure law suddenly surfaces. An example of this comes twice:

'Remove not the ancient landmark which your fathers have set' (Proverbs 22:28).

'Remove not an ancient landmark or enter the fields of the fatherless...' (Proverbs 23:10).

This clearly recalls Deuteronomy 27:17, 'cursed be he who removes his neighbour's landmark'. The importance of this is that it would be easy to steal someone's land by surreptitiously moving someone's landmark; nowadays this is done by a subtle relocation of fencing so that one's land is augmented at the expense of another's.

An important strand in Proverbs is the advice not to get involved with criminals.

'My son, if sinners entice you, do not consent. If they say, "Come with us, let us lie in wait for blood... "' (Proverbs 1:10).

The same advice in different phrasing keeps reappearing throughout the book, which lends an air of integrity for the book. This advice even extends to those who are liable to lose their tempers.

'A man of understanding remains silent...' (Proverbs 11:12).

'A tranquil mind gives life to the flesh but passion makes the bones rot' (Proverbs 14:30).

'If you have been foolish, exalting yourself, or if you have been devising evil, put your hand on your mouth for pressing milk produces curds, pressing the nose produces blood, and pressing anger produces strife' (Proverbs 30:32).

This all fits in with the thought that Wisdom, as personified, is modest and uses measured speech. Paradoxically, Wisdom cries out to attract people and yet there is restraint.

'Wisdom is too high for a fool; in the gate he does not open *his* mouth' (Proverbs 24:7).

'In the gate...[5] ' indicates where the elders and leaders used to gather to discuss important matters. But a wise person will observe caution when these debates begin; let the loud-mouthed ones carry on. We notice here that Wisdom has slipped into the masculine. This trait of reticence is evidenced in Job and also Confucius, who was inclined to observe caution when asked an awkward question.

In general terms, Proverbs equates fools with wickedness and wise people with virtue. This all ties in with those of easy mouth and those who are taciturn.

'Wise men lay up knowledge but the babbling fool brings ruin near; a rich man's wealth is his strong city, the poverty of the poor man is their ruin. The wage of the righteous leads to life, the gain of the wicked to sin...' (Proverbs 10:15).

The contrast is a strong one, between the idiot and the sage. Here we see the metaphor of wealth and poverty brought in to show the contrast between wisdom and folly. This is a clue that many of the sayings in this book are not to be taken completely literally. Much of it is figurative. The poetry of the book will be discussed later. In contrast with the Dhammapada, it seems that the simpleton can be helped to become wise, if only he will pay attention.

'"Whoever is simple, let him turn here." To him who is without sense she says, "Come eat of my bread and drink of the wine I have mixed. Leave simpleness and live, and walk in the way of insight."' (Proverbs 9:4-6).

In common with the Dhammapada there seems to be no graduation of wisdom. Either one is a fool or a wise man; there seems to be no mention of those who are some sort of happy average between these two poles. This kind of categorical thinking appears all through the book.

'The tongue of the wise dispenses knowledge; but the mouths of fools pour out folly... in the house of the righteous there is much treasure, but trouble befalls the income of the wicked' (Proverbs 15:2-6).

But whoever they are, wise or stupid, God is keeping an eye on them all the time; whether it is material wealth or spiritual richness, it is God who dispenses it according to each man's deserts. We do not have any specific mention of 'merit' as seen in Buddhism; even so, the thought-system of the Mosaic covenant is assumed all through the book. 'You reap as you sow'; your conduct produces an appropriate fate.

'Poverty and disgrace come to him who ignores instruction, but he who heeds reproof is honoured' (Proverbs 13:18).

In general terms though, there is nothing like the emphasis laid on merit as in the Dhammapada. This is probably because there is no assumption of Karma[6] and the personal effort involved in promoting oneself to heaven or Nirvana. Proverbs is almost certainly assuming predestination, which would mean that merit, in effect, would be meaningless.

Philosophy

As with many Hebrew scriptural texts, it would be artificial to try to separate Theology from Philosophy. The nearest we come to philosophy in the sense of what we see in the great Greek philosophers (and Chinese) is to be found in the wisdom literature of Proverbs, Job, Ecclesiastes, and also in the Apocrypha. But the Hebrews were so taken up with the imminence of God and the great covenants that speculation on philosophical matters was low on their agenda. We have already seen that free will and predestination were an issue for them, but not something to go into great details about. If asked the question about the ultimate truth, a Hebrew sage would probably say:

'Hear, for I will speak noble things, and from my lips will come what is right, for my mouth will utter *truth*, wickedness is an abomination to my lips' (Proverbs 8:6-7).

This is the crucial passage in which Wisdom, personified as a woman, appeals to all people to take her seriously. The ultimate truth, that is the standards of God, as given in the commandments, are the yardstick by which everything should be measured. Any other philosophy of life is not the truth and utter folly. We are advised to listen to the wise men and trust in God. The imminence of Wisdom is seen in Deuteronomy, right in front of one, unmissible and personally obvious.

'I have made them known to you today, even to you. Have I not written to you thirty sayings of admonition and knowledge, to show you what is right and **true** that you may give a true answer to those who sent you?' (Proverbs 22:19-21).

This is in fact saying that all forms of knowledge and truth stem from Wisdom, and she is the companion of God in Creation. This then is the fundamental truth that underpins every philosophy.

Literary worth

Proverbs is entirely expressed in poetry; there is no prose at all, which makes it a contrast with many other biblical books that are an admixture. Comparing it with the Psalms, one might say that the standard of poetry is not quite as high-flown, but of a very high standard. Often we have sustained parallelism, which is typical of Hebrew poetry.

'Riches and honour are with me, enduring wealth and prosperity; my fruit is better than gold, even fine gold, and my yield than choice silver. I walk in the way of righteousness, in the paths of justice, endowing with wealth those who love me, and filling their treasuries' (Proverbs 8:18-21).

This more or less sums up the sage's understanding of the mosaic covenant; do good and you will prosper. And yet the metaphor of earthly wealth illuminates the true wealth of spiritual rewards.

'Happy is the man who finds wisdom, and the man who gets understanding; for the gain from it is better than gain from silver and its profit better than gold. She is more precious than jewels and nothing you desire can compare with her. Long life is in her right hand; in her left hand are riches and honour. Her ways are ways of pleasantness and all her paths are peace. She is a **tree of life** to those who lay hold of her; those who hold her fast are called happy' (Proverbs 3:13-18).

The same metaphor concerning wealth appears here, with the added allusion to the Tree of Life as in the Garden of Eden, which again connects Wisdom with the earliest beginnings of Creation.

'Wisdom has built her house; she has set up her seven pillars. She has slaughtered her beasts, she has mixed her wine, she has also set her table. She has sent out her maids to call from the highest places in the town...' (Proverbs 9:1-3).

This whole passage has to be taken figuratively. Wisdom has built a temple and set up seven pillars. The seven pillars are highly poetic; it was believed that the three tiers of the universe were held up by pillars. In 1 Samuel 2:8

it says that the pillars of the earth are the Lord's and he has set the world on them. It is a poetic way of saying that God has founded the earth and made it steady; it has firmness, structural integrity and careful design work. These pillars are not mentioned in the Genesis account. The fear was that if God sent an earthquake, all the pillars would wobble.

'… who shakes the earth out of its place, and its pillars tremble…' (Job 9:8).

If Wisdom has killed animals, this indicates that the passage cannot be taken literally. It could mean that she has sacrificed something to God, but more likely it is the preparation for the feast that is coming. The feast is of course for all those who respond to the invitation to come and accept wisdom, for this is the true wealth. This is possibly the background thought to the Parable of the Great Feast, when the host has to send out to fetch in all manner of people. Also it gives fresh light on the Messianic Banquet as alluded to by Jesus[7].

There are several literary devices used in the Proverbs. There is an interesting use of an acrostic in the last few verses, 31:10-31. It begins with 'a good wife, who can find?' starting with Aleph, the first letter of the Hebrew alphabet, and going through to Tau, the last letter, with 'give her the fruit of her hands'. The passage does not seem to work too well with the 'words of Lemuel'. However, the description of a good wife balances well with the description of Wisdom as in the first nine chapters. The whole book is framed by this motif of the wise lady who cares for us, and whom we can trust. This again raises the question of how literally we should take the last passage; is Proverbs talking in literal terms about someone's wife? How many wives, in those days, plant a vineyard or go in for commerce? What is meant by 'snow' and 'scarlet clothing' for her household? 'She opens her mouth with wisdom' gives it away; this is personified Wisdom again, bringing the book to a closure. If her trainees wear scarlet, does that mean they are judges, and make all the right decisions? And snow; is that symbolic of cleanliness, purity and innocence? If this is a fair assessment, it shows that the book has some sort of framework or structure.

Obviously, most of the book is what appears to be random sayings, sometimes isolated and unrelated to their neighbouring remarks. No one has yet managed to see any logical progression in the layout of the sayings.

In spite of the obscurity of Proverbs, there are various sayings which have become famous; some quoted by Jesus himself. If one is kind to one's enemy 'you will heap coals of fire on his head' (Proverbs 25:22). In 16:18 we have 'Pride goes before destruction, and a haughty spirit before a fall'. This is the origin of our English proverb, 'Pride comes before a fall'. 'A soft answer turns away wrath, but a harsh word stirs up anger' (Proverbs 15:1) is another good example[8].

Another literary device is the so-called 'number proverbs'. Here is an example:

> 'Three things are stately in their tread, four are stately in their stride: the lion, which is mightiest among beasts and does not turn back for any; the strutting cock, the he-goat, and a king striding before his people' (Proverbs 30:29).

In Proverbs, we can find six such sayings: 6:16, 30:15, 30:18, 30:21, 30:24, 30:29. But the technique can be found elsewhere, in Job and other wisdom literature of the times. No one knows for sure what the intention was in doing it this way. It is just possible that the numbers used centre around three, four and seven, which would indicate the number of eternity, namely seven. This recalls the structure of the universe; if Wisdom is the basic factor in creation, then seven indicates or mirrors Wisdom. In Proverbs 6:16 we have six which becomes seven; is this saying, symbolically, that six is nearly right but not quite, and seven completes it, the things that the Lord hates? But there is no doubting the intention of humour when a proud king is associated with a strutting cockerel! Another amusing quip is 'Like a gold ring in a swine's snout is a beautiful woman with no discretion' (Proverbs 11:22). We must recall that the pig is seen as an unclean animal.

But some of the sayings are truly beautiful and profound. 'A word fitly spoken is like apples of gold in a setting of silver' (Proverbs 25:11). Also, 'Like the glaze covering an earthen vessel are the smooth lips with an evil heart' (Proverbs 26:23). It must have required someone with imagination and poetic soul to produce lines like this. One thinks of Solomon.

Linguistic considerations

Proverbs is written entirely in Hebrew and not very easy to translate; this is in contrast to books such as Deuteronomy, Samuel and the Kings which are relatively straightforward. There are many words and expressions which are obscure, partly because they are *happax legomena* (one-off words) and partly because their cultural background gives no clue as to their intended meaning. A few examples will suffice:

> 'The leech (?) has two daughters, "Give, give," they cry. Three things are never satisfied, four never say "Enough". Sheol, the barren womb, the earth ever thirsty for water, and the fire which never says, "Enough" (?)' (Proverbs 30:15).

Aluqah is thought to mean a 'leech'; it is probably an Aramaic loan word. It meant a vampire-like demon, which might fit better here. *Hon* is rendered as 'enough' but it has the implication of wealth, being satisfied. If we can see behind the metaphor, it conveys a very true issue; greed is never satisfied. Like Hell, dried up land and a woman desperate to have a baby; they go on demanding. How true!

> 'It is better to live on the corner of a rooftop (*pinath gag*) than to live in a house with a contentious woman (*haver*)' (Proverbs 25:24).

Not only is this rather amusing, but it conceals at least two cultural factors. The corner of a rooftop does not mean that one should live in an attic; the Israelite house would have a flat roof and one could spend all day and night (perhaps in a shelter) on top of the house rather than inside.

Also the *haver*, rendered as a brawling woman, carries the implication of 'association', in other words, a prostitute. This ties in with the strong advice elsewhere in Proverbs to steer clear of prostitutes. Again, as with the other women used metaphorically, the prostitute may not have to be taken totally literally. Stupidity is also personified as a woman, and forms a strong contrast with Wisdom and also the ideal wife. So this saying, which seems rather strange, is actually very much to the point. Keep away from folly.

And finally, a proverb that was used by Jesus for one of his parables is interesting:

> 'Do not put yourself forward in the king's presence or stand in the place of the great, for it is better to be told, "Come up here," than to be put lower in the presence of the prince' (Proverbs 25:6-7).

In Luke 14:7:11, we have a much fuller version of this motif. There are those who push their way to the front, only to be told to take a humbler place, and those who sit at the back and then receive an invitation to take a more exalted position. Luke takes it out of the context of a king's banquet, but of course, there is the assumption of the Messianic banquet in the background, with Jesus as the King. It fits in with Luke's theology very well: 'for everyone who exalts himself will be humbled, and he who humbles himself will be exalted' (Luke 14:11). It also fits in with the thinking of Proverbs, only there, it is the ones who shoot their mouths off that are ill-advised; those who are taciturn, like Confucius, are the real people to take notice of. This is the basis of our proverb, 'empty tins rattle most'[8].

Concluding remarks about the Proverbs

One of the least well known books in the Bible, Proverbs has nevertheless had its influence on later times, including Jesus. There is always the tension between the literal and figurative. This is a factor seen in many sacred writings, but the ongoing indication that much of this book is metaphoric, is the personification of Wisdom as an essential ingredient in the Creation. This is a profound thought which works its way through to the Christian era, with the understanding of God as the Holy Trinity.

The Aramaic Proverbs of Ahiqar

It is interesting to compare Proverbs with this Aramaic collection of proverbs dating from the time of the Assyrian ascendency, the reign of Sennacherib, which is contemporary to Hezekiah and Isaiah. Whether the one work copied the other is impossible to tell, but there is much material in common. The best-preserved version of Ahiqar has been found on the island of Elephantine in Egypt, and it dates from the fifth century BC, but there were other versions in circulation. What this demonstrates is the international nature of wisdom literature. The material was in the ether in the ancient Near East. The chief difference between the pagan wisdom and the Hebrew wisdom was the importance given to YHWH. We can see Proverbs against its background of the genre of wisdom in general, Egypt, Mesopotamia, and Assyria in particular. The text of Ahiqar is the one given in ancient Near Eastern Texts, by Michael Coogan, 2013.

Ahiqar begins thus:

'... She is precious to the god, her kingdom is eternal; she has been established by Shamayin, yea the Holy Lord has exalted her' (Lines 1-4).

This is talking about wisdom in much the same terms as Proverbs 8; the main difference is that Shamayin is 'the Lord of Heavens', namely Baal Shamayin is the backing for wisdom, as well as other gods. There is no mention of wisdom being involved in Creation, but it comes quite close to that idea since 'her kingdom is eternal'.

Line 5, 'My Son' is the same idea as in Proverbs: fatherly advice to someone lacking experience. 'Guard your mouth' and 'be discreet' is advice often found in Proverbs, and is contrasted with those who are loud-mouthed and slanderous.

A long passage discusses kingship and how one should not oppose one's ruler. One should tread carefully with a king. Compare this: 'a king's

265

tongue is gentle but it breaks a dragon's ribs... ' and Proverbs 25:15: 'with patience a ruler may be persuaded and a soft tongue will break a bone.'

With regard to one's parents, Ahiqar advises one to take pride in them:

'Whoever takes no pride in his father's and mother's name, may Shamash (the sun god) not shine on him, for he is an evil man'. Proverbs could be seen as intensifying this thought: 'if one curses his father or his mother, his lamp will be put out in utter darkness. An inheritance gotten hastily in the beginning will in the end not be blessed' (Proverbs 20:20-21). Not only is this more metaphoric, thus increasing the emotion, but is made into a useful parallelism.

The same advice is given with regard to false witnessing and telling lies, and also something is said about taking loans. Relevant to today is the advice to use corporal punishment:

'Do not withhold discipline from a child; if you beat him with a rod, he will not die. If you beat him with a rod you will save his life from Sheol' (Proverbs 23:13-14). Compare this with Ahiqar:

'Spare not your son from the rod; otherwise can you save him from wickedness? If I beat you, my son, you will not die; but if I leave you alone (you will not live). A blow for a serving-boy, a rebuke for a slave-girl, and for all your servants, discipline!' The thought is a little more extended in Ahiqar, to include all the household and not just one's own child. But the Hebrew tradition makes it more theological, with mention of Hell as a destination for one who is not corrected.

A 'number proverb' occurs in Ahiqar:

'There are two things which are good, and a third which is pleasing to Shamash; one who drinks wine and shares it, one who masters wisdom (and observes it), and one who hears a word but tells it not'. In other words, don't gossip, be generous with your liquor and use common sense. No one knows for sure what the significance of the number introduction to this proverb would be, but we notice that three is involved, another number deeply symbolic. Something similar to this occurs in Job 32:29, but the context and message is quite different.

One of the differences with Ahiqar is the use of short parables, rather like 'just-so' stories. One example will suffice:

'Once upon a time a leopard came upon a she-goat who was cold. The leopard said to the goat, "Why won't you let me cover you with my pelt?" The goat replied to the leopard, "Why should I do that, my Lord?

Don't take my hide away from me!" For (as they say) "A leopard does not greet a gazelle except to suck its blood."'

The lesson to learn from this would be; 'don't accept favours from someone who is known to be a predator or ferocious.'

The portion of Ahiqar is fairly short compared with Proverbs. It is quite possible that the Aramaic wisdom was originally much more extensive, but has been lost. The reason for the Egyptian version's survival is almost certainly because of the dry climate, which has preserved the papyrus roll. In Assyria, where this material must have originated, papyrus rolls scarcely survive. Clay tablets stand a much better chance, but even then, many of them are fractured. This is all evidence that Wisdom, as a literary genre, was widespread in the ancient Near East and also may have had some influence on Buddhism. But that, of course, is pure speculation.

Ecclesiasticus in the Apocrypha

This is not to be confused with Ecclesiastes which is canonical. Ecclesiasticus, like the Wisdom of Solomon, was rejected for the canon by the Jews. Even so, it is well respected and quoted frequently. An unusual feature is a prologue explaining who the author was, someone called Jesus ben Sirach. This Jesus is not to be confused with Jesus Christ. Jesus, or Joshua in the Hebrew, was a common name in Judaism. Ben Sirach modelled himself on Solomon, but comparing his work with Proverbs or even Ecclesiastes, reveals quite a difference in style, even if the subject matter of the sayings is much the same. The prologue states that the book stems from the time just after the return from the Exile; the grandfather of Jesus had begun the task of assembling proverbs. His son, Sirach, had continued the process and Jesus the grandson had completed the task. This would tally well with the knowledge that the work was originally in Hebrew, as fragments of it still survive; the main text is in the Greek of the Septuagint (the Greek version of the Old Testament). The second prologue actually states that it was originally in Hebrew, adding that in the thirty-eighth year when he came to Egypt, when Ptolemy Euergetes was in power, he found a book which he deemed worthy of translation, since the Egyptians seemed eager to learn. The only problem with this scenario is that in Ecclesiasticus 50:1 it mentions Simon the high priest, the son of Onias repairing the Temple, presumably after the ravages of Antiochus 4th Epiphanes. This must indicate the second Ptolemy Euergetes who ruled from 170 BC to 164 BC. This would be, presumably, long after the time of Jesus Ben Sirach (the grandfather), by about 350 years. Even so, with it having a Hebrew original, the work has, at least the most part, to belong to the time shortly after the Exile, before

Hebrew went out of use. Chapter 50 onwards has the appearance of being an addition, since verse 27 refers to Ben Sirach in the third person. Other than that, the book is of one style and seems to be from one author.

There is the same contrast between the wise man and the fool, not so heavily emphasised as in the Proverbs. There is no attempt at ameliorating this contrast; one is either wise or stupid. Again, Wisdom is personified as a woman, and is pictured as instrumental in Creation. Chapter 24 goes into detail about how she was integrated with the history of Israel, in an extended discussion of her beauty and wonder. In contrast to Proverbs, there is the occasional reference to historical events, such as Pharaoh hardening his heart and the covenant of Sinai (Chapter 17). The phrase, 'my son' occurs occasionally; it is not meant personally, but as a feature of style in wisdom literature. There is, however, a lengthy passage on the subject of children matching up to their parents' expectations (Chapter 22). This is typical of Ben Sirach; rather than disjointed proverbs not really relating to one another, he goes in for developed sermons and discourses.

On the subject of life and death, Ben Sirach has much more to say than Proverbs. He does not seem to mention Sheol or Heaven. Looking at Chapter 17 and other references, it seems that God created man from the earth and turned him back into it again, giving a limit to his lifespan.

'For all things cannot be in men, because the son of man is not immortal' (Ecclesiastes 17:30).

This would tend to the idea that one's spirit does not continue into the next world at death. This should be compared with 11:26:

'For it is an easy thing unto the Lord in the day of death to reward a man according to his ways'. This would tend to suggest rewards and punishments in the afterlife.

This prompts the question of what Ben Sirach thinks of those who were 'assumed'. Enoch is mentioned in 44:16, 'Enoch pleased the Lord and was translated... ' Also he was 'taken from the earth' (49:14). This stops short of saying he was actually assumed into heaven. When it comes to Moses, Sirach is even less specific, managing to slide out of it by saying 'the Lord himself is his portion and inheritance' (45:22). As for Elijah, another one 'assumed' into heaven, he admits that Elijah 'raised up a dead man from death, and his soul from the place of the dead[9]... ' (48:5). But of Elijah himself, he is stated to have been 'taken up in a whirlwind of fire.' There is no comment on this matter. With regard to Elisha there is the strange comment that 'after his death his body prophesied. He did wonders in his life and at his death were his works marvellous'[10]. So while Ben Sirach will admit that there is some kind of survival of the grave, he is still stuck with the traditional Hebrew view that there is nothing positive to look forward to. In his day, Ben Sirach might have seemed rather old-fashioned in his views.

> 'Weep for the dead for he hath lost the light… make little weeping for the dead, for he is at rest…' (Ecclesiasticus 22:11). Again, this is unspecific about the next world. He is content to say that people are buried in peace, even if their reputation lives for ever. (44:140).

An important section in Ben Sirach is the Praise of Famous Men, Chapter 44. It does not begin with Adam and Eve, understandably, as they have been commented on before. It starts with Enoch and traces the history of champions of the faith through the Patriarchs, Moses, Aaron, Joshua, the Judges, down to King David. There is a more frequent mention of covenant in this passage, which means that Ben Sirach does understand the basics of Hebrew faith and emphasises them rather than just assuming them. The list goes on down to Nehemiah and finishes with Simon the high priest in the Maccabean age. This is quite a development for a piece of wisdom literature. We can see in it the need for some kind of historical element, which is essential to the faith of Israel. Ben Sirach does it by citing all the important saints of the Israelite tradition, and even referring to those who are never mentioned but not forgotten:

> 'But these were merciful men whose righteousness hath not been forgotten… their bodies are buried in peace, but their name liveth for evermore' (44:14).

This appears to be Ben Sirach's answer to the future of man's soul; that one's reputation into the future is one's immortality. There is no mention of heaven.

This passage is rightly famous and has been influential down the centuries. It appears in a modified form in Hebrews Chapter11 (Chapter 24). The chief modifications – apart from some of the blatant exaggerations – is the emphasis placed on faith. All these champions of Israel were motivated by faith, which is emphasised at every turn. The list becomes less specific in Hebrews 11:33, but clearly it is commenting on the persecutions during the Maccabean age, (see Chapter 2). This 'cloud of witnesses' is the encouragement to cope with the present persecutions (probably under Nero) and see the positive side of it, that it is all part of God's discipline. Hebrews then actually quotes Proverbs 3:11-12[11]; this all goes to show the important contribution that wisdom literature made, and still does, to the shaping of the Jewish and Christian faith. One such factor is the practice of canonisation of individuals who have been martyred or are an outstanding example of the Christian life.

As a feature of wisdom literature, the so-called number proverbs appear in Ben Sirach; more this time – actually, seven of them – but not quite as striking or poetic as in Proverbs. More prominent are his extended discourses on various subjects, forming mini-sermons. One interesting example, which Mary Baker Eddy (Chapter 10) could have taken on board, is Ben Sirach's respect for doctors and medicine:

> 'Honour a physician with the honour due to him... ... for the Lord hath created him' (38:1).

It goes on to state that God provided drugs in plants, and the skill needed to produce them, but first and foremost, one should pray, just as the doctor will, for healing. It concludes with what must seem like a burst of jocularity:

> 'He that sinneth before his maker, let him fall into the hand of the physician' (38:15).

Another example of an extended discourse concerns a complete theory of sacrifice (Chapters 34 and 35). Wisdom literature does not normally concern itself with the ritual side of the Law, but here we have a certain rationale of sacrificing. If one is unjust, one's sacrifice is not accepted by God; if one's offering is dishonestly obtained, that too is worthless. The real peace offering to God, which has efficacy, is one's observance of the Law. Trying to bribe God is also nonsense. The true heart of the sacrificial mind is obedience to God's laws and serving him. This could be seen as an expanded thought on Proverbs 15:8:

> 'The sacrifice of the wicked is an abomination to the Lord; but the prayer of the upright is his delight'.

Another extended discourse comes in 44:1-33, just before the passage on the famous men. This one is all about the glories of nature. Every aspect of the natural world is drawn in, the sun, the moon, the stars, the rainbow, the snow, with a futuristic comment which is coming home to roost in our own times:

> 'There are yet hid greater things than these be, for we have seen but a few of his works' (Ben Sirach 43:32).

How true! The scientists are discovering all kinds of factors not realised in the ancient world, and yet strangely, many of them cannot see it as the works of God. But the wise man can see it thus:

'For the Lord hath made all things; and to the godly hath he given wisdom' (43:33).

If Ben Sirach were to be asked about free will and predestination, he would almost certainly have agreed with predestination. There is not much free will in this statement:

'As the clay is in the potter's hand, to fashion it at his pleasure; so man is in the hand of him that made him, to render to them as liketh him best' (Ben Sirach 33:13).

He goes on to say that there are two contrasts in life; good and evil, life and death, the godly versus the sinner, and the sinner versus the godly. There seems to be no grey area in between, something that we noted in Proverbs. This helps to explain that strange remark in 42:24:

'All things are double, one against another, and he hath made nothing imperfect'.

In other words, he is probably trying to say that for every plus in life there is a minus.

Everything is in balance with everything else. The use of the word 'double' looks as if it is a rudimentary way of talking about balance or contrast. But this brings us to the issue of theodicy; why is there any evil in the world. Ben Sirach is almost certainly saying that God has made everything, good and evil, and that includes people. This goes a lot further than Proverbs, in that there was the element of free will juxtaposed with predestination. Ben Sirach seems to have found the paradox between the two.

Ben Sirach has a lot to say about the rich and the poor. He has much sympathy with the poor and is damning about the rich and how they tyrannise the poor. An important passage comes in 10:12-18. It uses phraseology which reminds us of the Magnificat (Luke 1:46-55) when it compares the high and mighty with the lowly. In fact, the Song of Mary could be partly modelled on this passage in Ben Sirach, as well as the Song of Hannah (1 Samuel 2:1-10). It is interesting to note that Ben Sirach may not have noticed that 'Samuel' had a more positive notion of the afterlife:

'The Lord kills and brings to life; he brings down to Sheol and raises up' (1 Samuel 2:6).

271

On the assumption that this song is very early, long before the age of Solomonic wisdom, Ben Sirach seems to be much more pessimistic and negative about heaven. Even so, we need to evaluate a remark such as this:

'The prayer of the humble pierceth the clouds...' (Ben Sirach 35:16).

This has all the feeling of a euphemistic claim that in one's humility one can contact God in heaven. It does not go quite as far as saying that the humble will get to heaven one day, but it does tend to that view. There is another way of seeing this issue. In Chapter 51, the Prayer of Ben Sirach, death and hell are referred to as a present experience rather than the end of one's physical life:

'From the depth of the belly of hell...' and '... my life was near to the hell beneath... ' (verses 5 and 6). Is this meant figuratively rather than literally? In verse 12 he talks of his being rescued... 'for thou savedst me from destruction and deliverest me from the evil time...' He does not go on to mention heaven in contrast to hell, which is a surprise since he says that everything is 'double', which means that for every bad thing there is a good thing as a counterpart. When he talks about hell and choking fire on every side, he may not be talking literally, but metaphorically. This of course raises the question of how literally we need to take other matters in the wisdom literature of the Old Testament.

A general view of Ben Sirach, as a sage of the Post Exilic world is that he is heavily dependent on Proverbs. Much of his subject matter is simply a development of the ideas in Proverbs. Rather than disjointed sayings crammed together, he goes in for lengthier discourses, often expanding on a chosen remark from Proverbs. Also is the issue of desiring and seeking wisdom as one's main purpose in life. This comes out in the closing verses of Ben Sirach's prayer. It is the vision of Solomon, who in a dream was asked by God what he would like as a gift, and Solomon asked for Wisdom to rule his people. Ben Sirach is not attempting to be an ingénue monarch; he is a commoner ardently wishing to gain insight, and help others to come to a true understanding of life and the workings of God.

The Wisdom of Solomon in the Apocrypha

It is interesting to compare the Wisdom of Solomon with Proverbs. This work is regarded as very late by scholars, almost down to the time of Jesus; the reason for this is that it seems never to have had a Hebrew original, and Greek was its basic language. Some think that it was written in Alexandria by a diaspora Jew. It appears to have been written by one person as opposed to a being a miscellany like Proverbs. The tone of it, often using abstract and compound words, is typical of Greek rather than Hebrew or Aramaic. The book claims to have been written by Solomon, and indeed portions of it are the thoughts of a young and inexperienced king seeking for guidance for ruling his kingdom. Even so, most experts rule out Solomonic authorship. It was a feature of the Post Exilic world for writers to claim the authorship of certain ancient worthies, such as Moses, Enoch and others. The purpose of this pseudonimic approach is thought to be an attempt at concealing one's identity for fear of persecution, just as today writers use a pen name; otherwise it was an attempt at claiming authorship for one's book by giving it an air of antiquity. If this were so, then the writer of the Wisdom of Solomon did not succeed in his aim, as the book was eventually rejected for the Hebrew canon. It was and still is, accepted by certain elements of the Christian world, namely Roman Catholic and the Orthodox.

The thoughts and themes are much the same as in Proverbs, but rather than individual sayings just placed together without much thematic work, Wisdom goes in for extended sermons, quite often repetitious. The contrast between the wise and foolish, although there, is nowhere near as heavily emphasised as in Proverbs.

It is interesting that Chapter 2 takes a strand from Ecclesiastes, that of life being transitory and the advice to enjoy oneself while one has the chance. It is sarcastic about the righteous, regarding them as hypocrites, and subjecting them to shame and torture. This could be a recollection of what happened when the Greek king Antiochus 4th Epiphanes tried to stamp out Judaism by defiling the Temple. But the answer to all this is that although the faithful appear to be punished and die, in reality, they are rewarded by God in ways which the faithless do not understand:

'For God created man to be immortal and made him to be an image of his own eternity... but the souls of the righteous are in the hand of God and there shall no torment touch them. In the sight of the unwise they seemed to die... but they are in peace... for though they be punished in the sight of men, yet is their hope of a full immortality...' Wisdom 2:23-3:4.

This is quite a step forward from Proverbs, which has much to say about Sheol but little else. Now we are seeing, because of the reality of persecution, a stronger understanding of rewards in heaven after one's earthly life. This was the prevailing assumption at the time of Jesus and has been axiomatic to Jewish, Christian and Muslim thinking ever since.

For the ungodly, a different fate is described. He will see the ones that he scorned, rewarded and consoled by God, and realise where he has gone wrong. 'Their own iniquities shall convince them to their face' (Wisdom 4:20). The ungodly will have no eternal future; in contrast the righteous 'will live for evermore; their reward also is with the Lord... .they will receive a glorious kingdom' (Wisdom 5:15). Now we can glimpse what Jesus meant about the Kingdom of Heaven. It goes on 'he shall take to him... complete armour... he shall put on righteousness as a breastplate and true judgement instead of an helmet' (Wisdom 5:17). Now we can understand what St Paul meant when he talked about putting on the whole armour of God, in Ephesians 6:10. This incidentally is an indication that St Paul knew Wisdom and was quoting it as 'scriptural'.

In common with other wisdom literature, Wisdom is personified as a woman and celebrated as involved in the creation of the world, the establishment of calendars and the giver of immortality. Again this can hardly be taken literally, but as figurative. A good example of this would be where Solomon talks of marrying Wisdom like a wife; he would be less interested in having her as a sister. We see in 9:17 that Wisdom is in parallel with the Holy Spirit:

'And they counsel who hath known, except thou give Wisdom, and send they Holy Spirit from above'.

From this we can easily see how the early Christians soon equated Jesus with Eternal Wisdom and the gift of the Holy Spirit was the final seal on their understanding of God's will.

We have noted that wisdom literature is weak on the subject of historical factors. Claiming that the book is the work of Solomon is one way of attempting to address the matter, but not a very convincing attempt. However, Wisdom has a lengthy section of history, beginning with Adam and going on down to the Exodus and the Wilderness period. It is rather strangely done, omitting all names so that the story sounds almost hypothetical, except that the reader will know what the writer is talking about. The only proper name mentioned is the Red Sea, which helps us to locate it. The account is exaggerated and overdramatised with all kinds of additives that do not appear in Genesis or Exodus. This is a factor seen in the Koran (Chapter21) and the Masnavi (Chapter 17). One element that gives pause for thought is 'Whilst they slew their children in sacrifices' (Wisdom 14:23). This reminds us of the sin of Manesseh which was held to be the final straw which brought about the Fall of Jerusalem in 597 BC, long after the time of Solomon. Has the author of Wisdom given us a little anachronism?

Even so, the pattern of salvation is accredited to the lady Wisdom; 'she preserved the first formed father of the world', namely Adam, and continued to steer history right through. Even though the account reverts to 'thy Spirit' and also 'God', the writer does not really see any difference between them. It is one God who is in control of history; the writer is a rampant monotheist.

One strange element in the concluding verses of Wisdom is thus:

'For earthly things were turned into watery, and the things, that before swam in the water, now went upon the ground[12]. The fire had power in the water, forgetting its own virtue; and the water forgat his own quenching nature. On the other side the flames wasted not the flesh of the corruptible living things, though they walked therein; neither melted they the icy kind of heavenly meat, that was of nature apt to melt.' Wisdom 19:19ff.

This sounds like an attempt at elementary physics. Is this a reflection of Greek thought, or possibly also of Taoist philosophy? At one point, this seems to refer to the three holy children in the furnace. At another point, it seems to refer to the manna from heaven. Very strange! At the very least, it is talking, metaphorically of the reversal of all things, not just physical but values, ideas and human expectations; this is something that Isaiah would have appreciated, and also St Luke.

Final remarks on Wisdom Literature

It is interesting that it is principally with wisdom literature that we see the gradual emergence of an understanding of the afterlife. We start with Sheol, rather like as in Inanna (Chapter 22), and gradually progress to a realisation of Heaven, which Jesus assumed.

Notes for Chapter 15: Proverbs.

1. The Egyptian Book of the Dead (See Chapter25).
2. References to the tables of stone; for instance Exodus 34:1.
3. Hosea's wife; Hosea 1:2.
4. Baal and Astarte (Ashtaroth), the male and female principle in Canaanite practice (see 1 Samuel 7:4, for instance).
5. The 'gate': as seen in archaeological findings, the gatehouse of a city was a notable structure; it was where the elders met to discuss important matters, like a town council.
6. Karma is the Hindu word for reincarnation.
7. The Great Feast: Luke 14:7:24.
8. Also 'still waters run deep'.
9. Reference to Elijah in 2 Kings 13:21. Elijah was 'assumed' into Heaven.
10. Reference to Elisha in 2 Kings 13:21. Elisha was not assumed but buried.
11. Proverbs 3:11-12: ' My son, do not despise the Lord's discipline, or be weary of his reproof, for the Lord reproves him whom he loves, as a father the son in whom he delights.'
12. This sounds rather like Evolution; creatures coming out of the sea to inhabit the land.

16

The Kitab-i-Aqdas

The Most Holy Book

This work is one of the core literary productions of the Baha'i religion. A brief outline of the Baha'i history is now appropriate, if only to clarify a few details of its provenance. In 1844 a young Iranian merchant, named Sayyid 'Ali Muhammad Shirazi proclaimed himself as the **Bab** which means 'the Gate'. He gathered eighteen disciples, who became known as Babis, and sent them out to spread his message in Iran. In Islam, there is a certain messianic expectation; that the Mahdi will appear; the Bab claimed to be in receipt of divine revelations, which would place him on the same level as Muhammad; this would be the start of a new religious cycle, which explains why the Baha'is have their own calendar, starting in 1844.

This new message met with fierce opposition in Iran particularly but also in other Muslim countries. He spent much of his life in prison and eventually had to face a firing squad. On the first attempt all the riflemen missed; on the second attempt they managed to hit him. He left behind many converts and writings; he thought he was the Messiah, but there was no clarification about how he related to Jesus Christ.

The proper founder of the Baha'i faith was actually Baha'u'llah, which means the 'glory of God; ' his real name was Mirza Husayn 'Ali Nuri, the son of an Iranian nobleman, and an early convert to the Bab. He announced his claim to be the one foretold by the Bab and the inaugurator of a new religious dispensation, namely the Baha'i faith. This is something roughly analogous to the relationship between Jesus and St Paul. Baha'u'llah was the one who produced vast amounts of written material, which has become 'scriptural' for the Baha'is. The work analysed here is the Most Holy Book, which is probably the core of the Baha'i teachings. It was originally written in Arabic and appeared about 1873, but was not properly published until the end of his life in about 1890. It was Shoghi Effendi, one of his successors, who translated it into English. The version used here is the 1953 version, published by the Bah'ai World Centre, Haifa, which incidentally is the site of the tomb of the Bab and of Baha'u'llah, on Mount Carmel. The work is heavily dependent on the Koran and Muslim cultural assumptions in general. There are ideas taken from the Bible but there is no great emphasis placed on that. One might fairly say that Baha'i-ism is a moderated, even demythologised version of Islam. Unfortunately, even though many Muslims were attracted to this new faith, there was a ferocious reaction from the authorities resulting in heavy persecution. Even so, Baha'i-ism has spread throughout the world and has found favour in many countries, not least with the British.

Mathematical considerations

This centres on the introduction of a new calendar, something that the Bab inaugurated. It consists of nineteen months of nineteen days each, per year. This leaves us with four or five days that are for giving gifts. The number nineteen has significance for the Baha'is since there were eighteen disciples plus one, the Bab himself, we assume. The number nineteen has significance in the Koran; there are nineteen guards on the gates of Hell to stop people escaping once they are there. This makes for a very clumsy calendar[1], far more complicated than the Gregorian calendar, which almost everyone else uses. The months each have names that relate to divine attributes or spiritual qualities. The year begins on 21st March, the vernal equinox, which takes us back to Ancient Rome. There are nine holy days in the year, which include the birth of the Bab and of Baha'u'llah; none of them bear any relationship to Christian, Jewish or Muslim holy days. This pattern is not actually outlined in the main text of the Kitab-i-Aqdas, but is explained in the notes appended to the same volume.

Scientific matters

There is nothing relating to the sciences in this book. But Baha'u'llah has no objection to one learning such disciplines:

'We have permitted you to read such sciences as are profitable unto you, not such as end in idle disputation... ' (77, page 48).

277

There is no mention of biology or of the Theory of Evolution. This is something of a surprise, since it was a hot topic in the late nineteenth century. It may be that Baha'u'llah had no real opinion on it; he may have thought it irrelevant.

Historic-geographical information.

Unlike many other eastern religions, the Baha'i faith is to some extent grounded in time and place. This is not to the same extent as Judaism and Christianity, which rely heavily on historical and geographical realities. But we do have information about the Bab and the early founders, their place in history with regard to the situation in Persia and the relationship with Islam. It is also dependent on Messianism, which is a strong biblical tradition. The Kitab-i-Aqdas opens with what must be taken as an appeal to take the Bab seriously:

'The first duty prescribed by God for his servants is the recognition of him who is the Dayspring of his revelation and the fountain of his laws, who representeth the godhead in both the kingdom of his cause and the world of creation.' (1, page 19).

This does not actually name the Bab as such, but it is clearly referring to him indirectly.

There are references to Biblical incidents, which again ground it in real events.

'He it is who has caused the Rock to shout and the Burning Bush to lift up its voice, upon the Mount rising above the Holy Land... ' (103, page57).

Obviously this goes a little further than the original biblical text, but there is poetic license at work here; the metaphors are powerful, and there is a trace of parallelism as in Hebrew poetry.

Historical realities go a little further when the book addresses the Emperor of Austria, the King of Berlin, Queen Victoria, the rulers of America and the people of Constantinople, along with other less important countries. No one knows what reply was received but the message of peace and world unity was a valid one and is now even more relevant. There is no suggestion that this world is unreal. The Sufis were sympathetic to the Bab, but they had a totally different approach to the question of reality, see Chapter17.

It is clear that the Bab and Baha'u'llah were real historical people and not just imaginary; they are a part of recent history and moved around the orient to and from places like Mecca.

Philosophy

Baha'u'llah did not like 'idle disputations'. The Bab was unhappy about being asked any questions; Baha'u'llah by contrast has a question and answer section in this book. But by and large, one has to accept the dogmatic statements decided in advance by these people.

> 'Everything that is hath come to be through his irresistible decree... wherever my laws appear... they must be faithfully obeyed... ' (7, page 21).

This sounds like yet another authority system, not unlike a latter-day papacy, or the Mormons, or the Jehovah's Witnesses. In general, there is very little room for argument and discussion in Baha'i-ism.

Theological matters

The Kitab-i-Aqdas is almost entirely theological with ethical considerations included. It is a rampant monotheism; God is one and there is no other power or force available:

> 'There is none other God but Me, the Mighty, the All-wise' (39, page 33).

This rules out devils, evil spirits, Satan and bad angels. There is never any mention of such things in this book; there is mention of evil, but only as an adjective. This means that Baha'u'llah has demythologised the powers of evil, a very modern tendency, though not totally convincing. It follows from this that God plans and decrees everything. In a way this is a return to the faith of Isaiah:

> 'He of a truth, hath power to ordain whatsoever he desireth, and doeth as he pleaseth by virtue of his sovereign might' (20, page 26).

This clearly is the basis of predestination, an aspect of theology clearly stemming from Islam. Unlike Islam, there is no mention of free will in the Kitab. There are a few references to 'liberty' but that does not mean free will in the sense of the opposite of predestination. Liberty appears to be some sort of delusion under which ignorant people live their lives:

'We find some men desiring liberty, and priding themselves therein. Such men are in the depths of ignorance' (122, page 63).

'Liberty causeth man to overstep the bounds of propriety, and to infringe on the dignity of his station. It debaseth him to the level of extreme depravity and wickedness' (123, page 63).

The way this is phrased reminds us of the excesses of the French Revolution and also the American Revolution; situations where people having thrown off authority then descended into chaos. It would be a mistake to think that Baha'u'llah is totally negative on the subject of freedom; he can see that true freedom lies in obeying God. This reminds us of the Christian phrase 'whose service is perfect freedom[2].'

'The liberty that profiteth you is to be found nowhere except in complete servitude unto God, the Eternal Truth' (125, page 64).

'True liberty consisteth in man's submission unto my commandments, little as ye know it. Were men to observe that which we have sent down unto them from the Heaven of Revelation, they would, of a certainty, attain unto perfect liberty' (125, page 63).

In this way, Baha'u'llah has stumbled on to the paradox between freedom and predestination; although he does not actually use the word paradox, that is what it is. We are guided by God, but, paradoxically, we also have free will. 'Little as ye know it... ' is very apt; no one can analyse this piece of divine logic.

Consistent with this theological position, is the use of titles for God. They are reminiscent of the Koran and also of the Avestas of Zoroaster (see Chapter5). Here are a few examples:

Supreme Ordainer, All-knowing, Best-beloved, All-subduing, All-merciful, Omnipotent ruler, All-wise, Most Excellent, All-glorious, All-informed, Incomparable, All-perceiving, Most Compassionate and many more. One might conclude from this list that sin has no meaning and that punishment is senseless. But Baha'u'llah goes on to point out that God on the one hand is merciful, but can also hand out dire punishments.

'Whoso layeth claim to a revelation direct from God, ere the expiration of a full thousand years, such a man is assuredly a lying imposter. We pray God that he may graciously assist him to retract and repudiate such a claim. If, however, he persisteth in his error, God will, assuredly send down one who will deal mercilessly with him. Terrible indeed is God in punishing' (37, page 32).

This is a theological stance which worries people in today's world; the wrath of God. It receives various mentions in the Bible, but is juxtaposed with the love and mercy of God. This is again another paradox, but rather more comprehensible. It is bad conduct on the part of humans which elicits punishments, but how this relates to non-existent free will is a puzzle.

Laying claim to a revelation from God brings us to the messianic element in Baha'i-ism. The Bab proclaimed himself as the Mahdi, or Messiah, inaugurating a new world order. The Kitab-i-Aqdas goes into eulogies about this 'Messiah'. It calls him the 'Dayspring' in many places. The book actually begins with a call to realise that the Bab is the true representative of God:

'The first duty prescribed by God for his servants is the recognition of him who is the Dayspring[3] of his Revelation and the fountain of his laws. Who representeth the Godhead in both the Kingdom of his Cause and the world of Creation' (1, page 19).

If one accepts the Bab then one has 'attained unto all good; if one is deprived (notice the predestinatory tone here) of accepting him, regardless of how many good works he has done, has gone astray. We have to observe every ordinance of the Bab, termed the Desire of the World, other wise we shall be reckoned as abject and foolish. The Bab produced a book called the Bayan, which is still available, but Baha'u'llah took it upon himself to tone various things down a little. An example of this is that we can ask questions; the Bab forbade anyone to ask him questions! Baha'u'llah eulogises over the Bayan. Strangely, nowhere does he actually mention the Bab specifically by name, but indirectly.

'Whatsover ye understand not in the Bayan ask it of God... should he so desire, he will expound for you that which is revealed therein, and disclose to you the pearls of Divine Knowledge and wisdom that lie concealed within the ocean of its words... ' (180, page 85).

Jesus warned us of those who would claim to be the Messiah; the contrast is clear. Jesus allowed other people to come to the conclusion that he was the Messiah. He only claimed to be the 'Servant' and the 'Son of Man'. Jesus had modesty; the Bab must have had a massive ego. Yet we do not have any kind of incarnational theory or claim with regard to the Bab: there is no Transfiguration, no miracles, no Resurrection, no Ascension. Somehow the glory of God is seriously missing. What does it mean to call him the Dayspring? Clearly this reminds us of the early chapters in Luke – 'the Dayspring from on high hath visited us' – but what does this actually mean? A lot depends on whether we accept the Bab as a genuine Messiah; if he is an imposter, what does that mean for Baha'i-ism? Does it invalidate the whole thing?

There is only one place in the Kitab-i-Aqdas where any reference to Jesus is made, and that is an indirect one:

> 'By the one true God! Sinai is circling round the Dayspring of Revelation, while from the heights of the Kingdom the Voice of the Spirit of God is heard proclaiming, "Bestir yourselves, ye proud ones of the earth, and hasten ye unto him."' (80, page 48).

'The Spirit of God' is the phrase used to denote Jesus; it is often used in Islamic thought, and is found in the Koran with the same meaning. The mention of Sinai is of course referring to Moses, and here we see the Bab (Dayspring) at the centre of the Mosaic dispensation. Quite why Jesus is drawn into the argument at this point is not clear, and there is no evidence that Jesus ever said 'Bestir yourselves...' although it is not out of line with the thinking of St Luke. This would have been a good context to relate Jesus to the Bab, but this does not occur. We are left wondering how the two relate to one another. Also we wonder why Baha'u'llah does not state plainly what he thinks of Jesus.

Messianism in the Baha'i faith is a little more complicated than it is in Judaeo-Christianity. It would seem that the Bab prophesied the coming of Baha'u'llah and this is referred to in the Kitab-i-Aqdas:

> 'O people of the Bayan! Fear ye the most merciful and consider what he hath revealed in another passage. He said; "The Qiblih is indeed he whom God will make manifest; whenever he moveth, it moveth, until he shall come to rest." Thus it was set down by the Supreme Ordainer when he desired to make mention of this most great Beauty' (137, page 68).

The word Qiblih has a double meaning here; firstly it means Baha'u'llah himself, as the Bab's successor, and secondly the place which has been designated as the central spot of the religion. Just as Judaism centred on Jerusalem, and Islam on Mecca, so the Baha'is designated Haifa as the focal point. Both the Bab and Baha'u'llah are entombed there and it is the central point for pilgrimage; also one's prayers are directed to this town in Israel. It is on the slopes of Mount Carmel. All this strengthens the impression that Baha'i-ism can be regarded as a 'historical' religion, with its own saints, martyrs and important events.

The prescribed prayers are to be recited at the correct times:

> 'We have enjoined obligatory prayer upon you, with *rak'ahs*[4] to be offered at noon, and in the morning and evening unto God... we have

relieved you of a greater number... turn ye towards the Court of my most holy Presence, this hallowed spot... ' (6, page 21).

The Bab had ordered nineteen rak'ahs per day, but Baha'u'llah has reduced it to nine. Nine and nineteen have special significance in Baha'i-ism. There is much more flexibility over the timings of prayers; in parts of the world where days and nights are of unequal length, the use of clocks is allowed. The practice of congregational prayer is to be abandoned and prayer is to be done individually. Those who are ill, and women with child are exempted from prayer and fasting. The first month of the year is the fast: 21st March onwards. One can pray on any surface that is clean, and if there is no clean water available, there is no compulsion to wash beforehand. Thus the practices of Islam are eased considerably; even so Baha'i-ism can be seen as a derivative of Islam. The muttering of sacred verses in public is also forbidden; one should do it at home or in the sacred building.

Baha'u'llah is quite happy to endorse 'works-righteousness'[5]; to get to heaven, we have to observe the correct conduct and perform the prayers. There is to be a judgement:

'This is the infallible balance, established by God, the Lord of this world and the next. Through them the soul of man is caused to wing its flight towards the Dayspring of Revelation and the heart of every true believer is suffused with light' (148, page 73).

In other words, there is a wonderful future awaiting the true believer in the next world. Although Baha'u'llah does not actually use the words 'heaven' and 'hell', he does talk about them indirectly. For those who do not accept the Bab's teachings, 'a humiliating chastisement awaiteth in the life to come,' in other words, torment in Hell. One will receive what one deserves:

'He who dealeth faithlessly with God shall in justice meet with faithlessness himself; he... who acteth in accordance with God's bidding shall receive a blessing from the heaven of the bounty of his Lord... after this fleeting life, your souls soar heavenwards and the trappings of your earthly joys are folded up' (97, page 55).

This is works-righteousness at its crudest; there is very little mention of grace, and nothing on the subject of salvation by faith. God is stated as being merciful, but what does that mean if one's life is to be judged by strict justice in the balances?

One could ask how the Covenant is worked into the framework of Baha'i-ism. There is mention of the Covenant, as indeed there is in the Koran.

'These have violated the Covenant of God by breaking his commandments... these have erred grievously in the sight of God... ' (2, page 20).

This sounds like a reference to the Covenant of Sinai, and the thinking of Deuteronomy, a book that lays heavy stress on being faithful to the covenant of Moses. There seems to be no understanding of the other covenants in the Bible; the covenants of Noah, Abraham, David and of Jesus; perhaps Baha'u'llah does not understand them. Another reference to covenant occurs thus:

'Whoso faileth to recite (these verses) hath not been faithful to the Covenant of God and his Testament and whoso turneth away from these holy verses in this day is of those who throughout eternity have turned away from God' (149, page 73).

This reference to covenant is clearly nothing to do with the Bible; it is Baha'u'llah's covenant, something that he has concocted for himself. He does not go so far as to proclaim himself as yet another Messiah, but he must have had a massive ego, like the Bab! One wonders if he actually knows what covenant means, in the Biblical sense.

Something which receives a lot of emphasis in the Kitab is the concept of the 'veil'. This is a factor that goes back to the Temple in Jerusalem, in which there was a veil obscuring the view of mankind from the reality of God. Also at the lawgiving at Sinai, Moses had to put a veil over his face because of the glory of God shining through him. The concept of the veil is clearly related to the Old Testament dispensation. In the New Testament, St Mark, at the climax of his gospel, states that the veil of the Temple was rent in two, which indicates that through Christ's death, the blockage which obscures our view of God, is removed, and we all have access directly to God. St Paul takes up the same metaphor in 2 Corinthians 3:12-18. For those who are still working under the Old Testament, namely the Mosaic dispensation, there is a veil over their faces; they do not have clear access to God. But for those who have come to understand Christ, the veil is removed.

'But when a man turns to the Lord (Jesus) the veil is removed... and we all, with unveiled face, beholding the glory of the Lord, are being changed into his likeness[6]... '

The way that Baha'u'llah uses this metaphor is somewhat different; there are various permutations on it. With regard to recognising the true God, the veil is related to heathenism and idolatry.

'Fear God; and be not of those who are shut out as by a veil. Burn ye away the veils with the fire of my love, and dispel ye the mists of vain imaginings... ' (132, page 66).

'When my verses were sent down... we found you behind the veils... we have rent the veils asunder... pluck asunder the chains of vain imaginings... ' (165, page 79).

At this point vain imaginings seem to be associated with selfish desires. In another context, the veil is something to do with scholarship, as obscuring our minds from the vision of God.

'... the highest and last end of all learning be the recognition of him who is the object of all knowledge, and yet, behold how ye have allowed your learning to shut you out, as by a veil, from him who is the Dayspring (the Bab?) of this light, through whom every hidden thing hath been revealed... ' (102, page 57).

So scholarship, scientific enquiry and philosophy are likely to obscure one's acceptance of the Bab's message.

'Take heed lest pride deter you from recognising the source of revelation, lest the things of this world shut you out as by a veil from him who is the creator of heaven' (82, page 49).

So there is a subtle difference here between the biblical use of this metaphor and Baha'u'llah's. In the Bible, it is the Mosaic covenant which obscures our vision of God; in the Kitab, it is wordly values, vain imaginings, materialism and idolatry which obscures our vision of God. There is, of course, truth in both these views, but Baha'u'llah seems to avoid including the covenant of Moses in this metaphor. The reason why becomes clear when we come to assess the Baha'i ethical code. This is the new world order, as announced by the Bab. The ethics are closely integrated with his theology and cannot be divorced from it. His claim would be that if everyone followed the Baha'i code of conduct, there would be no more problems in the world. This may well be true, but what he does not explain to us, is how he is going to persuade everyone to do just that. In the Kitab (and other writings) there is no reference to or theory of sin. Further to that, the concept of original sin is missing. What this means is that one has an entirely optimistic expectation of humanity, that takes no account of the wickedness in the heart. For the Christian, this is an unpleasant reality; for the Baha'is it is some sort of humanistic wishful thinking.

Consistent with the concept of the veil is the element of secrecy, which is a strong strand in apocalyptic writing. It probably stems from the book of Enoch, but is also found in Revelation and the Koran. As far as the Kitab is concerned, it is the Bab who has brought the hidden matters out into the light:

'... the Dayspring of this Light, through whom every hidden thing hath been revealed' (102, 57).

It would seem that there is a book of hidden knowledge with God, and that the Bab is the one who is privy to its contents and can reveal matters to the believers.

The ethical code is worth considering; the details compare well with that of other religions. He makes no direct reference to the Ten Commandments; however, murder is forbidden, and attracts the death penalty. Manslaughter (provided that it was accidental) will require one to compensate the relatives of the deceased. Arson is forbidden; the arsonist is to be burned himself (62) (page 41). Adultery is forbidden; the punishment is a fine of nine mithquals of gold, to be doubled on the repeat offence (49) (page 37). Theft is wrong; a thief is to be exiled and imprisoned; on the third offence he is to be branded on the forehead and expelled altogether. We are warned about being soft and sentimental about offenders:

'We school you with the rod of wisdom and laws, like unto the father who educateth his son... ' (45, page 36).

It is also forbidden to carry arms unless essential. This must mean that a Baha'i will normally be a pacifist, unless in an extreme situation, he has to defend himself. If this dictum were to be accepted by the entire world, it would indeed be a changed world. There are also rules about cleanliness, smart appearance, length of hair. Incest and homosexuality are also a matter for regulation:

'It is forbidden you to wed your fathers' wives. We shrink for very shame, from treating of the subject of boys... ' (107, page 58).

There seems to be no mention of incest between brother and sister, aunts, grandparents, etc. as in the Mosaic laws. Baha'u'llah does not like to spell out pederasty in plain language. This was left to later Baha'i sages to ban homosexuality and offences against minors. With regard to marriage, the Kitab states that one can have up to two wives; this is a reduction from four wives in the Koran. The ideal has become monogamy in this religion:

'God hath prescribed matrimony unto you. Beware that ye take not unto yourselves more wives than two. Whoso contenteth himself with a single partner from among the maidservants of God, both he and she shall live in tranquillity… ' (63, page 41).

'It hath been laid down in the Bayan that marriage is dependent upon the consent of both parties. Desiring to establish love, unity and harmony amidst our servants… ' (65, page 42).

One is expected to marry a fellow Baha'i. Divorce is permitted but there are strict rules about alimony and compensation. The ideal is to live in union and harmony. There are also strict rules about inheritance, very largely derived from Islam, but not quite the same.

As far as Sacramentalism is concerned there is nothing said on this subject; this is consistent with Islam. The nearest we come to this kind of thinking is as follows:

'It is well with him who has quaffed the Mystic Wine of everlasting life from the utterance of his merciful Lord in my Name… a name through which every lofty and majestic mountain hath been reduced to dust' (150, page 74).

'… it behoveth whoso hath quaffed the Mystic Wine of everlasting life from the hands of the loving-kindness of the Lord his God, the merciful, to pulsate even as the throbbing artery in the body of mankind, that through him may be quickened the world and every crumbling stone' (173, page 82).

It is important to realise that this is talking metaphorically and symbolically. The Baha'i tradition forbids the consumption of alcohol, and also any other substance that will impair one's thinking, and that includes drugs like opium. The real meaning of the 'wine' in these quotations is the imbibing of the essential truths about God. The effect of it is to bring life to a dying world, through the inspiration of the Baha'is.

The same pattern of thought applies to water, for not only is it for washing, but enlivening the believers:

'The sincere among his servants will regard the precepts set forth by God as the Water of life to the followers of every faith, and the lamp of wisdom and loving providence to all the denizens of earth and heaven' (29, page 29).

So the instructions given by the Bab and his followers are couched in the same terms as the wine; the water gives life to the world. Also the lamp is another metaphor used.

> 'Beware lest ye be hindered by the veils of glory from partaking of the crystal waters of this living fountain. Seize ye the chalice of salvation... drink your fill in praise of him... ' (50, page 38).

Here we see the metaphor stretched almost to the sacramental level by the mention of a 'chalice'; but it remains a spiritual state and there is no actual ceremony analogous to Holy Communion. Consistent with this is the lack of *rites de passage*; there is no baptism, circumcision, marriage ceremony, or funeral as seen in many other religions. There are funerary guidelines found in Kitab 130, 128 and 129, pages 64 and 65. Cremation is not allowed; one is to be buried in a coffin of crystal, or some other durable material with graven rings on the fingers with inscriptions on them. The body is to be wrapped in five sheets of silk or cotton; failing that one single sheet will do. The burial should be within one hour's journey from the city. It should be interred 'with radiance and serenity, in a nearby place.' This is the nearest we come to any sort of ceremony in the Kitab.

Another powerful metaphor used along with the wine and the water, is the scent:

> 'From my laws the sweet-smelling savour of my garment can be smelled... Happy is the lover that hath inhaled the divine fragrance of his best-beloved from these words, laden with the perfume of a grace which no tongue can describe...' (4, page 20).

When he talks of 'the lover' he is referring to the true believer; this is seen in Sufi writings, the Masnavi, Chapter 17[7]. The 'best-beloved' is God. When he talks of 'grace' it is unlikely that he means it in the biblical sense, where it means the free love of God which is not merited but a gift in advance of anything we can do. It is interesting that the same metaphor is used by St Paul in 2 Corinthians 2:15:

> '... and through us (the believers) spreads the fragrance of the knowledge of him everywhere. For we are the aroma of Christ to God among those who are being saved and among those who are perishing, to one a fragrance from death to death, to the other a fragrance from life to life.'

Baha'u'llah does not go quite as far as saying that the scent actually sorts out the believers from the non-believers, but it is possible that he took the metaphor from St Paul.

Mythological matters

There is very little that could be called mythological in the Kitab. We have the assumption of heaven, earth and hell, though it is never clarified or expanded upon, or stated plainly.

> 'He... desireth to see in you the manners of the inmates of Paradise in his mighty... kingdom... your eyes may be preserved from beholding what is repugnant both to yourselves and to the dwellers of Paradise... ' (46, page 36).

He is only making passing reference to Paradise, as an assumption; the main point here is to behave in a decorous manner when having something to eat.

It would be fair to say that generally speaking, the Kitab presents us with a religion which has nothing miraculous, mythological or a strain on credulity. This is a surprise, since we understand that a miracle is claimed to have occurred when the firing squad attempted to shoot the Bab; they all missed. Sadly, on the second attempt, they succeeded. Other than that, the Baha'i tradition is rather short on the miraculous aspect of religion, and makes no attempt to connect itself with any of the miraculous material in the Bible. This might seem strange, until we recall that the mid-nineteenth century was a time of criticism of the miraculous and the resurgence of atheism, under the influence of the theory of Evolution. In this sense, Baha'i-ism can be seen as a child of its own age. Now, in the twenty-first century, the miraculous is being seen to be re-evaluated, as we see spiritual healing reappearing. But then, the same can be said of most other sacred writings; they are usually a child of their own age, something that is inevitable, since every writer is human.

Literary worth

We have already seen some very apt usage of metaphor in the Kitab: the veil, the scent, the wine, the water. Some of the most spiritually helpful metaphors come in the titles used for God. Possibly one of the most striking features is the use of indirect language, many examples of which have been seen already. One such not yet mentioned is 'the pen':

> '... whose names have been recorded by the Pen of the Most High... ' (24, page 27).

Here, as in many other contexts, Baha'u'llah is referring to himself – God's scribe, in other words. Whatever he writes is the infallible word of God. How big is his ego! It is the same literary feature as seen in St John's writings, 'the disciple whom Jesus loved', which stops short of saying 'myself'. With St John it was modesty; with Baha'u'llah it was thinly veiled boasting. To call oneself 'the Pen' of God is indirectly claiming to be the record keeper of God, inscribing people's names in those scrolls, which are kept secret until the final day of judgement. This reminds us of Enoch and other apocalyptic material.

The boasting becomes rather more crass as we read through the book. We have already noted the elaborate names for God; but then the suspicion grows that Baha'u'llah is not always talking about God, but himself! This explains what at first sight seem rather obscure remarks. We can recall that Baha'u'llah is not his real name; it is a title meaning 'The Glory of God'. To quote Shoghi Effendi:

'The greatest name is the name Baha'u'llah. "Ya Baha'u-Abha" is an invocation meaning, "O thou Glory of Glories!" "Allah-u-Abha" is a greeting which means, "God the all-Glorious". Both refer to Baha'u'llah. By 'the greatest name' is meant that Baha'u'llah has appeared in God's Greatest Name, in other words, that He is the supreme manifestation of God.

How literally we have to take this, is debatable. Clearly Baha'u'llah saw himself in massively elevated terms, in which modesty takes a back seat. On a figurative level, it may be that he is God's spokesman, just like the prophets of old, that is, assuming the validity of his vision. On a literal level, it is a massive claim, and when we look at some of the names he gives himself, it does indicate someone with a massive sense of self-promotion. Such titles as, Best-Beloved, Counsellor, Dawning-Place, God's Light, the Desire of the World and many others, indicate someone who is certainly superior to the Bab, and probably a way ahead of Jesus Christ. In his address to the rulers of America, he describes himself thus:

'The Dove is warbling on the Branch of Eternity... thus counselleth you He Who is the Dayspring of Names... the Promised One hath appeared in this station... ' (88, page 52).

The Promised One often occurs in the Kitab; since the Bab had made reference to someone who was to come, Baha'u'llah lays claim to be that person. Going further, he dubs himself as the 'King of Kings'. Again, writing to the earthly rulers, he says:

'He who is the King of Kings has appeared, arrayed in his most wondrous glory... take heed lest pride deter you from recognising the Source of Revelation... arise and serve him who is the Desire of all nations... ' (82, page 49).

This clearly evokes the promise in Isaiah, 'the King of Kings and Lord of Lords, the everlasting Father, the Prince of Peace.' Baha'u'llah is clearly claiming to be the fulfilment of this. As outlined in Kitab 143 (page 71), 'this wondrous revelation' the words of the Kitab are 'through him every Fountainhead, every Dawning-Place of Divine guidance is made manifest. Reflect O people on that which hath been sent down in truth... ' This was taken, by Baha'u'llah's successors as the summing up, completion and common denominator of all religions and philosophies. On that basis, we are told to:

'Consort with all religions with amity and concord, that they may inhale from you the sweet fragrance of God. Beware lest amidst men the flame of foolish ignorance overpower you...' (144, page 72).

We find that the Baha'is are amenable and tolerant towards all other religions; in becoming a Baha'i one does not have to give up being something else. On that basis, it is being claimed as a basic foundation of unity between all peoples, a concept much needed in this day and age. It was Shoghi Effendi that took this to its logical conclusion:

'To Israel he was neither more nor less than the incarnation of the "Everlasting Father"... to Christendom, Christ returned "in the glory of the Father", to Shi'ah Islam the return of the Imam Husayn; to Sunni Islam the descent of the "Spirit of God" (Jesus); to the Zoroastrians the promised Shah-Bahram; to the Hindus the reincarnation of Krishna; to the Bhuddists the fifth Buddha.'

Baha'u'llah never goes to this extent in the Kitab and yet the implication is there. To complete the picture, we have remarks about his 'Ascension'. He clearly shows concern about his departure from this world:

'Be not dismayed... when the day-star of my beauty is set, and the heaven of my tabernacle is concealed from your eyes. Arise to further my cause, and to exalt my word amongst men. We are with you at all times and shall strengthen you through the power of truth. We are truly almighty... ' (38, page 32).

He is talking about his death. He never talks in terms of 'Ascension' or 'Assumption'. But his followers did soon afterwards. This would seem rather strange, since he was buried, beside the Bab on the slopes of Mount Carmel. In effect he is claiming to be the Holy Spirit. His followers are clearly claiming him to be on the same level as Elijah or Moses (who were 'assumed').

General remarks about the Kitab-i-Aqdas

This work by Baha'u'llah is the scriptural basis for the Baha'i religion. Much other literature has flowed from it via himself and his successors. In common with most other holy writings, it is rambling, repetitive, and not very well organised. It is, however, versified, well annotated and cross-referenced. The English is clear and full of interesting metaphors, even if his method of entitling is indirect and possibly misleading. It is clearly the outpourings of someone who has had some kind of Theophanous experience. One can hardly deny that the Baha'i ethic, generally accepted throughout the world, would actually transform things. We would all be honest, peaceful, even-tempered, kind, hard-working, caring, family-orientated and respectful to God. But the big bit missing from this book is the reckoning with Evil; if personified this means the Devil; if demythologised, then this means that wicked streak in human nature, which is still there, despite centuries of attempting to eliminate it. So far, Baha'u'llah's appeal to the rulers of this world has met with no noticeable response. It is true that the Baha'i faith is spreading rapidly in many parts of the world, or at least, that is what they claim; it is still, however, early days. A century and a half is not long when dealing with religious reform. 'By their fruits ye shall know them'[8] is something that Jesus said; we have yet to see what fruits the Baha'is will offer. A lot also depends on how we see the Bab and Baha'u'llah; are they a pair of false Messiahs, religious frauds like so many others that have come and gone; or are they genuinely inspired by God? It is difficult to tell at this stage. One thing can be said; neither of them exhibited the glory, wonder and spiritual power as seen in Jesus. We hear nothing of miraculous healings or natural world miracles. More significantly, neither of them called himself 'the Servant', and allowed other people to apply exalted titles to them.

To omit the mysterious element in religion is a mistake. There is plenty to appeal to people on a rational, humanistic level but nothing to resonate with those deep, instinctive impulses in human nature. The miraculous, the numinous, the deep paradoxes of faith; these receive scant attention. One could almost call Baha'i-ism 'Humanism with God ensconced on top.' Time will tell us the validity of this new approach to faith.

Notes for Chapter16: The Qitab-i-Aqdas

1. The Baha'i calendar, described in detail on page 177 in the Qitab-i-Aqdas.
2. The Prayer of St Richard.
3. 'The Dayspring'. This appears often in the Qitab-i-Aqdas and is derived from Luke 1:78 in which John the Baptist is eulogised and also the coming of Jesus is in view.

4. Rak'ahs: the recitation of specifically revealed verses with genuflections and other movements. The Qitab-i-Aqdas goes into detail about it on page 167.
5. 'Works-righteousness' as discussed by St Paul in Romans and other places. Essentially, the Christian position is that we are saved by faith, as opposed to just doing good works.
6. The veil: 2 Corinthians 3:13-16.
7. The Masnavi, Chapter 17.
8. 'By their fruits you shall know them... ' Matthew 7:16-20.

17

The Masnavi

Rumi

This is a work that is not at all well known in the Western world. It has been termed 'the Persian Koran'; it is an important basis for the Sufi tradition, which is a part of the Muslim world. The Sufis are the mystical element in Islam. In the introduction to the first book, it states:

'It is the greatest creed and the most luminous of holy laws, as well as the most manifest of proofs of God... '

In general terms there is an emphasis on the divine origin of this material (see volume 2, page x). This actually stops short of claiming to be the **truth**, but the implication is there, even so. It is the writings of one Rumi, whose full name was Mowlana Jalaloddin Balkhi; Mowlana is Persian for 'Our Lord'. He was a Sufi of the thirteenth century AD living in Konya, (now in modern Turkey), but the book itself was started late in his life, about 1262, and there is the suspicion that it was not quite finished before he died. His disciples formed the Mevlevi Sufi order, known in some circles as the whirling dervishes because of their distinctive dance which is a part of their rituals. Rumi's death is commemorated annually in Konya, attracting pilgrims from every part of the world and every religion.

The English version used here is the new translation from the Persian, by Jawid Mojaddedi of 2004. The work is exceedingly lengthy, amounting to about 26,000 verses, and runs into three volumes. There is no attempt to review all of it; a selection will suffice. The whole work is in poetry, there being no prose whatsoever. It is framed in the 'ramal' metre, which goes like this:

-*--/-*--/-*-/

It also goes in for rhyming of this kind of pattern in couplets:

AA BB CC DD etc.

The English translation has lost the rhythm but the rhyming pattern is included.

In common with Jeremiah, Rumi had an amanuensis called Hosamoddin. The work may seem strange to many people, as 'scriptural' writing. It does not compare easily with the Bible or the Koran, or indeed any of the other sacred writings described in this book. It is however heavily dependent on the Koran, making many allusions to it; also the Bible is referred to, including Jesus in a sympathetic light. It is framed in parable-like stories, some short and some quite lengthy, often sounding frivolous and jocular, even 'off-the-wall'. But that is where one can easily form the wrong impression, for almost always there is a secondary meaning concealed somewhere. Sometimes the interpretation is actually stated; sometimes it is not made clear and the reader is left guessing as to the message. This policy is in line with Rumi's major theme in the Masnavi; that we must not be taken in by appearances. The whole of life can be seen as symbolic of something.

We begin with some of the short stories in the first volume and work on to some of the more extended ones.

The Song of the Reed (page 4)

This concerns a reed that has been uprooted from its home in the reed-bed, and feels the agony of separation:

'When kept from their true origin, all yearn for union on the day they can return' (page 4).

The reed goes on giving a sad tune, which helps to console those who are parted, and speaks of love, as the attraction to bring people together again. Love is described as a fire. The way back to union is a tortuous path but it is no use grieving. It goes on to talk of freedom from desire for gold. 'A greedy eye is never satisfied'. The cure for conceit and pride is love; thus we can soar heavenward. If we are not able to love, we are left with emptiness. The mention of a mirror on page 6 is interesting; it symbolises one's soul, one's eternity. On the face of it, this is a love-song, but beneath the surface, it is talking about one's separation from God, the true reality.

All else is unreal, but the soul will only be happy when reunited with God. There is sensitivity and depth in this poem.

The story about the competition between the Greeks and the Chinese in the art of painting and portraiture (page 212)

This is clearly some kind of fantasy, for the likelihood of Greeks and Chinamen coming together to have a painting contest, is very remote. However, it must have a secondary meaning. The sultan set them up with two rooms, adjoining one another, such that they formed a pair, one half for each group, and supplied plenty of paint. While the Chinamen went in for plenty of colours, the Greeks felt that colours would not succeed. They removed all the colours and polished all the walls. When the Chinese had finished they banged their drums and let the king see the work; he was stunned at its beauty. But when he went to the Greeks to see their work, he was even more amazed; the walls reflected because they had been polished. We assume that they were reflecting the work of the Chinese, although this is not actually clear from the account; but the walls were actually shining.

The poem goes on to explain in part the symbolism used here. The Sufis are the Greeks; they polish up their hearts to such an extent that they do not need theories, desires or emotions. We notice the mention of a mirror, which is a common factor in world mythology; it speaks of eternity, truth and facing up to oneself. It also mentions the 'hand of Moses', which, according to the Koran, turned white because of the light of God[1]. Exodus does not actually say this; Moses' hand went leprous briefly. While one's brain or intelligence goes quiet, one's heart is with God, and going further than that, actually *is* God in some way. It now mentions 'the veil', which is a New Testament and a Koranic theme. In one sense the veil is torn in two, giving us direct access to God; on the other hand, there is still a veil over the human heart, blocking the view to God. The Koran agrees that this veil is a reality, but the New Testament can see the paradox in this image. The poem then goes on to discuss the issue of 'certainty'. This is a factor of importance for all who are mystics. They do not need proof of God's existence or reality; they experience it all the time.

'When images from heaven shone to earth, their hearts received them, and they know their worth. Their place is loftier even than God's throne, God's seat of certainty they've made their own' (Line 3514).

We now have a mention of the 'seat of certainty', a place in Heaven where the righteous gather on judgement day, as stated in the Koran (55:45).

Here we have the awkward question of certainty as opposed to faith. It may be that in the next world there are certainties about God and Heaven, but in this world, we have to function on faith, which is not the same as certainty; we do not have proof of God, only trust. Rumi does not mention this, probably because he is convinced that he has proof of God in his own heart.

The Angels' Prayer about spending (page 137)

This is another example of Rumi referring to the words of the Koran, in which two angels pray to God to reward the spender in the marketplace, and award losses to the misers. This again may seem rather strange until we discover its secondary meaning. It means that those who are generous in their spending of commitment to and love of God will reap a boundless treasure. Those who are stingy with their faith, or who perhaps do not believe at all, will receive a paltry measure. This motif is that the more one gives, the more one receives. The argument hovers between the literal and figurative all the time.

'Give bread for God's sake, more will come to you, give up your soul, receive a soul that's new' (Line 2249).

'Your barn is emptied when you sow what's there but soon your field sprouts goodness everywhere' (Line 2250).

This reminds us of that line in the Old Testament, 'cast thy bread upon the waters and thou shalt find it after many days' (Ecclesiastes 11:1)[2]. It is unlikely that Rumi wants everyone to spend all their money and have nothing in savings in the literal sense, but figuratively investing in eternal values, there is no limit to how much one can commit.

As an illustration of how to do it, Rumi cites the story of the generous caliph. He was so generous that he eradicated need in the poor. His fame soon had people of all nationalities coming round; his generosity was just like God's own giving hand. He was kinder than Hatem Ta'i, who was a mythical figure of the orient, somewhat analogous to Robin Hood or King Arthur.

'Water of life and sea of kindness too, through him all humans were soon born again' (Line 2264).

This sounds like a reference to the river of life in Revelation[3] and also to St John's gospel[4] where Jesus states that one must be born again of water and of the spirit. Here it is claimed that one man's generosity could give everyone a fresh start.

The story of the Hoopoe[5] and Solomon (page 76)

This is a good example of the use of secondary meaning. It starts with Solomon, who was famous for his wisdom, attracting a flock of birds. This can hardly be taken literally; he speaks to them in their own language and knows them all personally. A close relationship develops. It starts with sharing a language, but does not stop there. Intimacy is beyond mere words; it is a matter of the heart.

'By verbal and non-verbal intimations our hearts give thousands of interpretations' (Line 1217).

When it talks of 'birds' it is really talking about Solomon's visitors, who impart to him all their secrets and skills. Then we have mention of the hoopoe who explains his skills; he flies high and looks down at the ground. He can see water lying beneath the ground level, what quality it is and where to dig a well. So when on a trek in the desert, one should have a hoopoe in tow. Solomon sees the sense in having a hoopoe in the caravan 'to lead men to water in the ground'. The hoopoe therefore represents a dowser, or someone like Moses who could strike a rock and find water. On another level of interpretation, this is saying that when we are lost, spiritually, we need guidance from someone who knows where to find inspiration. The Sufis knew that training and guidance in mystical experience was important and had to be done by someone who knew what he was talking about.

The story goes on to describe the crow's attack on the hoopoe. The crow, in jealousy, makes out that the hoopoe is making false claims and boasting. Solomon wants to know if all this boasting is untruth. After all, if the hoopoe can see so much from the sky, why did she not see the snare that she is caught in?

The hoopoe offers her neck to be chopped if she is lying. The crow represents the atheist who denies that God's will rules. She claims to see all the snares, unless of course they are withheld from her sight by fate. Fate also is the reason for one's denial of destiny. Here we see a poetic expression of predestination; that one's belief or lack of it is decided by fate, rather than free will. One can go through life looking carefully, but perceiving is another matter; not everyone interprets life in terms of God's guidance.

The story then goes on to cite the situation with Adam as he named all the animals in the Garden of Eden[6]. The assumption is one very often implied in the Hebrew tradition that one's name is a description of one's nature. It would seem strange to modern ears to call a child by a certain name and then expect him to fit in with that preconceived pattern of behaviour.

'Our names are like a seed that's been sown, before God is the fruit that's finally grown.' 'He names men thus according to their end while for the present state a name he'll lend' (Lines 1253–54).

Remnants of this kind of thinking still occur in modern life, with such names as Melissa, meaning a bee, and Eugene, implying exalted status.

Even though Adam was so perceptive as to name all the animals according to their potential qualities, the one thing he did not perceive was the folly of eating the forbidden fruit. But Rumi sees this as destined.

'So destiny can block the sun's bright light' (Line 1264).

Returning to the hoopoe in the snare, she says that even if destiny does land one in a nasty trap, there is the other side to it, namely, that there is compensation and rectification in the next life.

'If destiny should try to murder you first it makes sure that you'll be born anew' (Line 1268).

'By frightening you, know that he's being kind, in his safe kingdom space for you he'll find' (Line 1270).

This is saying, in metaphoric terms, that one can be as careful and observant as possible, and also discerning, but there is always that slip-up when one fails to notice the obvious, which so often happens. This can be seen as fate at work. It does not mean that God has ceased to care about us; it is just that his plan is beyond our comprehension at the time.

The Lion, the wolf and the fox go hunting (page 185)

This story is more like Aesop's fables than any other of Rumi's stories. The three of them went hunting as a team, on the assumption that together they would be more successful. The lion, possibly out of a superiority complex, resented the other two, but did not stop them coming along. Here is a poetic piece of personification:

'The moon is shamed by stars, in honesty, it lets them near through personality' (Line 3032).

As they went to the mountain, the three of them caught an ox, a goat and a fat hare, which they saw as a most useful catch. The fox and the wolf waited deferentially in the hopes of equal shares of the catch. But the lion was a mind reader and knew what they were thinking; he gave nothing away and just smiled. He said:

'I'll show you what you two have truly earned, beggarly misers. Then you will have learned' (Line 3045).

The account then breaks into its own interpretation: there are those who think ill of God, or do not believe. God is liable to chop their heads off. He is smiling even so, but planning a scheme – never take the smile on a lion's face literally. Material success leads us to complacency and conceit; poverty is a far healthier option.

The lion then invites the wolf to share out the spoils; it is a ploy to find out what he is essentially like. The wolf gives the ox to the lion, the goat for himself and the hare to the fox. Although this seems fair, the lion flies into a rage because the wolf has been disrespectful. The lesson is that if one is egocentric, God will not accept one into heaven. It is not entirely clear why egocentricity is related to the wolf's idea of sharing out the catch; after all, he did offer the largest animal to the lion-king.

After a temporary break, the story resumes with the lion giving the fox a chance to divide up the spoils. The fox offers all of the catch to the lion, for breakfast, lunch and supper. This apparently pleases the lion who gives all the catch to the fox. The lesson being that if one gives one's all to God, then the rewards will be all one's own.

'I'm yours, and all the prey can be your prize, step on the seventh heaven as you rise' (Line 3125).

The lesson is also to learn from other people's mistakes in dealing with God.

Tucked into this story is the **Story of the Lover tapping on the door, (page 188).** This at first sight seems irrelevant, however it is all about egocentricity and how it blocks our relationship with God. The man taps on his lover's door and the voice says, 'Who is it?' He replies, 'It's me.' But she tells him to go away at once. She takes this to be arrogance. Later on, he tries again, being more careful in his phrasing. His reply this time is 'None love, but you.' This gains him admission. The reason is that there is no room for two 'I's'; God is the 'I' and we are the object, but we can be included in him.

'Now you are I, please enter in this place because for two 'I's' here there is no space' (Line 3076).

It then goes on to relate how God is capable of doing anything; he can bring things from non-existence to existence. We then have a passage, which might almost have been taken from Buddhist philosophy[7]:

'So that the pure soul headlong then will race to non-existence's vast open space. A wide and vast realm of magnificence from which this false world gains its sustenance. Tighter than non-existence is thought's realm, that's why it causes griefs that overwhelm' (Line 3106).

This is talking in a different phraseology about Nirvana; the chief difference here is that God is causing it all to happen, as he says, 'Be!' or, 'exist.' The story of the lovers is only the framework for this parable, which attempts to show the unity between God and his ardent adherents. God is the real existence; our existence is entirely dependent on his. Any egocentricity simply destroys the relationship. This is the essence of Islam; the word means 'submission'.

The Grocer and the Parrot (page 19)

This story starts in rather a flippant mood but soon turns into something much more profound. The parrot lived with the grocer in his stall, and talked to everyone as well as the birds. One day the bird hopped down and spilt a flask of rose oil, and the grocer sat down in it, messing up his clothes. He flew into a rage, hit the parrot on the head and rendered him bald. The bird now refused to speak. All attempts at coaxing him to speak failed, even handing out gifts to the needy.

Then one day, a monk came past, with his tonsure; this made the parrot talk. 'How did you come to be a baldy? Did you overturn a bottle of rose oil?' He was assuming that the monk was the same as himself, having made the same mistake. But the lesson is that we must not be taken in by appearances. To take one instance; bees and wasps appear the same, but in fact one makes honey and the other scavenges for rejected food.

'With false comparisons this world is packed; notice how different each one is in fact' (Line 272).

'Like sweet and bitter water both being clear, who can discriminate between the two?' (Line 277).

Rumi then takes the example of Moses' staff, when he challenges the magicians of Egypt to turn their rods into snakes. While Moses' rod turned into a snake, theirs did not. Then later, when they did manage to do the trick, Moses' snake gobbled up the other snakes[8].

'The difference is vast, like night and day, their deeds contrasted, they were poles away!' (Line 280).

Rumi then does a sustained contrast between the genuine believers and the copyists, who are just hypocrites.

'Believers will be led to victory while hypocrites will pay eternally' (Line 288). This is an important strand in the Koran, that hypocrisy is a terrible thing.

So just as the parrot and the monk were both bald-headed, the one was a genuine believer and the other just aping and did not really understand what he was doing. Just as an assayer has a method for telling genuine gold from fool's gold, so God can place in your heart a way of telling the genuine from the spurious believer. This ability to tell the true from the false is a way into heaven. Other methods of approaching God fail as he turns them away. Good health and strength go together, but a healthy soul will make the body weak. The mystic method does weaken the body but there is compensation for it. Your body may be weakened and destroyed but a much stronger purer soul is the result. Rumi then turns to the metaphor of the journey of life; some are facing forward to the beloved, namely God; others choose to walk backwards, facing the other way and seeing themselves instead of God. It is not easy to distinguish the genuine from the false; 'the devils make themselves look just like me.' Just copying the methods of the Sufis does not produce a genuine believer.

'The actions of the genuine spread light, while false pretenders just distort what's right' (Line 322).

At this point Rumi recalls a certain Bu Mosaylem[9], who was a false prophet using the name Ahmad, just like Mohammet; but he was unmasked as a liar. The same difficult situation arose in the time of Jeremiah and he was seen as genuine when his prophecies came to pass. This is the 'litmus paper' that Deuteronomy[10] offers us.

So, from the comical story of the parrot, who amused everyone but actually was only copying everyone else, Rumi develops a full-scale discussion of the problem of discerning the true believer from the superficial copyist. It is interesting that this issue has been an on-going question in the Christian churches over the centuries; how can one tell a genuine believer from a poseur? In this life, it may be impossible to tell;

only God really knows how to analyse people. We judge by appearances; God judges by the heart and soul.

The Jewish King who killed Christians (page 23)

The identity of this king is not mentioned; he was opposed to Jesus, which means it could be one of the Herods before the Jewish monarchy finally ended. He was cross-eyed, seeing double; the implication in this was that although Moses and Jesus were essentially in agreement, the king saw them as opposed, and wished to support Moses.

A short parable then follows; a teacher told a cross-eyed boy to fetch a bottle. The boy did not know which bottle was meant; he was seeing double. The teacher did not realise the boy's problem, and told him to go and smash one of them. When the boy did so, both bottles disappeared from view. The lesson from this is that desire, lust and rage can make you cross-eyed, and fail to see things as they really are.

> 'Virtue's forgotten when your heart feels lust, veils block your heart and eyes like layers of dust' (Line 335).

So the king, consumed with hate, killed Christians on the assumption that they were undermining the teachings of Moses. 'Moses' faith I have to protect.'

The king had a vizier who was exceedingly crafty but convincing, and offered the king a way of rooting out all the Christians regardless of their public or private feelings. He planned to pose as a Christian, gain their confidence and then enable the king to expel them all. The Christians are deluded by his preaching, thinking he was Christ's deputy, but secretly the vizier was setting traps for them. Like wheat in a granary, a mouse was quietly nibbling away, removing the store. But there is no need to fear that little thief because our 'souls transcend to realms beyond compare where souls and bodies rest without care.' Rumi is now talking about the mystical experience of the Sufi, who is essentially safe in the hands of God.

The story now includes the **Tale of the caliph and Layli (page 28)**; a beautiful lady who has entranced Majnun[11], she comes out with a profound remark:

> 'To be awake to this world means to sleep; it's worse than sleep in fact, and much more deep. Asleep to God, awake to spectacles, this represents the worst of obstacles... .' Line 412.

Then there is a long discourse about life with its delusions and illusions and the call to rid oneself of jealousy. Rumi now returns to the vizier's jealousy; how he is envious of other people's faith and wishes to destroy it. At last, some of the Christians realise that he is not genuine. For six years he went on offering them immunity from the king's persecution, but secretly he was in contact with the king in order to complete the eradication of the Christians.

The Christians agree to have twelve leaders, but with the vizier as the leader of them all. He then writes separate letters to each tribal leader, but the contents of each letter are completely different and contradictory. Each group takes his words as the truth and gives him a reply accordingly. But the plot goes wrong; the 'idiots' find out and the 'wise' fellow is unmasked and made a fool of. It is God's policy of reversal; 'claiming to be wise they become fools.'[12]

The vizier then tries to devise another plot; he goes into seclusion like a hermit, which makes them all the keener to have his words of leadership back, but he resists all their persuasion. He tells them that silence is now the best policy, and to leave him alone to his meditation. At this point we have a telling remark on the subject of free will and predestination:

'Prophets in this world follow God's command while infidels receive in hell what's planned; in heaven, prophets have free will, that's clear, but fools will claim it for themselves right here' (Line 643).

The vizier refuses to come out of seclusion, preferring death. He wants to sit with Jesus in heaven. The plot now thickens; he calls each of the twelve leaders and tells them secretly that each one of them is his successor and God's own spokesman, and the other leaders are to be deputies. All this is to be kept hush-hush until the vizier is dead. Also he gives each one a scroll with contradictory instructions. After forty days, the vizier kills himself; everyone was mortified, but then the question of leadership begins to surface. The issue of unity is discussed – something relevant not only to Christianity but to just about every other religion. Each leader who has a scroll comes forth, claiming to be the true successor; soon there is violence and bloodshed, which means that the vizier has achieved his aim in the end, even if he is dead. The whole tale is a caution about being led astray by false prophets; the answer is to fix one's mind on the true Lord above:

'Why choose the dark when there's sun up there? Your heart will lead you to the mystic way... seek fortune from the ones who know their Lord' (Line 729).

Of course we do not need to take literally every aspect of this strange story. But the gist of it is that it is so easy to be led astray by convincing poseurs, and even idolise them. There is also the issue of unity; the underlying current in this is that Islam is claimed to be a united faith in contrast with Christianity, which has so many denominations and permutations. With regard to Jesus, Rumi appears to have respect for him and acceptance, although he does not actually state this clearly. At times one wonders if the vizier is not representing Jesus, with his forty days of seclusion and using a subtle method of handing on the succession. Then again, there is the implication of the disagreement over the successor to Mohammet, which has never been resolved and is the basis of the rift between the Sunis and the Shi'ites to this day. There are so many different levels of interpretation in this story, none of which needs to be taken simply at face value.

A guest came to Joseph (page 194)

We assume that this is recalling Joseph as in Genesis; a kind friend comes a long way to visit him with a gift. Joseph is not bitter about his brother's jealously; it was God's decree. His misfortunes in the well and in gaol were just a precursor to greater things later. Joseph wants to know what gift his guest has brought; after all, at the Resurrection, we shall all be expected to produce a gift. The guest produces a mirror; the only thing he could think of as being appropriate:

'I've brought this mirror so that when you see your handsome face you'll remember me' (Line 3213).

This introduces an interesting piece of philosophy; that a mirror shows up the opposite of itself.

'Defects reflect perfection's pure light, they mirror God's own glory and his might; all things thus make their opposites appear... in vinegar the taste of honey's clear' (Line 3224).

Thus non-being is the mirror of Being; food is the mirror of the hungry; tinder is the mirror of flame.

Thus we can come to terms with our own faults; imagining that one is perfect is a major error. Some people may appear to be pure and perfect, but beneath it all is filth. But the Sufi guide knows how to join us to God. We cannot cleanse ourselves; we need help from God. The process of purification is painful, and ongoing; it is a mistake to give up and do without help.

It is interesting that the mirror motif occurs again; in mythology, the mirror is symbolic of eternity, everlasting life, and facing up to realities about oneself. A short passage from volume 2, line 102 shows the importance of this metaphor:

'O universal mirror, I now see my image in your eyes so vividly. I said, "I've found myself at last today; I see in his eyes the enlightened way."' (Line 102).

A man from Qazvin gets a tattoo (page 183)

This is one of the more 'off-the-wall' stories in the Masnavi, but the meaning behind it is not too difficult to discern. The relevance of Qazvin, which is a town in northern Iran, is not clear; this story may be based on a real incident. Rumi claims that these people go in for a lot of tattooing.

Briefly, the story goes, that a man went to the barber and asked for a tattoo of a lion across his shoulder blades. As soon as the barber started sticking the needle in, the man started to object to the pain. He asked what part of the lion he was doing, and barber said it was the lion's tail. The man told him to leave out the tail and just do the rest. So the barber started on the lion's ears; this too received strong objection, so the ears were left out. The same happened over the lion's stomach. In the end the barber gave up in despair, wanting to know what kind of a lion would it be with no tail, ears or stomach. Then the message of the parable breaks through:

'Brother, you have to bear the needle's pain to flee your infidel self's poisonous reign' (Line 3015).

In other words, to achieve the ultimate goal of escaping one's own existence and selfness, and shine just like the sun, is a painful business, but worth it:

'If like the day you wish to shine so bright, burn up your being, for that's like the night... you've clung fast to the self of 'I' and 'you' although all wretchedness stems from these two' (Line 3015).

The parable also speaks of making a complete commitment and not just a partial one. Missing out the bits that hurt and trying to go the way of meditation in a half-hearted way, is no gain. One has to go the whole way and endure the suffering involved. If one clings on to the self, one will never escape one's own existence, and continue in wretchedness.

'You've clung fast to the self of 'I' and 'you' although all wretchedness stems from these two' (Line 3025).

306

It is interesting that here we see an element from Hindu thought, where in the Bhagavad Gita (Chapter 9), Krishna is giving guidance to Arjuna, that of escaping from 'selfness'. However, Rumi has no concept of reincarnation; he is firmly in the Islamic tradition, which assumes that we live once and then face judgement. Also we see an element from the teachings of Jesus, reminding us of 'take up thy cross'; the way to salvation is not easy, can be very painful, but in the end highly rewarding. The one thing missing from Rumi's writings is the element of messianism, even though he has a strong regard for Jesus.

The Prophet visits a sick Companion (page 125, volume 2)

This portion in the second volume is less of a story and more of moral advice. One of the Prophet's friends was very ill, so Mohammet came to visit him. We are now advised to visit the sick as a sound policy:

> 'There's benefit in visiting sick men; the good will soon come back to you again' (Line 2148).

We now see the reasoning behind it. The sick man might be a Sufi or a king; he may appear to be a physical wreck but beneath it he may be someone very worthwhile:

> 'There's treasure in this world, so don't despair. In every ruin you'll find treasure there' (Line 2152).

We now return to the theme of not judging by appearances. Even if the sick man is not somebody important, he may have some worthwhile features. One can make a friend of him, and even if he is not a friend, it may engender friendship:

> 'If he's a foe, good still comes from this act; kindness turned many foes to friends you lacked, or at least made their hate dissipate, because it is a balm which can heal hate' (Line 2155).

Rising above the plain level of visiting the sick, Rumi now makes the theme more general and more widely applicable:

> 'The gist is: be a friend to everyone, carve friends from stone just like the sculptor's done. And if they make your caravan grow longer, it can fight robbers off when it is stronger' (Line 2160).

In other words, we all need friends and allies, and a bit of kindness and caring can so easily be of advantage to one in difficult circumstances.

A Prince troubled a sleeping man(page 118, volume 2)

This is a really strange tale, and highly unlikely in literal terms, but the interpretation is much easier to assess.

A wise prince happened to see a man sleeping on the ground, and a snake was sliding into his mouth. The prince was too late to stop the snake sliding in, so he began to hit the sleeping man to wake him up. The man ran off, not realising the danger he was in. He hid beneath an apple tree. The prince persuaded him to eat lots of apples and went on beating him. The man wanted to know what he had done to deserve a beating, but the prince just kept on advising him to run. He fell on his face and had to keep on running until at last, he vomited. This had the effect of throwing up the apples and the snake too. Now he realised the reason for his ill-treatment. He was deeply grateful to the prince and thought of him as an angel or God himself:

'Blessed the moment I came in your view; I then was dead... now I've gained new life' (Line 1903).

The man is deeply appreciative of the prince's actions, even if they seemed brutal. The reason why the prince did not explain what he was doing, was because if he had told the man he had swallowed a snake, he would have gone into a panic and maybe died of sheer terror.

The lesson from this is that we do not fully realise the evil that is in ourselves, and God does not go into too much detail about how much danger we are in. Afterwards, when the danger is past, we can see what the problem was and feel deeply grateful; but that is what is required to remove the evil from us; a bit of rough handling and drastic measures from one who can see the problem and has the moral courage to do something about it.

Some concluding comments on the Masnavi

The Masnavi is not an easy corpus of literature to analyse. Almost all of it is not to be taken literally; there is so much of parable and symbolism in it, which gives it great depth and poetic value. One of the most valuable strands of thought is Rumi's insistence on not being taken in by appearances. This comes as quite a surprise, when he implies that the Koran is not to be taken too literally. In general terms, there is very little of the Doomsday mentality in the Masnavi; fear and damnation are much reduced. His emphasis is much more firmly on love; it is expressed in terms of romantic love but it is really talking about the closeness between God and the believing soul. A classic passage on this theme is found in volume 2 line 1533:

'Through love the bitter turns sweet, as we've told; through love all copper too becomes pure gold; through love the goblet's dregs turn clear and pure; through love the pain we feel becomes our cure; through love some even can revive the dead; through love the king becomes a slave instead.' And so it continues; profound words.

In this way, Rumi is very close to the New Testament, and indeed he refers to Jesus as the Messiah. Sadly, he does not make Jesus the central point of his theology. But there is something very close to the concluding thoughts in Revelation[13], where the Temple is provided and yet not needed because God's presence is with his people. Rumi transposes this thought to talk about mosques:

'Mosques are what the stupid venerate, while they attack the mystics with sick hate; donkeys, your mosques are only transient things! The real mosques are the hearts of mystic kings; the saint's heart is the greatest mosque around because that is the place where God is found' (volume 2, Line 3120).

It would be a mistake to take 'kings' purely literally; he means here the chief of the mystics. In fact very little in the Masnavi can be taken purely at face value. But the valuable element in this thought is that the close, loving relationship between God and the true believer is not tied to buildings or holy places. It is in one's heart wherever one goes.

We may be seeing an element of what we would now call 'demythologisation' in his view of the Koran. When talking about the Resurrection, he is not thinking first and foremost of the Day of Judgement. He is in fact thinking that every normal day is a resurrection when we wake up; a fresh start with God every time. An unusual reference to the crucifixion is also informative; it is for Rumi an inner matter which has its effect on one's soul:

'Spring sends God's kindness, but, lest men forget, Autumn shows them God's terror and his threat; the winter is the inner crucifixion, when, hidden thief, truth is made clear from fiction... poverty, hunger, handicaps and fear are sent so the soul's nature is made clear... the truth and falsehood have been muddled up, like putting real and false gold in one cup' (Volume 2, Line 2975 and going on).

With this we see a rationale for suffering, and an approach to theodicy.

Being close to God does not mean that life is all going to be plain sailing. There will be hardships, which are sent by God on purpose to clarify matters in one's soul. The falsenesses of life become more apparent; the deep truths about life and the next life become more obvious.

Rumi comes very close to an understanding of the paradox of Theodicy; for there to be anything good in life, there has to be evil, and vice versa. This juxtaposing is now applied to faith, and he comes very close to that comment in Mark 9:24; 'I believe; help my unbelief', a remark made by the father of a child with a demon[14].

'But let your heart express what's in its core! Your unbelief is faith, your faith God's light; the world through you is safe and bright' (volume 2, line 1788).

Here we see the tension between belief and doubt, which is the lot of many human souls; something which goes on in the Sufi method as well as everyone else. It is a valuable thing to express oneself openly without bottling up doubts, and even worse, pretending to believe when one does not.

With Rumi's approach to literalism, we are given an invaluable mode for coping with not just the Koran, but all the other scriptural material in the world. The question is, how literally do we take it; is it metaphoric, symbolic; has it got secondary meaning? This approach will help us with all those difficult passages, particularly in such a book as the Revelation. So for instance, when Rumi talks about 'height' he is not talking literally but figuratively:

'Height here is not a physical dimension; the soul's and wisdom's peak is the intention' (volume 2, line 1964).

This brings us to coping with the **truth**, which is what this book is all about. Rumi actually tackles this question head on with some very wise remarks.

'All men try to describe the mystery of truth, each one of them so differently' (volume 2, Line 2934).

Philosophers and theologians cancel each other out and others ignore what they are saying, but the truth is in there somewhere:

'About the true path each informs a bit, such that you might think they belong to it. They are not all correct in what they say and neither are they totally astray' (line2937).

So the truth is in there somewhere, but not one of them has the complete answer. Rumi then goes on to say that falsehood has its part to play just as truth does. In fact, truth would have no meaning if there were no falsehood. Even a lie can contain an element of truth in it, and the reverse is also true:

'The stupid man says everything is true; a man who says all's false is foolish too' (line 2953).

This too is a most valuable line of thought when dealing with the full spectrum of sacred literature from across the world. To say that there is something of value in each one is a fair comment; also there is the false element. The skill and the wisdom to assess and rationalise these matters is needed; how to assess historical material, how to cope with mythology and eschatology; how to evaluate the metaphoric language used, especially exaggeration. One may not necessarily become a Sufi, but we can learn a lot from the Masnavi.

Rumi's thoughts in relation to Jesus

In common with the Koran, the Masnavi makes various references to Jesus, in a sympathetic tone. The remarks mainly concern Jesus' ability to heal and raise people from the dead. Jesus is not described in relation to Satan, but rather to 'a fool', which might be a roundabout way of saying the same thing.

In volume 2, page 11, a fool finds some bones in a pit and asks Jesus to teach him God's Greatest Name so that he can raise the dead. The 'greatest name' is not explained; one would expect it to be YHWH. However, Jesus tells the fool to be quiet because he cannot use the name of God since he is not in the same league as Moses and other great prophets. The fool then tries to persuade Jesus to do the healing but he refuses. Jesus points out that the fool could take more care of his own life rather than worrying about someone else's. The general comment from God is that fools only produce thorns as opposed to roses. A remark which sounds like reincarnation states that fools will be reborn as snakes, and cannot be pure souls.

In volume 3, page 157, Jesus is running away to a mountain, to escape from a fool. The man following him is perplexed as to why Jesus should have to run away. There is the admission that Jesus is the Messiah, the king from the Unseen Realm, who heals the deaf and the blind and has the ability to raise the dead. He is also termed 'The Holy Spirit' as in the Koran. So why does Jesus have to run away? The answer is that he has tried to heal the fool and it did not work; this is why Jesus tries to escape from fools.

'Air steals flowing water bit by bit, and fools make faith evaporate
like it' (line 2595, page 158).

So the core of healing is faith, and if this is lacking, the cure will not work.

In volume 2, page 211, Rumi refers to the incident in St Luke where
Elizabeth and Mary meet and 'the babe (John the Baptist) leapt in her
womb'. John is honouring 'a great king inside you, a prophet of God...'
Mary admits to a strange sensation as well. Thus Rumi adds a little more
than is in the original story.

Then we have a fool who thinks this account is a mistake. He maintains
that Mary had gone away into solitude during her pregnancy and therefore
could not have met Elizabeth. We notice that there is no denial of Jesus
being born of Mary, although there is no mention of Bethlehem or the
stable.

Rumi explains this impasse away thus:

'Those with true vision easily can view remote things as though they
are present too; John's mother was to Mary visible and near although
that seems impossible'(line 3628, page 212).

Here we are verging on telepathy. But it is Rumi's chance to inveigh against
strict literalism, something that he applies to the Koran. So much of what he
says has to be taken figuratively, and we wonder how much of his comments
about Jesus are symbolic rather than literal.

The next reference to Jesus is somewhat indirect. In volume 3, page
225, The Holy Spirit appears to Mary while she is bathing. She was at first
afraid but took refuge in God, but she is reassured by the Holy Spirit that
there is no need to hide from him. It is God's Command. The phrase 'Holy
Spirit' is a euphemism for Jesus. With Mary bathing, we may see her being
cleansed and purified to have the baby Jesus. We note that it is not the angel
who speaks to Mary but a somewhat anthropomorphic appearance of Jesus
before he is born. This seems rather strange.

In general terms, Rumi is accepting of Jesus as the Messiah, a great
prophet and king, but does not go so far as to call him 'the Son of God'.
This is in accordance with Islamic tradition (Chapter 21).

Notes for Chapter 17: The Masnavi.

1. Exodus 4:6.
2. Ecclesiastes 11:1.
3. Revelation 22:17.
4. John 3:5.
5. The hoopoe: a brightly coloured bird with a long curved beak to probe the ground for

insects. It is found in Southern Europe, Asia, Ethiopia and Israel.

6. Genesis 2:19.
7. 'born anew': this may be an indirect reference to Karma as in Hindu tradition, but Rumi is not noted for any real assumption about reincarnation.
8. Moses' rod: Exodus 6:10. Actually in the story it was Aaron's rod that turned into a snake.
9. Bu Mosaylem; he was a contemporary of Mohammad, using the name Ahmad, which meant he was impersonating the Prophet. Bu was unmasked and exposed as a liar.
10. Deuteronomy 18:15-22 explores the whole problem of false prophecy.
11. Majnun: literally 'the madman' the name given to Qays, the lover of Layli after he fell madly in love with her.
12. Romans 1:22 'claiming to be wise they became fools'.
13. Revelation 21:22.
14. Mark 9:24.

18

The Book of 1 and 2 Kings

This work forms a complete contrast to many of the scriptural materials seen so far. The closest thing to it so far is the books of the Maccabees (Chapter 2). As far as our ten areas of truth are concerned, it is a far more balanced work, moving through most if not all of these areas. It is part of a much more extensive work, as the history of Israel moves on from the end of Deuteronomy, the conquest of Canaan, the establishment of the Hebrew kingdoms, the mistakes that were made leading to the downfall of both kingdoms, the fortunes of the Jews in the Exile. The writer or final editor's name is not known to us, but scholars have dubbed him 'the Deuteronomist.' This is because his style, theology and view of history is based on the Book of Deuteronomy (see Chapter 13). Although the Book of Jeremiah uses phrases and ideas echoing Deuteronomy, it is unlikely that Jeremiah himself actually wrote the Deuteronomic history; it is just possible that his scribe, Baruch, may have had a hand in it, but that is pure speculation. The reason for this part of the history being in two books is purely practical; it was to do with how much could be included in one scroll. Otherwise the one book just continues into the other. The first Book of Kings begins with the end of David's reign; as he lies dying, there are various abortive attempts at a *coup d'etat*, but Solomon emerges as the new king. We see the state of Israel in its glory days with a massive territory and wealth, coupled with peace on all frontiers. Gradually, as the books progress, we see the erosion of all this splendour, as the two kingdoms deteriorate and finally collapse, to be sent off into Exile. The final verses leave us with an inkling of hope, as King Jehoiakin is released from custody in Babylon and receives favours from the king. This gives us an end date for this work; about 560 BC when Amel Marduk had succeeded Nebuchadrezzar. The Book of Kings has had much influence on Jewish thinking in Post-Exilic times; probably more influence than many other Hebrew works. The Books of the Chronicles may have used the Kings as a source of information, but that is not certain; it is possible that the Chronicler did not know the kings at all. Also Josephus used them extensively as source material. It is a crucial work for this reason; that the whole issue of kingship with the Israelite people was a big dilemma. If God was seen as the king of his people, then what did it mean to have an earthly king? For many, it spelt trouble right from the start, and they were correct in their fears because it was the compromising attitude of the kings that led to the collapse of both kingdoms. For others, it was the basis for the prophecy of hope, that in the future there would come a Messiah, in the tradition of David, who would finally sort out their problems, not just of the Israelite people, but of the whole of humanity. Obviously the work is slanted to suit the stance of the Deuteronomist; careful analysis may enable us to see other aspects of the matter, as was possible with the books of the Maccabees (Chapter 2). The impression gained is that the Deuteronomist was a die-hard, heavily attached to the faith of the covenant of Sinai, totally averse to any compromise or dilution of the faith of Israel, and taking everything completely literally. Nowadays, we might call him a Bible Fundamentalist of the most severe kind.

Mathematical information

Kings is full of mathematical information, probably more so than many other scriptural works, within the Bible or in any other scriptural work. The main point of interest is the dating of the kings' reigns. Although sadly the Israelites split into two kingdoms, Judea and Samaria, the positive side of it for historical calculations, is that all the kings' reigns are correlated in detail, so that a complete chronology going back from the Exile to the time of David can be achieved. One example of this correlation will be enough, but the book is riddled with statements like this:

'In the fifteenth year of Amaziah to son of Joash, king of Judah, Jeroboam (the second) the son of Joash, king of Israel began to reign in Samaria and he reigned forty-one years... ' 2 Kings 14:23.

It has been pointed out that the chronology does not quite work out; this may be because regnal years were in many cases dated from the New Year Festival, which may have been some sort of coronation; also there may have been co-regencies. But from this we can calculate that Solomon was ruling about 922 BC. Before that, dating becomes much more sketchy, as inter-chronology does not occur, in fact everything in the second millennium BC is largely guesswork, dating-wise. Not only can we date the kings' reigns; we can also correlate them with the regnal years of other kings in neighbouring countries: Egypt, Assyria, Babylon and others.

Another aspect of mathematics comes with the construction of Solomon's Temple. There is much detail given of the dimensions of various artefacts, all in cubits. Here is an example:

'... he made two cherubim of olivewood, each ten cubits high. Five cubits was the length... the height of one cherub was ten cubits...' 1 Kings 6:23.

An interesting matter arises in 1 Kings 7:23 where the molten sea is described. It was ten cubits from brim to brim which means its diameter (it was round), and a line of 30 cubits measured its circumference. Pythagoras would have told us that this is impossible! If the diameter was ten, then the circumference would have to be ten times Pi, namely 3.14 which gives us 31.4 cubits. This could be seen as a pre-Pythagorean attempt at arriving at Pi.

One really significant date for the Deuteronomist is in 1 Kings 6:1:

'In the 480th year after Israel came out of Egypt, in the forth year of Solomon's reign... in the month Ziv which is the second month... he began to build the house...'

The writer sees this as very important and significant; we see the relationship between the forth year and 480. This is followed up in 6:37 with the completion of the Temple, which took seven years to build, in the eighth month, Bul, and Solomon's eleventh year.

This mention of 480 years going back from Solomon's time allows us to give an approximate timing for the Exodus, at about 1400 BC. This places it in the end of the eighteenth dynasty of Egypt, when someone like Thutmosis 4th or Amenophis 3rd were in power. Interestingly the reign of Akhenaten (1370 BC) comes just after this time; he was the Pharaoh who tried to introduce a kind of monotheism but failed.

Annoyingly we do not know the name of the Pharaoh who chased after the Israelites, but all this gives reality and substance to the account, when studying the kings. We are not dealing with imaginary or speculative matters, we are dealing with real figures, even if they may at times be a little distorted. In addition to this, there is just the possibility that these figures are partly symbolic; by the time we arrive at Revelation (Chapter 6) we become fully aware of the methods involved in Hebrew number symbolism.

Geographical factors

Again, we are told many details about the land of Canaan. We are told that Solomon ruled over a vast empire:

'Solomon ruled over all the kingdoms from the Euphrates to the land of the Philistines and to the border of Egypt; they brought him tribute and served Solomon all the days of his life' 1 Kings 4:21.

We notice that in the Maccabean account, the Jews had managed to extend their influence from the border of Egypt right up to Antioch, which is almost the same amount of territory; this is in fact saying that the glory days of Solomon were re-emerging. This does not mean that all these peoples became practising Jews, although some did, it would seem. The actual Hebrew territory was much smaller, according to the settlement of the twelve tribes, and even then, not all the indigenous peoples were displaced. The lesser kingdoms on the borders, it is claimed, became vassal states and paid tribute. One interesting situation was when Hiram King of Tyre, who had been a good friend of David, also befriended Solomon, and supplied materials for the building of the Temple. It may be that Hiram had respect for the God of the Hebrews:

'Hiram rejoiced greatly and said, "Blessed be the Lord this day..."' 1 Kings 5:7.

How literally we can take this, is a matter for debate, since Tyre and Sidon had their own collection of gods, which Solomon, strictly speaking was not supposed to recognise. Nevertheless, the two kings made a treaty and embarked on all kinds of lucrative projects, including fetching gold from the south. This all ties in with the visit of the Queen of Sheba, bringing gold from Ophir:

'Then she gave Solomon 120 talents of gold and spices... and the fleet of Hiram, which brought gold from Ophir... and almug wood and precious stones' 1 Kings 10:10-11.

There is some discussion as to exactly where Ophir was, but it must have been somewhere down the end of the Red Sea, adjoining Egyptian territory. There is much geographical information right through the chequered history of the kings, down to the collapse of the two kingdoms. A good example of this is:

'In the days of Pekah king of Israel, Tiglath-Pileser king of Assyria came and captured Ijon, Abel-beth-maacah, Janoah, Kedesh, Hazor, Gilead, and Galilee, all the land of Naphthali... ' 2 Kings 15:29.

Some of these places are not known for certain; but that does not matter, since at that time, the first readers would have known them. Hazor, however, is known to us for certain, and has been thoroughly excavated, revealing a blocked-up gateway that was intended to strengthen the town against siege. The book ends with a sad note:

'Nebuzaradan... brought them to the king of Babylon at Riblah in the land of Hamath ' 2 Kings 25:20.

This would be well to the north of Israel, on the Euphrates, and ironically the extent of Solomon's glory day kingdom.

But the geographical realities all serve to tie in with the dating and the reality of the events in the Book of Kings. It was all seen as the hand of God interacting with the fortunes of the Hebrew peoples; God was very real to them and active in day-to-day events and also certain special places.

Historical realities

Some of this has already been discussed. As historical account we have to bear in mind that the events recorded are with the slant of the Deuteronomist. Every king is judged by the yardstick of the Book of Deuteronomy: every king is either good or bad and there is very little in between. The writer expected everyone to be as single-minded and fanatical as such people as Jehu and Josiah. What we are lacking to a very large extent is the viewpoint of the foreign powers who were in contention with the Israelites. Still less do we hear the opinion of people like Ahab, Jeroboam and Manasseh. It is interesting to compare certain accounts and perhaps arrive at a slightly more balanced view of events. This is in contrast to the Maccabean situation, in which we do not have the Seleucid version of matters; the Seleucids clearly inherited the same sort of situation as the Assyrians and the Babylonians toiled under.

We can take a look at the account of Jehu, who assassinated Joram and wiped out the adherents of Ahab, all at the instigation of Elijah. The account occupies much space: 2 Kings 9:11 to 11:36 – quite a lengthy reign for those days at 28 years. This must indicate that he had much power in the area; even so, he was having trouble with Hazael the king of Syria (not to be confused with Assyria) who was marauding parts of the land. What is not recorded in Kings is that Jehu was having dealings with Shalmaneser 3rd of Assyria. Here is Shalmaneser's version of it, recorded in bas-relief on the Black Obelisk; the date would be 841 BC[1]:

'I received the tribute of Jehu son of Omri, silver, gold, a gold bowl, a gold vase, gold goblets.'

Shalmaneser is obviously stating things from his point of view, that Jehu is ingratiating himself. For what purpose? Almost certainly, Jehu is trying to make an alliance with the Assyrians in order to frighten Hazael; this sort of tactic was often employed. How literally do we have to take this obelisk? Did Jehu literally grovel on the floor, or is it symbolic? We know that Jehu was not the son of Omri – in fact, he was an upstart usurper – but seen from the Assyrian point of view he was a successor of Omri, Ahab and Joram. This shows that taking this obelisk completely literally is a mistake, just as taking everything in the account of the Kings completely at face value is also a mistake.

Why did the Deuteronomist omit this material? In general he approves of Jehu, as God says to him '... you have done well... ' with regard to removing Ahab and his influence. However, Jehu did not go the whole way and completely reverse the policy of Jeroboam, which involved setting up a breakaway kingdom and providing two golden calves for worship. In the next breath we see the result; Hazael king of Syria begins to attack Israel. We wonder why the Syrian invasions seem to be intermittent and only partially successful; the writer gives us the clue; that the king and the people prayed for deliverance. He does not admit that the king might have done a deal with Assyria. It is just possible, however that the Deuteronomist did not know of this arrangement with Assyria. It is also possible that he did not know about the Battle of Qarqar (853 BC) in which Ahab was involved.

The mention of Jehu in the Assyrian annals is interesting because it is the first actual clear mention, by name, of an Israelite king in a foreign record. This ties the event down to 841 BC, and that helps to give us a datum point for all the other kings and events, before or after.

Another such correlation comes with the Stele of Adad-Nirari 3rd, king of Assyria, circa 796 BC[2].

'He received tribute from Mari of Damascus... and also tribute of Joash (Jehoash) of Samaria... of the people of Tyre and Sidon...'

Clearly the Assyrians were extorting tribute from all the smaller kingdoms of the Levant. This Joash (Jehoash), who is not to be confused with the King of Judah of the same name, was rather more successful in managing to drive the Syrians back, recapturing many areas up to Hamath (2 Kings 13). Kings makes no mention of him giving tribute to Assyria, but it would explain why he managed to push the Syrians back; Assyria was helping from behind.

At last we get an admission that an Israelite king was paying the Assyrians:

'Menahem exacted money from Israel... from all the wealthy men to give to the king of Assyria. So the king of Assyria turned back and did not stay in the land... ' 2 Kings 15:20.

This ties in with the annals of Tiglath-Pileser 3rd of Assyria[3]:

'I received tribute of Kushtaspi of Kummak, Rezin of Damascus, Menahem of Samaria, Hiram of Tyre... (and a whole list of lesser kingdoms)...'

By this stage, the Syrian threat had almost completely subsided and Assyria was pushing directly into Israel. It was like a protection racket; pay up tribute or we will come and wreck your country.

The final collapse of the northern kingdom is described quite fully in 2 Kings 16. It seems that the penultimate king of Israel, Pekah, made an alliance with Rezin king of Syria and attacked Jerusalem. The response from Ahaz of Judah was to appeal to Tiglath-Pileser and do some more grovelling, even to the extent of having a copy made of his pagan altar for use in the Temple. The Assyrians came to his aid and Pekah with many of his people, were taken off into Exile. The Assyrian version of it is as follows:

'The land of Bit-Humria... all of its people to Assyria I carried off. Pekah, their king... and Hoshea as king, I appointed over them...' (then it lists the tribute he extorted)[4].

The land of Bit-Humria means the house of Omri; this shows the strong impression that Omri made on the ancient orient, as Pekah, who was no relation to Omri, was just another usurper. It cannot mean 'all' of the people because there is another deportation later. Kings does not admit that Hoshea was appointed by the Assyrian king:

'Hoshea, the son of Elah, began to reign... against him came up Shalmaneser king of Assyria and Hoshea became his vassal and paid him tribute. The King of Assyria found treachery in Hoshea... ' 2 Kings 17:1-5.

This is a bit later than Tiglath-Pileser's time. Hoshea had made an appeal to Egypt for help and the annual tribute money dried up. This precipitated the final siege of Samaria, but Kings does not mention that it was another Assyrian king, Sargon 2nd who carried this out, resulting in the rest of the people going into Exile[5]. Kings lists the countries where they were sent: Halah, at Habor on the river of Gozan and in Median territory (2 Kings 17:6). It is believed that they were lost to history. It is interesting how the one account supplements the other. One wonders if the Deuteronomist knew that Hoshea was the appointee of Tiglath-Pileser; or was the Assyrian king just boasting? The Deuteronomist describes Pekah in slightly more sympathetic terms than the other Israelite kings...' and yet not as bad as the kings who were before him...' 2 Kings 17:2. Maybe he does not wish to admit to such a humiliation; it would be like Adolf Hitler appointing Oswald Moseley as the occupant of Buckingham Palace!

Sargon's version of it is somewhat abbreviated, as seen from his Summary inscription 707 BC[5].

'I besieged and captured Samaria. I took as spoil 27,290 people who lived there; I organised a contingent of fifty chariots and I instructed the rest of them in correct conduct. I appointed my eunuch (a high ranking Assyrian officer) over them and imposed on them the tribute of the former king.'

Sargon goes on to describe a whole list of minor kingdoms in the area: Samaria was not the only city to be captured. Minor monarchs were dragged up and murdered or put in gaol, and whole peoples were exiled. Samaria was just a sideshow, it would seem.

Up till now, Jerusalem had managed to escape the ravages of the Assyrian juggernaut; but now, in the time of Hezekiah, king of Judah, all this was to change. We can compare the account in Kings with Sennacherib's own version of it (701 BC) of which there are several versions inscribed. He makes a long list of minor kingdoms that bought him off with tribute. This included Judah, which, he claims, was giving him dues and an annual tribute. Sennacherib managed to capture forty-six Judean cities and gave them to Mitinti the king of Ashdod, Padi the king of Ekron, and Silli-Bel the king of Gaza, so that Judean territory was much reduced. Hezekiah was boxed up in Jerusalem. Kings admits that he appealed to Sennacherib (2 Kings 18:14) and the tribute was 300 talents of silver and thirty talents of gold. Sennacherib's version agrees with the thirty talents of gold, but the silver was 800 talents and much more besides. This even included Hezekiah's male and female singers; we assume these were the choir people in the temple. Would Sennacherib have appreciated the Psalms being sung to him?

'He even dispatched his messenger to deliver the tribute and to do obeisance[6].'

But this is supposed to have happened after Sennacherib had departed on his return to Nineveh. Predictably, he does not mention the defeat during the night when the angel of the Lord slew 185,000 Assyrians in their camp. But Sennacherib offers no explanation as to why he did not defeat Jerusalem while he was on campaign. Kings does; it was the prayer of Hezekiah and the good offices of Isaiah giving him resistance that saved the day. It is difficult to see exactly what did happen when comparing the two accounts. We have to consider exaggeration in the Assyrian version; we have such swaggering phrases as 'Hezekiah was overwhelmed by the awesome splendour of my lordship...' but omits to mention what we see in the Kings. This is the third element in Sennacherib's failure to take to Jerusalem; Kings tells us of Tirhakah the king of Etheopia coming up through Egypt with various kings, including Cushites, to challenge him at Eltekeh. Sennacherib claims to have defeated them, but it may have been more like a stalemate, since he does not linger in that area for much longer. This helps to explain Sennacherib's abbreviation of his campaign in Judea. The incident in which the Assyrian officials try to frighten Hezekiah's officials on the walls of Jerusalem (2 Kings 18:19) may have been a half-baked attempt at avoiding a lengthy siege and come to an accommodation with Judea, which would have saved time. We also may have to admit to exaggeration in Kings; if the Assyrian army had gone down with an infection during the night, how many would have been left to retreat to Nineveh? There is clearly an element of truth in both these accounts, if carefully compared. But it is an interesting example of how history can be bent to suit the propaganda of either side. History is written by the winners, and we have two winners here. Sennacherib could not admit to being defeated, Isaiah could not admit to Hezekiah as being defeated, since he was a good king, and also Jerusalem with its temple could not be violated.

As an interesting sidelight to these events, Hezekiah had a water tunnel carved out as a precaution against sieges:

'... the deeds of Hezekiah... how he made the pool and the conduit and brought water into the city... ' 2 Kings 20:20.

Hezekiah's tunnel is still there to this day and there is an inscription on the wall inside, in ancient Hebrew script, describing how they carved out the rock with axes, from both ends and met up in the middle. Sadly the text is now incomplete, but it gives a vivid idea of how it was achieved. The tunnel does not go in a straight line; it must have taken great engineering skill to make the two ends meet up.

We have not, so far, unearthed an Assyrian version of the battle of Carchemish (605 BC), but that was another confrontation between Egypt and Assyria. 2 Kings 23:29 briefly mentions this incident, but not specifying Carchemish, when king Josiah was killed by Pharaoh Neco at Megiddo. This is quite an admission for the Deuteronomist, since Josiah was one of the best kings, who had enacted a complete reform following the discovery of the Book of the law in the temple. Many people assume this was Deuteronomy itself, but there is no certainty about this. By this stage we see the rising star of Babylon, which inevitably put a limit on Assyrian ambitions.

Esar-Haddon[7], a later Assyrian king, had ambitions to build himself a palace. It is described in much the same tones as Solomon's palace. He mentions Manasseh, king of Judah as being recruited to help in the supply of materials. This is not mentioned in 2 Kings 21. With the rise of Nebuchadrezzar in 605 BC, we see the final onslaught on Jerusalem. In the Chronicle of[8] Nebuchadrezzar, we have a passing account of his campaign in Syria and down to Ashkelon. The king in person was not in attendance at the siege of Jerusalem; this agrees with 2 Kings 24:10:

'At that time, the servants of Nebuchadrezzar, king of Babylon came up to Jerusalem and besieged it... '

Quite true: it was the king of Akkad who attacked Jerusalem, only to be joined later by Nebuchadrezzar. Jehoiakim, the Judean king surrendered and was taken prisoner and away into exile in Babylon. It even gives the dating: 604 BC, the month of Adar February to March and day two. A new king was installed: Jehoiakim's uncle, Zedekiah, probably on the assumption that he would play the 'Quisling', but he did not. This incurred another siege and the final destruction of Jerusalem and the Temple. In an administrative text of Nebuchadrezzar, mention is made of Jehoiakin, as a guest of the king, being apportioned a ration of fifteen litres of olive oil (half a Pi). Also a gallon of oil for the 'five sons of the king of Judah...' The book ends with Jehoiakin[9] being freed from prison, invited as a guest at the king's table and being given a regular ration, a sort of life-long pension; this was done by Amel-Marduk (561-599 BC), the biblical Evil-Merodach (2 Kings 25:27).

Enough has been said to give a balanced picture of events during the two Hebrew kingdoms. We are remarkably well supplied with information from a variety of sources. The general picture is that the glory days of Solomon, during which he was extorting tribute from every minor kingdom within range, gradually faded as the Syrians, the Assyrians, Egypt and Babylon increasingly encroached on the Israelites and eventually wrecked both kingdoms. It was a time of turmoil, scrambling for wealth and power, political and military ambitions and terror.

No historian can produce a history without source material. We have frequent mention of such written sources in the Kings, The Chronicles of the Kings of Judah and also of Israel. This is not to be confused with the two books of the Chronicles, which cover much the same period. It is quite possible that the Chronicler did not know the books of the Kings; he may have used separate sources. It would seem that in those days, each king had his own written records of his deeds, including Solomon himself, and the foreign kings too. Our Book of Kings admits that much information has had to be left out; each reign is *a précis*, in effect. In doing so, a one-sided picture can emerge. But this is often balanced by a similar account from Assyria. The general impression is that the people of faith, the Hebrews, were dealing with real events and personalities. Their religion was not just some sort of subjective, speculative faith; it grew out of historical realities.

One incident not reported in the Kings or anywhere else in the Old Testament is the battle of Qarqar, in 853 BC[10]. This concerned Shalmaneser 3rd of Assyria as recorded in the Kurkh Stele, how, in his western encroachments was confronted with a confederation of twelve kings, one of which was Ahab of Israel. Ahab is reported as contributing ten thousand soldiers and two thousand chariots. Shalmaneser claims this battle as a smashing victory; the reality was that it was a stalemate, and the confederation forced him to take five years in regrouping. This is a good example of how the Assyrians (and other powers) were given to exaggeration and boasting. One wonders why this incident is not recorded in the Kings. Would it have suited the Deuteronomist's argument? He might not have known about it, but that is unlikely. More likely, he disapproved of Ahab as a bad king, and did not wish to admit that he could firstly form a successful alliance with the neighbouring kingdoms, and secondly teach the Assyrians a severe lesson. History is always a matter of how you see it.

Another incident not reported in the Kings are the circumstances inscribed on the Moabite stone by King Mesha[11], relating to the time of Omri who founded Samaria. Omri was another self-proclaimed king, but he receives scant mention in the Kings (2 Kings 16:25-28); in fact we learn more about him from Mesha than from the Bible. It would seem that Omri had taken possession of Medeba and other areas in northern Moab, but Mesha reclaimed these parts for his own country. Many of the place names are also found in other parts of the Old Testament; Chemosh the god of Moab had observances in Jerusalem because Solomon was involved with many foreign princesses who brought their religions with them, including a Moabitess (1 Kings 11:1-8). It is a surprise that the Deuteronomist does not recount the reverses of Omri over Moab; it would have suited his argument. Perhaps he did not know about it; rather he was more interested in the fate of Ahab the son of Omri.

The Tel Dan Stele[12], describes how an Aramean (Syrian) king, possibly Hazael in the mid-850s slaughtered seventy kings or so he claims. This is the first incidental mention of David in a non-biblical text:

'… and the king of Israel formerly went up to my father's land… and I killed seventy kings, who harnessed thousands of chariots and thousands of horsemen. And I killed Joram the son of Ahab, king of Israel, and I killed Ahaziah the son of Joram, king of the house of David. And I set their land in desolation… and ruled over Israel.'

Unlikely! According to 2 Kings 9:21-26, it was Jehu who shot Joram in the back. The account is so vivid and personal that it has to be given credit. The demise of Ahaziah king of Judah was in much the same circumstances; Jehu shot him, and he was taken off to Megiddo and died there. Again, this account is quite credible. The only way the king of Syria could make such a claim would be by saying that Jehu was his secret agent, which is not out of the question, but somewhat unlikely. It would be fair to say that the Syrians made a nuisance of themselves towards the end of the Omride dynasty; it was more a case of marauding and extorting protection money. Some territory was taken by them, but this was soon recovered later. If we put the two accounts together, a more balanced picture emerges.

The earliest known reference to Israel in non-biblical records comes from the Marneptah[13] Stele in Egypt, about 1200 BC:

'Canaan is captive with all woe... Israel is wasted, bare of seed... all who roamed have been subdued...'

This it would seem relates to an earlier phase in Israel's history when they were just beginning to settle in the land of Canaan, and the nomadic era was still fresh in the minds of their enemies. They must have had a reputation not unlike that of the gypsies. This must be the era of Joshua and the Judges, long before the start of the Monarchy. We can understand why the Deuteronomist did not wish to give this impression of Israel being 'wasted'. It was a time when all was well in Israel, before the kings came along with their compromising policies with the foreign kings and their religions. On the other hand, this stele may be just another piece of exaggeration.

One may wonder what sort of madness this was, that all these large and tiny kingdoms should be constantly jockeying for supremacy. The Ancient Middle East sounds as if it was constantly in chaos with atrocities going on all the time. This may not be quite the true picture, for the Kings does admit that there were times of relative calm and prosperity. But as with all human affairs, the unspoken undercurrent was the money situation. In this case, gold, and by extension, silver. Where were the goldmines located? Egypt had them in the south; the Hittites had them in Asia Minor. Those nations with no gold resources had to either trade for it, or borrow it, or steal it. This goes a long way to explaining the aggressive attitude of Assyria and Babylon, and why they were intent on invading and defeating Egypt. It was all about greed and ambition. The Israelites were caught in the middle of it. It was rather similar to the situation in the Maccabean era. The end result for the Israelites was dispersal and exile; this was known as the Diaspora, scattering them to every country in the world.

Theological considerations

It is impossible to assess the history of this period without coming to terms with the theological aspects of it. The Deuteronomist is most emphatic about his theological stance; remarks pertaining to it can be found on almost every page. Every king is commended or condemned according to the Deuternomic yardstick. There are those who think that Deuteronomy was written late or even after this period, but that makes no sense in relation to the tenor of the Kings. The writer is constantly referring back to the basic standards set in Deuteronomy. It is not enough to say that the other parts of the Pentateuch could have been the backdrop of his judgements. We are assuming that there are three distinct areas of theology, which only occur in Deuteronomy. Firstly there is the issue of the importance of prophetic guidance. When we consider that the kings were quite careless about their adherence to true Israelite religion, and the priests also were not to be relied upon for a pure faith in the one true God, clearly a heavy emphasis on the prophets is unavoidable. Secondly, there is the issue of the Temple as being the only legitimate place for sacrificing, and this is combined with the covenant of David, which concerns the basis for Monarchy, and eventually the logic of Messianism. Thirdly, there is the covenant of Sinai, which concerns Israel's response to being rescued from the Egyptian policy of ethnic cleansing. Also there are the Ten Commandments, plus many laws that are relevant to a settled agricultural community as opposed to a nomadic desert way of life. In the logic of the Deuteronomist, these laws would have the element of prophecy, in other words, Moses was anticipating what would happen when Israel managed to settle in the Promised Land.

Prophecy

Deuteronomy 18:15-22 raises the question of the true prophets as opposed to the false ones. The only way one can tell them apart is to wait and see the result, possibly in the short term, and possibly in the long term. We have mention of many prophets in the Kings. Most notably there is Nathan, who was instrumental in smoothing the way for the accession of Solomon and his anointing. Then there is Elijah whose account occupies at least three chapters; this was the time of crisis when the true faith of Israel could have been destroyed by Ahab and Jezebel. This is followed by Elisha, who was instrumental in the accession of Jehu the reformist. Later we have the ministry of Isaiah in the reign of Hezekiah; this receives a lot of emphasis. With the Josianic reform we have a prophetess, Huldah, offering advice. What is strange is that there is no mention of Jeremiah the great prophet through the reigns of Josiah, Jehoiakim and Zedekiah. Could the Deuteronomist really have had no knowledge of him; or was Jeremiah himself actually the Deuteronomist and did not wish, out of modesty, to include his name in the Kings? The whole history of the monarchy is shot through with the influence of the prophets. Some are very important ones; others minor or unnamed ones. But the writer is convinced of their importance in preserving the true faith of Israel, and he is seriously upset by the fact that kings and their peoples ignored their warnings.

As an accompaniment and contrast to the prophets of God, are also the prophets of Baal who had the patronage of Jezebel. This comes to a head when Elijah lays down the gauntlet to Jezebel's protégées:

'Now therefore send and gather 450 prophets of Baal and the 400 prophets of Asherah, who eat at Jezebel's table' 1 Kings 18:19.

Elijah makes out that he is the only one left of the prophets of God; this is probably a bit of sympathy-gathering, since we have mention of other unnamed prophets in many places. The result of the showdown on Mount Carmel was that the true God of Israel was seen to be real and the Baals just a fantasy. When the prophets of Baal are put to death, Ahab seems to make no comment, but Queen Jezebel is furious. She threatens Elijah with death; she cannot accept the proof given on Mount Carmel. Eventually, Elijah is told to appoint Elisha as his successor; Elisha accomplishes the same kind of marvels as Elijah with the exception that he is not 'assumed' into heaven. But the contrast between the genuine prophets and the false pagan ones is a strong one.

As further proof of the reality of prophecy, the Deuteronomist furnishes us with a variety of prophecy-fulfilment situations. Some of them are trivial, almost irrelevant occurrences:

'And a certain man of the sons of the prophets said to his fellow at the command of the Lord, "strike me, I pray". But the man refused to strike him. Then he said to him, "Because you have not obeyed the voice of the Lord, behold, as soon as you have gone from me, a lion will kill you," and as soon as he had departed from him, a lion met him and killed him' 1 Kings 20:36.

But some are quite momentous situations with the prophets calling the trumps at national level. One such case is when the Assyrians are attacking Jerusalem and Hezekiah is in a panic. Isaiah issues the following oracle (not quoted in full):

'Thus says the Lord concerning the king of Assyria. He shall not come into this city or shoot an arrow here, or come before it with a shield or cast up a siege mound against it… for I will defend this city to save it, for my own sake and for the sake of my servant David' 2 Kings 19:32.

The fulfilment comes straightaway, for in the night 'the angel of the Lord went forth and slew 185,000… of the Assyrians… and Sennacherib departed and dwelt at Nineveh' 2 Kings 19:32.

We can guess what people like Ahab and other compromising kings thought about the prophets of God – they thought that they were a confounded nuisance!

'When Ahab saw Elijah, Ahab said to him, "is it you, you troubler of Israel?" And he answered, "I have not troubled Israel, but you have… "'

We can glimpse it from Ahab's point of view; here was a tiny kingdom surrounded by potentially hostile pagan kings. Even Judah was not sympathetic to him. It was an urgent matter to make alliances with as many nations as possible; this meant marrying someone like Jezebel who was a Tyrian princess. It also meant accepting to some extent their religious stance, and since Baal and Asherah were the centre of Canaanite practice, that would entail some sort of compromise. The purists like Elijah were seen to be disrupting this process. We can glimpse Jezebel's stance; she almost certainly thought that the God of Israel was a lot of nonsense. She might well have said that monotheism was obviously wrong and the covenant of Sinai was the result of Moses' ego-trip. As for the cultural aspect of it, she may have been very keen on Canaanite practice and thought the laws of Sinai as very puritanical and tedious. Just how nasty Jezebel could be emerges in the story of Naboth's vineyard in 1 Kings 21:1-14; this elicits a prophecy from Elijah that Ahab's family will be wiped out and Jezebel will be eaten by the dogs in Jezreel (1 Kings 21:23). The Deuteronomist takes great care to show how these remarks came to fulfilment; the story of Jezebel's death is recounted with great relish as the eunuchs throw her out of the window and her funeral was somewhat abbreviated since the dogs had done their work (2 Kings 9:30-37). In addition, the mention of 'dogs' gives us a slight sneer about her end, as a secondary meaning of 'dogs' in Hebrew is 'sodomite'. It was poetic justice that the dogs ate her, since sexual deviance was a part of Canaanite practice.

What is more difficult to assess is what the ordinary people thought of this paganising process of the compromising kings. It could be that the eunuchs throwing Jezebel out of a window was just what they had wanted to do for some time but had not dared. It is possible that Jehu's drastic reforms were well accepted by the people as they eagerly wrecked the temple of Baal and used it for a public lavatory (2 Kings 10:27)! Another incident in which a nasty queen is dispatched gives some indication of the attitude of ordinary people. Athaliah, who was the queen mother to Ahaziah, was plotted against and killed:

'All the people of the land went to the house of Baal and tore it down; his altars and his images they broke in pieces and they slew Mattan the priest of Baal before the altars... so the people of the land rejoiced; and the city (Jerusalem) was quiet after Athaliah had been slain... ' (2 Kings 11:18-20).

This is an indication that the ordinary people much preferred the religion of Moses and David but could hardly go against the policy of the king. They may have thought it was a price worth paying if the foreign powers could be persuaded to leave them alone. But the excesses of people like Jezebel and Athaliah were liable to stir them up to rebellion.

The strand of prophecy and fulfilment occupies much space in the Kings; this is seen particularly with the Elijah and Elisha sagas. There is much emphasis placed on this aspect; God is seen as speaking directly to such people; they are seen as very close to God. Also it is no accident that Elijah is portrayed as re-enacting and developing the scenes from Moses at Sinai. We can compare Exodus 34:1-9, in which Moses has a Theophanous encounter with God, with 1 Kings 19:1-15, in which Elijah also has a Theophanous encounter with God at Mount Horeb (which is the same place). This is the famous incident of the 'still small voice', which he instinctively knows is God in reality[15]. This is the new 'Moses'. This shows us the wonder and presence of God in the life of the fully committed believer. This is contrasted with the dithering of Ahab and the ferocious non-belief of Jezebel. The Book of Kings is a very powerful account. There is also the contrast between the God of battles and loud noises, and the God of quietness and inner realisation.

Another aspect of the prophetic phenomenon is the pairing of Elijah and Elisha. Elijah is commissioned to anoint Elisha as his successor (1 Kings 19:16:20). Here we gain the famous phrase 'to cast one's mantle upon', in other words to empower another person to carry on one's task. A comparison of the two prophets yields some interesting factors. Elijah goes to Zarephath[16], a town in Zidon, to be fed by a widow and in spite of the famine they are miraculously fed. Also the son of the house dies and Elijah brings him back to life. A parallel incident comes with Elisha, where another widow is in penury and only has a jar of oil, but the prophet manages to fill up an undisclosed number of vessels. This continues with the Shunemmite woman whose husband is old which implies that he is not capable of begetting a child. Elisha foretells that she will have a son; that son dies but Elisha raises him from the dead. Incidentally they found Elisha on Mount Carmel, the site of the famous Elijah sacrifice. Moreover, Elisha does a miracle not unlike the feeding of the 5,000 in the gospels (2 Kings 4:42). The Deuteronomist is pleased to emphasise for us:

> 'Now I know that you are a man of God, and the word of the Lord in our mouth is truth' (talking of Elijah 1 Kings 17:24). Of Elisha there is something similar:

> '"Behold, now I perceive that this is a holy man of God..."' 2 Kings 4:9.

At Elijah's parting, he struck the river Jordan with his mantle and the water was parted to allow them to cross over dry-shod. This is another incident recalling Moses with the Red Sea. After Elijah has gone, Elisha tries the same thing and it works (2 Kings 2:8-14). In between these two miracles, we see Elijah going up to heaven in a whirlwind. His followers imagined that he might have come down somewhere else and set out to find him, but with no result. This is the basis of the Assumption of Elijah, a theological factor attached to Enoch and Moses, and most significantly to Jesus at the Ascension. The basic factor in this is the matter of intercession; humanity understands that there are holy people in the presence of God, asking for forgiveness. Elisha goes on to perform many miracles, some of which involve food, but not all; there is a whole list of them in 2 Kings 4,5, and 6, including the famous incident of curing Namaan the Syrian of his leprosy. His request to have a double portion of Elijah's spirit is certainly well attested.

From the political point of view, Jehu seems to receive two anointings, one from Elijah and one from one of Elijah's protégés. This seems rather strange but perhaps there is purpose in this event being recorded twice. The Deuteronomist wishes to emphasise it, that it was by prophetic appointment and encouragement that Jehu carried out the purge to remove the influence of Ahab for good. We are treated to a most dramatic account of the revolution in which all of Ahab's friends and relations, including Jezebel, are bloodthirstily removed.

We have a most dramatic account of Elisha's funeral; it was not an assumption as with Elijah. However, as they put him in the grave, another corpse was thrown in with him. But the other man[18] sprang back to life and stood up. This might be seen as a sort of anti-climax after Elijah's fiery chariot; maybe people were expecting Elisha to be assumed as well. In 2 Kings 2:23, we have a mob of cheeky boys jeering at him, teasing him to 'go up' and calling him 'baldhead', which was in contrast to Elijah who was very hairy. But the boys came to an unfortunate end, which serves to emphasise that it is foolish to insult someone of that spiritual power, a high-powered prophet of God. But at this stage we see a contrast with the life of Elijah; he was always at loggerheads with the reigning monarch, but by the end of his ministry Elisha was being treated with great respect by King Joash, who wanted some prophetic guidance over his contention with the Syrians (2 Kings 13:14). We wonder what the common people thought of the prophets; they were thought to be mad, and yet people were inclined to respect them and offer them hospitality.

The Temple and the covenant of David

Of possibly more significance to the Deuteronomist is the Temple in Jerusalem and the covenant with David. Much space and detail is given to how Solomon is the heir to David's kingdom and status with God. With Solomon, this is the nearest thing we come to Sacral Kingship[14] in the Hebrew tradition. David had been a man of blood; it was Solomon who was charged with the task of building the Temple. No less than six chapters are devoted to the intricacies of building the Temple and the King's House; we marvel at the expense and the detail and the effort in obtaining the finest materials and artwork. But in 2 Kings 9 the die is clearly cast; be faithful to God or it will all go wrong:

> 'The Lord said, "... I have consecrated this house... and put my name there for ever... if you walk before me as David your father walked... keeping my statutes and ordinances, then I will establish your royal throne over Israel for ever... there shall not fail you a man upon the throne of Israel. But if you turn aside... and do not keep my commandments... but go and serve other gods... I will cut off Israel from the land... and the house which I have consecrated for my name I will cast out of my sight... and this house will become a heap of ruins."'
> 2 Kings 9:3.

It was not a prophet that gave the warning; it was God himself. How ironic! By the end of the book, all this came to pass with the Babylonian conquest and the ruination of the Temple. All this is given in detail in 2 Kings 25:8. The irony increases as we see before the end of Solomon's reign the rot beginning to set in. It was one thing to be friendly with Hiram king of Tyre; but another to give hospitality to people like the Queen of Sheba; but a very different matter to love many foreign women, a list of whom appears in Chapter 11. His wives 'turned away his heart'; in his old age, maybe, he became sentimental about the ladies with exotic foreign religions. 1 Kings 11:9 records God's disapproval of this compromising. The result was that the kingdom would be torn away from him and given to his servant. God honours his covenant with David, in that it will not happen during

Solomon's reign, but it is to be a crisis for his son, Rehoboam; even so, one tribe (which turned out to be Judah) is to be left for the sake of David and Jerusalem. Actually, it turned out to be the tribe of Benjamin as well. This gives us a hint as to the honesty of the Deuteronomist, in that he did not tamper with the prophecy.

So the pattern of increasing compromise and destruction of Solomon's fantastic kingdom inexorably progresses. Rehoboam, who took the wrong advice, precipitated the breakaway of the northern kingdom under Jeroboam. Again, the tearing of the kingdom is under the advice of the prophet Ahijah; so Jeroboam was paradoxically encouraged by God to do the wrong thing. The sin of Jeroboam, which reverberates right though the book, was twofold; firstly he made two golden calves, one for Bethel and one for Dan:

> 'Behold your gods, O Israel, who brought you up out of the land of Egypt' 1 Kings 12:28.

Secondly he established an alternative cultus at Bethel, as a rival system to the Temple in Jerusalem. This goes down as totally shocking in the Book of Kings. In a way, this was ironic; in the laws of Deuteronomy it never actually says specifically that Jerusalem has to be the place where God will set his name, but the Deuteronomist takes it as such. Also, he takes it to mean that there can only be one place for the Temple, as opposed to having various temples in different parts of the country, as had been the case before Solomon's building enterprises. This is a case of literalism plus a certain fanatical attachment to a particular place of worship. This attachment to the Temple in Jerusalem conditions all of the Israelite history down to the time of Jesus, and on into modern times, as Jerusalem is the focal point for three major monotheistic religions. As far as the Deuteronomist is concerned, the northern kingdom (Israel) could never do right, even if people like Jehu came along to clear out paganism:

> 'But Jehu did not turn aside from the sins of Jeroboam... the golden calves. And the Lord said to Jehu, "because you have done well in carrying out what is right in my eyes, your sons of the fourth generation shall sit on the throne of Israel." But Jehu was not careful to walk in the law of God... he did not turn aside from the sins of Jeroboam, which made Israel to sin' 2 Kings 10:28-31.

The whole history of the monarchy is peppered with judgements on each reign. Even the kings of Judah who still had the Temple, are criticised for the paganisation of the faith. Strangely, Elijah and Elisha are not criticised for doing a sacrifice at another place apart from the Temple, which would contradict Deuteronomy 12:14. But then he is in such awe of such people that sacrificing in the wrong place could probably be excused. The kings that really stand out as shining examples are Hezekiah and Josiah. According to 2 Kings 18:5, Hezekiah trusted in the Lord so that there was none like him, before or after, with the result that whatever he embarked on, went right, including the defeat of the Assyrian siege. Sadly, all the reforms of Hezekiah were swept away by his successor, Manasseh. According to the Deuteronomist, the sin of Manasseh was the last straw with God's patience, for the disgusting practices of the pagans were outmatched by Manasseh's activities. Just exactly what was the problem with Manasseh is not explained here in detail, but burning one's son as a sacrifice was seen as exceptionally horrific. Even the reforms of Josiah were not enough to stave off the inevitable; even so, Huldah the prophetess talked of amelioration in that Josiah would not live to see the collapse of the Judean kingdom. That would be a treat in store for his son, Jehoiakim. The sin of Manasseh was beyond all reason; somehow it ranked as dreadful as the sin of Jeroboam. Thus we understand the collapse of both Hebrew kingdoms.

The covenant of Sinai

The Deuteronomist is thoroughly committed to the Mosaic settlement, and often refers to the Sinai situation. Linking Elijah with Moses is just one aspect of it. But the main thrust is spelt out quite clearly when the northern kingdom went into Exile:

'Because they did not obey the voice of the Lord... but transgressed his covenant, even all that Moses the servant of the Lord commanded; they neither listened nor obeyed' 2 Kings 18:12.

As a kind of stiffener to this theology, it is worth noting that curious incident in 2 Kings 17:21-28. It would seem that the Assyrians transplanted foreigners from Babylon, Hamath and many other areas to take the place of the exiles. But lions appeared and killed some of them. This was taken to mean that the newcomers did not know the laws of the God of that land, so one of the priests that had gone into exile, had to come back and teach them the laws of God. This incidentally is a slight admission that the northern kingdom had not been as unfaithful to God as the Deuteronomist had depicted; the little details give a slightly different picture.

In addition to the covenant of Sinai, we also note other minor covenants surfacing. In the reign of Athaliah, Jehoiada the priest made a covenant with the guards to keep watch over the young prince Joash, to prevent him being assassinated. In 2 Kings 23:3, Josiah makes a covenant with all the people, leaders and commoners alike, to keep the laws of God. The arrangement was not a new idea; it was simply an extension, or renewal of the Sinai covenant. But the motif, or metaphor of covenant is very important in the Deuteronomist's theology.

The covenant also involved laws that would prevent the Israelites from compromising with the Canaanite religious practice. Deuteronomy goes into detail on the subject and this is reflected in many places in the Kings. The first two commandments are regularly ignored, with idolatry running rife and interest shown in foreign gods, especially Baal. Also some of the more disgusting aspects of Baalism, which are banned in Deuteronomy, are removed. Compare with Deuteronomy 23:17:

'And King Asa... put away the male cult prostitutes (dogs) out of the land, and removed all the idols that his father had made' 1 Kings 15:12.

As far as murder is concerned, there were some kings who seemed to want a massacre. Jehoiakim seems to be one of those, 'for he filled Jerusalem with innocent blood and the Lord would not pardon' 2 Kings 24:4. One might ask how Elijah and Jehu could justify killing the prophets of Baal and all of Ahab's friends and relations; but this was not innocent blood. According to Deuteronomy 17:1-7, anyone embarking on idolatry or worshipping other gods is to be put to death. It emerges as even more shocking and ironic that Naboth, who was innocent, was stoned to death for the sake of Ahab obtaining the vineyard. Manasseh, who was the most atrocious, went in for mediums and wizards, in direct contravention of Deuteronomy 18:10-12. We can trace many more such cases by comparing Deuteronomy with the Kings.

With the theology of the Deuteronomist, we see the clash between the purist religion of the nascent Hebrew nations and the indigenous religions of the native inhabitants. In theory it would seem a simple matter just to introduce a new religious regime, but life is not quite as simple as that. It is not so easy to rid oneself of one's parent religion in favour of something entirely new. This was seen at the Reformation in Western Christianity. The Protestants did not entirely free themselves from the backdrop of Catholicism. In addition to that the Israelites were constantly under pressure from foreign powers to take on board foreign practices as a concomitant of various alliances. In addition to that there was the often unspoken assumption of 'territory'; gods were assumed to occupy territory, and if one moved to another country, one would have to take into account the god of that land. It was the ancient version of 'when in Rome, do as the Romans do.' It would not have been easy to think oneself out of this pattern of thought.

But the net result of this decline and collapse of the two kingdoms was, on the return from the Exile, that the Jews went to another extreme, that of being totally strict and inflexible, to the extent of excluding anyone who was not properly Jewish, and enforcing in a literal and overpowering manner every word of the laws of Moses. This was a situation inherited by the Maccabees and also by Jesus himself, who tried to show them that the gentiles could be accepted, and that ferocious legalism was not the answer.

Mythology

It is difficult to separate the mythological aspects from the historical in the Kings. The account flows naturally from historical recording straight into the mysterious sagas of the two main prophets, Elijah and Elisha. The miraculous element is strongly emphasised and rationalising them away, which has been tried, is not altogether convincing. There are, however, a number of aspects that accord well with features of mythology as seen in many religious systems, the world over. We have the assumption of heaven, as Elijah goes up in a fiery chariot and a whirlwind; strangely there is no mention of *Sheol* or the underworld; one would have expected people like Ahab, Jezebel and Manasseh to have been sent in that direction.

Two cleansing agents universally mentioned are fire and water. These two appear at the sacrifice on Mount Carmel, where the god who answers by fire is the true God. In the cave, Elijah experiences a fire, after an earthquake. Chariots of fire are seen round Elisha (2 Kings 6:17) and indeed, the rallying cry at Elijah's assumption was a chariot of fire and horses of fire which separated him from Elisha (2 Kings 2:11). Elijah is noted as the one who can bring down fire from heaven (2 Kings1:10-14). One wonders if this is to be taken completely literally, or is it symbolic of cleansing the nation?

Death and resurrection is another important motif in mythology. With Elijah this is evidenced when he stays with the widow of Zaraphath; her son is raised to life with what might appear to be artificial resuscitation. A similar situation is found with Elisha with the Shunammite woman and her son. Also there is the incident at Elisha's burial, where a dead man springs back to life.

Related to this is the practice of sacrificing one's firstborn son if there is a dire situation. A good example of this is the incident when three kings, from Judah, Israel and Edom banded together to attack Moab. Mesha, the king of Moab, could see that a desperate situation faced him, so he sacrificed his firstborn son on the city wall, in full view of his enemies. To us that would seem insane, but to them it was the last resort when things were going wrong:

'And great wrath came upon Israel, and they withdrew from him and returned to their own country...' 2 Kings 3:27.

In modern terms we could render this as 'great consternation' or possibly 'deep revulsion', but it had the effect of demoralising the attacking army. Now we see the motive for child sacrifice that is so often mentioned in the Kings. There was a sacrificial place called the Topheth outside Jerusalem where children were burnt as an offering to a god called Molech. We do not know exactly what happened at this sanctuary; it may have been so disgusting that the Old Testament writers did not wish to go into details. The root MLK means 'king', and with the vowel transplant of O and E, derived from BOSHETH, meaning 'shame', it must have been some sort of regal offering in support of the king. This is an example of how a cultural, peri-mythological factor can have such a hold on people with a superstitious inclination. It is in practice very difficult to throw off an assumption like this, even if the prophets of God are denouncing it as atrocious.

There is also the miraculous element mostly associated with Elijah and Elisha but also with Isaiah, as Hezekiah is healed and Jerusalem is relieved from the siege. How far we would regard this as mythological is debatable; Kings is remarkably restrained on the subject of angels, evil spirits and other mythological factors. Many people would take the miraculous material at face value; some would say there is a strong element of exaggeration; other would say it is symbolic; others would say it is prophetic in that it points us forward to the ministry of Jesus. Whichever way one sees it, there is depth and an extra spiritual dimension given to the account of the two monarchies. History is not just a matter of recounting plain facts (if there are any); history is also about meaning and purpose. The miraculous element does just that; it points us to the fact that in spite of the degradation and compromising with paganism of the two kingdoms, God was nevertheless at work bringing healing and new life, and hope, through his spokesmen.

Philosophical considerations

The Book of Kings is not noted for its philosophical reasonings. If asked, the Deuteronomist would almost certainly have said that if you keep faith with God, he will keep faith with you. Also, that the opposite will happen. In other words, you get what you ask for. This is an assumption at the root of the covenant of Sinai, and is spelt out quite firmly in Deuteronomy 28. It is also an assumption that virtually every human soul has at the back of his mind: if you behave yourself, you will prosper and if you misbehave yourself, you will be punished. It is the Old Testament configuration as a basic cultural backdrop for everyone. However, we all know that life is often not quite as simple as that as the Book of Job points out – why do the innocent have to suffer? This question emerges slightly with the notion that the king, having done wrong, will not see the punishment in his lifetime, but his successor will have to face the music. We see this with Solomon and Josiah. God can hold fire a little but not completely, it would seem. It is the age-old question of theodicy[19], which no philosopher to this day has managed to answer convincingly.

As far as free will and predestination are concerned, the Deuteronomist never says anything of relevance to this issue. It could be said that since prophecy is the dominating factor in this history, then determinism is unavoidable. Indeed there is a certain inevitability in the course of the decline of the two kingdoms. Then again, there is the issue of free will. Some kings tried to halt the decline, and clearly had a certain degree of freedom to reverse the trend. How much political freedom they had is not clear, but they were living in an age where alliances were important to small kingdoms, when up against major powers like Egypt and Babylon. They were hardly free to do as they pleased in their own countries. An analogous situation nowadays would be that the major powers are preaching democracy and any small country that has to function on some other system of thought, is ostracised. Totalitarianism is right out of favour; even so, there are some countries that can only function on that kind of basis. As we saw in Deuteronomy (Chapter 13), there is a paradox over free will and predestination, never stated explicitly but there all the same. It would be fair to say that the same is true with the Kings.

In general terms, the Deuteronomist would be very much in favour of the idea that God is not just God, but the hand that guides history. His head office is in Jerusalem, which means that he is not just a remote idea up in the sky, but an active personal force at ground level. In addition to that he is very close to the single-minded fully committed believer, who fears him and yet loves him. God is very real and personal. This is in contrast to the many eastern religions where God, if he exists, is distant, unapproachable and irrelevant to the nitty-gritty of daily life.

Literary and linguistic considerations

The Book of Kings is a remarkable document stemming from the Iron Age in the Ancient Middle East. There are not many cultures that have produced such an account of that quality. We think of the Iliad and the Odyssey by Homer, and the Ramayana (Chapter 22); much of this has been regarded as mythical and not reliable as history. Recent thinking has been to take this literature more seriously, especially as ancient Troy has been discovered and excavated. The same is true for many aspects of the Kings; archaeology has shed much light on many aspects of this work. Much of it may be taken at face value, bearing in mind the slant of the Deuteronomist, which may be unduly pessimistic and severe.

One linguistic factor, which casts a slightly different light on matters, is the names of the kings. Many of their names are made up of some kind of compound using the name of God, YHWH. So Jotham, Jehoash, Jehoahaz all begin with JE, a particle of YHWH. Ahaziah, Zechariah, Zedekiah and many others end with IAH, which is another particle of YHWH. It would seem strange that paganising kings would retain 'Yahwistic' names. Perhaps they were more inclined to the true God than the Deuteronomist would like to admit. In general terms, the archaeologists have noted that Israelite cities are seriously lacking in figurines, statues and portrait art; this is in contrast to the other cities in the Ancient Near East. All the foreign kings form their names on their own gods, so it was the normal thing in those days to have one's regnal name formed according to one's protecting god. The exception to this could be seen in the names Omri and Ahab.

The Book of Kings is nearly all in prose; moreover, it is a prose that is not difficult to translate. The Deuteronomist wants his message and intentions to be quite clear. Difficult words or *hapax legomena* seldom occur. This is in contrast to some Old Testament books. There is a section of poetry where Isaiah gives an oracle; this is the same as in the Book of Isaiah. This comes in 2 Kings 19:21-28. It has some interesting parallelisms and it also has a superb irony:

'I will put my hook in your nose and my bit in your mouth and I will turn you back on the way by which you came' 2 Kings 19:28.

The point is that the Assyrians, being sadistic, used to take people into exile by putting fishhooks into people's noses to drag them along; now it will be the other way round.

In general terms, the Kings is a well-balanced piece of literature, with historical material mainly at the start and the finish and the prophetic sagas with their miraculous and semi-mythical material sandwiched in the middle, thus forming a rudimentary chiasmus[20].

With regard to figurative language, there is not much. One good example is in 2 Kings 21:12:

'Behold, I am bringing upon Jerusalem and Judah such evil that the ears of everyone who hears it will tingle. And I will stretch over Jerusalem the measuring line of Samaria and the plummet of the house of Ahab, and I will wipe Jerusalem as one wipes a dish, wiping it and turning it upside down...'

This is probably the origin of the metaphor 'to be wiped out', meaning totally destroyed.

The Chronicles: an alternative version

The Book of Kings has a parallel version also in two books; the Chronicles have a much larger scope and appear to continue into the Book of Ezra. One wonders if Ezra is not the author. For convenience we call him the Chronicler. He begins with Adam and works through to the end of the Exile when Cyrus the Persian Emperor announces a reversal of policy, in that everyone could have his own religion and return from exile. The second Book of Chronicles begins with the reign of Solomon, which is the approximate start of the first Book of Kings. The fact that there are two versions of this piece of history is useful; it shows how a writer can slant things to carry over his message. The message of the Chronicler is not totally different from that of the Deuteronomist, but different enough to shed a certain amount of light on certain incidents. The general impression gained is that the book was written by a priest or someone supportive of the priesthood, rather than a prophet. This does not mean to say that the kings and the prophets are omitted from the account, but they appear in rather a different light. The Chronicler admits to using various sources of information not mentioned in the Kings. Whether he knew the Book of the Kings is debatable, but he almost certainly used much of the source material used in the Kings. Many of the passages are word for word the same but this does not mean he has to have copied from the Deuteronomist; they had sources in common.

At the start of the account, we see none of the jockeying over the succession after David's reign. Solomon has a clean start and does not need to eliminate any alternative claimants or their supporters. This could be interpreted as making Solomon seem much more brilliant and the more obvious choice for kingship. God appears in a dream to Solomon twice; on the third occasion it is a reprimand for going after false gods; this incident does not appear in the Chronicles. In fact, there is no mention of him getting involved with paganism. Quite the contrary, he forbids the Egyptian princess to live in the city of David.

'My wife shall not live in the house of David king of Israel, for the places to which the ark of the Lord has come are holy' 2 Chronicles 8:11.

In fact he magnifies Solomon to a fantastic degree:

'Thus king Solomon excelled all the kings of the earth in riches and wisdom. All the kings of the earth sought the presence of Solomon to hear his wisdom' 2 Chronicles 9:22.

One wonders if this is not somewhat exaggerated; would Pharaoh, who thought he was a god, come to pay his respects to an Israelite king? Unlikely! Even so, the Queen of Sheba came to admire him.

With regard to the successors of Solomon, the Chronicler does not indulge in the snap judgement on each reign. He admits that Rehoboam was not faithful to God; most of the Judean kings are complimented on their adherence to the true religion. It is only when we get to Manasseh, Amon, and Jehoiakim that criticism begins to emerge.

He has a high opinion of kings like Jehoshaphat, Hezekiah, Josiah and others. Hezekiah is reported as having the Passover celebrated as a big event, something that seems to have lapsed over the years. He tried to summon everyone from the erstwhile northern kingdom and some of them came to Jerusalem. In fact it was such a success that the festival went on for an additional seven days. All this does not appear in the Kings. Moreover, the siege of Jerusalem is very much understated, with Isaiah just mentioned in passing and the angel of death briefly included. There is no mention of Hezekiah paying tribute to Sennacherib; quite the opposite:

'Hezekiah was exalted in the sight of the nations from that time on... '
2 Chronicles 32:23.

The way that king Uzziah is treated is also indicative. There is the account of him trying to offer the incense in the Temple, and when it was pointed out to him that only priests could do that, he was angry and objected. It was then that leprosy broke out on his head and he had to be quarantined for the rest of his life. This account does not appear in the Kings. In this we see that the priests had a special interest in retaining their privileges and were quite capable of overruling the king (2 Chronicles 26:1).

One wonders where the truth lies. Perhaps the Chronicler's brief account of the Siloam water system gives it away. He does not really understand that a tunnel was built with great skill (2 Chronicles 32:30) and this might mean partly that the book was written a long time after the time of Isaiah and partly that the writer had not actually visited Jerusalem. All this may indicate that his accuracy is not quite up to the standard of the Deuteronomist.

With regard to the northern kingdom, the Chronicler relates the schism under Jeroboam but after that, apart from a few cursory remarks about people like Baasha and Ahab, the northern kingdom might just as well not have existed. In fact the demise of the northern monarchy and the fall of Samaria are not mentioned. Instead we have a heavy focus on the kings of Judah and various attempts at drawing the northern territories in with the southern kingdom. Again this may indicate that the Chronicler was writing a long time after the Exile of the northern kingdom and had no clear idea of what had happened; also it may indicate that he did not know the Book of Kings.

Just as the northern kingdom is largely ignored, so too are the important prophetic activities, which do not play any part in the drama. The prophets do appear in places but do not seem to be so influential. Elijah and Elisha never appear at all; one wonders why not! Was the Chronicler worried about the miraculous and mythological material in the accounts? Did he think that the sacrifice on Mount Carmel was in the wrong location? Did he think Elijah should not have posed as a priest? It seems unlikely that he had no knowledge of these events, since Elijah was to become a major figure in the Jewish faith, on a par with Moses. It is also true that Isaiah is seriously understated in the Chronicles, and yet at the end in the closing verses, Jeremiah is quoted no less than three times, with heavy emphasis on the fact that the warnings given by the prophets had been ignored and scoffed at:

'He did not humble himself before Jeremiah the prophet who spoke from the mouth of the Lord' 2 Chronicles 36:12.

'... they kept mocking the messengers of God... and scoffing at his prophets... ' 2 Chronicles 36:16.

'... to fulfil the word of the Lord by the mouth of Jeremiah until the land had enjoyed its Sabbaths. All the days that it lay desolate it kept Sabbath, to fulfil seventy years' 2 Chronicles 36:21.

We can compare this with Jeremiah on the subject of the Sabbath, in Jeremiah 17:21. This is the explanation for the collapse of the kingdom of Judah, that the people had been ignoring Sabbath observance. This is a strand of thought that is hardly seen in the early parts of the Chronicles and not at all in the Kings. It appears in Jeremiah and also in the last few chapters of Isaiah.

Jeremiah throws extra light on the situation

Both the Kings and the Chronicles are seen in a modified light by assessing what Jeremiah offers. There is much historical material in Jeremiah, which does not receive a mention in either of the history books; some of it is virtually the same, and may have been copied by the Deuteronomist and the Chronicler. But the additional material concerns events during the reigns of Josiah, Manasseh, Jehoiakim, Zedekiah and Gedaliah, and gives far more detail about the catastrophic events leading up to the collapse of the Judean kingdom. It shows how much both the Kings and the Chronicles are condensed accounts, with much information omitted. This was probably

341

because of shortage of space. One vivid incident is when Jeremiah writes a scroll and it is presented to King Jehoiakim, who is sitting by a brazier. He does not like what he hears, takes a penknife and cuts off and burns the scroll piece by piece and then orders Jeremiah's arrest (Jeremiah 36:1-32). We can understand the king's dismay; he must have thought that Jeremiah was a traitor. We also see vivid accounts of how the false prophets tried to silence Jeremiah with his warnings; he was treated like an idiot and kept under arrest probably on the premise that he was sowing defeatism. There is an account of him writing to the exiles in Babylon, telling them to settle down and make the best of it; forget about returning to Jerusalem (Jeremiah 29). Gedaliah, the last ruler of Judah, receives only a brief mention in the Kings, but Jeremiah gives a much fuller account of the chaos in those last days before the Babylonians finally wrecked the Temple and the country. Also we have an account of how Jeremiah was pressganged into going to Egypt and continued to prophesy from there. This does not receive a mention in the histories.

All the writers are convinced that it was the sin of Manasseh that precipitated the exile of Judah. They record with horror the child sacrificing that went on in the Hinnom Valley at a place called the Topheth. Nobody cares to elaborate on what horrors occurred there. There were other kings who committed child sacrifice; their excuse would almost certainly have been 'it will persuade God to stave off our enemies'. But what or why was the sin of Manasseh worse than any others? No one wishes to explain it; perhaps they were so revolted that they did not wish to soil the pages of their books with anything too specific. It is possible, however, to figure out what was really going on, using two references from elsewhere: Psalm 106:37-39 and Ezekiel 16:20-21. The sacrifice of children is described using the word ZBH, zebhah. Normally, a sacrifice is termed HOLAH, which means a 'whole burnt offering'. From this we gain the word Holocaust; the entire victim was burnt up. But Zebhah is another kind of sacrifice in which the victim, normally an animal, is partly burnt or cooked and then eaten. To apply this word to the sacrifice of children would imply some sort of cannibalistic ritual. But this could explain the sin of Manasseh; he went over the top and had ritualistic cannibalism at the Topheth, an outrage that must have horrified practically everyone. On the assumption that this would push back his enemies, he was in effect inviting God to dispense with the kingdom of Judah.

We do not really know what the significance of the root MLK had; it means 'king'. The root TPHTH with the vowels of BOSHETH transplanted gives us the word TOPHETH. The root TPHTH is thought to mean a hearth, fireplace, or even an incinerator. From other sources (Canaanite) we find that other peoples committed child sacrifice by using a pit in the ground, filled with fire, and the victim was thrown into the flames, possibly dead, but also possibly alive, and the ritual would be accompanied with loud music and dancing. Whatever did actually happen in the Hinnom Valley, the place became a place of horror and revulsion right down to New Testament times. Incidentally, this idea of the Topheth may shed some light on the account of the three holy children being thrown into the fiery furnace; they, however, survived the experience (Daniel 3)[21].

Having said this, it becomes clear that many of the punishments prophesied by Jeremiah can be seen as ironic in relation to the excesses of Manesseh. The main passages are Jeremiah 19:1-13, 15:1-4 and 7:30-8:3. In each passage he is talking specifically about the Topheth. There will be so much death that no one will be left to bury them and the animals will eat them. There will be no more song and dance. In the siege, people will be forced to eat their own children. Dead men's bones will be dragged out and scattered about; this was a way of polluting or defiling a place of worship. The irony is clear: the people will receive what they asked for.

'… because of the sin of Manasseh… for what he did in Jerusalem' Jeremiah 15:4.

With this we see that various remarks in Jeremiah now have an extra sting:

'I brought them out of the land of Egypt, from the iron *furnace*' Jeremiah 11:4.

'I see a *boiling pot* facing away from the north… ' Jeremiah 1:13.

'They shall eat up your harvest and your food… they shall eat up your *sons and daughters*… flocks and herds, vines and fig trees… ' (the nation from afar) Jeremiah 5:17ff.

'Why are he and his children hurled and cast into a land which they do not know?… . write this man down as childless… for none of his offspring shall succeed… ' Jeremiah 22:28, talking of Jehoiakin having been sent off into exile.

'"The Lord make you like Zedekiah and Ahab whom the king of Babylon roasted in the fire…"' Jeremiah 29:22.

From this we can sense the consternation, horror and revulsion caused by the antics of Manasseh and his underlings, something that we sense from the Kings and Chronicles but is not really explained or elaborated upon.

Put together, the two histories plus Jeremiah give us a fascinating insight into life in the early Iron Age in Palestine. Obviously the bloodthirsty bits receive more attention; but then the same is true today with the media. It was a time when traditional superstitions were constantly rearing their ugly heads, while people who had a higher ethic from God were trying hard to overcome it. But the raw materials for a peaceful, ethical, democratic society were there in embryo; the sad thing is that it is taking so long to achieve. The Ten Commandments rear over us as a vital touchstone; persuading people to observe them is horse work but we all know it should be done.

Josephus on the Kings and the Chronicles

It is interesting to compare the version given to us by Josephus in his Book 8 of the Antiquities of the Jews. This was written in Greek a long time after the real events; nearly six hundred years elapsed before this connected and conflated account was offered. It was aimed first and foremost at the well-informed Roman reader of the Eastern Empire, and Josephus' slant is to explain the history of the Jews in such a way as to make them seem sensible, cultured and responsible, unlike the hooligans that started the revolt of 66 to 70 AD. One must ask how Josephus could write such a history so long after the events; he had much source material, particularly the Kings and the Chronicles, but other minor sources in addition. Some of them he actually mentions; Menander, Berosus, the Tyrian records and Herodotus. It is interesting that the famine at the time of Elijah is also mentioned in the works of Menander. In addition, Josephus does like to insert explanatory notes at times, for the benefit of his pagan Roman readership. But as a historian he is clearly doing his best to portray the truth, as he states quite clearly in Antiquities 8:8, page 243 of the Loeb Edition:

'These things I have given in detail because I wish my readers to know that we have said nothing more than what is true; and have not, by inserting into the history various plausible and seductive passages meant to deceive and entertain, attempted to evade critical enquiry, asking to be instantly believed... we ask that no hearing be given us unless we are able to establish the truth with demonstrations and convincing evidence.'

This sounds like a remarkably modern approach to historiography; Josephus is trying to give a well-balanced accurate account. Modern scholars might not agree with this claim, but it does seem as though Josephus did have extra sources of information, not necessarily written, with which he has supplemented his basic written sources. In the early parts of Book 8 he is heavily dependent on Kings, but as it progresses, the

344

Chronicles gradually assume more importance. What are the differences in slant in his account?

It would be fair to say that he does not disagree with the scriptural version of the history; what happens is that certain aspects receive more emphasis and others less emphasis. This tells us of how his mind worked and also what his readership was expected to accept as reliable.

Clearly, Josephus wishes to augment the glory days of Solomon. His Wisdom is stressed; how he produced 1,005 books of odes and songs, and 3,000 books of parables and similitudes. Even if we agree to the claims about Proverbs, Ecclesiastes and the Song of Solomon, this is a staggering amount of literary work, true? Is it possible that there is an element of exaggeration in this? Or are these figures in some way symbolic, as we see in Revelation? He is also credited with the gift of exorcism; a method using a herb which is still used 'to this day', i.e. 60 AD! Solomon's speech is amplified, the gifts he gave are exaggerated, and the gold and silver vessels for the Temple are a massive amount that would have filled the Temple and the Hinnom Valley below! He provided paved roads leading to Jerusalem. He is credited with the founding of Palmyra, something that could be true if indeed his empire extended as far as Riblah in Syria. All the same, Josephus is prepared to admit that Solomon in his dotage allowed himself to be taken in by the foreign cults of his wives, but this is understated.

When it comes to Rehoboam, Josephus plays down the enmity between the two kingdoms and plays up the treachery of Jeroboam and the nonsense of him making himself a high priest. This indicates Josephus' interest in priestly matters, since he himself was a Sadducee (theTemple party). When Uzziah tries to pose as a priest in the Temple, Josephus has an earthquake occur, but there is no mention of the king offering incense. He tones down the mention of idols and false shrines, and plays up how the northern kings were intent on destroying each other. This of course, was fair comment; their dynasty was inveterately unstable.

With regard to the prophets, the ministry of Elijah is included but somewhat toned down; the assumption of Elijah is omitted and the encounter with God in the cave is to some extent demythologised. The same would be true of Elijah's encounter with Ahaziah; the angel is left out and the passage somewhat ameliorated. In the encounter between Elisha and the Syrian army, there is a mist that allows the prophet to escape; they are not struck blind. Also there are no cheeky boys insulting him at his funeral. When the Assyrian army is defeated by plague in the siege of Jerusalem, this too is slightly demythologised; Sennacherib knew of this impending disaster in advance. This has the effect of somewhat reducing the impact of Isaiah's prophecy. Also, as Sennacherib is murdered by his two sons in his temple, Josephus reports that it did not allow them to take the throne; it was someone else, Esarhaddon, who became king, and the princes had to run off to escape retribution. This again would have the effect of slightly reducing the impact of Isaiah's prophecy. On the other hand, Josephus likes to work in some of the other lesser prophets, such as Jonah, Nahum, and Obadiah, who manages to hide 100 prophets in a cave to save them from Jezebel. Jonah is claimed to have been spat out of the whale on the shores of the Black Sea; how handy that would have been for reaching Nineveh! Josephus clearly takes this account as the literal truth, as opposed to symbolic.

It is interesting how Ahab is portrayed. Something that is latent in the Kings version, is Ahab as a weak and vacillating person, easily manipulated by his wife, Jezebel. He is easily taken in by false prophets, and he admits to shame over the incident of Naboth's vineyard. Ahab's guilt is played up. On the other hand, Ahab's ability to make alliances with neighbouring kings is shown, plus his leniency with his enemies. In general, Ahab is shown in a more agreeable light, in contrast to Jezebel.

One interesting detail concerns the death of Josiah, the great reformer. Josephus does not have Pharaoh Neco murder Josiah at Megiddo. He has an Egyptian officer take a shot at him and he is taken off to Jerusalem, mortally wounded. Jeremiah and Ezekiel are claimed to have composed laments over this tragedy. We notice that Ezekiel is not mentioned in the scriptural versions, neither is he noted as a poet. Jeremiah, however, is a major influence in the scriptures and Josephus shows him in a very sympathetic light.

The invading kings are shown as treacherous; this goes a long way to explaining why the Judean kings did not wish to enter into agreements with them. Sennacherib promises to go away, but breaks his word. Nebuchadrezzar to is shown as incapable of keeping a promise, and when he accuses Zedekiah of treachery, this comes out as a lovely piece of hypocrisy. Years later, when Nebuchadrezzar is succeeded by Evil Merodach (Amel Marduk), the new king feels guilty about his father's conduct, and releases Jehoiakin from prison and treats him well.

In general terms, Josephus does a little bit of rationalisation and demythologisation in places where the miraculous is claimed. He is all in favour of the prophets, and the kings are in general shown in a more favourable light. The same would apply to the priests, and he gives an entire expanded list of them right through the period in question. It is interesting that the cause of the Exile is not specifically accredited to the 'sin of Manasseh', which dominates the scriptures. Perhaps Josephus does not know why Manasseh was seen as worse than all the others. But it is worth mentioning two of those little sermonettes which tell us of Josephus' theological outlook. The first one, in Book 10, page 235, is his comment on the genuineness of Jeremiah and Ezekiel:

'... sufficiently clear to those who do not know, how varied and manifold is the nature of God and how these things which he foretells must come to pass, duly taking place at the appointed hour and should also make clear the ignorance and disbelief of these men... were taken off their guard, and so that any attempt to escape from it was impossible for them.'

In other words, you cannot thwart the purposes of God, and just ignoring his prophets is not going to alter the inevitable. Predestination is a fact! The Exile could not have been avoided.

The other sermon comes in Book 10, page 276:

'... how mistaken are the Epicureans who exclude Providence from human life and refuse to believe that God governs its affairs or that the universe is directed by a blessed and immortal Being to the end that the whole of it may endure, but say that the world runs by its own movement without knowing a guide or another's care...'

This again is related to Josephus' understanding of prophecy; that the world runs according to a plan, and anyone who cannot see it is foolish. The atheists and humanists of today could well take note of this passage. Josephus is generous in that he says 'if anyone wishes to judge otherwise, I shall not object to his holding a different opinion.' Doesn't this sound modern? But the same issues of belief and disbelief were current in the Ancient World as they are now. Josephus is saying that the fulfilment of prophecy is the clincher; one can see God's purposes being worked out by just taking notice of his prophets. This is an argument that the Romans would have appreciated, since they were obsessed with that kind of thinking. Sadly, it does not meet with the same response from people in today's world.

Footnotes for Chapter 18: 1 and 2 Kings

The following are taken from *Ancient Near Eastern Texts* by Michael Coogan, 2013.

1. Black Obelisk, no. 28.
2. Adad Nirari, no. 30.
3. Tiglath Pileser, no. 31.
4. Ditto.
5. Sargon 2nd, no. 32.
6. Sennacherib, no. 34.
7. Esar Haddon, no. 36.
8. Nebuchadrezzar, no. 37.
9. Amel Marduk, no. 38.
10. The battle of Qarqar, no. 25.

11. Moabite Stone, no. 27.
12. Tel Dan Stela, no. 28.
13. Marneptah, no. 24.
14. Sacral Kingship: the normal system in the Ancient Near East, where the king was equated with the national god.
15. 1 Kings 19:12.
16. 1 Kings 17:9-10
17. 2 Kings 4:12
18. 2 Kings 13:21.
19. Theodicy: the problem of evil. For a full discussion of this issue, refer to my previous book, *The Theology of Paradox*.
20. Chiasmus: a literary technique common in Hebrew literature; it takes the form of ABCBA for instance.
21. Daniel 3:16-25.

19

The Gospel of Truth

This is an early Gnostic work, only recently discovered in the Nag Hammadi desert of Egypt in 1945. It is one of many such works, lost for many centuries, and only known from the quotations and references in the early Church Fathers. It may be that there are many more waiting to be found by the archaeologists. The text, which was originally in Greek, is the English translation by Alan Jacobs, published in the book, *The Gnostic Gospels*, 2006. I have chosen this 'Gospel' from others, such as the gospel of Judas and the gospel of Mary Magdalene, because it actually claims, quite forcefully, that it is the **truth**. Actually, to call it a gospel is a misnomer, since it does not contain any record of the passion and crucifixion, let alone any of the teachings and miracles of Jesus. It can be fairly said to be a Christian work, and perhaps not as fanciful as some of the Gnostic speculators. Unfortunately, no author has been cited for this work; many of these so-called gospels try to claim inspiration from one or other of the original disciples, such as the Gospel of Thomas, but his one appears not to make such claims. What was the problem with Gnosticism? In general terms, it had difficulties with the Incarnation of Jesus Christ, making him out to be divine, but not fully human. This explains the reluctance to make any mention of the passion and death of Jesus. Also, the problem was that they indulged in all kinds of elaborate speculations on the creation, and the production, not of 'gods' but 'principles'. This was a convenient way to approach the question of theodicy, but the early Church saw this as some sort of sanitised paganism. The Gnostic speculators may have had the best of intentions in trying to bring some sort of amalgamation of basic original Jewish disciples' thinking and the fanciful mythology of the Greek world. It was all very interesting but total speculation and the church rejected it. Even so, to this day, outbreaks of Gnostic ideas keep appearing under different labels. Gnosticism was nothing new in the early centuries AD. Buddhism, which had been maturing for some time, must have had a massive influence on these Egyptian speculators. By and large, the vocabulary used is different, but the basic ideas are the same, even to the mention of reincarnation. As a Gnostic work, the Gospel of Truth seems not to be as extreme as some of the others; it is definitely a Christian work, and probably only narrowly escaped being burnt as many were in the early years of the Church. There are many parts of it that could fairly be said are spiritually helpful and might have become general reading in the Roman Empire. What a shame it tarnished itself with rather too much phraseology from the Gnostic speculators!

Mathematical information

There is nothing mathematical about this work at all: no dates, calculations of money or sizes of armies. The exception would be that God is thought to have a number, one hundred, applied to him (page209). This is not properly explained, except to say that when talking about the ninety-nine sheep that were left while the shepherd went to fetch the one that had strayed, that fetched it up to one hundred[1]. Also Abraham and Sarah were claimed to be ninety-nine years old when God promised the birth of Isaac; this meant that they would be 100 when he was born[2]. This is a piece of unsupported speculation.

'One hundred signifies soundness; it is our Father's number.'

Interestingly, the same idea occurs in the Bhagavad Gita (Chapter 9), with the mention of 100 yugas as applied to Krishna; this too is not properly explained.

Geographical information

There is none whatsoever in this work. The reason is fairly obvious; the writer spends all of his time discussing matters not earthbound. This is in contrast to the canonical Gospels in which the writers do clearly and deliberately tie things in with real places and dates.

Historical information

The same is true for history in this gospel; there is no human history included at all. It makes various references to pre-history, before the creation, but there is no clear scheme outlining how one principle developed into another principle. All the indirect references to Jesus Christ in this world are just such and no more. There is no attempt to tie the Incarnation in with actual times and places.

Philosophy

There is no philosophy, as could be seen from the productions of Aristotle or Plato; in fact, Jesus is portrayed as being at odds with the philosophers:

'Philosophers, wise in their own opinions, tried to refute him. He defeated them for they were ignorant, and in their folly they came to hate him' (page193).

This may also be a covert reference to the Pharisees, Sadducees and Essenes, each with their own systems of thought. Jesus was seen to be in contention with them.

Theologico-Mythical material

The book consists almost entirely of this kind of information. To put it into some sort of systematic order, we begin with God the Father who is uncreated, the flawless one. He is perfect, the unknowable, the inscrutable one; all things come from him especially the **All** whom he created.

It is not clear who or what the **All** is or was: a god, a principle, or some sort of power? But we can see the influence of Buddhism here. This word occurs in several Gnostic works of the period[3]; it is evocative, possibly pantheistic, but not clearly defined. There are mentions of the 'divine Mother'[5], the Holy Spirit, the Son, with none of which do we see the relationship with the Father.

Although the Father created all things, he did not cause **error**. This is the Gnostic approach to theodicy; how did evil come into the world? (page 191). Error appears to be personified (page 192):

'Error became enraged, persecuted and attacked him, but was nullified by his sacrifice.'

This is talking about the death of Jesus. There is one mention of Satan (page 211), but this is not related to error. The explanation for error could be something that the writer calls 'forgetfulness' (page 191). Jesus is the one who enlightens all those encased in darkness through forgetfulness.

So sin and distancing from God is not to do with bad behaviour; it is to do with ignorance, nescience and blindness. This is an interesting approach to theodicy:

'Nescience had caused anxiety and fear, a smutty fog that made people feel blind'[4] (page 190).

The fog or mist metaphor occurs more than once. The writer will not admit to God causing it:

'The Father didn't cause this error, although all emanates from him' (page 191).

So by this paradox, we have an answer to the problem of theodicy; it actually is no answer, because there is no clear explanation for why a perfect God can allow evil to occur in the creation. But we notice that evil has invaded the cosmos long before the appearance of the human race. In other words, evil is a cosmic problem, as opposed to a human problem.

With the Father is the divine Mother (page 201), Holy Spirit, and the Son. The relationship between these is not discussed except to say that the Holy Spirit is God's 'heart':

'The Father unveils his heart, the Holy Spirit. He reveals what is secret, his Son, so through his grace the aeons may know him... and abide in him... ' (page 210).

The mention of *aeons* now points out a thoroughly Gnostic concept, that there are divine entities who are not quite god and certainly not human. *Aeons* (Greek) actually means 'time-spans', in a literal sense, but that is not what is meant here. They are some kind of supernatural entity but created:

'Since our Father is unborn, he alone is the one who created for himself the name, before he created the aeons... ' (page 220).

It would seem that there are twenty-three aeons, though it is not explained how the writer arrives at that figure. They may be symbolic of something. We suspect that they live in some sort of 'intermediate realm', which would be between heaven and earth. We have mention of hell; heaven is not actually mentioned, but there is a thing called the 'Isle of the Blessed... their golden land' (page 226), which is a euphemistic way of saying the same thing. The Isles of the Blessed will be encountered when we look at the Egyptian Book of the Dead (Chapter 25)

We also have mention of the *Pleroma*[6]. Literally, this means fullness, completion, satisfaction, but here it has mythological overtones. It is not quite a personification but close to it. There are about eight mentions of the Pleroma. Page 224 comes close to defining it, or them:

'All the rays from our Father are Pleromas, and the source is the one who created them in his own self. He designated their fate; each is created so through their own will they may return.'

Christ is somehow associated with the Pleromas; he comes to preach about the 'splendour of the Pleroma, the magnitude of his Father and his divine sublimity' (page 224).

There is another entity called the Age, though how he is different from the Aeons is not clarified. There is also the All, who is very close to the Father but not quite so flawless:

'The Father... who created the All and contains the All and whom the All always needs, he held flawless within himself, which he didn't pass on to the All... ' (page 192).

There may be some confusion and contradiction in this; the All is associated with Jesus Christ as well, but not identical with him:

'It is necessary that the All shall aspire towards him, (Christ), for the flawlessness of the All is in him' (page 197).

The description of Jesus Christ is almost orthodox; there seems to be no denial of his humanity. He bore suffering and was crucified (page 197), was the good shepherd and rescued people from falsehood. How we take this remark is a point for discussion:

'He came in bodily form, without obstacles, for purity is unconquerable' (page 207).

What does 'bodily form' mean? It could imply that he only appeared to be human but was actually some kind of phantom, apparition or even theophany. 'Without obstacles'; what does that mean? It could mean such things as the normal hardships of life, or the problems that beset most ordinary people; but that is not clear. Here we see the possibility of the Gnostic influence on an early understanding of the Incarnation. More to the point, is a most telling remark about the significance of the crucifixion:

'The all-loving Christ was long-suffering in bearing the suffering of others, until he received that tome, since he knew his own death would bring life for the multitude' (page 195).

Here is a clear understanding of the Atonement, and going further, the 'tome', which ought literally to mean a document or book; in this case it means the 'testament', or 'covenant'. In the next verse, it talks about a householder leaving a will, which reveals his fortune. This thought ties in with Hebrews, where it states that Jesus had to die in order that the New Testament could be activated[7].

The other element in this is the mention of 'the secret'. This is not the messianic secret as seen in St Mark's gospel. It is the secret of self-knowledge and understanding: gnosis! When Christ came, he revealed the secret mysteries to those purified through his grace. He enlightened everyone and pointed out the Way of Truth. For those who can take this understanding on board, there is heaven waiting, but such people have to be 'called' in advance and known by God:

> 'Those whose names he knew in advance were summoned for the end. Thus the names the Father has uttered have understanding; the names of the uncalled remain nescient' (page 198)[4].

There is a thing called the Book of Life; if one's name is in it, one is saved. Clearly this is a doctrine of election and predestination: God chooses people beforehand. Even so, paradoxically, there is repentance, which appears as *metanoia*, a Greek word that means the same thing, literally, 'putting one's mind right'. There is an admission of a degree of universalism for Christ has 'rescued many from falsehood' (page 199). But conversely, those who are to be saved are kept secret with their names written in a book. In a way, the secrecy of Jesus' Messiahship is transmuted to a cosmic secrecy, which is only dispelled when the Christ comes directly from the Father. The redeemed remain in ignorance of their status until Christ comes to point it out to them:

> 'It was a miracle; they were within the Father while not recognising him, and they were able to walk on for they failed to understand or to know the One in whom they dwelled. If his will hadn't issued from him as revelation, the knowledge of how his various rays harmonise would have stayed in nescience' (page 199).

These are the chosen ones who come to realise they are saved. Strangely this reminds us of how Rama did not realise he was an avatar of Vishnu until the culmination of the Ramayana (Chapter 22).

The writer is quite clear that these are the words of truth, speculative as they may be. It was Jesus Christ who pointed out the Way of Truth in his teachings. But essentially, it was through the crucifixion that knowledge of the Father was given to the elect. St Mark would probably have agreed with this, as the rending of the veil in the Temple, coinciding with the crucifixion, had the effect of making access to God available, but, not for the chosen few – for everyone. The crucifixion did not lead to annihilation, 'because his way was practised. Those who practised rejoiced, discovering him in themselves' (page 192). For all those who diligently enquire, there is certainty; truth and the certainty that goes with it, appears at least five times in this gospel. Strangely, the resurrection is not mentioned; this seems to be a gap in the writer's thinking. This can be explained by saying that the writer did not believe that Jesus really died on the cross.

The final, essential element in the theology is the love of God, a strand which is found running through the Bible, and any system of thought worth having has to have this matter.

'… those who benefit from his unconditional love, which is constantly poured out, for he dwells in our midst' (page 226).

The gospel ends with these optimistic and spiritually enhancing words about God:

'He is goodness; his offspring are flawless, fit to bear his name. He is our Father; we are his children whom he loves!' (page 227).

This evokes all the covenant theology of the Bible, even if it does not actually use the word. There is that closeness to God, and the metaphor of the family and the father is most apt. It would be fair to say that 'love' is not well emphasised in this gospel; far too much time is spent on spiritual speculation about heavenly realms and aeons, but that is Gnosticism.

Literary worth

It would be fair to say that, in common with Gnostic literature, it is not noted for its literary brilliance. However, there are a few worthwhile metaphors worked in, though not exactly numerous.

'The knowledge of their Father comes as something of great worth, like a glorious sunrise' (page 205).

A sustained metaphor comes in page 216, concerning infinite compassion and unconditional love:

'Those whom he's anointed have become flawless; full jars receive ointment. The jar empties of ointment because there was a lack, and the salve was applied. His breath attracts healing, by its own power; for those without lack, no seal need be broken nor salve used...' (page 216).

This is a lovely metaphor using the figurative language of anointing.
Another bit of figurative language is based on incense:

'He takes notice of your works because his children are his incense, the grace of his face. Our Father loves his fragrance... it bestows perfume on his light and peace... the perfume but the breath, which attracts his fragrance... the primary fragrance that has grown cold... cold fragrance comes from duality, so faith comes and dissolves division' (page 212).

This is probably the finest sustained bit of figurative expression in this gospel; it speaks of God's children having a different quality, on a different dimension to the rest of humanity, which means that their good deeds carry weight with him.
Another short image concerns the Garden of Eden:

'He is good; he knows his plants because it is he who planted them in his own garden. Now his Eden is a haven of peace' (page 217).

A metaphor which points out the importance of knowing one's real self, and not sliding back into one's previous mentality goes like this:

'Don't return to the vomit you've thrown up. Don't be like moths or worms that cause decay, for you've already cast them out' (page 211)

It is all part of being certain that one has found the light and there is a certain spiritual superiority that goes with it.

'Utter from the heart, "I am the perfect day! And in me dwells the light which never sets."' (page 210).

On page 205 we have rather a weak paradox, but well in the tradition of Gnosticism:

'Striking blows or receiving them, falling from heights or flying in the air, being slain without a slayer, or slaying their friends, covered in blood.'

He is talking about those who are lost, 'full of agonising dreams', but when they come to know the Father, all these chimeras are dispelled, like waking up out of a nightmare. Although this is couched in figurative language, the paradoxical aspect of it is not strong here.

The whole work is poetic; there is no prose in it at all, and the translator has reflected that in his rendering of it.

General comments about the Gospel of Truth

A question which ought to be raised is, how literally do we need to take this gospel, and indeed, Gnostic material in general? Can we see it as the moderated mythological thought-patterns of the Graeco-Roman world? It is likely that some of the Gnostic philosophers took their own work literally; some may not have. One is struck by the fact that there were various thought-systems on the go, none of which entirely agreed with one another. Were they all trying to say something in their own way, which was not meant to be taken at face value? Take this example from page 192:

'As for the inscrutable, unknowable One, the Father, the Flawless ONE, who created the All and contains the All and whom the All always needs, he held flawlessness within himself, which he didn't pass on to the All; he wasn't envious; what envy could there be between himself and the All?'

Apart from the mild contradictions (which might be seen as paradoxes) in this, what is the writer trying to say? Is he saying that the Eternal God created everything but in so doing he remained perfect even if his creation had got faults in it? Where does envy come into it? Is this a mild way of saying that there is an eternal 'stand-off' between the Creator and the Creation? We may be seeing some sort of tension between a literal and a non-literal view of Gnostic material. The mistake made by them was to apply this to the life and ministry of Jesus, especially when it came to the passion and death of Christ. Once the sufferings and death of Jesus are denied or watered down, it undermines the entire process of Atonement. That was the big mistake made by the Gnostics and indeed many a modern 'passion-denier'.

As a Gnostic work, this one is not too ferocious. We do not see endless speculations about Demiurges and spiritual realities in the skies as some of the Gnostic theorists indulged in. This work needs to be seen against the background of the early AD centuries, in which there were all kinds of elaborate metaphysical theories circulating; a curious admixture of Greek philosophy, ancient pagan religions of the orient and especially Egypt, and influences from Hindu-Buddhism. The coming of Jesus Christ had a curious effect on this melting pot of ideas. Many of these mystery religions or fancy ideas tried to accommodate Jesus and offer an explanation in terms of their philosophy. With the Gnostics, who did not value the flesh, or this world, and had decided that the God of the Old Testament was a mistake, Jesus came as the revelation and intervention of the true, perfect God who was superior to all the other influences in the skies. His divinity was not doubted; his manhood was a matter of embarrassment to them. This was strange, since the Gnostics, probably taking their cue from various Eastern religions, had a strong idea of paradox in theology. Even then, not just the Gnostics, but everyone, had difficulties with the Incarnation; we still do to this day. It never occurred to them to see it as a profound paradox, and therefore way beyond any human explanation. The Gospel of Truth has an inkling of paradox but does not make a strong issue of it, as for instance occurs in Thunder[8].

Even if it is a mildly heretical work, it does have aspects of theological and spiritual worth:

'But the deepening of our Father's love is extensive and the concept of falsehood is non-existent in Him. It is faith that may fall but can again stand up in the knowing of Him... ' (page 214).

If the writer has a strong concept of God's love, and our need for faith, he can be forgiven for having a few cranky theories.

A few remarks on the main Gnostic theorists

The Gnostics of the early first centuries AD were mainly centred on Alexandria, or Egypt in general, and were probably the intellectuals of their day. It is interesting that the same kind of speculative theorising about the origins of the universe and of humanity was going on then, as it is now. Inevitably, it was very difficult to think oneself out of the basic mythological framework that they had; we too have the same problem. Basileides believed that there was a time when there was 'nothing' but conceptualising 'nothing' is a problem, since we all, then and now, live in a world which consists of 'somethings'. Then God enters the picture, who is 'non-existent', decided to make a world out of 'non-existents', by putting out one seed which contained all the germs to form a world. Here we see a watered down version of Greek and Egyptian mythology where the whole thing is far more crude. From there we have Archons and First Sonships, Ogdoads, Aether, Hebdomads coming down to the actual creation of the world. Somewhere in this domino-run of spiritual entities, the perfection of the original supreme God gets diminished and thus evil enters the picture.

All this is pure speculation and flights of fancy. Who is to know how many heavens there are? Basileides makes out there are 365 of them, because there are 365 days in the year. At least the Gospel of Truth is somewhat economical with this strand of Gnosticism.

Where does Jesus Christ fit with this scheme? It would seem that Jesus is someone separate from Christ. Jesus the man was born of Mary, but the Christ element only came upon him from the 'Hebdomad' at his baptism. So he was Jesus Christ all through the earthly ministry until it came to the crucifixion, whereupon, according to Basileides, he did a sort of phantom substitution with Simon of Cyrene; Jesus let Simon get crucified while he himself stood by laughing. So the human aspect of Jesus Christ was put to death but the divine aspect escaped back to heaven. There seems to be no mention of the resurrection. This dichotomising of Jesus Christ may have seemed to him as a clever rationalisation of the incarnation, but eventually it was condemned by the Chalcedonian definition; Jesus Christ was one person, not two[9].

There is much that we do not know about Basileides, but there was the tendency to speculate and theorise far too freely, just inventing ideas. Also, there was the element of magic, something that came out most strongly with Simon Magus.

Valentinus, a pupil of Basileides, comes out with much the same speculative ideas, just using a few different words, such as Aeon, Before-the-beginning, Primal –father, Abyss, Grace, Silence, Mind, Only-begotten and Pleroma. We notice some of these titles appear in the Gospel of Truth. With regard to the appearance of evil, it was Wisdom who produced an 'amorphous substance' which was imperfect; when she tried to rectify the matter with an appeal to the Father, it did not work, and thus evil is the fact that matter is wrong because of ignorance, grief, fear and bewilderment. We could compare this with the Japanese mythology in the Kojiki (Chapter 12), where similar things happen but much more crudely.

With regard to Jesus Christ and the Holy Spirit, they were reckoned to be two Aeons; they seem to have escaped the 'slip-up' made by Wisdom. Jesus Christ was invested with a special body that was animal in nature, but not the same as other humans. The basic thought behind this is that material things are corrupt and incapable of salvation; therefore Jesus could not have been truly human in the sense that everyone else is. So when he ate and drank, it was in a 'peculiar manner' and he never needed to go to the toilet! Again, Chalcedon emphasised that Jesus was truly and genuinely human and was not some sort of phantom.

Not stated in the writings of Basileides and Valentinus were the excesses of immorality indulged in by some of the rank and file Gnostics. When one believes that the material world is beyond redemption, what does it mean to adhere to good morals? Nothing! So they tore up the rule books and just did as they pleased – thieving, killing, fornicating and any other kind of vice – justifying it by saying it did not matter. After all, if one is convinced that one is 'elect' and has come to know the deep truths about God, what else matters in this world?

It is interesting that we are now going through another spell of 'Gnosticism' with the current mania over astrophysics. The vocabulary is obviously different, but the same basic questions are nagging at our souls. How did all things begin? What is there out in deep space? Was there a Big Bang? What was there before the Big Bang? What does 'nothing' actually mean? Does God exist or not exist? What about the origins of human life? Did it come from another planet? Are there other people on far away planets? Did spacemen visit this world a long time ago? It is all great fun to speculate, but there is hardly any fact any of this. So much of astrophysics is calculation based on wonderful assumptions. The truth of the matter is, that we just do not know what is or was going on in deep space; the whole thing is decorated with neo-mythological claims.

What this means is that human nature does not change, at least, not very much.

But the basic claims of Christianity, without a lot of decoration and fanciful theorising, are that there is One God, who may have company in the world of the spirit; there is One Messiah, the one whom God sent into the world to bring about a proper relationship with himself; there is one Spirit of God who actively guides us from day to day. Kept as simple as that, it is all we need to know.

The Corpus Hermeticum

This is a collection of Greek writings stemming from the late second century AD, although its precise date is a matter of debate. It is based on much older material coming from Ancient Egypt; much of this material is now lost, but scholars have been trying to reconstitute it. Some of this material will be reviewed in Chapter 25: The Egyptian Book of the Dead. The Hermiticum concerns the Egyptian god Thoth; he is transmuted into the Greek god Hermes, the messenger, who is the equivalent of Thoth. It is unlikely that this corpus was ever the 'Bible' of any particular group. It would be anachronistic to say that. However, its influence has been extensive, not least on the Renaissance and also the 'flower-power' movement of the late twentieth century. It is clearly an out-and-out Gnostic document, and is briefly described here as a comparison with the Gospel of Truth. It is not specifically a Christian work, though aspects of it do suggest a Christian influence. It is valuable as an insight into the religio-philosophical thinking in the Roman Empire; it has the gnostical elaborate speculation about the unseen world and yet does not indulge in too ridiculous a collection of ideas. The version used here is the *OMTO* of 2007, but it is clearly based on the classic rendering of it by G. R. S. Mead (1863-1933).

Although the corpus is in thirteen chapters and appears to be a conversation between different gods and people, there is a consistency of thought throughout. The writer(s) would claim that this book is the truth, like all the other scriptural writings studied. It begins with someone, whose name is not given to us, having a Theophanous encounter with some kind of celestial being called Poimandres[10], the Shepherd of Men. Apart from that, the work does not involve any human at all; it concentrates on the world of the spirit and how one can gain Gnosis, that vital ingredient which enlightens one and gains one salvation. We notice immediately that this is a reverberation of the Shepherd of Hermas, a Christian non-Gnostic work, which came close to being included in the New Testament. Also there are reverberations of the Sermon on the Mount, although the content of the two sermons is very different from the down-to-earth teachings of Jesus. Just how basic and realistic the motif of the shepherd can be, comes in the Birth Narratives of St Luke, where the shepherds have a vision of angels and visit the stable where the Good Shepherd of us all is found. Whether Luke saw it in this way is debatable, but it could be a 'side-swipe' at the Hermeticum. Also, the Son of God is mentioned in various places, not that this Son of God is equated with Jesus, but the inference may be there.

Although essentially a pagan text, the Hermeticum is clearly a sanitised mythology. God the Father is clearly understood and is equated with MIND; 'the All-Father Mind', who created all things. After that we have all kinds of philosophical principles that are not styled as gods or even angels. If the Greek text had been written in uncials, then the capital letters applied to these heavenly entities would not have been apparent; but the text is peppered with names, such as Reason, Archetypal Form, Providence, Necessity, Soul, Daimon, Cosmos and many more. Some of them seem to proceed from one another in a sort of chain reaction or domino run. The Judaeo-Christian tradition avoided this sort of thing; it has hordes of angels at work in the skies, but the Gnostics are quite happy with principles and philosophical concepts up above. But the Eternal Father does not proceed from anyone or anything; he is unmanifest and yet he is manifest; this is one of the useful paradoxes to be found in the corpus. 'He is the one of no body, the one of many bodies, no rather he is of every body.' (page 21). This comes very close to Pantheism. 'For all are He and He is all. For there is nothing in the world that is not He. He is Himself, both things that are and things that are not' (page 21). We might call this pro-Pantheism; and yet God is the eternal uncreated backstop. It might also be fair to say that with the emphasis being firmly laid on the unity of God, this could pass for Monotheism.

The Son of God receives various mentions in the Corpus. He appears, along with many other principles, from the Mind-God. His actual production is not explained, but it does not really refer to any incarnation, nor is there any attempt at equating him with Jesus. More likely another sort of incarnation is at the back of it; that of mankind being brought forth co-equal with the Father, as his own child, the image of God. Quite how it all went wrong is not clearly explained; the Garden of Eden episode is not included as such, but there was some kind of interplay between mankind and Nature and they were intermingled. This resulted in mankind being twofold in nature; mortal because of the physical body but immortal because of the essential spiritual element in him. Sin is essentially ignorance of God. To understand is to believe and vice versa. But any man can overcome this ignorance and become a 'god' again. If you are ignorant and mindless, you die and there is torment involved. This looks like a demythologised version of Hell, although Satan or the Devil are never actually mentioned. If you 'know', which means you have gnosis, you live and regain co-equality with God. You can know God by making yourself like God. It is not really explained how one acquires this Gnosis; there is no mention of the Messiah of God bringing this knowledge into the world.

This brings us to question of theodicy, which is a recurring theme in the Corpus. If God is good, which is claimed quite clearly, where did evil come from? At the outset, the Eternal Father is immobile; he does not change or develop. However, everything that he produces is mobile and therefore changes and by that definition cannot be fully God, even if they are divine principles. This idea can be found in the Tao Teh Ching (Chapter 10). But the divine principles emanate from each other, progressively becoming less and less perfect. So we begin with Energy of Growth and Waning, which lead to Device of Evils, then the Guile of Desires, until we come to the sixth one, which is Striving for Wealth by evil means, and then Ensnaring Falsehood. At each stage, the principle is de-energised, which means losing some of its power. So that is how evil comes into the world of the spirit; it means that evil is a cosmic problem, not just a human problem. We notice that the Fall, as in the Garden of Eden, is cleverly demythologised but also projected into the heavens. To counteract these faulted influences there are good principles available, such as Continence, and Sharing-with-all, and Truth, which will dispel the bad ones. This is when Righteousness chases away Unrighteousness. This is a kind of rebirth; on the face of it, it sounds like reincarnation, but it is not quite the Hindu idea; we can be born again and made into gods. That energy that was lost is now reinstated and we can be divine, just like the Father-Mind.

It is interesting that the Corpus makes some attempt at proofs for the existence of God; something which the Greek philosophers attempted but the Jewish scriptures never did. We are now accustomed to thinking of five main proofs on a philosophical level[11]:

The teleological argument; the argument from design[12]. This is gone into in some detail on page 20. Hermes phrases it thus: 'whereby is made this **order** of the cosmos and the cosmos which we see of order. This is his word for design. He then goes into details about the human body, which is an amazing description for twenty centuries ago; about how intricate and in perfect measure it is. It can only be explained by the creative work of God.

The cosmological argument, the argument from first cause[13] – this is endemic in the Corpus, for while God the Father is immobile, everything else is mobile. This concept comes out repeatedly, and is a way of saying, in different phrasing, that everything has a cause or causes, but there has to be something or someone at the start, who is uncaused, namely God.

The moral argument; the argument from ultimate perfection[14] – this idea was largely established by Kant, but traces of it can be found going back to Ancient Greece. It involves not just the thought that there is moral perfection somewhere, but also aesthetic perfection; since neither of these are to be found in the created world, they have to exist in the world of the spirit. The moral argument is not phrased in quite this way in the Corpus, and yet there is an awareness of it in this:

'... the power of our mind's eye to unfold and gaze upon the Beauty of the Good... Beauty that nothing can e'er corrupt or comprehend' (page33). We aspire to contemplate the Beauty of the Good. The word 'perfection' does not appear, but is very largely assumed.

The ontological argument[15], which was a major strand in Anselm's thinking, is clearly present in the Corpus. 'That than which nothing greater can be thought' is Anselm's phraseology. Hermes puts it like this:

'God is first "thinkable" for us, not for himself, for that the thing that is thought does fall beneath the thinker's sense. God then cannot be "thinkable" to himself, in that he is thought of by himself as being nothing else but what he thinks. But he is "something else" for us, and so he is thought of by us' (page 9).

Here we see the philosopher groping towards the thought that if one could think of something greater, that greater thing would be God. Another attempt at the same mentality is seen on page 19, where the question arises, 'Why can't God be obvious?' which means observable:

'For all that is made manifest is subject to becoming, for it has been made manifest. But the Unmanifest is for ever, for it does not desire to be made manifest. It ever is, and makes manifest all other things. Being himself unmanifest, as ever being and ever making-manifest, himself is not made manifest. God is not made himself; by thinking-manifest, he thinks all things manifest.'

In other words, if God were manifest, or obvious, he would not be God. By very definition, he is above and beyond the observable world. This is an attempt, arguing rather circuitously, at the Ontological Argument. One would hesitate to call it a bit clumsy, but all attempts at this line of reasoning come out as rather a strain on the logical powers of mankind. However, the same strand of thought keeps reappearing in different guises to this day.

The main way nowadays is with astrophysicists when contemplating deep space. We have heard all about the 'Big Bang', which is alleged to have started everything off in the universe. No one dared to contemplate what happened before the Big Bang. Now, it is being asked, what made the Big Bang happen and where did all the components come from; and before that and before that! It is the ontological argument in a different mode, but real enough in the heart of mankind. So God is no longer a Big Bang, he is something else – maybe a 'squeaky pop'! Interestingly, this question does arise on page 9: Hermes and Asclepius[16] together consider the vastness of space, maybe they did not think in terms of billions of light years; nevertheless, they sense that if space is boundless, then it must be some sort of godlike thing, or even God himself. How close this comes to the Big Bang mentality of today, in which God is pictured as the explosive start to all things!

In modern scientific thought, there is much attention drawn to the factors of positive and negative in atomic structure; in fact, all physical things are a subtle combination of plusses and minuses. The Corpus has an awareness of this with regard to creation. 'For it is the love and the blending of contraries and dissimilar that does give birth to light down shining by the energy of God... ' (page 41). Also of interest for modern thought, is the awareness of the earth as being spherical, even if heaven has seven layers and circulatory motion. Whether Hermes actually understood what he was saying here is impossible to assess, but of course, he is absolutely right about the opposites of life holding all things together. This is the basis of paradox. We see many paradoxes applied to God in the Corpus, a good example is on page 21:

'He is the God beyond all name; he is the unmanifest, he the most manifest; he whom the mind alone can contemplate, he is visible to the eyes as well; he is the one of no body, the one of many bodies, no, rather he is of every body. There is nothing that he is not. For all are he and he is all... ' and so it continues, a fine string of paradoxes.

This is only matched by some of the high-flown metaphors in the Corpus. Page 26 has a prolonged flow of metaphor as one approaches heaven:

'Be you then not carried off by the fierce flood, but using the shore current, you who can, make for Salvation's port, and, harbouring there seek you for one to take you by the hand and lead you to Gnosis' gates. Where shines clear light, of every darkness clean; where not a single soul is drunk, but sober all they gaze with their hearts' eyes on him who wills to be seen. No ear can hear him, nor can eye see him, nor tongue speak of him, but only mind and heart. But first you must tear off from you the cloak which thou dost wear... the web of ignorance, the ground of bad, corruption's chain, the carapace of darkness, the living death, sensation's corpse, the tomb you carry with you, the robber in your house, who through the things he loves, hates you, and through the things he hates, bears you malice'. This is a lovely summary of the main thrust of the Corpus, and as such is worthwhile as a work of literature.

Footnotes for Chapter 19: The Gospel of Truth

1. The Parable of the Lost Sheep, Luke 15:3-7.
2. Abraham's age; Genesis 17:1.
3. The Gospel of Thomas, for instance, page 20.
4. Nescience: failure to understand, ignorance, blindness, stupidity.
5. The 'Divine Mother'; this appears to be some sort of principle; it is not the Virgin Mary.
6. Pleroma; a Greek word meaning fullness, completion.
7. Hebrews 9:16.
8. Thunder: another Gnostic work with a unique element, that of a mysterious female deity. Thunder is noted for its use of paradoxes when talking about God. (pages 242-250).
9. The Council of Chalcedon ruled as heretical any dichotomy between the human and the divine in Jesus Christ. The Chalcedonian Definition, 451 AD: '... of one substance with the Father as regards his godhead and at the same time of one substance with us as regards his manhood; like us in all respects apart from sin... recognised in two natures, without confusion, without change, without division, without separation...'
10. Poimandres: the word poimen in Greek means a shepherd.
11. *Arguments for the Existence of God*, by John Hick. 1971.
12. *The Teleological Argument*, pages 1-14.
13. *The Cosmological argument*, pages 37-52.
14. *The Moral argument*, pages 53-67.
15. *The Ontological argument*, pages 68-83.
16. Asclepius was the Greek god of healing; an *asclepion* was a kind of hospital or sanatorium.

20

The Book of Enoch in the Pseudepigrapha

This is another apocryphal work belonging to the intertestamental period in the Judaeo-Christian scheme. It is in the same genre as the Gospel of Truth, in that it is the product of almost certainly a minority group with an eschatological mentality. The difference is that the Gospel of Truth was the product of a heretical group in Egypt, and lay hidden for centuries, only to be rediscovered in our own times. The Book of Enoch would hardly represent a heretical group, as it was never lost; it became influential by New Testament times and nearly became accepted for the canon of the Old Testament, but was rejected. It has many affinities with Ezekiel, but to compare the two, the difference in quality is quite noticeable. It is thought, with good reason, that it was originally written partly in Hebrew and partly in Aramaic, like Daniel. The date of its composition is uncertain, but it has to be before the Maccabean uprising but after the return of the Jews from Exile. It may be early in this time-slot; it was thought worthy of translation into Greek and Ethiopic, and those are the surviving writings of this work. The book is thought to be composite, probably an ongoing collection, but to read it, one is struck by the consistency of style and thought, in spite of various self-contradictions. Whoever it was, he was almost certainly one of the Hasidim, or proto-Pharisees, judging by his theology and general outlook. There is no doubt that Enoch had its influence on the New Testament writers and the early church Fathers, such as Justin Martyr and Ireneaus; it would be tedious to adduce all the literary connections; the classic one is Jude 6, which runs: 'the angels that did not keep their own position but left their proper dwelling have been kept by him in eternal chains ... until the judgement of the great day'. This is a thought that occurs in Enoch. The Book of Enoch was thus seen as scriptural in the early years of the church, but has slipped out of canonicity. Even so, in more than one place, it claims to be telling us the truth!

Who was Enoch? The whole book works on the presupposition of a certain passage in Genesis 5:1-32. The crucial remark, which is for us, somewhat cryptic, goes like this:

'Enoch walked with God; and he was not, for God took him.'

What does this mean? Later generations took this to mean that Enoch had been assumed into heaven, in the same way that Moses and Elijah had been. After all, they had had no funeral or tomb.
The writer of Hebrews includes Enoch in his list of worthies from the Old Testament:

'By faith, Enoch was taken up so that he should not see death; and he was not found, because God had taken him...' Hebrews 11:5.

For the Christians, this matter of 'assumption' was of much interest since it prefigured the Ascension of Jesus. The essential purpose of it related to intercession; that somebody from the world of humanity could be with God in Heaven and try to persuade God to be merciful. This throws light on the theology of Jesus as the eternal High Priest, interceding for us all. In addition, we can see how the Virgin Mary comes into the same orbit of thought.

Also, people noticed that Enoch was the seventh generation from Adam, which must, for them, have been significant. It went, Adam, Seth, Enosh, Kenan, Mahalalel, Jared, then Enoch. Also, Enoch was the grandfather of Noah. This must have been noteworthy for these ancient peoples. We also notice that at that stage of humanity, people live to astonishing lifespans; also there are giants, the Nephilim; also there are 'sons of God' who interbreed with the 'daughters of men', whatever that might mean. The question arises, 'do we have to take this completely at face value; is it to be taken literally, or figuratively?' The point being, that the Book of Enoch hardly ever works on the literal level; nearly all of it is dream-vision material, and the conclusion could fairly be drawn that one should take the whole thing as figurative, symbolic and non-literal. It looks as though Jude does take it literally, but that could be a big mistake. One needs to develop a certain skill in interpretation to make the best of such a book; a face-value approach simply makes the book seem absurd.

One interesting little matter arises in Genesis 5:23, in which Enoch is stated to be 365 years old when he dies; this is contradicted by Enoch 60:1 in which he is claimed to be 500 years old. Some have taken this to be a confusion with the age of Noah, who, in Genesis 5:32 is stated to be 500 years old. But whichever way one sees it, there is some sort of agenda going on here. At the very least, it could be a signal for the reader not to take these matters purely at face value. Furthermore, 365 may be symbolic for something; after all, there are 365 days in the year, and Enoch was very much interested in calendar calculation and celestial motions (Enoch 72-82). Later generations have puzzled over these astronomical ages for the Patriarchs; how could Methusaleh have lived to 969? Clearly there is some sort of agenda here, which we do not really understand. All sorts of clever rationalisations have been sought to explain it away. But the truth may be much easier and simpler, if we just knew how to interpret these figures as symbolic.

Mathematical matters

It is something of a surprise that a visionary book such as Enoch could include so much mathematical information, or rather, challenges. Numbers appear frequently, such as thousands of angels. There are seven archangels, then there are four archangels; can this be resolved? There are seven great mountains and seven great rivers (77:4), which are not actually named; there is no need to, for seven implies completeness, so the mountains and rivers complete the whole world. There are seventy shepherds as guardians of Israel before the Exile and thirty-five bad shepherds after the Exile. We note that thirty-five is a half of seventy; in other words, they were the failed ones. Now we see that to take his figures literally is wrong; they are symbolic. When he talks of shepherds, is that a code word for 'angels?'

Enoch's mathematical speculation is best seen in his cosmological section, Chapters 72 to 82. The sun has six portals for rising and six for setting. The use of 'portals' is a Hebrew way of avoiding any mention of the Zodiac, which is of course a pagan notion. He is insistent that the year consists of 364 days (not 365); he works it out as 52 x 7; therefore it has to be correct. But even with 364 days there is a dilemma; he raises the matter of intercalatary days; each month should have 30 days, but this does not work. Every quarter has to have an extra day added, thus; $30 + 30 + 30 + 1 = 91$. Multiply 91 by 4 and we arrive at 364. He goes on to work out how many days would be in 3 years, 5 years and eight years. All very interesting, but is it to be taken totally literally? After, we all know that the year is 365.25 days, and this was known in the ancient world. If you ignore this fact, the calendar becomes way out of line with the seasons very quickly. But the Essenes of Qumran did take it literally with the result that certain festivals always landed on the same day of the week, but it was a desperately clumsy arrangement. Enoch does not attempt to discuss such matters as leap year or the extra day to make up 365. If we take him as being symbolic here, what is he saying? He could be saying that everything in creation, including the heavenly motions, are regular and controlled by the angels of God.

Even more intriguing is Enoch's treatment of the length of days and nights. This is discussed in detail in 72:8. As we know, the further north one goes, the greater the difference between the length of day and night, until we come to the Arctic circle, where day can be continuous and also night, according to season. The way he describes the difference would suggest that he was living at 49 degrees north which would be somewhere in northern France, Germany or even Roumania, or even southern USSR. It is not impossible that, if he were a diaspora Jew, he could be describing the situation at this latitude! This might seem a little farfetched at that time in history. Otherwise, there is just the possibility of it being symbolic for something. We note that 49 equals 7 x 7, which might imply that the length of days and nights is a perfect relationship under the control of God's angels.

Enoch goes into detail about the phases of the moon (78:1-9 and 79:4). In 74:1-7 he goes into much detail about the lunar year, which is fascinating, to have these matters described in the thought-forms of Post-Exilic Jewish observation. He claims that the sun and moon are the same size; this is obvious to us on ground-level, but of course we now know that it only appears to be so, because the moon is much nearer to us than the sun. Even if he did not know such facts, he seems to have some kind of understanding of 'orbit' and 'circumference'. He does not attempt to discuss eclipses, which is rather a disappointment. As we know from the Antikithera mechanism, the ancients did have ways and means of calculating such things; it may have seemed to Enoch to be rather too paganistic to embark on. But the substratum of it is, that all the planetary movements are measured and controlled by God; they are not haphazard.

Geographical considerations

Enoch occasionally makes mention of real places, such as the land of Dan and Mount Hermon. The Great Sea, (77:6), i.e., the Mediterranean is mentioned, and is the Erythrean Sea(32:2), which is the Greek name for the Persian Gulf and the Indian Ocean. This may be an indication of the book being written, or at least edited, in the Greek era, which would mean 300 BC and onwards. But as with the mathematics, this may be purely symbolic.

Enoch has a fascination for meteorology, the weather and the climate. In 76:1-14 we are told that there are twelve winds that produce the weather and the climate; from all four quarters come three winds each from its own portal, each giving its own results. It is interesting to hear that there is snow, hoar frost and cold; this in itself might suggest that the writer is living in a northerly country rather than Israel. Meteorological matters occur in more than one place, which suggests that he wishes to emphasise that the elements are under the control of God and his angels. They all have their laws to conform to. Each element, such as the wind and the frost, has some kind of spirit or angel driving it as seen in 60:11-24. According to 69:15, there is a 'secret oath' relating to all of creation. The oath, termed *Akae*, was handed to Michael the Archangel, who now reveals its power. It is the fact that everything in creation, including the weather, carries on regardless:

> 'Through that oath the stars complete their course, and he calls them by their names, and they answer him from eternity to eternity' Enoch 69:21.

This, it would seem, is Enoch's version of the covenant of Noah, that of the continuity of nature and the fact that the seasons will never fail. When discussing Noah, that covenant is not actually mentioned; this 'oath' appears to pre-exist the Flood. This implies that God established his goodwill for his creation right from the start, and the covenant of Noah was more of a reaffirmation of this oath, rather than a new idea. In fact, the word 'covenant' only appears once in this book, and in another context altogether.

Scientific information

Some of this has already been mentioned in the section on Geography. But Enoch has a few remarks to make about Biology; he notes how the trees behave in winter and summer, the deciduous trees shedding their leaves. There are fourteen trees which are coniferous. This again might be an indication of him living in a northerly situation; that is, if we take him literally. In the next breath he describes how the trees bear fruit, which is an indication of God's consistency from year to year and faithfulness in creation. This is again the message of the 'oath'.

Enoch is also interested in metallurgy. In various places he mentions the different ores and metals that can be obtained, not just for fabricating weapons, but for ornaments and women's makeup. In 8:1, it is Azazel, a wicked angel, who shows mankind how to work in metal. But in 65:15 it is an angel who is pre-eminent who produces the ores from the ground. Again we can see that all these matters, scientific or otherwise, are essentially controlled and provided by the world of the spirit. It is not just the clever invention of mankind.

We have already seen how astronomy and astrophysics are a major interest to Enoch, for the same reasons. It is interesting that while the sun and moon each have a chariot to carry them across the sky, there is some awareness that the moon has no light of its own. He does not go quite as far as to say that it is reflected light from the Sun but he is nearly there (78:8 and 10). This would be highly advanced thinking for those times. Also he says that the sun is seven times brighter than the moon. Is it? Never mind; we can see the symbolism in it; that the sun is 7 times (notice the perfect number) more powerful, influential and commanding than the moon. Or to put it another way, the Light of God always overpowers the light of the sinister, evil, and malevolent. The moon was always thought of as sinister. In this we see an intriguing consommé of ideas, mythological, factual and proto-scientific; for us, fascinating; for them, only common sense.

Another intriguing claim is found in 54:7; when the day of judgement arrives, God will open up the waters that are above the firmament and also the waters beneath the earth. They are taken to be masculine (above) and feminine (below). All these waters will be joined together to destroy all life on earth. This is talking about the Flood as with Noah. But the idea of the waters being masculine and feminine is suggestive that heaven and hell are in some kind of reciprocal relationship. We see this motif at the end of the Ramayana (Chapter 22). At the very least, it indicates that God is in control of the whole thing, heaven, hell and anywhere else.

In Enoch 43:1 we almost have the give-away interpretation:

'And I saw other lightnings and the stars of heaven, and I saw how he called them all by their names and they hearkened unto him. And I saw how they are weighed in a righteous balance according to their proportions of light...' We notice the metaphor of the scales, as in the Egyptian Book of the Dead (Chapter 25),

This rudimentary attempt at astrophysics is in effect telling us that God has it all worked out in the right proportions, and that they all have a 'parabolic meaning' (verse 4). This is a strong indication that large amounts of Enoch must be taken as symbolic.

History

There is no direct historical account in Enoch. There is one mention of the 'Medes and the Parthians' in Enoch 56:5. This might suggest a date after the collapse of the Medo-Persian Empire, around 300 BC, when Persia was transmuted into the Parthian Empire. Again, this might be some sort of symbolism, and cannot be taken literally. It might even be a genuine prophecy.

What we can take as literal to a certain extent is the resumé of Israelite history from Cain and Abel down to the Maccabean age. This is an extended section from Chapter 85 to 90. None of the actual names are stated; we have to infer from our knowledge of the Old Testament regarding who is what. It is all done as an extensive allegory. We begin with two bulls, which symbolise Cain and Abel. All the 'goodies' are bulls in the Patriachal age, and any other animal is a 'baddy'. After Abraham, who is a white bull, the people of God become sheep and carry on as innocent, trusting, peaceful souls down to Judas Maccabeus. We have the Exodus, the Sinai event, the settlement in Canaan, Saul and David, the Temple built as a 'tower', Elijah's assumption 'to be with me'. Worth noting is that all the sheep that are lost to marauding wolves, are recorded in 'the book' (89:71), the purpose of which will be seen later. Strangely there is no explicit mention of the two kingdoms; one wonders if there is a reason for this. Perhaps Enoch prefers the version of the Chronicler to that of the Deuteronomist. The Exile comes, but only a quarter of the Jews return to rebuild the city and the Temple. Then we have the Persian period and into the Hellenistic era.

'And I saw that twenty-three had undertaken the pasturing and completed their several periods fifty-eight times,' Enoch 90:5.

What does this mean? It is typical of this genre of writing to use esoteric number systems. Does this mean that there were twenty-three High Priests from the end of the Exile to the Maccabean Age? That is just possible. But what does 'their several periods fifty-eight times' mean? At the very least, it is foolish to try to take this as literal history. In many ways, this resembles Daniel's dream-visions. If we try to take them too literally and locate each feature to a known event in history, it does not quite work. This may be an indication that Enoch was genuinely a dreamer, just as Daniel was.

With the Maccabean age, Enoch expects the Messianic age to come in, as indeed so did Daniel. However, Enoch has another resume of history, done in the Apocalypse of Weeks. This comes in Chapters 93, and 91. It is based on the seven days of the week, except that it goes on past seven to ten and even 'many weeks without number for ever.' So, week one marks the birth of Enoch, even though he was the seventh, i.e., seventh generation from Adam. Week two was an age of wickedness ending in the Flood. Week three is the election of Abraham. Week four is the Ten Commandments and the Tabernacle. Week five is the Temple. Week six is the assumption of Elijah and the Exile; again no mention is made of the two kingdoms. Week seven is an apostate generation ending with what appears to be the Messiah; this sounds like the Maccabean situation. None of this is precisely dated and no names are actually identified. It all relies on our knowledge of the Old Testament. Going on from there, there is an eighth week of righteousness, which sounds like Judas Maccabeus with his sword. Also it refers to the rebuilding of the Temple; could this mean Herod's building schemes? In the ninth week righteous judgement is to be revealed to the whole world; is this the coming of Jesus? In the tenth week comes the apocalypse, the judgement on the whole earth. 'The first heaven shall pass away and a new heaven will appear...' Enoch 91:16. Now we see the context and implications in Revelation, where the same thought is included. Also we see the Messiah termed a Lamb (90:38); the metaphor is taken up in the New Testament and is a major piece of imagery in Revelation (Chapter 6).

After that there will be many weeks without number and all shall be goodness and righteousness and sin shall no more be mentioned for ever. Is this the Christian era? It would be lovely if it were; so we end on a note of optimism. Most apocalyptic writers have some sort of time-scheme from the beginning to the end, with the Messianic age somehow fitted into the scheme. Enoch is unusual in that he has two contrasting schemes, but they amount to the same message; that the course of history is mapped out and controlled by God. This may not appear so, since the people of God are constantly under pressure from evil influences both abroad and at home. Thus Enoch points out that this is all part of the plan; it is not that evil has gone out of control and is just killing off the faithful. The People of God will survive, either on earth, or in heaven, and one day there will be a reckoning and everything will be put to rights.

When we come to Judas Maccabeus, he is a lamb who grows a great horn! Clearly the metaphor has slipped a bit. Moreover, he is termed 'a great sword' (90:19).

Mythology

This is the main vehicle of expression in Enoch. His book hardly ever touches on earthly realities, except for what we have already seen. He is thoroughly immersed in speculations about the other world of the spirit. It is no use trying to turn his visions into some kind of systematic order. As we all know from dreams, they are haphazard, chaotic and sometimes frightening. But, in common with the Gnostic material, speculation is rife as to what goes on in the next world. In 70:1-4, he is translated, or assumed to be shown all kinds of futuristic things, only to be told to go back to earth for a year (81:5) in order to instruct his son, Methuselah, in the truth. Then presumably he must return to heaven. It is difficult to separate this from theology, for the two matters are interlaced. But essentially, there are squadrons of angels with all kinds of funny names. This occurs more than once and the lists of names do not always coincide. Nevertheless all these names have some kind of meaning.

In Enoch 6:7-8 we have 200 angels descend on Mount Hermon, with the express intent of finding girls to marry and getting them with child.

It was like a well-ordered[1] army, with twenty leading angels organising ten underlings. The chief was Semjazaz and then follows a list of all their names, with meanings attached; a selection will give some examples. Tamiel means 'perfection of God'; Kokabiel means 'star of God'; Barakijal means 'lightning of God'. Semjazaz seems aware that this interference with the ladies is something naughty and does not wish to take the responsibility, whereupon they all take an oath to bear the responsibility communally. The result was that a race of giants appeared and terrorised the earth, causing mayhem. Then the four archangels, Michael, Uriel, Raphael and Gabriel, realised what was happening and informed God about the wickedness going on. God replied that Noah was to be told to hide himself and prepare for the Flood, because everything will be destroyed. With this interesting elaboration on Genesis 6, we see a mythological explanation for theodicy; that evil came into the world via certain hooliganistic angels! This in fact contradicts Genesis 2, in which the disobedience of mankind was the root cause of evil in the world.

In Enoch 69:1-2 we have another list of fallen angels with Semjaza as the first, but now twenty-one of them. The names are somewhat different, and the last one is Azazel, who is encountered in many places as a kind of Devil. This time we have chiefs over hundreds and fifties and tens, sounding even more like a well-organised army. Now we see why St Luke described the angels as 'a multitude of the heavenly host' which implies an army, Luke 2:13. This passage in Enoch sixty-nine goes into more detail about how badly behaved the angels were, pointing out that Gadreel was the one who led Eve astray. This is all very fascinating but pure speculation and fantasy.

The normal assumption in the Ancient World, about a three-tiered universe appears frequently in Enoch, with much elaboration. Heaven is not just one, but it goes up in stages, to the heaven of heavens. This is where 'the Head of Days' (God) sat on his throne of glory and the angels and the righteous stood around him,' Enoch 60:2. We have frequent mention of the pillars of the earth, and columns of fire going down into the abyss. He has a vision of hell; also clefts in the ground and valleys of fire. There are dark hollows in the underworld where the souls of the dead are gathered, awaiting the day of judgement (Enoch 22:3-4), crying out to heaven for release. But the fallen angels are chained up in the fiery prison for ever. All very lurid and frightening! But we must remember that this is mythology and not to be taken literally.

Much is said about fire. In mythology, this is an agent of cleansing; the implication is that hell is there for purifying and refining the dross from human nature. This is clearly explained in Enoch 10:5-17, in which the earth will be cleansed from all evil. It is talking about the Flood, but paradoxically, it is fire that will be cast upon the earth. Water also, is another cleansing agent; this is how the world is given a fresh start. In Enoch 66:1-3, there are angels in charge of the waters under the earth; they hold them in check for the right moment to bring about the Flood. How this works in relation to hellfire below the ground is not explained. But the waters contain Leviathan and Behemoth, the primeval monsters, the former female and the latter male. Even so they do not seem to mate. The metaphor of fire and water may sound contradictory, but Enoch actually admits that they are the same thing:

> 'Because these waters of judgement minister to the healing of the body of the kings and the lust of their body; therefore they will not see and will not believe that those waters will change and become a fire which burns for ever,' Enoch 67:13.

The Garden of Eden and the Tree of Wisdom are often mentioned. The elect will live in the Garden of Life; it is called the Garden of the Righteous (Enoch 60:23). But in the future, the whole earth will be replanted with trees and be full of blessing; also vines and olives. In Enoch 32:1-6 we hear about the Tree of Wisdom and how beautiful it is; how Adam and Eve ate the fruit and realised that they were naked. The trees have a special significance for Enoch; they exude all kinds of lovely fragrance, incense and many other scents. The Tree of Life, in particular, gives off wonderful odours, but the fruit is to be reserved for the day of judgement (Enoch 25:1-7). Then the Tree is transplanted to the Temple. In 14:10 we have a vivid description of the Temple, made of crystal, with flames of fire, with a lofty throne inside with the Great Glory seated on it. The trees are also involved with the 'blessed place', which is in the 'middle of the earth'. This is a circumlocution for Jerusalem, which as far as the Jews were concerned, was the centre of the earth. This is a precept that worked its way into Christian thinking; we recall that the Mappa Mundi features Jerusalem as the central point.

Looking at the mythology in this, the tree is an important symbol in world mythology. It occurs in virtually every system of mythology the world over. Its branches stretch up to heaven, its roots stretch down to hell and its bole is plain for all to see on the earth level. It is the ongoing connection between all three layers of the universe. In Enoch, with the trees giving off scents, particularly incense, this is symbolic of the presence of God. Incense, which gives off an aromatic smoke, like a sacrifice, implies God's presence. The removal of the Tree of Life to the Heavenly Temple tells us that Wisdom, understanding and the truth about life is elevated to the presence of God. But at the day of judgement, when we can all eat the fruit, the problem begun in the Garden of Eden will be reversed and all of mankind will come to understand the final truths about God. The mention of crystal is also mythological; Enoch is economical on the subject of gemstones (though notice 18:7). But in world mythology, jewels, glass, mirrors and crystal and translucent stones like alabaster and jade are all symbolic of everlasting life and eternity. So to have the Temple built of crystal is in symbolic terms saying, 'God's presence with us is everlasting and permanent'. Also the fact that there is fire all over it means that it is cleansed from all impurity.

The metaphor of God sitting on a fiery throne in the sky is also seen in Daniel 7:9. Many have taken this literally, believing that there is an old gentleman sitting on a chair up in the sky! But we must recall that this is mythology combined with heavy figurative language. What does it signify? It means that God is the everlasting king of the universe; he is the ultimate source of authority and the basis of all justice and fair play. He allows wickedness to continue to spoil matters in the world of humanity, but eventually, there will be a reckoning and the righting of all wrongs. This is why Enoch is emphatic that the earthly rulers, the kings and the mighty, who have misruled and caused so much trouble, will be abased and have to beg for mercy:

'And all the kings and the mighty and the exalted and those who rule the earth shall fall down before him on their faces...' Enoch 62:9.

This reminds us of Antichus 4th Epiphanes, but this does not have to mean that Enoch was written at that time; it could also remind us of the Assyrian and Babylonian kings who were such tyrants[1].

Another element of mythology is the appearance of the sword:

'Because the wrath of the Lord of Spirits resteth upon them and his sword is drunk with their blood,' Enoch 62:12.

The sword symbolises justice, the righting of wrongs, the enforcement of law and order. Taken literally, this remark is lurid and frightening, and yet we need to see beneath the imagery, which is a superb piece of hyperbole. God comes to defeat evil with great power and rescue those who are being tyrannised. In Enoch 17:3, the fiery sword is accompanied by a fiery bow and arrows and their quiver, and lightning. All this is saying the same things only in different metaphors.

Some of the mythological phrasing in Enoch is of the highest and most inspiring quality:

'I saw all the treasuries of the winds; I saw how he had furnished with them the whole creation and the firm foundations of the earth. And I saw the corner-stone of the earth; I saw the four winds which bear the firmament of the heaven. And I saw how the winds stretch out the vaults of heaven, and have their station between heaven and earth; these are the pillars of the heaven... .. I saw... there are seven mountains of magnificent stones... .one was of coloured stone, and one of pearl, and one of jacinth (jasper)... and the summit of his throne was of sapphire...' Enoch 18:1-9.

Superb imagery! People have taken this kind of thing literally, but it is not realistic to do so. It tells, in symbolic language, that the world is steady on its course, held firmly by God; he is ultimately in charge, and he is everlasting. Put like that, it is all very banal; put in Enoch's words, it is fantastic.

Another mythological element, not normally seen in world mythology, is the matter of the 'heavenly tablets' or 'books'. Enoch makes much mention of them[2]:

'... I saw the Head of Days... on the throne of his glory, and the books of the living were opened before him... ' Enoch 47:3.

This is a recurring theme; the tablets or records concern the deeds of mankind. They are all written down in heaven so that when judgement day comes, the eternal judge can produce the evidence. Again, this can hardly be taken literally. What it means is that God knows and recalls everything; it is not possible to deceive God and pretend to be innocent when one is guilty. This is in contrast to an earthly judge who might be deluded into making a wrong decision. This is an element heavily worked into the message of Revelation (Chapter 6); there are numerous augmentations of the scrolls, but it is the same theme, that God will not make any mistakes when it comes to the great judgement.

An interesting connection with Proverbs (Chapter 15) concerns Wisdom. As with all the Wisdom literature, Wisdom is personified as a woman. Here she is looking for somewhere to dwell. There is nowhere on earth for her to live. So she returned to her place in heaven and 'took her seat among the angels,' Enoch 42:1-2.

Theology of Enoch

Much of this has been touched on before, largely because it is unrealistic to try to separate it from the mythology of the book. Enoch is aware of the overwhelming power of the One God, who goes under various titles, such as 'the Head of Days'. He is in control of everything, and knows in advance the course of history.

'Thou knowest all things before they come to pass, and thou seest these things, and thou dost suffer them...' Enoch 9:11.

The obvious conclusion we draw from this is that predestination is a reality. However, Enoch never actually states this in so many words. It is, however, a prevailing assumption in the apocalyptic genre of this period. The fact that Enoch is a dream-prophet also strengthens this view. Nothing is said about free will.

This inevitably raises the question of why there is any evil, assuming that God is essentially good. Enoch's answer is that there was a collection of angels who went wrong, by taking a fancy to some of the human girls. This introduced wickedness to the world. Also there is a bad angel called Azazel, but there is no attempt at explaining how he comes about. This is the root of the problem of Theodicy, and like the Book of Job, there is no neat solution to why evil should occur.

As far as mankind is concerned, Enoch believes that we all started as innocent:

'For men were created exactly like the angels to the intent that they should continue pure and righteous, and death, which destroys everything, could not have taken hold of them...' Enoch 69:11.

In effect this is saying that no one need have died if we had all behaved ourselves. But there is more to it than that. The context here is an angel called Penemue who instructed men in the use of pen and ink and paper 'and thereby many sinned from eternity to eternity to this day'. So sin has something to do with learning, knowledge and written communication! How strange! Another angel, Gadreel, was the one who led Eve astray. We can see the drift of this line of thought; mankind was not to be blamed for disobeying God at the beginning; we were induced by fallen angels to go wrong. But in Enoch 98:4 we have the opposite thought:

'Even so, sin has not been sent upon the earth, but man of himself has created it...'

This appears to be a contradiction, but it need not be. It can be seen like this; historically and socially, mankind introduced sin; mythically and theologically, it was a spiritual failure coming from the other world of the spirit. Both are true in their own way; we can see in this a paradox.

For those who have sinned, there is condemnation and punishment. This will all happen on the day of judgement at the end of time. However, Enoch does allow for forgiveness:

'And all… shall rejoice, and there shall be forgiveness of sins, and every mercy and peace and forbearance; there shall be salvation unto them, a goodly light,' Enoch 5:6.

In case one were thinking that it would only be the pious Jews who would be saved, Enoch does display a certain amount of universalism:

'He shall be the light of the Gentiles[3], and the hope of all that are troubled of heart. All who dwell on earth shall fall down and worship before him and will praise and bless and celebrate the Lord of the Spirits,' Enoch 48:4.

Here he is talking about the Messiah. The book is not all about doom and damnation; here is a positive, optimistic view of the future in the Messianic kingdom. Now we know where St Luke found the phrase 'a light to lighten the Gentiles', as well as in Isaiah.

This brings us to consider the messianism in Enoch. The Messiah is usually called the 'Elect One' but also goes under various other titles, including the Son of Man and also 'My Son'. On judgement day, the Messiah will be asked to sit on the throne of glory and make rulings. He will dethrone kings and mighty men; echoes of St Luke again! The Messiah has been chosen by God, which explains the term 'elect one'; his dwelling place is 'under the wings' of God. He has been anointed, which implies the title 'Christ'. There is an ongoing theme of a secret that is with God and concerns the Messiah. There are secret books and tablets and they appear to conceal the reality of the Messiah; also, he will reveal all the secret treasures of God, on that crucial day. This ties in with the thought that Noah had to hide himself and also Enoch. Much play is made of secrecy and revelation at the right moment. This is a strand of thought worked with great effect in the Gospel of St Mark; the messianic secret. Enoch, it would seem, is given a preview of these secrets and of the day of judgement:

'… I saw all the secrets of the heavens,… and how the actions of men are weighed in the balance. And there I saw the mansions of the elect and the mansions of the holy…' Enoch 41:1.

The weighing of souls in the balance is not a new idea here; it is evidenced on the tomb walls of the Pharaohs; like the Egyptians, Enoch is a specialist in speculating about the afterlife. It is interesting that 'mansions' are stated as the homes of the righteous who are saved. This may help to explain why Jesus, in St John's gospel, says that 'in my Father's house are many mansions[4].' Here, it is just as cryptic as it is in Enoch. Jesus may have been saying, in a roundabout way, 'Why don't you go and read it up in

Enoch?' The word 'mansions' in the Greek is *monai,* which literally means, 'stopping places'.

But this brings us to an important aspect of Enoch: the resurrection. The word itself is not actually used, but in many places, the dead, who have been waiting in Sheol, are roused from their slumbers to face judgement day:

'And in those days, the earth shall give back that which has been entrusted to it, and Sheol shall give back that which it has received and hell shall give back that which it owes.' Enoch 51:1. This is Enoch's way of saying that those who died unfairly, under persecution, even though they were well behaved, will be compensated in the next world. This is his answer to the nagging question of 'why do the innocent have to suffer?' which is the sharpest end of Theodicy.

'And the righteous and elect shall be saved on that day... and the Lord of Spirits will abide over them, and with that Son of Man they shall eat... and the righteous and elect shall have risen from the earth and ceased to be of downcast countenance. And they shall have been clothed with garments of glory...' Enoch 62:13.

Here we see the idea of the messianic banquet 'with that Son of Man they shall eat': this is a theme again which appears in the Gospels, and explains why Jesus refused to eat anything at the Last Supper[5]. Also they have garments of glory; is this a possible explanation for that unfortunate man who was turned out of the feast because he did not have his best suit on (Matthew 22:11)[6]?

With regard to covenant theology, Enoch does not embark on this to any great extent. The only direct mention of a 'covenant' comes in 60:6, in which the righteous, on the day of judgement, will receive a covenant, but the sinners will receive an inquisition. Enoch does not go into detail about what this covenant consists of, or any details, which would make one wonder if he knows what covenant theology is. When it comes to the covenant of Noah, which is unavoidable in the context, he talks in terms of 'the oath', which is kept secret before the Flood[7]. This means that God has promised to keep the natural world going on continuously, even before the Flood. There is no mention of the rainbow or Noah's sacrifice, or any details about the ark. It is just possible that this book was intended for a Gentile readership, which might not have understood the Biblical assumptions about covenant.

The Book of Enoch stands out as typical of the eschatology of his times. It was a mental framework which was almost certainly stimulated by the Persian Zoroastrian thinking, worked its way into post-Exilic

Judaism and was a powerful assumption at the time of Jesus. The fact that Jesus assumed all this kind of material as normal thinking, underlines the fact that he was genuinely human. It would have taken a lot of mental effort to think himself out of this kind of thing. Nowadays, we think of eschatology in different terms; not so much to do with angels and demons, but in terms of the sun coming to the end of its life, Big Bangs, Black Holes and Quasars. One wonders where the truth really lies! But we too would have difficulties in thinking ourselves out of the astro-physical assumptions of our day and age.

Philosophy

Much of Enoch's philosophy has already been considered with his theology. But when considering the **truth** he also wishes to imply that his book is the TRUTH:

'The chief over the angels said, "Enoch, why dost thou ask? And why art thou eager for the truth?"' Enoch 21:6.

'And Michael said unto me, "Enoch, why dost thou ask me regarding the fragrance of the tree, and why dost thou wish to learn the truth?"' Enoch 25:1.

The implication in this is that this book contains the truth about heaven and earth and God. Put in simple terms, there is God, and fallen angels, and sinful mankind. But there are a few who are righteous. When it comes to the day of judgement, all will be put to rights; evil will be destroyed and good will be triumphant. This is leaving out all the decorations and elaborate phrasings. Enoch, in a way, represents all of humanity, in that we would all like to know the truth about God and peer into his eternity. We would all like to know what life is in aid of and where we are heading. The evolutionists can only offer an answer on a physical and social level. We all need to know the truth on a spiritual level, because most of us are aware that the universe is not just purely and simply a physical phenomenon. It has a spiritual basis to it and we would all like to have it explained to us by someone who does understand how it all works. This book is an attempt, using lavish mythological language, appealing to our deepest instincts, to show that the secrets of God for now are retained, but will be revealed at some time in the future. This will come with God's personal intervention with the coming of the Messiah. In common with many, if not all, scriptural writings, the truth is being sought, but there are many different ideas on what it actually consists of.

As Literature and Language

Since, as it is believed with good reason, that the Book of Enoch was originally written in Hebrew and Aramaic, we are only seeing it in translation. However the Greek does give a fair impression of how it was. Much of it comes in snatches of poetry, and the parallelisms are noteworthy, but not perhaps as accomplished as what we see in the Psalms or Isaiah;

> 'And there I saw another vision, the dwelling-places of the holy,
> And the resting places of the righteous.
> Here mine eyes saw their dwellings with his righteous angels,
> And their resting places with the holy.
> And they petitioned and interceded and prayed for the children of men,
> And righteousness flowed before them as water.
> And mercy like dew upon the earth,... .' Enoch 39:1-5.

Wonderful phrasing and sentiments! The eschatological vision of Enoch clearly builds on what we see in Daniel, but is not quite of the same stature or conviction. When we compare it with Revelation, there is no comparison; St John has produced a fantastic vision of the end of the world, and he has worked in the Messiah as having arrived and done his eternal task. In Enoch, the Messiah, although known about, has not yet actually set to work; he is still a secret in the heart of God. But much of the imagery used by St John can be seen as derived from Enoch.

A lovely simile combined with a metaphor, comes in 42:3:

> 'Wisdom returned to her place, and took her seat among the angels. And unrighteousness went forth from her chambers; whom she sought not she found, and dwelt with them, as rain in the desert and dew on a thirsty land.'

In common with many holy writings, Enoch indulges in a lot of repetition. The same idea comes round repeatedly, that the righteous will be saved and the wicked destroyed. There never seems to be any admission that one might be a mixture of good and evil; never any grey areas. Perhaps this is a symptom of the general policy of exaggeration in the book and in general in eschatology.

Most of the book can be taken on a figurative level, but perhaps not all. There is an interesting play on words, which only works if one assumes it was originally Hebrew. This occurs in Enoch 6:6:

'The angels *descended* in the days of **Jared** on the summit of Mount *Hermon*... .because they had **sworn** and bound themselves by mutual imprecations upon it.'

The root YARAD which means 'descend' is punned with Jared, the father of Enoch, and the root HRM which means 'curse' is punned with 'Hermon'. It is a double paranomasiae[8]. It is also in the tradition of Jeremiah who went in for puns. This confirms that this section was originally in Hebrew.

Concluding thoughts on Enoch

This kind of literature is at present out of fashion with modern thinking. Eschatology was for many peoples in the past, a major driving force and caused much fear of hellfire and damnation. What we need to remember is how literally we need to take all this kind of thing. If it really is the literal truth, where is heaven located, where are the pillars of the universe and where is hell? Physically, this is most misleading. Spiritually, the message of people like Enoch is highly relevant to every generation of believing souls. The eternal 'back-stop' is there and there is eternal justice waiting to correct all wrongs. To put it in demythologised phrasing, 'we all need to be aware that we are responsible for our deeds and will have to face up to the eternal judge somewhere in the future.' In other words, one's misbehaviour will catch up on one, even if one tries to pretend it will not. The other important factor is God's personal intervention in this world. In Enoch it is all wrapped up with images of angels, good or bad, and Azazel who is a Devil, and also of the expected Messiah. Taken completely literally, this can all be very frightening, but so often we have seen God's intervention in human affairs to be far more subtle and less judgemental than Enoch would have us believe. The reality of eternal justice is at the heart of it. This is the final substratum of the book, and others like it. We may see it against the backdrop of persecution, such as was experienced in the Maccabean age, but this is only an assumption. Persecution of the Jews, and indeed of anyone because of their religion, can happen at any time. This raises the question of why should a law-abaiding, god-fearing person have to be put to death in torment? Enoch has the answer; it will all be straightened out on the day of judgement. Eternal and everlasting justice is the key to the whole understanding of this book.

Footnotes for Chapter 20: The Book of Enoch

1. Luke 1:51-53.
2. This idea seems first to be mentioned in the Psalms; 56:8, 69:28, 139:16. It infers that God has all our deeds and fortunes recorded somewhere, so that he cannot be deceived.

The Apocalyptists developed this idea to be a factor on the day of judgement. This idea may have stemmed from Ancient Egypt as in The Egyptian Book of the Dead (Chapter 25).

3. It is quite possible that Luke (or Simeon) derived this phrase from Enoch. See Luke 2:32, and Isaiah 42:6.

4. John 14:2; **monai** means 'stopping places, resting places, even bed-and-breakfast'. We notice that the same idea comes in the Egyptian Book of the Dead (Chapter 25).

5. Matthew 26:29, Mark 14:25, and Luke 22:15 especially, where Jesus refused to eat the bread.

6. Matthew 22:11. This may indicate that Jesus knew the Book of Enoch.

7. Also, it may indicate that 'Enoch' was clever enough to avoid an anachronism; that the concept of covenant only came in with Noah, two generations later! This is in contrast to Joseph Smith!

8. Paronomasia; a pun, a play on words..

21

The Koran

This corpus of scripture is the basis of Islam, one of the three main monotheistic faiths in the world. The book is the collected visions of one Mohammed, who was born about 570 AD and died in 632 AD after an eventful life which saw the founding of Islam. In about 610 AD he began to have visions of the Angel Gabriel in a cave; the messages from God were written down and edited by his followers, there being very little time in which oral transmission could have been a factor. Muslims take this material as the word of God and the absolute truth. They also accept the Bible as scriptural, with certain reservations about the New Testament. In general though, the Koran is a reconnection with the faith of Abraham and Moses, but with a very strong apocalyptic framework. This was something that the early founders of Judaism did not have; it is thought to have gathered momentum with the Jewish involvement with Zoroastrianism. It is interesting to compare the Koran with Enoch and other what are considered as Post-Exilic eschatological works. There is much in common; even so, the Koran only refers to Enoch once, calling him Idris[1], and that in a context which is not eschatological.

It is unusual for the origins of a scriptural work to be so well authenticated and seen in a particular historical setting. Others of this background would be the Book of Mormon, *Mein Kampf* and the Epistles of St Paul. But all of these are markedly different. The background is Mecca in the seventh century, at a time when original Arabic pagan faiths were declining and monotheism, whether of the Jews or the Christians, was gathering acceptance quite rapidly. The book is written in Arabic and is still recited and learnt by heart by devout Muslims. The modern translation used here is the Pelican Classic version by N. J. Dawood of 1956 (several editions), which is a masterly attempt at rendering the Arabic in an idiom comprehendible for modern English without too much paraphrasing. Many who are not necessarily Muslims, regard this work as one of the world's great classics. If seen against the general background of apocalyptic literature, whether included in the Bible or on the periphery, it is far easier to understand what is going on here. We recall that there is the urgency of being prepared for the final judgement day, which could happen at any time; there is the exaggeration element seen in so much of the biblical material; there is the secrecy element; also the strong connection with man's primal origins as seen in the Garden of Eden. In contrast, however, the Koran does not indulge in endless speculation about the names and numbers of angels; mythology is present but not overdone. Neither is there the phoney mathematical calculation concerning the last day. In common with just about every scriptural corpus, the Koran attempts to cope with the problem of theodicy, not in any systematic or head-on-collision approach, but quite consistently.

One of the Koran's notable features is its repetitive style. The same basic statements about God and mankind appear on almost every page. This of course is nothing new with regard to sacral writing; it is clearly a method used to emphasise certain important matters. Mohammed was, and still is, dubbed the 'Last Prophet', although usually in the Koran he is entitled the 'Apostle'. As a prognosticator about the future, he is not noted as particularly fulsome. As an apocalyptist, with a simplified and direct message about the day of judgement, he is fully focussed and highly dogmatic.

Mathematical, Scientific, Geographic and Historical information

There is absolutely no mathematical or scientific information in the Koran. Even when talking about celestial bodies, there is never any attempt at figures or explanations. The only thing that could remotely come under this heading would be the mention of certain months of the year, such as Ramadan[2], but they are never located or calculated.

With regard to historical information, the Koran makes much mention of personalities in the Old and New Testament, as basic to the faith of Allah. Sometimes key events in the Old Testament are amplified and decorated. Most of the major characters in the Old Testament are mentioned in a sympathetic way, but the emphasis is placed firmly on Noah, Abraham and Moses. A good example of this would be with the Joseph sagas in the chapter entitled 'Joseph' (page 38). With regard to geography, there is much mention of Egypt, including Pharaohs, and many of the towns in Palestine, some of which are not readily recognisable in relation to the Bible. Two examples of this would be Aad and Thoud, which we take to be Sodom and

386

Gomorrah. In this way, the Koran has a firm historical and geographical basis in real earthly terms, which is a strong feature of Judaism and Christianity. This is in contrast to many eastern scriptures, which have the bare minimum of anchorage in earthly realities, if any at all. In addition to this, the Koran refers indirectly to important events in Mohammed's life; actual names and places are euphemistically mentioned. The Koran does not embark on a specific connected account of the prophet's life, but hints at significant events, such as battles with the Meccans. Occasionally real places are mentioned; an example of this would be Safa and Marwa, which were sacred mountains in the pagan Arab religion. The Koran says they are beacons of Allah, and the pilgrims can walk round them without feeling guilty; this is clearly an example of a pagan feature being adapted to work with the new faith of Islam. In general terms, however, the pattern of Mohammed's life does not really impinge on the central message of the Koran, which is essentially theological.

Theological message

The theology of the Koran is essential for an understanding of Islam, both in its nascent phase and in today's world. The central message, which is hammered home on almost every page, is neatly summed up in The Hordes, page 278:

> 'The trumpet shall be sounded and all who are in heaven and earth shall fall down fainting, except those that shall be spared by Allah. Then the trumpet will sound again and they shall rise and gaze around them. The earth will shine with the light of her Lord, and the Book will be laid open. The prophets and witnesses shall be brought in and all shall be judged with fairness; none shall be wronged. Every soul shall be paid back according to its deeds, for Allah knows of all their actions. In hordes the unbelievers shall be led to Hell... and they will stay there for ever. But those who fear their Lord shall be led in bands to Paradise... and dwell in it for ever.'

There will come a day of Resurrection when everyone, including those who are living and dead, both angels and humans, will be assembled; this is the great day of judgement, the hour of Doom, heralded by a blast on the trumpet. Souls will be weighed in the eternal scales of justice:

> 'Then he whose scales are heavy shall dwell in bliss; but he whose scales are light, the Abyss shall be his home... it is a scorching fire' (The Disaster, page 29).

387

Everyone will be sorted into three groups: those on the right will be the blessed, those on the left will be the damned, and those to the fore will be foremost and come near to Allah. The fate of the damned is truly horrific; their crime is essentially that of idolatry, which means in effect that they ignored Allah and went in for falsehood. Hell is a terrifying fire, where they will have to drink boiling water and eat the fruit of the Zaqqum[3] tree and there will be no relief from the scorching heat. As for the blessed, they will go to the Garden where everything is peace, beauty and bliss. Rivers run through it and one can recline on couches all day with beautiful virgins serving up delicious food and wine that does not render one intoxicated.

To avoid being consigned to hell, it is a simple matter of accepting the teachings of Islam. Those who do not, have damned themselves and it is their own fault if they descend into hell. However, there is time, in this life to repent:

'For those that do evil and later repent and have faith, they shall find your Lord forgiving and merciful' (The Heights, page 253).

Almost every chapter begins with the statement that Allah is compassionate and merciful. This means that there is hope for everyone, as long as they do not leave it too late.

The other side of the matter is that Allah knows every detail of one's life, both public and secret, and decides on one's destiny. Predestination is an ongoing strand in the Koran. This inevitably means that one does not arrive at hell or heaven by some sort of coincidence:

'Thus we put unbelief in the hearts of the evil-doers' (The Poets, page 204).

This may sound unfair, but the Koran stresses that Allah does not wrong people; they wrong themselves. This must indicate the element of free will, or choice. It would be fair to say that free will, though implied in many places, is not a particularly noticeable factor in the Koran. However, the concept of merit is very strongly emphasised, and this must, logically imply the freedom to choose the right path and do good deeds:

'Deeds of lasting merit shall earn you a better reward in his sight and a more auspicious end' (Mary, page 36).

This inevitably raises the issue of grace versus works-righteousness. It would seem that St Paul's detailed analysis of the dilemma does not have any influence here. If asked, Mohammed might well have said something to this effect; that those who have faith and do good works will be saved:

' I swear by the declining day that perdition shall be the lot of man, except for those who have faith and do good works, and exhort each other to justice and fortitude' (The Declining Day, page 27).

There is never any attempt at evaluating this phrase, which recurs very often in the Koran. Is it essentially faith that is the key to salvation, or is it good works? Mohammed would probably say that both are needed. He does not attempt to tease out the paradoxical element in this contradiction[4].

It is clear that Paradise is the counterpart of the Garden of Eden. The Koran takes the early Genesis chapters of Creation completely literally, as Muslims do today. It is assumed that at the very beginning of mankind, there was innocence. 'We moulded man into a most noble image'. Sadly, this went wrong; this was because of the 'mischief of the slinking prompter who whispers in the heart of men... ' Men (page 23). This is a demythologised version of the temptation in the Garden of Eden. The Koran is aware of the reality of devils who turn humans away from the right path, even if they think they are rightly guided themselves. There is much mention of Satan in the Koran. He was the one angel who refused to worship Allah and thus was in revolt against the truth. The equation between Satan and the serpent does not really surface much, but it was Satan in the Garden who instigated human perdition. The other side of this is that man's soul is prone to evil (page 42), with the proviso that Allah has mercy on some and saves them in spite of their human weaknesses. The purpose of creating mankind was to give him some sort of trial or testing. We must add to that the realisation that Allah actually puts unbelief into men's hearts. Thus we see there is a compound approach to Theodicy; partly it is a cosmic problem, with a fallen angel in the other world, but also it is a basic problem in human nature; also, Allah actually decides on who shall suffer and who shall not:

'We have made all things according to a fixed decree; we command but once; our will is done in the twinkling of an eye' (The Moon, page 112).

At the same time, everyone's deeds, actions and thoughts are noted down in the Book. This implies responsibility for one's sins; it will all be quoted on the day of judgement. There is much mention of the 'Tablets', or the 'sealed book', which are kept secret until the hour of doom. The secrecy element was noted in Enoch, and now comes to prominence in the Koran. In Revelation it is highly dramatised with angels opening up the seals. Only Allah has knowledge of what is hidden (page 65).

In case one is thinking that the slightest little fault will land one in hell, it is not quite as drastic as that. It seems that Allah does not worry too much about the trivial human failings; it is far more important to have the correct *belief* or *faith*. This raises the question of what will happen to the Jews and the Christians, for they are monotheists and in theory ought to be accepted by Allah. The Koran is in general sympathetic to these people, whom he terms 'the People of the Book,' but with reservations:

> 'If the People of the Book accept the true faith and keep from evil, we will pardon them their sins and admit them to the gardens of delight. If they observe the Torah (Laws of Moses) and the Gospel and what is revealed to them from Allah, they shall be given abundance from above and from beneath. Some of them are righteous men; but many of them do nothing but evil' (The Table, page 384).

Generally speaking, the Koran accepts that some Christians are acceptable; it does not go into details about exactly how or in what way they are acceptable. It is likely that it concerns faith and belief in God. The Koran is most categorical about the fate of the hypocrites; those who pretend to have faith and make bogus claims, but actually do not mean a word of it. They will face hell-fire along with the infidels. This strand of hypocrisy is to be noted in the gospels. In general terms, the Koran is accepting of the gospels, as being just a continuation of the faith of Noah, Abraham, and Moses.

This brings us to consider another important theological factor, that of covenant. The Bible is based on it; it is not possible to understand the Bible unless one takes into account the various covenants as described. The Koran often mentions the covenant in many contexts, but there is no attempt at explaining or describing it. There may be an assumption that it is all the same covenant throughout the Bible. The reality is that the various covenants in the Bible are different. To summarise briefly; the covenant of Noah[5] concerns all of creation with a promise that all people will be fed and cared for by God, regardless of their moral worth. The Koran would appear to disagree with this important theological element. It would seem that Allah only loves the righteous; he does not love the unbelievers, the proud or the treacherous. The opposite is seen in the gospels, where Jesus specifically makes friends with the sinners. In fact, the Love of God, which is a dominant theme in the Bible, is much reduced in the Koran. In fact the word love itself is rather scarce[6].

The covenant of Abraham[7] is more specific; it concerns one man and his wife and family, as the beginnings of the Hebrew nation. It is essentially a matter of Abraham trusting in God; there is very little that could be called a moral or ritual code. In that regard, the Koran is in agreement with those early chapters in Genesis; that the essential thing is belief rather than observing a massive list of rules and regulations. The Koran does not embark on endless lists of rules; there is a certain amount of it towards the end which will be discussed later. It would be fair to say that Mohammed wishes to reconnect with the faith of Abraham, and indeed the centre of gravity in the Koran lies heavily on the early theology of the Hebrews.

The covenant of Moses[8] rests on the Sinai event, and the escape from Egypt. This matter is also heavily emphasised in the Koran and taken very seriously. The covenant of Sinai was a conditional one; the essence of it was, and still is, that one receives what one merits. If one indulges in bad behaviour and disobedience to God, there is disaster awaiting; if one obeys God and follows the rules, all will go well. At that point, there is nothing on the subject of Heaven and Hell. The Pentateuch concerns itself entirely with the fate of the Israelite nation in this world, not the next. The Koran takes this motif and extends it to both worlds; things will go wrong in the this world and more importantly in the next world if one does not believe in Allah. If one is damned in the next world, there is no reprieve; there are even guards at the gates of hell, nineteen keepers[9], to prevent one from escaping one's eternal fate. We recall that the Bab had a group of nineteen apostles at the start of the Baha'i ministry. At this point, the Koran in a way agrees with the Mosaic covenant, for there is always the possibility of a change of heart, repentance and being forgiven by God. This is stressed in the closing chapters of Deuteronomy[10].

The covenant of David[11] concerns the kingship arrangement in ancient Israel, a factor which has reverberated down to present times, with the view that the head of state (king, president or prime minister) has a responsibility, personally to God, for the course of the nation. This covenant was also prophetic in the sense that it pointed forward to the coming of the Messiah, the king of Israel, who turned out to be Jesus of Nazareth, the ultimate king. This element does not figure in the Koran, even if David and Solomon are seen as faithful and amongst the redeemed. Furthermore, there is no trace of future Messianism in the Koran. This was a matter to be adjusted later with the belief in the coming of the Mahdi (as seen with the Baha'is), but it is not an element in the Koran.

However the Koran does look back on Jesus Christ and calls him the Messiah, the son of Mary, in what appears to be rather a sarcastic tone (Repentance, page 316).

'Unbelievers are those who declare, "Allah is the Messiah, the son of Mary."' (page 379).

Clearly the Koran has a problem with Jesus, even if he is a true apostle. The root of the problem lies in that metaphor used by the Christians, 'the only begotten Son of God' (see St John 1:14), and also the Chalcedonian definition. The Koran is quite emphatic that Allah cannot 'beget', by which it is taken to mean, produce a son by the normal means of procreation. There are many places where this matter is mentioned. One can understand

and sympathise with this view; after all, the early Christians were only trying to find a metaphor that would associate Jesus with God in a way that was above and totally different from any other prophet that had been experienced.

This is an example of how a metaphor which was reasonable at one time in history, becomes a problem for people in another setting. The background of this, which helps to explain the Muslim antipathy to Jesus as being seen as God, was that at Mecca, the pagan Arabic faiths had Allah begetting three daughters:

> 'Ask the unbelievers if it be true that Allah has daughters; while they themselves choose sons. Did we create the angels females... surely they lie when they declare, "Allah has begotten children."' (The Ranks, page 170).

In this we see that there is confusion over the pagan idea of 'god-production' and the Christian understanding of the Incarnation. It is also symptomatic of the tendency in the Koran to take everything completely literally. For the Christians, 'beget' was never taken as the literal truth; it was always metaphoric. Unfortunately this has been a bone of contention between Islam and Christianity right up to this day.

The covenant of Jesus, the New Covenant, which is never mentioned in the Koran, works on a different level as compared with the earlier ones. Jesus declares forgiveness, reconciliation and love for all of mankind, regardless of their quality or moral worth. The faith of the church and the love of God is extended to all people; the sin of the world, which is essentially separation from God, is taken away by his atoning death. It would be fair to say that the Koran does not understand this. In general terms, Islam is a reversion to the basics of Hebrew faith in the early years.

The Koran does not seem to have any difficulty with the virgin birth, or the ascension, or the miracles of Jesus. Mohammed actually says that he himself does not do miracles, and in fact makes no claim to be anything more than an 'apostle'. He would never claim to be the Messiah. However the crucifixion does raise a problem for him:

> 'They declared, "We have put to death the Messiah Jesus, the son of Mary, the apostle of Allah". They did not kill him, nor did they crucify him, but they thought they did' (Women, page 372).

Here we see a possible trace of Gnostic thinking, that Jesus only appeared to die on the cross, but the thought is not fully developed or explained.

In general terms, it would be instructive to sum up the Koran's view of covenant in these terms:

'Each soul is the hostage to his own deeds' (The Cloaked One, page 56).

With this we see an eternal truism; that one gets what one deserves. It is an important instinct in all of us; good behaviour deserves a reward and bad behaviour deserves a punishment. Sadly, life is not always as simple as that, as Job found out to his cost.

This brings us to consider the metaphor of the 'veil', which is a Biblical theme and also appears in the Koran. Continuing the theme that Allah causes people to disbelieve, it says:

'But we have cast veils over their hearts and made them hard of hearing lest they understand your words' (Cattle, page 416).

This is a somewhat mixed metaphor but the meaning of it is plain. A veil, which usually obscures one's vision, also blocks up one's ears and hardens one's heart. This is an interesting indirect admission that not everything in the Koran is to be taken totally literally. This was an issue seen in the Gospels and in St Paul's writings. In the Koran it is applied to men's failure to accept its teachings and disbelief in general. In the Bible it also has this meaning, but in addition, it means that access to God is obscured, just as Moses had to wear a veil when he had conversations with God. On that issue, the Koran actually says that we do not have direct access to God:

'The Merciful, with whom no one can speak' (The Tidings, page 53).

This serves to confirm the impression given in the book, that Allah is too distant, exalted and transcendent for mortals to converse with. This actually ignores what happened with Moses and other prophets who had direct conversations with God. In St Mark, it actually says that the veil of the Temple is rent in two, which is a metaphorical way of saying that all people can have personal access to God.

To sum up the theology of the Koran, it would be fair to say that Mohammed has a very strong impression of this world and the next, and that to get it right for the next world, one has to believe the correct teachings and follow a moral path. A good quotation would sum it up:

'Such are they (those who reject the prophets) who buy the life of this world at the price of the life to come' (The Cow, page 333). Very telling words!

Philosophy

Much of the Koran's philosophy is bound up with its theology. There is no doubt that this book claims to be the truth in many places:

'Men, the Apostle (Mohammed) has brought you the Truth from your Lord. Have faith and it shall be well with you' (Women, page 373).

This does raise the question of what to do about those who do not accept the Koran. We are told to bear patiently with unbelievers:

'Bear patiently with what they say (the infidels) and leave their company without recrimination. Leave to me (Allah) those that deny the truth...' (The Mantled One, page 59).

We are ordered not to use force; if the infidels are inclined to make peace or establish a treaty, then go along with that. Wait for them to break the truce. But there is also a case for violence:

'When the sacred months are over, slay the idolaters wherever you find them. Arrest them, besiege them and lie in ambush everywhere for them' (Repentance, page 313).

'Make war on them (the idolaters) until idolatry is no more and Allah's religion reigns supreme' (The Spoils, page 309).

So warfare is to be justified; not that one would start the contention, but if the other side starts it, one is justified in annihilating them. With this we see the determination not to compromise the values of Islam, just as the Jews at the time of Judas Maccabeus were determined to prevent any kind of accommodation to Greek values.

As far as moral values are concerned, the Koran has a certain amount to say but nothing like as much as came in afterwards. We can tell the book was written by a man because it is completely orientated to a man's point of view. Even so, men and women are able to enter Paradise; it says nothing about what luxuries the women will receive. So women have to be obedient to their husbands and are to receive a beating if they refuse. A man can have up to four wives, some of which could be slave girls. If a divorce becomes necessary, it has to be done fairly, with a proper financial settlement and the woman's future secured. Adultery merits a hundred lashes, not for the man but for the woman (page 209). Adulterers are to marry each other, in other words, they will get what they practised. There is a certain amount of advice on a woman's costume, but not on a man's. There is nothing said about wearing a burkha. When it comes to making a will, all members of the family, including the women, are to receive a portion of the estate. There is a whole list of prohibitions on the matter of consanguinity, though strangely, cousins are not forbidden to marry, as in Christianity.

There is a ban on drinking alcohol, gambling, usury, and the use of 'arrows'[12]. This we take to mean some sort of game of dice or coin tossing. Breaking an oath is a serious matter. Fasting in Ramadan is ordered, although if one is ill, or on a journey, the rules are relaxed. There is nothing said about drug taking. The general impression is that the Koran is more humane and considerate than what was probably going on in the pagan Arab world. This is a process that was probably seen in the age of Moses, when comparing his laws with that of pagan customs. A useful quotation probably sets the tone for the whole of the Koran's moral philosophy:

'A kind word with forgiveness is better than charity followed by insult. Allah is self-sufficient and indulgent' (The Cow, page 353).

Consistent with this is the Koran's philosophy on wealth and poverty. One of the main features of one's moral conduct is the giving of alms; this became one of the main tenets of Islam. It is stated that whatever kindnesses one shows, or help given to the poor, will be recompensed in the long run by Allah. One might say that this is some kind of proto-socialism, which ought in theory to produce a kind of Welfare State in an Islamic country.

There is a strong call for Unity in the Koran. It does not like schisms and sects. In theory, Islam should be all one opinion and united. This is an element of philosophy that has come to the fore in recent years; there is now a strong urge to bring about world unity, which is obviously coupled with the abolition of warfare.

The Koran's overview of human history is clearly that it all began in the ideal state of a wonderful garden (Eden), and will end with another beautiful garden (Paradise). The gardens stand like bookends, holding all of human history in between.

The Koran as literature

The whole book is in prose, and deliberately so:

'We have taught Mohammed no poetry, nor does it become him to be a poet... an eloquent Koran to admonish the living...' (Ya Sin, page 174).

The intention here is to make the message of the Koran more clear and direct than if it were in poetry. The feeling that the whole book is to be taken word for word literally pervades the whole text. Even so, there are passages that give a good turn of metaphoric language which can only be taken figuratively. There is a good hyperbole in The Cave, page 98:

'If the waters of the sea were ink with which to write the words of my Lord, the sea would surely be consumed before his words were finished, though we brought another sea to replenish it.'

'If all the trees in the earth were pens, and the sea, with seven more seas to replenish it, were ink, the writing of Allah's words could never be finished' (Luqman, page 187).

Another one on rather similar lines comes in The Imrams, page 404.

'As for those that… die unbelievers, no ransom shall be accepted from them; although it be as much gold as would fill the entire earth.'

There are also some quite unusual similes to be found.

'He that gives his wealth for the cause of Allah is like a grain of corn which brings forth seven ears, each bearing a hundred grains' (The Cow, page 353). This reminds us of the Parable of the Sower in the gospels.

'Such men are like rock covered with earth; a shower falls upon it and leaves it hard and bare.' (The Cow, page 353). Another one sounding like the Sower.

'This present life is like the golden robe with which the earth bedecks itself…' (Jonah, page 65).

'… Rivers of unpolluted water, and rivers of milk for ever fresh; rivers of delectable wine and rivers of clearest honey…' (Mohammed, page 122). This is a metaphoric description of Paradise.

Paradise is often described, not always in such lofty metaphor. This is a feature of the Koran, its repetitive style. In contrast to hell, the hour of doom and Paradise are referred to on almost every page. This is clearly a method of hammering home its message, emphasising the core of the teachings of Islam. Much emphasis is laid on the Koran not being merely an invention of Mohammed. It is termed the Glorious Book, not so much because of its literary worth, but very much because of its theological message, which is a guide and joyful news to true believers.

The original language, Arabic, shows through in a few places. The intention was to write it all in Arabic:

'We have revealed the Koran in the Arabic tongue that you may grasp its meaning. It is a transcript of our Eternal Book, sublime and full of Wisdom' (Ornaments of God, page 146).

The eternal tablets, or books that are only known to Allah, are now produced for mankind to read. The Koran is taken to be the actual words of God by the Muslims. In addition to this there are two books, which are carefully kept records of the good and the bad, that will be produced on judgement day. There is Sidjeen, which has all the names of the sinners, and also Illiyun, which has all the names of the righteous, only to be seen by Allah and his closest confederates (The Unjust, page 49).

This ties in with the thought that Islam, and its prophet, were specifically aimed at the Arab peoples:

'There has now come to you an apostle of your own... ' (Repentance, page 325).

One might infer from that that Islam is only relevant to the Arab peoples; even so, Islam has had a policy of converting all kinds and conditions of mankind and has become a dominant factor in many non-Arabic countries.

Just occasionally the Arabic raises an interesting linguistic teaser. In The Cow, (page 335), two Arabic words are quoted as a play on words juxtaposed with Hebrew.

'Do not say to our apostle Ra'ina, but say Undburna. In Arabic, Ra'ina means 'listen to us' and Undburna means 'look upon us'. But in Hebrew 'Ra'ina' means 'Our evil one'. The expression was used as a derisive pun.

Another Arabic survivor is the Qiblah, in the Cow,(page 338), which means the place towards which one turns to say one's prayers. At the start, Muslims had to face Jerusalem but this was later changed to Mecca. So for many people in Western Europe it would be just about the same direction. We notice that the Baha'is have taken Haifa as their Qiblih.

In Ta Ha (page 225), we have the strange word Samiri. It was the situation over the golden calf when Aaron blundered while Moses was up the mountain. The people took their jewellery and threw it into the fire to melt it down. The Samiri did the same. But no one knows who they were; they are not mentioned in the account in Exodus. Just occasionally we have an obscurity like this, as does occur in the Bible.

In general terms, from the literary point of view, the repetitious nature of the book takes up rather a lot of space; much more could have been made of the imaginative turn of figurative language which occasionally surfaces.

Mythology in the Koran

In general terms the cosmology of Islam is the same as for all peoples in the Ancient World, and often reflects the residual assumptions of the pagan Arabs. It was seen as a three-tiered universe: heaven, earth and hell. There is not much embroidery on this concept; the exception being that there are seven heavens, and seven earths, and there are seven gates, which are guarded by the keepers of hell. Hell is termed 'the Abyss', which betrays a Greek influence. The pillars of the world are mentioned in passing. There is a Zaqqum tree growing in hell. Hell is a very hot place; there is fire and molten brass, but also, paradoxically, hot water. Paradise, by contrast, has cooling streams and there is no fire. We can see the implication in this: fire and water are the two main modes for cleansing, found in virtually every world mythology. If one were to be cleansed or refined by fire or water, one would be prepared for God's forgiveness. The difference there, is that the Koran does not allow of one to be reformed enough to escape from Hell; one is doomed eternally. With regard to the connection between earth and Heaven, in this mythology very little is said about trees. However, there is a reference to ladders;

'Allah is the Lord of the Ladders, by which the angels and the Spirit will ascend to him in one day; a day whose space is fifty thousand years' (The Ladders, page 57).

This indicates the way in which souls ascend to God. The Spirit, as quoted here, refers to Jesus, which means that the Ascension is taken seriously in the Koran. Strangely the Resurrection of Jesus is never mentioned, but then the Koran does not think that Jesus was actually killed.

Concluding remarks about the Koran

There are two crucial issues involved here. Firstly, the question must arise as to how literally we must take the Koran. It is a fair comment to say that the many references to hell and damnation are deeply frightening, and for many people this will persuade them that this book is not the truth. The question arises, if God is compassionate and merciful, how can he consign anyone to hell on a permanent basis? We noted that with all the other eschatological works considered, that there is a heavy degree of exaggeration which is intended to arrest people's attention and induce them to make a decision; also to see that the work of God and Christ are not purely and simply a local and earthbound matter; it has cosmic consequences. This would surely be true for the Koran. But what is the book actually saying, apart from trying to stir people into accepting the religion of Islam? It is saying that the clash between good and evil is going on between peoples of different qualities in this life; but also it is a cosmic problem. The final answer is that God will intervene and the contest between good and evil will be brought to a conclusion in dramatic terms. The state of innocence, which characterised the beginnings of humanity, will return with another Eden, but in the skies, and not subject to failure or wickedness. Thus we may tentatively demythologise the apocalyptic material, the Koran included.

How do we know we can demythologise it? The Koran makes its own admission that it can be done. Consider this remark:

'It is he who has made the night a mantle for you and sleep a rest. He makes each day a resurrection' (Al-Furqan, page 208).

This is a poetic way of saying that from day to day we have to 'die' but be raised again each morning. Resurrection is something that happens every day as a part of our normal routine. If we apply this to the general picture of the Koran, which mentions either directly or indirectly the Resurrection of all people, both living and dead, it means, or implies that God's judgement is upon us from day to day. It is a thing called guilt for the wrong we do; there is condemnation. Sometimes it is us ourselves who feel guilty; sometimes other people point it out to us. There is such a thing as repentance, which is important for us all, for a soul twisted with unrelieved guilt is in torture. The problem is that guilt can be ongoing and even permanent; this is seen in the Koran. The New Testament, however, tells us that there is everlasting forgiveness, which is provided by the work of the Messiah.

This brings us to the second issue with the Koran: the Messiah. The Koran is somewhat ambivalent about the Messiah, even if it knows that the Messiah is a necessary feature of the world of faith. If the Christians had not used the metaphor of 'begetting' in attempting to explain the relationship between God the Father and God the Son, there might never have been a problem. The Muslims and the Christians could have been one and the same thing. But metaphors, rightly or wrongly, can cause all sorts of differences of opinion in the household of faith. The result has been that Islam, via the Koran, has without doubt connected itself to the faith of Abraham and the early patriarchs, including Moses. The centre of gravity is clearly on that era in theological understanding, even if New Testament people and images are quoted. In that sense, it is the Old Testament restated forcefully, but with no understanding or development into the New Testament. The same could fairly be said about the Book of Mormon and the teachings of the Jehovah's Witnesses, not to mention a few others. If that were the sum total of faith, namely the Old Testament, that would be fair enough; but it would leave us with an incomplete religion, despite the fact that the apocalyptic element is heavily emphasised. The essential issue with the New Testament, is that we are forgiven right from the start, regardless of anyone's moral worth; this is effected by the coming of God's Messiah, God in person into this fallen world, to bring about a new relationship of trust and love between God and his creation. On this basis, the apocalyptists are right to use grand exaggeration and high-flown metaphor; the work of redemption is not just like playing tiddly-winks; it is salvation worked out against the background of the entire cosmos. Thus the humble carpenter from Nazareth comes out as a magnificent super-hero, defeating sin and death, and drawing us all into the presence of the Almighty Father.

Footnotes for Chapter 21: The Koran

1. Idris, equals ENOCH (see chapter 20)
2. Ramadan: A month that occurs at different times in the year because it is governed by lunar movements.
3. Zaqqum tree: A kind of tree that grows in Southern Arabia; it has very bitter fruit, nasty to the taste. This tree has acquired mythical overtones, and is seen as growing in Hell and reaching up to ground level.
4. The paradox of faith and works. St Paul in Romans explains the importance of salvation by faith, with good works following on from that.
5. The covenant of Noah: Genesis 9:8.
6. The Love of God is central to the covenant theology of the Bible.
7. The covenant of Abraham: Genesis 12 and following.
8. The covenant of Moses: Deuteronomy 7:9.
9. The 19 keepers to stop people from escaping from Hell. This is reflected in the 19 original Babis, as seen in chapter 16.
10. Deuteronomy 30ff.
11. The covenant of David: 2 Samuel 23:5.
12. 'Arrows': a method of divination

22

The Ramayana

Valmiki

This intriguing corpus of literature from ancient Hindu tradition is ascribed to someone called Valmiki. It was written in Sanskrit in the years approximately 700 to 500 BC, which makes it roughly contemporaneous to 1 and 2 Kings and the great prophets of Israel. Whether there is any knowledge the one of the other, is hard to say; evidence of such a thing is more or less non-existent. Even so, the Ramayana does raise the same sort of theological and philosophical questions. The answers, if they can be found, are somewhat different, but not entirely. The difference chiefly lies in the approach taken. Valmiki's account of Rama and Sita is couched in the medium of sustained epic; it is a romantic tale of two lovers, a prince and a princess, who encounter all kinds of difficulties but in the end win through and are justified. To find literature of similar method and genre, one has to consider the *Iliad* and the *Odyssey* from Homer, possibly also the Norse mythological tales. Otherwise, this work and the Mahabharata, another Hindu epic of the same type are really beyond comparison in world literature.

The version used here is the recent translation, by Arshia Sattar, (1996) published by Penguin Classics. This is a masterpiece of translation; it is not easy to translate ancient Sanskrit into modern English; Sattar has made a considerable achievement by making paraphrasing and colloquialisms where appropriate but otherwise retaining the essence of the text. The initial difficulty lay in deciding what was actually authentic material as opposed to spurious. The edition is not over-critical, but there are elements which circulate in Indian folklore which have been rejected as not being original.

The result of Sattar's painstaking work has been a connected, dramatic story which is highly readable, and can be seen as every bit as exciting as some of the hyped-up sci-fi material which is in circulation today.

It is not easy to compare a work such as the Ramayana with the sacred literature of other cultures. There is a certain assumption at the back of it, which is consistent with Hindu thinking, that this world is not actually real. Everything is some sort of illusion; the real world is up in the skies with the gods. This would doubtless please people like Mary Baker Eddy. But on that basis, it is difficult to evaluate a work like the Ramayana when we have material like the Koran, the Bible, and the Chinese scriptures, which are intended to be taken very largely as literal and real. Even so, the same nagging questions at the back of every human being's mind are in evidence no matter what sacred literature is evaluated. Where do we come from, what is life all about, and why do we have to suffer?

Mathematic and Scientific aspects

There is absolutely no attempt at any mathematical calculation in the Ramayana. The exception to this is the mention of distances, measured in *yojanas,* which approximate to about nine miles; but when this is used, it is normally in some sort of massive exaggeration of distance, and not meant to be taken literally. There is no attempt at any kind of dating; the story is not anchored in actual historical events, even if the idea was originally derived from a real historical situation. There is frequent use of numbers with esoteric loading, such as seven, but this is never meant as a mathematical reality; it is all part of the hint of eternity and a perfect universe. The impression given is that the story is an eternal one, which is meant to teach us lessons about life and death. In addition there is nothing scientific in the Ramayana; even if the monkeys are told to go and fetch medicinal herbs to heal the wounded princes, the way it is dramatised rules out any kind of literal acceptance. The fact is that the Ramayana is working on an altogether different level from the realities of this world.

Geographical realities

Here we see rather more of reality. The story begins with the town of Ayodhya, which is the perfect Utopia, and a wonderful king in charge. There is frequent mention of the Himalayas, the Ganges and other rivers, various mountains such as Kailasa, but, most importantly, the island of Lanka, which has been known as Ceylon but is now Sri Lanka. With this start for the story, the rest of the place names become increasingly imaginary and probably deliberately so. We float off from earthly realities into mythical and heroic epic tales. It is the human situation magnified and writ large against the entire cosmos. In a way, this is the same method seen in Revelation.

Historical realities

If there are any residual historical realities in the Ramayana, they are well hidden and of no real relevance to the story. It is a gripping tale of epic proportions but in no way is it even intended to be an accurate account of historical events, such as we see in the books of the Kings. The tale can be briefly summarised as follows:

The king of Ayodhya, Dasaratha, had four sons: Rama, the eldest and most accomplished in virtually every field and the obvious choice for the next king; Laksmana, his half-brother who was devoted to him; and Satrughna; and Bharata, whose mother had extorted a promise from king Dasaratha. When it came to appointing a new king, Rama found that Bharata's mother had managed to wangle the succession in favour of her son. Rama, Sita (his wife), and Laksmana went off into the forest to live the ascetic life and leave Bharata to take on the kingdom. He did not actually want to, but Rama gave him permission to be his regent while he was away for fourteen years[1].

While they were living in the forest, Rama fought and killed a whole collection of *raksasas* (malevolent beings, semi-divine, evil spirits), including Surpanakha. The King of the demons, Ravana, was outraged and enlisted Marica to help him take revenge. Marica lured the princes away and Ravana came and abducted Sita away to Lanka. Torn with grief, Rama wandered until he met Hanuman, the monkey (god) who introduced him to Sugriva, who should have been the king of the monkeys except that a usurper, Vali, had taken his kingdom. Rama killed Vali and restored Sugriva as the king of the monkeys. This way, the monkey-tribes were enlisted to help Rama recover his wife.

The monkeys went out all over India seeking Sita. Hanuman found out where Sita was, went to the seaboard and leapt over on to Lanka. He found Sita, reassured her that rescue was coming, caused mayhem in the city and returned to Rama with the information. The monkey army, with bears too, converged on the seaboard. The monkeys built a bridge over the straights and the army poured across to the island. Ravana was advised several times to concede and hand Sita back, but being obstinate he refused. There was an almighty battle of apocalyptic proportions and Ravana was killed. Sita was restored to her husband, and all the monkeys that had been killed came back to life.

The story concludes with Rama and Sita being restored to their kingdom; in other words, they start with Utopia and regain Utopia at the end. This is a pattern seen in the Bible, but expressed in rather different terms. The Garden of Eden is one man and his wife; the kingdom of Ayodha is a king and queen and a whole horde of contented subjects. This is the same image but in different terms. The basic story comes round at least three times, which is a way of emphasising the outlines of it. By the end, we have Rama's twin sons, who are brilliant vocalists, chanting the Ramayana and enchanting all the hearers.

The Ramayana is very lengthy and I have chosen to concentrate on the closing chapters, from chapter five of the section called Beauty, and into War with its 14 chapters, plus the Epilogue.

Ravana is using every means of persuasion to cajole Sita into submitting to him. She is constantly pressurised into forgetting all about Rama, but she refuses. Part of her argument is that a mortal, such as herself, cannot marry a raksasa. Meanwhile, Hanuman is hiding in a tree by the asoka grove[2], listening to all this. But there was one raksasa called Trijata, who was not happy with this situation; she had had a dream in which Ravana was destroyed. At this point, we have a précis of the story, yet again. She advises them to come to terms with Rama and ask for forgiveness. Just as Sita was on the verge of suicide, Hanuman is considering what to do; Sita notices Hanuman perching in a tree and they begin to talk. After reassuring herself that this was a real monkey as opposed to an appearance of Ravana, she was so heartened. Hanuman tells that Rama and his army are on their way and deliverance is imminent. Sita refuses the offer to jump on Hanuman's back and leap over to the mainland; she wants the final showdown with Ravana. Before setting off again, Hanuman decides to wreck the palace on Lanka; this makes Ravana rage with anger. He sends champion after champion to try to kill Hanuman, all to no avail. In the end Hanuman allows himself to be taken prisoner on purpose so that he could confront Ravana; he takes the opportunity to advise Ravana to return Sita, whereupon Ravana flies into a rage and orders the monkey to be killed. However, Vibhisana, the crown prince, could see that this was unethical, and points out that a messenger should never be killed. So instead, they set fire to Hanuman's tail. He breaks his bonds and goes all over the city setting fire to it, then plunges his tail into the ocean. After reassuring himself that Sita is safe, Hanuman leaps over the ocean and reports all that has happened, including the fact that Sita is still alive and faithful to her husband. The stage is now set for the invasion and the rescue of Sita.

As the army approaches the straights, the question arises as to how the monkeys will cross over. Hanuman assures them that a bridge will be built; and indeed it is built.

Meanwhile the raksasas in Lanka are giving Ravana dutch courage.

Vibhisana however, is a little more inclined to caution; his advice is to hand Sita back and come to terms. But Ravana rejects this wise counsel. This results in Vibhisana going over to the other side; he approaches Rama and offers to be his ally. This is greeted with some suspicion at first but soon they decide to trust him, giving him the promise of the kingdom of Lanka when Ravana is dispatched. As the army arrives on the island, two monkey spies are sent to work out the strength of Rama's army; but Vibhisana realises who they are, Suka and Sarana, and they are sent back with the repeated advice for Ravana to give up, but he refuses in a rage. His next ploy is to enlist a magician called Vidyujjivha to simulate Rama's death, and so destroy Sita's confidence. But Sarana reassures her that Rama has arrived and the battle is about to commence. Sarana pays a secret visit to Rama's council and finds out his strategy. There is yet another attempt at persuading Ravana to come to terms, this time by Malyavan, a wise lady, but Ravana was even more obstinate. Then the battle begins[3].

The siege of Lanka begins, with Rama and Laksmana opposing Ravana at the north gate. The monkeys and the raksasas lock in battle, going on all day and into the night. It escalates with the appearance of Indrajit, Ravana's terrifying son; he can operate invisibly, firing arrows that turn into snakes, and wounding Rama and Laksmana. The brothers are bound together and fall on the ground, but still only just alive. The raksasas think they are dead; this idea was given to Ravana who is delighted with Indrajit. Sita is taken to the battlefield to view the 'dead' brothers, but Trijata reassures her. After she has gone, the two brothers regain consciousness; the king of the birds, Garuda, heals them and redoubles their strength. Soon the battle recommences with a champion called Dhumraksa rallying the raksasas, but Hanuman kills him. Another champion, Akampana emerges, but he too is killed by Hanuman. Then a third champion, Prahasta, appears, but is also killed by Nila. Ravana then decides to join the fray; he fells Nila and then turns on Laksmana, wounding him. It is Rama and Hanuman who then attack Ravana, but they allow him to escape back to Lanka.

Ravana, now desperate, decides to enlist the help of the giant Kumbhakarna; it takes a supreme effort to wake him up, but eventually he comes on to the battlefield, terrifying the monkeys, wounding Hanuman and capturing Sugriva. In the end it is a mighty arrow from Rama that splits the giant's head and fells him. Ravana is thoroughly dispirited by the loss of his brother.

Then another all-out battle begins. Another son of Ravana, Narantaka, joins the fray, but he too is cut down by Angada, and three more of them attack Angada, all to no avail. Then Antikaya, another brother, tries his luck but he is felled by Laksmana. Now it is Indrajit's turn, using the same trick as before, that of making himself invisible. But Rama and Laksmana pretend to be killed and collapse, wounded. Hanuman is sent off to the herb mountain, Himavat, to bring back medicines, which he does; the two princes and the monkeys are restored to health and vitality. During that night, the monkeys do another raid on Lanka, setting fire to the city. Ravana is infuriated and sends for Kumbha and Nikumbha his nephews to lead another battle which turns out to be even more frightful. But the giant's sons are killed as well. Then Ravana sends out Makaraksa to try and kill Rama and Laksmana, but Rama shoots them both with his terrible arrows. Then Indrajit decides to try again; this 'dirty-tricks' merchant decides to conjure up Sita sitting in his chariot, and then kill her with Rama watching. This demoralises the monkey army and Rama too; but Vibhisana, who knows the tricks involved, revives their spirits by saying it is all an illusion. He advises Laksmana to go to the temple where Indrajit is sacrificing, and attack him before he can finish the ceremony. After an epic struggle lasting hours, Laksmana manages to sever Indrajit's head with an arrow; once again Laksmana's wounds are healed by herbs. Ravana is enraged again, all ten of his heads; he decides to join the fray himself despite many portents of defeat. Then a personal encounter between Rama and Ravana take place. Laksmana receives a spear wound in his chest, but is not killed. Rama is infuriated. Once again Laksmana is revived with herbs from the herb mountain. The gods give Rama a special chariot to counter Ravana and the battle begins again. After a massive duel, Rama manages to sever Ravana's head with an arrow; but another one grows, and another and another. At last, Rama takes out a special arrow and shoots the monster in the chest, killing him. That finishes the opposition; the war was over; evil is defeated. Vibhisana is able to receive his kingdom in Lanka.

Hanuman then goes to Sita and announces the victory. Sita is brought back to Rama; but there is a problem. Rama is suspicious that Sita may have been compromised in Ravana's house. The only way to settle the matter is with a trial by ordeal; a fire is built and Sita steps into it. In the nick of time, an assortment of gods, including Brahma, come to the rescue and Sita is saved. It is then that Rama is told that he is a god, not just any old god, but the lord of the worlds, an avatar of Vishnu, and just about everything else. The whole purpose of his incarnation is to defeat Ravana. So now he can return to heaven. The family is reconciled. Rama still has to sort things out with Bharata who is still holding the regency, but that is quickly resolved as they return to Ayodhya.

Hanuman goes on ahead to tell Bharata the news and he is overjoyed. Then commences another recapitulation of the epic. Bharata hands back the kingdom to Rama; there is a coronation and Laksmana is given the title of regent. Everything in his kingdom is just perfect.

The epilogue brings in a sad note to conclude the epic. Sita is now known to be pregnant. But there is a shadow over the whole thing; common gossip in the town is saying that Sita must have given in to Ravana. Rama feels he has to take this seriously; he takes advice from the princes and decides to banish Sita from the kingdom, to go and live with the sages in the forest. Laksmana takes her and leaves her with Valmiki (the author of the story) and he takes her in. Six months later, Sita gives birth to twin boys, Lava and Kusa.

Rama decides to do a horse sacrifice[4]. He always takes a golden statue of Sita with him everywhere he goes. During the sacrifice, Valmiki appears, with the two boys who sing beautifully the epic of the Ramayana. It enchants everyone and eventually Rama discovers that these two boys are his sons, by Sita. Rama wishes to clear Sita of any accusation; she appears briefly on a throne but disappears again into the earth. For many years Rama rules wisely and the kingdom is fine; eventually the time comes for Rama to 'die' and go back to heaven. Also a sage appears and tells them that Laksmana will have to die, killed by Rama. Instead, Laksmana goes off to the Sarayu River and is assumed into heaven, to become once more one quarter of Vishnu. Knowing that he is about to die, Rama anoints his two sons as kings. Next day, Rama goes forth in a massive procession to the Sarayu River[5] and is met by Brahma. He is assumed into heaven; many of his followers are also assumed, but into a realm called Santanika, which is just a little less that Brahma's heaven. And so the story ends.

So the whole purpose of Rama coming as an avatar of Vishnu was to defeat the evil influences that were tormenting people on earth and then eventually return to heaven, bringing with him all kinds of animals, subjects of his realm and sages too. It is a powerful story, full of romance, excitement and tension. The only matter that spoils it is that Sita and Rama are not fully and finally reunited and content with each other. In that sense, it ends on a note of sadness.

The human race is hardly ever involved in the story, only indirectly. The main thrust of it concerns avatars such as Rama and Laksmana, powerful spiritual realities from heaven and also the animal kingdom, chiefly the monkeys and bears who are understood to be the children of gods.

Literary factors

The Ramayana is first and foremost a superb work of literary worth. It has hardly anything to do with actual human history; it is all about gods intervening in the problems of this world. One of the most noteworthy factors is that Rama, for nearly all the story, does not realise that he is an avatar of Vishnu; this is a superb piece of sustained irony. On a second reading, all kinds of factors make additional sense: his superb righteousness, his kindness to the animals, his skills in just about everything, and his good looks. It requires the gods, after the battle is won, to tell him of his true status, something which Ravana had suspected but did not wish to accept.

Another feature is the rising climax in the entire story, as it proceeds inevitably from the Utopia of Rama's father's kingdom, with the evil influences at work in the world. Little by little, the tension mounts as Rama defeats one after another, and the chief of the demons, Ravana becomes increasingly annoyed. The escalation in tension comes to a head as the monkey army arrives on the seashore and builds a bridge over to Lanka. Then we have the final battles, as magical weaponry becomes increasingly devastating, up to the final killing of Ravana. Here the story reaches its climax as Sita and Rama are reunited. But what happens then? Here we have a massive anticlimax as Rama feels suspicious about Sita's integrity; although she is proved innocent, nagging doubts still spoil the situation, and in the end, she has to go and live the life of a hermit with Valmiki. So the climax is there, but somehow it is not quite all that it should have been. Even the end of his life and the assumption[6] into heaven does not mention Rama being reunited with his wife. It is smashing victory tempered with a little sadness, a superb use of climax and anticlimax.

It would seem that the Ramayana was originally (in Sanskrit) framed in poetry, which explains why the twins could chant it with their superb voices. However, Sattar has rendered it in prose. This has not destroyed the poetic nature of the work – there are many passages that could be termed 'super-prose' – and the poetic original clearly shines out and lifts us up to flights of imagination not usually found in normal prose. Here is just one such passage, full of beauty:

'The ocean had submarine mountain ranges and its unplumbed depths were as dangerous as the realm of the *asuras*[7]. The waves rose and fell with the wind, filled with the fish and serpents that lived in the waters. Drops of water gleamed like sparks from a fire. The waters were like the sky and the sky like the waters. You could not tell the one from the other. Sky and water mingled, the only difference being that one was filled with stars, the other with precious gems. Waves filled the sea as clouds fill the sky and waves crashed against each other, making a noise like drums on a battlefield. The monkeys watched in wonder as the waters were tossed by the wind and seemed to fill the sky' (page 517).

This passage captures exactly the fascination one feels when watching the sea in all its moods. This passage is one of the more restrained ones; there is not much of hyperbole here, but the use of simile and metaphor are superb.

This brings us to the use of exaggeration in the Ramayana. Of all others, the most prominent feature in the work is the use of hyperbole. Everything is overstated; it lifts us from the banality of normal life and reminds us of the beauty of heaven. Figures are elasticated and so Rama rules over his kingdom for ten thousand years! There are literally millions of monkeys in the army, with the bears in addition. The raksasas of Lanka seem to be an endless stream of evil spirits and Ravana's heads, which are supposed to be only ten, go on regrowing up to a hundred; in addition to this he has twenty arms; one wonders how his shoulders would have coped with such an encumbrance! The distance from the coast to Lanka can only be about fifty miles and yet Hanuman claims he can leap ten thousand *yojanas* (90,000 miles) across the straights. Hanuman can open his mouth to ten *yojanas*, and then to twenty and then to thirty and eventually to 100 (900 miles!). The monkeys have huge bodies the size of mountains; Hanuman is capable of carving the peak off a mountain and hurling it at his enemies. There are endless amounts of jewels – gold and silver in the palaces – and princes hand out gifts without much limit. The weaponry is always some sort of gift from a god and is therefore magical. Arrows never seem to miss their target; spears always do their work. All this assures us that we are not dealing with banality here; we are on an eternal level with spiritual powers that mankind is aware of, but is not in possession of.

There must also be a certain degree of humour in the story; at least from the western point of view. We always see monkeys as comical characters, and this may be partly true in India. But we must recall that the monkey-god, Hanuman, is also the god of the wind and is to be taken seriously. One must smile, however, as the monkey army reaches the seaboard and is in need of food. Dadimukha, Sugriva's uncle, gives them leave to search for food in his grove. They leap and babble and giggle, since they were drunk, and make a huge commotion. In their frantic efforts to find food, they rip the place apart. This can only be seen as a comical interlude. The elephants are enjoying themselves; they decide to trumpet in time with the peacock's calls! Sugriva, the king of the monkeys, is too busy making love to Tara that he fails to listen to Laksmana's request.

A joke, which concerns a king who only pursues pleasure and neglects his duties, 'is like a man who goes to sleep in a tree and wakes only when he has fallen out of it.' The hint here is that he will lose his kingdom if he does not apply himself to the important issues.

Another element is the mirror-image factor. We notice that Ravana's palace and gardens are just as beautiful and dazzling as the palaces of the righteous kings. This would seem rather strange since Ravana is such a villainous character; however, the implication in it is that both Rama and Ravana are in some way favoured by the gods. Good versus evil is paradoxically a balancing act between one power and another, but the whole matter is watched over and nudged into correctitude by one god or another. If Ravana is an inversion of the righteous king, with the normal world as a sort of battleground or boxing ring, then the whole story is just that; the question of right prevailing over wrong.

Related to this is the element of rightful claims running through brotherly love. Rama's first call on his father's kingdom is set aside and Bharata, reluctantly takes on the task as regent. The monkey kingdom has a similar situation: Vali has taken the kingdom away from his brother, and Sugriva, dispossessed, is reinstated by Rama. The same happens with Ravana and his brother Kiskindha; he actually turns against his brother for being so obstinate and joins the enemy. At the end of the war, when Ravana is killed, Kiskindha is installed as the new king of Lanka, now an ally of Rama. Of course, the other brotherly situation is between Rama and Laksmana. Though being half-brothers, they are devoted to each other. It never occurs to Laksmana to mount a claim on the throne, and when it becomes apparent that his death is necessary to ensure Rama's future, he does not hesitate to comply, faithful to the end.

The first and last chapters of the Ramayana are claimed to be additional to Valmiki's original text; even so, the whole scheme makes a gripping tale full of theology and Hindu philosophy.

Theology and Philosophy in the Ramayana

As with many sacred texts, it would be artificial to attempt to separate theology and philosophy overmuch. The Ramayana is not specifically a theological doctrinal text; however, Hindu theology is assumed at almost every moment. It is very different from the monotheism of the West, but even so, the same basic drives in human nature are to be found with answers supplied in mythological and metaphorical terms. Brahma is the original of the gods, the grandfather, and then there are hordes of gods that are different aspects of him. It is important to understand the concept of *avatar*[8] in the Ramayana. Rama is the avatar of Vishnu, one of the Hindu trinity, even though he does not realise it until they tell him at the end. Most of the story concerns Rama as a human prince; that having been said, he has all kinds of spiritual and mystical gifts and is thoroughly righteous. He never seems to do anything wrong or wicked; even when he displays suspicion about Sita's purity, and it appears to be cruel, it is for a very good reason. He is justified in this action when the gods swoop down from heaven to save Sita from being burned in the fire of the ordeal.

Hanuman, the monkey god, also behaves like an animal. We need to realise that the boundary between human, animal and god is not at all clear or well defined. They can change appearance at will in order to deceive people. Ravana, who is a wicked character, can change his appearance, and so can many of the raksasas. In addition to this, there are all kinds of spirits, whether good or evil, or something in between. Yaksas, danavas, gandharvas, siddhas, caranas, kinnaras and asuras, all of these are spiritual influences, which in the West might be called devils, imps or goblins. The whole epic is the interplay between these entities, which are hard to define.

An important theological statement about them comes as thus (page 541):

> 'Brahma created only two ways of life, *dharma*[9] for the gods and *adharma* for asuras and raksasas. When *dharma* vanquishes *adharma*, it is the krtayuga and when *adharma* triumphs, it is the kaliyuga . When you (Ravana) conquered the world, you allowed *adharma* to flourish and this made our enemies (Rama) stronger. The *adharma* you nurtured now works against us and strengthens the gods...'

In this we see some sort of balancing going on between good and evil. When evil prevails, which is what has happened when Ravana made a nuisance of himself, the good influences are stirred up to counter it and defeat it. This, in a way, must be the Hindu answer to the question of Theodicy; if Brahma is essentially good, why is there any evil in the world? The answer is that there are nasty characters like Ravana living in a stronghold, just waiting for a powerful god to come along and defeat him. In this way, life holds a promise of ultimate rectification by the powers of the good gods. There is no underestimating Ravana's powers; he has magical abilities and so have his underlings. His palace is just as attractive as that of the good rulers like Rama's father. One can easily be taken in by evil; one can easily be sucked into it against one's better judgement, like Sita. But anyone with a degree of self-control and determination can resist temptation and live in hopes of being rescued by the god who loves one.

So people are either righteous or non-righteous. There seems to be very little in between. But at this point it is important to consider the meaning of the word *dharma*[9]. It is just as hard to define as the Hebrew word *hesedh*[10]. One might take a liberty and say they are virtually the same, except that *hesedh* is involved with the concept of covenant, and this does not appear in Hindu thought. Even a Hindu like Sattar finds *dharma* difficult to express in English, since it has such a wide range of meaning: righteous conduct; moral correctitude; mutual consideration; respect for the gods; antagonism to evil; allowing others their rights and privileges; gentleness; love; being the ideal son, brother, husband, wife; never being nasty to anyone; and above all **truth,** which is of importance for this work. All these might pass as a fraction of its meaning.

Often Sattar does not attempt to translate it, but just leaves it as it is in the text. Relevant to this is the concept of 'righteousness'; nowhere does righteous behaviour receive a definition. There is nothing analogous to the

411

Ten Commandments, but a lot is assumed. Respect for one's parents, and for the gods, and the sages; an austere life are important factors. Murder, theft and adultery are seen as wrong. There is a heavy emphasis on purity and modesty. These values are not really so different from the Judaeo-Christian code of conduct, but the motivation behind it is somewhat different.

Sacrifice is seen as highly effective, something that cannot fail to buy favour with the gods. There is one clear reference to a sacrifice, which might have been some sort of *yagya*[11] ceremony. It would appear that a 'horse' sacrifice is highly effective; a black horse is allowed to roam free for a year and then at a special ceremony is sacrificed[4]. Rama executes such a ceremony at the end of the book. In addition to this, there are 'austerities', which are practised by sages and hermits in the forests. Rama and Laksmana indulge in this kind of life pattern. It means living like a yogi with matted hair and eating very little. Even Ravana, who is hardly to be termed righteous, as he is *adharma*, goes in for austerities. They are assumed to have a lot of buying power with the gods. One does not dare to trifle with the sages; they are analogous to the prophets like Elijah in the books of Kings.

The underlying assumption in Hindu thought is the concept of *karma*, or reincarnation. This means that one's conduct in this life decides what one will be reborn as in the next life. This ties in with the connectedness between gods, humans, animals and devils. In the epic, there is no firm dividing line between these entities. Animals talk to humans; gods turn into animals; devils can change their appearance and pose as something else. It reminds us of the 'Just so' stories and also the Garden of Eden. When Sita is considering her misfortunes, she speculates that in her previous life she must have caused the break-up of someone's marriage – poetic justice that she has been forcibly separated from her husband.

An important underlying assumption in the Ramayana is the feeling of destiny. Occasionally it breaks the surface in a passing remark, but the whole tenor of the epic involves Brahma's plan to defeat evil by sending Rama into the world as a human and bringing Ravana out into the open in a pitched battle. Everything is predestined with that all-important victory in mind. That is not to say there is no free will, but that is definitely not remarked upon clearly. In a way, this is analogous to the coming of Jesus as the Son of God to defeat evil and provide a rescue for everyone. The difference is that Brahma has any amount of offspring, male and female, and Rama is not really fully human. He is an avatar which means that he is god, in the appearance of a human, but not fully human. The same goes for Laksmana. Also with Jesus, the victory was about defeating evil by means of humility and obedience; with Rama it is about having an all-out bloodthirsty battle.

This brings us to the issue of literal versus figurative. Is the battle with

Ravana to be taken literally? We notice that there are seven sessions; Ravana is defeated at the climax of the campaign on the seventh day. Can all those magical weapons be taken at face value? At times it sounds like machine guns and bazookas mowing down thousands of monkeys and raksasas. Do we demythologise this and say that the love between husband and wife can overcome all kinds of problems and wickedness in life? Doubtless the Hindus will themselves be divided on this issue, just as the Christians are over the Garden of Eden. But it is fair to say that the Ramayana was never meant to be an accurate record of actual historical events, in the way that the Kings and the Maccabees were.

Another theological issue arises out of the question of kingship. There is much emphasis laid on the institution of monarchy in the Ramayana. Not just the humans, but the animals of various kinds all have their own kings, and of course Ravana is the king of the raksasas. When Rama eventually claims his kingdom in Ayodhya, everything works out to be wonderful.

'The earth yielded her bounty, trees produced fruit and flowers... no one ever heard the wailing of widows, nor was there any fear of disease or poisonous snakes. There was no cruelty or injustice and the old never had to do the work of the young. There was happiness everywhere and dharma flourished... people were never violent towards each other. Everybody lived for a thousand years and had a thousand sons. They knew neither disease or unhappiness... the rains always came at the right time and the touch of the wind was always pleasant... everyone abided by dharma and there was no unrighteousness...' (page 657).

There are various elements in this that remind us of sacral kingship as understood in the Ancient Middle East. The strength and divinity of the king was directly connected with the success of the harvest and the well being of the people in general. Admittedly we do not have the rising of the Nile connected with the Pharaoh and his rituals, but the same mentality is at work here. The monarch is seen as a major factor in the control of the elements and the supply of food, plus the security of the nation. Sacral kingship has not been noted as such an important element in Hinduism, when we compare it with China, Japan, Egypt, Mesopotamia, Greece and Mesoamerica. Even so, the same instincts in human nature are seen at play here.

Since we have such an emphasis on kingship, there is much less emphasis on priesthood, and still less on prophecy. A small exception to this is when Narada knows the future. The priests are there but seem to play only a small part in the story. There seem to be no prophets at all. What happens instead is that the sages, who live an austere life in the forest, almost certainly take their place. It is not that they foretell the future or accuse people of misconduct, but they seem to act like a magnet, attracting other people to come and take a spell at meditating or living the simple life with matted hair and ragged clothing. These are the holy people who are heading for heaven; their austerities gain merit and buying power with the gods. They live a calm and placid life, not given to outbursts of emotion. One of the traits in having the dharma is keeping one's temper. Various casual remarks in the book reveal that anger or losing one's temper is a bad thing; it has to be conquered. The Biblical equivalent of this would be people like Elijah and John the Baptist who live a solitary life devoid of luxuries.

Occasionally we find there is a little philosophic-moral sermon, which illustrates the Hindu pattern of thought. One such comes on page 519:

> 'Wise men say that war should be sought only after the first three options have been tried and failed. My child, force will only succeed if it is used correctly after proper deliberation, according to the rules, or if the enemy is destined to die, or if he is engaged with other enemies, or if he is unaware. How can you think of attacking someone who is vigilant, who is supported by a huge army, who is determined to win, who has conquered his temper and is invincible?'

We notice that aggression has to be disciplined and properly thought out. It is no good attacking someone who is stronger than oneself. We notice the irony in 'has conquered is temper'; this is on the eve of the attack on Lanka, and Ravana has already lost his temper and will go into tirades of fury as the battle progresses. In this we see the Hindu virtue of non-violence, unless it becomes unavoidable. Rama, of course, blazes with anger, but he has been provoked and in any case he is righteous from the start, so it is justifiable wrath. Therefore it does not count as adharmic. On the other hand, Ravana and his henchmen fight unethically. They cheat; Indrajit makes himself invisible so that one cannot fire back at him. Deceit and trickery give us much justification for Rama's victory. Ravana is a bully and a coward and deserves to be silenced. The Ramayana does not miss an opportunity to emphasise Ravana's debauchery: as Hanuman inspects the palace on Lanka, he sees scores of beautiful ladies and a severe shortage of men. This indicates how lustful Ravana is. With all these ladies to amuse him, he still wants to take Sita as his wife, thus committing adultery. When Hanuman is taken prisoner, Ravana wants to kill him; only the decent raksasas object on the grounds that one should never kill a messenger, even if one does not like his message. When Vibishana deserts his brother and comes to join in Rama's army and there is a debate on whether to accept him, Rama points out that one should always accept a fugitive.

Before the battle starts, we have a passage that is deeply ironic spoken by Malyavan, Ravana's grandfather (page 541):

'A king who is learned in statecraft can rule for years and keep his enemies at bay... .He declares war or peace according to circumstances and through that he increases his own power. A king should wage war only against those who are weaker. He should make alliances with his equals and with those that are superior to him. An enemy should never be underestimated.'

Very sound advice; but Ravana is not really listening; he certainly does underestimate Rama's ability in battle and fails to realise that the gods are backing him. Also he ignores many portents of defeat that keep appearing; these are signs that the gods are not in favour of one's cause.

It is clear that the bond of marriage is to be taken very seriously. The relationship between Rama and Sita is the ideal love match and partnership. Fidelity is heavily emphasised; it is a match made in heaven, and the wife is his partner in the *dharma*. If the husband dies first, the wife should ask herself what she has done to bring this about. This goes a long way to explain the practice of suttee[12] in which widows were expected to climb on to the husband's funeral pyre. We notice that Sita actually does step into the fire to prove her faithfulness to Rama; the gods intervene and save her from burning.

Mythology in the Ramayana

Certain elements in this area have already been mentioned in passing. When we compare the mythology included in the Ramayana, it has much in common with that seen in nearly every other religion. It is somewhat artificial to separate mythology from theology here.

In many world religions, there is the motif of death and resurrection, usually of a champion god. This is clearly an important element in this book. Rama 'dies' several times and Laksmana too. They are not really dead but severely wounded; Hanuman brings herbs and revives them. At the end, both Rama and Laksmana are assumed into heaven; they do not actually die since they are immortal, but they appear to die. Sita is on the verge of suicide over the separation from her husband, but is persuaded to take fresh hope at the last minute. Many of the monkeys are killed in the battle, but with one word from the friendly gods, they all come back to life. This, it would seem, does not apply to the evil army. Vali is presumed dead but reappears to oust Sugriva as the monkey king.

The three levels of the universe are often mentioned too. Heaven, earth and hell are assumed, although hell is not specifically mentioned. This assumption of the three-tiered universe was important in the Ancient World, and still is for many people nowadays. The question of the connection between the levels is always a matter of speculation; but the Ramayana mentions various ideas on that line. The bridge between the mainland and Lanka is a concept normally used for earth to heaven. Lanka is not exactly a hell, but it is full of devils and the chief ogre, Ravana. When Rama is assumed into heaven, he is reunited with Vishnu's body, but his followers, freed from their earthly bodies, climbed into fabulous chariots and went to a heavenly realm called Santanika, second only to the realm of Brahma himself. The idea of the chariot matches what happened to Elijah. It is just possible that Valmiki took the idea from the book of Kings.

Related to the three worlds is the motif of the tree. Its roots are going down into the ground, towards hell; its bole is plain enough in the world of men; its branches extend up to heaven. This motif is not heavily emphasised in the Ramayana, except to say that Hanuman hides in a tree (the Simsapa tree) as he overhears Ravana trying to seduce Sita. In effect this is saying that the powers of good were watching over Sita and looking for an opportunity to console her. Other than that we have vast forests of trees in India, this is the home of the sages and gurus who are heading for heaven because of their austere life. We do not have the tree of life here as in the Bible, but the implication is that these wise people have a deep understanding of life and death and of heaven, since they lead the simple life among the trees. When Sita is abducted, Rama goes from tree to tree asking of her whereabouts:

'O Kadamba tree, have you seen my beloved?... bilva tree, where is she?... O palm tree, take pity on me... Rose-apple tree... tell me where she is? (page 293).

As a substitute for trees, the mountains are often cited[13]. Hanuman and other monkeys, have a habit of carving the top off a mountain and hurling it at their enemies. Sometimes the rivers play the same symbolic part, especially the Ganges, which is thought to flow through all three worlds. There is the added assumption that they will purify one. Also the Sarayu[5], emphasised as pure and clear, is a river used as people bathe before going up into heaven.

There is also the ongoing hint of eternity on almost every page. Everywhere there are jewels, crystal, silver and gold, even in Ravana's palace. Gold is obviously symbolic of kingship and authority. We seem not to have mention of glass, mirrors and mercury; perhaps these were unknown in India at this time. But all of these things speak of incorruption, everlasting life and eternity. We begin with a jewel-studded palace at the start, which is a hint that Rama and his family are more than just ordinary humans. We end with a return to Ayodhya and its magnificence. Rama hands out precious jewels as gifts; symbolically, this is conferring eternal life on people. In between, we have Ravana's palace, the last word in luxury with all its riches. The hint here is that evil is not just a passing error or a human mistake; it is an eternal issue, just as righteousness is too.

The appearance of swords, spears and arrows is also symbolic of eternal justice, the righting of all wrongs. The sword stands for justice, the rectification of all evil; in the Ramayana it is also symbolic of purification, which is not really very different. In many cultures, arrows and spears take the place of swords, but not so here; all three are important weaponry. It is ironic that Ravana, the devil, has the same weaponry, on the assumption that right is on his side; but we all know he is deeply mistaken. Both sides have special weapons given to them by the gods, including Brahma, but Rama has the trump card in weapons and therefore wins the duel with Ravana. In a way this is saying that both good and evil have everlasting spiritual force, but also that good will prevail in the end.

Many of the arrows have snakes attached to them. The snake in mythology is symbolic of death, but also life and fecundity. It is a paradoxical creature; but there are dozens of snakes in the story, some of them oozing out of Ravana's heads.

One surprising element is the frequent mention of Doomsday in the Ramayana. It is well accepted that all things had a beginning with Brahma a long way back in the past. But Hindu thought goes along the lines that the world is eternal and will not come to an end. This book, however, talks about the end of the world as a well-accepted assumption, although it does not go into details about it.

We do not seem to have mention of angels; perhaps the gods in heaven are the substitute for them. But we do have mention of various grades of devils or evil influences. Their levels of wickedness are outlined in some detail, but Ravana is clearly at the bottom of the list in terms of virtue. Some are benign and some are malevolent; others are a paradoxical combination of both. It is rather like reading about the pixies and goblins in Norse folklore. The siddhas and the caranas are benign; after that, there are asuras, going downhill, daityas, and danavas; then raksasas, yaksas, and nagas; at the very bottom come the pisacus and yatudhanas. The nearer the top they come, the more they resemble the gods; some of them try to rival the gods. In the Ramayana, the raksasas, though they are Ravana's allies, are not totally evil. In fact some of them have some sort of conscience and they know how to fight ethically; others, however, do not. What it means is that the graduation between good and evil is not quite as straightforward as one would hope. This aspect is not mentioned in respect of the human race; it is a spiritual problem, which means that good and evil are not only interwoven and interplay with each other, but it takes someone of Rama's spiritual authority to kill them and finally defeat Ravana, the chief monster.

It would be fair to say that the main theme in the Ramayana is about justice and truth prevailing over falsehood and filthy trickery. That is the essence of the main plot: Sita, the faithful wife is abducted by a monster. Right must be re-established. Rama has to assemble an army, attack the monster and reclaim his lawful wife. It is a powerful tale in which right and wrong are writ large against a background of gods and devils. Much of this story is couched in mythological and cultural assumptions.

One interesting element is the contrast between Rama and Sita; although they are the ideal couple, Rama comes from heaven, as an avatar of Vishnu, and Sita comes from the earth, and when she departs, she goes back into the earth on a throne. Is this symbolic of saying that heaven and earth are ideally in a partnership of love and trust? Sadly, the Ramayana is shot through with generous amounts of grief; occasionally we have joy and triumph, but all too often, Rama is sobbing for his wife, and Sita is pining for her husband. Is this a symbolic way of saying that heaven and earth are strongly attracted to one another but there is always some sort of feeling of suspicion, on the part of heaven, that earth may have been compromised somehow, with evil? Normally, the general assumption in the Ramayana is that women are in an inferior position to men. A woman's place is with her husband and she has to look up to him as a god. Even so, she is a partner with him in the *dharma*. This is obviously a cultural assumption, which still prevails to this day in India, even if Mrs Ghandi managed to attain the rank of Prime Minister. Behind it may be this theological idea that heaven and earth are essentially one and inseparable, even if there is some sort of distancing between them. This may be a profound paradox in the Hindu soul.

Although most of the book is couched in elaborate mythology and metaphor derived from it, there are moments when some sort of demythologisation breaks the surface. The *dharma*, however difficult that is to define, is stated to establish the truth; the world is established in truth, and truth controls the world. This is a philosophical way of omitting mention of gods and allowing abstract ideas to be the basis of life. It is interesting that the Brahmins (the top layer of the caste system) are dubbed as the philosophers; they go in for rationality. There is mention of atheism (page 209), which is an interesting admission for a culture that is so steeped in spirituality. Before becoming too critical about the mythology of the Ramayana, it is a sound policy to consider what deep truths are being portrayed in symbolic terms.

Concluding remarks on the Ramayana

This is a powerful story that explores so many personal relationships plus elements of royalty and divinity. The bond between Rama and Laksmana[14], and also Bharata are deeply emotional, and rank with the situation with Jacob and Esau. Dasaratha, the ideal king, degenerates into a silly old man, rather like Solomon. Sita is the perfect wife, something that is outlined in Proverbs. The chariot going up into heaven appears in various places. One wonders if the Old Testament has had any influence with Valmiki; it is not out of the question. The friendship bond between Rama and Sugriva reminds us of David and Jonathan; there is no mention of a covenant between Rama and Sugriva, but the Hindu cultural equivalent, that of walking round a fire, is described. One is fascinated by the many casual remarks that indicate cultural factors: the sages living in the forest; their hair matted and them wearing doeskins; the lotus pattern of holding one's hands in a sign of respect; touching someone's feet. Most intriguing of all is the mention of one's left eye twitching which is taken to be a bad omen!

Inanna: her descent into the underworld

This Epic, coming from Uruk in Mesopotamia, may be the earliest known production of its kind. It hails from 2,500 BC, was written in cuneiform script on clay tablets, and has only recently been translated. It is very short in comparison with the Ramayana, but even so, it belongs with the same genre in that it tackles the deep questions of life and death. Most of the epics from early Mesopotamia are short; the ones from Greece, the *Iliad* and the *Odyssey* are lengthy. But that makes no difference. The same basic questions in the human soul need to be aired and an answer attempted. The version here used is by Eleanor Allitt, published in 2010 on demand-worldwide.com.

A short outline of the story goes thus: Inanna, a beautiful young woman from Uruk, was the daughter of the moon and great granddaughter of the sky god, An, and Nannu, mother of heaven and earth. She was destined to become queen of heaven and earth. While she was bathing in the sacred river Abzu, the God of Wisdom, Enki, noticed her and invited her to up to heaven for a meal, and bestowed on her the perceptive ear, the power of attention and the art of kindliness, wisdom, truth, priesthood, but also descent into and return from the underworld. The people of Uruk were delighted to see her with such gifts. One day she heard a voice calling her to visit her sister in the underworld. One day when Inanna was out walking, she noticed a shepherd called Dumuzi. It was love at first sight; he came to her house and they were betrothed, and they had two sons, Shara and Lulal.

Inanna became aware of the underworld calling her; the call became increasingly insistent. So she took with her seven holy gifts and bade farewell to Dumuzi. She took her friend Ninshubur along, and she would have to report to Enki if Inanna did not return after three days. To enter the underworld, there were seven gates guarded by Neti with a bunch of keys. One by one Inanna had to surrender her seven holy gifts. Her reason for penetrating this world was that her sister, Erishkagal was in there mourning her husband who had died. By the time Inanna reached the core of the underworld, she was naked. Erishkagal rose from her throne, and, summoning the Anunni, the seven judges of the underworld, they found her guilty and hung her on a hook on the wall.

Since three days had elapsed, Ninshubur went to Enki to plead for Inanna's life. Enki produced the food and water of life and gave it to little flying insects that could get through the gates of the underworld and revive Inanna, using the food and water given by Enki. But the seven judges held on to her; she would have to supply someone to take her place if she wanted to return to earth. Inanna did not want to nominate Ninshubur, or her sons, but Dumuzi who was sitting on his throne, was found guilty so they took him. But Dumuzi appealed to Utu, the god of justice, and his hands and feet were turned into snakes' heads and feet, but this was to no avail; a wind carried Dumuzi away. This caused enormous grief for Inanna, and Dumuzi's sister, Geshtinanna; they did not know where Dumuzi had gone. But the fly did know; when they found him a deal was struck. Dumuzi would go to the underworld for half a year; Geshtinanna would go for the other half of the year. Erishkagal was satisfied with this arrangement and Inanna was released by the gatekeeper. She returned to earth as Queen of Heaven and Earth.

We might recall that Abraham, who came from that part of the world, might well have known this myth; he almost certainly knew the Epic of Gilgamesh, which includes the Flood. Certainly it explains the early Hebrew impression of Sheol, a dark, shadowy existence down below. It was only later, we assume, that the impression of Hell as being torments in flames came in under the influence of Zoroastrianism. But the myth of Inanna does concern itself with the basic question of life and death; what happens when we die? Is it fair that one should die or is there a way of sidestepping it? Who is in control of all these things?

In addition, there is the motif of the God of Wisdom imparting wisdom to the Queen of Heaven and Earth. Even so, she has to explore the underworld and receive the food and water of life. With that she has understanding of life in all its aspects and eternal life at that. We notice that the dividing line between life and death is not clearly or finally demarcated. People in hell are still 'alive' and capable of coming back to earth, or at least, communicating across the divide of these kingdoms. This reminds us of the Parable of Dives and Lazarus.

But the core of the story, like any 'just so' story, is to explain the alternation between winter and summer. So Inanna only has her husband for half a year at a time; nature goes quiet for six months at a time. Here we see the connection between kingship and the fertility of the land. This was a very important strand in ancient Middle Eastern thinking, and also surfaces in the Ramayana. There is also an element of it in Greek mythology, with the story of Persephone. There is even the implication of it in the life and ministry of Jesus, since the resurrection is located in the springtime; life comes back to the natural world, even if it is located in the northern hemisphere.

The motif of resurrection is central to many myths the world over. Inanna goes down into hell, which is a euphemistic way of saying that she dies, but that is not the end. She is still alive, even if from the earthly point of view she is dead. But then she is ransomed from hell by the substitution of her husband, Dumuzi and his sister. The motif is profound; it comes in the rituals of sacral kingship, in which the king was supposed to 'die' like the autumn, but be 'raised' again like the spring. In the Ramayana, Rama and Laksmana 'die' more than once but are brought back to life with magic herbs; the monkeys that were killed in battle, all come back to life. What this is saying is in effect, that life is precious; it ought to last for ever. It will last for ever, even if we go to a different world, if we have the right sort of help from the appropriate god.

In common with all world mythologies, there are the symbolisms of eternal life worked into the story. So Inanna has a golden breastplate and ring, semi-precious and precious jewels like amethyst and lapis lazuli, plus her royal crown and robe. Also Dumuzi has snake hands and feet, which paradoxically betoken life and death in the same person.

Underpinning all this is the general assumption of the three-tiered universe, heaven, earth and hell. We notice that that all-important figure seven appears more than once. Inanna has seven gifts and there are seven judges of the underworld. The connection from earth to hell is down a perilous narrow subterranean passageway, something that the Greeks and Romans believed, except that they had the river Styx at the bottom. The connection to heaven is not clearly explained, except that Inanna and her friend have access to Enki without much difficulty. But what the story is really saying is that there is a god (or goddess) who has experience of all three worlds, and allowed himself to 'die' in order to satisfy the call of the underworld. Because of this experience, the implication is that there is life in continuation for us all. Now we see the importance of the death and resurrection of Jesus; he is the true Son of God who invaded all three realms of the spirit and provided eternal life for us all, something that was not specifically tied to the seasons of the year.

The Iliad by Homer, as compared with the Ramayana

Of much the same genre as the Ramayana and the Epic of Inanna, the *Iliad* is by far the most widely known of epics in world history. Its partner and completion is the *Odyssey,* also by Homer. This classical Greek literature, written in iambic pentameter, is thought to stem from the period about 750 BC. The internal evidence is that the action takes place in the late Bronze Age as it merged into the early Iron Age, which would place it at about the time that the Philistines were clashing with the Israelites about 1,000 BC. But that does not mean that Homer has to have written it then; he could have composed this drama much later, based on oral tradition and folk memories. It is enough to say that the *Iliad* is roughly contemporaneous with the Ramayana but postdates probably all of the classic epics coming from Babylonia. The version cited here is the Penguin Classics edition, as translated by E. V. Rieu in 1949. As literature, the *Iliad* is difficult to undervalue; Homer is an accomplished poet who has been imitated by many literary geniuses down to the present day. Although this work was never regarded as 'scriptural' in the way that other epics have become, even so, in Greek culture, the *Iliad* and the *Odyssey* became a basic inspiration and touchstone for that people and for the Romans who simply took the whole thing over lock stock and barrel. It is claimed that Alexander the Great[15] kept a copy of the *Iliad* by his beside. Homer's mastery of language and metaphor can be demonstrated with three short quotations:

'But Idomeneus was not to be scared off like a little boy. He waited for him with the self-reliance of a mountain boar when he is caught by a crowd of huntsmen in some lonely spot and faces the hue and cry with bristling back and eyes aflame, whetting his tusks in his eagerness to take on all comers, hound or man.'

'But the dart rebounded. As the black beans or chickpeas on a broad threshing floor leap from the flat shovel, with the whistling wind and the winnower's force behind them, the deadly arrow bounced off… and sped into the distance…'

'The Trojans came on like an angry squall that swoops down from a thunder-laden sky to strike salt water, bringing indescribable turmoil to the moaning sea, where the great waves hiss and arch their foaming backs in a never-ending procession.'

Superb turn of sustained metaphor! This is augmented all through by the interplay of gods and humanity on the battlefield. It is done slightly differently as compared with the Ramayana. The gods are not unanimous about who should win the conflict; sometimes they favour the Trojans, sometimes the Achaeans. Zeus himself is ambivalent about the whole thing, and changes sides in a whimsical fashion. As one side gains the upper hand, the gods come to the rescue of the losers. In this way, the sustained conflict sways to and fro, keeping up the suspense. Sometimes the gods offer an omen to warn or encourage the warriors, sometimes they come as some sort of 'avatar', in deep disguise to affect the flow of the battle. Athena appears as a herald and at one point comes with a 'tarn cap' of invisibility; this reminds us of Wagner's operas. It would be fair to say that Homer himself, unlike Valmiki, does not appear to favour one side against another. The Trojans are not dubbed as thoroughly wicked, like Ravana and his hordes,and neither are the supporters of Agamemnon. Both sides are accorded a degree of stupidity. Agamemnon was an idiot to antagonise Achilles, who now hangs about sulking and will not join in the fray until it is almost too late. Paris was an idiot to abduct Helen; he must have known that her husband, Menelaus would come calling to retrieve her. Paris is labelled as laid back, a womanising ninny, and not pulling his weight in the battle. In fact the Trojans in general are depicted as softies. All this contrasts magnificently with the champions on the battlefield.

The folly of the Trojans is underlined in various ways. The elders advise that Helen should be given up, in order to avoid a conflict, but this is ignored, like Ravana. The action begins with a truce in which two champions are nominated to settle the dispute; but one of the Trojans lets loose an arrow, thus breaking the truce! More than once, champions face each other on the field but this does not seem to settle the matter. One is left with the impression that the war is more than just a dispute over an abducted wife.

The way in which the battle is described would give the impression that the whole thing is glorious. In fact, the attitude of the warriors, which is virtually suicidal at times, certainly gives that impression. But does Homer think the same way himself? On page 112, he lets drop a brief comment like this; 'Athena, (goddess of war) ... equipped herself for the lamentable work of war with the arms of Zeus...' What Homer is saying here is that the whole thing is futile but even so, the mentality of aggression goes right to the top, in the mentality of Athena and Zeus the top god himself. Even if war is ridiculous, it is an inevitable aspect of life. This contrasts with the Ramayana in which war only happens when there is a firm reason for it, and the story is punctuated with spells of peace and well-being. And even today, with all our efforts at establishing world peace through the United Nations, warfare still surfaces, as does cruelty, aggression and all the futility that accompanies it.

In contrast with the Ramayana, the *Iliad* appears to have some sort of relationship with actual historical events. For a long time, people thought that the *Iliad* was pure imagination on the part of Homer. However, recent thought has changed on the matter; it is thought that we have located Troy (Ilium) in northwestern Turkey. Sadly, the wall thrown up by the Achaeans has not been found; the book itself explains that Zeus made sure it was swept away. We know about King Minos of Crete and Agamemnon of Mycene; in fact an artistic impression of Agamemnon in gold has been unearthed. This means that the *Iliad* is dealing with historical realities to some extent, although to read its pages, it is clear that the whole thing is dramatised, sensationalised and exaggerated. This, however, is nothing strange in ancient literature. It was their way of emphasising matters that they saw as important. This is probably in contrast with the Ramayana, in which no real history is intended; it is almost entirely symbolic of the conflict between good and evil. What is Homer trying to say? We have the contrast between the swashbuckling, swanking attitude of the contestants, and the piles of bodies littering the shore – what a nonsense! We have champions knocking someone over on the battlefield, and then spending time removing his armour as a prize of war; greed outweighs the urgency to bring a decisive result to the conflict. In this case, it is not good versus evil; it is stupidity versus stupidity. And all this is augmented by the interference of the gods, who cannot make their minds up over the rights and wrongs of the matter. Did Homer think the gods were a coterie of idiots too? Possibly!

But one element that characterises both works is the factor of grief. Rama grieves for Sita; Menelaus grieves for Helen; Achilles grieves for Briseis; the Achaeans are pining to go home after this prolonged campaign, but cannot afford to lose face by abandoning their mission. Many fathers grieve over their sons being killed in battle. The whole work has a substratum of sadness that never really finds resolution, even if the gods do bring people back to life.

As works of literature, the Ramayana and the *Iliad* are both masterpieces of climax and suspense. On a grand scale, and even on a small scale, the *Iliad* may have the advantage. When Hector is killed, his wife, blissfully unaware of it and busy preparing his bathtub for his return, only realises later than all the rest of Troy, that he is dead. This is a superb piece of ironic suspense. But as the Ramayana brings the whole story to a conclusion, though not quite a happy one, the Iliad leaves us in mid-air. It is not quite an anticlimax, but what we would now call a 'cliff-hanger'. We are left with a sort of gentlemen's agreement that hostilities will be suspended for the duration of Hector's funerary arrangements, but no conclusion over what will happen to Helen or the settlement of the dispute. In addition, the death of Achilles is quite confidently foretold, but this does not materialise in the account. The result of this has been various spurious attempts in later years by lesser authors, to complete the story; it is like Schubert's unfinished symphony. Even so it is a powerful story as it stands.

There are several elements in common with the Ramayana. There is the prophetic element, though not heavily emphasised, with the admission that there is false prophecy too. There are frequent mentions of Fate or Destiny, but this is balanced by remarks about Luck or dodging destiny.

There is the brotherly love element: Achilles and Patroclus are like brothers. This reminds us of David and Jonathan. In fact, when the funeral pyre of Patroclus goes up in flames miraculously (page 418) this reminds us of Elijah on Mount Carmel; did Homer derive this idea from the Book of Kings[16]?

Various aspects of mythology are seen in the *Iliad*. There is mention of a golden rope from heaven to earth (page 145). There is much mention of Hades as the destination for all those who die. No one ever seems to go to heaven. At one point there is an oak tree in which the gods meet to discuss matters (page 133). At the demise of Patroclus, his ghost comes to Achilles in the night and goes into details about his admission into Hades. If he cannot have a proper funeral, he will be stuck on this side of the River Styx. He needs to be buried instantly so that he can be admitted; also he wishes to be buried with Achilles in the same urn (or possibly ossuary). One important element in mythology is gold, silver and jewels. Although we have hardly any mention of jewellery in the *Iliad*, there is much mention of glittering armour with gold and silver. In reality, an armourer would hardly have increased the weight of the armour with soft and heavy metals like gold and silver. Achilles is given a special set of weapons from Hephaistos[17] before facing up to Hector. Hector's spear hits Achilles' shield and is stopped by the gold trimmings in it – hardly! In this we see that symbolism has taken over from reality; gold is symbolic of royalty, imperishableness and eternal life, silver is too. For this reason, we must ask, how much of the *Iliad* is symbolic as opposed to literal history. Judging by the hyperbole of certain elements in the account we can conclude that while the drama is based on real events in the past, it is also a comment on human nature then and now[18].

Perhaps the final comment on human nature comes right at the end. Priam and Achilles actually have a sympathetic (if confidential) conversation and agree a twelve-day truce while Hector's funeral is completed. This just goes to show how people can come to their senses, perhaps belatedly, and show a certain degree of decency. One is bound to ask, at the end, why they did not decide to settle their differences in a reasonable fashion a long time before so that many decent men did not have to die, and so many parents, wives and children did not have to be bereaved! Perhaps this is Homer's comment on human nature. We should certainly ask ourselves this question in relation to the death toll in the twentieth century!

Norse Mythology as compared with the Ramayana

This corpus of material stemming from the culture of the Vikings is fascinating to study and compare with works like the Ramayana, Revelation, Inanna and the *Iliad*. Obviously the climatic background makes an important difference to the basic assumptions underlying the stories. This is a world of ice, snow, glaciers, forests, stormy seas, high snow-capped mountains and gloomy caverns. It is a far cry from India and Sri Lanka. The whole layout of the myths is approached in an obviously different way; even so, there are many similarities which make one wonder if ideas were borrowed or in general circulation in the Ancient World.

We are only aware of a fraction of the Norse mythology; much of it has been lost. What we do have is the written records of certain bards, such as Snorri Snurlason, an Icelandic poet, who produced written sagas in the twelfth to the thirteenth century AD. But Norse oral traditions had been in circulation for many centuries before. The Romans came up against this material when they clashed with the Germans. Apart from fragments of runic material, none of the myths were in writing until well into the Christian era. There is no doubt that the Norsemen regarded their myths as the truth, but it would be difficult to describe it as 'scriptural' in the sense that we now understand the word. We can now read these tales in such editions as the *Penguin book of Norse Myths* by Crossley-Holland. This rendition is very much a paraphrase, and is often colloquial English; this does not detract from the dramatic, highly-charged sagas of the gods and their exploits. It would be fair to say that the prevailing atmosphere is one of gloom, doom, revenge, nasty bargaining, bloodshed and hate. There is nothing that equates to the love God as seen in the Bible, except in so far as the gods indulge in erotic fixations on the goddesses. This always results in some sort of violence.

It would be helpful to begin with the differences from other mythologies. The Norsemen believed the universe was a three-tiered system, just as everyone else did. However, it was more complicated than that, for there were nine worlds. This gives the effect of the figure nine being used freely, just as the Jews and almost everyone else used the figure seven. The Japanese used the figure eight (see Chapter 12). Heaven consists of Asgard, where the Aesir live; Vanaheim, where the Vanir live; Alfheim where the light elves live; and Valhalla for those who die in battle. Ground level, middle earth is Midgard, where the humans live; Nidavellir, where the dwarfs live; Jotunheim where the giants live; and Svartalfheim, where the dark elves live. In the underworld, there is Hel, where the dead go, and Niflheim, which is a lower hell. It is principally three layers with different compartments. All this is held together by a massive ash tree called Yggdrasill, which pervades all three layers. Coiled round the whole structure is a massive serpent, Jormungand, who bites his own tail. The whole corpus of sagas is characterised by the interplay of gods, giants, elves and dwarfs. The human race is hardly ever involved except in a few instances. The stories centre round Thor with his hammer, Odin with his one eye which sees everything, and Loki who is a naughty god. If we wanted to identify the Devil, that would be misleading. Hel, the goddess of the underworld is not Satanic, even if Hell is rather like Sheol, a shadowy hopeless place for those who fail to die in battle. Rather more like the Devil is Loki, the Trickster god, who is sly, nasty, cheeky and goes in for vandalism; but he is very much one of the gang in Asgard and only has to run off when he causes the death of Balder.

Balder appears to be the only god who is not only beautiful but good-natured and admired by everyone. His mother goes round extracting a promise from everyone and everything that they will not injure Balder. Sadly, she neglected to tackle the mistletoe, and crafty Loki managed to find this out. He then took a sprig of mistletoe, put it into the hand of his blind brother and aimed it at Balder, with the result that he died. Does this remind us of Achilles with his heel? Balder had to go to Hel and rot but we are assured that he will be raised to life again when Ragnarok comes. This is the Norse version of the apocalypse and the end of the world. However, this will not really be the end because Odin knows that there will be a fresh start. Another echo of Christian teaching is the story of Odin hanging on the tree for nine nights, with his side pierced by a spear, in order to learn the wisdom of the dead. One wonders if this was borrowed from the Christian gospels!

Creation is also a subject for explanation. The backdrop of it is clearly Iceland because we have ice and flame, land that is molten and glowing. This rules out places like Norway and Sweden. We begin with a giant called Ymir, who is evil. Out of him grew a man and a woman (Adam and Eve?) and he also had a son. We have a scheme of the first, the second and the third day! Eventually Odin, Vili and Ve killed Ymir and used his flesh to form the world and his bones to form the mountains, and his blood to form the seas and lakes. Ymir's skull became the sky. Then they made the sun, moon and stars from sparks. Ymir's brains became the clouds. Then the sons of Bor made the first man and woman (again?) and Odin breathed into them the breath of life. The man was called Ask and the woman Embla. There were two kinds of gods, the Aesir who looked after mankind and the Vanir who were the fertility gods. Odin and his brothers were the chief creators and everything and all forms of life, including dwarfs, elves, pixies, goblins and giants stem from him. How much of this reminds us of Genesis; also certain aspects of Japanese mythology?

In common with the *Iliad* and the Ramayana, the gods are capable of coming down to Midgard in disguise. This is the Nordic version of 'avatar'. There is one occasion where Loki turns himself into a fly in order to invade Thor's hall, and then cut off all his wife's hair, as some sort of practical joke. This reminds us of Inanna. Always there is the inference that the gods are in the right and are fighting evil as seen in the giants. But the difference between good and evil is not as clear as in the Ramayana, for the Nordic

427

gods can be just as deceitful, cruel, lecherous and generally wicked as any of the others. The elves and dwarfs however, are not characterised as evil, but willing to produce anything craftwise for a fee. They are the clever ones who produce jewellery and useful artefacts. All these classes of people have hordes of wealth – gold, silver and jewels – which is symbolic of eternity and monarchy.

The value of life is also the substratum of many of the scenes in Nordic mythology. There is a goddess, Idun, who has a basket of golden apples, which when given to the gods, prevent them from aging; if the apples are denied, they start to wither and wrinkle up. A giant called Thiazi steals them and Loki has to employ one of his tricks to recover them. Anyone who dies either goes to Valhalla or Hel; they are not really dead. In Valhalla they fight all day long and get killed; then rise up again to have their feast in the evening. Life is indestructible; the motif of resurrection is an important substratum. We even have somebody with eight heads which means that if one is chopped off, another grows in its place; think of Ravana.

The gods would hardly be able to join the Salvation Army; they have drinking contests and drink themselves into a stupor. This is also seen in the *Iliad*, but not the Ramayana. The gods usually have some sort of arrangement with the animals: Thor has two wolves pulling his chariot and Rama has an alliance with the monkeys and bears. But the *Iliad* does not seem to involve the animals at all.

An important element in many mythologies is the champion with his magic weapon, which is supposed to win every battle. With Thor, we have his famous hammer, Mjollnir, which can smash anyone's head in. On one occasion he found a sleeping giant and sank his hammer into his head, but the giant woke up and seemed unperturbed. A crisis occurred when a giant called Thrym managed to steal the hammer, which meant that the giants would breed out of control and rule the world. This is where Loki's cunning comes into play: Thor dresses up as Freyja whom Thrym wants to marry and the hammer is handed over, the disguise is thrown away and Thor smashes all the giants to pieces in the wedding hall. We notice that Rama has his special bow and arrow and Ravana his magic spear. The substratum of this all is the element of magic. But the hero always wins through. Justice prevails in the end; the substratum of all this is the assumption of everlasting and eternal justice.

One important difference with the Norse mythology is that the sagas are not really a connected account. With the Ramayana, it is a full-scale epic coming to a climax and an anticlimax. The same is true with the *Iliad*. With the Norse material, the stories do not progress along a line such as the fortunes of Thor, even if he is one of the main characters. One could see the death of Balder as the climax, but not a very convincing one; the destruction of a good and beautiful god is not a particularly pleasant ending, even if we know he will be raised again at Ragnarok.

The coincidence of so many features in mythologies from differing parts of the world must be of significance. It is not realistic to say that they all borrowed ideas from each other. For instance, how could the Norsemen and the Japanese both have the same idea of the rainbow being the bridge between heaven and earth? More likely these features are the instinctive responses in the soul of mankind. In a wonderful way, our mythologies describe ourselves as well as speculate on such matters as creation, the end of the world, destiny, love, hate, warfare. This is particularly noticeable with the Nordic material; reading the sagas we can so easily picture the Viking ruffians who gloried in aggression and cared nothing for avoidance of death. We can also glimpse the settled life of the farmers and fishermen who had no ambition to go marauding and colonising. The same is true with the *Iliad*; we can gain a most instructive picture of life in Mycenean Greece and its outlying colonies in Asia Minor. They too were an aggressive gang who knew that wrongs must be righted. And the Ramayana; a culture in ancient India is shown to us with the yogis, the avatars, the righteous princes and kings. Their attitude to aggression is somewhat different and it is a more cautious attitude towards warfare, only to be undertaken under certain conditions. But we can well imagine the cultural background that produced the new religion of Buddhism. Mythology tells us so much about ourselves, our habits of thought and our expectations. Anyone who tries to take this material literally is missing the point; the truth about the human race is writ large in grandiose metaphor and drama.

Notes for Chapter 22; The Ramayana

1. This reminds us of the fourteen years that Jacob had to work for his two wives (Genesis 29:21).
2. Asoka: a kind of tree. There was a king called Asoka who was an early champion of Buddhism in India, some time after the Ramayana was written.
3. The obstinacy of Ravana is a dramatic feature of the saga, and reminds us of Pharaoh's obstinacy at the Passover(Exodus 8).
4. The horse sacrifice was believed to be a particularly effective sacrifice.
5. The Sarayu River is a tributary of the Ganges and is used for sacral bathing.
6. Rama ascends into heaven in a chariot. This reminds us of Elijah's assumption, 2 Kings 2.
7. Asura: a kind of evil spirit, something like a goblin or imp in Western thought.
8. Avatar: a kind of incarnation, in which the god appears in physical form, human or animal.
9. *Dharma*: this has a wide range of meanings: righteousness, good conduct, family cohesion, respect, patience and much more.
10. *Hesedh*: a crucial Hebrew word meaning deep committed love in the Covenant relationship.

11. *Yagya*: a kind of ceremony outlined in the Rig Veda, in which soma, an intoxicating juice was consumed.
12. Suttee: the Hindu tradition in which a widow was expected to be burned on her husband's funeral pyre. The practice was abolished by the British in 1829, but this did not stop the practice entirely.
13. Mount Meru a real mountain in the Himalayas, but with mythical overtones. A replica of Mount Meru is often seen on the top of a Hindu temple.
14. Brotherly love and attachment are emphasised in the Ramayana and the *Iliad*. This reminds us of David and Jonathan, 1 Samuel 19.
15. Alexander the Great is known to have placed a high value on the *Iliad* and the *Odyssey*.
16. The miraculous production of fire reminds us of Elijah on Mount Carmel (1 Kings 18:19).
17. Hephaistos: in Greek mythology, he was the blacksmith, the sparks from whose anvil gave life to the human race.
18. Mycenean Greece: Mycene and Knossos as well as other cities of the same era, have been excavated, telling us much of how these people lived and what they thought.

23

St Luke

Of the four canonical gospels in the New Testament, St Luke stands out as probably the most carefully thought out and schematised. It is clearly a two-volume work, of which the Acts of the Apostles forms a sequel. No one nowadays seriously questions the authorship of this work; it is the Luke that accompanies St Paul on his journeys. He must have known St Mark and all the other disciples. He sets out to give an orderly account of the amazing events surrounding the earthly ministry of Jesus. Early tradition has it that Luke was a doctor; all the best doctors in the Roman empire were of Greek extraction, and the impression given is that he is a well-educated, thoughtful person, wishing to inform properly anyone who wishes to know the truth about Jesus. Theophilus may be an actual person or a title because the word means 'lover of God'. Even if he was a Greek, he is well versed in the Hebrew traditions and the Septuagint (the Greek translation of the Old Testament). He may have been a gentile proselyte who was attracted to Christianity at an early date. No one is really sure of the date of composition of the gospel, but Luke admits to having researched other sources of information with care. It is now widely accepted that Mark's gospel came first, and that Matthew and Luke copied from him. There was also another source named Q (German for *Quelle*, meaning ' source'), which was not known to Mark; also another source termed L which was material which only appears in Luke. Where this material came from is beyond us to ascertain; the material does contain some of the most iconic accounts in the Bible, such as the Prodigal Son, and the Good Samaritan. No one really tries to discount these as the authentic thoughts of Jesus.

Historico-mathematical information

These two issues must be taken together. Unlike many writers, Luke firmly anchors the start of the Messiah's ministry in the dating of the Roman Empire. He begins in 1:5 with 'In the days of Herod, king of Judea'; this is talking about Herod the Great who reigned from 37 BC and died in 4 BC. So Jesus was born just on the tail end of Herod's reign. In 2:1 we have Caesar Augustus ordering an enrolment for the purposes of taxation. That places Jesus' birth in the period 27 BC to 14 AD; Herod and Augustus were very much in alliance and collaboration; it gave Herod a free hand in his kingdom. Also we have mention of Quirinius as governor of Syria. Quirinius can be evidenced from Josephus' writings and also an inscription found in Antioch may refer to Quirinius as the leading military official. He is also mentioned in Suetonius as active in the reign of Tiberius[1]. He is known to have instigated a census in 6-7 AD but there is nothing said about one before 4 BC. However it was typical of the Romans to enforce a taxation census, probably at regular intervals, such as ten years. This all rings true. Then in Luke 3:1ff we have mention of the fifteenth year of Tiberius Caesar; since he reigned from 14 AD to 37 AD, that places the start of Jesus' ministry as something like 29 AD. Pontius Pilate was the governor of Judea because Archilaus, Herod's son, had been deposed for incompetence in 6 AD. We have a stone inscription to verify the historical reality of Pontius Pilate. Herod (Antipas) was the tetrarch of Galilee, and his brother Philip held the region of Iturea and Trachonitis, and Lysanias was the tetrarch of Abilene. An inscription mentioning 'Lysanias the tetrarch' has been found in Abilene, dated 15-30 AD. There is no reason to call into question any of this historical material. The only thing missing is a datum point in history; the Christian era had not, at that stage, been envisaged. The only datum point available was the AUC reckoning, which was based on the foundation of Rome, but Luke does not use this and neither does he use the Seleucid system based on Alexander the Great. This is why there is a certain amount of vagueness about the birth and start of Jesus' ministry; even so, Luke sets out quite clearly to anchor the work of Jesus in a specific historical setting, with dates implied though not actually stated in terms of the official Roman dating system.

An indirect appeal to actual history is found in the Parable of the Pounds Luke 19:13. It concerns a candidate for royal status who has to go off to have his entitlement confirmed in a foreign land. This is exactly how Herod the Great managed to keep his kingdom; also his sons were sent off to Rome to be educated and then sent back to take up their stations as kings and tetrarchs. Almost the same parable comes in Matthew 25:14, but it does not include the royal appointee element. Luke must have been fully aware of how young hopefuls of the royal household managed to acquire a kingdom;

it was happening all the time; what one had to do was to ingratiate oneself with the current Caesar.

Geographical factors

In common with the other gospels, Luke includes many places and territories by name. He allows the reader to understand Jesus as excising his ministry all over that part of the world, not just in Galilee, but Samaria, Judea, the Decapolis, Tyre and Sidon. This is less noticeable in the other gospels. Also he mentions place-names that do not appear anywhere else. Emmaus, Nain, Olivet are such. Some of these places are known to this day, others only sketchily. But it all gives realism to the account. This is deliberate; Luke wants us to see that the Messiah is not just a theoretical idea or some sort of philosophical construct; he was a real person with a real human family; he had a real impact on the Jewish people of his day.

Theology in St Luke

Luke's theological outlook is not greatly different from that of the other gospel writers. The best way to glimpse his slant is to study the birth narratives in Chapters 1 to 4 and in addition the material in his special source termed L.

The birth narratives concentrate on the two ladies, Elizabeth and Mary and their miraculous conceptions. Elizabeth and Zechariah were aged and past childbearing age. This reminds us of Abraham and Sarah, and how a new covenant was given; indeed we have a reference to the covenant of Abraham in Luke 1:72-73. With the birth of John the Baptist, we see a new covenant being inaugurated, even if John is later dubbed as the least in the kingdom. In Luke 7:33, John is acknowledged as the messenger who has to prepare the way for the Messiah, but even then, anyone belonging to the kingdom is greater than he[2]. Then we have the conception of Jesus, which is even more miraculous than John's; this is explained as the work of the Holy Spirit. All through Luke's gospel, the Holy Spirit is mentioned as an important aspect of God's intervention in this world.

Both conceptions are announced by the angel Gabriel; is this a mythological way of saying that both babies were not just a matter of human conception, but of cosmic significance? As it turned out, John brings the Old Testament to a conclusion; Jesus brings in the New Testament. Both are balanced and contrasted, and yet both testaments need each other to make sense of each other. From the Old Testament point of view, the four parents are thoroughly committed to keeping to the rules and regulations.

433

Elizabeth and Zechariah are both righteous before the Lord, walking in all the commandments and ordinances of the Lord blameless. They are 'squeaky-clean' in today's parlance. Indeed, it is again emphasised in 1:75, how the family will serve God in holiness and righteousness all the days of their life. It is emphasised that Mary is obedient to God; it is pointed out that she has got no husband and is a virgin, which is an indirect way of saying that she was pure when Jesus was conceived. In Luke 2:22, it is stated that Mary went through the purification process by performing a sacrifice in the Temple. Jesus himself, as a young boy, is pointed out as filled with wisdom and in favour with God and also with men. This is in spite of him being a bit naughty about staying behind in the Temple when his parents set off for home.

In common with the other gospels, Luke is at pains to show that the prophets of old are coming to fulfilment. 'As he spoke by the mouth of his holy prophets from of old...' Luke 1:70, sets the tone for the whole gospel. He is particularly fond of Isaiah and he has John the Baptist specifically relating himself to Isaiah 40:3-5;

'In the wilderness prepare the way of the Lord, make straight in the desert a highway for our God. Every valley shall be lifted up and every mountain and hill be made low; the uneven ground shall be made level and the rough places a plain. And the glory of the Lord shall be revealed, and all flesh shall see it together, for the mouth of the Lord has spoken.'

Mark and Matthew make the prophetic quotation much shorter, probably on the assumption that their readers will know the passage; Luke cites it much more fully, possibly on the assumption that his readers will not be familiar with it, in other words, gentile converts.

In other places, Luke is far subtler about his prophetic realisations. The Song of Mary, known as the Magnificat (Luke 1:46), is clearly modelled on the Song of Hannah in 1 Samuel 2:1-10, and to some extent on a passage in Enoch[3]. As it happens, Hannah, the childless wife is more closely matched by Elizabeth, but the general thought is the same – giving thanks to God for one's baby.

Also, the thought that God helps the poor and puts down the pompous (1 Samuel 2:7) is a major theme in Luke; it comes out in Luke 1:51-53, the proud are abased and the humble are exalted. Even more subtle is the use of Micah 7:20 which says, 'Thou wilt show faithfulness to Jacob and steadfast love to Abraham, as thou hast sworn to our fathers, from the days of old.' This reverberates in the closing verses of the Magnificat and the Benedictus in Luke 1:73 '... the oath which he swore to our father Abraham...' Even more subtle, and easily missed by the casual reader is this sort of thing:

Jesus was born and laid in a manger. In the opening verses of Isaiah, it says, 'The ox knows its owner, and the ass his master's crib, but Israel does not know, my people does not understand' (Isaiah 1:3). How true! This fact repeatedly appears in the rest of the gospel; the leaders of the Jews do not really understand what is going on, and reject Jesus. This factor is underscored by the puzzlement of his parents; Mary had to ponder all these things in her heart (Luke 2:19), and when Jesus is found chatting to the theological experts in the Temple, his parents were again amazed and could not comprehend his remark, 'I must be in my Father's house...' (Luke 2:50); 'They did not understand the saying which he spoke to them'. This boy was a puzzle to them all, and this comes round repeatedly right through to the end of the gospel. Another subtle prophetic realisation comes with the account of the widow of Nain, whose son was raised from death by Jesus. This reminds us of both Elijah and Elisha who raised the sons of two widows. It is a roundabout way of saying that Jesus is in the same league as the great prophets of old.

But Luke is at pains to show that Jesus was fully human, as opposed to some divine apparition or angel. He was circumcised; hardly something one could perpetrate on an angel! He was a bit of a scamp, dodging off from his parents – typical of young boys! He comes to John the Baptist to be baptised. He is cited as being about thirty years old. We are given a complete genealogy going back from Joseph to Adam, and if we count carefully, it is seventy-seven generations. An auspicious number indeed – one wonders where Luke managed to locate this information. It does stress, however that Jesus is descended from King David, and also Mattathias[4], the chief of the Hasmonean family, and also Zerubbabel[5], the would-be royalist returnee from the Exile. Of the twelve tribes, he is descended from Judah, and thence from Abraham and back to Seth and Adam. The implication in this is that he belongs very firmly to the human family; however he has an unmistakable streak of royalty in him. If we compare this with Matthew's genealogy, which is based on Joseph rather than Mary, he makes it forty-two generations from Abraham, including David and Zerubbabel, and all the Judean kings before the Exile, but not, however, the Hasmonean kings. What is this saying? That Jesus was clearly Jewish as opposed to gentile, and clearly of royal stock coming from David and Solomon. We notice the esoteric use of number seven in both arrangements. We also notice that in Matthew, Herod is stirred up to attempt to kill Jesus, but this element is missing in Luke. Instead, we have John the Baptist arrested for criticising Herod Antipas about his adulterous and incestuous behaviour with his sister in law.

Consistent with his humanity is Jesus' humility. He is born in a stable, like an outcast. His parents are of low estate, in spite of their genealogical connections. Mary calls herself the handmaid of the Lord. Their first visitors were shepherds; they were regarded as of very low social standing. There is no mention of the Magi coming from Persia. Jesus is noted as being obedient to his parents.

John the Baptist also is some kind of social failure; he was the subject of great expectations (Luke 1:66), and yet he goes off into the wilderness to live like a hermit; only later does he emerge at the Jordan to start his ministry of baptism. He is quickly equated with Elijah with his shaggy hair and teetotal approach to life (Luke 1:15-17).

The Messianic expectation is never very far beneath the surface in Luke. The phrase 'looking for the redemption of Jerusalem' occurs in 2:38, and reappears in Luke's writings. This expectation had been augmented by successive tyrannies: the Seleucids, the Hasmonean dynasty, the Herods and now the Romans. The Jews were asking, 'When will this all end? The Messiah must come soon to relieve us of this problem'. They were looking back to the glory days of David and Solomon. Anyone who looked something like a military deliverer was quickly hailed as the answer. Remarks such as 'he will be great... and the Lord will give to him the throne of his father David, and of his kingdom there will be no end... ' and '... for he has visited and redeemed his people Israel... ' and also 'this child is set for the rising and falling of many in Israel... ' were enough to raise many people's expectations[6]. The very name Jesus, in Hebrew, Joshua evoked the great hero who was the successor to Moses and conquered the land of Canaan. So it is no surprise that '... the people were in expectation and all men questioned in their hearts concerning John...' (3:15). At first they thought John was the Messiah, but he denied it. So their expectations landed on Jesus instead.

As a contrast to the humility and obscurity of Jesus, Luke makes sure that we see Jesus as the Son of God; this thought comes round no less than four times; three blatantly and the fourth indirectly when Jesus talks about 'My Father's house'. It is dramatically and publicly pronounced at the baptism as the Holy Spirit comes down in the form of a dove. This again is a subtle reference to an Old Testament situation; when the Flood subsided, it was a dove that gave Noah the indication that it was safe to come out of the Ark. What is this saying, symbolically? Is it saying that now we are starting again with a new regime with God; rescue has arrived and the ones who are saved can emerge and begin all over again? Or is it saying that the Covenant of Noah is now coming to fulfilment, just as the Covenant of Abraham, of David and the Sinai Covenant are as well.

This brings us to another important strand in Luke's theology, the work of the Holy Spirit. More than any of the other gospels, the Holy Spirit is emphasised. 'Filled with the Holy Spirit' appears several times in the birth narratives; Zechariah prophesies, with the Spirit, John is to be filled with the Spirit; Simeon is inspired by the Spirit. This theme recurs often in St Luke.

If we look at the L source, the material peculiar to Luke, we see these factors coming out with emphasis. Luke is particularly concerned about the poor, needy, widows, the sick, the women folk, the outcasts of society, the criminals and foreigners; in fact, anyone who does not fit in with the respectability of the Jewish legalists. That is not to say that this element is absent from the other gospels; it is just more heavily emphasised in Luke. In his first sermon at Nazareth, we have the mention of widows; this issue reappears regularly. The widow of Nain (7:11-17), the parable of the Unjust Judge in which a widow pleads her case (18:1), and the incident of the Widow's Mite in 21:1, although this also appears in Matthew[7]. It is just possible that this is another subtle prophetic fulfilment; in Isaiah and Jeremiah, Israel is often depicted as a widow because of their faithlessness, but this will all be reversed with the coming of the Messiah (Isaiah 47:8).

The lepers, who also were outcasts of society, are mentioned in his first sermon. In 17:11 we have ten lepers cleansed in the land of Samaria. The one who did come back to give thanks was actually a Samaritan. One of the most famous of Luke's parables is the Good Samaritan. The poor are constantly on his mind; not only in his first sermon, but in his version of the Beatitudes it reads 'blessed are the poor' and 'blessed are you who hunger'. The parable of Dives and Lazarus is a stark comparison between wealth and poverty and how it will all be reversed. So we see the parable of the Rich Fool where it says, 'a man's life does not consist in the abundance of his possessions' (12:15). Self importance is also criticised: it is unwise to take the chief seats at a party in case someone more important comes and one is displaced; when giving a party, why not invite the poor and disabled instead of one's rich friends. Luke is not happy with surfeiting and drunkenness. This all completes the thoughts in the Magnificat, that the rich will be sent empty away.

As far as a light to lighten the gentiles is concerned, Luke clearly shows that foreigners are welcome in the new kingdom of God. The widow of Zaraphath (another prophetic realisation), Naaman the Syrian, and the men of Nineveh (from Assyria, the arch-enemy) are all in favour. At the healing of the Centurion's servant in 7:1-10, Luke points out that he is worthy and helpful towards the Jews, having built them a synagogue. In fact, gentiles from every direction of the compass will be coming and accepted (13:29).

Luke must have been in favour of gender equality. In the infancy narratives, the account centres on Elizabeth and Mary as an essential element in the story of salvation. Much mention is made of the ladies who followed him on his journeys; Joanna, Susanna, and Mary Magdalene whose healing is specifically mentioned. The account of Martha and Mary is cited for the importance of not being too busy to listen to God's words. Jesus' feet are anointed by a fallen woman, an unnamed woman in the crowd blesses him (11:27), and a woman cured of an infirmity is dubbed as a daughter of Abraham. On his way to the cross, Jesus tells the daughters of Jerusalem not to weep for him, but for themselves. An important contingent who are witnesses to the crucifixion and the resurrection are an assemblage of women. It is strange that Luke, according to church tradition, never married, but he must have been in favour of social equality, which for those days would have seemed exceedingly trendy, and for some people quite threatening.

But added to this, he is not very pleased with those who are in authority. Pontius Pilate is noted as committing an atrocity with the Galileans, and also as a weak and indecisive judge who is swayed by the mob. Herod Antipas is dubbed 'that fox' who was committing incest, and who treated Jesus with disrespect. He sent him off with 'gorgeous apparel'. How do we interpret this; that he dressed him up in purple to go back to Pilate; this would have been a capital offence, impersonating royalty; in other words, he tried to frame Jesus. One of the parables includes an Unjust Judge. The Pharisees, who thought of themselves as the leading lights in Judaism, are constantly shown up in a poor light, as in the parable of the Pharisee and the Publican. It is a Pharisee who is dubious about the anointing of Jesus' feet; he is given a pep-talk on the subject of forgiveness.

Just as his parents were careful to keep to the rules, so too is Jesus. So for instance, the cleansing of the Temple in 19:44 is shortened and toned down by comparison with the other gospels. Jesus does not turn violent and make a whip. The cursing of the fig tree is omitted; it is the only destructive miracle on record, but Luke avoids mentioning it. At the trials, Pontius Pilate no less than three times states that he can find no fault in Jesus and wants to release him. Quite clearly he is being framed by false witnesses who mendaciously claim he was telling people not to pay their taxes. Herod Antipas also cannot find any fault in him, but treats him with contempt. The contrast between Jesus and Barabbas the thief and insurrectionist is quite stark, and the irony is that the criminal gets off and the innocent is condemned. At the end of the crucifixion scene, the Centurion concludes that Jesus is an innocent man, or a righteous man. This could be Luke's way of telling us that the Roman system of justice was seriously faulty. As Jesus is placed in the tomb, there is no attempt at embalming him, since as the Sabbath was about to come at 6 pm, they had to rest according to the Law (23:56). Here we see the contrast between Jesus' followers observing the rules, and the authorities who tried every nasty trick to incriminate him and force a death sentence quite unfairly. On the other hand, Jesus gives us plenty of indication that mercy and forgiveness are on offer. So, when one of the thieves on the cross repented, he was forgiven and promised Paradise in the next world. In the parables there is much about forgiveness: the Unjust Judge, the Unjust Steward, the Friend at Midnight, the Prodigal Son, the Pharisee and the Publican. All tell of God's mercy. The incident of Zacchaeus, the tax collector, is cited; with the reputation they had, of swindling the public and the authorities, here is someone who is repentant and forgiven. When Jesus is arrested and Malchus' ear is damaged, Jesus heals him; the last of the healing miracles, which indicates that he had nothing against his enemies. In the last few moments of his life, Jesus says 'Father forgive; they know not what they are doing' (23:34).

Thus we see that the configuration of Isaiah, that everything in the Messianic age will be reversed; the rich become poor, the high and mighty are abased, the sick and the dying are given new life. The whole of his gospel speaks of this; principally with the special source called L but also the material borrowed from Mark and possibly also Matthew. There are a few other issues that Luke likes to emphasise in addition to this.

The temptations clearly show that the unseen world of evil spirits are trying to derail Jesus' ministry. In Luke 4:13 it states that the devil 'departed from him until an opportune time', in other words, temptation was still going to occur, right up to the very end. And the final temptation was on the cross, when everyone was coaxing him to break free and assert his messiahship. But Jesus is aware of this and knows how to deal with it. A most significant remark comes in 10:17 where he states that he has seen Satan fall like lightning from heaven. This follows the apocalyptic view that Satan is a fallen angel. Whether Jesus means that it is happening now, or that he saw it before the beginning of human history, in his capacity as God's instrument in creation, is not clear. But Satan is seen as active at the Last Supper, when Jesus says that Satan wants to sift Simon Peter like wheat; in other words, test his faith. But Jesus has prayed for him. Even so, he knows that Peter will give way to temptation and learn a sharp lesson about the need for repentance. Strangely, in Luke 9:22, following the incident of Peter's confession, there is no mention of Satan speaking through the mouth of Peter, as is seen in Matthew 16:16-23. In Luke 17:1, Jesus says, 'temptations to sin are sure to come...'; evil is a reality but we have to be realistic about it.

Another important element is Luke's emphasis on the reality of the resurrection. It is a lovely touch how the women who followed him were the first to become aware of his rising again. The men-folk thought it was a fiction. When he showed himself to them later on, he says, 'See my hands and my feet, that it is I myself; handle me, and see; for a spirit has not flesh and bones as you see that I have...' and he then eats a piece of boiled fish. The importance of there being witnesses is stressed, not just for the crucifixion which meant he really did die, but also for the resurrection which meant he really did rise again. The issue of disbelief is raised: 'they still disbelieved for joy'.

This brings us back to Jesus as a prophet. His foreknowledge of the death and resurrection is stressed in the teachings of the gospel. Also the little details about how he knew about the upper room and the man carrying a pitcher of water, which would lead them to the right house, are all indicative of his status as a genuine prophet. To us, a man carrying a jug of water would seem[8] normal, but in those days, it would have been a woman's task to cart water into the house. This is another example of the reversal of everything in the messianic age. Luke continues this element of the continuation of prophesy in the acts, where we see New Testament prophets at work.

One rather strange difference of opinion between Luke and the other two Synoptics comes at the Last Supper. Jesus blesses the cup of wine first but refuses to drink any himself. The blessing of the bread comes after the cup. We notice that he stresses more clearly that he will not eat or drink any of it until the messianic banquet in the Kingdom of God comes. The same element is seen in Mark and Matthew, but it is not so heavily stressed. One could explain the cup and the bread in this way. At a Passover meal, there might be anything up to four blessings of the cup and the bread, or possibly more. So in the middle of the meal, a cup could be blessed followed by the bread[9]. Maybe this is a trivial point but Luke may be inferring something all the same. Is he saying that Jesus has to die first, before he can feed the whole world? It would tie in with the thought that he would have to die first before the Kingdom of God can fully come in. This is actually what did happen; after he had died, and rose again, he ate a piece of fish. Also, with the two people on the road to Emmaus (a very special story only found in Luke), he has a meal with them, after he has suffered[10].

Looking at the material peculiar to Luke is very instructive; it tells us what his bias is. That does not mean that he has to have invented all this material. Much of it ties in with what we see in the other gospels, but he has a way of citing material in such a fashion as to emphasise the matters that he felt ought to come out in relation to Jesus. All the gospel writers do this, some more blatantly than others. That does not mean that he disagrees with the other writers. To take an instance, the Messianic secret, which is dominant in Mark, almost disappears in Luke, but not completely. Also Mark's emphasis on the world of the spirit is downplayed, but it does not disappear altogether. Matthew's emphasis on Jesus as the Eternal Judge and the coming of judgement day is also toned down. Luke's apocalypse is there but nowhere near as vivid and frightening as in Matthew. The same is true with Matthew's resurrection account. It is massively exciting, dramatic and loaded with mythology, but Luke's resurrection is calm, unspectacular and focussed on the witnessing of the event. Luke has a way of including these matters, but in proportion to other issues. Luke's approach is often more subtle, which will suggest that he must have been a very clever person.

One theological issue that is not peculiar to Luke is the importance of the Sabbath. One might have thought that, assuming he was aiming at a gentile readership, the Sabbath would have not had much meaning for them. Very much to the contrary. Looking at the Cornfield incident when the disciples plucked wheat on the Sabbath, Luke slightly abbreviates Mark's version, omitting any mention of Abiathar the priest (which is understandable), but comes to the same conclusion, that 'The Son of Man is Lord of the Sabbath' (6:5). Matthew also abbreviates Mark's version but adds rather more from his own source, termed M. This account is followed by the healing of the man with a withered hand, on the Sabbath. Luke repeats the story quite faithfully this time; he steps up the emotion by saying that the Scribes and Pharisees were 'filled with fury'. Jesus points out that mercy and caring for people is more important than sticking rigidly to the rules. 'Is it lawful on the Sabbath to do good or to do harm, to save life or to destroy it?'[11] In Luke 4:31 we have another Sabbath incident, of a man with a withered hand, followed by the healing of Peter's mother in law. Luke has quite faithfully taken this from St Mark. But Luke is not completely dependent on Mark for his interest in the Sabbath; in Luke 13:10-15 we have a woman who is bent double and Jesus cures her. But the ruler of the Synogogue objected. Jesus calls him a hypocrite. If you can feed your animals on a Sabbath, why not release this lady from her bondage to Satan? This is an even more outright and deliberate teaching about the Sabbath, found only in the L source.

What is the substratum of this piece of theology? After all, the gentile readers presumably would have found the Jewish Sabbath observance rather strange; one was not allowed to do any work at all, with a few exceptions outlined by the Rabbis. One would then, as now, find that excessive to the point of folly. What is Jesus saying when he claims to be the Lord of the Sabbath? If we assume, as the first disciples almost certainly did, that Jesus was pre-existent with the Father at creation and also at the giving of the Ten Commandments, in effect it was Jesus who gave us the law of the Sabbath. So then, if it is his law, he has the right to alter, amend and modify it. It is no surprise to find that in Luke's gospel, Jesus is actually called 'the Lord' (e.g. 17:5 and 22:61) which is tantamount to calling him God. So from God's point of view, and man's point of view, the Sabbath needs to be used with common sense and moderation. This view of things now pervades virtually all of life in the world. Everyone knows the importance of one, or even two, days a week off from work, and in addition the necessity of having a holiday; just working flat out all the time is destructive for physical and mental health. We have the Jews to thank for that approach to life.

Philosophy in St Luke

His philosophy is very much bound up with his theology, and it is perhaps artificial to try to separate the two. Luke's attitude to society is remarkably 'modern' in tone. He is clearly in favour of equality. He might almost be a non-violent version of 'Liberty, Equality and Fraternity', which is what the French attempted to achieve. In today's parlance, he might be seen as a leftist, probably comfortable as a Socialist, and quite happy to criticise authority. This is most noticeable with the gender equality that he clearly advocates. The ladies have as much, if not more, to offer than the men. That would have seemed outrageous to many in the ancient world. He is also sympathetic to the working man, the slaves and labourers. In 10:7 he remarks, 'the labourer his worthy of his hire'.

If asked about free will and predestination, Luke would almost certainly have said that the life and ministry of Jesus was predetermined. This comes out in Luke 22:22, 'for the Son of Man goes as it has been determined'. However, in the next breath there is the concession to free will: 'but woe to that man by whom he is betrayed'. In other words, Judas was not forced to betray him; it was his choice. The fact that there were three temptations to go wrong indicate that Jesus had the freedom to choose. If he had had no such freedom, then the temptations would have been meaningless. The disciples, by association, are also predetermined. Following the apocalyptic tradition that people's names are inscribed in heavenly records, which means they are saved in advance[12], this is a mythological way of saying, 'You were chosen beforehand, and it was not a matter of your free choice'.

Luke would almost certainly have found himself comfortable with the modern policy of One World. He stresses that the gospel is for the Gentiles as much as for the Jews. This is the international way of thinking which would tie in with socialism. He records how this way of thinking annoyed the Jews to the point that they attempted to lynch him.

With regard to the question of theodicy, the problem of evil, Luke would almost certainly say that dualism was the answer. Satan is often mentioned in many contexts; not that Satan is an alternative god. Luke would also claim to be a monotheist if he had any regard for Isaiah, but strangely, God allows Satan to interfere with people's health. How often do we have it said that someone's illness is some sort of bondage to Satan? Coming from a doctor of the ancient world, this is significant. It means that then, as now, the medics are aware that disease is not just purely and simply a physical matter; there is also, almost always a spiritual aspect to it. Unfortunately we are not fully informed of what methods the doctors used in those days, but we know that they had a thing called the asclepeion, which in modern parlance would be a sanatorium or health centre. Some of their procedures were quite sophisticated, and may have been just as effective or perhaps even more effective than today's invasive methods. But as we all know, healthy mind almost always leads to healthy body. That is a modern philosophical dictum, which would hardly be denied by Luke.

Mythology in Luke

It is noticeable that Luke, of all the Synoptics, places less emphasis on mythological thought. It is not completely absent from his gospel, but is clearly toned down. Matthew would rate as the most mythological thinker of the three, and Mark somewhere in between. It would be an interesting thought to consider if Luke was the demythologiser of the ancient world. His stance might come somewhat close to humanism, except that he has a strong impression of God bringing his Kingdom into this world. We notice that at the crucifixion, there is no earthquake, neither is there one at the resurrection. We do not hear about angels at the tomb, just men in dazzling white clothing. This reminds us of the two men with Jesus at the transfiguration; are they meant to be Moses and Elijah, as opposed to being angels? We notice that there is no mention of an angel at the temptations. Luke is economical on the subject of angels; we only have Gabriel appearing in the birth narratives, and the whole company of heaven visiting the shepherds. However, an angel does appear to comfort him, in the Garden of Gethsemane (Luke 22:43), which does not happen in Mark or Matthew, or even in John.

As far as truth is concerned, Luke would definitely claim to be offering the truth about Jesus to the Roman world; and since Jesus is termed 'the Lord' that would mean the truth about God as well. It would be fair to say that he does try to portray the amazing events surrounding Jesus in a fair and rational way, without undue exaggeration. Jesus himself does not indulge in too much exaggeration in his teaching, something that we do see in Matthew. It would be fair to say that Luke is honest in his inclusion of material, which other gospel writers probably baulked at. The Parable of the Unjust Steward (16:1-13) is a problem and has been for all Christians over the centuries. It is not easy to interpret and is probably the most difficult of all the parables. When Jesus told it, the effect was that the Pharisees concluded that he was deranged – that was an easy way out of the problem. But a close inspection of the parable reveals that there are hidden depths in it that defy[13] easy human rationalisation. We can applaud Luke for his honesty in including it. There are times when the truth is difficult. One can study my treatment of this parable in my first book, *The Theology of Paradox*.

Literary and Linguistic matters

Luke's gospel is a companion volume to the Acts of the Apostles. It is in Koine Greek, which was the *patois* of the eastern Roman Empire, but in contrast with other New Testament writers, Luke's Greek is quite elevated and polished, probably the best Greek in the book. It forms quite a contrast to Mark's pretty basic and John's fairly simplistic Greek. This supports the idea that he was a gentile, but probably a proselyte to Judaism. He seems to be well versed in the Septuagint, the Greek translation of the Old Testament. It is possible that he did not understand the Hebrew as he usually omits any original Aramaic words, which can be found in Mark and Matthew. In fact, it might be fair to say that he thought of his two books as a continuation of the classic Hebrew view of the pattern of salvation, but as applied by continuation into the gentile world. Many of his passages remind us of some of the classic accounts in the books of Samuel and the Kings. It is no surprise to find that his poetic renditions are meant to evoke the Song of Hannah and others. He has Jesus pointing out that all these happenings are a fulfilment of the old prophecies; but his use of the prophets on the one hand can be fairly obvious; on the other hand, they can be really quite subtle. It is there for anyone soaked in Judaism but not too heavy-going for anyone who wished to convert to Christianity.

His style is quite distinctive. He does not go in for too much repetition, which is in contrast to many sacred writings. Where repetition is required, he varies the wording or the setting so that it does not become tedious. 'And it came to pass' is used as a cliché to connect us to the Old Testament phraseology, but it is not overdone, as in the Book of Mormon (Chapter 11). When quoting Mark or Matthew, he often tidies up their wording or abbreviates things a little, for the sake of space, we assume. In his own source, termed L, there is the suspicion that this was an oral source and as such it displays rather more of his own turn of phrase. Some of the most iconic of all Jesus' parables are Luke's own material: the Prodigal Son and the Good Samaritan. These are really the nitty-gritty of Christian love and caring.

Concluding remarks about Luke

Because there are four canonical gospels, each written with its own bias and axe to grind, this does not mean that one is correct and the others wrong. Each gospel offers us a slightly different view of Jesus. Just as 1 and 2 Maccabees portray the Hasmonean upsurge in a slightly different light, so too does 1 and 2 Kings and 1 and 2 Chronicles and the four gospels also offer different insights. The picture of Jesus comes up in 3D; it might even be fair to say 4D. In Christian symbolism, Luke is portrayed with the face of a man[14]; this is very appropriate. He has a human interest, he knows about the realities of those who are underprivileged and rejected. He is thoroughly down-to-earth and realistic about Jesus. He offers us a few insights into his childhood, which are largely absent from the other gospels. He does not get carried away with a lot of spurious and exaggerated material, which was almost certainly current at that time. The apocryphal gospels must have been a temptation for inclusion, and Matthew appears to lean in that direction. But Luke is almost certainly thinking of the impression it would make on the average logical, reasonable, decent-minded Roman gentleman of his times. Such a person would hardly have been impressed by the exaggerated material about Jesus in his infancy[15]. It is now thought that the apocryphal gospels surfaced after the formation of the canonical gospels, and whether that is true or not does not matter. The truth was that there were all kinds of rumours and accounts about Jesus in circulation, some of them wild and some of them well supported by solid witnesses. Luke goes to the trouble to sort these matters out and give us a balanced and reliable account; in that task, he does admirably well.

The proto-gospel of James, as compared with the early Chapters of Luke

This work goes under various titles and has been known all through church history and taken seriously by various elements in the Christian world. The author is claimed to be James – not the disciple, but the half-brother of Jesus by a previous marriage of Joseph. Joseph is portrayed as an elderly widower who is chosen by lot to take on this girl Mary who is a ward of the Temple. It is thought that the book was in circulation by 150 AD, but it never received canonical status. This did not stop some elements in the church from taking it seriously, but it has never been given the status of being doctrinally binding, since it is clearly somewhat fanciful. It is of relevance to St Luke because it concerns only the origins of Jesus and John the Baptist; it does not go on to describe the ministry or the passion. It is described here as an example of what Luke may have been faced with when selecting reliable material for his Gospel; there were many such 'gospels' in circulation, of varying quality. This one, allegedly by James the half-brother of Jesus, is comparatively sane when seen against some of the others. Some of its material is quite intriguing, but always there is the element of exaggeration and the difficulty of evaluating it.[15]

To give a brief outline: a wealthy man called Joachim and his wife, Anna, were advanced in years and had not been able to produce a child. This was regarded as disgraceful by the Jewish leadership and they were both deeply upset about it. Joachim went off into the wilderness to pray and Anna dressed up in mourning like a widow. However, angels came to both of them and announced that they would have a child. When Joachim came home to his wife, she told him the good news, but of course the inference was that it was a miraculous conception. Anna gave birth after seven months to a baby girl to be called Mary. They waited until she was three years old and then presented her at the Temple to be a ward, rather like Samuel. At the age of twelve, the priests decided that she should be married; this was done by lot, and the lot fell on Joseph. He had to take the Lord's virgin into his safe-keeping, not so much as a full-blown 'wife', but as a 'daughter'. Joseph had to go away to do his construction work. In the meantime, Mary was employed in making a veil for the Temple. It was then that the angel of the Annunciation came to her; then she went to stay with her cousin Elizabeth for three months as her pregnancy developed.

On coming home, Joseph saw that Mary was pregnant and went through the obvious shock and questioning about how this could be. But the angel reassured him and issued the name Jesus. When the authorities realised the situation they were indignant, but both Mary and Joseph insist on their innocence. They are both required to drink 'the water of refutation', which must have been some sort of endurance test, but no sin was revealed. Then we come to the birth of Jesus in a cave in Bethlehem. Joseph found a midwife and the birth was accompanied with a marvellous light. Salome, on hearing of the virgin birth, wanted to ascertain the truth of it. She inspected Mary and received a shock: it was true. Then the wise men appeared, after seeking advice from Herod. The star is described and the three gifts. When Mary heard of the murder of the babies, she hid Jesus in the manger. Elizabeth, however, took John into the mountains to avoid the hit squad. There was angelic protection in action. When Herod could not find John, he badgered his father Zacharias, and in the end had him murdered in the sanctuary. When the priests realised what had happened, they appointed Simeon in his place, the very one who gave us the Nunc Dimittis. This is where the account ends; there is nothing about the visit to the Temple when Jesus was aged twelve, nor the Baptism, nor anything of his ministry.

We notice that the same ingredients are included as in the birth narratives in Luke – the aged couples that are desperate to have a baby. Could we take this as symbolic of the Old Testament desperate to be transformed into the New Testament? Anna's conception is just as miraculous as Mary's. Great emphasis is placed on the purity of both women and of the two men involved. This is a factor seen with many great spiritual leaders in other parts of the world. There is a need for one's messiah to be above and beyond human corruption, and that would include his mother, in this case his grandmother Anna, also.

An intriguing element in the story is when Joseph observes that 'time gets stuck'. All movement is suspended as Jesus is born. It is just like when a film abruptly stops and then starts again. What is this saying? Does it imply that the Lord of time and space is coming into this world?

We see that important urge in human nature to find out what happened before, the causation of things. Mark's gospel starts abruptly with no explanation of where Jesus came from. John's gospel gives us a prologue about Jesus being the *logos* of God, the everlasting Word. People must have been asking, 'Where or how did Jesus appear?' 'Was he an angel or a ghost or what?' The answer is attempted by Matthew and Luke. This gospel of James cleverly combines the two accounts, but strangely there is no mention of the shepherds in the fields as the first visitors to Jesus. Instead, we have the midwife and Salome who wishes to be certain that Mary is still a virgin. In this we see a curious paradox, that she has had a baby but is still 'pure' in terms of Jewish thinking at the time. But the upshot of it is that Jesus is really human, born of a woman, even if there was glory shining in the cave.

From this we can conclude that James, the alleged half-brother of Jesus was not a Gnostic. For an outline of Gnostic thought, one can refer to Chapter 19, the Gnostic Gospel of Truth. He can fairly be called proto-orthodox, in that Jesus is portrayed as really human and yet heralded by the angels and arrived in glory despite his humble circumstances. So too with Mary, as she is portrayed as just a simple girl doing work for the Temple just as other girls did. But she too has an angelic announcement as she is conceived by Anna.

It is easy to write this material off as fanciful and worthless, but the trouble is, where do we draw the line? It is interesting that the account of Zacharias (Zechariah) being murdered in the sanctuary appears to be known about by Jesus! There are two references to this incident, apparently coming from the Q source, which is not noted for being too fanciful. Luke, in 11:52, records Jesus as admonishing the lawyers, and blaming them for the martyrdom of the prophets from Abel at the start down to Zechariah. Abel is dubbed as innocent, and Zechariah is claimed to have been murdered by the Pharisees. This is perhaps putting it rather strongly; in James' version, it is Herod's hit squad that commit the atrocity. Even so it will all come home to roost in this generation.

What this indicates, if anything, is that the relationship between the canonical gospels and the apocryphal gospels is not really a straightforward matter. We think we know who influenced whom; but nothing is totally certain. We do not really know how much borrowing went on, how much copying, how much rumour-mongering, and how much invention. In the end, we have to trust the early church fathers in their wisdom, for deciding what material is reliable and what is spurious.

Footnotes for Chapter 23: St Luke

1. Suetonius; The Twelve Caesars, page 133.
2. Luke 7:28.
3. The same thought occurs in Enoch; see Chapter 20.
4. Mattathais, the father of Judas Maccabeus. See Chapter 2.

5. Zerubbabel: In 1 Chronicles 3:19 he is clearly of royal lineage. Haggai and Zechariah make several mentions of him.
6. Luke 1:32.
7. Mark 12:41
8. Luke 22:10.
9. Luke 22:17.
10. Luke 24:13.
11. Luke 6:6-11
12. This idea of heavenly records is found in Enoch (Chapter 20), and the earliest traces of it may be found in the Psalms.
13. Luke 16:1-8.
14. Revelation 4:7. The four living beasts represent the four gospel writers.
15. There were many such spurious 'gospels' in circulation. Many of them were destroyed and others keep appearing with the efforts of the archaeologists.

24

The Epistle to the Hebrews

This letter, which is addressed to the Jewish people and possibly early converts to Christianity, has been attributed to St Paul. But in recent years, scholarship has brought this into question, since the style and thought forms are somewhat different from what we assume to be the genuine epistles of Paul, which dominate the latter part of the New Testament. Essentially it does not matter who wrote it; the theological message is just as valid as if Paul had written it. It may have come from one of Paul's associates, which could explain why it was included in the canon of the New Testament. There was a reluctance to include anything that was not known to be apostolic; this means that the letter must stem from the early years of the Christian Church, maybe within the first twenty or thirty years, when Christianity was beginning to emerge as a separate entity from Judaism. The fact that it is a letter addressed to the Jews is probably quite incidental; its theological message and application is just as relevant to anyone of any religion that follows some sort of sacrificial mentality, combined with meritology, in any age or situation. It has universal application. It is essentially a theological tract attempting to justify why Jesus had to suffer and die, a question which many an enquirer would pose.

Historical, geographical and mathematical aspects

There is very little of these elements in the Hebrews, which is rather unusual for the Judaeo-Christian scriptural material. In 13:23 we are told that Timothy has been released from prison, and this brings us down to earth with a bump, for he was one of Paul's associates on the early missionary journeys. Also there is mention of Italy, but that does not have to mean that the epistle was written there. The main historical element lies in that classic passage in Chapter 11, where the writer reviews all the champions of faith from Abel, through the Patriarchs, to Moses, the Judges and onwards[1]. The passage is clearly inspired by that passage in Ecclesiasticus 44–50 and is patently the New Testament equivalent of it. It is clearly an encouragement to bear up under persecution, which was happening in the early years of the Church. In addition to this, there is much reference to the wilderness period, when the Israelites moaned and groaned at Meribah. Other than that there is no direct or firm historical connection in the book.

Mythological assumptions

Hebrews has much to say about angels but seldom mentions the Devil. He would be making the same assumptions about the three-tiered universe as almost everyone in that day and age. The apocalyptic mentality of the age was happy to speculate about angels, archangels and all kinds of spiritual entities and heavenly principles. This was in contrast to the polytheistic pattern of thought, as seen in Greek, Roman and Hindu thought, that there was a supreme god who fathered hordes of secondary gods. If one were a Judaic monotheist, one would have one God and hordes of angels instead; also some fallen angels which would explain the existence of evil in the world. But Hebrews does not embark on this aspect of theology, namely theodicy. Nearly all of Chapter one is taken up with emphasising that Jesus was not just another angel or heavenly appearance; not an avatar as the Hindus might have said. He is way above the angels, being right next to God in the top rank. Here we have the 'sonship' of Jesus emphasised; not that he is a run-of-the-mill son of God which all believers become, but 'son' in a special way, not available even to the angels. Hebrews quotes a whole list of Old Testament references to support his argument, all of them coming from the Psalms. His method of using scriptural proofs may seem a little strange to us in today's world, but we must realise that he is speaking to those who were soaked in the Psalms and took them literally. So while the angels are 'ministering spirits sent forth to serve', which is fine in its own way, Jesus is above and beyond all that. This is where the pre-existence of the Messiah Jesus comes into play; he was with the Eternal Father right at the beginning of all things, 'upholding the universe by his word of power'. Then he came into the world to address human failure and then returned to the Father eternally, 'having become as much superior to the angels as the name he has obtained is more excellent than theirs'[2].

In this we see Hebrews' attempt at coping with the Incarnation. Wisely, he does not attempt to explain it in terms of human logic; something which is not possible anyway. It sounds a little like adoptionism at times; 'the name he has obtained' might suggest that Jesus had to earn it by some sort of merit pattern. Such a phrase would be an encouragement to those in later years who embarked on an adoptionist heresy, but Hebrews probably never thought of it like that. What he is trying to say, as a counterblast to the Gnostics of his day, is that Jesus was not just some sort of heavenly apparition, like an angel or some sort of spiritual principle; he was really on earth as a human being, and the phrase 'in the days of his flesh'[3] is important. He was not just pretending to die; the crucifixion was not just a piece of theatre. He had to die just like any other human person in order that the New Testament could come into force.

The sonship of Jesus naturally raises the question of the sonship of all of us. That is the relevance of 'what is man that thou art mindful of him?' (Hebrews 2:5), 'or the son of man that thou carest for him?' Why is Hebrews saying this? We must recall that Zeus, in Greek theology, hardly cared anything for mankind; in fact, he detested us. The relevance here is that Hebrews is saying that Almighty God does care about us, to the extent that he sent his Eternal Son into the world to sort things out and take control of everything. Hebrews has to admit, quite fairly, that 'as it is, we do not yet see everything in subjection to him'[4]. To this day, the Jews will say that Jesus cannot have been the true Messiah since the world is still bogged down with evil and things going wrong. One could reply to this by saying that things appear to go wrong, but the deeper truth is that God is in control of history and he has a mysterious way of transforming wrong into right. This is a paradox that is a spin-off from the Incarnation. The prime example of it is the case of the treachery of Judas Iscariot – a filthy treacherous act that resulted in Jesus being put to death. This was perfect for God's purposes; out of it came the Resurrection and salvation available for all of the human race. Hebrews takes a slightly different line in his answer; he says that because Jesus was tempted and suffered, he is able to help us now with our earthly problems. This means that the failures encountered in this life are transformed into successes, a paradox which underlies the whole ministry of Jesus. It is all about sonship. As Jesus was a 'son', so also his brothers and sisters in the faith become adopted by God:

'Here am I, and the children God has given me' (Hebrews 2:13). We all become the children of God. This is where mythology fades away and the metaphor of sonship becomes central.

Theological main themes

Certain elements of the theology of Hebrews have already been touched on, and this is unavoidable since theology and mythology are not normally separable in the Bible. But the main theological theme now takes shape in

Chapter 3 and onwards. He claims that there are two covenants and two priesthoods associated with each one. There is the juxtaposition of Moses with Jesus: Moses was a faithful worker as a servant; Jesus was faithful as a Son. This typifies the two covenants, the one given at Sinai and the one given by Jesus. This is not to deny the other covenants in the Old Testament; namely that of Noah, of Abraham, and of David. They too all receive a mention in various places. But the core of the matter in Hebrews is the contrast between the giving of the Law at Mount Sinai and the giving of the New Testament. With the first situation, God's gift of the covenant, was met with hardness of heart and disbelief on the part of the Israelites. They provoked God by playing up awkward; this is typified by the Meribah incident. The result of this was that even though they eventually physically gained the Promised Land, they did not really enter into a full relationship of peace and trust with God. This is termed God's rest and it is related to the Sabbath. Hebrews is quite emphatic that this time round, with a new covenant being given, there is another chance to enter into God's 'rest'. He quotes Psalm 95 not just as a warning but as a way out of the impasse caused by the Israelites being difficult. This time, 'today', do not mess things up. Take the opportunity and accept this new covenant that Jesus has brought in. 'Today, when you hear his voice, do not harden your hearts...' comes round various times. This is Hebrews' way of emphasising the matter: do not miss out on the opportunity to enter into a full and wonderful relationship with God, as the Israelites in the wilderness failed to do. Since Hebrews is speaking first and foremost to the Jews who were objecting to Christianity and also to early converts from Judaism, he does not widen the matter out to involve the Gentiles, something that St Paul almost certainly would have done.

Working in with the two covenants is the metaphor of the two kinds of priesthood. There is the earthly priesthood, which although it was ordained by God and nominated Aaron as its founding member, it is only of any efficacy within the covenant of Sinai. The priest has the task of offering sacrifices to clear guilt, but since he is only human himself and subject to human failure, there is a limit to what this system can achieve. It really needs someone who is free of guilt and has withstood temptation to make a truly effective sacrifice. We notice that in the Exodus account, it was Aaron who instigated the making of the golden calf that horrified Moses; Hebrews does not mention this but any Jewish reader would have immediately thought of this incident. It means that Aaron and his sons were not perfect by any manner of means. Now comes the relevance of Jesus, the eternal high priest, who was perfect. Hebrews gives this a firm theological basis by reference to the encounter between Melchizedek and Abraham in Genesis 14:18, an incident that pre-dates the Sinai covenant and refers us indirectly to the covenant of Abraham. In this account, a priest appears, from a place called Salem, which we now see as Jerusalem, and a sacramental ceremony is enacted. It involves bread and wine, which reminds us of the Christian Eucharist. Since Melchizedek appears to have no earthly parentage, Hebrews takes this as him being some sort of unbegotten heavenly figure; in other words, his priesthood is not of this world but eternal. The way that Hebrews argues this will probably cut very little ice with modern minds, but in the ancient world, where one's parentage and family line were seen as very important for one's identity, this logical development would have meant quite a lot; certainly to the Jews, but also to various Gentile peoples. The name Melchizedek reverberates right through Chapters 5, 6 and 7, thus giving it a massive emphasis. Hebrews quotes Psalm 110 as a proof text that is meant to convince his readers: 'thou art a priest after the order of Melchizedek'. How is this concept of any meaning to us now? What Hebrews is saying, if we can try to render it in modern terms, is that Jesus is not just an earthly representative of man to God, as we see in the priesthood of Judaism and of other world religions. Jesus is actually an eternal priest who was interceding for us before he arrived on earth as well as after he ascended. This now ties in with the eternal sonship of Jesus; it is another metaphor but amounts to much the same thing. There is some element, some facility, some aspect in the nature of God that allows him to relate to the human race in a sympathetic way; he understands our weaknesses and he makes allowances for our stupidities. This contrasts strongly with the pagan view of God. Zeus was not inclined to care about the fate of mankind, and he was quite annoyed that any of us survived the Flood. When it comes to a battle, such as the siege of Troy, he is not bothered about the outcome; he changes sides on a whim. This is not the God of Love, as shown to us in the New Testament.

Hebrews shows how the Old Testament of Sinai was a preparation for the New Testament. In the old arrangement, the high priest (Aaron) enters the Holy of Holies once a year but Jesus enters the 'Holy Place' once and for all. Since he is perfect, his offering of himself is totally effective and brings about a new relationship between God and mankind. Hebrews is playing on the fact that in the pagan world whatever sacrifice is enacted it had to be perfect: the victim had to be without blemish, the priest had to be washed and prepared, and the ritual had to be absolutely followed correctly. If anything went wrong, such as the animal wanting to turn back, the whole process had to be started all over again. But the truth was that no humanly-performed sacrifice was ever completely perfect, since we all have our failings, priests included. But the contrast with Jesus was that he was perfect himself, not having sinned. He had been washed in the River Jordan at his baptism; the victim, himself, was perfect and did not try to turn back; the altar and the temple also was not made with hands, in other words, perfect. This means that the sacrifice of Christ is totally effective with God and brings about everlasting cleansing of the human conscience. The metaphor is a powerful one, but Hebrews does let drop that this is all symbolic (Hebrews 9:9); even so, this does not prevent it from being the truth. In fact, it is probably nearer to the truth as figurative language as opposed to literal.

We then encounter the theological matter of **typology**, something that is not normally discussed nowadays. Typology means that matters arising in the New Testament can also be traced in the Old Testament, rather like a mirror image. The question arises, what was the point of having the Old Covenant with its rituals, if it was not really effective? Why bother? Hebrews gives us the answer: 'they serve as a copy and a shadow of the heavenly sanctuary'. In other words, it was a 'type' of what was to come. It had the effect of preparing people's minds for the ultimate sacrifice of Christ. Now that this has happened, the old order is going into obsolescence; not that it was wrong, but that it has been brought to completion and superseded. This means that the rituals and ceremonies of the Temple are now unnecessary. Hebrews does not quite go so far as to say that all the pagan sacrificial systems have been rendered obsolete, but that is the implication in this remark:

'It is impossible that the blood of bulls and goats should take away sins' (Hebrews 10:4).

This was quite a courageous and *avant guarde* thing to say, in a world, both Jewish and Hellenistic, that all their sacrifices were a waste of time and resources. We may recall that some of the mystery religions of Ancient Rome involved the Taurobolium[5], a ceremony in which a bull was bled to death over someone in a pit beneath, as a sort of baptismal initiatory ritual. Hebrews must have been aware of such procedures, but he is saying it is all complete nonsense. Of course, in the modern world, most people would take that remark as fairly obvious.

Continuing the metaphor of the covenant (Hebrews 9:11), spins out the implications of it rather cleverly. When God made the covenant or testament of Sinai, there had to be a sacrifice to ratify the arrangement. In fact, any covenant in those times had to be accompanied by a sacrifice, but Hebrews does not include that thought. Now, when Jesus gives us the New Testament, there must also be a sacrifice, the shedding of blood will bring the covenant into force. While the testator is still alive, the will does not come into force. Only when the testator dies, does it become active and the beneficiaries receive the benefits. This is Hebrews' way of explaining why Jesus had to suffer and to die. 'Without the shedding of blood there is no forgiveness' (Hebrews 9:22). This is a clever way of extending the metaphor of covenant, not exactly mixing metaphors, but showing another permutation on it. The Hebrew word *berith* means an agreement, treaty, alliance, and the phrase 'to cut a covenant' implies the cutting of an animal at a sacrifice to seal the agreement. But the Greek word *diatheke,* which is used to translate *berith* has the same meaning of a treaty, but with the additional implication of a 'last will and testament', something that is not implied in the word *berith*. So when Jesus said 'this is my blood of the New Testament', he was in fact[6] saying, 'I am now giving my life so that everlasting forgiveness will come into force, and will be available for all who accept it'.

Hebrews does not go on to speculate on what might have happened if Jesus had not been crucified, it would be the same sort of guesswork as speculating on what would have happened if Jesus had succumbed to the temptations. But Hebrews does take a stern line on the subject of us believers falling away after we have accepted God's forgiveness. He says that the sacrifice of Christ is, in effect, cancelled out and we are back where we started:

'For if we sin deliberately after receiving the knowledge of the truth, there no longer remains a sacrifice for sins, but a fearful prospect of judgement' (Hebrews 10:26). This is the encouragement to hold fast to one's commitment of faith, and not to waver or give in to pressure from one's persecutors. The question arises as to how literally do we take this? The early church did, and were very strict about it. If one sinned after baptism, one was assumed to be damned and certainly not re-admitted to the church. This had the effect of people postponing baptism until they were on their deathbeds, for fear of sinning after baptism. But now, the churches take a more moderate view of this matter. If one sins after becoming a Christian, there is confession and absolution, regularly offered, both publicly and privately. The implication is that anything serious such as a mortal sin can be removed from one's conscience and does not have to involve eternal damnation. There is all the world of difference between committing a minor fault and deliberately causing a major offence; the word 'deliberately' is important here.

This is where the apocalyptic element comes into Hebrews. He can see 'the day' drawing near, in other words, the second coming of Christ. This was something that the apostolic church was acutely aware of in the early years, although Hebrews does not emphasise this matter overmuch, at least, not as much as St Paul would have done. But of course, this element reappears in the Koran, heavily emphasised, and has received a renewed impetus in recent times in the Christian churches. Many take it literally; others see it as symbolic or figurative.

But the nub of Hebrews' theology comes in 4:14. This speaks of proximity to God and everlasting mercy:

'Since then we have a great high priest who has passed through the heavens, Jesus the Son of God, let us hold fast our confession. For we have not a high priest who is unable to sympathise with our weaknesses, but one who in every respect has been tempted as we are, yet without sinning. Let us then with confidence draw near to the throne of grace that we may receive mercy and find grace to help in time of need.'

If we can unravel the metaphors here, it means that because Jesus came as a mediator between God and mankind, and as he suffered the same human lot as us, he therefore understands what we have to face in this world and makes allowances. There is something in the nature of the Eternal Father that knows what it is like to be human and that is the basis of forgiveness. That is the importance of describing Jesus as the eternal high priest; he is the final connection and basis of understanding between God and mankind. So Jesus, when he ascended, entered into the presence of the Eternal Father on our behalf. Jesus only had to do this once, not repeatedly like an earthly priest. The heavenly eternal priesthood is an ongoing continuing process that forms the connection between God and mankind (see Hebrews 9:23-28).

Because of this, we can now have complete confidence in our Christian conviction, in the face of adversities. Hebrews now cites all those examples from the past, from Abel down to the present day, in which faith has been the conviction of things not seen, or proven. This occupies all of Chapter 11 down to 12:1. All these people of the Old Testament managed to trust in God without knowledge of the Messiah, we who do now have the Messiah can look to him for inspiration. It is a complete joy to accept the sufferings that Jesus did. There is no point in being downcast or demoralised. After all, if we are the sons of God, we can expect him to discipline us just as any responsible earthly father will discipline his child. Here we see the metaphor of sonship being extended a little further. From this point on, Hebrews gives an outline of the Christian life and conduct; if we are the sons of God, then as brothers (and sisters) we should love one another.

In common with all New Testament writers, Hebrews is keen to show that the ancient prophecies have been fulfilled, and also will continue to be worked out in the life of the church. The main use, as early in the book, is to establish the true nature of Jesus as the Son of God. This then slides into justifying the priesthood of Jesus, something that is latent in the gospels but not fully developed. The nearest we come to it is in St John Chapter 17, the great high priestly prayer. Then we have the covenant theology which is basic to the Bible altogether, and explains the use of the terms Old and New Testament. In addition, his frequent reference to Abraham in relation to Melchizedek and also his concern 'with the descendants of Abraham' (Hebrews 2:17) is an indirect reference to the covenant of Abraham. As for the covenant of David, the fact that Hebrews uses the Psalms extensively, as backing for his arguments, shows indirectly an understanding of the status of David and the implication of Messianism. This comes out strongly in his reliance of Psalm 110. Apart from the mention of Noah in Hebrews 11:7, the covenant of Noah is largely understated in Hebrews.

We also have an interesting permutation on the quotation of prophecy. One might call it indirect fulfilment of prophecy, that of typology. This element, which is peculiar to Hebrews in the Bible, does not rely on literal quotations from specified prophets. It opens up the view that everything in the life of Jesus was in some way or other foreshadowed in the Old Testament. This pattern of thought has been developed in many ways with some interesting results. Two examples will suffice: Joseph in Genesis, who was a dreamer who had to go down to Egypt, and then another Joseph, also a dreamer, who had to take the infant Jesus down to Egypt, in the early chapters of St Matthew. The Israelites had to cross the River Jordan; Jesus was baptised in the same river. Many more such coincidences could be found, but the chief one, which pervades the whole book, is the priesthood of Aaron and how it foreshadowed the eternal priesthood of Jesus. It means that fulfilment of prophecy is not just a matter of quoting important writers from the past; it is 'events-fulfilment'. That is the importance of typology.

Literary and Linguistic considerations

It is clear that Hebrews was well versed in Hebrew and Greek. When it comes to the citation of Melchizedek, he parses the word correctly, pointing out that *Melchi* means 'my king' and *zedek* means 'righteousness', and *salem* means 'peace'. It means that this strange figure, coming from what we take to be Jerusalem, prefigures the eternal prince of peace coming from the presence of God. This cleverly carries the implication of Messianism without actually stating it plainly. His clever extension of the meaning of 'covenant' into the Greek *diatheke* with the implication of 'last will and testament' is also an indication of a fertile mind. In general, his use of Greek is quite sophisticated, unlike some New Testament writers. He is also clever enough to allow his theology to be extendable; he is first and foremost speaking to the Jewish community and recent proselytes who were still immersed in the rituals of the Temple worship, using the motifs of priesthood and sacrifice, and yet the metaphor is capable of being applied to non-Jewish ritual situations, such as the Greco-Roman system of worship. We can, quite legitimately, extend the thought to all religions, which involve sacrificing and some form of priesthood in any part of the world. Would this imply that in the modern world, where blood sacrificing is now largely a thing of the past, that the message of Hebrews is of very little relevance today? Not so: in our own times we have seen millions put to death in two World Wars and various ethnic cleansings. The term 'sacrifice' has actually been applied to such outrages, not to mention the term 'Holocaust' which actually means 'a whole burnt offering'. What would Hebrews have said to this? He might well have said something to the effect that the final, conclusive and totally effective sacrifice was done by Jesus himself, and that all our bloodletting in modern times is not making a jot of difference in relation to God's forgiveness. So why did God allow such things to happen, a question posed by many a sufferer in the wars? At this point we might say that typology is not just a thing of the BC period; it recurs in all kinds of ways in the AD period. What is the purpose of it? The same as before; to be a visual aid, a reminder of what Jesus had to suffer, a warning about how low mankind can sink when we ignore God, a pointer to the final Day of Judgement, when the Messiah will reappear. All these are possibilities stemming from the thought-pattern of Hebrews.

Hebrews' use of sustained metaphor is one of the main characteristics of the book. He does it in such a way as to verge on the literal element. He may have pictured Jesus as literally the Son of God. We, today, cannot do that; it has to be figurative. God does not have a wife or a partner in the way that humans do, still less like Zeus with the ladies. In addition to this, the metaphor of 'beget', while being useful in the early years of the church, has come to cause a problem, as the Koran quite rightly emphasises that God cannot beget as in the human or animal world; he creates but he does not reproduce himself. This is an example of how a metaphor in one situation can be helpful but can also become a problem in another situation. But Hebrews supplies us with four more metaphors which are equally helpful. In Hebrews 1:3 Jesus reflects the glory of God, which means that he is a kind of mirror so that we can see God without actually having to stare straight at him, which is impossible. Also, Jesus 'bears the very stamp of his nature'. This was in the days before postage stamps, and actually refers to the striking of coins in the mint; it speaks of the offset imprint of God in a precious metal. The shortcoming with this metaphor is the implication of idolatry, if we take it literally. Another useful metaphor comes in Hebrews 1:3, where Jesus 'sits down at the right hand of the majesty on high'; the image is one where a champion or hero of the kingdom is invited to become the king's 'right hand man', his chief adviser, the one most trusted to advise the ruler. Nowadays we would call him the Prime Minister. Yet another undeveloped metaphor comes in 'the name he has obtained'; for the Hebrew people, one's name was of much significance; far more than it is for us now. All names had meaning, as seen with Melchizedek; one's name described one's nature. There was power in it. As St Paul would say, 'at the name of Jesus, every knee shall bow'[7]. It was like when an important dignitary is announced and everyone bows or curtsies in response. It is a shame that Hebrews did not give more development to these and other potentially helpful metaphors.

Of course, his chief metaphor is Jesus as the high priest, which again, almost verges on the feeling of being literal. But not quite. Hebrews tempers this with other aspects of the ministry of Jesus. Jesus is the sacrificial offering, the altar, the Temple and he is also the veil of the Temple, his very own flesh, which is rent asunder to provide access to God's forgiveness. If this is a highly mixed metaphor, then so be it; but it also has the effect of preventing any one metaphor from monopolising the total truth. Each one is valid in its own way; paradoxically, Jesus is all of these things in one. It is very cleverly done and just because it is figurative language does not invalidate the basic truth behind it.

Philosophy

It is quite unusual, when considering the whole range of sacred texts, that Hebrews does not baldly make any direct claim to be in possession of the *truth*. It would be fair to say that he assumes that his theology is true, but he never states this openly. Perhaps the nearest we come to any such remark, is in Hebrews 11:1, where he says, 'now faith is the assurance of things hoped for, the conviction of things not seen.' This is in itself a nice piece of Hebrew parallelism, even if it is in prose. It is in fact saying that the believer can be certain in his own mind about the truth of God's active intervention in world history and in one's own life. Also lacking is any reference to the dilemma between free will and predestination, something that St Paul certainly did explore. As a philosophical tract, Hebrews is not really in that league; even so, much is assumed.

The importance of good moral conduct is stressed, and this is related to the metaphor of sonship, and also the intervention of spirits from the other world (Hebrews 13:1-2).

One major substratum of Hebrews is the assumption of the value of life. That life might be human or animal. His chief metaphor for life is 'blood'. This is a fair assumption since in Leviticus it actually says that the blood is the life of a creature[8] (Leviticus 17:11). The assumption goes further, that giving of life has some sort of purchasing power with the unseen forces in the next world. This relates to an important assumption in the human mind, that to give something away implies something back in return. If one gives something, perhaps of great value, to God, then one assumes that God will make some kind of concession. Sacrifice, then and now, involves four major elements; firstly, the clearing of guilt; secondly, persuading the deity to grant some kind of concession; thirdly, to express gratitude for a concession given; fourthly, to seal an agreement, either between people or between God and people. In relation to this, we can see that the first one is heavily stressed in Hebrews, and also the fourth one, in terms of sealing the New Testament. The other two, though not absent, are not so heavily emphasised. In Hebrews 13:15 he says, 'through him then let us continually offer up a sacrifice of praise to God, that is, the fruit of lips that acknowledge his name.' We notice the return to the metaphor of 'name'. This is the thanksgiving element; here 'sacrifice' has lost its literal meaning and is now applied to praising God in the Christian worship. With regard to obtaining a concession from God, there is a tiny but important reference in Hebrews 4:16, where he says, 'let us then draw near to the throne of grace, that we may receive mercy and find grace to help in time of need.' In other words, because Jesus gave himself, we now have clear access to God's mercy when things go wrong in our lives. On this basis, Hebrews not only frames his tract on the metaphor of sacrifice, but also opens up the possibility of transmuted sacrifice. This means that sacrifice does not have to mean killing an animal; it can be done in various ways such as singing hymns and doing good deeds (Hebrews 13:16). It would be wrong to call this demythologisation; maybe, secular application, or possibly transferred method?

Concluding remarks on the Book of Hebrews

In assessing this book, it must be remembered that it is very much couched in the mindset of the first century AD, with a heavy Jewish emphasis. Many of the arguments may seem somewhat strange by today's preconceptions. Hebrews was assuming that the things that go wrong in human life can be rectified by the process of sacrifice. He is trying to tell us that the Old Testament configuration of blood sacrifice is now obsolete, even if it was ordained by God at Mount Sinai; the sacrifice of praising God and doing good works is now the true sacrifice which brings about a renewed relationship with God. But this is only effective because Jesus himself, the true Son of God, has given himself completely, and is the final, ultimate and totally effective sacrifice. For those who think that sacrifice is some sort of superstitious practice belonging to the Stone Age, there is this caution; blood sacrifice still goes on in some areas and religious practices, even if Hebrews has quite rightly told us that it is to no avail. But there are many situations in modern life where some kind of transmuted sacrifice is very much to the fore in people's thinking. We have only to think of two World Wars and the loss of life, on the assumption that this will bring about a better world. But has it? That is debatable. Sacrifice is still a reality, even if it takes different forms now.

Hebrews is conscious of living at a nexus in world history. Just as the Sinai event was seminal and crucial in world affairs, so too is the appearance of the Son of God, Jesus. But this nexus was related to the eschatology of the day, largely derived from Daniel, Ezekiel, Enoch and other less influential writers. Hebrews is saying, in effect, that religious awareness and closeness to God, does not require a physical, literal sacrifice: a Temple, an altar, or a victim. He does not comment on church buildings, cathedrals or basilicas. This is possibly because church construction had hardly begun at that stage in the Apostolic Church. But the implication is that essentially, these are no longer the core of one's faith. God is in one's heart and soul, an indestructible element in anyone's life. For those who are fixated on church architecture and religious artwork, this is fine as far as it goes, but such things can so easily become some sort of idolatry. One's true focus is on God himself and his Messiah, Jesus.

And finally, the mightiest paradox of all in the Christian system of thought. We can dump sin, misery and shame, and concentrate on JOY. Just as Jesus endured the cross and the result was everlasting joy and triumph, so the same can apply to us. Out of pain comes victory; out of shame comes conviction of being saved. The Christian faith is essentially a joyful matter, not a misery session. This is in contrast to practically every other system of thought in the world.

The Epistle of Barnabas in relation to Hebrews

This late first century work has various features in common with Hebrews, and in some ways it can be seen as a development of many of the thoughts in Hebrews. It is unlikely that it was written by Barnabas, the companion of St Paul, but it may have been someone who carried on their tradition of thought. It must have been written after the destruction of the Temple in AD 70, and probably before the Romans built a pagan temple on the same site, thus preventing the Jews from doing a rebuild. Other than that, there is nothing in this so-called epistle to anchor it to any known times, places or personalities. It was written in Koine Greek. The text is taken from Ehrman's book, *Lost Scriptures*. For some time in the Patristic era, this work was taken as scriptural, but fell out of usage and acceptance. It disappeared from circulation only to be rediscovered in the late 19th century in a library in Alexandria. One could call it proto-orthodox; there is nothing heretical in it and it serves to support many of the themes in the New Testament. Having said that, there are some rather strange biological statements that one might regard as less than literal.

The main relevance to Hebrews lies in Barnabas' development of typology. He is not so much interested in sacrificing and priesthoods, which is understandable if the Temple and the Jewish system of sacrifice was a thing of the past. But this is a telling remark (Barnabas 6:15):

'For the dwelling place of our hearts, my brothers, is a temple holy to the Lord.'

That is a very apt summary of the thinking of Hebrews, and comes to complete relevance after AD 70. In a way, Barnabas completes the argument set out in Hebrews. In Barnabas 7:6, we have the procedure for the Atonement: taking two goats, one to be sacrificed and the other to be sent off into the wilderness. Hebrews never draws this element into his theological line. Barnabas does not mention Azazel[9] (an early understanding of the Devil), but does include extra details not found in Leviticus:

'... shall spit on the goat, and wrap a piece of scarlet wool round its head... and remove the wool, and place it on a blackberry bush...' Barnabas 7:8.

This is all very inventive, but may have been an unofficial variation on the Atonement ritual at that time. But now comes the typology. The goat sent off into the wilderness is Jesus; he is crowned, and wears a scarlet robe. Placing the wool in the blackberry thorns indicates that anyone who wishes to remove the scarlet wool must suffer scratching from the thorns. This means that anyone who wants to touch the Kingdom must take hold of Jesus through pain and suffering. All very imaginative!

Another issue, that of circumcision, is raised; something that Hebrews omits to mention. Barnabas is clever enough to see that true circumcision is not just a matter of cutting off a piece of flesh: 'For he has said that circumcision is not a matter of the flesh' Barnabas 9:4. What about one's hardness of heart and stiffness of neck? Circumcision is really about listening to God and responding correctly. This is something that Hebrews would have agreed with.

Then we come on to the dietary laws of the Pentateuch. Barnabas says, 'the commandment of God is not a matter of avoiding food; but Moses spoke in the spirit' Barnabas 10:2.

So, for instance, not eating pork, means do not eat like a pig, which is greedy and only acknowledges its master when it becomes hungry. Not eating the eagle, the hawk, the kite, or the crow, is commented on, although Leviticus 11:13 makes a much longer list of such birds. This is because they are scavengers, waiting about for some other animal to leave them something to eat. We must not be scavengers. We must not eat the lamprey-eel, the octopus, or the cuttlefish; this does not appear in Leviticus and may be Barnabas' own invention. The reason given is that they are cursed and hover in the depths, not swimming like other fish but lurking about in the mud in the ooze. We must not eat the hare (Leviticus 11:6) because such people corrupt children! The rabbit is permitted. We must not eat the hyena – another invention of Barnabas – as those that do are adulterers and perverts! Hyenas are supposed to change from male to female; is that true? As for the weasel (would anyone think of eating one?), it conceives in its mouth (does it?) and it is said that we must not be lawless like that. This may be a reference to oral sex. Even if this is somewhat fanciful and based on mistaken ideas about biology, we can see that the process of making all the food laws symbolic as opposed to being taken literally, is thoroughgoing. Incidentally, this does not quite square with St Peter's vision in Acts 15, in which all foodstuffs are stated to be 'clean'.

Something that surfaced in St John's gospel, is the incident in Numbers 21:4-8, when the snakes bite the Israelites and Moses makes a bronze serpent and brings people back to life. This is made out as a type of Jesus on the cross, bringing people to eternal life.

The issue of the true people of God surfaces in Barnabas and he maintains that the Jews are not the true people of God and that the Christians are the true ones. He justifies this by citing the blessing of Jacob in Genesis 48:14, where Jacob blesses Ephraim and Manasseh, the two sons of Joseph. Jacob crosses his hands so that the firstborn, Manasseh, has an inferior blessing to Ephraim, the younger, saying that the greater will serve the lesser. This is typology with a political agenda (Barnabas 13:5)!

Another aspect of working with typology comes in Barnabas 15:1-9. He does not try to make the Sabbath purely symbolic this time. He takes Genesis as literal but in a different sense; he makes it mean that when God finished his work in six days, this means that God will finish his work in 6,000 years. A day equals 1,000 years, quoting Psalm 90:4 to support it. When we get to 7,000 years, then the world will be put to rights and lawlessness will cease. Moreover a new world will begin and everything will have a rest when the eighth day arrives. He does not actually mention the return of the Messiah, except to say that the eighth day is for the resurrection and the ascension. The implication in this is that Saturday is no longer observed as a day of rest, but he does not actually state it in so many words. This is an interesting permutation on typology. It also betrays a certain influence from Zoroastrianism, which saw world history as divided into portions of a thousand years, a theory which does not appear in the New Testament.

Barnabas goes on to tell us that there are two paths of teaching and authority: the path of light and the path of darkness. The angels of God are supervising the ones, and the angels of Satan the other. We are told not to mix with people of the wrong path; we are either the one thing or the other and not something in between. This is a motif hardly seen in the New Testament unless we take the Parable of the Wheat and the Tares at face value[10]. But it is seen in The Proverbs (Chapter 15) and other wisdom literature and also the Dhammapada (Chapter 14). Moreover, Jesus himself made a point of mixing with the bad element, on the assumption that those who are sick actually do need a doctor. This may be one reason why Barnabas was omitted from the New Testament.

In general terms, however, Barnabas is valuable as we see that even at that stage in the Christian era, people were trying to avoid taking everything completely literally in the Old Testament. The idea that much of it is symbolic or typological is useful. This has of course become one of the main issues at the present, how to interpret the Old Testament, and indeed the New. There are those who wish to take everything completely at face value; they are called 'Bible Fundamentalists'. It is a mistake to assume that they are stupid; they are found in all grades of intelligence, churchmanships and levels of theological knowledge. The chief problem lies in the issue of how we interpret the Creation stories in Genesis. But that is not the only problem. A balanced and reasonable view sees much of the material in the Bible as factual, symbolic and figurative. That does not mean that portions of the Bible that are not factual are therefore not the truth. As we have seen, the truth can be conveyed in various dimensions as outlined in Chapter one. It is a mistake to assume that the truth can only be contained in literal material such as mathematics and science.

Notes for Chapter 24: The Hebrews

1. A normal pattern seen in many apocryphal works, using symbolisms.
2. Hebrews 1:4.
3. Hebrews 5:7.
4. Hebrews 2:8.
5. The Taurobolium: a bull sacrifice used in the religion of Cybele and Attis; also Mithras.
6. Mark 14:29.
7. Philippians 2;10.
8. Leviticus; 17:14.
9. Azazel: first seen in Leviticus 16:8 in the ritual for the Atonement. One goat is sacrificed and the other goat is sent off into the Wilderness to Azazel, who is an early understanding of the Devil.
10. The Parable of the Wheat and the Tares, Matthew 13:24.

25

The Egyptian Book of the Dead

As far as we know, the Egyptian religion did not have a Bible as such, in spite of all their elaborate ideas on the subject of gods, Pharaohs and tombs. The nearest we can come to anything 'scriptural' must be the Egyptian Book of the Dead. This was a part of the work of Thoth, the messenger, scribe and controller of time, who produced sacred literature. The Corpus Hermeticum (Chapter 19) is another part of this type of literature, although it is very different from these funerary texts. These were the inscriptions found on the tomb walls, the mummies and the papyrus rolls that gave elaborate ideas on funerary procedures and the afterlife. There were many of these papyri but the best preserved of them so far has been the Papyrus of Ani which was discovered in 1888 and bought by the British Museum. It survived in the ground from about 1500BC to 1400 BC and is a remarkable document from the Theban period. It is seventy-eight feet long and fifteen inches broad. Ani was a royal scribe and his wife, Thuthu, was a priestess of Amen Ra at Thebes. They would almost certainly have regarded this sort of document as theologically and spiritually authoritative, but whether we can term it 'scriptural' is a good question; it may be somewhat anachronistic to term it thus. However it throws much light on the religious thinking of the ancient world and compares well with other pre-historic material such as The Epic of Innana (Chapter 21) and the Holy Kojiki (Chapter 11). Also various features can be seen surfacing in the Old Testament; after all, the Hebrews were probably in Egypt at about this time in history[1].

The references here are taken from E. A. Wallis Budges' excellent version, *The Egyptian Book of the Dead*, 1895. It is a masterpiece of accurate translation followed by construing, with the actual text in hieroglyphics for us to inspect.

Mathematical, geographical, scientific and historical material

There is nothing historical or scientific in this book. If there is anything mathematical, it could be said that there is an awareness of the world being millions of years old, and this is emphasised quite heavily (pages 253, 338, 336, 342). Also there is the notion that the world will have no end; in other words, it will go on for ever (page 275). With regard to geography, there are many locations in Egypt mentioned, some actual and some mythical, and some of them are of relevance to the main theme. The main geographical assumption, which is essential to the whole matter of funerary procedures, is the fact that the sun rises in the east, proceeds across the sky to the west and then is assumed to go under the world, through the underworld, only to reappear in the east next morning. This is linked to the course of one's life, that as one dies, one goes down through the underworld and then one rises again. This is their version of resurrection; an essential theological notion in Egyptian religion. Strangely there is very little mention of the rising of the Nile, which was also essential to their thinking, plus the fact that the Pharaoh's life was integral to the annual inundation.

Theological assumptions

In this papyrus we are seeing something of the Egyptians' elaborate ideas on life, death and afterlife. Essentially, they believed that the spirit of mankind did not die but carried on into the afterlife to face judgement. We may be seeing only a fraction of their total beliefs. After all, this papyrus is only a 'snapshot' view of their theology in the Theban period. We know that earlier and later ideas could vary considerably. Over an empire that lasted 3,000 years with all kinds of vicissitudes and influences, we can hardly expect exactly the same beliefs to prevail from start to finish. We see a certain amount of disagreement and uncertainty about what the gods did or did not do. Some of the ideas persisted well into Christian times and the Coptic Church[2] seems to have assimilated some aspects into their theology. It is no surprise that the Gnostics, who mainly hailed from Egypt in Roman times, had such elaborate, speculative ideas about God and heaven.

To summarise briefly, there were hundreds of gods, associated with just about every aspect of life and death. The chief god was Amun, and this helps to explain our Biblical word 'Amen' meaning 'truly', in fact there was another god called AMEN, but his function was different. The name actually meant 'hidden one' but he had nothing to do with funerals. There is little said on the subject of how gods are produced. There is one comment to the effect that Ra (the sun god) was produced from the buttocks of the cow Mehurt (page 285). The god Shu is claimed to have sprung from unformed

466

matter (page 340). Thoth is claimed to be 'self-produced' but this is not explained. Khepera, the god who is associated with Ra as he rises in the morning is said to be 'self-created'. It is interesting that he is said to go through 'evolutions' (page 246); does this mean that evolution was thought of long before Charles Darwin? Elsewhere, we have a god who managed to give birth to himself! But this is an ongoing question in any mythology – how or where to do gods come from? It is essentially the ontological theory in anthropomorphic form. Mostly the gods are well intentioned and 'good' as opposed to 'bad'. But there is someone called the 'Evil One' (page 327 and 340), in addition to which there are 'fiends' that we take to be evil spirits and also 'shining ones' (page 326). These spiritual entities are not necessarily located in one and the same place; they can appear in heaven or the underworld. Osiris is the one who will destroy all fiends wherever they may be found (page 329). Ra too opposes them, and there are battles between good and bad spiritual entities.

The main purpose of the Papyrus is to smooth the passage of the soul into the afterlife. We see Ani at the end of his life, becoming associated with or even identified with Osiris. This is a kind of apotheosis that most Egyptians would have aspired to. But first he would have to go through the underworld, just as the setting sun, Tmu, went down each evening. There is a process of purification as one approaches the underworld. It can be termed 'the cutting off of the corruptible' (page 283) or 'the destruction of faults' (page 286). In the underworld there is a northern door at which one hopes to gain admittance to the Hall of Double Law or Truth, sometimes called the Hall of Double Right and Wrong, or even The Hall of Hearts. The judges are there with a pair of scales; Anubis actually holds the scales: on one scale is a feather and on the other side is one's soul. If one's soul is too heavy, with guilt, the scales will tip (page 345). Thoth is there to record the results. Anyone who fails the test might be eaten by a female monster called Amam, otherwise, some might even be 'blotted out' (page 203). At all costs one will hope to keep one's heart, the ab (page 312) or not let one's head be cut off (page 317). There is also a process called 'passing through seven Arits'. We translate these as 'mansions' (page 291). Alternatively, one might pass through twenty-one Pylons (page 298).

Once purged, and having passed through the judgement hall, one enters a doorway and rises up to heaven. This is where one joins in with Ra as he sets out on his daily course across the sky.

We have a detailed description of the boat. It is painted green and is seven cubits long (page 328). It has eight oars, each shaped like a serpent's head, with a hawk's head on each handle, and it also carries a flight of steps. On the stern and the bows is written, 'The god therein is Un-nefer'. This means 'good being' and it is actually Osiris (page 322). There is an island where the dead go to live and reap their harvest (page 365). A Bennu bird is often depicted; this is a symbol of the soul of Ra. iI was a kind of Pheonix[3]. The boat, which is termed a 'sektet boat' sails over the sky into a lake of fire. It has a rudder that is steered by Horus, and it is towed along in spite of having sails (page 307). The descriptions are not completely consistent.

It is important that one is purged before reaching the company of Ra in his boat. Before gaining access to the underworld, there is a procedure that could be termed 'a negative confession'. The dead man reels off all the sins that he has not committed. Ani reels off thirty-three offences that he is innocent of, or so he claims. Here is a sample (page 347):

> ' I have not done iniquity... I have not robbed with violence... I have not stolen... I have done no murder... I have not defrauded offerings... I have not plundered the god... I have not been an eavesdropper... I have not multiplied words exceedingly...'

We notice that the alleged non-offences are moral and ritual. The list is far more fulsome than the Ten Commandments, but there is no doubt that Moses would have known of these funerary inscriptions. We also notice that being taciturn is a virtue, something that appears in the Proverbs (Chapter 15) and in the Analects (Chapter 7).

All this indicates the importance given by the Egyptians to the belief in life beyond the grave and resurrection. Also stressed is the importance of arriving at one's funeral with a clear conscience; something that still persists in the Christian tradition with deathbed conversions and the last rites. All this explains the time and expense invested in carving out rock tombs and making mummies. Often mentioned in passing is the food offerings involved in the rituals; it was thought essential to feed the dead person after he had gone, even to the extent of taking the food on board the boat as it went across the sky.

There were elaborate beliefs about one's *ka*[4] (the double) and *khat*[5] (the physical body), the *sahu*[6] (the spiritual body), the *ab*[7] (the heart), the *ba* (the soul)[8], the *khaibit* (the shadow)[9], the *khu*[10] (one's intelligence) and the *sekhem*[11] (heavenly form). These are mentioned in the texts but not really explained in any great detail. The Egyptians would not have thought it necessary to describe these matters in detail. The physical body had to be preserved in full, otherwise it could not come back to life and be resurrected. Texts do not actually describe the process of embalming, but we know from other documents and examination of mummies, how it was done.

Once one had been accepted and had a boat ride across the sky, one would be admitted to one of two places: The Isles of the Blest, which were modelled on the islands in the Delta, Goshen, which was washed by the Nile; or the Sekhet Aru, which can be rendered as 'the Elysian Fields' where one could reap and sow just as in earthly life, eat bread and drink ale and feel quite normal. All this would be up in the skies.

With Moses having been raised in Egypt at the time when The Book of the Dead would have been in full use and widely known, it would be no surprise if this corpus of literature had a certain influence on the Bible and later Christian practice. As we see from Genesis, there was a primeval ocean that pre-existed the Creation of the world. This is also assumed in the Egyptian material. The ladder, which was needed to reach up into heaven, and is depicted in the artwork, also appears in Genesis, when Jacob had his dream with angels ascending and descending on it. The pillars which held the sky up, often mentioned in The Book of the Dead, are also referred to in the Old Testament, and the Song of Hannah is one example where it is pointed out that the pillars belong to YHWH (rather than Ra or Amon, for instance) 1 Samuel 2:8.

The Egyptians occasionally mention the 'second death' but do not really explain it. In Revelation, however, we have a fresh mention of the second death but it is more fully explained. The idea that one's conduct and moral worth is recorded by Thoth and used in evidence against one when it comes to judgement is also noted in the Old Testament and in 1 Enoch. By the time we arrive at Revelation, it is angels unfolding scrolls when the judgement comes.

The idea that one needs purification to enter into the presence of the gods and be found not guilty continues into the Christian era with such things as the last rites and the doctrine of 'Purgatory'. But the major influence from the Book of the Dead is the assumption that the physical body will have to be raised at the resurrection, as well as one's spirit. This helps to explain how we have traditionally buried people. The idea of cremation, although being forced on us through lack of burial space, is still not a comfortable thought for many people. Still there are people who put grave goods in the coffin, in spite of the Christian assumption that this is not necessary.

Footnotes for Chapter 25: The Egyptian Book of the Dead

1. The date of the Exodus is approximately 1400 BC, which means that the Israelites would have been aware of such literature and its contents.
2. The Coptic Church, the Egyptian Christians, took on various ideas from the Hermetic literature, the most notable one being ideas on Hell and torment in the next world. See page cxxxi in Wallis Budge.
3. The Bennu bird was a mythical bird like the phoenix. The early Christians took the phoenix to be a symbol of the Resurrection.
4. *Ka*, or double, means ghost, image, genius, character. Food had to be provided in the tomb or the *ka* would fade out. The statue of a man was inhabited by his *ka*. Special priests and chapels were provided for the *ka*. Another word, Ren, meaning 'name' is

associated with *ka*. We might call it 'one's reputation'. The ancients believed that there was power in one's name. So, for instance, 'at the name of Jesus'.

5. *Khat*, the physical body, which had to be mummified to prevent it decaying.

6. *Sahu*, the spiritual body, which germinates and receives knowledge, power and glory.

7. *Ab*, the heart, the seat of the power of life, good and evil thoughts.

8. *Ba*, the soul, shown as a human-headed hawk, which will revisit the body in the tomb, and re-animated it. It was closely associated with *ka*, and would fade out if not properly fed. Its permanent place is with the gods in heaven.

9. *Khaibit*, the shadow, which could have an independent existence, and detach itself from the body. It also eats food in the tomb.

10. *Khu*, one's intelligence, shining and glorious, one's spirit that goes up to heaven to Ra and Hathor.

11. *Sekhem*, heavenly form, or power associated with *khu*. All of these terms indicate the importance of the Egyptian belief in life beyond the grave. How distinct these concepts were is debatable. Some of them are used in parallel, as synonyms, and there may not have been any hard and fast distinction between these factors.

26

The Guru Granth Sahib

This sacred scripture is the basis for the Sikh religion. This was an attempt at finding some sort of accommodation between Hinduism and Islam, and as a syncretistic scheme it has had perhaps more success than others. In the sixteenth century, contemporaneous with the Protestant Reformation in the West, Guru Nanak had a Theophanous experience, on the basis of which he produced the Guru Granth, or at least, parts of it. There is a strong resistance to the Guru Granth being circulated either in Gurmukhi, its original language, or in translation. It is now possible to find portions of it via the internet. The text used here is the translation by Singh Sahib Sant Singh Kalsa. The complete Guru Granth is very lengthy, 1,430 pages, and no attempt here is made to assess all of it. In keeping with the mood of this religion, I am restricting myself to thirteen pages from the beginning. I understand that there would be little point in reviewing any more, since the book is highly repetitive and the main gist of it can be gleaned from the first thirteen pages. The tenor of the book is all about praise to God, and on that basis it is on the same lines as the Psalms of David and the Gathas of Zoroaster. But there is nothing historical, geographical, mathematical or scientific included at all. The main focus is on God, and everything else is purely incidental.

Theological Truth

There is One Universal Creator God, whose name is Truth who is beyond description; he cannot be described in words (1:4, page 2).

'Just how great his greatness is... this is known only to those who have seen him. His value cannot be estimated; he cannot be described. Those who describe you, Lord, remain immersed and absorbed in you' (So Dar 1, page 9).

This is monotheism, which was an appeal to the Muslims. However, there is another aspect to this. Nanak talks about One Divine Mother who conceived and gave birth to the three deities: the Creator of the world, the Sustainer and the Destroyer (1:29, page 7). In other places he talks about Shiva, Vishnu, Brahma and Krishna, and 'the Guru'. Does this mean Nanak himself, or God? This is not clear. He may not be talking literally about these Hindu gods, only figuratively. But even then, that would be enough to upset the Muslims. We may be dealing with a situation of henotheism, rather than monotheism, something similar to Zoroaster's ideas in that there was only one god worthy of worship and all the others could be downgraded to being devils and angels of one kind or another. It may be that Divine Mother can be seen in the same light as Holy Wisdom in the Hebrew scheme of things, namely as figurative, and not an infringement of monotheism.

But this one god is a god of truth, and of beauty, and of love. He hands out blessings:

'His blessings are so abundant that there can be no written account of them. The great giver does not hold anything back' (1:24, page 5).

But there is also a concept of justice; the metaphor of the scales is used as also the concept of the records kept (as we see in Chapter 20: The Book of Enoch)[1].

'Good and bad deeds... the record is read out in the presence of the Lord of Dharma[2]...' (1:38, page 8).

'Priceless is the divine court of Justice. Priceless are the scales and priceless are the weights' (1:25, page 5).

Here we see an element from the Egyptian Book of the Dead (Chapter 25) even if the metaphor is not quite the same. In contrast to the Koran (Chapter 21) the judgement or justice does not appear to be too threatening or heavily emphasised. It could be seen as a watered down version of the day of judgement. There seems to be no mention of torments in hell, even though there is mention of the underworld. Looking at it positively, there is much mention of being absorbed into God.

'They alone understand, whom you inspire to understand; they continually chant and repeat the Lord's praises. Those who serve you find

472

peace. They are intuitively absorbed into the Lord's name' (Raag Aasaa Fourth Hehl 1:2, page 11:12).

God, it would seem has a name, the Jewel of the NAAM. The way to salvation is to meditate on the NAAM and have faith. Faith is heavily emphasised; it is also admitted that there are those who fail to do so, and are therefore separated from God. It does not specify what becomes of them, except that they 'aimlessly wander for ever' (1:1, page 1). Also, there is a sound vibration that brings one into touch with God:

'In the realm of Wisdom, spiritual Wisdom reigns supreme. The sound current of the NAAD vibrates there, amidst the sounds and the sights of bliss' (1:25, page 7).

In other places, all one has to do is 'listen' for the problems of life to be removed:

'Listening, pain and sin are erased. Listening... truth, contentment and spiritual wisdom. Listening... take your cleansing bathe at sixty-eight places of pilgrimage. Listening... reading and reciting, honour is obtained. Listening... intuitively grasp the essence of meditation... listening... pain and sin are erased...' (1:9, page 3).

This is Nanak's answer to the problem of pain, namely theodicy. But the ultimate explanation, which is the logical concomitant of having just one God, is that God causes everything, good or bad, through predestination. Everything is commanded by God, there appears to be no Satan trying to contradict God's decisions:

'By his command, some are high and some are low; by his written command pain and pleasure are obtained. Some by his command are blessed and forgiven; others, by his command wander aimlessly for ever. Everyone is subject to his command; no one is beyond his command...' (1:1, page 1).

In contrast to this, we have mention of merit:

'Pilgrimages, austere discipline, compassion and charity... these by themselves, bring only an iota of merit...' (1:20, page 4).

This would imply some sort of buying power with God, which again implies free will. But these matters are not heavily emphasised, as they are in Hinduism and Buddhism.

Philosophy

Relevant to the concept of merit, is the question of karma, i.e. Reincarnation. Nanak seems to assume this as a basic thought-pattern in India. He calls it the 'wheel of reincarnation', which sounds like Buddhism[3].

'By the karma of past actions, the robe of this physical body is obtained. By his grace, the Gate of Liberation is found'[4] (1:3, page 2).

The assumption of karma, is a kind of background cultural assumption, but Nanak is saying that God, inside one's soul, can free one from it and there is no need to be born again successively[5].

'The Lord shall dwell within your mind. Within the home of your inner being, you shall obtain the Mansion of the Lord's presence with intuitive ease. You shall not be consigned again to the wheel of reincarnation'[3] (4:2, page 13).

One could gain the impression that moral conduct is not directly related to salvation. In 1:17 (page 4) it talks about theft, murder, lying, slandering, but there is no code of conduct as seen in the Ten Commandments or the Noble Eightfold Path (see Chapter 14). The crux of the matter seems to lie in calmness of the mind, meditation and listening; these are the matters that bring one into God's presence.

Nanak's estimation of human nature is probably a little pessimistic. He talks about the human race as 'poor helpless creatures' (2:3, page 9), and 'I am a mere insect, a worm'. But this is consistent with his understanding of God as overpowering, controlling everyone's destiny.

Mythology

In common with Buddhism, there is nothing specific said about Creation, nor any Creation myth. Nanak says that the age of the earth is beyond calculation:

'What was that time, and what was that moment? What was that day, and what was that date? What was that season, and what was that month when the Universe was created?' (1:20, page 4).

Only God knows how it all came about. This is of course a challenge to all the modern scientific attempts at dating the earth and indeed the solar system. He talks about the planets and the galaxies, but does not try to analyse them in scientific terms. Nanak goes on to assume that there are three levels: heaven, earth and the underworld. We realise that this assumption went on after it was discovered that the world was round. The conclusion must fairly be drawn that Nanak is talking figuratively and not literally. Nanak goes further and says that there are 18,000 worlds (1:21) and the Universe is limitless. A remark, which is highly relevant to today's astrophysicists, would be 'the limits of the created universe cannot be perceived... many struggle to know his limits but his limits cannot be found' (1:23, page 5), which means in effect that the more we discover, the more we realise there is to be discovered. There are nine treasures and eighteen supernatural powers held by God in the palm of his hand. Again, these are not described in detail, but they are almost certainly figurative language (page 10), and we notice what is almost certainly the use of symbolic figures.

Nanak talks about there being nine continents, but does not tell us their identities, and four ages. As with some of this material already, there is the feeling that this is exaggeration and hardly to be taken literally. The connection between heaven and earth is seen as a ladder (1:331, page 7) but of course this is figurative. It is almost certainly derived from Egyptian thinking. It also reminds us of the staircase as mentioned in the Rig Veda[6].

There are also six schools of philosophy and six teachers and six sets of teachings. But the teacher of teachers is the One, who appears in so many different forms. We notice that the seventh one is God himself. Nanak does not go into details about their names and functions.

There is also 'a mythical bull who is the dharma[2], the son of compassion'. This bull patiently holds the earth in its place, so it is claimed (1:15, page 3). Again this is almost certainly not to be taken literally. The bull is symbolic of Krishna in Hindu thought, and is also significant in Zoroastrian thinking[7].

Significant is the mention of Nanak being a sacrifice. This reminds us of Amida and Perusha in Buddhist and Hindu thought. Going further, Nanak is termed a 'slave' or 'servant'. 'Nanak your slave begs for his happiness' (page 13). This too reminds us of Jesus who called himself the Servant. How literally we can take this is a good question; there is no mention of Guru Nanak allowing himself to be put to death, let alone being the essential element in the salvation of the world. Even so, there are various factors in this that remind us of Christianity.

The impression gained is that although Nanak includes a lot of mythological ideas, none of them need to be taken at face value. They are all poetic and expressive of God's wonders and the inability of humans to comprehend it all.

Literary skill including artistic ability

The whole book is intended as a liturgical manual; everything would be chanted to the accompaniment of musical instruments. Unfortunately the quality and expertise of this is missing in a plain rendition on paper.

But Nanak's literary skill is quite accomplished. Consider this:

'Make contentment your ear-rings, humility your begging bowl, and meditation the ashes you apply to your body. Let the remembrance of death be the patched coat you wear, let the purity of virginity be your way in the world, and let faith in the Lord be your walking-stick' (1:27, page 6).

'Let self-control be the furnace, and patience the goldsmith. Let understanding be the anvil, and spiritual wisdom be the tools. With the fear of God as the bellows, fan the flames of *tapa*[8], the body's inner heat. In the crucible of love, melt the nectar of the Name, and mint the true coin of the *shabad*[9], the word of God' (1:37, page 8).

This can only be described as lovely figurative language. It reminds us of St Paul with the whole armour of God[10].

In common with Lao Tzu (Chapter 10) and the Dhammapada (Chapter 14), Nanak is quite fluent with paradoxes when talking about God. This is because he knows it is impossible to describe God:

'You have thousands of eyes, and yet you have no eyes. You have thousands of forms and yet you do not even have one. You have thousands of lotus feet and yet you do not have even one foot. You have no nose, but you have thousands of noses' (Raag Dhanaasaree, First Mehl 1:1, page 13).

As a piece of literature, this is most appropriate. It is unfortunate that there is so much repetition in the Guru Granth, but then, it is not intended to be a systematic theology book. It remains a liturgical book, and must be judged in that light. The only other scriptural materials with which it can be compared would be the Gathas of Zoroaster (Chapter 5) and the Yengishiki (Chapter 12). With regard to the Psalms of David, there is the added element of historical and geographical material which is clearly related to the important events and places in Israel's history; also there is the prophetic element in the Psalms, which never seems to surface in Eastern religions.

Concluding remarks on the Guru Granth Sahib

One would have to admit that this is only a 'snapshot' view of this book, but that is fair enough for two reasons: firstly, the Sikhs do not feel happy about allowing their holy book to be generally available (one is amazed to find that it is on the internet!), and so I have taken just thirteen pages as a sample; secondly, it would seem that the rest of the book is virtually the same material in repetition, so there is little point in trying to assess all of it. But the sample taken is a fair indication of Sikh thinking.

Although much of Sikh theology is very close to Christianity, there is one vital element missing, that of Messianism. There is no mention of Jesus or of any other Messiah or Mahdi. If one were to try to make Nanak out to be a Messiah, this will not work. Firstly, he made no claim to be any such thing, in spite of thinking of himself as a servant and a sacrifice. Secondly, none of his followers regarded him as such. In fact the whole concept of Messianism is absent from Sikh thinking, as indeed any kind of Sacral Kingship.

There is much to commend the Sikh system of thought, if indeed it can be termed a system. One would suggest that they could agree with the last line of a certain hymn which goes, '*God is Love, his the care...* and finishes with *God is Good, God is Truth, God is beauty, praise him*'[11].

Footnotes for Chapter 26; The Guru Granth Sahib

1. The scales of eternal justice: this goes back to Ancient Egypt (Chapter 25), with the weighing of souls depicted on the walls of the tombs and described in the Egyptian Book of the Dead.
2. *Dharma*; a key word in Hindu thought and also Buddhist. It means truth, justice, righteousness, good conduct, the right approach to life.
3. This sounds like the 'Wheel of Becoming' an important element in Buddhist thought; as one moves from one form of life to another, governed by one's conduct in a previous life.
4. This sounds like an element in the Bhagavad Gita, in which one is born into a family appropriate to one's previous attitude to life (see Chapter 8).
5. Sikhism is one of the three escape routes from karma, Buddhism, Jainism and Sikhism.
6. The Rig Veda depicts the connection between heaven and earth as a staircase; see IV Canto, Sookta 8, page 90).
7. The Potent Ox of Days, is a title given to Ahura Mazda in the Gathas, Chapter 5.
8. *Tapa*, in Sanskrit means, 'heat, ardour, inner heat'.
9. Shabad the word of God.
10. Ephesians 6:11.
11. Hymn 502 in Songs of Praise.

27

Drawing Conclusions

Having reviewed many scriptures from just about every religion and sect in the world, it is apparent that the quality and quantity varies greatly. It is unrealistic to attempt to include every piece of scriptural material and so this book only contains a selection. From the Bible itself, a selection has had to be made. It is not easy to evaluate these written materials; one is bound to allow one's own cultural and doctrinal assumptions to influence any comment one might make. A lot must depend on what one expects from a scriptural corpus; is it the basis of one's personal faith, or a cultural backdrop which may not have to be taken too seriously, or is it the absolute truth to the exclusion of all others?

Each and every one of these scriptures makes a claim, often directly and sometimes indirectly, to be the truth. Those that do not make such a claim are in the minority, and even then, there is the inference that they contain the truth. But the differences of opinion, not usually stated baldly, but implicit in their statements, must rule out the possibility of them all being correct. Some of them must be wrong in some way, and by implication, possibly the religion of which they are the substratum.

One of the fundamental questions concerns the reality of life on this earth. Are we to say, like Mary Baker Eddy (Chapter 9), and many Eastern thinkers, that this world and humanity is just an illusion, a fiction, or even a delusion? That would leave us with the obvious conclusion that it is the other world of the spirit, that is the real world. Conversely, for those of an atheistic or agnostic frame of thought, there is the idea that this world is real enough, but the next world is pure fiction, fantasy and imagination. There seems to be no way of breaking out of this dilemma. For the Christian, following the assumptions in the Bible, there is no escaping the challenge to face up to both worlds as real; this earth with its people is a fact; the next

478

world, for which we have various bits of evidence, is also a reality waiting to be encountered. Religion has been criticised as being 'escapism'. This could be a fair comment for those whose religion is all about cancelling out the realities of this life, going along in some sort of mental coma, and ignoring all the problems. But that is not the Christian approach.

It would be fair to say that many Christians have tried, and still do try, to cross out the realities of life. Mary Baker Eddy is a case in point, but it is not necessary to embark on Christian Science to hold this kind of view. The early church came up against this matter from the start. There were the Gnostics who not only devalued the physical existence of this world, but went further and tried to make out that Jesus was not really human. He was seen as an apparition, pretence, even a cinematic projection, but not a real human being. Outbursts of Gnosticism still occur to this day, often in different guises or vocabulary. 'How could Jesus have suffered? If he was God, how could he have died?' But this goes against the plain intention of the gospel writers. He really did suffer and die, and was raised, not just as a ghost but as real flesh. For those who deny the reality of this life, all one can say is that whether or not it is real, is not actually saying anything; the plusses and minuses of life are still there as a challenge to be faced, even if one does think of oneself as a piece of fiction.

On this basis, we have to recognise that the Old Testament, the New Testament and the Koran clearly relate themselves to actual historical, geographical realities. In addition to that there is the mathematical element of dates, times, seasons and measurements. It is fair to say that some of these figures are symbolic, and it takes a certain amount of common sense to tell what is happening in any given context. Even if the Koran is rather more meagre on these matters, it still anchors itself in the realities of Genesis, Exodus and so forth; it borrows from the factual elements of the faith of Israel, every bit as much as Christianity does. The other material from the Eastern world does not do this. Even with the Avestas of Zoroaster and the Ramayana of Hinduism, which might have had a slight historical anchorage, the main thrust of the matter is in the mind and not earthbound.

Symptomatic of this approach, to see religion as purely in the mind, has been the recent trend amongst certain Western scholars to question the existence of such people as Abraham, Moses, and even Jesus himself. It goes further, Shakespeare too is not allowed to be Shakespeare but possibly Roger Bacon. In twenty centuries' time, we will probably be told that Winston Churchill cannot possibly be Winston Churchill! Is this sort of approach actually saying anything? Another symptom of it is the mania for demythologisation by Rudolph Bultmann and others of the same thinking. We have seen in the Bible itself traces of the demythologisation process at work; doubtless there is an element of truth in it, but it is a long way from being the complete truth. We need to accept that to explain any great alterations in people's religious thinking requires a towering figure that can stun people into changed thoughts. Moses, Jesus and Mohammed are such highly influential people; if they had never appeared there would have been no change in people's thinking. There is no point in trying to rake up evidence from the past. The evidence is in front of us in our own times. The introduction of new prayer books in Christian worship has been in the face of opposition from deeply entrenched attitudes. The old prayer book of Cranmer is still seen as something approaching scriptural. It took a great deal of effort and compulsion to make people accept the first prayer books of Edward VI. The truth is that it takes an overpowering event or personality to bring about changes in people's religious patterns. The inception of the faith of Israel could not have been achieved without a towering personality, such as Moses. To persuade certain Jews to cut loose from their legalistic faith and embark on a new direction called 'the Way' (now known as Christianity) cannot have been the result of some vague opinioniser with a few easy platitudes. Jesus must have been an overwhelming personality to have made the disciples do what they did, and face years of persecution. Historical realities cannot be sidestepped or airbrushed out. We can admit to a certain amount of distortion in the relating of history, as there is always the element of exaggeration and also understatement. But so many of the matters related in the Bible can be supported (directly or indirectly) by archaeological findings and literary evidence from those times. History is real, even if the human mind does have to distort it and interpret it[1].

Does this mean that the non-historical religions have no value? That would be unfair; they all have something to offer in their own way. Even if it is not historically based, that does not have to invalidate what they have to say. From the Western point of view, it is regretted that we do not know more about people like Siddhartha, Mahavira, Confucius, Guru Nanak, Zoroaster and Lao Tzu. They too in their lifetimes must have been towering figures to introduce a religion that has persisted down to modern times. But the message they offer does not rely on historical, geographical or scientific realities, and in some cases, does not depend on a clear understanding of God. The inner world of the spirit is important; meditation is an important factor. Symptomatic of this is the Buddhist attitude towards Creation; how do we know how everything got started? That is irrelevant. We are faced with a situation here and now and the methods for dealing with it are within our capability. The inner life of the soul is important[2].

This is not to say that the Western religions are devoid of inner, or mental activity – far from it – but we can see that there needs to be a balance struck between objective and subjective religious faith. If one is given undue emphasis, one's faith can easily become unbalanced and unstable. The result has been that within many Eastern faiths, people are able to think what they like, speculate to their hearts' content, and never state anything with any great firmness. An example of that would be with Shintoism, where it is claimed that there are no dogmas or hard and fast theological claims. You can think what you like. Christianity, or certain sections of it, has been heading in that direction for some time, but not all the way. It would be fair to say that one of the problems with Western religions has been their propensity to serve up hard and fast doctrines, dogmas and patterns of liturgy which have become quasi-scriptural. This has led to all kinds of intolerance and strife, very often over issues that are not specifically clarified in the Bible, and are some sort of theological guesswork or philosophical wrangling that are a long way from the essentials of the faith. Great cruelties have been perpetrated on people; one wonders how this can be squared with the love of God. One can be thankful that such extremes of dogmatism in the Christian world are now very much abated; one would hope that the fanaticism seen in other parts of the world could also be calmed down somehow. It may be that we have the great dictators of the twentieth century to thank for showing us how wrong, self-seeking, and totally unfair, ultra-indoctrination and brainwashing can be. We are now in the mood for questioning everything, and that is a healthy approach; but there is also the need to find something firm to hold on to. We all have the urge to find the truth somewhere; this applies to peoples of all religions and political philosophies. But how do we know where the truth really lies? Too often we assume that the truth is just one thing and that anything which contradicts it must be untruth. There is the need to see that sometimes the truth is held in paradox. This means that two contradictory statements may both be true in their own way, but cannot be resolved. This gives us a genuine paradox.

Mythology[3]

Before forgetting what this word actually means, it is important to recall that 'myth' does not mean a 'lie' or even a 'misapprehension'. A myth is some kind of attempt at explaining the origins of the universe and the human race, life on this planet and going further, the end result. We begin with Creation and end with un-creation. They stand like bookends holding the processes of history together. Even religions with no concept of history, still have this arrangement; this may be evidence that there is some awareness or need for history in spite of their religion not being really dependent on it. Strangely, but interestingly, the same kind of language and metaphors are found in all parts of the world. The details may differ but the essentials remain the same. How can we explain this? Does it mean that in remote pre-history mankind disseminated the same ideas all through the globe? This is somewhat unlikely. More likely is the factor of instinct. Just as people the world over value life, property and the person, they also need to answer some deep questions about life. Why are we here? How did it all begin and how will it end? Why do we have a tough time of it in life? What will happen when we die? These are instinctive reactions in any thinking person, and the myths are there to offer some answers. In another sense the myths are only describing ourselves, our emotions, our needs, our fears and our hopes. It is not enough to say that the myths are nonsense; they spring from deep instinctive urges in the human soul.

It has been said that since Darwin proposed the theory of evolution, that the myths have taken quite a knock. Nothing could be further from the truth. With regard to the Genesis accounts of creation, in relation to evolution, this has produced mainly three opinions: firstly, the out-and-out disbeliever who is confident that Genesis is wrong; secondly, the diehard Bible fundamentalist, who objects to being descended from a monkey, and rejects evolution outright; thirdly, a variety of stances in between, which seek to bring about some sort of compromise or co-ordination between the two, namely that Genesis is right on a symbolic level but as far as biology is concerned, life on this planet developed over millions of years. Who can tell where the truth lies? Was anyone there with a camcorder to record these events millions of years ago? I take the stance that none of them is completely right: there are problems with evolution, even if certain aspects of it may hold good; there are problems with fundamentalism, and even more difficulties with the notion that the world is only about 6,000 years old. The compromise position is nothing new, as we saw from the Norse sagas (Chapter 22), and that too has its problems.

The fascinating thing is that as the old myths have come under fire and lost their hold on peoples' imaginations, we see new myths multiplying at an astonishing rate. The chief myth, which seems to dominate almost everyone's thinking, and that includes the fundamentalists too, is the theory of Evolution itself. A lot of people take it as the gospel truth and assume it to have been proved. If one questions it, one is immediately labelled as a crank. This is totally unfair; evolution is still very largely a matter of guesswork and speculation, and there is nothing absolutely proven about it. It is just possible that it will one day turn out to be some sort of mirage or delusion. Let us just remember that at one time people thought that because the sky is blue, it meant that there was an ocean up there. That was their mirage; we have our own mirages nowadays.

In addition to this we have the astrophysicists probing into deep space, in the hopes of finding life on other planets or indeed the origins of the universe. A massive number of strange assumptions seem to guide their investigations. One wonders if, should some sort of life form be found on another planet, it would resemble our version of life; it might take a mode or form that we do not recognise as life as we know it. In the programme *Star Trek*, which is pure fantasy from start to finish, it is interesting how

482

strange little men on other planets seem to be cleverer than us, more dictatorial, more vicious than us, and what is more, they all seem to speak English with an American accent! Clearly, what is happening here is the projection of human traits up into the skies, and this is a process that has been going on all through the pagan eras of humanity. All this can be seen as myth in the making. Furthermore, it is clear that as the awareness of God has diminished in the modern world, something else is being sought as a substitute. This comes out very strongly in a book like *The Chariots of the Gods* by Von Daniken; the visitors from outer space were actually some sort of god. One wonders how many people accept this sort of thinking. Of course it is sheer speculation and can easily be rebuffed. The same goes for UFO's; there are panics over these strange appearances, but whatever they are, some sort of hoax or illusion, they have nothing to do with outer space[4]. The scientists are desperate to probe the so-called Big Bang, which again may turn out to be another complete illusion. There is questioning now over what might have happened before this alleged explosion; seldom does anyone dare to suggest that God provided all the materials, forces and ignition to start the universe off. What is happening here is the same as what Anselm propounded in his ontological proof for the existence of God. 'God is that than which nothing greater can be thought'. When we unwrap this thought, it means that however far one goes back into the origins or greatness of things, there is always that question, 'Where or who did it come from?' The only difference here is that nowadays we confuse ourselves with radio telescopes and claims to have received messages from millions of years ago! It is all expressed in modern thought-forms and vocabulary, but is essentially the same mental process as it ever was. No; myth is not dead; it is simply working on a different wavelength, a wavelength which is providing us with fewer answers to life than the old myths did.

Returning to the myths of old, which are not dead by any manner of means, there are various elements in them that are the same from every culture on earth. The first element is the awareness of nothingness at the start; this is very difficult for us to assimilate in a world that consists of somethings all the time. It is only in recent years that the scientists have been investigating the concept of anti-matter. But since we are probing outer space with its vast distances measured in millions of light years, an impression of nothingness is growing on us. Then we come to the beginning of creation, which is usually started by a pre-existent top god of some description, an eternal being who is superior to creation. Nearly every myth indulges in a whole family of gods, a pantheon, emanating from the top god. The major exception to this was the Hebrew insistence on there being only one God, who did not have a family in the skies. Instead, he had troupes of angels, but they were created as opposed to being 'born'. Many of the gods in the pantheon did similar functions but under different names, such as Thoth the Egyptian god being equivalent to Hermes, the Greek messenger boy (Chapter 19). It is easy to see how human traits are projected into the skies, and in effect people were worshipping themselves. Some of the accounts of the gods are really crude and disgusting. On that level, it is easy to discount these lurid myths, and yet, they tell us a lot about human nature, its aspirations, fears, and failures, and the culture that produced them.

The gods then indulge in conflict. There is usually at least one champion like Thor, sometimes more than one. He or they are usually locked in battle with someone evil, but we all know who will win eventually. It is like the modern crime programmes or the cowboy films; this is the modern permutation on it, and is just as mythical. Many myths bring the conflict to a conclusion with some sort of apocalypse or doomsday. The Hebrews handled this slightly differently in that the conflict was between the good angels and Satan, the fallen angel with his gang of 'baddies'. In the end, the good angels will win and the world will return to a state of innocence, which was how we all started in the Garden of Eden. All this is bound up with Messianism, another factor to be discussed later.

Another factor in every myth is the indestructibility of life. People and gods get 'killed' but they only go to another realm, such as heaven or hell. They are not snuffed out, and the Egyptian idea that one might be rubbed out is very unusual. That leaves the way open for resurrection, which is a strong element everywhere. This tells us that life is precious and it ought to last forever. There are various symbolisms in attendance for eternal life. Gold, silver, jewels, mirrors, crystal, and glass all speak of the indestructibility of life, and these are applied to humans, gods and devils alike. The snake is a universal symbol; it is paradoxical in that it symbolises death and life and also fecundity. In areas where there are no snakes, something else like an octopus is a substitute. The tree too is an important symbol; the world tree occurs in many mythological systems, and is important for the question of how there is any connection between heaven, earth and hell.

This brings us to the concept of the three-tiered universe. Obviously this aspect of mythology has taken more of a knock than most other elements. Now that we have visited the moon and have space stations in orbit, the flat earth mentality and the three shelves cannot be literally maintained any longer. But this does not mean that this idea is worthless; on a figurative level it still has much to offer. People still have an understanding of heaven and hell, even if from a geographical point of view, they are not physical locations. Talking of hell, today is politically wrong (!) but even so, everyone knows what it means and understands the threat involved. Heaven is however still in favour, and most people would like to think they will graduate to this state at the end of their lives. Clearly, no one thinks that heaven is a shelf up in the skies anymore; it is metaphoric, but even so, it is a powerful assumption with people, even if they would not claim to be a fully committed religionist. This all goes to show that mythology is far from dead; it is now being seen for what it really is, namely figurative language. For those who would try to demythologise these matters, heaven is now held to be 'in God's presence' and hell is the opposite, 'being separated from God'. Thus the traditional mythology still has relevance for us today.

An important aspect of mythology is the concept of everlasting justice and fair play. It is an instinctive response in human nature, that when something unfair occurs or something is out of balance, then it has to be rectified. We see this in virtually every mythology, that when some misdemeanour has been perpetrated, then somehow the matter has to be corrected. So when Loki engineers the death of Balder, the gods hunt him down and bind him, and the final rectification is known to be Balder's return to life for the unfairness of his murder. We see this in the moral argument for the existence of God, propounded by Kant, that there is a sense of ethics in everyone. That does not have to mean that we all have the same moral values, but we all do have values of some kind attached to the three main areas of morality, namely, the value of life, the value of property and the value of the person, which includes sexual values. This is one way in which mythology connects with everyday conduct. One might say the reverse is true; perhaps it is a matter of 'chicken and egg.'

It is worth noting that mythology in the Bible is not confined to the early chapters of Genesis. Just as the writers switch from prose to poetry without any signal, so the same applies to mythology. In Genesis, we slide gradually from the mythical material in the Garden of Eden, into the Tower of Babel and Noah's Flood. These could be called 'peri-mythological' since they may be based on real occurrences in ancient Mesopotamia. Then we flow into the accounts of Abraham and his battles with the kings of Shinar. This sort of thing often happens in the Bible and it requires a certain amount of common sense to see what is going on. Just because a certain passage may be classed as mythical, does not mean it is to be discounted. As we have seen, mythical material almost always has a lot to say at the figurative level, and just because it is not strictly literal on the historical level, does not prevent it from being deeply truthful. When dealing with the question of theodicy, we have noticed that it almost always reverts to the mythical mode of expression. No one ever seems to think that the problem of evil is purely and simply a product of human nature. The problem is seen as an eternal one and the only way to describe it is in terms of angels and devils (if one follows the Hebrew tradition) or gods of different attitudes in conflict with one another.

The same vagueness over the historical as opposed to the mythological is seen in other scriptures too. In the Japanese material (Chapter 12) it is very largely about the gods and their antics in the remote past. But mixed in we have references to real territory in the Japanese islands, and the story gravitates to the arrival of the Japanese Emperor. History and mythology are combined in a subtle way. In the Ramayana (Chapter 22) we see the same method at work, for as the main story is about good and evil on a mythical level, we have yogis, kings, devils and monkeys interwoven with it. It might be fair to say that for the people in the ancient world, there was no clear distinction between history and myth, and that would be particularly true in the east.

This must lead us on to some thoughts on Jesus in relation to mythology. The gospel writers, especially Mark, make it quite clear that Jesus is conversant with two worlds at once, the physical and the spiritual. He has command over the evil spirits and is in some sort of duel with Satan over temptation to do wrong. He talks about heaven and hell, Paradise and Gehenna, quite freely on the assumption that everyone would understand such phraseology. Does that mean that we have to take him literally and assume all these things, including the Devil? Some will say yes to this; if it was a part of the faith of Jesus, then it should be a part of one's own spirituality. There is a lot to be said for this stance. However, we must recall that in his incarnation he was fully human. This would entail having the same instincts, worldview and spiritual awareness as anyone else in that time in history. We would hardly expect him to arrive and tell everyone that there were no devils, and that the earth was not three-tiered and that the world circulated round the sun. No, he was a child of his own age just as we are. And yet, on the other hand, he was the Messiah of God, which meant that in a very special way he understood the essentials of God's intentions in a way that no one had ever done before and has ever since. He was there to assure us that God is basically and essentially love, not hate. Going on from that, seeing that there is pain and evil in the world, it is not just an unfortunate mistake – it is there for a purpose. On this basis we can see beyond the tension between history and mythology that the basic truths about life are above and beyond any vehicle of human expression. It is a matter of instinct combined with revelation. These matters are glimpsed in other scriptural materials, but are expressed much more clearly in the Bible.

To conclude on the matter of mythology, it is only a natural impulse in human nature to attempt to rationalise, explain, and make an application to life regarding the world we see around us. One cannot escape wondering what it is all about: a world with humans, animals and plants all interrelating with one another. Add to that there is the sun and moon and millions of stars that are not only of great beauty but must ask the question; what is it all about? What purpose does it have? What is it leading to? These questions were acute enough in the ancient world where gods and demons were believed to be playing tricks on us. But now that we are probing into space and are aware of distances in millions of light years, probably going on for ever, with black holes, and red giants, and quasars being described (one wonders how much of this is pure speculation on the part of the scientists), the question becomes even more acute. Are we really alone in the universe? Modern mythology likes to invent some form of life on other planets, but so far, there has been no solid evidence for this, and it may be that increasingly we become aware of being all on our own. So in a sense, we may be back to the ancient view of things, that this world is the centre of the universe after all – not geographically, but spiritually, ethically and eternally. That will leave us with the question of God's reality. Essentially, it is not a matter of proof, despite the well-known 'proofs for the existence of God'. God, or gods, were an essential part of every mythology, but now it seems the reverse is happening. God is not some sort of backstop hiding behind an alleged Big Bang. Now, God is an essential spiritual element that underpins the entire creation, something that the Bible said, but it was obscured by mythology. No longer is he an old man sitting on a chair up in the sky. He is ancient, fair enough, but also modern and futuristic. We have the scientists to thank for disentangling God from his creation and also from our mythologies.

Literary considerations

There is no doubt that some of the scriptural material reviewed in this book, is literary expression of the highest order, some of it less so. This may be stated regardless of one's stance on the merits of any given religion. The Ramayana, the Bhagavad Gita and Revelation stand out as world classics, each with merits of their own. On that basis alone, it is worth studying them and allowing them to speak for themselves in their own way.

It is a common feature seen in holy writings that repetition seems to play a very important part. This occurs in Ezekiel, Mary Baker Eddy, and certainly in *Mein Kampf*. Some see it as detrimental to the general effect; but the motive must surely be to provide emphasis and also, in the case of Hitler, to reinforce one's dogmatisms. In the modern world, publication is relatively cheap and the writer can afford to make emphatic repetitions, but in the ancient world, where papyrus scribal work was expensive, repetition must have been at a huge cost. This must underscore their need for emphasis. Repetition does not indicate a lack of mental ability or recollection of what one wrote a few pages back; it is a part of stressing one's deepest feelings.

Another aspect of nearly every sacred text is the element of hyperbolic language. Exaggeration is an accepted feature of poetic work, and the Bible is full of such features; so too the works of Zoroaster (Chapter 5 and the Ramayana, Chapter 22). While this is acceptable in poetic forms, we have to recognise that the same mentality occurs in prose material as well. In

Revelation (Chapter 6), for instance, we have prose and poetry intermingled, with massive hyperboles at work. What is the purpose of this? It must be that ordinary banal language is not enough to deal with the great issues of life and death, the activities of God and the beauty of the universe. Just as the world of the spirit is above and beyond us to assimilate, so too the extremes of human vocabulary are needed to attempt to describe what is happening on a spiritual level. It is to no purpose to say that exaggeration is a form of untruth; almost always the truth is underlined and emphasised by being hyperbolised. After all, if truth is a major aspect of God's nature, no amount of human vocabulary can do it justice. Truth needs to be writ large against the skies and the background of the entire cosmos. It is not something banal, trite and commonplace. The major and all-embracing truth seen in almost everyone's scriptures is that ordinary life is not enough in itself to explain itself. This was the mistake made by the Marxists (Chapter 3). It needs the element of the divine to give it any sense of purpose and direction. That is why we talk about God, or gods.

Another symptom of this attempt at talking about the divine is to use obsolete or semi-obsolete language. The Hebrew of the Old Testament, the Arabic of the Koran, the Gurmukhi of the Guru Granth and the Persian of the Avestas (Chapter 5) all show the same tendency. There is the feeling that because God is ancient, therefore antique language must be used in order to carry any conviction. We have only to recall how there was much resistance to Tyndall's translation of the Bible into English, let alone translating the Mass. We tend to forget that the Roman Mass stayed in Latin until the mid-1960s, and there are still those who support the Latin Mass Society to this day. In fairness, the Latin Mass, if properly performed, exudes an ambience that modern languages do not. The problem is essentially about describing or discussing the eternal God in human terms. This is a problem that Jesus himself had; how to represent God in terms that humans could understand, but even then, they had difficulties in taking in what he said. The answer was, to give them parables.

It is interesting that the parables of Jesus are his way of describing the intervention of God in this world, by the channel of Messiahship[5]. They are also a method for relating spiritual realities to everyday matters and tensions, such as wealth and poverty, acceptance and rejection, preparedness and not being ready. This is a literary mode that Jesus did not invent for himself. We see various parables in the Old Testament prophets, and in addition there is almost certainly some influence coming from the Jataka, tales that are basic to Buddhism. Because he borrowed the idea, does not mean it is worthless. But he does transform them and they carry a kind of eternal, indescribable feel to them, which is absent from lesser storytelling. There are various strands of thought in his parables, but the one most relevant here is the motif of the master or king setting his people to work, going away, and then coming back to conclude the business. Sometimes it is his son who is sent to assess the workmen. But the conclusion is usually the same; there are some who respond positively to the master and settle up with him honestly, and others who resist him and play up awkward. That is precisely the reception that Jesus had during his earthly ministry; some were attracted to him and others reacted badly and rejected him. Telling such issues in a story means that people of all levels of intelligence can comprehend him, as opposed to giving people a clever flow of high-flown philosophical discourse. This brings us to the chasm between good and bad.

This too is a feature of many sacred writings. We can see it as an aspect of exaggeration. Hardly anyone wishes to admit that there is a grey area with most people being an admixture of good and bad. It is seen in the wisdom literature from many parts of the world. One is either wise or a fool, and in some cases, it is not possible to transfer from the one to the other. This kind of chasmic, categorical thinking is all very dramatic and clear-cut, but is not entirely realistic. It may be a spin-off from the understanding that there are good gods and bad gods, good angels and fallen angels. There never seems to be an angel who is a happy average. We also have the distancing between the elect and the non-elect; it does not seem possible to be somewhere in no-man's-land. This is another trait in the parables of Jesus; that one should make one's mind up about being in favour of the Kingdom of God, or not, as the case may be. There is no room for ditherers. This may seem difficult for us who try to be good but are aware of our faults, but there is probably sound reasoning in this from God's point of view (if that can ever be assessed). We may notice that the whole of creation is based on the polarity between plus and minus, from the tiniest of atoms up to the largest structures. Everything in creation is dependent on the attraction in differing modes and circumstances, which produces in turn the vast array of all kinds of material. So there is purpose in having polarity; everything depends on the opposition of plus and minus. Somewhere in the purposes of God, the chasm between good and bad, white and black, is fundamental to life and death[6].

Another all-pervading aspect of scriptural material is the element of personification, an important technique in any literary work. This is fairly obvious with the pagan pantheons, how the gods represent the varying aspects of human nature, and also human aspirations. This is particularly so with regard to wealth; gold, silver and jewels are applied to gods, kings and champions. Also the sexual element is a strong drive, showing up in the characters of Baal and Asherah, Odin and Freyja, Apollo and Dianna, and Izanagi and Izanami. The Hebrew version of this, which did not allow for any pantheon, was to personify Wisdom as a sensible woman, in contrast to the loud-mouthed, pleasure-seeking female who is labelled as a prostitute. This method is not confined to Hebrew thinking. Sometimes we have the question of theodicy itself outlined in personification. In Japan, it is a god and a goddess, Izanagi and Izanami who walk round a pillar and make a mistake, which causes all the wrong things in life to occur (Chapter 12). They try to correct it but it is the goddess who is essentially blamed for life's problems. That much it has in common with the Garden of Eden, except that Adam and Eve are not divinities.

In the Ramayana (Chapter 22), we have the intriguing approach of using the animals in sustained personification. Even if they are gods in some sort of disguise, the monkeys show traits of loyalty and courage alongside the heroes like Rama and Laksmana. In the Norse material, the animals are important elements in the story even if they are not given a clear personality; they seem to be a vital part of each god's act. In India we have a whole array of spiritual beings somewhere in between the 'goodies' and the 'baddies'. They seem to vary greatly in their moral attitudes; they seem to be the equivalent of the dwarfs and elves in Norse tradition.

But the tension between good and evil is an essential ingredient in any storytelling. It comes out in just about every theatrical or media production today. This ranges across cowboy films, farce, kitchen sink drama, detective novels, police thrillers, soap operas, spy thrillers and many more. The chief difference nowadays is that the villain is not always seen as such at the start, but does emerge at the end. Justice has to prevail, something that in real life is not always completely obvious.

Mathematical truth

This approach to truth has become of the greatest importance in the modern world. That does not diminish the importance it had in the ancient world, although they may have seen it in a rather different light. We are aware of the excellence of mathematical skills in Mesopotamia, Egypt, China and Greece. We are stunned by the ingenuity of the Antikithera mechanism, which must have required a genius to devise it; one thinks of Archimedes. One might not expect sacred writings to become involved with mathematics and yet in various scriptural texts we see the use of numbers. In a world where there was constant uncertainty over a datum point in history, it is plain that much thought went into dating events by the regnal years of kings, not just Jewish kings but others too. We take for granted that everything can be related to the birth of Christ, and that is our datum point, in spite of efforts to sidestep this matter. With regard to Eastern religions, there is a constant uncertainty about dating of such people as Confucius and Lao Tzu. Even if their dates were firmer, it would not have any real bearing on their message.

It is quite likely that in the ancient world, numbers were not seen as exactitudes as we do now. The fact that in the Hebrew alphabet the letters each carry a number value ought to indicate that numbers were regarded as symbols or some sort of code, rather than as sums and calculations. This becomes quite obvious when studying Revelation (Chapter 6), for we suspect that all those numbers, some of them fantastic, are some sort of symbolism or code. This does raise the question of how to understand numbers that appear in other parts of the Bible, and indeed other sacred writings. We are amazed to hear that Abraham was ninety-nine when God gave him the promise of a son, Isaac. Is this biologically possible? The clue may be that when Isaac was born Abraham was then 100; we know from Enoch (and the Ramayana) that 100 is the number for God. Is this saying that Abraham's life is now coming to fulfilment with the promise being honoured by God? Number symbolism may be the answer to those astonishing ages that people attained to; Noah at 500 and Methuselah at 969, for example. Sadly we do not have the key to resolving these matters; people of the ancient world may have understood immediately what the encoding meant.

There is also the factor of measuring up the dimensions of the Temple and also of population census. Here we might expect something literal to occur, but the way it is presented in Ezekiel and Revelation would give the impression that it is all symbolic. We can include in this the dimensions of the Tabernacle used in the wilderness. If we interpret it just at face value, it looks very strange indeed, possibly it is all symbolic. When it comes to David doing a population census, God is shown to be unhappy about this, that the children of Israel can be numbered. Why was this? Was this because God had promised Abraham that his seed would be without number? There is certainly something strange going on over calculation and numbers in the Hebrew tradition.

In a subtle way, calculation is related to the concept of predestination. This is a factor seen in virtually every scripture discussed. There is the feeling of the inevitability of the march of events. Even Confucius, who was not really interested in gods, had a sense of predestination. The Ramayana too has this strand. In the Bible, it is heavily underlined with its insistence on the importance of prophecy. The correct fulfilment of prophecy presupposes predestination. This is clear enough in the Old Testament, with the messianic material in the prophets, but we notice that the New Testament re-asserts the importance of prophecy. It was Daniel who dealt out actual time schemes and schedules and this was copied by people like Ezra and Enoch. The apocalyptists had elaborate schemes about epochs and the end of the world, all related to 'weeks', which was a way of relating it to the Sabbath. This comes to completion in the book of Hebrews (Chapter 24). Again, it is possible to see this all as symbolism, and yet, one is left with the impression that the events of the Maccabean age were seen as the almost exact fulfilment of Daniel. How literally do we take three and a half? This became a sort of bogey number in the intertestamental period. Half of seven – that means something bad, incomplete, worrying. It starts in Daniel, runs through the Maccabees, then into the gospels and then into Revelation. Clearly, it is symbolic by this stage, and yet, at one point it must have been the literal truth. This may be a good example of how a number starts out as a face-value factor, but develops into some sort of symbolic factor. We are constantly up against this factor, not only in the Bible, but in the Kitab-i-Aqdas (Chapter 16) with its use of nineteen, the Japanese use of eight (Chapter 12), and the Norse use of nine (Chapter 22).

The substratum of all this mathematical usage is almost certainly the feeling that eternity is somehow calculable, quantifiable, and predictable. It certainly was with the Mayans with their ingenious calendar work. Are we seeing the basic awareness that God is reliable, not vague, and something that can be recorded in solid figures? We certainly get that feeling from the Antikithera mechanism, for all those planets and heavenly bodies worked into its system, would have been seen as gods, following predetermined paths through the skies. Perhaps this is the fundamental relevance of mathematics to religious faith. Just a thought: why does Enoch state that the number of God is 100? 100 is ten squared; ten is the number of fingers on the human frame. What do fingers do? They make things, man's creativeness. So God's creativeness is not just ten but ten squared, ten augmented, a complete number. There are so many possibilities in this that could be explored. But the conclusion is that mathematics cannot be underestimated in the general picture of scriptural material.

Artistic truth

It may have occurred to the reader that this aspect of reality has not been mentioned since the first chapter. There is a reason for this; that all the books cited so far have not been artistic renditions, in the sense of pictorial art, sculpture, architecture or music. They have always been a preparation of words. Is this a fair assessment? We notice that in the Masnavi, the Sufi scriptures (Chapter 17) that there is a painting contest between the Greeks and the Chinese, but like all Sufi material it is highly symbolic and not to be taken at face value. Even so, the realisation that artworks can be an aspect of religious expression is important.

To compensate for this, it is clear that the Biblical material, especially before the days of printing and also of widespread literacy, has been decorated with artistic renditions of great beauty. So for instance, the Lindisfarne gospels; the same is true for many mediaeval manuscript versions of the Bible. Stained glass windows have played an important part in reinforcing belief. Many Christian traditions have not found it necessary to take the second commandment totally literally. We can have pictures and statues of the saints and Jesus without it becoming idolatrous. The Koran too has had ingenious artistry worked into it, usually some sort of abstract design and not people with faces. All this is an admission, or rather an indirect statement that eternal truths are not just words that lead to belief, but matters of great beauty. This helps us to understand the pagan world to some extent[7]. They tended not to have written scriptures as the focus of belief. They went in for statuary and visual representations of their gods. From the Western point of view, it sounds like idolatry, but the Buddhists would claim that their images of Siddhartha, every one of them being different in some way, are there as an aid to meditation. The same would be true for the Eastern orthodox churches with their icons.

Similar remarks may be made about music. The written material studied here contains no music, strictly speaking. But many, if not most, religions have some kind of musical traditions to support belief. We immediately think if the Psalms, and indeed there are remarks in the text which indicate some sort of musical interpretation. Unfortunately, we do not have an insight into what they mean; for instance, what does *selah* mean? Literally, it means 'rock', but what does that mean in terms of singing or playing an instrument? In the Ramayana we have Rama's two sons singing the epic to everyone's delight. Sadly we do not know what it would have sounded like. In *Mein Kampf* there is reference to Wagner's operas; also we know that the Nazi rallies had various parade songs such as the Horst Wessel song, but they are not integral to Hitler's book. The importance of music in worship cannot be underestimated. It heightens the emotion and allows the worshipper to release spiritual energy in a way that other modes do not. We note that as the Last Supper was ended, they sang a hymn before going out to the Mount of Olives.

With regard to architecture, this is another important avenue for expressing religious faith. A major feature of the faith of Israel was the Temple of Solomon, and we have a detailed description of its fittings and the artistry in metal and wood that went into it. Ezekiel takes up the same strand of thought over the rebuilding of the Temple. When it comes to the New Testament, Herod's Temple is still in the process of being built, but even so it is most impressive. It is only when we see the scale model of the Temple in Jerusalem that one marvels at the skill and ingenuity that went into erecting it. Matching this is the knowledge that the pagan world also went to great lengths to build fantastic structures. The 'seven wonders of the ancient world' were largely religious structures. Many of the ruins of their temples can still be seen; the only one surviving intact is the Pantheon in Rome; it was transformed into a church and is little altered[8]. Many Hindu and Buddhist temples can be seen in the east. The Hindu temples often have an impression of Mount Meru on top, the mythical mountain mentioned in the Ramayana. In the west we have the legacy of the Gothic cathedrals; one has to ask, how did they do it? We suspect that each building had its own collections of symbolisms worked into the structure. Many of them were cruciform; sometimes the Chancel is slightly tilted to one side, suggesting Jesus' head sagging over when he died. In Durham Cathedral, it is speculated that the structure is devised to symbolise the womb of the Virgin Mary. So much of religious faith and commitment can be shown in the quality of architecture.

So too with the element of portraiture, whether it be a picture or a statue. Another important element creeps in here. Just as the pagans saw their gods in terms of their own physical appearance, so too the Christians tend almost always to picture Jesus as one of themselves. A visit to France will reveal that statues of Jesus seem to resemble Napoleon 3rd, with a goatee beard! Englishmen like to picture Jesus as an Englishman. The accepted picture of Jesus for the Mormons shows him as a benign Aryan! What is this saying? There is that tendency to claim Jesus for ourselves and forget that he was Jewish. So in a way, he becomes someone totally familiar with us as opposed to someone foreign; he is part of the soul of the Christian community. The same tendency was seen in ancient Greece, where Apollo was the idealised athletic young man with no clothes on; so too with Venus and many others. A visit to India will reveal the same thing; statues of gods looking like the idealised Indian men and women. We tend to see divinity in our own terms of reference. Perhaps the exception to this must be the deification of Lenin and Stalin, embalmed and on show in the Kremlin. They may have been cosmetically tidied up, but they were a reasonable likeness. So too the statues of them all over the communist world. This is a factor in common with the mythologies; we project our own likeness and nature into the skies and turn them into gods. In a way, we are worshipping ourselves.

Messianism

This is an important element in any understanding of sacred literature and indeed of any religion. There is the ever-present need for the divine to be represented in real terms in the world of humanity. This results in messianism, but it takes various different forms with varying degrees of efficacy. Probably the earliest known prototype of messianism may well be with the faith of Abraham. He had an encounter with Melchizedek, and although he may not have realised it, this was the precursor of the ultimate high priest, Jesus Christ. Although most of the Old Testament makes little use of this motif, the early Christians sprang upon it and showed that Melchizedek was a 'type' of Jesus; this comes out in the book of Hebrews very strongly (Chapter 24). Most of the Old Testament messianic material is prophecy about the ideal king who will rescue the people of Israel from a whole array of foreign tyrants. Since Judaism, on the official level, never recognised Jesus of Nazareth as the true Messiah, they are still waiting for this to happen.

With the Koran also we see that Jesus, though highly regarded as a prophet (he is termed 'an apostle' and 'the spirit of God'), is not regarded as the Messiah, or Mahdi. The Muslims also are still waiting for the Mahdi to appear, although the expectation for most of them is not as acute as in the Biblical material. When the Bab appeared in the nineteenth century and claimed to be the Mahdi, the Muslim world in general refused to accept him; this also applied to his follower, Baha'u'llah, who thought of himself as superior even to the Mahdi (Chapter 16). All this clashed with Muslim thinking and the result has been another splinter-group religion, namely the Baha'is. There was no doubt that with both these claimants, their humanity was never in doubt, but their claims to messianic status and divinity were seen as spurious. The Muslims, at present, would probably claim that the Koran, as given to them through Muhammad, is all they need for a connection with Allah. Muhammad is seen as the final prophet, but not seen as the Mahdi. Another aspect of this is Sufism, the mystical element in Islam. The author of the Masnavi, Rumi (Chapter 17), never makes any claims about being the Mahdi or Messiah. He is venerated annually at Konya in Turkey, but no one has actually tried to elevate him beyond just being the founder of Sufism.

One might have thought that in Eastern religions there would be no inclination towards Messianism. However, this is a mistaken view. It just takes a different form. For the Hindus there are many avatars, these are gods who appear in human or animal form, usually to help people on earth. The classic one studied in the Ramayana (Chapter 22) is Rama himself, who is an avatar of Vishnu. All through the epic, Rama does not seem to realise that he is a god in human form. His humanity is a little in question; he is always 'righteous' even when he does something that we would call dubious, such as being suspicious of Sita's integrity. In fact he is so idealised that he almost becomes unrealistic. But his true purpose is to defeat evil, in the form of Ravana. Only at the end, when the gods intervene, is he made aware of his true status. It is rather a different logic to that of the humble carpenter of Nazareth. Rama has all the advantages of being heir apparent to an idealistic kingdom. Another approach to Messianism in the Hindu tradition is found in the Bhagavad Gita. Here we have Krishna talking to a princely soldier, Arjuna, and advising him to fight the battle, contrary to his inclination to refuse. In this situation, Krishna is definitely a god, but is not in any physical form, such as human flesh. The conversation is all very mystical and informative of Hindu thought, but the possibility of Krishna coming as a real human being to share the human lot, with all its problems, is not there. Even so, this is another attempt at Messianism.

With Buddhism there seem to be two approaches to Messianism, both highly theoretical and philosophical. There was a king called Amida (Amidabha) who accrued massive amounts of merit which are available to help ordinary people towards salvation. This reminds us of Jesus in the mediaeval view of the sacrificial theory of the atonement. The difference is that Amida was never a real historical person; he was just a metaphor or theory. Not that that would worry the Buddhists since history is of very little account. The other approach is regarding Siddhartha himself. He was clearly an earthly figure, being born into a royal family. But he managed, through meditation, to find Nirvana and then make it available to anyone else who wanted to find it. This does not mean that he is the Son of God, or some sort of divine apparition. Even so, there is the concept of Bodhisattvaism, which comes a little closer to Messianism in the Western sense. But then there have been thousands of Bodhisattvas who have come in mercy to help people find salvation. But none of these are termed the Son of God. The Dhammapada (Chapter 14) does not go into any explanation of these matters.

With Confucius and Lao Tzu we clearly see two human figures who made no attempt at claiming divine status, in fact they claimed nothing for themselves. Confucius claimed that his wisdom was heaven-sent, but then, Solomon would have said the same thing. Later generations were to elevate them to divine status and make statues of them and worship them. None of this is mentioned in the Analects (Chapter 7) or the Tao Teh Ching (Chapter 10). Messianism in China is now more likely to concern Mao Tse Tung; although he was clearly human, he is still some sort of everlasting touchstone in the new permutation of capitalism in China. Some people have actually been known to picture him as being with the angels in heaven. As the epic of the Kojiki (Chapter 12) draws to a close, we see Amaterasu, the sun goddess, produce the Mikado, the Japanese emperor, installing him at the shrine of Ise. While the Japanese emperor is known to be human, his divine status has had to be renounced since the defeat of 1945.

With the Christian approach to Messianism, we see the insistence on Jesus being both fully human and fully divine at the same time and in one person. In terms of human logic, this is impossible, and it is one of the greatest paradoxes in any religious faith, not just in Christianity. In the early years, there were many who could accept Jesus as fully human but not divine, or vice versa, fully divine but not human, or even more intriguingly, fully human and nearly divine, but not actually God. These problems were sensed in the gospels themselves and in the New Testament generally.

Each gospel writer has his own way of expressing it, not in philosophical jargon but in real terms. St Mark is the one who comes very close to stating it plainly, and said that Jesus was human, but was able to dominate the world of the spirit. In other words, he was conversant with both worlds at once, human and divine.

Relevant to Messianism is the factor of sacral kingship. This was an important strand of belief in the ancient world but is now virtually dead, at least in its traditional form. Where it does appear in today's world, it is normally in some kind of secularised form and omits any connection to monarchy. The most readily recognisable ones have been Adolf Hitler, Stalin, and Mao Tse Tung. The scriptural texts studied in this book have reviewed Mein Kampf (Chapter 4) and the *Little Red Book* (Chapter 3). It is in *Mein Kampf* that we see the Nazi thinking on the subject of leadership; it was a kind of messianism minus God and minus the monarch. It was a messianism for the benefit of the German people at the expense of others whose racial background was not too pleasing to Hitler. Other than that, scriptural material on the subject of sacral kingship is rather scarce. The surviving records from Meso-America give us some indication of how the Mayans and the Aztecs approached sacral kingship, but the Egyptians, who had the most extreme case of sacral kingship, have not left us anything that might be called 'a scripture' on the subject. It is all a part of the human instinct to equate one's earthly ruler with one's heavenly ruler. We all need to have some sort of ultimate representative of God in some earthly shape or form, preferably a much-respected human.

Related to Messianism is the 'qiblih' mentality. This is a borrowed a word from the Baha'i thinking. The qiblih has two meanings: one, Baha'u'llah himself, and two, the place on earth where the god is located, physically. For the Baha'is it is Haifa; for the Muslims it is Mecca; for the Jews and Christians it is Jerusalem; for the Mormons it is the Temple in Salt Lake City; for the Japanese it is Ise; for the Chinese it is Peking; for the Sikhs it is Amritsar; for the Hindus it is the river Ganges; for the Buddhists it is Benares; for the Nazis it was Nuremberg. There is that tendency to locate God geographically, usually with a magnificent Temple. There are those who take this very literally indeed; the Temple of Solomon in Jerusalem was taken to be God's dwelling place on earth. We have Revelation (Chapter 6) to thank for pointing out to us that the real meaning of this is metaphorical; the real and everlasting Jerusalem is not on earth, but in heaven with God; and that paradoxically, since God's presence is everywhere in heaven, there is no need for a physical Temple.

Following this understanding, there are many Christian groups (and others) that do not allow their thinking to revolve around the earthly Jerusalem. They know that it is all figurative; there is no need to build a cathedral over the tomb of Jesus, if such a place could ever be determined. Christians of other stances have gone to great lengths to take the earthly Jerusalem as literally vital to their system of thought. So the church of the

Holy Sepulchre has been in dispute between the Roman Catholics and the Orthodox for a long time. Christians of other stances find that absurd, if not comical. But it goes further than that. The whole issue of relics flows from the qiblih mentality. People find that they have to have something physical to bolster up their faith. Splinters of the true cross, bones from the martyrs, Madonnas that weep or move – all this means a lot to some people. This tendency is not confined to Western religion; we find that Siddhartha's tooth is preserved somewhere. The whole issue of relics is interesting but wide open to fraud. But it all ties in with the need in human nature to have something tangible to hold on to. The same tendency is seen with the need to hold on to the written word in various scriptures. Modern scholarship has devoted much time and thought into the question of authorship and authenticity of the Biblical material. Why is it necessary to question who wrote which epistle? It is all a part of the tendency to hold on to something that can be accepted as real. In the final analysis it does not matter who wrote what; it is the content of the writing that is the crucial issue. What does it say, and what effect does it have on the reader? The reason why so many ancient (and certain modern) texts have gained acceptance and stood the test of time, is because they have resonated with something in the human soul, some need, some instinctive knowledge of God. In a way, the scriptures authenticate themselves, and the basic truths about life and death are handled in such a way as to give insight to those who already have that inclination in their souls.

Human failure

It would be fair to say that practically all world scriptural material has an element of awareness of human failure, inadequacy, something lacking in relation to the divine. The theological word for this is 'sin', but unfortunately this word has become far too tied up with sexual misdemeanour and that is a distortion of its true meaning. This is why I tend to avoid using the word, to avoid its pejorative overtones. What it does mean is that humanity is aware of a distancing between God and mankind, a failure of understanding, some sort of breakdown in relationship. If this situation had not occurred, there would actually be no need for religion, but so far, there has been no culture or society on earth that has managed to do without religion. The Communists have tried, but it has simply resulted in some sort of substitute, and now we see those countries sliding back, or rather forward, into a renewal of faith. If everything in the Garden had been rosy, if no one had ever hurt anyone, ever taken advantage, or ignored the honest impulses in human nature then there would not have been any need for some sort of reconciliation or repair work. As it is, we all have that feeling that all is not right with the world, and that a better world could be achieved somehow.

Lao Tzu in his Tao Teh Ching (Chapter 10) approaches this on a philosophical basis. He maintains that originally there was complete harmony between heaven and earth because everyone followed the tao. But then people began to stray from this and a breakdown in communications between the divine world and humanity and also between humans themselves, brought in disharmony. Lao Tzu does not explain how this happened. There is no 'Garden of Eden' story to illustrate it. But his answer to this problem is for everyone to be nice to each other, thus restoring harmony.

The Genesis account in the Bible follows another method of in fact saying the same thing. Adam and Eve were naked, which is symbolic of their innocence in the remote past. But it all went wrong because they thought they knew better than God; they ate the forbidden fruit and their innocence was destroyed. To augment the problem they began to blame each other and then the serpent for beguiling them; at that stage the serpent is not identified as the Devil, but that equation was to come later. At least three major world religions and a collection of splinter groups, have worked on this hypothesis, even if some of them see the story as symbolic. Once there was an age of innocence but it all went wrong. Even the Communists would probably subscribe to this idea by reference to Rousseau with his thoughts on the 'noble savage'.

The Indian religions, Hinduism and Buddhism do not seem to go in for such a motif; at least there is no echo of it in the scriptures studied so far. Even so, there is still the awareness of human failure and unworthiness and the need to be cleansed. There is the awareness of purity and the need to attain it. So the Hindus feel they have to bathe in the Ganges, even if the water is filthy. The Buddhist monks shave their heads. The Parsees (the successors of Zoroastrianism) have fire altars and expose their dead to the vultures for the sake of cleanliness. The Muslims must wash before saying their prayers. The Jews and the Christians have baptism. The Shintoists have white paper and water at their shrines. The Taoists picture the Jade Emperor as having a piece of white jade on his forehead, symbolising purity. There are people who are obsessive about washing and cleanliness. In many of the myths, there is reference to crystal and glass, which also symbolises purity as well as eternity.

In the myths, the gods too are aware of their inadequacies in relation to the top god, whether it be Zeus or Odin or Brahma. In fact we can see human factors simply writ large in the heavens, unworthiness and moral failure being the most notable. This leads us on to the issue of life and death itself.

From earliest times, mankind must have sensed the awkward question, 'why do we have to die? Life is precious; it ought to last for ever'. The Epic of Inanna (Chapter 22) very aptly describes how Inanna felt she had to go into the underworld, against her finer feelings. She was not dead really, but down below in Sheol there was gloom, silence, rot and despair. As thoughts developed, the motif of hell became increasingly complicated, speculative and frightening. So too did the motif of heaven, but not so frightening. Every human soul has this three-tiered impression deep in his subconscious. It has nothing to do with the physical world. It is instinctive and closely related to the issue of unworthiness. There have been two substantial ways out of this problem: firstly, was to earn a passage upwards by gaining merit, and secondly was to expect the unseen world to come in mercy and resolve the problem in real terms. One way or another, the human soul would find peace of mind. The main monotheistic religions have allowed both methods to interplay; the Protestants laid a heavy emphasis on justification by faith; the Roman Catholics tended to give merit a strong influence on people.

The other awkward question, 'Why do we have to suffer?' is allied to the death question. This question, called theodicy has dogged humanity since the dawn of time and reappears in some shape or form in every religion, with some attempt at an answer. But a conclusive answer has not yet been found. Some of the answers offered carry no long-term conviction at all. So *Mein Kampf* has an explanation which goes on the racist line: everything in life would be wonderful if the pure-blooded Germans were the dominant force in life. Everything is less than wonderful because of so-called inferior races, notably the Jews, with their allegedly tainted blood, ruining everything. The trouble was that millions would have to be shot or enslaved in order to achieve this imaginary goal.

The Communists sought to blame the exploitative element in human society, the capitalists and the imperialists. Chairman Mao seems to think that if the Chinese peasants were able to rule the world our problems would all be solved! But life is not as simple as that; just illuminating the 'bad' people does not work, any more than it did with the Nazi policy. The thing in common between the Nazis and the Communists is the assumption that evil is a purely this-worldly issue, that there is nothing spiritual about it at all. Human failure can be removed with a clever social policy, they would claim. But the evidence is that this approach is a non-starter.

All the other scriptural works assume, or even state quite plainly in picture language, that evil is a cosmic problem, way above the control of humanity. It is no use trying to tell everyone to be nice to each other; this does not work. The prevalent assumption is that there are evil influences at work. In the West, this is augmented into ideas about Satan, under various names and personifications, serpents and dragons. Evil is aggressive; it requires the counter-balance of good spirits, angels, and good gods to cope with the problem. In the East, they still understand the spiritual side of evil; just look at Ravana, and Yama the god of the dead, the good and bad kami in Japan. If evil is a spiritual and a cosmic matter at that, then the solution to it must also be a cosmic one. As far as the west is concerned, that means the active intervention by God at some kind of judgement day. This also brings in the relevance of Messianism, God intervening in real terms in this world. The solution to theodicy, however it is caused and for whatever reason, lies not in the capability of human nature. It requires someone like Rama, who is 'perfect' even if he is imaginary, or Jesus, who can effectively fight against evil, to make any serious impression on the spiritual side of evil.

The Question of Theodicy

The question of human failure cannot be easily disentangled from the problem of divine failure. The essential question has always been and still is, if there is a good god, why is there any evil in the world? Or more acutely, why does the innocent have to suffer? This is the root question that the atheists usually wave around as some sort of magic wand to advertise disbelief in God. Every religion of any type has some kind of approach to this question but as yet there is no convincing answer to it. It is possible to offer seven major solutions to this problem, all of which find some kind of representation in the scriptural material reviewed so far. Sometimes it is clearly on a pictorial level; at other times, it is highly theoretical.

Firstly, we can see that the pagan pantheon idea is quite an easy way out of the problem. There is a top god, usually the father of all and he usually sets the standard for all the rest. From him proceed any number of offspring who vary greatly in quality. Some of them are kindly, reliable and decent; others are less so. Some are capricious, nasty-minded and aggressive. There seems to be no clear explanation for how the top god can produce someone who is not of the same quality as himself. The Holy Kojiki (Chapter 12) of Japan is probably the nearest we come to an 'explanation', which states that damaged gods are produced because the god and goddess who mated did it wrong, inadvertently. The goddess spoke first which is supposed to explain the problem; it should have been the god who spoke first. But on a superficial level, the pagan multi-god concept offers an easy answer to the problem of evil and why humanity has to suffer. On a deeper level, we are still left wondering how a good god can produce something that is evil. The chapter that gives the most light on this aspect would be Chapter 22, which investigates the Hindu system, the Norse and the Greek epics.

Secondly, we can see that the pantheon idea became sanitised and the crudities were reduced if not removed altogether. So the top god is still there but the hordes of underlings become principles and theoretical entities. This was seen in the Gnostic work, The Gospel of Truth (Chapter 19), and the Corpus Hermeticum (same chapter), with the use of the term 'pleroma' and many others. The difference between the good god and the evil influence in the world, in this case, was caused by someone with a bad memory, in other words, carelessness. But there are all kinds of excuse methods at work. But the classic way out of it is seen in the Jewish adaptation of paganism. God is seen as not alone in heaven; instead of godlets or principles, he has hordes of angels. Most of them are helpful to mankind, but there was one, before the Creation of the world, who 'fell' and disagreed with God. He became Satan or the Devil, or various other names. So by this method, the evil in the world can easily be explained by this contention in the skies. Again, on a superficial level, this seems to answer the question; all our sufferings are caused by the malfeasances of the Devil. Even so, we are left with the question of why or how God allows a fallen angel to interfere with human life. These matters are assumed in the apocalyptic works such as Enoch (Chapter 20), the Koran (Chapter 21) and Revelation (Chapter 6). The answer to that is that for the time being, God allows this situation to persist, but eventually there will be an apocalypse and the evil will be rooted out.

This leads us on to the third solution, that of Dualism. This is represented here by the Avestas of Zoroaster (Chapter 5), as the clearest example of this scheme. This is the juxtaposition of two gods, one good and one bad, who are in perpetual contention with one another, and the battlefield is the soul of each and every person. This is not to say that there are no other gods, but they do not have any influence on the matter and might as well not exist. Traces of this idea can be found in many religions, sometimes slipped in as incidental. But with Judaism, Islam and Christianity, dualism has been an important substratum right up to the present day. The difference is that the Devil has never been allowed to be taken as a god; he is always, in spite of his spiritual power, in the final analysis under the one true God. Some of the Christians using a process called demythologisation, are trying to play down the reality of Satan on the grounds that it is 'sub-Christian', whatever that might mean. Even so, dualism leaves us with the question of how or why two opposing spiritual powers managed to appear in the first place. Some of the Zoroastrians pictured the two gods as twins who came from the same 'father' called Zurvan. This is all very mythological, but still leaves us with the question of how Zurvan could have produced two offspring so completely different.

This leads us on to the fourth possibility, that of pure monotheism. This is where Zoroastrianism came very close to monotheism but not quite. With pure monotheism, which is assumed in all the Hebrew, Christian and Muslim scriptural material, the assumption is that the One God is good, even if he does something that us humans might see as bad. That throws the question back on humanity. Even if the problem of evil is a cosmic matter, it is also essentially a case of mankind going wrong. This is where the

Garden of Eden motif is essential; it makes no difference whether one takes it literally or symbolically. What it is saying, in effect, is that the evil in the world is caused by mankind not taking any notice of God's instructions. This brings about a distancing between God and mankind and that explains all the problems we have in this world. It also implies that it is beyond the capability of mankind to rectify the problem. But the idea of an age of innocence in remote pre-history is a strong one and by no means confined to the Judaeo-Christian scheme of things.

The fifth possibility is to say that there is no God, which means atheism. This is by no means purely a modern idea, but has become more prominent in recent times. The Communists in the twentieth century tried to exercise statecraft on the atheistic assumption, but the problem was that something or someone else had to be found as a substitute for God. Some sort of ultimate reference point is needed, and that element has to be 'good' or 'fair' otherwise we have chaos on our hands. We notice that in the *Little Red Book*, (Chapter 3), religion is absent from Mao's remarks, but even then, we have that intriguing tale of the two mountains being removed; the angels had to intervene and there was some form of God after all. In the long term, atheistic social and political policy has been seen not to work. Somebody or something else has to be found to take the blame for this world's problems.

The sixth possibility is to say that there is no evil. This is not quite the same as saying there is no Devil, but it comes fairly close to it. The best example we have of this is Mary Baker Eddy's works (Chapter 10), which deny the existence of pain, and in fact the reality of this life altogether. But a strong assumption in people's minds is that suffering is a direct result of some kind of moral failure; you reap as you sow; you have problems in this life because of something bad you did before, perhaps in an earlier life. All things come home to roost somewhere or some time. If we try to deny the existence of evil, we then have to explain such phenomena as Adolf Hitler, Iddi Ahmin, and various serial killers on a lesser scale.

The seventh possibility is to try to forget the issue altogether. It is not really a genuine solution but many people try this approach. I call it 'cartouchism' which means that we draw an elliptical line round it, like the ellipse round the Pharaoh's name in the tomb. This way we isolate it from the main system of thought and sideline it, trying to ignore the problem. A classic example of this is the Buddhist Wheel of Becoming, in which all stations, good, bad and indifferent are contained in a circular rotating motif, but the main thrust of Buddhism is about escaping from it to Nirvana, which is a comfortable mental state that is morally neutral. Cartouchism is not confined to Buddhism by any manner of means. This idea too has its shortcomings: it only takes a major catastrophe nationally or in one's personal life, and the clash between good and bad re-emerges painfully.

It seems that we have to have a theory about everything, and that includes the problem of evil. Trying to ignore it does not work for very long; neither do any these other ideas. Most religions with their theoretical systems, are some kind of subtle blend of one or more of these seven ideas. Only to look at the wonders of creation elicits the question, 'what does it all mean?' We all assume there has to be some significance in it. Even the modern astrophysicists with their immense calculations and speculations, cannot leave out the question, 'what is it all about?' This is why we have all kinds of speculation about little green men from faraway planets; it is some sort of democratic projection into the skies. We cannot have gods, but we can have clever little men like us, who might respond to a radio signal! The thought that humanity might be unique and the pinnacle of creation in this universe, seems difficult for them to assimilate. But it is a distinct possibility that just as there is One God, so there is also only one humanity, and the ancient and basic question returns; 'how are we to relate to this God, or vice versa, how does he relate to us?

Sacrifice[9]

This leads us to the next question: how do we relate to the divine? In trying to find the truth, we cannot avoid noticing that an important element in every religion has been and still is the factor of sacrifice. In the ancient world it was taken for granted that sacrifice had to be performed to keep the gods happy. Failure to do this would invite disaster in various forms. Most of the major religions have now side-lined sacrifice in the sense of killing an animal or destroying goods, but the memory of sacrifice is very important, and the transformation of sacrifice into something more symbolic or personal is still a crucial factor. But whether one's sacrifice involves the spilling of blood, or of giving away money, or of some kind of commitment to a worthwhile cause, makes no difference: the urge to do it is just as important. There is that sense of giving thanks, even if one's belief in God is vestigial; there is that sense that in order to receive one has to give, or vice versa, having received, one ought to give something back. It is some sort of reciprocal arrangement.

Many of our scriptural texts actually mention sacrifice as a normal procedure; sometimes it is just assumed. Rather unusual is Mary Baker Eddy, (Chapter 10) who is not in favour of any ritual activity, neither is there any mention of sacrifice in any sense in her writings. She might well have said that the whole business is an illusion, at least the idea of trying to propitiate gods or God. Some of the Gnostic material too, such as the Gospel of Truth (Chapter 19), does not refer to sacrifice, which in a way, shows that Eddy was on the same line as they were.

It is interesting to see that in a modern work such as *Mein Kampf*

(Chapter 4), the motif of the scapegoat is an important assumption. This strand, which is detailed in Leviticus but is by no means confined to the Old Testament, illustrates the human urge to victimise someone or a group of people, on the assumption that this will solve our problems. In the case of the Nazis, it was the Jews as a race. This was combined with Bolshevism, but there were other targets as well, such as the gypsies. It was assumed, quite gratuitously, that the removal of such people would make for a better world. Ironically, and paradoxically, the opposite was the truth; the removal of Nazism is now seen as an urgent matter!

We have not studied the Capitalist mentality as they do not really have any 'scriptural' material unless one upgrades Adam Smith's *Wealth of Nations*. But the entrepreneurs of this world have their own approach to sacrifice; in starting up an enterprise it is always on the basis of advancing a generous amount of money or the equivalent on the assumption that this will bring great returns. Unbridled capitalism can result in horrendous exploitation, which amounts to the sacrifice coming from other people. This in turn explains the rise of communism. But that too has its own system of sacrifice. We have heard of the Five Year Plan and other such schemes, which meant that the peoples of China, Russia and others, were worked into the ground on the assumption that this would produce a better world. It was compulsory sacrifice, coupled with victimisation of anyone who disagreed with the government.

Sacrifice in its many forms is still with us today, and the most poignant one in recent times has been the loss of life in the twentieth century due to two world wars and various ethnic cleansings. Millions have had to die on account of the crazed ideas of certain crackpots. It is worth considering that just as blood sacrifice has all but died out from the ancient world, the modern world has substituted much greater hecatombs and on much shakier premises. The ancients thought they were pleasing their gods; the moderns thought that God was on their side but the motive for sacrifice was to defend one's own living space, a far baser motive.

But sacrifice is in effect the human counterpart of theodicy. We live in a world that is an interplay between plus and minus, gain and loss, success and failure. Why God created it thus is a puzzle to us all, but the truth is that if there were no such thing as plus and minus, nothing would ever happen. It is the tension between plus and minus that holds the tiniest atoms together to form molecules; it is the tension between gain and loss which allows great empires to run their course and then meet their downfall. At every level in the created world, we see life and death in a constant interplay; this way we avoid stagnation. This is something that Lao Tzu understood (Chapter 10) even though he had no atomic theory to consider. This of course has much relevance to the problem of theodicy: 'Why do we have to suffer?' Why not ask the corresponding question, 'Why do we have to have pleasure?' Life is an admixture of the two. It relates to plus and minus, gain and loss, success and failure. Without these two 'poles' there would be no values, no sense of direction, no ultimate aim of mankind. The seven strands that attempt to cope with theodicy all have the tendency to find someone or something to blame. The exception to this is the 'cartouche' approach, which in effect means 'bury your head in the sand'. Hardly anyone sees the matter in a positive light, that pain and pleasure, loss and gain are there for a purpose. These matters prevent humanity from going into stagnation and just drifting along aimlessly. That is what would happen if everything in the world were lovely, easy, painless, and perfect; we would all sit back and rot, not just physically but mentally and spiritually.

So how does sacrifice relate to theodicy? Given that theodicy is God's method for keeping things moving, developing and reaching out for an ultimate goal, sacrifice is mankind's method for working in with this pattern. From earliest times, humanity must have realised that for there to be life there has to be death, and vice versa, for there to be death there has to be life. The two things interplay with each other in the same way as the two elements in theodicy. So the giving of life has the effect of stimulating new life or fresh growth. Even on a basic level such as pruning bushes in the garden, this truism is known to all gardeners. If you leave the rosebush alone, it will go into suckers and eventually become a tangled mess. If you prune it carefully, it will be a disciplined and beautiful flower. This is true of so many plants. Take plenty off and it will stimulate new growth. This is an uncomfortable thought when it comes to pruning or culling the human race, but strangely, the urge is there. It does not even take God to persuade us to go in for genocide, but that is in effect what happens. We can see that from the tragedy of two World Wars that the long-term result has been firstly a fresh spurt in population growth (and that is quite paradoxical), but also a fresh approach to morality in various aspects. Did we have to have two world wars to persuade us to found and give full support to the United Nations? It certainly looks that way. Did we have to have the Third Reich to point out to us the senselessness and iniquity of anti-Semitism and other racial prejudices?

We have to be careful of moral arguments drawn from naturalistic assumptions, but this is regularly done without much thought. A case in point is how Evolution, as a theory, has stated the concept of the survival of the fittest. The truth or falsehood of this is not being debated here; what is debated is why it should be enlisted to justify the subjugation of so-called inferior races, and going further, the liquidation of those who are thought not fit to live. So, the Third Reich decided that the Jews should all be dispatched, on the premise that the world would be a better place without them. Other 'inferior' races could be allowed to live, but reduced to slavery, which meant that the Slavic races, Poland, Russia and others could be dispossessed and simply exploited. This was all supposed to be in support of Evolution, in other words, helping it along in an active way. Paradoxically, but predictably, the Holocaust has given the Jews a fresh impetus and purpose in life. Now that they have re-established their homeland in Palestine and are a major influence in world affairs despite their small numbers, it all goes to show that persecution generally has the opposite effect.

Moral factors

So far we have just assumed the moral dimension in all these discussions. But the moral dimension is obvious and sometimes implicit in every religion of any kind. Sometimes ethical and ritual prescriptions are seen as separate; sometimes, as for instance in Islam, ethical and ritual aspects of the faith are the same. But morality, as something distinguishable from ritual procedures, has three main foci; the value of life, the value of property and the value of the person. The value of life is chiefly seen in the ban on murder and related matters. The value of property is seen in the ban on theft and related matters. The value of the person is a much wider concept, which includes sexual values, and a whole range of personal values concerning everyday conduct. It is not easy to separate these criteria since they are intertwined and interrelated. They will be discussed in more detail below. It does not mean that every culture on earth has exactly the same laws and customs; very far from it. But the values underpinning the laws and customs are the same. This is to say that all of humanity has some sense of ethics; in other words, right and wrong. It is just that the details and implementation of them varying widely. The differences have gradually been diminished in recent times because of globalisation. But we all have some sort of sense of balance, fair play and justice.

On this basis, the argument for the existence of God, using the moral argument can be a powerful persuader. It was Kant who elaborated on this theme, but the rudiments of it go back much further in the history of philosophy. Briefly, if everyone has some sense of justice, then it is a short step to say that somewhere there must be an ultimate source of justice, above and beyond the failures of human nature. That source is God. It is a then a short step to suppose that if one observes the ethics given to one, for instance the Ten Commandments, then there will be a reward somewhere. If it is not in this life, then it will be in the next life. We notice that this is already following the thought-pattern of the Mosaic Covenant. This was made explicit in Deuteronomy and played out in 1 and 2 Kings (Chapter 18). It is easy to see how the Mosaic Covenant has been fundamental to Judaism, Christianity and Islam, since they all refer back to Moses and the Ten Commandments, but what about the Eastern religions that do not function on the basis of 'covenant'? Of course, they do, in a way, but it is not stated in the same metaphors or vocabulary. The whole concept of 'merit' as seen in Hinduism and Buddhism, presupposes some sort of concept of covenant, some sort of 'deal' going on between this world and the next. You do good works in order to achieve salvation. The same can be traced in Chinese religion in the way that one can be in harmony with the Tao if one's conduct is appropriate. This has been reinforced by the influence of Buddhism in China and Japan. Somewhere, instinctively, humanity assumes that to do good will result in good fortune and a happier life, and to do bad things will result in the opposite. Unfortunately, as we all know, life can sometimes give the lie to this idea, as seen in the book of Job, but there is a way out of this, by saying that there is compensation in the next world. This assumption was seen in 2 Maccabees (Chapter 2).

There is also another aspect to morality, that of development. It may be fair to say that in every age and culture we are constantly learning a higher ethic. A good example of that would be the story of the 'sacrifice of Isaac'. Abraham had the feeling (he thought God was prompting him) that he should sacrifice his first-born son. In those days that would have been a perfectly normal procedure; a way of giving thanks for the arrival of the firstborn and a way of ensuring that there would be more sons to come. This was at a time when human sacrifice was thought of not as murder, as we would think nowadays, but as essential to honour the gods. But God intervenes at the last minute and prevents Abraham from killing his son. What is this telling us? That human sacrifice is wrong and should not be perpetrated any more. In other words, Abraham and his people were learning a higher ethic. The same can be said for us in our times. Before the antics of the Third Reich, it was quite the normal thing for the white races to regard the others as inferior and to treat them as such. Joseph Smith goes even further and assumes they are 'under a curse' (Chapter 7). It seldom occurred to people that this was wrong and completely unfair. But having seen the depths of cruelty and barbarity inflicted on innocent people in the Holocaust, this has brought it home to us how unfair and horrendous racial discrimination can be. This does not mean that everyone has given up being racially prejudiced, but the main thrust nowadays is for equality and decency towards those who have been kept down. The same goes for warfare. Going back to 1900 it was commonly assumed that to have a war was perfectly acceptable as long as one observed certain ground rules, notably, one does not start a war oneself. But two world wars and with massive loss of life and destruction of property, culminating in a nuclear stalemate, has brought it home to us all, not just the futility of war (as seen in the Iliad, Chapter 22), but also the iniquity of it. Now the majority of governments go out of their way to prevent or smother conflict; the United Nations is at last being taken seriously because we all know the consequences of another all-out conflict that may involve nuclear weapons. This is another case of us learning a higher ethic.

The recent troubles in the Middle East may again be the next lesson we have to learn in the realm of ethics. The gratuitous bloodshed being perpetrated by certain fanatics is almost certainly motivated by a literal acceptance of certain statements made in a certain religion (Chapter 21). There is some kind of assumption that this conduct will evoke the return of the Mahdi, or Messiah. Are we to learn from this that a literal interpretation of sacred literature needs to be tempered by reference to basic truths, one of which is the commandment 'Thou shalt not commit murder'?

Given this process of ethical development must make us wonder what other moral criteria are waiting for us to learn. It is not easy for us to stand back from our own culture and see the wrong things that are going on, and there is always an excuse for carrying on as before. What will people be saying about us in twenty centuries' time, assuming we have not blown ourselves to smithereens? Will they regard us as collection of cruel idiots? They might say something like, 'Why did they spend billions on space exploration when there are people starving to death, and others in pain because certain diseases are not being tackled seriously enough?' They might say, 'Why did they forget about God and assume that they could solve their problems with some kind of clever social policy?' Who knows what they will be saying!

But the truth of the matter is that we have to have an ethic of some description, otherwise we have chaos. Moreover, the ethical code has to be given to us by a higher authority than ourselves; otherwise people will just ignore it. That is one of the problems nowadays with people who cancel off the concept of God and think they can still have a consensus morality. The way to do it is to assume God, as the giver of laws and final backstop of justice. That way there is no need to argue over it. We see this in the Ten Commandments, God is effectively saying, 'Here are my instructions; stick to that, otherwise you will have trouble.' It is worth remarking that the Ten Commandments are a bare minimum statement; there is a lot more to ethics than just observing the Ten Commandments, but they do form a foundational basis for the whole of humanity, regardless of one's religious superstructure. This would apply to the Humanists and others whose notion of God is not the orthodox conception. We can take a look at the Ten Commandments in some detail but not in any particular order.

A modern application of the Ten Commandments

'Thou shalt not commit murder'. Here we see the value of human life writ large; one should not put another human to death deliberately. But of course, over the centuries, the definition of murder has altered and is still mutating.

In the ancient world, murder gradually became applied to human sacrifice. By the time of the Roman Empire, we see the Caesars actually persecuting those who perpetrated it. In our own times, we are at last seeing it applied to killing in warfare; now many people see killing in a battle as iniquitous. Going further than that there is the dilemma over when abortion should be permitted – at what point does a foetus become classed as a living human soul? Difficult! Also the dilemma over euthanasia is a red-hot issue. I do not have any ready-made answers to this question, but we can see how this commandment is being developed and reapplied in today's world. It does raise the question of how literally we have to take such a law.

There is all the appearance of a finer conscience stemming from this law on the sanctity of life. Cruelty in its various forms is now out of favour. Torture too, though not common in times gone by, is completely out of the question. Corporal punishment too is banned. The main thrust (allegedly) behind Health and Safety is the preservation of life and health. In this way, 'Thou shalt not commit murder' is being applied far more rigorously than ever before. But strangely, suicide is now legal and assisted dying for terminal cases is now available in some countries. This simply serves to illustrate that human nature is seldom completely consistent on any matter.

Looking at it positively, it is more to the point to ask, 'How can we save life, enrich it, reduce pain and suffering?'

'Thou shalt not steal' clearly refers to property rather than life. The sixth commandment does become involved if it is robbery with violence. Most reasonable people have respect for other people's property. In today's world, it is honesty by compulsion rather than by conscience. The banking system has devised a device using plastic cards which means there is far less room for perpetrating a swindle. Even so, there are criminals around with ingenious ways of pulling a 'scam'. Some of the financial frauds are so clever that an ordinary jury has difficulties in seeing what has been perpetrated. But 'theft' now involves more than just refraining from stealing someone else's property. It extends to being careful with anything belonging to someone else, whether borrowed, or just interfered with or held on trust. Even such a thing as vandalism is heavily frowned upon; the property damaged may belong to the community and has to be repaired with public money. A certain amount of thought often has to be given as to where to draw the line; walking off with someone's pencil inadvertently is strictly speaking theft, but is it such a big issue, when we consider that some companies hand out pens and pencils as freebies. This brings up again the question of how literally to take this commandment. Chairman Mao said that it was a crime to take even a needle or thread from the masses; but then he managed to appropriate the freedom of the entire Chinese nation. Things need to be seen in proportion.

Looking at it positively, we can ask, 'How can we give, help, encourage?'

'Thou shalt not commit adultery' is somehow very largely ignored in modern Western society. We must remember that in some parts of the world, this is still taken very seriously. This law relates to 'stealing' and also to the person, in that it involves sexual values. There is the issue of how to define adultery. The ideal situation in the west is for one man and one woman to commit themselves to each other in a bond of trust. Formal marriage as such is now taken far less seriously than it used to be. But in some polygamous cultures, it is not thought of as wrong for a man to have several wives. The Koran (Chapter 21) says that a man can have up to four wives; other cultures in Africa can sanction many more wives. This is not seen as adultery. On the other hand, if a married woman has a liaison with another man, then there is trouble. What is the core of the matter? The core of the matter is the deception going on in the marriage. If a husband is having an affair and is deceiving his wife, then that is what most people would say is unacceptable. Moreover it will be even less fair if the family income is being diverted away from the wife and children to broker another (illicit) family. In that sense, it involves the eighth commandment, in other words, dishonesty and deception, deception over money or property.

But the intention behind this commandment is now being seen as more extensive than just relationships between husband and wife. There are many relationships that we form in day-to-day living; business partnerships, sports clubs, commitment to some kind of cause. Obviously there is the element of betrayal if someone deceives a close colleague or friend, taking advantage of goodwill and turning it into disappointment for the other person. An example would be if two people were in business together and the one decided to defraud the partnership and perhaps start up another arrangement with another business. That would be an example of deceit with the intention of furthering one's own interests at the expense of another's.

To look at it in a positive light, let us have honest dealings within the family and the marriage, and with others with whom we form relationships, and leave out sexual exploitation in the many forms it can take.

'Thou shalt not bear false witness'. This clearly relates to court procedure. Obviously it is wrong, if called as a witness, to hand out a false accusation that will land the defendant in trouble. This, in the past, might have involved the death penalty or a tough prison sentence. But taking it further, many people see this as a prohibition on telling any lie at all, in court or anywhere else. We must ask ourselves, what about a 'white lie'? Suppose someone is dying of cancer; is it ethical to tell him that he is actually getting better and there is nothing to worry about? The bitter truth may make things a lot worse for him. There is also the issue of lying by just not saying anything at all; if one knows about something that is likely to cause upset and injury, it is a good idea to keep quiet?

These are matters for the individual conscience and the use of common sense.

But the truth is an important issue for us all, and this is the motivation for this book itself. How do we know which religion or political theory is correct? What criteria can we use? We notice that virtually every text studied claims to be the truth. The whole purpose of philosophy is to discover the truth. So on this level, the truth is God, in an important way. Falsehood is to be shunned. Deception, whether of deceiving oneself or someone else, is wrong. There is an instinctive element in human nature that requires the truth to be sought. This is not just on the trivial level of lying oneself out of trouble, but on the ultimate level of wanting to know the essential truths about life and death. We cannot just ignore these matters.

Looking at it in a positive light, it is almost always simpler in the end just to tell the truth.

'Thou shalt not covet' means being envious of someone else's property. This is clearly related to theft, but can go further and result in murder. This is where the commandment becomes much more personal and internal. The very motivation for theft and murder are being tackled. Jesus went so far as to say that even if one thinks about stealing, murder or adultery, one has done it in one's heart. This is a good example of how he would exaggerate in his teachings, thus making it impossible for anyone to think of themselves as perfect. Indeed this does raise the question of how literally one needs to take this commandment, or indeed any of the others. Obviously there is a difference between just admiring someone else's property and burning with desire to steal or destroy it. This is a case of not allowing one's emotions to run away with one's conduct. This is an example of how 'Thou shalt not covet' can be applied in a modern context, keeping one's emotions in check against getting carried away and perpetrating some sort of rash conduct.

Looking at it in a positive light, it would be better to offer something that might enhance another person's property.

Starting at the other end with the first commandment, we see that the early ones are related to theology rather than ethics, that is, if the two can be separated. 'Thou shalt have no other gods before me' tells us that in effect, we need to make our minds up where our true orientation towards the truth is to be found. This law does not deny the existence of other gods; we know that there are many different religions and many different gods contained within them, plus the secularist gods such as alcohol, drugs, gambling, 'pop idols' and many others. It is difficult to go through life without becoming involved with one lesser god or another, but here, God is saying, 'Get your true focus on the ultimate truth; leave out the distractions of man-made gods and secular obsessions.' This commandment is relevant to us all, regardless of our stance on religion. Even the atheist needs to consider where the ultimate truth is to be found, and not get distracted by one mania after another. The same applies to the heavy religionist; he too needs to raise his sights to the ultimate truths and not allow the trappings, the superstructure and the traditional dogmas of religion to shorten his vision.

Looking at it positively, we need to concentrate on the deep and ultimate issues of life, rather than be distracted by trivial matters.

The second commandment, 'Thou shalt not make a graven image', may seem rather strange to many today. But there are people, chiefly the Jews and the Muslims, who take this totally at face value, and will not have any statues or pictures of people. This was of considerable importance in the ancient world because most religions were dominated by idolatry; every temple had a statue of a god of some kind. In today's world, which is saturated with pictures and representations of people and animals, the question of taking this literally is a difficult one. Art, in its various forms would be much the poorer if we had no films, magazines with illustrations, no television with people shown on it, no cinemas with film stars exciting us. But idolatry is not purely and simply a matter of making a statue and regarding it as a god. Idolatry is a spiritual problem in which all kinds of obsessions, fancy notions, elaborate theories get in the way of a direct understanding of the ultimate truth, namely God. It is so easy to reduce God to some sort of human picture, or expect him to conform to our expectations. For many, God has been pictured as an old man sitting on a chair up in the sky; we have the Book of Daniel to thank for that metaphor. But such an image cannot be taken literally. Admittedly we have to think of God in terms of something. For many people, evolution has become a god, a complete explanation for everything. The astrophysicists too, with their probing into deep space, are trying to find 'god' by which I mean the explanation for life itself. But this is all idolatry. It is mankind fabricating God in our own image, but the opposite is the truth; God fashions us in his own image. And for those who have trouble in understanding God at all, the truth is that he came in person at a special time and place and showed himself to us as his Messiah. That is the idol that we are allowed to have; God gave it to us himself. That is the opposite way round from us concocting an image of God.

Looking at it in a positive light, God allows us to have one image that will cancel out all the false ones. That image is Jesus himself.

'Thou shalt not take the name of God in vain'. This has traditionally been taken to mean a ban on swearing and bad language. Most of our current swearwords are related to God, the Devil or sexual matters. Many people find it offensive, and that includes many who would not claim to have much religious faith. In the New Testament, the chief complaint about Jesus was that he was a blasphemer; in other words, he laid claim to be God. This is an important aspect of the third commandment and clearly more to the point than just using expletives. In the ancient world, it was nothing unusual for an important person to decide to claim divinity. Alexander the

Great is a case in point. The Roman Emperors regularly did this, although it is unlikely that many people took them literally. The Dalai Lama is claimed to be a god, but how literally is this to be taken? In the twentieth century, Adolf Hitler, though not overtly making such a claim, certainly behaved as such and his followers regarded him is such a light. But behaving like God is not confined to demagogues. Anyone who makes decisions and indulges in behaviour that betrays a lack of humility and concern for humanity, throwing his weight around and behaving like a 'control-freak', is in fact doing this. How often do we hear the phrase 'Oh he thinks he's God', in other words, orders everyone around, makes gratuitous executive decisions and generally bullies everyone around. That is the true blasphemy; a serious lack of humility. That is very important in relation to today's emphasis on democracy. Clearly, foul language is an annoyance to many people, but then there are times when one has to give vent to one's emotions without actually physically harming anyone.

Looking at it positively, it is a healthy policy to show a generous degree of humility, and willingness to serve and help people as opposed to being pushy.

'Remember to keep holy the Sabbath day'. This is clearly related to the Creation in Genesis Chapter 1, in which God rested on the seventh day, namely Saturday. A literal approach to this would mean that everyone would stop work at 6 pm on a Friday evening and start again at 6 pm on a Saturday evening. The Jews do observe this, some more strictly than others; also the Seventh Day Adventists. But many religions keep another day of the week as holy; the Christians have Sunday and the Muslims have Friday. Of what relevance is this commandment for the modern world? Things such as power stations, blast furnaces, supermarkets, hospitals, to name but a few, have to keep going all the time, and thus they are manned by shift workers. But having a rest, a holiday, a change that is as good as a rest, is very important. It is damaging to health to go on working continuously. We all know that it is psychologically important to have a holiday; everyone values the regular festivals in the year coupled with bank holidays, plus one or two days off in seven. They are of course associated with religious commemorations, but people of all or no faith find it necessary to have a break.

As the laws of Moses received more detail, there was the law of the Jubilees, which meant that every forty-nine or fifty years, there should be a rest period; in other words, an augmented Sabbath. This meant that not just the humans, but the natural world, the fields, the crops, should have a chance to recover their strength. For centuries, farmers used to allow their fields to lie fallow, to regain their nutrients. Nowadays, many farmers smother their fields with chemicals instead. The wisdom of this is already being questioned. In general terms, there is much awareness of the need to avoid the over-exploitation of the natural world, coupled with concerns over global warming. It is clear that all this is a natural development of the fourth commandment. In other words, 'do not over-exploit things'.

Looking at it positively, which is implicit in this commandment anyway, take plenty of rest, do not become overtired and allow the natural world to recoup its strength.

'Honour your father and mother'. Most people do have this emotion in their lives, regardless of their stance on religion; it is a natural impulse. But a lot depends on how literally one must take it. It does not actually say 'obey', although in the wisdom literature we have reviewed (Chapter 15), there is a heavy stress on taking one's parents' advice seriously. In China, it goes further: one must obey one's parents, even if they are going senile and talking total rubbish. Obviously there has to be a balance struck here. Any responsible parent will not obstruct a child's ambitions in life; the freedom to leave home and make a career at something is important. It would be fair to say that the Biblical view of the parent-child relationship is that the child is only 'loaned' by God to the parent; the parent does not own the child like some sort of property.

But the extended implications of this commandment are possibly more important than the literal ones. We were confronted with Rehoboam's folly: he was nowhere near as wise as his father, and he took the advice of the young men with disastrous results (Chapter 18). In general terms, whether it is our parents or just experienced people in general, it is wise to take seriously their advice, which is normally on the side of caution. Those who ignore the voice of experience are taking a massive risk. This of course is regularly done. Politicians often ignore the lessons of history; Hitler is a case in point with regard to Russia. The whole point of studying history is to warn us of the pitfalls of the future; history is thus our greatest parent. We all know that history has a nasty habit of repeating itself; it need not do that, if we were to learn our lessons and accept sound advice from those with experience.

Looking at it positively, which is the tenor of the sixth commandment, it is wise to take into account the advice of those with full experience of life, rather than be carried away with a bright new idea. This sounds like conservatism, but then, so often this has turned out to be true.

It can be seen from this that the Ten Commandments are basic to so many aspects of life, not just at the time they were issued, but in the modern world too. There is the literal level, much of which is still of great importance to us all, such as murder and theft. But there is also the transferred or expanded level, which means that Moses was far-sighted enough to see that all of these commandments had many further implications that are also of great value to us all. The situation over the environment is a case in point, in fact, later in the Pentateuch, this issue is in many places discussed; care for

515

the natural world. We notice that the first five commandments are mainly 'Godward' and the rest mainly social or manward. There is a balance to be struck between honouring the 'father' and caring for humanity. This crystallised into the two great commandments that Jesus gave us. 'Love the Lord your God' comes a little later in Deuteronomy; 'Love your neighbour' comes in Leviticus. Jesus turns the 'Thou shalt not', negative approach into a positive one. It is all very well to be on the defensive all the time, just avoiding bad behaviour; there is the need to think positive about life and reach out to other people, offering help and caring. This is all very down to earth; there is nothing fanciful, theoretic or even mythological about it. It is a basic code for civilised life, and that tells us that essentially, religion is about the realities of everyday living. It is not essentially about fancy speculations, clever theories and the denial of the realities of life.

Ritual prescriptions

Ritual in the ancient world very largely centred round some form of sacrificial activity. It was the book of Hebrews (Chapter 24) that provided the logic of abandoning sacrifice, since Jesus himself had performed the ultimate sacrifice. This meant, and still means, that anyone sacrificing today is not actually making any impression on God. It might be making an impression on humanity, possibly a negative impression, but not making any difference with the world of the spirit. That does not mean that worship and liturgy has disappeared, far from it. The Japanese have their Shinto shrines, the Buddhists have their meditations in their monasteries, the Hindus have their temples and festivals, the Jews have Passover and Yom Kippur, the Muslims have Ramadan and other observances, and the Christians have the Eucharist. These observances have their customs and regulations and convey something spiritually valuable to those who have faith in such procedures.

The truth of the matter is that we all need some sort of ritual to accompany life. This may take the form of the regular festivals which punctuate the year, or the day of rest once a week, or the *rites de passage* which many religions have, such as baptism, bar mizbah, weddings and funerals. Just a plain passage through life with no kind of ceremony is not enough for most people. The Communists discovered this on trying to rule out religious ceremonies; they had to invent observances such as May 1st to fill the gap. Then there are the lesser rituals in life, such as wearing clothing which more or less conforms to the normal fashion, or table manners, or traffic regulations, or certificates for achievement, or installing a new Lord Mayor or head of state. There are all sorts of minor rituals that are not strictly ethical but we just take for granted as the rich pattern of life. Allowing such things to occupy centre stage to the exclusion of all else can become counterproductive. It comes down to not seeing the wood for the trees. But the basic essentials of loving God and loving one's neighbour can still be kept in mind in spite of the complications in life. It is fair to conclude that we all need something symbolic, not literal, and capable of lifting us out of the banality of ordinary life. Life has to have shape and meaning; if we do not allow God to give us it, then we have to improvise it for ourselves.

Notes for Chapter 27: Drawing Conclusions

1. See Chapter 22, 1 and 2 Kings.
2. See Chapter 14, The Dhammapada.
3. See Chapter 11 in The Theology of Paradox.
4. It is interesting that so far, none of the men in the space stations have reported seeing any UFO's; this would tend to the view that the phenomenon is terrestrial, some kind of mirage, hoax, testing of futuristic weapons or illusion.
5. See Chapter 10, on Parables, in The Theology of Paradox.
6. See Chapter 2 on theodicy, in The Theology of Paradox, in which a full discussion of the Problem of Evil is set out.
7. The Aztecs are the exception; they had many sacred texts but nearly all of them were destroyed by the Spaniards under the assumption that their scriptures were the work of the Devil.
8. The Pantheon in Rome is the only complete building surviving from the Roman Empire. It is a remarkable structure; the dome is made of pumice, which greatly reduces the weigh in order to avoid collapse.
9. The rationale for sacrifice is detailed in Chapter 4: *The Theology of Paradox.*

28

Towards finding the Truth

It has been said that there are only two certainties in life: firstly, that one will die and secondly that one will pay tax. After that, anything could happen to us and there is no guarantee about anything good, bad or indifferent. To cope with this, we all need to have faith in something, whether it is a career, a marriage, our children, our nation or arts or sciences. It is unusual to find someone who has no faith in anything at all, no interpretation of life, no target, no symbolism. But this raises the question of finding the right thing to have faith in. Obviously, faith can attach itself to something wicked, cruel, destructive, selfish. We saw this with *Mein Kampf* (Chapter 4). Faith can also indulge in some sort of exaggeration of an element of truth; we saw this with Mary Baker Eddy and her cranky health ideas. Faith can attach itself to some sort of answer to all our problems, some sort of messianic answer, the centre of which could be a complete fraud. We saw this with *Mein Kampf* (Chapter 4) and the Qitab-i-Aqdas (Chapter 16) and the Book of Mormon (Chapter 7). Faith can be carried away with something completely fanciful and speculative. We saw that with the Holy Kojiki (Chapter 12), the Gospel of Truth (Chapter 19) and the Ramayana (Chapter 22). Faith can attach itself to something frightening and eschatological, such as Revelation (Chapter 6) and Enoch (Chapter 20) and the Koran (Chapter 21).

It would seem that every scriptural production has some sort of shortcoming. This is inevitable since they are all the product of humanity in relation to the divine. The human element produces some sort of distortion; the divine element still manages to show through in spite of our failings. This is also true of the Bible; it is a fine example of divine guidance interplaying with human weakness. Examples of this can be seen in the way the great prophets are called. Jeremiah admitted that he was only a young man and not up to the task, but God put the right words in his mouth. The case of

518

Jonah is probably the most stark in this respect. Here was a prophet who actually tried to run away and avoid his commission, but events caught up with him and he found himself delivering his message even though he did not feel at all confident about it. The truth catches up with us regardless of our human weaknesses.

Although there are elements of truth contained in worldly scriptures, the whole unmitigated, undiluted truth is not to be found in any of them. We can return to the thought at the conclusion of Chapter 1; the truth is not a piece of paper, but it is a person, first and foremost God himself and then, by extension into this world, his Messiah, Jesus. Obviously, this Messiah has to be reported and recorded by the gospel writers, who themselves are only human. This means that there is bound to be an element of distortion and interpretation in the way they portray Jesus. The way round this has been to have four different versions of the same thing. The synoptic gospels concentrate largely on the public side of Jesus' ministry; St John takes a more interpretative approach and gives us more of the private and intimate side of Jesus in relation to his disciples. It is foolish to say that one is wrong and the other right; both aspects show us Jesus in a slightly different light. John admits that if everything were to be recorded about the ministry of Jesus, the world would not be able to contain all the books. This means that all four writers have had to make a careful selection in relation to each one's interest. The paradox is that, on the one hand, the truth is above and beyond all human recording and calculating; on the other hand, four scriptural writings have attempted to portray Jesus in human vocabulary and thought forms. Each gospel has its own strengths and weaknesses. When put together, Jesus comes up in 3D against the background of first century Israel as a backwater of the Roman Empire.

It will be helpful to make a short critique of each gospel and see how they contribute to our understanding of Jesus. It is worth remarking that no other major religious figure in history has been described by this method of four different versions, produced by his early followers. We can take each gospel in turn and evaluate them in a constructive way.

St Mark

This comes first because with modern criticism it is thought that this gospel was written first and the others copied large portions from it. There is a tradition in the Church that it was St Peter, in his last days, who gave Mark the information he needed. There is no certainty about which gospel came first, but the primacy of Mark is probably a fair assumption. Essentially, for our purposes, it makes little difference which one was written first.

Mark is noted for his emphasis on the 'Messianic Secret'. Jesus does

519

not go round making great proclamations about how he is the Messiah of God. He allows other people to come to that conclusion. He is constantly telling people to keep quiet about the miracles. His reason for this may be twofold. Firstly, he did not wish to be cornered into some sort of politico-military revolt of the kind that were two a penny in those days. All of them ended in disaster. Secondly, the notion of secrecy, as we saw in Enoch, was an important ingredient in the arrival of the day of judgement. Jesus almost certainly knew the book of Enoch (Chapter 20) and felt that his messiahship was to be fully demonstrated at the end of his ministry. This is what Mark succeeds in showing us; at the moment of Jesus' death on the cross, the veil of the Temple is rent asunder. The metaphor is a powerful one; it demonstrates that through Jesus giving his life, we all have unimpeded access to God, the unmitigated truth about life and death.

Another major theme in Mark, is his insistence on Jesus being in control of factors in this world and the unseen world of the spirit at the same time. This gospel has been termed 'the spiritual gospel' for that reason. His healings concern physical and spiritual illnesses; physical illnesses are clearly related to the workings of Satan. He has power over all kinds of disorders, including the elements.

Another important theme in Mark is to show how Jesus began by reaching out to the Jews but increasingly found that a mission to the gentiles was far more viable. He appears not to be too happy about this, but is forced to the conclusion that the leadership of the Jews have made their minds up to reject him, and more than that, to make sure he was removed from the scene.

Mark is in unison with the other gospel writers in that the fulfilment of prophecy was a vital element, which ought to have made the Jewish leadership take Jesus more seriously. So many times Jesus performs miracles that remind us of Elijah and Elisha. There is the raising of the dead, Jairus' daughter, and the feeding of the five thousand. He calls himself the 'Servant' which recalls the servant material in Isaiah. Jesus calls himself the 'Son of Man' which evokes Ezekiel and Daniel.

A notable strand in Mark is Jesus' advice 'do not be afraid'. This is in the face of people being frightened out of their wits at the events unfolding. In fact the gospel, strictly speaking ends with 'for they were afraid'. Ironic; they need not have been if they had taken his advice. But this was symptomatic of how he was systematically misunderstood and ignored from start to finish.

Mark himself is clearly the John Mark who accompanied St Paul. Mark may well have been an eyewitness himself to all these amazing events. He may have been the young man who ran away naked in the Garden of Gethsemane! Another way of seeing that incident is to recall that there was another naked young man in a garden at the beginning of history, another events fulfilment. He may also have been an employee of the fishermen on the Sea of Galilee; his gospel very largely centres around the fishing exploits of the first four disciples. Much of his material is so vivid that it can only be seen as eyewitness reporting. There is that sense of urgency and immediacy in his gospel; the present tense seems to dominate the account, and the word Euthus ('immediately') occurs many times. St Mark's gospel is a gem of undecorated realism and may be taken as very close to the real earthly Jesus.

St Matthew

This gospel is thought to have been written much later than St Mark. It is usually said that the writer knew St Mark's gospel and copied large amounts, often abbreviating them, one assumes, for the sake of space. But he has other information from elsewhere; Q (*quelle*) is a source in common with St Luke but not found in St Mark; M is a source peculiar to St Matthew. Whether Matthew is actually the tax collector that Jesus called to be one of the Twelve Apostles, or not, is not clear. Matthew would hardly disagree with the other gospel writers, but he has various issues worth emphasising.

He is intent on showing that Jesus was descended from Abraham through King David to Joseph, his earthly father. In fact the birth stories centre round Joseph rather than Mary, and bring in the Magi from the East. It is assumed that Persian Magi were minor royalty. They arrive seeking the 'King of the Jews' and want to worship him, bringing expensive gifts appropriate for royalty. Thus the kingship of Jesus is emphasised. This is given further emphasis in the climax of the Passion, where the phrase 'King of the Jews' comes round no less than four times. The crown of thorns, the reed in his hand, which must symbolise a sceptre, all add to this strand. Matthew touches on the same theme from time to time; the two blind men are calling out for the Son of David (Matthew 20:32); at the Triumphal Entry to Jerusalem, the crowds shout 'Hosanna to the Son of David!' and the prophet Zechariah (9:9) is quoted 'your king is coming to you' (Matthew 21:5).

The Sermon on the Mount is of great importance in Matthew's scheme. Here we see the new 'Moses' going up the mountain. This is not Mount Sinai and the mountain is actually not named, but traditionally it is identified as Mount Tabor. But this is a very different law; gone is the negativity of the Ten Commandments; it is all about blessing from God. But the new law is far more demanding than the old one. One has to be correct on every detail, and outdo the Pharisees in virtue. All the old rules are intensified to an impossible pitch. Hypocrisy is frowned upon. The air of authority in his teaching is unmistakable and on a different level to the legalists of the Jewish faith. Even so, he is seen as fulfilling the Mosaic Law:

'Think not that I have come to abolish the law and the prophets; I have come not to abolish them but to fulfil them' (Matthew 5:17).

This leads us to another important strand in Matthew, that of Jesus being a great prophet in the tradition of Elijah. Paradoxically, it is John the Baptist who is identified with Elijah; even so, Jesus is also associated with Elijah. That strange scene at the crucifixion, when the bystanders misunderstand what he is saying, '*Eli, Eli, lama sabach-thani,*' and think it is an appeal to Elijah to come and rescue him, completes the association. The soldiers who assault Jesus after the trial, clearly assume that he is a prophet, and as such, is psychic:

'Prophesy to us, you Christ, who is it that struck you?' (Matthew 26:68).

Otherwise, Matthew shows much interest in the ministry of prophecy and goes on to imply that the twelve disciples are also prophets. 'He who receives a prophet because he is a prophet shall receive a prophet's reward...' (Matthew 10:41). This is in the context of the disciples being commissioned for ministry.

Consistent with this is Matthew's strong interest in the fulfilment of prophecy. It is a wide-ranging use of Old Testament, especially Isaiah, and often rather wooden in the way he does it. There is none of the subtlety seen in St Luke. One might conclude that Matthew was what we might call a 'fundamentalist' in today's terms. One puzzle is '"He shall be called a Nazarene"' (Matthew 2:23); no one knows where he found this prophecy. It is possible he is quoting an apocryphal work now lost; otherwise, he may have just made it up. Interestingly, Matthew's rationale for the messianic secret as seen in St Mark, is explained by reference to Isaiah 42:1-4: 'He will not wrangle or cry aloud, nor will anyone hear his voice in the street...' We notice that his use of that passage is something of a paraphrase, and the added element, which appears rather differently in Isaiah, is that the gentiles will benefit from his justice. Isaiah has it phrased as 'the coastlands', which in his mindset means the far-flung parts of the world. This is an interesting example of how a prophecy can be slightly adjusted to further a theme (see Matthew 12:17:20).

In this way, the tension between the mission to the Jews, as opposed to the gentiles is more heavily stressed in Matthew. As Jesus sends the twelve out on their mission he tells them to go only to the 'lost sheep of the house of Israel' and keep away from the gentiles and the Samaritans (Matthew 10:5). But the tipping point comes in Matthew 15:21, where a Canaanite woman begs to have her daughter healed. At first Jesus tries to ignore her and the disciples try to send her away. Then comes what to us might seem shockingly racist, '"It is not fair to take the children's bread and throw it to the dogs."' But Jesus relents and the girl is healed. Was he just testing her? Or was this the moment that he realised that the gentiles were far more inclined to accept his ministry than the Jews? In general terms, Matthew's gospel is more Jewish-orientated, in contrast to the others.

It is no surprise to find that Matthew is the most inclined to the eschatological mentality. So many of his parables concern the day of judgement and the separation of the good from the bad. His apocalypse, found in Matthew 23:4, which is delivered from another mountain, namely the Mount of Olives, is the most fulsome and frightening of all the gospel apocalypses, unless one includes the Revelation of St John. And the eternal Judge, Jesus himself, is a major theme in Matthew. It comes to a head in Matthew 25:31 when the Son of Man comes in his glory and eternal punishment is waiting for the bad, but eternal life for the good. This is much more strongly put than in the other gospels. It is no surprise that Jesus is made to wear a SCARLET robe (Matthew 27:28); Roman judges wore red, just as ours do nowadays. This symbolises Jesus as the eternal judge.

Consistent with Matthew's eschatology is his description of the resurrection. It is the most exciting, loud, demonstrative of all the gospel accounts, with earthquakes and lightning, with the guards falling down as if dead. Clearly this is meant to tie in with his apocalypse, and the hint is that the eschatological words of Jesus have come to fulfilment at the Resurrection. This is contrasted with the feeble attempts on the part of the Jewish authorities, to stifle the Resurrection (Matthew 28:12). This all goes to augment the power and wonder of the climax of the book.

Of the four gospels, Matthew is the most eschatological, and mythologically inclined, but this is tempered by so many down-to-earth day-to-day realities in the ministry of Jesus. We have to ask ourselves, what is being said with so much mythology? Surely, Matthew is trying to show us that Jesus was not just an ordinary rabbi or teacher like all the others, but the significance of his ministry was universal and groundbreaking, above and beyond the banality of routine life.

St Luke

Much has already been said about this gospel in Chapter 23. It is generally accepted that Luke, like Matthew, knew Mark's gospel and used it as a source of information. Also there is that unknown source Q (*quelle*) and Luke's own particular material called L.

Luke is more interested in the family connections of Jesus, Zechariah, Elizabeth, John the Baptist, and concentrates on Mary's side of the birth stories. This is consistent with his emphasis on the womenfolk's role in the gospel. He is in general sympathetic to the underprivileged people in Jewish society: the beggars, the lepers, the shepherds, the widows, and the poor. This goes further for he shows how Jesus reached out to the Samaritans and the gentiles in general; all the sort of people that the Jewish leadership disdained. We notice that the great sermon is not on a mountain, but on the same level as the people, not just the Jews but people from Tyre and Sidon. The association with Moses and Elijah is weakened but not absent. Both of them appear at the Transfiguration, but in a prophetic role, outlining the end of his ministry.

Luke is not so fulsome in quoting the prophets; this element too is toned down, but not absent. His references to the prophets is done in a much more subtle way. A good example of this would be found in Luke 9:54 where the disciples ask if they can call down fire from heaven on the Samaritans. This may seem a little strange until we realise that Elijah did just that in 2 Kings 1:9-16. Prophetic fulfilment is there for anyone who knows his Old Testament. Luke's reason for doing this could well be that he was writing mainly for a gentile readership, who might have found the Hebrew prophets of less interest.

The eschatological element too is much toned down in Luke. His apocalypse (Luke 21:5-28) is much the shortest of the three synoptic gospels, and has a more positive tone, and is far less damning. We must beware of false Messiahs. The END is a time of hope when we must look up, raise our heads because our redemption is drawing near (Luke 21:28).

Luke wishes to emphasise the innocence of Jesus. There are no less than four trials at which Jesus could not be found guilty. But because of the weakness of Pontius Pilate, Jesus is handed over to be crucified and Barabbas the murderer and insurrectionist is set free. This piece of harsh irony serves to highlight the failures in the Roman legal system. It is the centurion, as Jesus dies, who says: 'Surely this man was innocent' (Luke 23:47).

One of Luke's ongoing themes is that of forgiveness. It comes out in the most important parables, such as the Prodigal Son, and at the cross where the penitent thief is pardoned (Luke 23:43).

The account of the Resurrection in Luke 24:1-11 is very restrained. This is consistent with his lack of emphasis on the mythological and spectacular. Luke wishes to stress that Jesus really did rise from the dead, not just as a ghost, but real flesh and blood.

None of these matters would have been denied by Matthew and Mark, but it is all a question of emphasis, and what each writer is trying to portray. It does not mean that one is right and the other is wrong; there is an element of truth in all these things. It would be fair to say that while Matthew is writing first and foremost for the Jews, Luke is thinking of the Gentile readership, but like all generalisations, it is not the entire truth.

St John

There is no certainty about when this gospel was written; most scholars imagine it was written some time after the other three, whilst some people regard it as the earliest. It is quite possible that John is the apostle John who was very close to Jesus, 'the one whom Jesus loved'. If that is so, those long discourses may be almost a verbatim account of what Jesus said.

John wishes to stress the pre-existence of Jesus, the *word* of God. He did not just stretch back to Abraham, or Adam, but before all creation. He was God's instrument in creation, the true light and the life. John does not attempt to give details about birth narratives; perhaps he knew of them from the other gospels. He wishes to show the eternity of Jesus as well as his earthly life.

Jesus is also seen as the sacrificial victim, the Passover lamb. 'Behold the lamb of God who takes away the sin of the world' (John 1:29), is an important statement. This is reinforced by the fact that many of the scenes in John are related to the Passover festival in Jerusalem. This is especially so at the trials and the Crucifixion, as John times Good Friday to coincide with the Day of Preparation when the Passover lambs would have been prepared. '"Not a bone of his body shall be broken,"' reminds us of the rule at the Passover that when eating the Passover meal, the bones should not be broken (John 19:37). The following day, the Sabbath coinciding with the Day of the Passover, infers that God's work, the Messiah's work has come to completion, as in the six days of creation. Related to this is the high priesthood of Jesus, which comes out in the prayer in Chapter 17. In general terms, the priestly aspect of Jesus is somewhat understated in this gospel.

The kingship of Jesus, however, is heavily underlined. However, it is not an earthly kingship, which involves armies and violence. This comes out when Jesus is in conversation with Pontius Pilate. The phrase 'King of the Jews', or variants on it, comes round no less than six times, and when the signboard is put up, it is in three languages, and Pilate refuses to alter the wording to reduce the impact of them. The paradox in this is that although he was the King of the Jews, he was also the king of the entire universe. He was forced to wear a crown of thorns and was dressed in a purple robe, which then, as now, indicates royalty.

Jesus as a prophet is also a theme in St John, though not as heavily stressed as the other matters. Jesus foretells his own death and resurrection in such a way as to leave his disciples puzzled, for instance, in John 14:18. Another example comes in John 12:23: '"the hour has come for the Son of Man to be glorified..."' A direct statement of Jesus' prophetic role comes in the incident with the Samaritan woman at the well: '"Sir, I perceive that you are a prophet"' (John 4:19). John's approach to the fulfilment of prophecy is somewhat different from that seen elsewhere. He is not quite so wooden and literalistic as the other gospel writers. There is a degree of subtlety about it, but he is still intent on showing how Jesus fulfilled the ancient prophecies.

But the main thrust of John's gospel is that he takes five selected miracles and each one is related to the important 'I am' statements. This provides us with a completion of God's identification at the Burning Bush, 'I am that I am'. Jesus fills this out with, 'I am the Light of the world', or 'I am the Resurrection and the life'. The seven statements comprehensively portray the whole of Christ's ministry and relationship not just with the disciples but with the whole of humanity. That there is power in that statement 'I am...' is seen in John 18:6 where the soldiers fall to the ground, assumedly with shock. Also the effect on the Jews is quite astonishing, when Jesus says, 'Before Abraham was, I AM'. It all relates to the question of identity, a theme seen in the other gospels, but heavily underlined in St John. That is the purpose of the great statements that underpin the messiahship of Jesus.

In contrast, the Jews are constantly making a serious misunderstanding of Jesus, his identity and his status. There is the literalistic hang-up, in which they cannot understand how he can give them his flesh to eat (John 6:52); they cannot see that it is figurative and a truth on another level. But so often, Jesus transforms the literal to the figurative, which ties in with transforming the Old Testament into the New, as seen in the miracle of the water into wine in Chapter 2. Eyesight is transposed into not just seeing, but being enlightened. Life itself is transposed into risen life with the resurrection of Lazarus. But the chief priests are so enraged that they try to murder Lazarus (John 12:10). Here we see a strong contrast; Jesus gives us life; the chief priests are intent on taking it away.

In today's terms, John's frequent mention of 'the Jews' in an unfavourable light, can be easily taken as anti-Semitism. But he hardly meant it in such literal terms in his gospel. He admits that many of his countrymen were strongly in favour of Jesus; it was the sectarians, such as the Pharisees, the Sadducees and chief priests who were dismissive and increasingly infuriated with him. There were many in the halls of power who accepted Jesus (John 12:42) but had to keep it quiet because they did not want to land in trouble. When he says 'the Jews' we could fairly paraphrase it by saying 'the Jewish leadership'. To us nowadays, this antipathy seems incomprehensible, and even St Paul agonised over it. St John resorts to the prophecy of Isaiah for an explanation:

'Therefore they could not believe. For Isaiah again said, "He has blinded their eyes and hardened their hearts, lest they should see with their eyes and perceive with their heart, and turn for me to heal them"' (John 12:39).

This contrasts strongly with the healing of the blind man; while the blind beggar receives his sight, the arguments and confusions still rage among the Jews. This is compounded by the fact that Jesus, as with many of his other miracles, did it on a Saturday, the Sabbath. This, to us, would seem a trivial matter, but to the heavy literalists, this was about as heinous as high treason. But the reader can easily see that there is deep symbolism in doing a miracle on the Sabbath; it was the last day of creation when everything came to completion. So, God was completing his work with the extra blessing and demonstration of his love on a Saturday morning.

This contrast between the literal and the figurative is an important element in St John. It is paradoxical that there is so much figurative and symbolic material in John's gospel, and yet, there are realities that are missing from the other gospels. So, the Pool of Siloam, where the blind man had to wash, is a real place which Hezekiah constructed and can be visited today (Chapter 18). Also the pool of Bethesda with five porticos, has been unearthed by the archaeologists, 40 feet below ground level. Also the Pavement, Gabbatha, the Lithostroton, has been discovered, below street level, and interestingly in the stonework, there is a Basilinda, a kind of game played by the Roman soldiers, which involved dressing a slave up as a king and mocking him. Is that what they did to Jesus? It may be, paradoxically, that we are nearer to the literal truth, in places, in St John, than in many other contexts in the gospels. In turn this may indicate that John himself was an eyewitness to so many of the incidents in the ministry of Jesus. This gives an extra significance to this statement at the end of his gospel:

'This is the disciple who is bearing witness to these things, and who has written these things; and we know that his testimony is true' (John 21:24).

Finding the truth in completion

There is clearly a certain amount of tension between the literal truth and the figurative truth. This emerges in many of the scriptural works reviewed. Even with the eastern religions, the historical and geographical elements cannot just be ignored. There is a need for one's religion to be related, even if loosely, to earthly realities. But with the Judaeo-Christian approach, earthly realities are indispensable. Theology and metaphor grow out of history and geography. This of course, causes a problem with the Creation accounts in the early part of Genesis. Taking these completely literally, involves one in all kinds of problems. In common with so many other world mythologies, so much of the text is metaphorical and figurative, and it cannot be taken as scientific or sociological fact. The difficulty comes in knowing where to draw the line. The Bible does not tell us when it switches from historical fact to poetic rendering; from the literal to the figurative. We have to use common sense, but that is not too surprising, since Jesus very often did not tell people what to think, but asked them to use their brains. Human common sense and discernment has its part to play, and this is seen quite clearly in the way the gospel writers each bring their own point of view or focus of interest into the portrayal of Jesus.

The truth is that we all, of whatever religion, have trouble over finding the ultimate truths about God. This is because God is on a different level to us and our human minds cannot take in the greatness of his reality. But real he is, even for those who are in denial of him. And the most revealing account of him comes from his own Messiah, Jesus the carpenter from Nazareth. It is St John who relates Jesus' identity directly to the Burning Bush incident, when God gave Moses this conundrum, 'I am that I am'. But the completion of it comes in the fourth gospel, where the great 'I am...' statements fill out the conundrum and give us a comprehensive understanding of the work of the Messiah, in terms of this world. The way it is written is not in literal language; it is figurative and yet that does not prevent it being the ultimate truth. Jesus can hardly be literally a vine or a piece of bread. But the metaphors used are powerful, emotional and all encompassing. They bring to completion not just the Jewish faith of the Old Testament, but also all the other religions of the world, in their attempts at understanding the realities of God. So often, they have some kind of attempt at Messianism, with a great prophet, or a great teacher who is seen as uttering deep truths about God. But none of them come up to the greatness of the Messiah from Nazareth. There is no comparison. But Jesus brings to fulfilment all their hopes and attempts at understanding the divine. We can demonstrate this by briefly reviewing each scripture in relation to Jesus.

The Holy Kojiki (the basis for Shintoism)

This work is noteworthy for its understanding of the complexity of creation, in that the ultimate God has agents in the work of creation, rather than doing it all himself. Within this is an understanding and partial explanation for the problem of theodicy. At the end of the myths, the Japanese Emperor, the Mikado, emerges as the offspring of Amaterasu; this means that one's earthly ruler is the same as one's heavenly ruler, but only, it would seem, for the Japanese people, as opposed to the whole human race. The Israelites, who were not living on an isolated island, saw that their monarchy, when it came to relations with other nations, was relevant not just to themselves but the gentiles as well, and this helps us to understand the developing concept of Messianism. But the completion of it came with Jesus the Son of God as the Eternal King. Here we have the universal king who is on the one hand, king of his own people, the Jews, but also the king of us all.

The Analects of Confucius and the Tao Teh Ching by Lao Tzu (the basis for Confucianism and Taoism)

The positive element in both these is sound advice for anyone in a position of power or influence. This applies chiefly to earthly rulers and bureaucrats. This advice is only common sense and would hardly be denied by any responsible person. The mentality of caring for people, being responsible, not using violence, being honest, thinking of the best interests of the nation is to be applauded. But we see this in the leadership of Jesus; he never resorted to hectoring, bullying, and cared for everyone, especially the outcasts. He was prepared to lay down his life for his friends. We wonder if Confucius or Lao Tzu would go to that extreme.

The Dhammapada (one of the bases for Buddhism)

One of the essential elements in Buddhism is the gaining of merit in order to achieve an improved life in this world, and hopefully Nirvana in the next world. The historical Siddhartha is not a god or a messiah in the western sense and is not referred to in the Dhammapada. The concept of someone who has accrued merit on behalf of others is there, but not on the basis of a historical figure. There is a lot to be said for letting go of worldly values and concentrating on matters of the spirit and preparing oneself for the next world. But Jesus would take it further and say that not only should one renounce the world, but take up one's cross, because giving of oneself is the surest way to receive eternal triumph. That does not mean isolating oneself from the world; it means involving oneself in a positive way to care for people, the opposite of greed and self-interest. Obviously, St Paul would have something to say on the subject of merit; essentially we are saved by faith. Even so, Jesus did talk about rewards for those who made the full commitment to the kingdom of God.

Bhagavad Gita, by Vyasa (one of the bases for Hinduism)

The emphasis on love, between Krishna and his followers is valuable, but the limit comes when someone does not love Krishna; that person is not loved. But Jesus takes this further, and shows that he loves everybody, regardless of their moral worth. Krishna makes massive claims about what he is; in fact, he is just about everything, good, bad and indifferent included. But Jesus is sparing in his claims and usually allows other people to make the identification. When people label him as Satan, he is most offended. So there are some things that Jesus is not; evil things. So there is a stand-off between good and bad, in the Christian world. The renunciation of worldly values and commitment to yoga are worthwhile elements, but then again, such values were given to us by Jesus.

The Gathas (the basis for Zoroastrianism and Parsi-ism)

This system of thought has had much positive input into later Judaism and then into Christianity. In its day, it may have been seen as another variant on monotheism. The dualism between the good god and the bad god is a little strange since the good god is claimed to have created the bad god. But Jesus constantly makes the assumption that there is only one God and the bad influence, Satan, is not a god, but ultimately subordinate to God. This version of dualism has been an important strand in Christianity right through its history, even if nowadays, people are trying to modify it somehow. Zoroaster constantly has eulogies for God and conceives him as being flames, light and glory, another influence seen in the New Testament. So while the Gathas have much to commend them, Jesus lifts Zoroaster's thoughts to an even greater height.

The Kitab-i-Aqdas (one of the bases for the Baha'i faith)

This is a very modern system of thought, based on the appearance of two gentlemen who regard themselves as one the Messiah and second, something even more exalted. Jesus actually warned us about spurious claimants to that status. The Christians are under the impression that the Messiah, on his return, will be with power and glory and the authority to judge the world and remove all the evil. So far, these two Persian gentlemen have not succeeded in doing this. The thoughts and morality in this book are very largely commendable, as is the attempt to start a new world order. But so far no new world order has materialised. One is somewhat perplexed about the exalted titles they give themselves; is this inflated ego-ism? Jesus was the opposite; he was very modest in his claims, but also accurate and focussed with his 'I am...' statements. None of this materialises in the Kitab-i-Aqdas.

The Masnavi by Rumi (the basis for the Sufi faith, a sub-set of Islam)

The most striking feature of this material is the heavy symbolism, which can be beyond easy interpretation. While it is true that many issues in the Bible are not completely crystal clear, in general terms, the Hebrew and Christian scriptures are fairly straightforward; at least, the essentials are not beyond the comprehension of almost everybody. The essentials of Sufism are the mystic closeness of the believer to God; this is something that Jews and Christians would hardly wish to deny. But to express it in such difficult images does raise an important question; why does it have to be so hard? Rumi does not make any claim to be the Messiah, which is fair enough.

The Ramayana, by Valmiki (one of the bases of Hinduism)

As a stunning epic in the mythological mode, this is a world winner. But here we see Rama, an avatar of Vishnu organising the attack and defeat of evil. This is all imaginary and symbolic; but with Revelation we see the Lamb, the Messiah augmented into epic proportions, based on the real life and ministry of Jesus of Nazareth. Something imaginary and spectacular is brought down to realities by the Messiah in his struggle against evil. It is not a matter of bloodshed and cruelty; it is a matter of humility and resistance to doing wrong. In this way, Jesus brings the Ramayana to a fulfilment that even Valmiki would not have guessed at.

The Gospel of Truth (one of the Gnostic writings)

This kind of thinking, which clearly has a relationship with the Hindu-Buddhist tradition, indulges in massive speculation about the other world, spiritual beings and has little relationship with earthly realities. This is an element that keeps reappearing through history and is by no means missing from the theological horizons of today. But the reality in earthly terms, of Jesus of Nazareth brings us down to earth with a bump. He is real, we are real, and God is real. There is a need for us to beware of endless spiritual speculations which are mostly, if not all, pure fantasy.

Science and Health by Mary Baker Eddy (one of the bases of Christian Science)

This is a good example of the re-application of Gnostic ideas, or rather the misuse of very ancient ideas, in a modern setting. There is clearly an important element in the process of healing, which requires the patient to believe that he is being healed. This comes out in the gospels as much as anywhere else. One has to trust one's doctor or spiritual healer. But to carry the matter to an extreme which says there is no pain or sickness, and that it is all imaginary, plus the whole of earthly life, is pushing things a long way. Jesus never told us that this life, with its pains, is pure fiction; very much the opposite, he told us to face up to pain and suffering, take up the cross, but transform it into something triumphant. In this way, Jesus is the corrective to Mary Baker Eddy.

Mein Kampf **and the** *Little Red Book* **by Adolf Hitler and Chairman Mao respectively (the basis of two political creeds, Nazism and Communism)**

Both of these are a good example of attempting to solve this world's problems by resort to a drastic political programme. Both of them have come to grief in our own times, and the basic reason is that they both ignore the element of the divine; God intervening in this world. This would be Messianism, except that both doctrines have to find another Messiah apart from Jesus. Hitler promoted himself to Messiah, and Mao became the Chinese Messiah, and for many, still is. But what Jesus showed us was that evil in this world is not purely and simply an earthly matter; there is a strong spiritual dimension to it. Any method that stands a chance of defeating wrong in this world, has to take into account the spiritual side of human nature, plus the fact that evil is not just a this-wordly matter, but a cosmic collision. For that reason, it needs someone of the stature and spiritual authority of the true Messiah to solve this world's problems. That Messiah is Jesus himself.

One factor, which becomes apparent in reviewing the sacred scriptures of the world, is that there is almost always a large gap between theory and practice. The written authoritative word is one thing, but the implementation of it is usually something different, some sort of distortion of the scriptural basis. Is this avoidable? Probably not. We have only to see how differing versions of Christianity interpret the Bible into alternative practicalities, sometimes the exact opposite of each other. This book has focussed on the written word, allowing each one to speak for itself, as far as possible. Admittedly there is always something lost in translation, but we are fortunate in having many up-to-date renderings available, which give an accurate impression without too much paraphrasing.

Another important factor in reviewing different scriptures is the fact that one's own cultural and religious assumptions will always colour one's assessments and judgements. It is not possible to think oneself out of one's own mind-set. One is always a child of one's own age, regardless of how much one may try to be objective. The same was true for Jesus, for if the Incarnation was genuine, he would be assuming the same mythical and theological ideas as everyone else in his day and age. In our own times, many of these assumptions are still with us, albeit in partially demythologised forms. I make no apology for being a British, middle-of-the road Christian, born and raised in an Anglican environment. There is no point in my trying to be something else just for the sake of trying to be objective. To compensate for this, I have tried not to offer too many judgemental remarks and have left many questions open for the reader to think through for himself and make his own decisions. I believe that this is what Jesus would have done; he was not inclined to dogmatise, but allow people to come to their own conclusions on matters. At this point I feel I can state a few things I can agree with across the varied scriptural materials on offer.

1. In the Taoist philosophy, there is the TAO, the Way, which is beyond definition. It is subtle and all pervading. The minute one tries to define it, it disappears. How like YHWH this is. I like the array of paradoxes that go with the concept of the TAO.
2. With Confucius, there is so much that agrees with the New Testament morality about gentleness and caring. If all political and religious leaders were so minded, it would be a world transformed, with kings and presidents putting the best interests of their subjects first.
3. With Mary Baker Eddy, I have to agree that a positive approach to health is the key to life. Pills and surgery have their place but essentially one has to believe that one is fit and well, and not go cringing through life imagining all kinds of disorders.
4. With the Gnostics, of which there are many different variants, it is important to see life on this earth as real and not imaginary. Life in the next world is also a reality but on a different dimension and it is foolish to think we can speculate freely on such matters.
5. On the subject of merit, which is endemic in many eastern religious and not a few western believers too, it is important to say that while merit has its place, and indeed Jesus himself talked about rewards, essentially, it is not within the ability of humanity, whether individually or communally, to save itself. There is the need for a merciful, loving superior spiritual force, namely God, to rescue us from the failures of this world.
6. This brings us to the question of Messianism, which is the final and ultimate channel through which the Eternal God intervenes in world affairs and humanity can respond to his outreach. Those religions which involve some sort of messianic thinking, such as Shintoism, Baha'i-ism, Islam and Judaism to name a few, are correct in their approach. Unfortunately, we have to beware of imposters, who are two-a-penny, nowadays as at the time of Jesus. As far as I am concerned, there is only one true Messiah and that is Jesus of Nazareth, and if and when he does reappear, I would be delighted, but also cautious until I saw evidence of the genuineness of this new claimant.
7. Valuable is the concept of closeness to the Almighty through some kind of meditatory method. This would apply to Buddhism, Hinduism, Taoism and Sufi-ism. A quietness of the mind surrounded by the love

of God brings great benefits to the believing soul. Worldly values pale into insignificance. The mistake however is to allow oneself to become completely detached from the real world. The reality is that this world has to function on the basis of wealth, sweated effort, trade and co-operation. So a balance needs to be struck between worldly and spiritual values. Sadly, many of our scriptures do not include this thought.

8. I like mythology. I like the imagination that goes into it, the exaggeration, the power of metaphor and high-flown expression. I do not like that attitude today which says that all religious or theological statements must be banal, prosaic and plain poverty-stricken. We need angels and devils, heaven and hell, the Cross and the Resurrection. These are the things that lift the human soul above the banality of daily life and give us eternal hope. Some would ask, 'Is this the truth?' But who knows what the truth is; Pontius Pilate certainly did not!

9. At the same time, we must keep our feet on the ground. Historical, geographical and mathematical realities cannot just be thrown aside. The true Messiah came at a specific time and place in human history, but all the other aspects of truth, as outlined in Chapter 1, tied in with his coming, and he summed them all up. There needs to be a balance struck between the earthly and the heavenly here; that is the deep paradox in a well-balanced religious faith; can you cope with life real on earth and also with the realities of the world of the spirit?

10. This brings us to the final paradox, which is writ large across the full spectrum of religious expression and scriptural material. It is the paradox of God being imminent, personal and close to the believing soul from day to day, a God with which an ongoing conversation can be had. Clearly this is an aspect of Messianism, but this closeness was available long before the true Messiah arrived. On the other hand, God is entirely other than this world. He is not a part of his own creation; he is above and beyond it, and even then he underpins the whole of reality. There is that sense that he is distant and the human mind cannot cope with his glory. This is a paradox which does a kind of seesaw motion between eastern and western religion, but even so, this is not a complete generalisation. The Bible itself contains elements of this dilemma and this comes to a climax in the first chapter of St John, where the Eternal Father, who cannot be seen by humanity, is nevertheless made known to us in the coming of the Messiah. I like this paradox; it is fundamental to many aspects of faith and practice.

At the same time, there are various things that I do not agree with, contained in various scriptural materials.

1. Many, if not all, of our scriptures, make a stark dichotomy between the

good and the bad. There seems to be no grey area in which people are an admixture of good and bad. It seems to be all or nothing. Is this an entirely fair assessment of human nature? This seems to augment itself into salvation and damnation.

2. Any scripture that advocates or glorifies violence, cruelty and unfair treatment must be treated with suspicion. This would include *Mein Kampf* (Chapter 4),the Book of Mormon (Chapter 7), the Holy Kojiki (Chapter 12), and to some extent the Ramayana (Chapter 22), and portions of the Bible. The world has had to learn from the mistakes made in the twentieth century, that aggression, cruelty, torture and discrimination may give a temporary advantage but in the long run, do not achieve anything. The real conflict is not people against people, but us against the spiritual forces of evil. This is something that St Paul in Ephesians would agree with, and also The Bhagavad Gita (Chapter 9). In fact, in the Iliad, the futility of warfare is mentioned.

3. One of the major shortcomings of many of our scriptural materials is the 'one author' situation. Many books only contain the slant of one author, which does not allow the ideas of someone else to form a contrast. The gospels overcome this problem by giving us four different versions of the same thing. The Maccabees give us two versions of the same thing. In the Pentateuch, which is believed to contain four sources of material woven together, we see differing accounts of the same events. This is important so that the reader can gain a balanced view of things, rather than just the one impression. The worst case of 'one author-ism' is the book of Mormon.

4. Another problem, which is probably less prevalent across scriptural materials, is the matter of obscurantism. The worst case is the Guru Granth, which is included in this work, but it is almost impossible to obtain a copy, on the grounds that it is far too holy for widespread dissemination. But the same tendency lingers on over the matter of old-fashioned or obsolete language. For many this may enhance the originality and authority of the written word, but for most of us, it simply makes the material more difficult to understand. I would maintain that if one's scripture is claimed to be the truth, then it ought to be readily available to everyone, since everybody should be entitled to discover the truth about life and eternity.

5. Another shortcoming, which does not apply to every scripture, is the lack of moral relevance to everyday living. Some scriptures do give us clear ethical guidelines but others do not. What is the point of indulging in elaborate speculations about the world of the spirit, unless it results in a code of conduct that enables people to live together in harmony and by extension, a pattern for world peace?

What I like about the Bible

When comparing scriptures from almost every religion in the world, it is plain that the Bible stands head and shoulder above all the rest of them. Here are some reasons for saying this.

1. The Bible has a clarity of message, and consistency which is not found elsewhere. Admittedly it has difficult passages, but in general terms the message is very clear indeed, that there is a God of love who cares for this world, in spite of its failures, and that this will all come to a glorious conclusion in his good time.
2. The Bible is a balanced work of literature. By this I mean that it is not a 'one genre' work as some are. There is a healthy working relationship between prose and poetry, mythology and history, legal material and inspiration, and different relationships with God, expressed in terms of 'covenant'.
3. The Bible is not a 'one author' work, but is the product of many different authors in widely separated times in the ancient world, and with their own slant. The result is that there is something in there for everyone, of whatever inclination he may have.
4. I like the way the Bible is structured. We begin with Creation and end with a glorious finale, summing up the whole of history and Creation. It is like two book-ends, holding the whole of human history together. This structuring indicates that history is not just a matter of one dispute after another; history is guided and shaped by the Eternal Hand.
5. The Bible also shows a progression in religious awareness. This is framed in the metaphor of covenant, which is fundamental to Judaeo-Christian thinking. It starts with the Covenant of Noah and culminates in the New Covenant at the Last Supper. At each stage another element of spirituality is brought in, the personal and family relationship to God with Abraham, the national and legalist element with Moses, the issue of kingship, which implies Messianism with King David, and finally, to sum it all up, what Jesus brought to us as the ultimate relationship with the Eternal Father.
6. An issue that began with Judaism and reappeared with Christianity is that not all portions of the Bible are of equal authority. The Pentateuch is supreme, the Law, then the Prophets on a lower level of importance and then the Writings on a third level. We could go a step further and say that the apocryphal material is a fourth level, but the Jews rejected them as sub-canonical. The same thinking applies to the New Testament; the gospels are of the first importance, and then the epistles. The material from the Apostolic Fathers comes next, some of which very nearly was included in the New Testament Canon; for instance, the Shepherd of

Hermas and the Epistle of Barnabas. This scheme of authority never seems to appear in the scriptures of other religions.

7. The Biblical writers do not shrink from employing elements from all our areas of truth, as discussed in Chapter One. One might say that the Bible is slightly weak on philosophy and artistic truth, but these matters are not completely absent. The result is that its portrayal of God's love in relationship to this world is a comprehensive one, and there is enough there to appeal to virtually every human soul, of whatever inclination they may be. To term it the 'Book of Life' is something of an understatement. All aspects of life whether human or divine are writ large and interwoven; all human emotions, all divine activities, love and hate, joy and sorrow are interplayed. When we compare it with what is almost certainly a forgery, or something that is a purely human concoction, the contrast is blatant. The Bible is the real thing.

8. The Bible is rich in different levels of interpretation. It would be fair to say that every time one reads a certain passage, say a Chapter from the gospels, one sees something different in it. Different possibilities and slants appear; this is the hallmark of a truly great piece of literature. A Buddhist would say the same about a work like the Dhammapada (Chapter 14), but one does not have to be a Buddhist to appreciate this factor. Neither does one have to be a Christian to see the greatness of the gospels.

Postscript

To return to our original thought on the subject of Sherlock Holmes, it is interesting that only this year (2015) yet another permutation on the great sleuth has been produced. It is a fascinating juxtaposition of the modern and the Victorian. The 'sci-fi' element is much toned down except that we have Holmes arriving in a jet plane. The costume drama element combined with the snobbery of the big country house is much more prominent. Also more attention is paid to minor characters such as Mrs Hudson, Mrs Watson and Mycroft Holmes.

Of relevance to this book is the way that a certain degree of exaggeration and augmentation has been worked in. This is a constant factor in our selection of sacred writings. Holmes' powers of deduction are augmented almost to the level of him being psychic, and his conceit is even greater than ever. This is backed up by his highly acute abilities in sensory perception.

Far more important is the way that reality and imagination are interplayed. The subjective and the objective are very cleverly interrelated. It starts with the brainteaser of how a woman who shot herself could go on to shoot her husband and various other people. This is one of the main strands in the book. Then it graduates to the issue of Moriarty and the incident at the Reichenbach Falls. Is this real or is it just all in the mind? This is one of the main themes of the drama, the tension between reality and unreality. There is that theme in Conan Doyle's stories of how there is nothing supernatural, no ghosts. This comes out especially in *The Hound of the Baskervilles* for instance, but also very strongly in this latest production. However, we are all haunted by something from the past, some sort of misconduct, moral failure or 'guilt-glug'. Ghosts are real, sometimes in the literal sense, but more often in the figurative sense.

The importance of this for us, when trying to assess any scriptural material, is that we must bear in mind the tension between the literal and the figurative truth, the objective and the subjective. This aspect occurs at all different levels of reality. It is one thing to say that a book is the truth, but another thing to assess the truth in what respect, or at what level. This is why, on reading any scriptural material, one must ask oneself what kind of literature this is, what genre, and what is the intention of the writer. Also one may ask in what way it resonates with human nature.

It became clear towards the end that this latest Holmes drama had at least one substratum; female emancipation. This was a theme not exactly absent from the original stories, but certainly not too heavily emphasised. This is a good example of how any writer has his own axe to grind, and will shape his story to convey his idea.

But the strongest substratum, and this may be understating it, is the issue of the tension between good and evil. Like any pantomime, cowboy film, soap opera, detective 'who-dunnit' or novel, the 'goodies' have to win and the 'baddies' have to be caught out. The fact that Moriarty was dead, or supposed to be, is irrelevant. He still goes on in Holmes' mind. It is the mythological clash between right and wrong, with no compromise between them. We see this in so many of our scriptural choices. The tension maybe purely on a human level; more often it is dramatically portrayed on a cosmic level with angels and devils. It is something that we cannot get away from; it is a part of human nature. The final resolution of it is that good prevails. In the drama, Watson appeared just at the right moment at the Reichenbach Falls to allow Holmes to prevail, and Moriarty went over the edge. Holmes followed later but was portrayed as flying away rather than plummeting into the Abyss. This is all very symbolic and mythological, but real enough at a certain level.

The whole picture left us wondering where reality is actually to be found, and that is also one of the main issues between religions of all kinds; what is objective and what is subjective. It is the age-old tension between the physical and the spiritual world. Time is tied in with the physical world, our calendars, time sheets, life-spans and all other matters relating to them. Time is not tied into the world of eternity. God can intervene in our time-scheme, but he is not subject to time himself. The same could be said of all great religious leaders or innovators, and their scriptures that we are left with; there is the temporal aspect in their writings, but also the spiritual, and that is the hallmark of any authoritative writing.

We can conclude with a very telling remark as the drama came to an end and Holmes faded from the screen;

'I've always known that I was a man out of his time!'

Index

Select Bibliography

Primary Scriptural material

The Bible (Revised Standard Version).
The Apocrypha edited by R.H.Charles.
The Pseudepigrapha edited by R.H.Charles.
The Little Red Book; quotations from Chairman Mao Tse-Tung, 1966.
Mein Kampf, by Adolf Hitler.
The Analects of Confucius.
The Bhagavad Gita, by Vyasa, translated by Eknath Easwaran.
Science and Health, by Mary Baker Eddy.
The Tao Teh Ching, by Lao Tzu, translated by Hua-Ching Ni.
The Hua Hu Ching, see above.
The Holy Kojiki and the Yengishiki, Cosimo Classics, 2007.
The Dhammapada, translated by Gil Fronsdal.
The Gathas; the Hymns of Zoroaster, translated by M.L.West.
The Kitab-i-Aqdas, by Baha'u'llah, translated by Shoghi Effendi.
The Masnavi, by Rumi, translated by Jawid Mojaddedi.
The Gospel of Truth, translated by Alan Jacobs, 2006 (in The Gnostic
     Gospels).
The Corpus Hermeticum, the OMTO version of 2007 based on the work of
     G.R.S.Mead.
The Book of Enoch, in the Pseudipigrapha.
The Koran, Pelican version by N.J.Dawood, 1956.
The Ramayana, by Valmiki, translated by Arshia Sittar. 1996.
The Guru Granth Sahib.
The Egyptian Book of the Dead, translated by E.A.Wallis Budge.

Secondary material, not necessarily scriptural

The Book of Odes collected by Confucius.
The Aramaic Proverbs of Ahiqar.
Ecclesiasticus (Apocrypha).
The Wisdom of Solomon (Apocrypha).
The Iliad, by Homer.
The Proto-gospel of James.
The Antiquities of the Jews by Josephus.
Inanna; her descent into the underworld by Eleanor Allitt.
Lost Scriptures, by Bart D. Ehrman.